THE GAMES CLIMBERS PLAY

*To the Editors, Writers, Photographers and
Illustrators of the world's mountaineering journals
and magazines. Long may they continue to record
the affairs of the mountaineering world and
preserve its literary traditions.*

EDITED BY KEN WILSON

The Games Climbers Play

with cartoons by Sheridan Anderson

Inspired by the essay 'Games Climbers Play'
by Lito Tejada Flores

BÂTON WICKS · LONDON

Also in this series:

The Games Climbers Play. Volume 2:
MIRRORS IN THE CLIFFS
Edited by Jim Perrin

Published in Great Britain in 2006 by Bâton Wicks Publications, London

First edition 1978 (Diadem, UK hbk) and 1981 (Sierra Club Books, US tpbk)
Reprints: 1981 (Diadem hbk), 1984 (Sierra Club Books, tpbk), 1986 (Diadem hbk),
1995, 1998 and 2000 (Bâton Wicks UK, tpbk and Menasha Ridge Press US tpbk)

All trade enquiries in the UK to: Cordee 3a De Montfort Street, Leicester LE1 7HD

British Library Cataloguing in Publication Data
ISBN 1-898573-01-8

Printed and bound in Singapore by the Kyodo Printing Company

CONTENTS

Part 1: The World of the Rock-Climber

Part 2: The Alpine Odyssey

Part 3: Style and Character

Part 4: Ethical Discussions

Part 5: Expeditions

Part 6: Some Part-Time Games

Part 7: Epics, Risk, Falling, Death, Obituary and Retirement

Part 8: Mountain Rescue and Access Problems

Part 9: Mountain Education

PHOTOGRAPHS*

Cover photo: Leo Houlding making the first ascent of Trauma (E9/7a) high on Dinas Mot, North Wales in 1999, one of the hardest traditional climbs in Britain. The name stems from an incident during an earlier attempt. An old in-situ piton snapped (when used for resting) and Houlding took a sizeable fall down the slabs of Lorraine below. On his next attempt he made 6c moves to place (blind) the high nut runner seen here, then climbed down to the stance to test it. He then attempted the crux taking several short falls before retreating and leaving the runner in place. The picture shows Houlding engrossed in the crux moves during his successful ascent a few days later. When removing his gear afterwards (by abseil) he was 'surprised' to find that the critical runner lifted out easily. *Photo: Ray Wood*

1.   John Long on Pinch Overhang near Fort Collins. *Photo: Michael Kennedy*

2.   Cerro Torre – the epitome of the challenging mountain. *Photo: Daniele Chiappa*

3.   Nearing the top of the West Face of Cerro Torre. *Photo: Daniele Chiappa*

4.   John Syrett climbing Encore (E2, 5c) one of the many bold and uncompromising gritstone climbs on Almscliff, Yorkshire. *Photo: John Harwood*

5.   Dale Bard leads Butterballs (5.11), the final pitch of Nabisco Wall on the superb Cookie Cliff, Yosemite Valley, California. *Photo: Gene Foley*

6.   Chamonix's Bar National, for years the spiritual home of English-speaking alpinists. *Photo: John Powell*

7.   Helmut Wagner encounters tough conditions on the North Face of Les Droites in the Mont Blanc massif, during an early repeat attempt in 1964. *Photo: Heli Wagner*

8.   Malcolm Howells, Martin Boysen, Joe Brown and Mo Anthoine bivouacing during the first ascent of Trango's Nameless Tower in 1976. *Photo: Tony Riley*

9.   Reinhold Messner – the central figure in Himalayan climbing during the 1970s. *Photo: Messner archive*

10.   Messner's frostbitten toes after his enforced traverse of Nanga Parbat in 1970. *Photo: Messner archive*

11.   The scene of the Cairngorm Tragedy in 1971 when six teenagers died in a blizzard while trying to traverse a high mountain plateau during an official Edinburgh Education Authority winter expedition.

*All photo captions are written in 2006, with the benefit of hindsight, twenty-eight years after the book was first published.

MAP AND CARTOONS

All by Sheridan Anderson unless otherwise stated

FOREWORD

AL ALVAREZ

In recent years climbing has been going through one of its curious, periodic changes of life which Chairman Mao would have called 'a great leap forward'. In simplest terms, this means that the apparently impossible is once again obligatory for any young tiger wanting to make his mark.

This time the change has not been brought about by one great climber who floated up routes neither his predecessors nor most of his contemporaries even dared to peer at, as Joe Brown did in England in the 1950s, or Bonatti did in the Alps. Today there are a number of exceptional young climbers who, having cut their teeth on the Brown routes which scared my generation witless, now compete with each other on increasingly absurd blank faces of vertical or overhanging rock. The kind of moves which were once thought feasible only as boulder problems to be solved a few feet above solid ground or top-roped on tiny sandstone crags are now the exposed cruxes of the new climbs. In Yosemite and, even more, in Britain – where fresh rock is hard to find – routes which used to be climbed artificially now go free.

None of this has happened simply because the new generation of climbers has at its disposal an equally new generation of sophisticated protection – particularly, nuts and cams of imaginative shapes and sizes and names – which provide an illusion of security where none was previously possible. There has also been a physical break-through. The top climbers train like Olympic gymnasts; for all I know, they train with Olympic gymnasts. They also have indoor climbing walls on which they can practise daily, despite rotten weather or winter darkness. Soon after Chouinard's chrome-moly pitons appeared in England, Peter Crew remarked to me laconically, 'They mean there's no longer any such thing as impossible rock'. Today's top climbers have the same attitude, but it is founded on their extraordinary physical confidence rather than on artificial aids.

The attitude seems to be contagious. In the Alps the hardest routes are now climbed in winter and often solo, whilst in the Himalaya and Karakoram huge, steep and highly technical faces are done Alpine-style by small parties who tote their own gear above Base Camp.

The progression from hard to harder seems natural enough and the

11

elaborate ethical discussions which have accompanied it – 'To chalk or not to chalk?'; 'When is a free ascent not a free ascent? When you rest in slings' – make it seem simple as well as logical. This, however, is misleading. The further climbers push the limits of their capabilities, the higher the risk, no matter how fit they are or how brilliant the protection they use. If you stick your neck out far enough, a qualitative change takes place; the psychology of the game alters.

Risk, of course, has always been one of the abiding satisfactions of the sport, however strenuously we all deny that to outsiders, pretending we do it for the view or the loneliness or the sense of physical well-being. 'Life is impoverished,' wrote Freud, 'it loses in interest, when the highest stake in the game of living, life itself, may not be risked.' To put yourself into a situation where a mistake cannot necessarily be recouped, where the life you lose may be your own, clears the head wonderfully. It puts domestic problems back into proportion and adds an element of seriousness to your drab, routine life. Perhaps this is one reason why climbing has become increasingly hard as society has become increasingly, disproportionately, coddling.

Risk, however, like fear, is a taboo subject; nobody wants to talk about it. But that, of course, doesn't make it go away. Instead, it gets in obliquely in a widening, deepening flood of black humour, a spirit of pure anarchy which goes with the almost surrealist difficulty of the hardest new climbs.

Naturally enough, none of this has found its way into official expedition books or the national press, which still tend to treat the sport as, at best, a rather hearty form of grand opera. The new style of mountain literature flourishes almost exclusively in the trade papers – particularly *Mountain*, *Ascent* and the journals of the Climbers' and Scottish Mountaineering Clubs. In all of them everything you ever wanted to know about the latest climbs (but were afraid to ask) is juxtaposed with that black gallows humour which seems to erupt spontaneously whenever climbers get back down to earth and try to remember what happened to them.

It is this odd and special mixture which Ken Wilson has recreated in this anthology. It should be read not only by climbers but by anyone who wants to know what happened to what the boys in the business used to call 'the Spirit of the Hills'. The answer this book suggests is that it is still alive and well, but now living not all that far from the spirit of Vietnam and Watergate.

AL ALVAREZ
Hampstead, London 1978

INTRODUCTION

In compiling this anthology of recent mountaineering writing, I owe much to Michael Ward's *The Mountaineer's Companion* (London, 1966) – a blend of essays, illustrations and poetry that formed an eloquent statement on the origins and appeal of mountaineering and the instincts of its participants.

But the mountaineering world that Ward reflected a decade ago has changed radically. An intellectual mountaineer with finely tuned tastes, immersed in Alpine Club history and the great explorations of the Himalaya, Ward tended towards a traditional view of the sport. I have found that my selection has been very different – perhaps more youthful and irreverent – a rather evolutionary depiction of climbing.

The essay 'Games Climbers Play' by Lito Tejada Flores, which appeared in first issue of *Ascent* in 1967, charted an altogether more logical concept of the sport than anything hitherto conceived. I was able to use it to provide a firm ideological base for the magazine *Mountain* which I began editing in 1968. Therefore it seemed natural when assembling this collection, to return to Lito's essay to give the book its title, its keynote chapter and central theme. As a companion scene-setter, I have chosen Ed Drummond's remarkable saga of adventure on the Troll Wall – 'Mirror Mirror' – a mannered description of an epic so prolonged as to stir even the most cynical spirit.

Thereafter this book, like Ward's, is organised into sections covering well-known subjects. Rock-climbing has been given a great deal of space, reflecting a fresh new optimism on the crags. Alpinism and Expedition activity follow but with less prominence than in Ward's book, in which the subject (following the historic 1950s ascents) was thoroughly examined.[1]

I resolved to select writings as far as possible from the magazines and journals of the last twenty years, leaving much interesting work from books to be examined in some later volume. This policy has led to the assembling of some very disparate items that are placed, with supporting cartoons, in interesting juxtapositions to the larger articles.

In this way it has been possible to cover a number of peripheral facets of the sport, alongside Lito's games: Regulation and Access; Risk, Death and Obituary; Mountain Rescue; Ethics. Finally there is a section on Mountain Education that is, I hope, sufficiently general to have a wide interest.

---

[1] Himalayan political restrictions during the late 1960s (linked to the border tensions between India and China) resulted in a paucity of expedition accounts at that time. That period was followed (early 1970s) by the Himalayan Big Wall era that provided a mere handful of few memorable accounts.

The concluding essay, as if to defy my stated theme, is old (1941), taken from a book and entitled, ironically, 'Beginnings'. It is Colin Kirkus's description of his first adventures in the sport, as fresh and relevant now as on the day it was written. Hopefully it will serve as a reminder of the simple pleasures and adventures that the sport holds for all of us – its fellowship, its excitement, its fun and its power to produce deep inner satisfaction.

After twenty-eight years *Games* remains relevant for today's readers because of the many acclaimed articles within its covers. As a statement of its time a general revision seemed unwise. As with all sporting activities performance has improved though vituouso efforts remain rare. In alpinism improvements in clothing, equipment and food make things possible that were much more problematic in the 1970s. The primitive challenges of rock climbing have been largely tamed by equipment improvements. Sport climbing, bolts, and competition climbing have changed the scene to some degree, particularly by bringing a higher level of fitness and stamina. Cheap travel allows winter activity in warmer rock venues and alpine activity in places like Patagonia and the Andes can stretch the season. Deep water soloing and bouldering (now virtually a sport in itself) are important reinvigorated trends. Yet on-sight traditional climbing, with its still bracing challenge – either on new routes or personal first ascents – remains an important preoccupation for many climbers, even some of those who concentrate on other styles. Aid climbing, particularly in Yosemite, has also rejuvenated itself.

Of the other subjects Mountain Training, in an increasingly litigious world, is the one that has changed most but the central tenets remain the same – the lessons of the Cairngorm Accident remaining relevant to today's instructors, administrators, educationalists and guides. 1970s efforts to stem the tide of certification bought only a brief respite. While still not cramping the style of ordinary climbers, the instructional world has been colonised with badges for every level of activity, however mundane. University clubs (a major recruiting ground for the sport) are now struggling to maintain their freedom to train.

Despite all these protective measures the key theme of the sport – to extend oneself whilst using skill and judgement to manage the risks – remains the same for most climbers, always with an eye to not taking oneself too seriously and remembering that fun and good companionship remain essential elements in the mix. We also draw sustenance from the marvellously wild environs in which we are privileged to conduct our activities.

The climbing world in the 21st century seems less irreverent than it was in the 1960s and 1970s. Today's consumerist, politically correct and conformist society is clearly having a homogenising effect on the climbing scene and its current publications and in that respect there will be elements in *Games* that will grate in certain quarters. Maybe they always did?

KEN WILSON   1978 / 2006

GAMES CLIMBERS PLAY

LITO TEJADA FLORES

Reality is the apparent absence of contradiction
Louis Arragon, Le Paysan de Paris

I

What I should like to propose in this article is not a new answer to the basically unanswerable question, 'what is climbing?' but rather a new way of talking and thinking about it. Climbing is not a homogeneous sport but rather a collection of differing (though related) activities, each with its own adepts, distinctive terrain, problems and satisfactions, and perhaps most important, its own rules. Therefore, I propose to consider climbing in general as a hierarchy of climbing-games, each defined by a set of rules and an appropriate field of play.

The word *game* seems to imply a sort of artificiality which is foreign to what we actually feel on a climb. The attraction of the great walls, above all, is surely that when one is climbing them he is playing 'for keeps'. Unlike the player in a bridge game, the climber cannot simply lay down his cards and go home. But this does not mean that climbing is any less a game. Although the player's actions have real and lasting consequences, the decision to start playing is just as gratuitous and unnecessary as the decision to start a game of chess. In fact, it is precisely because there is no necessity to climb that we can describe climbing as a *game* activity.

The obstacles one must surmount to gain the summit of Indian Rock in Berkeley or the Hand at Pinnacles National Monument are scarcely of the same order as those defending the West Face of Sentinel Rock in Yosemite or the North Face of the Eiger. And the personal satisfaction of the climber upon having solved each of these problems could hardly be the same. As a result, a handicap system has evolved to equalise the inherent challenge and maintain the climber's feeling of achievement at a high level in each of these differing situations. This handicap system is expressed through the rules of the various climbing-games.

It is important to realise at the outset that these rules are negatively expressed although their aim is positive. They are nothing more than a series of 'don'ts': don't use fixed ropes, belays, pitons, a series of camps, etc. The

17

purpose of these negative rules is essentially protective or conservative. That is, they are designed to conserve the climber's feeling of personal (moral) accomplishment against the meaninglessness of a success which represents merely technological victory.

Let us take as a concrete example the most complex game in the climbing hierarchy – bouldering. It is complex by definition since it has more rules than any other climbing game, rules which prohibit nearly everything – ropes, pitons, and belayers. All that is left is the individual standing in front of a rock problem. (It should be noted that the upper belay belongs to practice climbing, that is, training for any of the climbing-games). But why so many restrictions? Only because boulders are too accessible; they don't defend themselves well enough. For example, it would be an absurdity to use a ladder to reach the top of a boulder in Fontainebleau, but to use the same ladder to bridge a crevasse in the Khumbu Icefall would be reasonable since Everest defends itself so well that one ladder no longer tips the scales toward certain success. Thus the basic principle of a handicap is applied to maintain a degree of uncertainty as to the eventual outcome, and from this very uncertainty stems the adventure and personal satisfaction of climbing.

More generally, I discern a complete spectrum of climbing-games, ranked according to the complexity (or number) of their rules. The higher one goes on the scale, the more inaccessible and formidable become the climber's goals, and, in consequence, he need apply fewer restrictions to conserve the full measure of challenge and satisfaction inherent in the climbing-game he is playing. At the top of the hierarchy we find the expedition-game, which, although complicated to organise and play, is formalistically speaking, the simplest game of all, since virtually nothing is forbidden to the climber. The recent use of aeroplanes and helicopters exemplifies the total lack of rules in the pure expedition-game.

While variant games have arisen in isolated and special circumstances in different countries, one can distinguish the following seven basic climbing games.

1. The Bouldering Game
We have already discussed bouldering, but one should note that the basic bouldering rules eliminate not only protection but also companions. The boulderer is essentially a solo climber. In fact, when we see solo climbing at any level of difficulty it represents the application of bouldering rules to some other climbing-game. Aside from that, this game is found in every country where climbing exists, although the number of climbers who specialise in it is relatively small.

2. The Crag Climbing Game

Crag climbing as a pure game form has doubtless reached its highest form of expression in the British Isles. It is practised on cliffs of limited size – routes averaging one to three pitches in length. Because of their limited size and the large amount of time at the climber's disposal, such routes are not imposing enough to be approached with the full arsenal of the climber's tools (though they may contain moves as hard as those of any climb). Fundamentally the game consists in climbing them free with the use of extremely well-defined and limited protection. The use of pitons is avoided or, in special cases, standardised at an absolute minimum. Pure crag climbing is scarcely practised as a game in this country except in areas such as Pinnacles National Monument, where the rock is virtually unpitonable. There are, however, a number of areas in the States, such as the Shawangunks, where the crag game could be played with more rigour.

3. The Continuous Rock-Climbing Game

This is the game that most California climbers know best. It differs from the crag game in allowing the full range of rock-climbing equipment to be used at the discretion of the climber as well as allowing the use of direct aid. Fundamentally this game should be played on longer, multi-pitch climbs whose length puts a kind of time limit to the mechanical means that a climber can employ and still reach the top. Shorter climbs should still be approached as more complex games with stricter rules.

4. The Big Wall Game

This game is practised not only on the bigger Yosemite walls but in the Dolomites and elsewhere. It is characterised by the prolonged periods of time spent on the walls and by the fact that each member of the party does not have to climb every lead (e.g., different climbers may prusik with loads on different days but are still considered to have done the entire climb). The full technical and logistic equipment range is allowed. In the modern big wall game fixed ropes to the ground and multiple attempts to prepare the route are no longer allowed (see part II), and a rigorous distinction is still made between free and artificial moves and pitches.

5. The Alpine Climbing Game

In alpine climbing the player encounters for the first time the full range of hostile forces present in the mountain environment. In addition to problems of length and logistics he meets increased objective dangers in the form of falling rock, bad weather and extreme cold, and bad conditions such as verglas. All this leads to a further relaxation of formal rules since success in the game may often include merely surviving. In alpine climbing the use of pitons is avoided wherever possible because of time loss in situations where speed means safety, but where pitons are used there is a tendency to use them as holds also. Thus the rules of this game do not require one to push all leads free. The restrictions upon the player are more determined by the nature of the mountain and the route than by a set of rules which he accepts in advance.

6. The Super-Alpine Game

This is the newest climbing-game to appear and is not yet completely understood. It rejects expedition techniques on terrain which would traditionally have been suitable for it. Its only restrictive rule is that the party must be self-contained. Any umbilical-like connection in the form of a series of camps, fixed ropes, etc., to a secure base is no longer permitted. This rule provides a measure of commitment that automatically increases the uncertainty of success, making victory that much more meaningful. Often the major alpine routes under extreme winter conditions provide suitable terrain for super-alpine climbs. Some of the early, classic super-alpine routes were the South Face of Aconcagua, the ascent of Cerro Torre by Egger and Maestri, and the first winter ascent of the Eiger North Wall.

7. The Expedition Game

I have already mentioned the lack of rules in this game, but I wish to point out that there are still differences of personal involvement on the part of the players from expedition to expedition. For example, members of the Austrian Broad Peak expedition who packed all their own loads up the mountain were, in a sense, playing a more difficult game than the usual Himalayan expedition that moves up the mountain on the backs of its Sherpas.

It should be noted that the above ordering of climbing-games is not an attempt to say that some games are better, harder, or more worthwhile in themselves than others. One remembers that the very purpose of the game structure is to equalise such value connotations from game to game so that the climber who plays any of these games by its proper set of rules should have at least a similar feeling of personal accomplishment. Of course, each type of game will still have its own proponents, its own classics, heroes, and myths.

The real purpose of ranking climbing games into such a hierarchy, however, is not to make judgements about a game or its players, but rather to have a useful scale against which to discuss climbing ethics, since unethical behaviour involves a disregard of certain rules.

II

Within our new framework we can now clear up certain misconceptions about climbing ethics. Ethical climbing merely means respecting the set of rules of the climbing-game that one is playing. Conversely, unethical climbing occurs when a climber attempts to use a set of rules appropriate to a game higher up on the scale than the one he is actually playing (i.e. a less restrictive set of rules). Applying this idea to the bolt controversy that has animated ethical discussions among climbers for the last several years, we can see that there is nothing unethical about bolts *per se;* it is merely that their use is prohibited by the rules of certain climbing-games and not by others. In certain games the question becomes meaningless for, as Bonatti points out, on a major mixed face no amount of bolts can guarantee success, whereas an excessive number will insure defeat through lack of time.

I have assumed so far that the rules for various climbing-games were fixed. Of course, this is not the case, as both the games and their rules are undergoing a constant, if slow, evolution. The central problem of climbing ethics is really the question: who makes the rules for these games? and secondarily: how do they change with time?

On reflection, it seems to me that the rules of various climbing-games are determined by the climbing community at large, but less so by climbers approaching the two extremes of ability. One of these elements is composed of those fainthearted types who desire to overcome every new difficulty with some kind of technological means rather than at the expense of personal effort under pressure. The other group is the small nucleus of elite climbers whose basic concern is not with merely ethical climbing but with minimising the role of technology and increasing that of individual effort in order to do climbs with better *style.* But before talking about style and the role of the elite climber in climbing evolution, I want to expand my idea that the majority of climbers are responsible for deciding the rules of a given climbing-game.

No matter what their origin a set of rules must be consecrated by usage and general acceptance. Thus, the way good climbers have always done a climb becomes the traditional way of doing it; the rules become classic and constitute an ethical minimum for the climb, defining at the same time the climbing-game to which it belongs. But what of new climbs? At any moment there are relatively few members of the climbing community capable of doing significant first ascents; these will be members of the creative elite we have already mentioned. The question arises: should the style they use on a first ascent determine the rules for succeeding ascents? I think not (although their approaches and attitudes will of course serve as guidelines for following parties). Examples of cases where the first ascent has not set the pattern for succeeding ascents are almost too numerous to list. Just because Jeff Foott made the first ascent of Patio Pinnacle solo or because Bonatti soloed the South-West Pillar of the Drus, following climbers have felt under no obligation to stick to the difficult rules of the first ascent; or just because the first ascent of the Eiger North Wall was made in a storm, no one has seriously suggested that later parties wait for bad weather to go up the face. A kind of group prudence is at work here, rejecting individual solutions whose extremism puts them beyond the reach of the majority of competent climbers climbing at any given period.

What, then, is the role of the small minority of extremist climbers in the evolution of climbing-games? To understand it we must first develop the idea of climbing style. Style may be defined as the conscious choice of a set of rules for a given climbing-game. Thus, if a climber follows the accepted rules for a given game he is climbing both in classical style and ethically. Bad style and unethical climbing are synonymous and represent the choice of rules from a simpler (higher) game, such as alpine climbing with expedition style. On the other hand, a climber can choose to climb with better style and still be climbing ethically by choosing rules from a game lower down in the hierarchy than that which he is playing. A fitting example would be the way John Gill has applied bouldering rules to certain crag climbing problems, doing extremely hard, unprotected moves high off the ground.

In this way the creative nucleus of elite climbers can express itself by climbing with better style than the average climber (like aristocrats playing a more demanding game than the democratic majority), which certainly provides enough room for personal expression, yet seems to avoid the traditional aristocratic role of leadership and direction. In fact, these climbers lead the majority only indirectly – their responsibility is not to determine and set ethical standards (rules) for the majority but rather to demonstrate the feasibility of new standards by climbing with consistently superior style. Thus, they stake out the possible directions for the evolution of climbing-games. And this, aside from suffering the wiles of equipment-mongers, is the only way that such changes can come about.

Let me give a concrete example. The most evident is the way in which the rules of the big-wall game have evolved in Yosemite Valley under the influence of the best climbers of the day whose primary concern was to do their own climbs in the best style possible rather than to impose an arbitrary set of rules on all climbers. After the feasibility of doing the bigger Grade VI walls without siege tactics had been consistently demonstrated, climbers were impressed enough to accept this approach as a basic rule to such an extent that today even strangers to the Yosemite climbing community (such as the two Frenchmen who did the Nose of El Capitan in the spring of 1966) follow it as a matter of course.

In a less dramatic way the rules of all climbing-games are changing constantly, becoming ever more restrictive in order to preserve the fundamental challenge that the climber is seeking from the inroads of a fast changing technology. The present *laissez-faire* of the uppermost games is disappearing slowly as the complexity of rules shifts up the spectrum. The eventual victim, of course, will be the expedition game which will disappear completely as super-alpine climbing takes its place. This is not only the newest but, in a sense, the most creative climbing-game, since here the nature of the obstacles encountered is so severe that it will be a long, long time before technological advances even begin to encroach upon the climber's personal satisfaction. The possibilities, on the other hand, are immense. One can even visualise the day when, with ultra-modern bivouac gear, a climbing party of two sets off to do an 8000m peak just as today one sets off to do a hard route on the Grand Teton or on Mont Blanc.*

Here, I think, this article should end. Not because speculations about the future of climbing are either futile or uninteresting, but because we have already wandered far enough from our original subject. That climbing will continue to evolve is a certainty, although it is far less certain that the idea of climbing-games is the best basis for looking at this evolution. But surely this, or any, new framework for thinking and talking about what we are actually doing when we climb is at least a valid step toward the future.

from ASCENT *1967*

MIRROR MIRROR

ED DRUMMOND

We reached Oslo in two days, nudging in under the shrouds of cloud spreading a thin fine rain upon toast-faced Norwegians and palefaces alike. It was the first rain for a month. Burning up to Romsdal on the bike, I found my cagoule was promiscuous in the rain, but Lindy, at the back of me, kept

---

*This has developed differently with high peak fees forcing out small expeditions in favour of large guided parties and the use of much fixed rope (hardly climbing progress). A similar situation developed on Mont Blanc in the early 19th Century where a vested interest of local guides enforced a costly form of climbing that stifled innovation.

dry and fed me on chocolate and made me hum with her big hugs. I couldn't lean on her as I could my cold companion of other years who pulled on my neck: my rain-slimed haul bag, my meticulous Humpty Dumpty. She was continually delighted at new waterfalls; her oohs flew to my ears and near the end of the journey, my goggles crying with rain, I raised a soggy arm at the alp of cloud shearing up a white mile. 'That's the wall,' I roared. She gripped her hand on my arm, and yelled about the coming bend.

Where am I? I'm cold. Thin mists shift past, touching me. Where is she? She must have got out of the bag. I shake my head out, struggling to look. There is another near me, raw-red in the white air. Hugh! A dream. I'm not on the Romsdalhorn. That was a week ago. Lindy isn't here. This is the wall.

So. Three nights. Almost 1000ft. Our second ledge, Luckys. Seven pitches and a paper-dry cag. Hugh's still in the bag, sleeping the sleep of the just, sound as a foetus, on his first wall. During the past three years I had, in three summers and a spring, snailed the mile-long approach scree twenty-three times and twenty times I came back. Not this time. The Northern European Wall; The Mourning Wall; The Rurt Wall, (Realised Ultimate Reality Troll); The Lord of the Walls; The Drummond Route (if we said nothing they'd call it this); The Royal Wall, naw, what has Robbins ever done for you? You'll never level with him.

On our first cralk up to the wall – the scree is so steep that it's like trying to ski uphill – we had climbed the first slabs, 200ft or so, gritty, nasty, wobbling to extreme. There had been the snow pitch, cricket size, and the jokes about forgetting the ice axes, using skyhooks and étriers as we had no crampons and the ice was marble. Then the 'schrund and my little leap; it was all fun. After three trips we'd brimmed the hauls and I'd climbed the third, a squirrelly free up a great crooked slab, funnelling to an upside-down squeeze chimney that made me squeak. Then we went down, Lindy, who'd come up to watch, and I, slowly, like two old people, while High flew off to the river where he swam among the salmon; the fishermen had all gone home. We just promised us a swim when it was all over.

Returning, two days later, Hugh went first and the hauls went after, quite a while after. His first haul; his first artyfishyl; first hamouac; first air jumar (barring one from a tree in Mexico). Hugh was, slowly, going up the wall. So it was noon when I set out on the fourth pitch.

And it was seven in the evening when Hugh's jumars gritted their teeth to follow. What passed in those seven hours is unforgettable: my mouth, sock-hot; my larynx strangling for spit; a fine trembling as of a thin wind trembling through me. It began with a layback of twenty feet, wonderful but for the iron stone around my neck – it was a struggle, favourite uncle, was it not? Then the footholds faded away and I muttered on nuts under this thin roof until the only way up was up.

There was a crack, not a crack crack, but a line, a cra ...; the start of a crack say. At any rate the bolts were in the haul bag and this was the third pitch of the N.A. Wall as far as I was concerned. My rurps curled up when I banged their heads and refused to sit still. After five fingernail knifeblades I got out my hook and sat on that, about as secure as the last angel to make it onto that pin head. Then I struck dirt. Now dirt is okay if you can get dug in. I began and ended with a knifeblade which dangled sillily from my waist, and I was glad that it was not me that was holding the rope, for after four hours and forty feet I might have been caught napping. But Hugh wasn't and as it was I only went fifteen feet for the hook stuck and though it trembled it snapped not, O Dolt.

So then I had to free that bit, but after that it eased some. Nuts hammered in the dirt and at long last a ding dong bong. Hotheaded I'd reached a ledge, feeling a bit sorry for myself. 'No Ledges' we called it and it all hung out. There we had a pantomime in hammocks by headtorch which was really not in the least bit funny. Hugh, as chattery as a parrot, floated above me in his one-point. He even said he was comfortable and had the cheek to take a shit. By a battery *son-et-lumiere* I watched his anus line an angry eye; no voyeur but it might look my way. However, he missed me, my arms full of ropes like some deeply confused spider.

'Ed! Come on, it's light.'

Oh, God, awake already.

'Look at the sun.'

Why don't you go back to sleep?

'Unh uh.'

There and then I decided that if he was unable to lead the next pitch, then that was it. I'd led every pitch so far (didn't you want to?) and it was unthinkable that I'd lead all of them. Not bloody likely. I'd make that clear. I tortoised out. What are you smiling at? Rather him than me. I've had about bloody five minutes bloody sleep. 'Right, coming.'

It was strange to be there, sitting up in the hammock, feet stirring in the air over the side, opening the haul, fingers weaseling in the cold stuff bags, tramp-thankful for food in the hand. Eating quietly we heard the whipcrack of breaking ice in the gloomy cwm below and I'd yell 'hello' with a dervish fervour (wake up, Drummond, grow up, you can't go back). The echoes yodelled and I'd say to Hugh, 'He's there.'

'Who?' he'd ask.

'That bloke,' I'd tell him. 'Listen.' And I'd do it again and we'd both cackle like kids with a home-made phone.

By 7 am I was ready to belay him. I wasn't laughing now. One more pitch and there would be no retreat. I moled into the cold rope bag, my arms up to my elbows, fingers fiddling for the iron sling. I had a krab, empty, ready on the belay to receive it. My fingers curled in the sling; I moved my arm gracefully, slowly, (I was cold) to clip it into the krab before passing it up to him. If I drop the iron sling we'll have to go back down. From the end of my arm my little family of fingers waved at me. And it went, there, no, once, twice, there, oh, down, out, there, and under and into the heart of the icefield, clinking like lost money.

I couldn't believe it. Hugh was silent. I kept saying I was sorry. I didn't mean it. Not this time (How do you know?). I couldn't believe it. Hugh said nothing.

'I've done it now.'

Instantly, 'How long will it take you to get back up?'

He's got you now.

I got back by noon, gasping. I'd come down to earth. A 600ft abseil, my figure-of-eight sizzling my spits at it, and then a free jumar all the way back. I was furious. 'Right, belay on.'

His pitch was perfect after a bit. Dirty at first, then a cool, clean fist-lock crack. Iron out in the air like a bunch of weapons, he groped at the sky like something falling. All around a sea-sheer swell of wall, untouchable. Him the one sign of life.

Then the rain came. A dot in the eye. I heave for my cagoule, one eye on Hugh, an invisible drizzle blackening the rock. New noises fizz in. Twitters of water and Hugh is yelling for his cagoule, but I point out the time and that he's leaking already. Well, for a couple of hours I kept pushing boiled sweets in my mouth and Hugh kept on moaning and kept on. After 150ft he had to stop and pin himself to the wall.

Early evening. There he hung, wringing himself like fresh washing. Thank God he had no cagoule, or we would both have been up there for the night, him perched above, if not on, my head like a great wet heron. The waterfalls would weep all night. 'Why wait for Godot' I yelled up. He said, 'Eh?' so I said, 'Come on down, let's piss off.'

We stripped the ropes off the hauls, tied the lot together and down we went, happy as nuns in a car. A slalom down the scree and back before dark. Back in the camp hut we listened with Lindy, gladly, to the rain hissing outside while we kissed at a smug mug of tea and drooled on the food to come. That night I slept like a child.

Eight days later, well pickled, we humped up the boulderfields in epileptic sunshowers, snagged at by cold-cutting winds. The days were getting shorter.

The bergschrund had rotted back and we had to go down inside the mouth. Our ropes were twenty feet up the slabs, strung taut to a peg. I manteled up on this mica jug, massaging off the dust, feeling sick with this white pit under me, thirty feet deep, rocks in its dark, lurking.

When I had the end of the rope I dangled a bong on and looped it to him. Three times I threw and three times I missed; each time the bong tolled dolefully. 'Hey, our funeral knell,' I yelled, but he wasn't impressed.

Two and half jumehours later Hugh brooded on the haul eggs, sucking the sacred sweet, as I botched up the freeasy and awkwaid of the next pitch. When I warbled down about the ledge I'd found, he said he'd kiss me, but on arrival he didn't hold me to the treat. In fact, the first thing that he said was that the next pitch looked a bit steep for him and ordered me to do it. But since it was dark I could wait until tomorrow. Under the tube-tent, scarfed in cigar smoke, we crept to sleep like refugees.

Pitch 7 took me all the next day. It is 156ft long; our ropes were 150ft long, at a stretch. That last six feet to the belay cracks saw me lying flat on my face on the ledge, hammering like front-crawling. Hugh climbed up from his end, pulling the haul bags (one at a time, and there were three, each weighing over fifty pounds) onto his shoulder and then weightlifting them up so that I could get them through the pulley. Hugh studied Law at university.

So. Three nights. Almost 1000ft. Lucky's Ledge is no longer important. A stab of butter, a jab of honey; the pumpernickel crumbling among your fingers, a steamy censer of tea, packing your bags, hurrying as a jostle of cumulus smudges out the sun and the stove starts to fizz the drizzle.

As I remember we made three pitches that day in a rain as insidious as gas. For two or three seconds, suddenly the valley would come like an answer, and we would stumble into conversation, then numb up, sullen with wet clothes and cold, clubbed feet. In the downpouring darkness I jumed up to Hugh, squatting on blocks, owl aloof. While he belayed me I hand-traversed down to a ledge on his left, where I backheeled and rubbled away for over half an hour, making the bed. We couldn't find pin placements for the tube tent, so we hung our bivi bags from the rope and crept into their red, wet dark.

Sneaking out the next day at noon like shell-less tortoises, I realised as we both emptied a gallon of fresh water from our bags, that it might be better to have the opening at the front rather than at the top of the bag. A point that had escaped me as I tried out the bag on the floor in front of the fire at home. Sneer not. Wasn't the first Whillans Box a plastic mac and a pram? The Drummond Cot would have its night in time. Well, we strung the tube tent as an awning, lit the stove, and wrung our pulpy feet out, sitting in the cloud, machine-gunned by water drops from the great roofs that crashed out over 200ft wide, a thousand feet above our heads. We wriggled a little in the tent, slowly gulping lumpy salami, a bit stunned, stuttering with cold.

At about four we took the hood off our heads and saw the valley for the first time in twenty hours: the curve of the railway line, the thin black line of the road, pastures of grass, the glitter of the river, the big stacks of corn like yellow firs. The red tractor a slow blood drop. Then we heard yells, names, my name, and saw a spot of orange jump at the toe of the scree. It was Lindy calling, calling, and I called for my favourite team: 'LindyLindy LindyLindy,' and the wall called with me. Hugh even asked if I was going out that night.

Morning. The fifth day. Cornflower blue skies, fiord-cold in the shade, and above us brooded a huge wing of white granite, its edge a thin black slab about as long and steep as the spire of Salisbury Cathedral. I had seen this from the scree. We go that way.

Two skyhooks raised me off the rubble, and dash, wobbling, for ten feet without protection – a necessary enema after the thirty-hour sit-in. Then I'm staring at a poor flare where I belt a nut. Little chains of sweat trickle down my back. I'm struggling to free climb and Hugh's not even looking. Jerkily I struggle to a ledge, not a word of wonder escaping his lips as I braille for holds and shake onto this ledge with a flurry of boots. With time against us I was doing all the leading. Hugh sat still on his stone throne while I squirmed about, greasing my palms with myself. Still, a cat may look, and he was the one rock, the one unshakeable, all the way there and back.

Abseiling down in the dying day, the bergschrund breaking its wave beneath my feet 1500ft below in the cold ammonia air, the tube tent was a rush of bright flesh, raw on the ledge, and Hugh, his back bent, peering, was a black bird feeding at it. After a soup supper, watched by the smouldery eye of Hugh's cigar, I blew my harmonica, and brought tears of laughter to our eyes. We were doing okay. Hugh even said he liked to hear me play.

Two days later we were barely 300ft higher, and what I could see was not pretty. It looked as though, during the night, someone had pumped Hugh's foot up. His skin transparent as tracing paper, the foot was a mallet of flesh, the toes tiny buds; thalidomide. I didn't want to say too much. Perhaps the strain of his jumaring had done it, or the rotting wet when we were at Lucky's taking the waters. It was early yet; we had a long way to go. He said he just needed to rest it.

The ledge was lovely and I was glad to linger there. We spread ourselves around, Hugh blowing gently on his foot while I had a bath. A snip of cotton for a flannel, line for a towel, and a nip of antiseptic to give my spit a bit of bite. With behindsight I don't recommend the antiseptic neat, my dears. Let me tell you it wasn't a red face I had. The funny thing was it didn't hurt at the time I dabbed it, lovingly, my back turned while I blinked over the drop; but the day after, well, as they say, there hangs a tale.

A week later, his feet out like two heady cheeses in the dim pink light of the tent, Hugh has the mirror. He's checking on the stranger – the first time in twelve days, squeezing his pimples, humming some Neil Young song. For four days we've been in and out of this womb tube, harassed each time we go outside by the web of stuff bags breeding at the hole end. They are our other stomachs. We feel in them for our pots, our pottage, and our porter (although the porter is water since we've finished the orange). Cosmetics ended, we turn to draughts, drawing a board on the white insulating pad and inventing a set of signs for pieces and moves. So we pass an hour; doze, shift, fidget, sleep, talk, warn, fart, groan or cackle, plan, doze, and watch the light dissolve like a dye in the darkness. Snuggled together we are pre-eminently grateful that there is another here at the end of the day. We don't talk about failing and I hardly think about it now we've been here so long it's a way of life. The pendulum's done now and the only sign I'm waiting for is a weather one. The valley in my mind is out of sight.

In raggy mists we moved quickly, leaving our hauls on the bivouac ledge. Hugh, some deflated astronaut, swam slowly up on jumars as though someone had taken the gravity away. Breezes whiffed up my cuffs and my icy cagoule etherised the back of my neck. After those two pitches I frog-legged left, my numb hands bungling on the flat holds, to reach a little ledge from where I would go down to pendulum. After each pitch I was getting a bit desperate with the cold and I'd can-can to keep warm. Hugh, only forty feet away, was a white ghastly shadow.

Below us, Norway was at war. A volcanic pit of bursting water; the cwm boomed, a vat of slashed air. Stones howled around us and avalanching crashes trembled the wall. And me. Nothing could be seen in the gassing mist. No pendulum today.

Going back to our home, Hugh passed out into the cloud first, using the haul lines as a back rope to the bivouac ledge, which would otherwise had been impossible to return to because of the overhanging wall. When I got down he'd a brew ready which lit a fire, briefly, inside me. My thanks that it wasn't snowing just about made it.

During the night it snowed.

In the morning it was still falling, so we rolled over; better sleep on it. In the fitful sleep of that day I had my dream! The editor of *Mountain* had arrived at the foot of the scree and, with a foghorn or some kind of voice, had managed to wake me, telling me that he had come all the way from

England to let me know what a great job I was doing for British rock-climbing (he never mentioned Hugh), and also how we were, contributing to better Anglo-Norwegian political relations.

By the time I awoke he was gone but Hugh hadn't; he was just vanishing down the hole at the other end. My watch told 4am – the night had gone. I oozed out of my pit to find lard-pale Hugh with the blue black foot, sitting stinking in a skinful of sun. For half an hour we wallowed, exposing ourselves to the warm air. New creatures we were, able, if not to fly, at least to jumar, up there. And up there, today, I had to swing for it.

I try, flying, at thirty feet below Hugh, then fifty feet, then eighty feet, then at over 100ft and I'm a bit too low so I jume up to about ninety-five. 'Ed Leadlegs,' I tell him but only the wind hears me. I'm getting a bit tired; Hugh has given up asking me how I'm doing and he is just hanging, staring, his pipe alight – the wind brings a tang of it to me. No doubt he's thinking of his girl in Mexico.

The white wall is so steep here that I can barely keep hold of it when I crab myself right for the big swing. But my first swings wing me out into space away from the wall and I have to pirouette to miss smashing my back. This is ridiculous. Like a spider at puberty I toil but spin not. It's after 2pm, Lindy will be here soon.

When I've fingernailed back as far right as I can (and this time I manage about four feet more) I'm nearly eighty feet away from the groove that I'm trying to reach.

I'm off, the white rushing past; out, out, away from the wall, way past the groove, out – I tread air, the valley at my feet. Hugh moons down, he's yelling something – can't hear a word he's saying – rushing, coming back, crashing in, wall falling on top of me, I kick, jab, bounce my boot, bounce out, floating, an easy trapeze. Then the unknown groove is running into my open arms and I strike at a flake and stick. Fingers leeching its crack.

I hung a nut in (my jumars attaching me to the rope are pulling me up), then I get an et. and stand in it. The nut stays put. Jumars down. Now put a knife under that block. The press of the block keeps it in as I weigh in on it. Out flips the nut. Whoops. I know I'm going to get there. I can't see Hugh but I know he's there. A tiny nut like a coin in a slot. Watch me. The knifeblade tinkles out. Thank you. The nut gleams a gold tooth at me. There you go. To climb is to know the universe is All Right. Then I clink a good pin in at a stretch. Can't get the nut now (it's still there). And then I'm in the groove, appalled at the sheer, clean walls around and below me, baying for breath, my heart chopping through my chest.

We have lost 100ft, but gained a narrow track of cracks that will, I believe, lead to the 'Arch Roof', the huge, square-cut overhang that from the valley looks like an old press photo of the Loch Ness Monster. I saw a crack in 1970 through binoculars going out through the top of his head. 'Loch Ness Monster sighted on Troll Wall.' I'd out-yeti Whillans yet. Just before dark Hugh lands and goes on ahead to order dinner; we're eating out at the Traveller's Tube tonight, a farewell meal. The pendulum being done, our time was going and so must we.

But it snowed for two days.

On the thirteenth day the sun rubbed shoulders with us again, and Hugh jumared up at a snail sprint. He found that the yellow perlon he was on had rubbed through to half its core, so he tied that out with an overhand before I came up at a slow rush. Halfway up I worked loose a huge detached flake which had hung 100ft above our tent; it took me five minutes so we had no need to worry. We watch it bounce, bomb-bursting down to the cwm, and the walls applaud.

The crack above the pendulum's end was a nice smile for standard angles except where a ladder of loose flakes is propped. Bloody visions slump at the belay below me. Silence. Care. The hauls zoom out well clear.

The next two pitches, up a bulging, near-blind groove, were ecstasy. I had to free climb. The hooks were only for luck, and I was quick in the blue fields. Above, suddenly, two swifts flashed past, thuds of white. 'That's us,' I yelled to myself. Lindy may not have been here, but there she was. I could hear her, naming my name, and I flew slowly up. Four fine patches of ledgeless pleasure that day. In the dark Hugh jumared up to the Arch, me guiding his feet with my head torch.

But that night the sky shone no stars. Packs of black cloud massed. Not enough food to eat. A sweet or two. No cigar. And too late to fish for hammocks. All night, four hours, I squirmed in my seat sling. I speculated on recommending to the makers that they rename it the Iron Maiden, but it was too suitable an epitaph to laugh about. My hip is still numb from damaged nerves.

Came the morning I was thrashed. The sun did not exist. The roof over my head was a weight on my mind. Suddenly, over Vengetind the weather mountain, clouds boiled, whipping and exploding in avalanching chaos. Over Lillejfel, a low shoulder on the other side of the valley cauldron, a dinosaur mass of white cloud was rat-arrowing toward us. We could hardly run away; we were so cold and hungry we could hardly move.

I was scared as I moved out under the Arch, a clown without props, all these things were real, there were no nets here, only dear patient Hugh blowing on his fingers.

No man walks on air was all my thought as I melted out of sight, upside down for forty feet, my haul line dissolving in the mist. I couldn't feel that

I was connected to anything solid. Fly sized, I mimed away under three giant inverted steps, lips. Not a single foothold, not a toehold in a hundred feet. Just over the final lip, in a single strand of crack, I pinned myself to a wall of water and started to land the hauls.

They must have seen me coming. I couldn't believe it. Raindrops ripped into me, making me wince. The cold rose an octave, catapulting hail into my face. The wind thrummed a hundred longbow cords. I could hardly see through my chinese eyes. Only while I hauled could I stop shaking. My fingers, cut deeply at the tips, were almost helpless. People at upstairs windows watching a road accident in the street below. My feet were dying. My silent white hands.

Hugh came up for air, grinning. He'd had no idea down there. Up here he had the thing itself. Murdering, washing out more than ears. I led off, hardly knowing where, except that we couldn't stay there. I could only just open my karabiners with two hands. Sleet had settled thickly on the bunches of tie-offs. Both of us were really worried. Hugh cried up after an hour that he was getting frostbite. What could I say? I had to find a place for the night.

If you ever go there and have it the way we did, you'll know why we called it 'The Altar'. I remember the rush in the drowning dark to hang the tent, the moss churning to slush beneath our feet. Back to back, our backs to the wall, we slumped on three feet of ledge for three days. We had nothing to drink for the first two of those days; our haul bags were jammed below us and we were diseased with fatigue. Lice trickles of wet get everywhere.

I remember Hugh drinking the brown water that had collected in his boots, instantly vomiting it out, and me silently mouthing the gluey water from my helmet. You didn't miss much. Hugh. He shared his food with me, some cheese and dates and a bag of sweets; rare fruits. After a day he had to piss and used quadrupled poly bags which I politely declined to use; I had no need. A day later my proud bladder was bursting. But sitting, propped in a wet bed of underwear, I was impotent. For over two hours I strained and grunted in scholastic passion. Hugh said it was trench penis. A sort of success went to my head, however, or rather onto and into my sleeping bag. After that I felt like some great baby, trapped in his wet cot, the air sickly with urine, and sleep would not come.

To get more room, both of us, we later confessed when there were witnesses present, developed strategies of delay while we shuffled the status quo. 'Could you sit forward a minute?' or, 'Would you hold this for me?' At times I'd get Hugh to tuck my insulating pads around me to bluff off the cold stone. It was deeply satisfying to have someone do that. Grizzly, bristly Hugh: what a mother.

We wondered if this could continue for more than a week. But we didn't wonder what would happen if it did. We never talked about not finishing. (We were just over 1000ft below the summit.) It was no longer a new route to us. It was not possible to consider anything else as real. There were no echoes from the valley. There was no valley. There was no one to call your name. No wall now; unhappy little solipsists, all we had was each other.

We began to get ratty, like children locked in a bedroom. An elbow scuffled against a back once or twice as we humped back to stop the slow slide off the ledge. A ton of silence rested on us like a public monument, for hours on end. I felt that this was all sterile. I ate food, wore out my clothes, used up my warmth, but earned nothing, made nothing. The art was chrysalising into artifice. A grubby routine. Trying not to die. Millions have the disease and know it not. My sleep a continual dream of hammering: banging in pins, clipping in, moving up, then back down, banging, banging, taking them out. A bit like having fleas. Searching for an ultimate belay. Unable to stop: the Holy Nail. My Dad, my dad, why hast thou forsaken me? At times I was pretty far gone.

But it wasn't all self-pity. We talked about the plight of the Trolls and could clearly see a long bony hairy arm poking under the tent, handing us a steaming pan of hot troll tea, and although nothing appeared in our anaesthetic dark, the idea lit a brief candle.

Three days later we were released.

Lindy yelled us out. A giant marigold sun beamed at us. Everywhere up here – and we could see hundreds of miles – was white, perfect, appalling. Across the river I could clearly make out scores of tourists, a distant litter of colour in one of the camping fields opposite the wall. Cars flashed their headlamps and horns bugled as we struggled into view and flagged them with our tent.

Then, quickly, the charging roar of an avalanche. I flattened to the wall. And then I spotted it, a helicopter, gunning in a stone's throw from the wall, a military green with yellow emblems. A gun poked from the window. 'Hugh, they're going to shoot us,' then, tearing his head up he saw it: an arm waving. We waved arms, heads, legs; danced, jigged, yelled, while they circled in and away like something from another world. Later we learned that it was Norwegian television, but we fluttered no blushes on the wall. The spell of our selves was broken.

Five hours later, after a long lovely 130ft of aid, intricate and out in space, I was on the final summit walls, the last roofs wiped with light, 700ft above me.

All that night, while a white moon sailed over our shoulders, we perched on our haul bags and cut off the blood to our already damaged feet, too exhausted to know. Sharing our last cigar while the nerves in our feet were suffocating to death, we shone in our hunger and smiled a while.

As soon as I put my weight on my foot in the new dawn I knew I'd had it. Hugh's foot was an unspeakable image, and I had to tell him when his heel was grounded inside his boot. He could hardly have his laces tied at all and I was terrified that one of his boots might drop off.

All that day the feeling was of having my boots being filled with boiling water that would trickle in between my toes and flood my soles. Then a sensation of shards of glass being wriggled into the balls of my feet. And upon each of my feet a dentist was at work, pulling my nails and slowly filing my toes. Then nothing but a rat-tatting heart when I stopped climbing. I would tremble like water in a faint breeze. I knew it was hypothermia. We had had no food for three days. Maybe it was two.

All the last day we called, a little hysterically I think, for someone on the summit; they were coming to meet us. Sitting fifteen feet below the top, with Hugh whimpering up on jumars I heard whispers... 'Keep quiet... wait until he comes over the top'.

There was no one there. Only, thank God, the sun. It seemed right in a way to meet only each other there. At the summit cairn Hugh sucked on his pipe while my tongue nippled at a crushed sweet that he had found in his pocket. We dozed warm as new cakes, in a high white world, above impenetrable clouds which had shut out the valley all day. We were terribly glad to be there. After midnight we collapsed into a coma of sleep, half a mile down in the boulder-field.

We met them the next morning, quite near the road; it must have been about half-past eight. They were coming up to meet us. Lindy flew up the hill to hug me forever. I was Odysseus, with a small o, I was Ed, come back for the first time. Hugh grinned in his pain when I told the Norwegian journalists that his real name was Peer Gynt, and that he was an artist like Van Gogh, but that he had given a foot for the wall, instead of an ear to his girl.

On our last hobble, he had, before we met the others, found himself dreaming of the walks he used to have with his Dad, as a child, into the park to feed the ducks, and of the delights of playing marbles (we were both pocketing stones and rare bits from the summit on down). When we arrived in Andalsnes with our friends, I saw the apples burning on the boughs, glowy drops of gold and red (the green gargoyle buds, the little knuckle apples had lit while we were gone); and the postbox in its red skirt shouted to me as we turned the corner into town. Bodil washed Hugh's feet, sent for her doctor, and everyone in our house was alive and well. Only the Troll

Wall gave me black looks, over the hill and far away at last. Black iceberg under eye-blue skies.

Back in England my feet were as irrefutable as war wounds. I was on my back for a month, and I had the cuttings from the Norwegian press, as precious as visas. But nowhere to get to.

from ASCENT *1973*

ANDERSON

'THIS NEW GUY IS REALLY FOULING UP OUR
CLASSIFICATION SYSTEM!'

PART 1

THE WORLD OF THE ROCK CLIMBER

One of the dominant themes in all the activities that comprise mountaineering has been the surge in the popularity of rock-climbing. This trend has been particularly marked in the last decade and for an increasing number of climbers, the pursuit of excellence in the art of free-climbing on very hard rock has become the main objective of their climbing ambitions. Despite this, the schism that has so often been predicted between the rock-climber and the mountaineer has not really developed as each discipline still has so many common participants.

Nevertheless rock-climbing now enjoys a prominence in the sport that is unchallenged, at least in the English-speaking part of the climbing world. It is natural, therefore, that the first, and major section of this book should be devoted to the writings of the rock-climber. The following essays should demonstrate that he is no less able than the great mountaineer/writers of the past in committing the drama and interest of his experiences to paper.

Note for 2006: In 1978 the British interest in American big-wall climbing was at a high level. The Americans in turn had (following visits to Britain by Robbins, Chouinard, Barber, Bridwell, Donini, Wunsch and Erikson) adopted British nut protection techniques which Chouinard and Frost adapted and improved. This in turn threw the American focus back from aiding big walls to smaller scale free climbing. The stage was being set for the explosion of free climbing on the big walls that was to follow in the 1980s and 90s in which the arrival of Friends (designed by Ray Jardine and manufactured by Mark Vallance) also played a key role.

At this time John Gill had championed an intense interest in bouldering in the United States that went beyond similar practices at Fontainebleau and locations in Britain. Gill's single-minded concentration tended to isolate bouldering as an activity on its own. In this respect the articles of Bernard Amy and John Long will seem very prescient to today's bouldering aficionados.

THE BAT AND THE WICKED

ROBIN SMITH

You got to go with the times. I went by the Halfway Lochan over the shoulder of Ben Nevis and I got to the Hut about two in the morning. Dick was there before me; we had to talk in whispers because old men were sleeping in the other beds. Next day we went up Sassenach and Centurion to spy on the little secrets hidden between them. We came down in the dark, and so next day it was so late before we were back on the hill that the big heat of our wicked scheme was fizzling away.

Càrn Dearg Buttress sits like a black haystack split up the front by two great lines. Centurion rises straight up the middle, 500ft in a vast corner running out into slabs and over the traverse of Route II and 200ft threading the roofs above. Sassenach is close to the clean-cut right edge of the cliff, 200ft through a barrier of overhangs, 200ft in an overhanging chimney and 500ft in a wide broken slowly easing corner. At the bottom a great dripping overhang leans out over the 100ft of intervening ground. Above this, tiers of overlapping shelves like armour plating sweep out of the corner of Centurion diagonally up to the right to peter out against the monstrous bulge of the wall on the left of the Sassenach chimney. And hung in the middle of this bulging wall is the Corner, cutting through 100ft of the bulge. Dick and I lay and swithered on a flat stone. We wanted to find a way out of Centurion over the shelves and over the bulge into the Corner and up the Corner and straight on by a line of grooves running all the way over the top of the Buttress, only now it was after two in the afternoon.

But we thought we ought just to have a look, so we climbed the first pitch of Centurion, fifty feet to a ledge on the left. The first twisted shelf on the right was not at all for us, so we followed the corner a little farther and broke out rightwards over a slab on a wandering line of holds, and as the slab heeled over into the overlap below, a break in the overlap above led to the start of a higher shelf and we followed this till it tapered away to a jammed block poking into the monstrous bulge above. For a little while Dick had a theory that he felt unlike leading, but I put on all the running belays just before the hard bits so that he was in for the bigger swing away down over the bottom dripping overhang. We were so frightened that we shattered ourselves fiddling pebbles and jamming knots for runners. We swung down backwards in to an overlap and down to the right to a lower shelf and followed it over a fiendish step to crouch on a tiny triangular slab tucked under the bulge, and here we could just unfold enough to reach into a V-groove, cutting through the bottom of the bulge and letting us out on a slab on the right just left of the Sassenach chimney.

And so we had found a way over the shelves, but only to go into orbit round the bulging wall with still about forty feet of bulge between us and the bottom of the Corner now up on the left. The way to go was very plain to see, a crooked·little lichenous overhanging groove looking as happy as a hoodie crow. But it looked as though it was getting late and all the belays we could see were very lousy and we might get up the groove and then have to abseil and underneath were 200ft of overhangs and anyway we would be back in the morning. We could just see the top of the Corner leering down at us over the bulge as we slunk round the edge on the right to the foot of the Sassenach chimney. A great old-fashioned battle with fearful constrictions and rattling chockstones brought us out of the chimney into night, and from there we groped our way on our memory of the day before, leading through in 150ft run-outs and looking for belays and failing to find them and tying on to lumps of grass and little stones lying on the ledges. When we came over the top we made away to the left and down the bed of Number Five Gully to find the door of the Hut in the wee small hours.

We woke in the afternoon to the whine of the Death Wind fleeing down the Allt a' Mhuillin. Fingery mists were creeping in at the five windows. Great grey spirals of rain were boring into the Buttress. We stuck our hands in our pockets and our heads between our shoulders and stomped off down the path under our rucksacks into the bright lights of the big city.

Well the summer went away and we all went to the Alps. (Dick had gone and failed his exams and was living in a hole until the re-sits, he was scrubbed.) The rest of the boys were extradited earlier than I was, sweeping north from the Channel with a pause in Wales in the Llanberis Pass at a daily rate of four apiece of climbs that Englishmen call XS (X is a variable, from exceptionally or extremely through very or hardily to merely or mildly severe). From there they never stopped until they came to Fort William, but the big black Ben was sitting in the clouds in the huff and bucketing rain and the rocks never dried until their holidays ended and I came home and only students and wasters were left on the hill.

Well I was the only climber Dougal could find and the only climber I could find was Dougal, so we swallowed a very mutual aversion to gain the greater end of a sort of start over the rest of the field. Even so we had little time for the Ben. We could no more go for a weekend than anyone else, for as from the time that a fellow Cunningham showed us the rules we were drawn like iron filings to Jacksonville in the shadow of the Buachaille for the big-time inter-city pontoon school of a Saturday night. And then we had no transport and Dougal was living on the dole, and so to my disgust he would leave me on a Wednesday to hitch-hike back to Edinburgh in time to pick up his moneys on a Thursday. The first time we went away we had a bad Saturday night, we were late getting out on the Buachaille on Sunday and came down in the dark in a bit of rain. But the rain came to nothing, so we made our way to the Fort on Monday thinking of climbing to the Hut for the night; only there was something great showing at the pictures and then we went for chip suppers and then there were the birds and the juke-box and the slot machines and we ended up in a back-garden shed. But on Tuesday we got up in the morning, and since Dougal was going home next day we took nothing for the Hut, just our climbing gear like a bundle of stings and made a beeline for Càrn Dearg Buttress.

This time we went over the shelves no bother at all, until we stood looking into the little green hoodie groove. It ran into a roof and from under the roof we would have to get out on the left on to what looked as though it might be a slab crossing to the bottom of the Corner. I was scheming to myself, now the groove will be terrible but nothing to the Corner and I will surely have to lead the crux, but Dougal shamed me with indifference and sent me round the edge on the right to find a decent belay under the Sassenach chimney. There it was very peaceful, I could see none of the tigering, only the red stripes down the side of Càrn Mòr Dearg running into the Allt a' Mhuillin that was putting me to sleep if there hadn't been odd faint snarls and scrabblings and little bits of rope once in a while tugging around the small of my back. But once Dougal was up he took in so much slack that I had to go and follow it myself. Half-way up he told me, you lean away out and loop a sling over the tip of a spike and do a can-can move to get a foot in the sling and reach for the sling with both hands as you lurch out of the groove and when you stop swinging climb up the sling until you can step back into the groove; and his sling had rolled off the spike as he left it, so I would have to put it on again. I came out at the top of the groove in a row of convulsions, which multiplied like Asdic as I took in the new perspective.

Dougal was belayed to pitons on the slab under the Corner. The slab and the left retaining wall went tapering down for twenty feet till they merged and all heeled over into the general bulge. Above, the Corner balanced over Dougal like a blank open book with a rubber under the binding. The only big break in the bareness of the walls was a clean-cut black roof barring the width of the right wall. The crack went into the right wall, about six inches wide but tightly packed with bits of filling; and thus it rose in two leaps, thirty-five feet to the black roof, then out four horizontal feet and straight up thirty-five feet again; and then it widened for the last thirty feet as the right wall came swelling out in a bulge to meet the top of the great arc of the sky-line edge of the left wall. And if we could only get there then all the climb would surely be in the bag.

Well I had stolen the lead, only some time before I had been to a place called Harrison's Rocks and some or other fellow out of London had made off with my PAS. Now PAS are the Achilles' Heel of all the new men, they buckle your feet into claws and turn you into a tiger, but here I had only a flabby pair of *kletterschuhe* with nails sticking out on both sides of the soles, and so I worked on Dougal to change footwear at which he was not pleased because we stood on a steep slab with one little ledge for feet and a vision before us of retreating in our socks. We had two full-weight ropes. Dougal had one rope that was old before its time, it had once been 120ft long but it lost five feet during an experiment on the Currie Railway Walls. (This last word to sound like 'Woz'.) A Glaswegian who was a friend had one day loaned us the other, and so it was even older, and he mentioned that it had been stretched a little, indeed it was 130ft long, and so Dougal at the bottom had quickly tied on to an end of each rope which left me with fifteen feet on the one to get rid of round and round my middle to make the two ropes even. This was confusing, since I had a good dozen slings and karabiners round my neck and two bunches of pitons like bananas at my waist and a wooden wedge and a piton hammer swinging about and three or four spare karabiners and a big sling knotted into steps.

But I could still get my hands to the rocks, and I made slow progress as far as the black roof. I left about six feeble running belays on the way, mainly so that I would be able to breathe. And as there seemed little chance of runners above and little value in those below and nowhere to stand just under the roof and next to no chance of moving up for a while, I took a fat channel peg and drove it to the hilt into the corner crack as high under the roof as I could and fixed it as a runner and hung the knotted sling from it and stood with my right foot in the sling. Thus with my hands in the crack where it came out horizontally under the roof, I could plant my left foot fictitiously away out on the left wall and peer round over the roof into the Corner above. Deep dismay. The crack looked very useless and the walls utterly bare and I shrunk under the roof into the sling. Shortly I leaned away out again to ponder a certain move and a little twist and then something else to get me ten feet up, but what would I do then, and then the pre-pondering angle sent me scuttling back like a crab into shelter. In a while I got a grip and left the sling and heaved up half-way round the roof and sent a hand up the Corner exploring for a hold, but I thought, no no there is nothing at all, and I came down scarting with a foot under the roof feverishly fishing for the sling. And there I hung like a brooding ape, maybe there's a runner ten-foot up or a secret keyhole for the fingers, but how are you ever to know for sitting primevally here, so for shame now where's your boldness, see how good your piton is, and what's in a peel, think of the Club, think of the glory, be a devil. I found a notch under the roof in which to jam the knot of a sling which made another runner, and I tried going up a few more times like a ball stopping bouncing until I realised I was going nowhere and trying nothing at all. So I jacked it in and left all the runners for Dougal and Dougal let out slack and I dribbled down to join him on the slab.

Here I sat a while and blew, then I took my coat of mail and put it on Dougal and Dougal wanted his PAs back and we untied to swop our end of rope so that Dougal could use my runners and I tied myself on to the stance while Dougal rotated into the tail end of the longer rope and the time went by. But Dougal caught it up a little by rushing up to the black roof while I pulleyed in the slack. And here we had a plan. Just above the lip of the roof, the crack opened into a pocket about an inch and a quarter wide. There should have been a chockstone in it, only there was not, and we could find none the right size to insert. If there had been trees on the Ben the way there are in Wales there would have been a tree growing out of the pocket, or at least down at the stance or close to hand so that we could have lopped off a branch and stuck it in the pocket. But here we had a wooden wedge tapering just to the right size and surely it once grew in a tree and so maybe it would not be very artificial to see if it could be made to stick in the pocket. Blows of the hammer did this thing, and Dougal clipped in a karabiner and threaded a sling and the two ropes and pulled up to stand in the sling so that he could reach well over the roof and look about at ease. And sure enough he could see a winking ledge, about twenty-five-foot up on the right wall.

Now Dougal is a bit thick and very bold, he never stopped to think, he put bits of left arm and leg in the crack and the rest of him over the right wall and beat the rock ferociously and moved in staccato shuffles out of the sling and up the Corner. I shifted uneasily upon my slab which tapered into the overhangs, making eyes at my two little piton belays. As Dougal neared his ledge he was slowing down but flailing all the more, left fingers clawing at grass in the crack and right leg scything moss on the wall. I pulled down the sleeves of my jersey over my hands and took a great grip of the ropes. Then there came a sort of squawk as Dougal found that his ledge was not. He got a hand on it but it all sloped. Rattling sounds came from his throat or nails or something. In his last throes to bridge he threw his right foot at a straw away out on the right wall. Then his fingers went to butter. It began under control as the bit of news 'I'm off,' but it must have been caught in the wind, for it grew like a wailing siren to a bloodcurdling scream as a black and bat-like shape came hurtling over the roof with legs splayed like webbed wings and hands hooked like a vampire. I flattened my ears and curled up rigid into a bristling ball, then I was lifted off my slab and rose five feet in the air until we met head to foot and buffered to a stop hanging from the runners at the roof. I could have sworn that his teeth were fangs and his eyes were big red orbs. We lowered ourselves to the slab, and there we sat in a swound while the shadows grew.

But indeed it was getting very late, and so I being a little less shattered heaved up on the ropes to retrieve the gear, leaving the wedge and the piton at the roof. We fixed a sling to one of the belay pitons and abseiled down the groove below with tails between our legs and a swing at the bottom to take us round to the foot of the Sassenach chimney. By now it was dusk and we thought it would be chaos in the chimney and just below it was very over-hanging, but I knew a traversing line above the great roof of Sassenach leading to the clean-cut right edge of the cliff. My *kletterschuhe* kept slipping about and I was climbing like a stiff and I put in two or three tips of pitons for psychological runners before I made the fifty feet of progress to peer around the edge. But it looked a good 200ft to the shadowy screes at the bottom, and I scuffled back in half a panic out of the frying pan into the chimney. Then two English voices that were living in a tent came up the hill to ask if we were worried. We said we were laughing but what was the time, and they said it would soon be the middle of the night, and when we thought about the 700ft of Sassenach above and all the shambles round the side to get to our big boots sitting at the bottom of the cliff, we thought we would just slide to the end of the rope.

So I went back to the edge and round the right angle and down a bit of the wall on the far side to a ledge and a fat crack for a piton. By the time Dougal joined me we could only see a few dismal stars and sky-lines and a light in the English tent. Dougal vanished down a single rope while I belayed him on the other, and just as the belaying rope ran out I heard a long squelch and murky oaths. He seemed to be down and so I followed. Suddenly my feet shot away and I swung in under the great roof and spiralled down till I landed up to my knees in a black bog. We found our boots under Centurion and made off down the hill past the English tent to tell them we were living. When we hit the streets we followed our noses straight to our sleeping bags in the shed, leaving the city night, life alone.

The next Sunday we left a lot of enemies in Jacksonville and took a lift with the Mountain Rescue round to Fort William. They were saying they might be back to take us away as well. We had thick wads of notes but nothing to eat, and so we had to wait in the city to buy stores on Monday, and we got to the Hut so late that we thought we would house our energies to give us the chance of an early start in the morning. Even so we might have slept right through Tuesday but for the din of a mighty file of pilgrims winding up the Allt a' Mhuillin making for Ben Nevis. We stumbled out, rubbing our eyes and stood looking evil in the doorway, so that nobody called in, and then we ate and went out late in the day to the big black Buttress.

This time we went over the shelves and up the hoodie groove no bother at all. It was my turn to go into the Corner. By now I had a pair of PAs. I climbed to the black roof and made three runners with a jammed knot, the piton and the wooden wedge and stood in a sling clipped to the wedge. Dougal's ledge was fluttering above but it fooled nobody now. At full stretch I could reach two pebbles sitting in a thin bit of the crack and pinched them together to jam. Then I felt a lurch in my stomach like flying through an air pocket. When I looked at the wedge I could have sworn it had moved. I seized a baby nylon sling and desperately threaded it round the pebbles. And then I was gracefully plucked from the rock to stop twenty feet under the roof hanging from the piton and the jammed knot with the traitor wedge hanging from me and a sling round the pebbles sticking out of the Corner far above. I rushed back to the roof in a rage and made a strange manoeuvre to get round the roof and reach the sling and clip in a karabiner and various ropes, then trying not to think I hauled up to sit in slings which seemed like a table of kings all to come down from the same two pebbles. I moved on hastily, but I felt neither strong nor bold, and so I took a piton and hammered it into the Corner about twenty feet above the roof. Happily I pulled up, and it leaped out with a squeal of delight and gave me no time to squeal at all before I found myself swinging about under the miserable roof again. The pebbles had held firm, but that meant I hung straight down from the lip of the roof and out from the Corner below so that Dougal had to lower me right to the bottom.

By now the night was creeping in. Peels were no longer upsetting, but Dougal was fed up with sitting on a slab and wanted to go down for a brew. But that was all very well, he was going home in the morning, and then coming back for a whole week with a host of terrible tigers when I would have to be sitting exams. So I was very sly and said we had to get the gear and climbed past the roof to the sling at the pebbles leaving all the gear in place. There I was so exhausted that I put in a piton, only it was very low, and I thought, so am I, *peccavi, peccabo,* and I put in another and rose indiscriminately until to my surprise I was past Dougal's ledge and still on the rock in a place to rest beside a solid chockstone. Sweat was pouring out of me, frosting at my waist in the frozen mutterings flowing up the rope from Dougal. Overhead the right wall was swelling out like a bull-frog, but the cracks grew to a tight shallow chimney in which it was even blacker than the rest of the night. I squeezed in and pulled on a real hold, and a vast block slid down and sat on my head. Dougal tried to hide on his slab, I wobbled my head and the block rolled down my back, and then there was a deathly hush until it thundered on to the screes and made for the Hut like a fireball. I wriggled my last slings round chockstones and myself round the last of the bulges and I came out of the Corner fighting into the light of half a moon rising over the North-East Buttress. All around there were ledges and great good holds and bewildering easy angles, and I lashed myself to about six belays.

Dougal followed in the moonshade, in too great a hurry and too blinded and miserable to pass the time taking out the pitons, and so they are still there turning to rust, creeping up the cliff like poison ivy. Heated up by the time he passed me, Dougal went into a long groove out of the moon but not steep and brought me up to the left end of a terrace above the chimney of Sassenach. We could see the grooves we should have climbed in a long line above us, but only as thick black shadows against the shiny bulges, and so we went right and grovelled up in the final corner of Sassenach where I knew the way to go. The wall on the left kept sticking out and stealing all the moonlight, but we took our belays right out on the clean-cut right edge of the cliff so that we could squat in the moon and peer at the fabulous sights. When we came over the top we hobbled down the screes on the left to get out of our PAS into our boots and back to the Hut from as late a night as any, so late you could hardly call it a bed-night.

Some time next day Dougal beetled off and I slowly followed to face the examiners. The tigers all came for their week. On the first day Dougal and the elder Marshall climbed Sassenach until they were one pitch up from the Terrace above the chimney, and then they thought of going left and finished by the new line of grooves. Overnight the big black clouds rolled over and drummed out the summer and it rained all week and hardly stopped until it started to snow and we put away our PAs and went for hill-walks waiting for the winter. They say the grooves were very nice and not very hard. All that was needed to make a whole new climb was one pitch from the terrace above the chimney, until we decided that the way we had been leaving the terrace as from the time that Dick found it when we first climbed Sassenach was not really part of Sassenach at all. By this means we put an end to this unscrupulous first ascent. The next team will climb it all no bother at all, except that they will complain that they couldn't get their fingers into the holds filled up with pitons.

from THE SCOTTISH MOUNTAINEERING
CLUB JOURNAL *1960*

THE GREATEST CLIMBER
IN THE WORLD

BERNARD AMY
translated by Beverly Davitt

*He who has the greater virtue does not act and has no goal.
He who only has the lesser virtue acts and has a goal. Tao te ching*

Although no-one had ever really known his proper name, everyone called him Tronc Feuillu. It must have been something like Tron Fo Oyu, but his fellow countrymen pronounced the name too quickly for a European to grasp it properly.[1]

This surname, however, did not in any way describe his actual person. Tronc Feuillu was a long, thin man, with the face and hands of an ascetic. His head was shaved. From somewhere behind his flat eastern eyes came an expression which was at the same time severe, ironic and gentle. He was more like the trunk of one of those trees found in the Southern Hemisphere which, having survived the flames of a forest fire, seem to have acquired power over death.

Tronc Feuillu was a member of the Japanese delegation at the international gathering at ENSA. Although he was the most outstanding person in the team, he was not the leader. However, his companions spoke of him with a respect which his technical abilities alone did not entirely justify. When questioned, they seemed rather vague, and talked of 'supreme wisdom' and 'a technique beyond technique', which explained nothing. To those who would have liked to know more, Tronc Feuillu's companions replied: 'The facts will speak for themselves. You will have to wait to see how he does the route he has planned.'

'*The* route? Is he only going to do one?'

'Yes, definitely'.

Three days later, the weather became fine. The Japanese launched a direct attack on the North Face of Mont Rekwal, the highest route and without doubt the most difficult in the range. Led by Tronc Feuillu, they avoided the route known as The Clock by using a variation famous ever since. No-one

---

[1] 'Tronc Feuillu' in fact means 'Leafy Trunk', hence the refences to trees. Unfortunately, 'Leafy Trunk' does not sound anything like 'Tron Fo Oyu'. *Translator's note.*

has been able to follow it again. The most skilled European and American alpinists have attempted it, but not one has been able to cover more than the first thirty feet. Tronc Feuillu succeeded in climbing a smooth rock wall, 250ft high, where there was no ledge, nor even a crack wide enough for foot or hand. He did not use pitons, nor did he protect himself with running belays. He and his three companions – who appeared transfigured by their brilliant leader – climbed that long passage without hesitation, 'without any apparent effort, as if the passage in question were just a simple one', reported a British team tackling The Clock at the same time.

The event aroused much comment. First the British, and then the other climbers who had been on the face at the same time, enthused over the sureness and skill of the Japanese, and particularly over the mastery of Tronc Feuillu. The Japanese leader became *the* personality of Chamonix. But his admirers hardly had a chance to approach him. He fled from the public, with its noisy adulation. He countered all curiosity by displaying a total indifference towards image, publicity, notoriety, and ego-tripping. Thus, even though he had just completed a very important route, he displayed a calm detachment, a refusal to become prey to the mad frenzy which the slightest sign of a corner of blue sky above the Aiguilles inspired in others.

For he did not set out on another route. Not that he spent his time in Chamonix. The fine weather continued, and he was quite happy to disappear for the entire day, without anyone knowing whether he went off to climb on his own, or to stroll in the Alpine meadows. His companions completed other routes, three of which were first ascents of the highest order. Tronc Feuillu did not accompany them. Some alpinists were amazed at such disaffection. They even went so far as to suggest that a deep fear experienced on Mont Rekwal prevented him from making a further ascent. Although he must have known of this, he seemed completely disinterested. As for his compatriots, they insisted that Tronc Feuillu formed an integral part of their team. 'It is enough,' they said, 'that through his meditation he inspires our achievements.'

One rainy day when the Chamonix crowd was passing the time, impatiently, in cafes, Tronc Feuillu ventured out to the Drugstore. He was talking, discussing, looking surprisingly relaxed. No-one recognised in him the austere character of the past few days. Someone managed to question him about his extraordinary climb: 'How did you go about it? What were the difficulties? Was it possible to use pitons? How did you cover the first forty feet? Do you know that only one climber has since managed to cover that part and come back down it again?'

Tronc Feuillu allowed the questions to continue, and then replied: 'At the end of that section, I perceived on the top of Mont Rekwal one of the most beautiful snow-flake patterns that I have ever seen.'

His audience took this to be a witticism, all the more so since Tronc Feuillu himself broke into laughter. 'He doesn't like questions,' we said. 'He wished to send the other about his business. It was a fitting answer.' And there we left it.

Towards the middle of August, there was a period of fine weather. I was able to do some good routes. Then I returned to Chamonix to rest for a few days. One morning I watched the sun rise in a perfectly clear sky above Mont Blanc and the Aiguilles. The streets were almost deserted. Everyone was up in the mountains. Standing in the *Place de la Poste*, I tasted that moment, certain that a beautiful day was about to unfold. I was going to be able to enjoy it without any reservations, to abandon myself to idleness while still retaining on my fingertips the memory of the rock and the wind from the heights.

Tronc Feuillu came out of his hotel. He was carrying a small bag, and I guessed that he was going for one of his mysterious walks. He passed quite close to me, stopped, and abandoned his usual silence:

'Aren't you going out climbing?' he asked.

I looked at him and smiled:

'Well, you know, just because it's a fine day...'

'All the same, we don't often get it as fine as this...'

'True, but it's not always necessary actually to touch the rock to enjoy it!' My reply must have pleased him. Against all my expectations, he invited me to accompany him.

Tronc Feuillu led me along paths quite unknown to me. I thought at first that he was taking me along the Blaitière path. However, he turned off very soon towards the heart of the forest. With amazingly sure steps, he followed the faintest of tracks into copses, across thickets, and thence along new tracks. From time to time, we came across broad paths, but Tronc Feuillu seemed to avoid them quite systematically. He managed it all so well that in the end I hadn't the faintest idea where we were. The high slopes which we were climbing appeared to us across the trees. They enveloped us completely, and it seemed to me that we were gradually becoming lost in a labyrinth. I allowed myself to be led along, happy to discover a mountain so unfamiliar to me.

I had placed myself behind my guide, making sure that I followed his every step. He was moving forward at a regular pace. I could not see his face, but I guessed it to be lost in a dream which, however, still permitted him to find his way through the network of tracks, copses and paths which we were following. Finally, we emerged in a clearing on a shelf of the forest. The morning sun poured into it. The earth was covered with grass still heavy with dew. The droplets were sparkling in the light. They formed quite regular patterns, leading one to believe that a master gardener had arranged them thus by using a very special rake.

Jutting out from the grass were several rocks, scattered in little groups. One of them dominated all the others. It was an enormous, monolithic block, at least twenty feet high, and made of beautiful ochre-coloured granite, already warm from the sun. It was so compact and solid that it was difficult to believe that it had once rolled down from the scree above. I had never seen such a fine block. Or perhaps it was our walk that predisposed me to regard it as perfect.

The side facing the sun was dry. The air nearby quivered in the heat coming from the rock. I couldn't help thinking of a perfect climb across that sun-drenched rock face, a climb that would lead me to the summit of the block. To touch a fine rock is most pleasant and reassuring. I had a strong desire to go and touch this rock. But Tronc Feuillu stopped me with a gesture and, almost sharply, asked me to wait. Placing his bag on the ground, he took out his PAs and put them on. Without knowing whether this was the object of our coming here, I understood that my companion, like myself, had thought of climbing the block. Was he really considering doing so by means of the only visible face? The face looked utterly impossible to me.

He made his preparations slowly. Having changed his clothes very carefully, and having wiped the soles of his shoes and smeared his fingers with resin, he sank into an endless period of meditation. I saw his muscles slacken one by one, his whole body relaxing. His breathing became more and more regular. His gaze would move across the carpet of grass which separated us from the rock, stop at the rock face, and return again to the grass.

Fascinated by such immobility, I watched without daring to move. The nearby forest and the great slopes all around were silent and yet I could tell that they were filled by the same spirit which at that moment animated Tronc Feuillu. As though he were talking to himself, I heard him murmur: 'If I could go as far as the stone without disturbing a single dewdrop, the stone would no longer exist. And I should be at its summit.' Then, after a long silence, he spoke again: 'To be at the summit of the rock, you must be the summit of the rock, and thus of stone.' I realised that he was speaking on my behalf, for he had long ceased to need to himself. I thought back to the North Face of Mont Rekwal, the Japanese variation and the feat of Tronc Feuillu. I wondered if he was about to prove that same mastery.

He ceased to be immobile. He was deep in a trance, but without seeming to be in the power of any external forces. It was more a surfacing, and externalisation of his own powers. He moved towards the rock. His feet did not crush the blades of grass but gently parted them. He placed his hands on the rock, and then, without a single irregular movement, as though it had been the easiest of climbs, he reached the top. Holding my breath, fearing that I might break what seemed to be a spell – but would Tronc Feuillu even have heard me? – I saw him grasp the upper shelf and install himself there with ease. The finest climb that I had ever seen! The elegance of his move-ments was such that it erased the very inertia of those movements. Tronc Feuillu was even more clever than I had been told!

As he stood up on the summit, he turned his face towards the sun, and I saw his features illuminated by the bright light.

Each of us wears on his face a mask with hard, bitter features, marked at times by cynicism or despair. Each of us wears it to a greater or lesser degree of transparency. When I saw the face of Tronc Feuillu, I thought that he had succeeded in giving his mask perfect transparency. But at the same time I realised that I was mistaken. He had gone even further: his mask no longer existed. The sun was lighting up a man both terrifying in his lack of personality – he was pure, vast thought – and fascinating in the immense internal peace which filled him.

The moment did not last. Tronc Feuillu was already leaping towards the hidden face of the block, disappearing and joining me once more – with a laugh. Indeed, my amazement must have been rather ridiculous. But it was in the most serious of tones that he asked me whether I, in my turn, would like to climb the block. My silence must have answered for me. Without more ado, he changed his clothes again, and indicated that he was returning to the valley. I followed him. Later, as though he were continuing a con-versation (which in fact we had never begun), he started to talk. Without interrupting our walk, and without turning round, he said:

'Usually, that sort of thing is not expressed in words. But I know that you need words. And what you said to me earlier in the square in Chamonix makes me think that perhaps you will understand… and yet the words you need already exist within you. I can remember having read in a book: "If one really wishes to master an art, technical knowledge alone is not enough. One must go beyond the technical to the point where the art becomes an *art without artifice*, which has its roots in the subconscious" … I could use more impressive words, tell you that we cannot attain perfection by piling feat upon feat, or by making the greatest possible use of our muscles and senses, but that, on the contrary, we must use the basic link that joins our own essence to the essence of our art. But why say that which cannot be said!'

We continued to walk down towards the valley. Tronc Feuillu preceded me. I heard his words, and I should have liked to see his face once more. But he did not stop, and in places I almost had to run to keep up with him. He was silent for some time. I dared not question him. Later, he continued.

'What you have seen me do is for some only the beginning of climbing. In my country, we say "the ultimate state of activity is inactivity"... I'm going to tell you the story of a climber named Chi-Ch'ang. He lived in a Chinese province, but there can be few climbers in my country who do not know his story. Chi-Ch'ang would have liked to be the greatest climber in the world. He was highly skilled, but would have liked to reach perfection. Finally, he discovered that the greatest master-climber in the country was a certain Wei-Fei. It was said that Wei-Fei was capable of drawing himself up smooth, vertical stretches of stone, no matter how high up. Some people had seen him climb overhangs of solid rock where no holds were apparent. Chi-Ch'ang made his way to the distant province where Wei-Fei lived, and became his pupil.

'The master kept him there for several days, then explained that he would continue his instruction when Chi-Ch'ang had acquired the art of not blinking. Chi-Ch'ang returned to his home and lay down on his back beneath his wife's loom. He wanted to be able to keep his eyes fixed on the loom pedal, without closing them when it passed in front of his face. Day after day he practised. When two years had passed, he was able to refrain from blinking even when the pedal pulled out one of his eyelashes. From that moment on, neither blasts of wind filled with snow or dust, nor the lightning on the mountain ridges, could have any effect on him. Indeed, nothing could make him blink. He even slept with his eyes open. One day, whilst he was contemplating the village fields, a spider spun her web between his lashes. Chi-Ch'ang knew he was ready, and returned to the Master.

'"This is but the first stage," Wei-Fei said to him. "Now you must learn to see. Come to me again when that which is minute appears obvious to you, and when that which is small appears huge."

'Chi-Ch'ang returned to his province. On a river bank he found a perfectly smooth pebble, adorned by a lichen which could hardly be seen. He placed it near to the window of his room, sat down at the other end and, day after day, practised looking. Two weeks later, he could see the lichen quite clearly. Soon, it began to look larger. After three months had passed, it seemed in Chi-Ch'ang's eyes as large as a flower. Its slightest detail was familiar to him. He spoke to the other members of the family of the astonishing complexity of the leaves of the lichen, admiration filling his voice. The seasons passed. Chi-Ch'ang hardly noticed, if at all. The occasions on which he left his room were rare. Each day his wife cleaned the pebble, lest a speck of dust should settle on it and disturb his contemplation. After three years, the lichen seemed to him as large as a tree. For the first time, Chi-Ch'ang diverted his gaze from it to the pebble. Its dimensions seemed those of an enormous block. He rushed out of the house: horses seemed as big as mountains, pigs the size of hills; chickens looked like castle towers. Chi-Ch'ang went then to the climbing school where he had originally trained, and came upon a smooth stretch of rock that no one had ever climbed. The slightest roughness on its surface seemed to Chi-Ch'ang on that occasion to take on the size of a considerable hold. He climbed it easily. Without waiting any longer, he returned to Wei-Fei. This time, the master had to admit that his pupil had succeeded.

'Thus Chi-Ch'ang had spent five years in the initiation to climbing. He felt that from then on all feats would be possible. He decided to undergo a series of tests. He began by climbing quite easily some of the routes that had been Wei-Fei's speciality. Then he covered them again, carrying a bag filled with stones, heavy enough to unbalance him on the ground. On his head he placed a cup full of water: not a single drop was spilt. A week later, he chose an overhanging wall so split and cracked that it threatened to crumble away. He began to climb, and such was the swift sureness of his movements that each stone, when pushed off balance by one movement, found itself immediately readjusted by the following movement. At the end, Chi-Ch'ang reached the top of the wall without a single rock having fallen. Wei-Fei, who had witnessed the feat, could not help but applaud.

'From that day on, Chi-Ch'ang knew that he had nothing more to learn from his master. He could return to his village: no-one could equal him. And yet, he did not feel satisfied. A final obstacle stood in his way: Wei-Fei himself. Full of bitterness, Chi-Ch'ang realised that he could not set himself up as the greatest climber in the world. He was his master's equal, not his superior. The two continued to climb together.

'One day while they were climbing a long dihedral, roped up together, Chi-Ch'ang made a belay on a terrace which had a large number of rocks scattered on it. Lower down, Wei-Fei was climbing. Without hesitation, Chi-Ch'ang pushed one of the rocks into space. But for some time the old master had been able to read his pupil's mind; Chi-Ch'ang, without realising it, had lost some of his confidence. Wei-Fei saw what was happening, dangled on the rope at once, and avoided the falling rock by swinging right round the outside of the dihedral, then returned to his original position. Chi-Ch'ang had fixed the rope instinctively, so that he would not be pulled down by Wei-Fei's weight. He threw more rocks but his companion avoided them all. Then he selected a large, sharp-edged piece of rock and cut the rope with it. Wei-Fei found himself without any support, completely at the mercy of his enemy. "This time I have won," muttered Chi-Ch'ang. He pushed a final stone. But at the very moment when Wei-Fei was about to be dragged into space, he leaped on to one of the smooth faces of the dihedral and clung there for a brief moment. At the same time he pushed the stone away with one hand. The stone, deviating from its original trajectory, crashed against the rock, carving out a tiny hold as it did so. Wei-Fei dropped on to it. Before Chi-Ch'ang realised what was happening, the master had reached the bottom of the dihedral.

'Aware then that he would never succeed, Chi-Ch'ang felt full of remorse. As for Wei-Fei, he was so pleased at having exhibited his genius in such a magnificent way that he felt no anger at all towards the person who had wanted to kill him. The two men reached the summit without a rope, and wept as they embraced one another. Wei-Fei realised, however, that his life was in danger from that day on. The only way to avert the danger was to direct Chi-Ch'ang's attention towards another object.

'"My friend," he said, "I have passed on all my knowledge to you. But neither you nor I possess the ultimate knowledge. If you wish to know more, you must cross the Ta-Hsing col and climb to the summit of Mount Ho. There you will find the old master Kan-Ying who never has had and never will have an equal in our art. Compared with his, our skill is like that of a child. He alone has something to teach you."

'Chi-Ch'ang set off at once. After a difficult journey which lasted a month, he arrived at the summit of Mount Ho. He stopped, removed his walking shoes and put on his climbing boots. Then he set off for the grotto where the hermit lived. Kan-Ying was a very old man. His eyes were very gentle. His back was bent and his white hair reached right down to the ground. A man so old would surely be deaf. Chi-Ch'ang went up to him and shouted: "I have come here to make sure that I am the greatest climber in the world." And without waiting for a reply, he rushed up a large block of marble, polished by the elements, which overhung the entrance to the grotto. When he had climbed down again, he noticed that Kan-Ying was smiling indulgently.

'"What you are doing is really quite easy: what is there to admire about the act of climbing on rock? The route is there to be followed, a rock to be climbed. Come, I'm going to teach you something better."

'Annoyed at not having impressed the old man, Chi-Ch'ang followed him until they reached a col which gave access to a face of rock and ice rising to a dizzy height. Kan-Ying began to tackle an ever-narrowing traverse dominated by a high wall of rock which had been smoothed by falls of ice. Up above, a formidable sérac barrier hid a part of the sky from them. They were prevented from seeing the foot of the rock face by the overhanging rock which jutted out beneath them. Kan-Ying proceeded without hesitation. Suddenly he pulled Chi-Ch'ang towards him. With a terrible noise, a huge part of the sérac above fell down around them, surrounding them with a cloud of finely crushed ice. Chi-Ch'ang realised that a slightly overhanging rock was protecting them, and the avalanche would have swept him away if Kan-Ying had not intervened. For a moment his gaze followed the falling blocks of ice. The void beneath him took on a new dimension. A nausea which he had never felt before took hold of him. But Kan-Ying left the shelter of the rock quite calmly and carried on.

'The winding track had disappeared. There was now only a simple narrow ledge of rock along which Chi-Ch'ang moved very slowly. He reflected that he had done well to change his boots before arriving at the grotto. And yet, there was Kan-Ying before him, bare feet clad in old sandals, walking as if he were on a footpath. Chi-Ch'ang would have felt humiliated by this if his mind had not been otherwise occupied. Both had left the shelter fortuitously provided by the overhanging rock – but *was* it only by chance that they had been there at that moment? – and now nothing was protecting them. Chi-Ch'ang began to feel uncertainty overtake him. If just one block of ice were to fall, it would be the end, he thought. Suddenly, Kan-Ying stopped, and turned towards Chi-Ch'ang;

'"Now, show me your skill! You see that overhang beneath the sérac barrier? You have just enough time to reach it before the next avalanche."

'Chi-Ch'ang was too proud not to accept the challenge. He left the holds on which he had stopped and began to climb towards the sérac. But hardly had he, with the greatest difficulty, moved forward one metre, when he heard a cracking sound above him. He climbed down again hurriedly, and without even stopping at Kan-Ying's side, he continued until he reached the shelter of the overhang once more. One of his legs had begun to tremble and he had no control over it. The old man had not moved and laughed as he watched him:

'"The glacier does not move forward when it is not time for it to move forward. Come back up here and follow me!"

'Chi-Ch'ang moved across again. They continued until they reached a traverse which was a continuation of the first one. This permitted them to skirt a spur which plunged into the abyss. Kan-Ying reached the very edge of the spur. A magnificent needle of rock jutted out before them. It was only two rope-lengths away from the climbers, but the precipice made it inaccessible. Up above, the sharp narrow edge of the spur jutted out, supporting fragile groups of rocks over the void.

'"Now," said the hermit, "permit me to demonstrate the art of true climbing."

'"But you are only wearing sandals," said Chi-Ch'ang in a weak voice, "you will never cross those overhangs."

'"Who mentioned overhangs? For the finest movements, one needs the finest summit. Don't you think that that aiguille is worth more than the spur we are now on?" Chi-Ch'ang looked once more at the abyss which separated them from the aiguille and, not having understood, turned to Kan-Ying.

'"But there is no arête, no face which leads to the top!"

'"Boots? Rock? As long as one needs the soles of one's boots and rock to climb, one knows nothing of this art. The true climber does not need tools, or even rock."

'The old man seemed to find before him imaginary holds, then to carry out a succession of incredibly precise movements. Chi-Ch'ang thought he heard the almost inaudible sound of non-existent boots making contact with rock that had no substance. Then he saw Kan-Ying stand up on the tip of the needle. And then he knew with complete certainty that he had witnessed the supreme manifestation of an art in which he had wanted with all his heart to excel.

'He spent nine years on the mountain with the old hermit. What discipline he underwent during those years, nobody ever knew. When he came down again to return to his village and his home, everyone was astonished at the change which had taken place in him. He no longer had the determined and arrogant air about him which he had had previously. His face was wooden and without expression, like that of an idiot. His former master, Wei-Fei, knew that he had returned and came to see him. Straightway, he understood.

'"I can see now that you have become a great climber. And from this moment on, I am unworthy of roping myself up behind you."

'The people of the province welcomed Chi-Ch'ang as the greatest climber in the country. And they waited impatiently to see feats which would confirm his brilliance. But Chi-Ch'ang did nothing to satisfy their waiting. He never returned to the rock faces which he had formerly visited so often. He had not even brought back his climbing boots which, brand new, he had taken away with him nine years before, saying as he went that they would be the instruments of his glory. And to those who begged him to explain, he would reply, in a jaded voice:

'"The ultimate stage of the spoken word is silence. The ultimate stage of climbing is not to climb."

'The most subtle ones amongst them understood what he meant, and admired him: but many, misled by the lack of expression on his face, thought that he was rather simple, and went away again without understanding why he enjoyed such fame.

'All kinds of stories about him began to circulate. Moved by jealousy, superstitious people, or those prepared to make use of the superstitiousness of others, passed round the story that, while on Mount Ho, Chi-Ch'ang had learned all the black arts, and that even now the migrating birds would avoid flying over his roof. Climbers, however, convinced of the supreme wisdom and unequalled skill of Chi-Ch'ang, said that no evil spirit ever haunted his house. It was, they added, the god of climbers who came to visit the Master's soul and to discuss with him the merits of fabled climbers of old.

'Chi-Ch'ang paid no attention to the stories that were told about him. Old age crept softly upon him. His face had lost all expression. There was no outside force which could disturb his complete impassiveness. He was so well attuned to the secret laws of the universe, so far removed from the uncertainties and contradictions of the material world, that in the evening of his life he no longer made any distinction between "I" and "he", or between "this" and "that".

'The multiplicity of the senses had vanished for him: his eye might as well have been an ear, his ear a nose, his nose a mouth. Forty years after his return from Mount Ho, Chi-Ch'ang departed peacefully from this world, as a puff of smoke disperses in the sky. During all those years he had never made a single reference to the art of climbing, nor had he touched a single rock. It is said that, shortly before his death, he paid a visit to a friend who had a luxurious home. As he crossed the threshold, he indicated the door-frame which was hewn from free-stone, and asked his friend:

'"Pray tell me, what is the material of which this doorway is made?" Then, straight away, seeing his host's climbing boots in the corridor, "What strange boots! What can they possibly be used for?"

'His friend, quite stupefied, realised that Chi-Ch'ang was not joking. He turned towards the Master, and could only say to him, in a trembling voice:

'"You must truly be the greatest master of all time to have forgotten what stone is, and what the instruments of climbing are."

'It is said that in the days which followed, the painters of the region threw away their brushes and the artisans were ashamed to be seen with their tools...

'... So there is the story of Chi-Ch'ang who wanted to be the greatest climber in the world,' concluded Tronc Feuillu. 'Draw what conclusions you will. But before we reach Chamonix, let me just add this: the climbers of your mountains have often tried to define climbing. They have talked of a sport, of a drug, of a way of forgetting, of an escape, of a religion, a philosophy, an ethic or a moral. Some of them, those who have understood a little better, have mentioned a way of life. The truth is at the same time contained within all these words and in none of them... Arrange them around a circum-ference: alpinism must be in the centre. It is the duty of everyone to put it there, indeed it is the duty of everyone to put there his own alpinism. Yes, every climber, unaided, must aim for the centre... As they say in your language: "as sure as I am called ..."'

He turned towards me, smiling broadly, like someone about to crack a good joke.

'... just as sure as you call me Tronc Feuillu!'

I have never known his real name.

from MOUNTAIN 24 *1972*

Author's Footnote. This tale was written after a story by Natashima Ton which appeared in *The World of Zen* by W. Ross, and the introduction by D.T. Suzuki to the work of E. Herrigel, *Zen Buddhism in the Noble Art of Archery*.

PUMPING SANDSTONE

JOHN LONG

Some years ago, John Gill published several explanatory-philosophical articles on specialised bouldering. During this time the aces of the climbing community were pursuing the last of the natural big walls, with the extreme-type movements of Gill's fancy being predominantly overlooked. Shortly thereafter the paradigm shifted to free climbing, with the rising standards usually demanding some bouldering from those in pursuit. Today (with the assistance of considerable hearsay, fable and actual documentation) the accomplishments of Gill are gaining notice and, in turn, his feats provide much in the way of inspiration for those who have tasted them.

Sixteen years ago, Gill demolished the current free standards by soloing 'The Thimble' in the Needles of South Dakota. Few even knew of it then and only a handful now. Through the years I had caught a glimpse of the odd scope of Gill's exploits, though no first-hand knowledge existed. My first exposure to any Gill propaganda occurred some half-dozen years ago. Someone, somewhere along in my climbing career, had produced a picture of himself posed on the crux of a supposed Gill problem. His motive seemed twofold: to astonish us with his performance and to verify his good taste. He failed at both. The photo was cropped at boot level – a feeble attempt to conceal his feet firmly anchored to the turf. Eye level graffiti told of his true location. To be sure, the stone above this trickster's fingers appeared quite smooth, only to become smoother as memory became coloured by imagination.

Reliable friends had forewarned me of the absurdity of Fort Collins bouldering, this being but one of Gill's many playgrounds in the 1960s. Driven from Yosemite by summer heat, and from Tuolumne by a funky social scene, we headed east for Colorado and our first peek at the boulders. Under the guidance of John Bachar we visited the notorious Eliminators, Mental Block, Torture Chamber, Sunshine Boulder and more, the likes of which had haunted us for some time. John, one of America's foremost free-climbers, had frequented Fort Collins for three summers, systematically bagging almost every problem there. Knowing this in advance I banked on a personal advantage, assuming that John could reveal the keys to sequence-solving, enabling us simply to work on the moves.

The difference between these boulders and others is the rock – Dakota sandstone – which holds no secrets in sequences, these usually being solved via long moves between unreliable holds. Dynamic techniques play no small part in their execution. Hence, Bachar's presence served us little pragmatic value, save for the reefers he continuously scrolled.

Anyway, these outrageous problems were proof positive that Gill had indeed mastered the intricacies of dynamic movements. The Mental Block has six standard classics, four of which involve considerable gunnery to succeed. The Eliminators – Left, Centre and Right, are all dynamic problems. This is unique considering that most bouldering is intentionally static movement, with dynamics being avoided and sometimes even scorned as a false technique. For those with an aversion towards lunging, Fort Collins is to be avoided as static efforts will generally ensure certain failure regardless of strength.

After experiencing Fort Collins a second time, I concluded that exposure to Gill was obligatory – but how? Dave Breashears, my only contact, was in Canada, which vetoed any possibilities for a proper introduction. I briefly pondered requesting Pat Ament to introduce us but surmised he would charge me. A childish attitude, but stuck I was, so I simply looked up Gill's Pueblo number and, as a relative stranger, called him up. Acknowledging my wonderment, he immediately arranged for a guided tour of the 'more outstanding areas'. When we talked later to verify the plan, he mentioned an itinerary he had drafted, the details of which, I imagined, would surely prove my undoing. As we finally approached the door of Gill's two-storey Pueblo abode, my mind was void of expectations, as the endless tapestry of fable coupled with my own experiences had left me somewhat numb. As time passed we learned that Gill was exempt from all the preconceived notions that climbers and books had transposed upon him. Soon enough we were venturing through colourful sage, scrub oak and assorted cacti *en route* to the 'Fatted Calf' boulder. Just then, I believe, John began to display that unmistakeable smirk which reminded me of an old film I'd seen of Mohammed Ali watching amateurs box.

I spent half my energy attempting the numerous problems on the Fatted Calf. Gill's smirk only grew as he knew all too well to what I aspired – to bag all the problems in the shortest time possible. At this I failed. One problem (described on pp145–6 of Ament's book, *Master of Rock*) proved responsible for a host of holes in my fingers. No description could justly portray the absurdity of this leap.

Soon after we were swinging from the razor edges of the Ripper Traverse, a paramount of finger strength. This problem seemed so severe that to reverse it would certainly usher in some type of injury. If one could harness the torque involved in crossing the Ripper, one could conceivably turn coal into shining gems. Shortly thereafter, John rigged a top rope on the sensational Little Overhang, perhaps the most enjoyable problem I climbed that day. A series of swinging aerobatics led twenty feet to the crux move to the top. Once there I wobbled over to unclip the cord from the anchor – a fixed blade behind a loose block. Shocked, I reflected on how marginal my climbing had been, and remembered the barrel cactus at the base. Laughing over my cowardice we were off to lunch and then to a third area.

This final tour involved more looking than climbing, as by this juncture my hands felt as if they had been stroked with a bastard file. This area, referred to as the Badlands in *Master of Rock*, had the most unlimited possibilities conceivable. Following a warm-up on the Penny Ante boulder we crossed a quick-sanded creek bed to the final problem of the day – the phenomenal Juggernaut. Not having enough energy even to come close, I became stupefied by the bizarre and unique sequence involved in ascending it. Completely spent, we left the lost canyon, talking of a future visit.

A month later I returned with John Bachar, both of us having tuned up considerably during that time. On this second tour the problems became more realistic, though still the hardest both John and I had seen. Heavily psyched, we warmed up on Saturday for our appointment with Gill on Sunday. The training had paid off as we both managed problems that had thwarted us previously, most pleasurable being the Ripper Traverse, Gill's way (from right to left). Exuberant we retired in lieu of the following day.

On Sunday we drove straight to the lost canyon for a swing at the Juggernaut. Warming up again on the Penny Ante I mostly loafed while Bachar familiarised himself with the problems. Gill slipped on his boots for the first time and powered over several B1s. With this as inspiration we headed for the Juggernaut.

In the weeks previously I had devised a way to train for this climb (thirty feet) by swinging from the support beams of a basketball backboard. The aim was to limit the lower body swing by levering off one or the other arm. With the top rope set I tried it and, deliberating past mistakes, managed to succeed. I stood, then sat on the small summit, astonished. I yearned to write home, but realised I had none – my folks left no forwarding address after moving in 1975. Shortly after, Bachar succeeded and we spent the remainder of the day exploring for new problems and attempting several. I think we only did one of the many we saw. We left the lost canyon talking of yet another visit.

from CLIMBING *January 1978*

I FEEL ROCK

PETE LIVESEY

MORATORIUM

El Cap's East Buttress route starts high above the [Yosemite] Valley at the end of a ledge system on the mountain's right flank. It's a beautiful sunbaked route on a bulging rounded buttress of fine weathered yellow rock.

If you're waiting there to start the route, it's slow because there are usually several Japanese teams hurling themselves at the first pitch like demented bananas. So have a look over the end of the ledge.

Below, in deep-contrasted shadow, is a tremendous corner sweeping down for 600ft. Continuous – with smooth wide walls, one overhanging and one just leaning back – the hair-like corner crack makes no secret of its challenge.

If you're into laybacks, then this is it, you've found it at last – the spiritual home of laybacks, whence came all the other little laybacks in the world. In all this climb's length there is just ten feet of bridging on the second pitch: the rest is just pure apelike joy in every conceivable kind of layback position.

The start is ten minutes from the road and blatantly obvious. Senses are immediately stirred by the incredibly harsh light-and-shade chequer work of the corner's beautiful slabs, features obliterated by deep black shadow on brilliant sunlit stripes. It's hard to be single-minded enough to concentrate on the first pitch of laybacking – but there it is, there's no other way.

Laybacking is a strangely committing kind of climbing. It always feels like that's it, once you start. You just stand there looking at it, building up for a rush, and although you know the crack will take good protection, you can't see where to put it once you're arched up in a layback position. There's always a tendency to get going and forget the protection.

As the Editor would say:

'Just lay back and enjoy it.'

REED PINNACLE DIRECT

The first pitch is a wicked curved slash like a sabre scar, but it's just my size. forty feet up, twenty feet to go, and I put a chock in. Handjam-size, number 9, pick it out on a tatty white tape and throw it in.

I threw it in: it went right in, two feet in, krab and all, out of reach. I was broddling round with my longest wire, and was just pulling the tape out, when I saw one of those sights you just don't want to believe or accept. In the crack behind the nut was a hand, yes a hand. It still had chalk on, and grubby fingernails.

Not only was the sight of a hand completely unacceptable to me, but also it was dragging the nut away, my nut, into the depths of the mountain. I instinctively let go of the tape, and I remember thinking that dozens of climbers have probably lost their hands that way, best to let it have the nut and clear off. At the top of the pitch I grabbed the tree, tied on and checked to see if my feet were still there – you never know with hands in cracks what they're after.

Behind the tree was a perfect dark chimney parallel to the cliff face. Creeping out of the base at ground level was a giggling Yank with my nut.

The next pitch looked potentially even more horrific. A slab of rock weighing a few million tons had split, leaving a curly crack, then one side had slipped a couple of feet so that the curls on one side were out of phase with those on the other. Could it be a giant American meat grinder?

Our fears were allayed. The crack proved to be perfect jamming – just throw a fist or a finger in, and let it slide down until it jams. Easy, just like that for 120 perfectly vertical feet.

The last pitch was another leap into the unknown. Run into the back of a twenty-foot-wide cavernous chimney and bridge out of its roof, funnelling up into a narrowing fissure, squeezed out into space on a fist jam; layback and mantelshelf on to it, another jam for fingers only, and grab the top.

CLAWS

The trouble with Kilnsey is that the reasonably-angled slabs turn out to be overhanging, and the steep wall leading to the roof overhangs seriously.

So the concept of the route was all right. The discreet wall trending to the shallow delicate groove-line – in turn becoming a cobra-headed corner, curving, poised. All right when it was a germ of an idea that quickly grew to a route that had to be done, a last great problem that we naively thought everyone was after.

But when it came to cleaning it, that's when realisation dawned. Trying to reach in. Spinning on the long rope; flailing with a wire brush at the head-wall; looking down at the rope shaking in space some twenty-foot clear of the 'slabs' below. Bouncing around trying to get in and grab a piece of rock to clean – and that flicking rope cleaned out its own gully up above, the falling debris knocking bits off cheekbones and arms. And waking up from unconsciousness on the ground, with a red-hot figure of eight still melting the rope.

It was ridiculous, but too late. We'd blabbed, but now we were set.

Discreet walls were first. I never want to see another wall as discreet as that. Small hidden holds ten feet apart with smirches, flickets and wrinkles in between, but where to go? Half lines leading to whole truths. And I follow one and see another, go again – and now suddenly I can say the climbing is unreasonable, but I think we mean the climber has lost the reason. So I hang on half a wire nut and smash hell out of my number 1 Clog, and make it thread a hole it wouldn't before. And I feel safe now, perhaps it's not so unreasonable – but it's too late, because Ron is pulling me down with plenty of reason bottled up in his paws.

At the thread Ron loses his reason, sees it is unreasonable, grabs the thread, rests, then spies a reason, a line of reasons leading to the groove. He likes the groove because it's hard, all go, but not unreasonable – and at the top, a perfect perch, two by one, two nuts and a peg.

Above, the cobra was wet, and to pin it down would have been too much, and the elder I was resting on broke off, so we broke off.

And we waited for the drought and with the waiting lost all reason, rushed past the thread and barely made it, strength failing fifty feet out. The elder was weak and needed tying up to a stopper thread.

I become an overhanging gardener and look for sheep to heal or pines to plant out – but there aren't any here, and I have to think about the cobra's head yet to come. I've seen this bit before, from my rope before it cleaned me off, so I climbed with confidence. Safely past the cobra's still-weeping eye, sneak left but can't rest beneath a wall that's not the one I knew on the rope. The wall has Aero-bubbled rock bulging up to back-to-jugs fifteen-foot above. Deep breaths, nine or ten – I like to think it re-aerates my blood, but in reality it's a simple task I can concentrate on – nine or ten, then go. Just-made-the-jugs, but perhaps it was a do-it-better-next-time move; it was, however, still the longest stretch I can do.

Up, and I persuade the second not to bother – I want it to be my experience for a year or two. I abseil down, as far out in space as possible.

WELLINGTON CRACK

There's not much to recommend Wellington Crack to the seeker of the aesthetic in climbing. The ugliness of the situation [Ilkley Quarry] is enveloping, the crack itself more of an evil unnatural slit – no comparison with the perfect Yosemite crack carefully dividing and apportioning sweeps of clean rock.

No, if any beauty is to be found in Wellington Crack, it can only be through feedback from the body and its movement.

From bottom to top the crack demands unending attention to movement that is at the same time delicate yet strenuous, dynamic yet slow and balanced. Every foot requires something different of the climber. Every movement of every part has to be considered. Every movement is deliberate and worthwhile. A knee or an arm too far out and the layback doesn't work, or balance is lost. Too far in, and you begin to swing outwards slowly but irrevocably: in three or four seconds finger friction will be lost, and you'll be away.

You'll realise the reason at the top, take pride in five minutes of perfectly controlled movement, and the graffiti and litter and tourists' dogs are unimportant.

LUNATIC FRINGE

Barry Bates's routes are all alike – sort of thin cracks that split smooth walls with no footholds.

Having fingers the same shape and consistency as Chouinard 5½" Stoppers is a distinct advantage on these routes. For the rest of us, it's just a 150ft exercise in every conceivable kind of finger jam, finger layaway and a half-a-handjam.

Feet are a kind of embarrassment: there appears to be nowhere to put them, and if you start worrying about it, your hands fall out. I finally worked out that the best scheme was to hide them away underneath your knees and hope they'd get up the route on their own.

It's not a straight-in crack. It's angled slightly and this makes the climbing a little easier, all kinds of peculiar finger jams surprisingly sticking in place.

The rock is magnificent, even for Yosemite – one of those routes where you get back down and say: 'Did I do that? Let's do it again.' But you don't, because somewhere in your inner mind is a subconscious but compelling chink of cool beer cans – or half-gallon buckets of sherbet ice cream, if your name's Ron Fawcett.

SOUTH FACE OF KOH I PARAU

You've not come here for a weekend's cragging. The route is 11,000ft up a mountain in the middle of the Persian desert – just getting there is about as difficult as getting into Yorkshire.

If the inscrutable Eastern customs officers don't stop you, or the swarms of Kurdish brigands brewing up on glowing camel-shit cakes don't over-power you on the slopes of the mountain, then the ten-foot tabby cats called mountain leopards will certainly have you on top.

But the route is something else – a slender, almost vertical 1500ft pillar of limestone, featureless from a distance but, on closer inspection, revealing a texture like Aero chocolate. Rough little bubbles that allow you to claw the rock like a cat.

Once you've learnt the clawing technique, the climbing becomes superb – just pitch after pitch of seemingly runnerless rock, and you simply claw your way up it.

The situation is a spacewalk: 10,000ft below, like a relief map, lies the barren ridged desert, stretching away to the oil rigs of the Persian Gulf ghosting up from the haze.

FAIRVIEW DOME – REGULAR ROUTE

To the unsuspecting British climber the High Sierra is unbelievably beautiful. Gentle forest trails and the occasional road wind across an 8000ft plateau, dark sweet-smelling pine alternating with areas of sunbleached bare granite – acres of glacier-scoured rock sprouting the occasional lonely, twisted Jeffrey Pine.

In the distance are a dozen or so domes of brilliant white granite rising in perfect curves from the forest. The tallest is Fairview Dome, an 1800ft sweep of granite, perfectly circular, with curves that ensure its place as the most perfect and biggest breast in the world. There's no way you can drive past without fondling its smooth slabs.

So gentle at first that it's easy walking; almost imperceptibly steepening until the slab is a steep slab and friction is not enough, and the eye is drawn to the line, the only line, a pencil-line crack creasing the surface of that cuppable tit.

Find the line, follow it, and be drawn through the slabs to the wall, through overlaps and roofs, the line still faithfully leading to the only possible finishing point on this mountain.

Higher, the walls gradually curve back again, easing off for three pitches before the last final thrust of what one can only call a nipple, whether it looks like one or not.

Do you know what it feels like to sit up there on the biggest tit there is, looking down on a pine-chested woman with eleven more tits all around you? Outasight, man.

L'ANGE (THE ANGEL)

If you think you've ripped off the French in Chamonix, then it's only fair to let them do it to you – they've got a special place for it, the Saussois.

It's just Stoney Middleton with French-speaking routes; sort of smoother, more subtle, more elegant. The French will laugh at your efforts to climb the routes in English: you see, the French still regard a fifi hook for a rest as free climbing, while you end up with dislocated fingers after failing to make decent hooks out of them. It's worth being sand-bagged to climb in English, though, just for the experience of swinging up highly overhanging and improbable walls on superb hidden finger-jugs, or to be confronted suddenly on an overhang with a thread that you can crawl into for a rest.

L'Ange is the ultimate test of these techniques; nowhere is there a poor hold, just steep sustained strenuosity up a highly improbable line. Protection is superb except at the start of the overhanging section, which is de-pegged. thirty feet above and fifteen feet out in space is a large jugular thread, ready threaded.

Just rush up this technical steep bit until good holds start you curving backwards up the roof. In such a haven of runners, that section is truly exciting. Next come two or three resting pegs, though it could be done without if you hadn't been to the pub the night before. That's the other place the French are out to rip you off – but we beat 'em.

When the landlord realises you're English and not just noddy Frogs, he produces a free round of strong green liquor from a bottle wrapped in a towel. When you've drunk it, he whips off the towel to reveal a pickled python, and you're supposed to rush off to be sick.

Not so our team – the landlord's jubilant garlic grin turning sour as John ordered two beers and another round of snake juice, s'il vous plaît. The angel, it seems, is no match for the devil.

DARKINBAD THE BRIGHTDAYLER

A foreboding, harsh grey cliff glowering at an equally angry-looking sea. A 150ft sheet of smooth wall is dominated by a leaning headwall seamed with ridiculous-looking grooves [Pentire Head, Cornwall]. The start of Darkinbad does little to ease your mind – a lurch from a boulder on to a wall of no return.

Then suddenly things change, and the whole wall is a mass of tiny twisted cracks and holds, each one containing hundreds of friendly acrobatic shrimps

– it's alive. Everything is enjoyable, you're among friends – millions of climbers whiling away their time on a vast handhold sanctuary.

Just wander up that vast wall, always heading for a shallow alcove below the nastiest of the hanging grooves above. You set out up the groove; steady laybacking to a roof where you gradually realise that you're trying to layback with your feet above your hands and there's no horizon left.

The shrimps above are disturbed by a blind hand creeping over the roof, feeling around, finding a flat hold with a useful crack down the back; a body and legs follow, and all end up teetering on the flat hold with the useful crack.

The rest is a foregone conclusion, and you can lie in the sun in perfect Japanese film-maker's grass until your second gets annoyed and begins to drag you over the edge, like a fish catching an angler.

from CRAGS 7 *1976*

SURELY WE'RE OFF THE ROUTE?

KEVIN FITZGERALD

In the old days there were never any difficulties walking about in Wales, or, if there were, I have forgotten them. Somewhere around ten o'clock, and after a leisurely breakfast, people began revising the overnight plan to run round the Horseshoe in favour of what was called 'a quick look at the Glyders' or 'an easy half day on the Rivals' or even just 'going out'. That was best of all: 'going out'. One stayed in slippers, with some gear thrown into the back of the car for the look of the thing. On a day like that one usually went straight to Bangor or Llandudno, or possibly to Mrs. Williams' Cottage to eat bacon and eggs. It was never anyone's business to inquire into destinations or what had been done. 'Had a good day?' they asked at The Gwryd. 'Wonderful,' you said.

How different it all is now, what with all this actual climbing, and struggling about inside networks of ropes, and listening to people holding forth about 'the personal challenge' or 'finding out about yourself as you face the rock'. But one must try to keep up, especially in one's last decade, and that means taking to the rocks: walking is more or less *out* for the moment, or seems to be.

Happily, the preparations are simpler now. There was a time when the talk was all of 'confidence in your boots my dear chap. That's all you need'. One never, of course, had the slightest confidence in one's boots. They were huge, bent double as the pressures came on, and always did the one thing they were supposed never to do, slip violently, and with sparks, off any and every hold. It was possible to slide without warning down fifty or sixty feet of the Ordinary Route on 'The Slabs' if you were foolish enough to have confidence in your boots.

Things got a lot worse with the arrival of the Vibram Sole. With these on your feet you could slip gracefully on boulders, wet grass, any path or mountain track, and while looking for the start of North Buttress. If, unhappily, you found that dreary start you could slip at each step up that first long groove and, once or twice, all the way down it as well. The firework display as you did this no longer occurred, which perhaps was a genuine step forward. You never hear anyone today remarking that, 'he doesn't really climb awfully well, you could read a guide in the evening by the flashes under his boots'.

All of a sudden proper things to put on climbing feet came into general use, bringing, for people like me, the appalling realisation that matters could be postponed no longer, that it was now possible to reach the top of a climb and that 'going out' was to mean in future actually doing something and no longer, as a friend of mine put it, 'fulfilling the Fitzgerald role of standing at the foot of climbs, complaining'. It was a serious day for me when the shops began to stock close-fitting moulded rubber *kletterschuhe*, PAs and comfortable walking boots. A decision had to be made at last, 'Stay away from it all or buy something reasonable to put on your feet'. And so it came about that just as my contemporaries were beginning to accept offers of board and lodging, ('You're not as spry as you were, dear'), from their grandchildren, I began a new and frightening life.

As was right and proper, and in accordance with tradition, the first 'new life' climb was that little thing of Geoffrey Winthrop Young's. You know it, of course? Climb into the heather, move across the traverse, move up the little wall at the end of that, walk along the terrace, and that's it. I had often watched my friends, ('we've only got twenty minutes and we must do something') run along the Miner's Track, leap over the pipeline, swarm up G. W. Young's climb, run down the far side of it, run back to their cars, and hurtle off to Manchester, while I was more or less getting into position to read in comfort while keeping an eye on events. Now I was on the ground gazing uneasily at my leader some five or six hundred feet above me. It seemed quite strange that I could hear his voice, especially as he had a bad cold and was whispering.

'Come on up,' he said, using the vernacular of the cliffs. I put a tentative *kletterschuhe* on the rock and felt my whole body being pushed away by the heather and bracken.

'Surely we're off the route,' I said.

'We'll be on it when you're on it,' said my companion, who, I now realised, was just above my head.

I tried again. To my horror I found myself off the ground and 'committed', as I have now learned to say. Soon, or fairly soon, I had reached the first stance and was being given a first lesson in modern rope work. This involved, as you all know, tying me, the climbing rope, the spare rope, the safety back rope, the red tape sling, the old fashioned rope sling, eight karabiners, the top of my trousers and the rock face into one vast, utterly comprehensive figure-of-eight.

'You'll be all right there for a bit,' said my leader, stepping straight out into nothing, turning in mid-air and clinging lightly to the smoother part of a polished slab. 'You'll enjoy this move,' he said, disappearing.

It is not an exaggeration to say that I have seen the traverse on G. W. Young's route *done* at least a dozen times. I've seen Longland do it, Hilton Jones do it, Moulam do it, Chris Briggs do it, even Doug Verity do it. Now the others made a gentle step out, paused while they lighted pipes, took off jerseys, put away books, took the paper off sweets, and then with steps reminiscent of the Pavlova of my youth moving into her swan routine, feet practically twinkling, hands as sinuous as any priestess of Isis, they slid along the face of the cliff. But when you are there, if you're me, it isn't like that at all. Far below is the cruel ground, far away to the left and almost out of sight is your leader, and the step you have to make is into the void. They tell you, 'Make the move and it all comes right'. So it does actually, but at the time I thought it better to stay for a little while in my net of rope dwelling on my past life. After a bit I undid everything and leapt forward. Years before I had lost my trousers on Pulpit Route on the Milestone. This time I arrived on the traverse with all my clothes on and it seemed that I had become a climber.

You will have read somewhere that you may be sure your Sin will find you out and quite soon I was to discover the truth of that statement. A long time ago I wrote for this Journal a piece called 'The Assault on Slab Recess Route' and now it was to catch up with me.

'There's a little thing called Edge Route, just beside your Slab Recess,' said my friend, 'and now that you are climbing you ought to do it.'

Well, it's easy is Edge Route. The start presents no difficulty, then there is a big ledge to stroll along; in two places it must be all of three inches wide. After that all you have to do is, 'to stand well out and walk up the edge to the loose block'. You are not allowed to clutch the loose block when you reach it, you have to do the thing called 'skirting it'. This is by no means what you have always thought; anybody interested in the general idea of skirting anything is not to be found on or near Edge Route. No, skirting the loose block means letting go of everything and, with a gay little smile, walking round the thing. There is nothing after that except a wet holdless slab. It is half way up that that you hear your quavering voice moaning, 'Surely we're off the route,' to which comes the firm reply from your leader, 'Stand out a bit more'. Perhaps it should be mentioned that if you stand out while doing the skirting operation you fall backwards over the edge.

We did Flying Buttress on the Cromlech soon after Edge Route. You can't go wrong on that one, just follow the rope, preferably with your eyes shut. As we were very short of time we had to cut short the comparatively simple operation of climbing the crag in favour of the 'easy walk off' half way up. Anyone who has ever reached that dangerous agglomeration of steep loose rock, wet grass, and unexpected chasms known as 'easier ground' knows what an easy walk off is like. Everyone relaxes, the rope is removed and coiled, hands are thrust into pockets and 'starting off down' begins. After the first couple of paces I always find myself calling out, 'Surely we're off the route,' and always I get the same reply. 'Oh, anywhere you can find a way does.'

It took me a day or two to get over the descent from Flying Buttress, just long enough to prepare for Kirkus's Route in the Moelwyns. That's a walk up, really. All there is after the chimney which gets you off the ground into 'commitment' is a straddle across the abyss, a little wall or two, a well sheltered slab on jugs, another wall, and what is called an exalted top pitch. It was on the slab that I said to my leader the standard piece about being off the route.

'Nice, isn't it? Just severe in wet weather, but beautiful today,' was his reply.

'But there aren't any holds where I am', I remember saying.

'Put your left foot out, Kevin, and trust your boots', came the reply, and my mind went back twenty years. I got up but I suppose if it had really been twenty years earlier there would have been a lot of sparks.

So here I am, a climber in spite of myself and with the delightful Great Slab in Cwm Silyn at last behind me. There cannot be very much in front. I went for a walk the other day; I like to torture myself once or twice a year on what A. D. M. Cox perfectly and unforgettably once called 'the aptly named Pig Track'. Above Bwlch Moch a stranger said:

'It's fine in these hills, but you must take it easy if you're not used to them, they're deceptive.'

We sat down and he told me about the joy of it all, the companionship. the beauty, the difficulties, the dangers. He never mentioned women or food so I knew he wasn't a climber. I got tired of it after a bit and got up.

'Where are you going?' he asked me. 'You must keep to the paths up here you know, you can't be too careful.'

As the stranger spoke there flashed across my mind a vision of all the great ones with whom I had walked, attempted to climb, or even climbed. What a splendid sight they made, Hilton Jones, who began my ruin, Tony Moulam, Jack Longland, Alan Hargreaves, Lorrie Richardson, Maurice Guinness, Garym Thomas, Trevor Matthews, Glyn Roberts, Doug Verity, Mervyn Hughes, Ray Greenall, Alf Bridge, Joe Kretschmer, Eric Mensforth and, always in the forefront of my mind, David Cox. I pointed straight under my feet and spoke my last words to the stranger, 'Down there,' I said, 'on to the Miners' Track.'

At that he gave me the title of his, perhaps my last climbing article:

'Surely that's not a route', he said.

I gave him the kind of wave which I hope summed up all I think and thought about the long happy years in Wales. 'It'll do for me,' I said to the sky, and I 'started off down'.

from THE CLIMBERS' CLUB JOURNAL *1968*

LAZY MEN'S WAYS

ALLAN AUSTIN

'Four hours,' I said to Claude as I wheezed my way to a standstill, adding a couple of extra pullovers before roping up, for it was cold up there, 'I have promised to take Jennie climbing this afternoon.' The route as far as Cenotaph Corner is an undistinguished affair and, except for the so-called 'Traverse on Jams', presents little in the way of interesting rock, steep, sound or otherwise. This Traverse on Jams came as something of a shock, for being a gritstoner I naturally regard hand-jam pitches as being my cup of tea. This one wasn't. The wall was very steep and smooth and was broken about three-quarters of the way up with a little black overhang. The traverse ran along the wall immediately below this overhang, using the crack in the angle, presumably for hand-jams. I may be thick, I know I am, and my best friends fight to confirm it, but I swear the man has not been born who could hand-jam that crack; it was so thin I could only just get my fingers in, and thick though they be, they are not appreciably thicker than J.B.'s hand, so I had to hand-traverse it. Now those of you who know me will realise that I am not built for hand-traversing, the seat of my gravity being too low. Nevertheless I overcame all nature's obstacles and rounded the corner, where the crack took an upward turn. 'Aha', I thought, 'the rope will jam in the crack if I don't wedge a stone in.' So I wedged and continued into the chimney to belay. It was on the very last swing that the rope jammed – shoddy workmanship no doubt – so back I went to the corner. Six times I returned along that by now well-known traverse to the corner to free the rope, and in spite of repeated wedged stones it managed to stick. It is only ten to twelve feet to the corner, but six times ten or twelve comes to a sizeable amount. I was clapped out. Fortunately the next two or three pitches were not difficult, and I managed to coast round until we reached the 'meat' of the route, the crossing of Cenotaph Corner.

It is an impressive viewing spot, this stance on the edge of Sabre Cut. One sits there in perfect comfort, peeping round the corner across a wall of appalling verticality. There are no overhangs round there, nothing but a piton some seventy or eighty feet above in the exit cracks of the Left Wall to break the clean awe-inspiring sweep of its smooth walls. Once started out, the impression of smoothness quickly disappears and the wall becomes a warm and friendly place, rough and spiky with lots of holds. Not many are large, most are very small, but always they are sharp and comforting.

The pitch looked a long one, but like all long journeys it had to start with a first step. So I stepped. Down to the ledge I went, then twenty feet vertically up the wall via a thin and very strenuous curving crack to a sizeable flake runner. It was all very-protected and I enjoyed it. The cold was gone now and the sun shone directly into the corner. I felt warmer and more comfortable. Two or three parties were congregating in the amphitheatre at the foot of Cenotaph, and several more were toiling up the slopes below. I was the only person in sight wearing an anorak, and I felt slightly superior, having been up here when it was still cold. From now on the pitch was sheer delight, interesting climbing on good holds, safe, and on a superb piece of rock, and when I reached the Corner, along the last twenty feet or so of semi-hand-traversing, I felt almost sorry to arrive. But here I was and it behoved me to find a stance, especially as one of the parties below had decided to do the Corner and were not casting very friendly glances in my direction. So I started looking. The Corner in its middle section seemed sheltered and friendly with lots of holds, and knowing that one is not going to climb the difficult part at the top removes all the tension and everything seems comfortable and easy. But when one has said that, there's no more. There is certainly nothing remotely resembling a stance. Finally I settled on a spot. On the face of it there was little to choose between this spot and anywhere else in the Corner, but deep inside I had found a fine crack where I planted a fat channel peg. This was the stance.

I clipped in a big karabiner, added a few threads, and started to make myself a stance. It was hard work, twisting and turning, getting cramp, steaming up my glasses and using all the surplus rope in a complicated system of stirrups, slings etc. in which I vainly hoped to find comfort. Stances in étriers may be O.K. for hardened Alpinists, but for me this one was purgatory; somehow I was slowly being bent double and at the same time twisted in two. I felt like a worn-out corkscrew. The stance across the way on Cemetery Gates, usually numbered with the more precarious and uncomfortable stances in Wales, began to look more and more inviting. Claude took his time, obviously savouring to the full the delights of this pitch, and it seemed to me, deliberately delaying the time when he would occupy my place in the sun.

He is a patient sort of lad, is Claude, and he made sure he was well and truly belayed before he allowed me to strip off my cradle. The confusion had to be seen to be believed. At one time, although we had started out with 320ft of rope, all of it was used up in a massive series of knots and in general chaos. But at last order emerged from the chaos and I could start. Ah what bliss to be out of that little corner of hell! It will be realised that by now we were extremely unpopular with the party below, the leader of which had been up the first twenty feet a good half-dozen times. Still, the sun was beating down and I have no doubt that they were enjoying their enforced idleness with a spot of sunbathing. There were plenty of idiots to watch that day.

A ledge ran across the right wall of Cenotaph to the stance on the Gates, and the only difficulty seemed to lie in the twenty-foot gap before the ledge started. Fortunately a narrower rounded gangway, perhaps a couple of inches wide, sloped up to the near end of the ledge and bridged that gap. Before starting I went up the corner a little way and clipped one rope onto a large solid-looking chock just below the niche. The last time I had been here some years ago this stone had lived at the bottom of the wide crack, but since then some public-spirited climber had moved it to the top of the crack, almost to the crux in fact. It may be a cad's trick, but I was grateful and silently thanked my unknown friend. On my first attempt the sins of my past, or maybe Claude's, caught up with me and instilled momentary paralysis when I reached the end of my rope, all six feet of it, with the rest still tied onto Claude's belay. I regained the corner and, a few minutes later, temper and the rest of the rope, and sallied forth again. The required technique for climbing the gangway is unusual and worth describing. One starts one's feet off along this gangway giving them a couple of seconds' start over the body. This is then set in motion, being dragged along the wall by pulling on tiny pockets which crop up at intervals along the way. The position is such that it looks as though one is about to sit down, whereas in fact one is about to stand up, or would stand up if one could. Not only is the position undignified, but it is extremely strenuous, particularly so for a man of my build, when a considerable strain is imposed upon the fingers. Nevertheless it is a fine piece of climbing, blending precarious and unusual moves on steep rock with plenty of exposure. Once on the ledge I was able to regain my composure and proceed in a more leisurely fashion, still climbing, even though on a ledge, to the stance.

A party on Cemetery Gates had beaten me to the post; they already had two men there, but I smiled persuasively and offered to hold the rope while the leader led on to the top, thus freeing his second to bring up the last man. I noticed the second looking somewhat askance as I used him as a sort of belaying-pin, but it was in a good cause. I don't suppose he was very comfortable anyway. Eventually they went and Claude could start to free himself from his cage and all the angry glares from below, and start across.

While this was going on and I was paying out one rope and bringing the other in because Claude had left himself a back rope, I became aware of a white face and a pair of hands below: another party on the 'Gates'. I observed that the leader's eyes were bulging, his fingers were shaking and he was showing signs of considerable strain. I thought he would have difficulty in completing his climb. No sooner had the thought crossed my mind than he enquired in a breathless sort of way about the chances of a top rope. I apologised and explained that I was fully booked at the moment; however, if he cared to hang on for a few minutes ... I then offered him the use of the slack rope that dangled from my waist if things got too bad, and turned my attention back to Claude, who was by now approaching 'easier' ground. Suddenly he paused in mid-stride, so to speak, and his face paled as he looked towards his staunch belayer. I looked down. There was a sort of flash and there the other leader was, hanging from my free rope. Fortunately the rope was well belayed round my ample middle and Claude's expectation of being suddenly plucked from the rock remained unfulfilled. In the space of a couple of seconds he disappeared below at an ever increasing speed to the sound of a high pitched humming-cum-whooshing sound, until he was held by his second on a runner. There was much noise and commotion below as the rest of the team fielded their man. I was fully engaged in assuring Claude that he wasn't forgotten, that I wouldn't let him fall and that I was quite safe. Scarcely had we got Claude settled in on the stance when there was a cry from below: 'Any chance of a top rope, mate?'

Finally motion was restored and I moved off onto the next pitch. From the rib I stood looking across into Ivy Sepulchre. I could see straight away that this would be a gripper, a piece of information I lost no time in passing on to Claude. This cheered him up no end, as he was already sharing belays he didn't trust with a party he expected to come to grief on the next pitch. The wall was steep and loose, with the holds resembling autumn leaves on a wire fence. There was no lack of them, holds I mean, but I wasn't impressed – it looked a thoroughly nasty pitch. I seem to remember reading about a 'small superlative class of climber specialising in unsound and uncertain holds... rotten rock, overhangs etc.' This is it, the typical pitch. Still, it is the only rotten pitch on the traverse and makes one appreciate the rest, and anyway I managed it without pulling anything off. The stance in Ivy Sepulchre was a splayed-out, sliding-off affair and Claude refused to share it when he arrived, racing off round the corner onto the big roomy terrace affair that is the next stance. A few minutes more and we reached the top.

It had been a really enjoyable few hours. The crossing of Cenotaph in particular, on a sunny day such as ours, is superb.

from THE CLIMBERS' CLUB JOURNAL *1963*

SUMMERTIME

JOHN CARDY

It was midnight as the car headlights momentarily pierced the clear starry sky before they tilted down into the shadowed pass and began their familiar winding descent into the depths. They halted by the stream and we got out and breathed the chill air that told of green mountain sides and grey rock. Over the hill, felt but not seen, was the big cliff waiting for tomorrow. We slept a dreamless sleep while it waited.

The next morning was the sort you get when you haven't been in the hills for a long time. The hillsides were a riot of grey and yellow in the early morning sun, the sky an achingly pure blue. As soon as we could we were climbing up the narrow, gated road and trying to find a place to park the car. There were people here, many people, but they didn't count. This was the day of days and nothing else mattered.

Well we sweated and panted up the track like everyone else I suppose, and dutifully drank our lemonade halfway there, and all the time the cliff was getting bigger and bigger and looking just like a photograph of itself, so often studied in the long winter months. Then suddenly it was real, it was just across the water, suddenly I realised that all those corners and slabs were the routes, on them if you could see well enough were all the tiny edges and roughnesses that go to make a climb. This image before us would not blur on closer inspection. Its secrets, for it had many, were ours for the climbing. By now we were jogging round the scree almost under the crag and I was lost in the impossibility of the gully wall of the Pinnacle above. Then we drew in under the shadowed walls of the East – still, perhaps, a little damp here and there? Everything above was so big and just a little frightening, we spoke in hushed voices as we quickly sorted out the gear and scrambled up to the belay. We had chosen Diglyph to start on, a thin looking crack that splits the wall right of Chimney Route. This was Charles' climb, he had been here before, he would lead the crux pitch. Quickly, impatiently, he belayed and sent me off up the first easy pitch. This was it then, first pitch on Cloggy. How would it be? The rock leans and is awkward. I scrabble into a niche. A nut, a bridge, the corner shuns me, the holds seem green and slippery, I step left and mantelshelf onto the belay ledge. Done. Charles comes up more elegantly and sets off jamming up the crack above.

I see his feet resting minutely on the rugosities above my head, my mind contracts with fear at having to follow such a pitch, and I look longingly at the deep security of the chimney alongside. But the ropes go tight and I follow. Half blind to the climb I throw my hands into the crack, struggling fearfully. There is a niche then a peg and then things are not obvious. I lunge upwards, find a spike and climb more easily to the belay. Charles is in a little corner that proves awkward to get out of. Then I am moving up the groove above, lurching from foothold to foothold and fiddling in little nuts, still gripped with the fear of the last pitch, but stifled under a blanket of concentration and a desire not to fall off. Where it ends I move out onto the right edge and everything swims in a new perspective. Away, to the right and below me stretches the vast unbroken smoothness of Great Wall. Beyond, dwarfed figures crawl out of Curving Crack and Vember. Was this not Cloggy, the best place to be alive on a day like this? Why then this fear, this feeling of mindlessness? I leaned back on the jugs and drank in the pure exposure. It would be all right now.

I belayed in the recesses of Continuation Chimney and Charles came up with a big grin on his face. Soon we were up into the sunlight playing on the easy walls and slabs above, and out onto the stony wastes of the Eastern Terrace. Now in those days Charles was ambitious and in no time at all he had driven us over the stumbling boulders of the summit plateau and we were clattering down the terrace under the Far East. The bulges above seemed full of ropes and climbers, but after a bit we discovered they were all on Woubits so we went right down to the end and eventually found a peg belay at the foot of The Mostest. We stared up at the buttress and divided the steep bit into my pitch and his, mine the delicate pitch out over the bulges into the bottom of the big bottomless corner, and his the corner itself, then up and round the black roof and out into the sunshine above that now seemed so remote. So he started off up the first easy pitch while I sat and stared at the flat lake and thought of all the places I'd like to be, but it didn't matter.

The pitch actually was easy apart from a funny little slab and soon all the loose jugs ran out and I joined Charles in the dank mossinesses of a cave. Here the bulges loomed indecently close overhead and over them we knew lurked our big corner. The only way out was by a crack going off up left to end at a little pinnacle which gave at least the promise of a runner. After a brief pause to attend to other needs, I found a jug and pulled over the initial bulge into a bridge in the groove above. The crack gave good jams and soon I was standing on the pinnacle with a nice full weight runner at my feet. So far so good, but now things got awkward. Fifteen feet to the right was a bulging rib round which, the guidebook assured me, I should swing, to embark on a difficult traverse across a wall. The immediate problem was getting there, as all the holds seemed to dwindle in size as I got further and further from the security of the pinnacle. After several breathless quivering retreats I felt the need for a runner above my head. A slot was duly found for a nut. With this protection I kept going until I was in the groove left of the rib, back in balance but not standing on very much. But I could see a great nutting crack above, so I mantelshelved onto a foothold at waist height and was soon slotting in big nuts in the roof above my head and generally feeling a lot better. Now I don't like blind moves around anything and this one around the rib seemed blinder than most, so I wasn't in any particular hurry, to leave my cosy little corner and big nuts. But I had to try something so I tried too high and of course it was hopeless, there was nothing there, so I told Charles so. However he was being as non-committal as I was, so I peered round the overhang to the left and sought guidance from above. Fifteen feet away a grinning face on Woubits suggested that I tried lower down and referred me to the originator of the climb who was standing watching on the opposite buttress. This did not help at all and I felt even more of an impostor in this hard man's country, but I tried a bit and put my left hand in the nutting crack and leaned out and round until my right hand fell into a jug. Now there are some people who, their hand falling into a jug, just pull and stand up and say it's all over, what were you worrying about. But not me, and I had a nasty feeling that once I'd pulled on the jug I wouldn't be able to stand up and it wouldn't be all over, and what's more I wouldn't be able to get back. So I hid back in the corner of sight and Charles made more non-committal noises below.

Well this might have gone on all day had not the rival team appeared on the terrace below and directed a few well chosen words in my direction concerning their displeasure at finding us on their route. At last I had a reason for committing myself apart from a totally selfish desire to get up the route, so I justified it to myself and thought: 'Go on you coward, what's climbing for if it isn't the glory of self-commitment?' – and this time I pulled on the jug and it wasn't all over, it was only just beginning, but it was great. Twenty feet away was the corner and in between was a wall with the holds in all the right places. A line of small square footholds rigorously poised on the lip of the dark green bulges below, and six feet above, a scattered sequence of little flakes and finger jams. After each move I stood in balance on one foot, face pressed close to the rock, eyes working out the next move, then wandering downwards past Charles' white upturned face to the ridiculously foreshortened view of Mick crawling up the initial slabs. The whole thing was superb, and the sense of elation heightened as I moved further and further from the last runner. At the right moment a little nut appeared, to safeguard the final rather loose moves up to the stance. This stance is a feature of the climb, as it isn't really a stance at all but a couple of big footholds stuck in the bottom of the corner before it peters out into the general overhangs below. But if it were on a peg route you'd say it was great, you could hold a beer party on it. So I wasn't grumbling, it all added to the atmosphere of the place, and I battered in a fat angle and leaned objectively back on a nice tight belay to see where the ropes hung when I took them in. Anyway I was very happy by then because I'd done my bit and I was really looking forward to following the next pitch.

Charles came up and appeared around the bulge. He thought the traverse was good too, but he wasn't as happy as I was because he had to lead the next pitch. But of course being Charles he did it all right and was soon trying to get out left under the roof past the famous wedge. Several things have always puzzled me about this wedge. Did Brown always carry wedges with him on first ascents? Or did he have to retreat from that point the first time because he didn't have one? One thing for sure, he must have used it for aid, because there is a perfectly good protection peg a few feet lower down. Fifty feet above me, Charles was rapidly coming to the same conclusion, though in slightly different circumstances. He had just succeeded in moving past the wedge without using it, and was embarking on the groove above, when there was a sort of squawk and a scuffle, and a hand shot down into the karabiner, rapidly followed by the rest of Charles. After a few seconds' breathless agitation a sling was slung and I could let the ropes go slack again. Next time he made it all right and soon the ropes went tight and I could relinquish the stance in favour of Mick who was rapidly approaching up the pitch below. The corner was surprisingly easy, the holds being perfect for bridging, but I found the traverse under the roof very nasty and was very glad to use the wedge. Bridging up the groove above was glorious, nothing but the thin thread of the path an immeasurable depth beneath. That climb was almost the mostest, but there was the next day.

There was time for another route, but the sun was warm and the thought did not arise. Instead we strolled down the Eastern Terrace, back under the climb where the other team was still in action, and down to the car where we just sat by the stream and stared at the hills and the sky, drunk with happiness. And of course later on we celebrated in the pub where everyone was, who had done much harder routes than we had, but somehow it didn't seem to matter one little bit.

Sunday was fabulous as well. We went up to Cloggy again, sweating up the dry dust in the morning heat, until there was the cliff again, sheer and black, its facets catching the early sun, across the still green water. Already there were climbers, minute flies crawling around its base and tentatively committing themselves to its walls.

We walked past, staring at the routes of yesterday, and wondering half hoping, half dreading, if today would be as good. At the foot of the East was Mick, winding himself up for Troach, his face a study in advanced grippery. But at some stage in the proceedings last night we had decided to do Slanting. It may even have been my idea. Anyway there it was, so we slid down under Middle Rock and dumped the gear at the foot of the West. This looked all overhanging and we couldn't see where anything went, but then a party we thought were on Great turned out to be on White, and we realised that our route started much further right. So we plodded on up the stony terrace to where the overhangs got so big above you had to look down. Further up a rope was dangling. A party on Mynedd? No, it is our route. A big team had just spent half an hour lassoing the peg and were attempting to leave the ground. Apart from wishing I had a camera I was very glad of an excuse to get out of the climb. The whole thing looked much thinner and more serious than I had expected. The first pitch, which is technically the crux, overcomes the huge initial overhangs at their right hand end, just before they peter out into the smoothnesses of Bloody, then embarks on an almost horizontal traverse immediately above them, aiming for the slanting slab proper, which is miles away round the corner, right in the middle of the cliff somewhere. But there was a great queue for White, and we thought Bloody was wet, and by the time we'd realised that Bloody didn't actually go up the wet bit, a couple of mates had rolled up and booked it, so that was that. Anyway Charles volunteered to second the first pitch, which was the thing I was really frightened of, so I couldn't really do anything apart from uncoil the ropes and sit and wait.

The leader in front eventually reached the peg on the lip and started across the slab. He made it look very easy and found a few runners so I felt a bit better. About the same time Charles discovered a peg halfway out across the roof, so we wouldn't have to play at cowboys either. The afternoon wasn't really too far gone by the time the route was free and I was slowly gyrating from the peg halfway across the roof. From here there was no difficulty in reaching a long sling which the previous party had just happened to leave dangling from the top peg, in return for our giving their second man a back rope on the traverse. All too soon I had sorted out my gear on the peg and was preparing to face the rather terrifying prospect of a 5b slab. I stepped out of the sling and was immediately gripped. You are supposed to go hard left from here but it looked very smooth and rounded and anyway a few feet above was a 'flower' growing out of a crack in the slab. A couple of inept upward lurches later it was in my hand, and strangely

enough there proved to be a neat hole in it just large enough to take a
karabiner. Well I didn't feel like going back down to the traverse line now,
so I kept going up and left to where I'd spotted a big foothold under the
next roof. I padded up to it and with my hands on great undercuts behind
the overlap everything seemed more reasonable. A few steps left and down
brought me to the grass patch that is the base of operations on the crux.
Rather pleased at having avoided one of the hard bits I began to wonder if
the big team had missed anything else, like protection. It didn't take much
looking for. I've since heard that it's supposed to be the belay peg on Gael,
but since it is immediately above the crux of Slanting it would take a very
hard man to resist its security. Well now I was doing the crux on a top rope
which seemed quite a good idea, and it just remained to do it. So I climbed
down to the lip of the overhangs and dug my fingers in the grass the way
everyone else obviously had, and had a look at it. Slowly I worked out the
sequence of moves out from security and learned how to reverse them. Then
it was time for the big push so first I rested my face against the rock and
breathed its sweet smell and pretended I was somewhere else, but I wasn't,
so I went out and this time I made it, feet bridged out and leaning out as far
as I dared to give enough friction on the sloping holds. The feelings on
completing a move like this cannot be described in words.

A brief rest then a look around the corner at the rest of the pitch. The
angle fell back and straightforward climbing on rather doubtful rock led to
a grassy ledge. It was a good thing that it didn't get hard again anyway, for
it was completely unprotected and I was virtually soloing above the biggest
overhang on the crag. I moved back right along the ledge to protect Charles
and belayed. But I couldn't relax here the way I had on The Mostest, because
we still had the big pitch to come. A route like this is much more of a team
effort, and leader and second must share the seriousness of the position.
Charles came up and made suitable noises on the crux but I wasn't worried
as he had fixed a back rope through the peg.

While he was climbing there was opportunity to admire the view and in
particular the antics of an orange anorak which seemed to have been in one
position on Troach for quite a long time.

Meanwhile, back at the belay, it was time to do a few calculations.
According to the guidebook the big pitch is 180ft. Now if you're slick at
arithmetic you'll realise that we couldn't really do that on 150ft ropes
without stretching them quite a bit, which might tend to pull the leader off
on delicate stuff like this. The party in front, who were on 200ft ropes (bought
especially for Great Wall, it is rumoured) took great apparent delight in
informing us that there was no possibility of belaying halfway, and therefore
we would have to move together for thirty feet. It's all right, they said, the

first bit's only VS. But such things happen only in fairy tales and bar rooms, so we weren't too worried. When Charles arrived he belayed at the other end of the ledge and I moved past him to look at the next bit. Out to the left, set in space, was the slanting slab proper, its outside edge overlooking the big emptinesses which, before Mynedd was put up, was called the empty quarter of Cloggy. I was on a level with the bottom of the slab and an exposed little gangway led across to it. A sling flicked over a bunch of spikes above gave confidence for an awkward step up, and I was on the slab. It was quite a place. But, hard under the big overlap of the right wall, were holds and even protection, so I padded up until it got hard and anyway I reckoned I'd done my thirty feet. So I looked for the biggest foothold around and buried a couple of pegs in the brown crumbly rock under the right wall. When Charles came past he intimated in the way that only Charles can that he wasn't happy. Such admissions from Charles are so rare that I began to think he didn't like my belay or something, so we groped about for ten minutes in the crack and came up with a chockstone someone had left lying there along with all the empty fag packets and broken false teeth.

Well I think that this chockstone might just have stood an inward pull, but he seemed happier now and couldn't delay it any longer so he set off up the big pitch at last. Soon he was out of sight again, leaving me to my thoughts in the middle of that big slab and the oppressive overhangs above. Down there by the lake people were half naked in the late afternoon sun, but I just shivered and changed feet on the stance from time to time to restore the feeling of reality. The ropes were still for a long time then slowly, a foot at a time, they crept out. Once I caught a glimpse of a red sling waving in the sun immeasurably far above the overhangs, but that was all, and all I could do was follow the line of the ropes up the slab to where a bunch of perlon swung from the right wall, then out across under the overhangs to the edge where he had disappeared an indefinite time ago that might have been seconds or hours. With five feet of rope left there was a faint cry and he was up.

It was sustained that pitch, and hard too, just round the corner out of sight where there was a narrow little white slab on the edge of it all, and it got thinner and thinner and more and more irreversible until there was a big overlap and you thought this is the end but reached over the top half hoping, and there was a jug and a pull and a heave and you could stand on holds again. Above it was still hard but now you could see the sun on the arête twenty feet away and so you went across the breath-catching wall above the big roof to a final glorious pull into a world of big green ledges and easy grey slabs.

At the top we didn't want to go down but just sat and looked at it all, and we were glad it was done but we didn't want it all to be over.

from CAMBRIDGE MOUNTAINEERING *1970*

THE GREAT WALL

ED DRUMMOND

'You've just got to climb it now.' That was all the man said: Boysen slipping quietly off to climb. Seal cold in my shorts I was feeling a little blue. Below us Llyn du'r Arddu flashed black glass. On the line of the mountain the toy tiny train crept, its gasps of steam signalling like heartbeats.

'Come on lily legs.' Crew didn't like to be kept waiting; it was him holding the rope.

Above me the wall beamed gleamy with rain, bald as a whale. Easter Sunday 1967. I gulped to see there was a line; my pub outboast still stoodered. This wasn't funny.

A paraphernalia of cameras, wormy ropes, comments, draggles of steel krabs, oh, and a talisman rurp I'd hidden in the pocket of my shorts; he said I wouldn't need any pegs. The camera shot me in black and white, glossing over my burning cheeks. My knees were news in wild Wales. Boysen was slinking up his route on velvet feet.

On blunt finger-tips to a jingle of krabs, I footjigged the first wall to the small overhang. 'That's as far as Banner got,' floated up. I can rest there thought I, peering, manteling.

I could not and, mouse nervous, I not-rested for an hour, Crew spearing me from below. 'I didn't have a runner there.' But I did, after an hour, and then I rose again. Ten feet. There was a quartz break and I took one too and looked around.

I could just make out Llanberis smudged between hills; woman and child would be up now asking where I was. Below me a delighted Pete was blowing advice to a numbed Boysen. Above me was a peg; with an open eye. If I could poke my finger in, he certainly wouldn't be able to see. If I had a ten-foot arm.

I lift up to the left, 'Clements fell off that way,' bless you sir – a five-foot arm – my fingers start to finger the slippery dimples, toes walking backwards. A ten-foot arm.

Then he tells me he moved right, 'then a quick layback and then up to the peg'. I note the connective; he didn't say a quick layback up *to* the peg, so what happens when I get to that 'and'? Climbers arriving below would ask how long I'd been there. I felt established as a kind of gargoyle. Stuck.

AfivefootarmsuspensionbridgingyourlifeinyourhandatthreefootarmIdon't havetofalloffSolesstickonicenice. Made it, snug as a nut, my *doigt* in the peg. While I'm not-resting at the peg he tells me he used it. I'm getting to like him.

Now you're big enough to fly, jugs come lovely, hands full of rock up I go like a slow balloon, pink knees bumping up after me. Two rusty pegs peep; 'That's as far as Brown got.' Uncle Joe beams at me from his advert and Pete sounds a long way away.

Now once upon a ledge in the middle of Great Wall I sat on a jammed half arse and dangled. A tidal wave of rock swelled out all around. Above me a twenty-foot groove groped to a slim bulge; above this straggled a ragged crack. Where this began was a tiny sling, waving to me. Suddenly hungry I took off my sock and lowered it on the slack to the deck where someone put a block of my dates in which I pulled up to suck. For a while I'd turned cold. While someone else held the rope Pete ran on the spot for warmth. Climbers below moved off home silent as fish.

I was delighted now to bridge, push, flow, no runners since the ledge, warmer. The little sling was trying to reach me. Boysen, perched, smoking, watching.

The bulge slid into my arms, frigid with cold. It was staring me in the face. Thirty feet above a runner, only noholds here. Sixty feet is long enough to see where you're going. The noholds in front of my eyes float up, slowly. First you see them, then you don't.

PAs on wheels I move quickly, fingers whimpering. The little sling stops to tickle my chin and I put a krab on it and hum. One thin nut on eyelash tape. Then I put my foot in the noose.

Down I glide, invisible, in the lift, and slip among the staring crowd on the street. He's still up there. He must be holding on to something. Then he moves jerkily. Suddenly no one is talking, upturned white faces eating the sight alive. You blink and stop breathing. He stands in the sling. 'This is like cracking a safe,' he yells. We look at each other. He's all right. I'm all right. Pete shouts something up.

Now the crack grins for two sweet nuts. Elephants bounce past trumpeting. I would like to put my fingers in its mouth, free as air, but I'm saving that for a sunny day. Then the crack shuts up and it shut me up until he said there was a peg behind a hidden flake to the right. After that parabola there's just a human sucker move with a ledge after, just lying there waiting for you to stand on it. Pancake hearted I plopped a fist in five feet above, just as my feet skedaddled. I'm not usually lucky.

It was too late for him to follow now, and I sat chilling, the silly rurp still in my pocket, while he abseiled down to unstick my runners. 'Well done

Scream,' he'd said. Five years ago. He was still in love with that wall. Lovely
boy Crew, arrow climber. Wall without end.

from HARD ROCK *1974*

SNOWDON, WHITSUNTIDE

The mountain bared itself.
Cold, nude, not to be moved.

Carrying well-dressed men with quiet wives
and two children;
hugging couples in city shoes
they placed like chess pieces on the polished rocks;
striding, whippet-kneed climbers
with ropes on their shoulders
and one or two elderly gentlemen, sticked and piped
and steady as clocks,
the broad path ambled over grassy spurs
until it stumbled, slowly rearing, to strike the sky.

On the dead-limb-fidge we step by step.
Lakes, below our feet, ink-drops; the blink of sheep
in the distance.

Under the summit gulls hung, glided, battled back
then rode out like witches over the lip of the precipice,
rattling their calls against the bleak faces
and down dank gullies, juggling and tumbling on
the updraught
as if they were laughing,
while we laboured slowly upwards
into the clouds.
The train coughed past: glassed-in faces, newspapers,
cameras eyeing the sky
and sudden gulfs;

puff-puff-puffing, Britain's last rack railway
groaned iron-stubborn.
We pushed for the hotel.

Steaming teas, late apple, people
eating like eagles
before the arrival of nightfall.

Outside, the smithereening wind
Was about its business of chilling and uplifting
detached objects,
licking clean the tops of Easter,
inviting us.

LLYN DU'R ARDDU: THE BLACK LAKE

The cliff fangs
Over the cym and barren mountain flanks.
Only the lake holds back the monarch of rock.

A take-it-or-leave-it-lake, like a work of art.
You can spit spray, flower squalls,
Gallop away with long white manes in a wink,
Yet stary, rippling into sleep
And dream you are a mouth, sprinkled with stars.
In winter you sing, organpiping icicles
on the silent stones.
Sometimes you sit still all day and think blue.

You are a wound
In the mountain's side, leaking the sky.
Streams come and go, fish swim,
and in your depths where the passing birds reflect,

trembling,
I see myself

Ed Drummond

NERVE WRACK POINT*

PAT AMENT and TOM HIGGINS

Higgins: Life-giving sunlight, positive and harsh on the polished rock, soft and trembling in the grasses. The streams, in their persistent way, oblivious to us, finding the sea. Tuolumne, place of lush, blooming swaths of meadow, of granite domes surrounded by alpine peaks. Summer after summer, a handful of climbers come here for the exhilaration of moving on high-angle faces, of teetering a little breathless and spellbound near a sky so blue it seems almost black.

After a short hike, Pat and I are able to get a close look at the southern margin of Lamb Dome, a crackless, 600ft wall. We scramble on to a ledge at the base of the wall.

Climbing this season in Tuolumne has new meaning for me. As I discover more and more my friends, this place, and myself, challenge and difficulty become less insistent, fellowship and encounter more important. I have thoughts of the descent: returning together from the summit, holding and knowing a chosen experience, a chosen day.

It is good to be with Pat. The morning is exquisite. We sort gear and lace our shoes. Feelings are right. We are eager and yet relaxed. Each of us knows the other to be a capable climber. Perhaps I sense a bit of uncertainty in Pat. He is wondering if this will be a non-competitive ascent.

We rope-up.

Pat chalks his fingers. I burrow behind some boulders and a tree and secure the belay.

After forty feet of thin, 70° face climbing, he moves left ten feet to what looks like a crack but isn't. He is able to get a bolt in with half-an-hour of touchy hammering while stemming between two jaw-breaker-sized knobs. Twenty-five feet higher, a second bolt. He places the third bolt on a headwall. More thin climbing runs the rope out and takes him to a minimal belay stance. We are happy and loud and imitate the antics of T. M. Herbert, that light soul, a miracle of nature, able to laugh and make silly the sometimes snarling ways of climbers.

I follow the pitch. At the belay stance, we begin to realise the seriousness

*The spelling of the word Wrack is that used in the original text (Editor)

of our undertaking and talk of possible ways to go. The angle of the face appears slightly less to the right. It is forty feet to the first decent knob. A bolt... maybe... will go there. I work my way up, avoiding anything too hard to reverse. A new route will be a clear-cut achievement for me after months with Vista where any accomplishment can be easily undone.

I find another crack that isn't a crack, pound the tip of a piton into it, nest another pin behind that one, and tie them off. Contortions. Ament slides his hat off and pushes his fingers through his hair which is a pile of spaghetti stranger than Manzanita. Face climbing without cracks is like roulette. What next?

'We should name this Nerve Wrack Point,' Pat suggests. Lamb Dome. Some name for a dome. Lambaste ... Lambent ... lament ... lame ... lame-brain...

Ament: I wonder if we will get off in a day. Setting speed records. It's like making love and trying to see how fast you can do it. Higgins is on a nubbin and pressed against the rock... like a butterfly. I study his techniques and strategies, hoping to remember them.

Higgins: Pat blasts loose with a war whoop that sounds like the San Andreas fault shifting. We try to make the difficulties disappear, but they won't. 'Exfoliating' I screech.

Ament and his travelling medicine show. Riding freights. Cutting records. Walking a tightwire over some canyon in Colorado. Running from the law. Having three affairs all at once!

Ament: Higgins is balancing on an edge. I ask him how it looks.
'Think I see a place where I might be able to get a bolt in.'
'Wish Peggy had come climbing with us.'
'Look at that blue hat. He sleeps in that thing.'
Higgins has a way of getting people outside of themselves. I find myself looking at me.
'It's stupid to push it much further without some protection,' Tom says.
'The point of climbing isn't to try to get killed.'
Tom's footwork is wild. He gets the bolt in, standing on nothing. An endurance test follows: a five-nine traverse to the right; two more bolts, the remainder of our supply, widely-spaced, on the limit of his reserves.

Higgins: Pat is unpretentious and serious in his appraisal of the situation. While I am climbing, he feeds rope carefully. When I look down, I see his body erect, set for a fall. The smiling is put aside.

Ament: Tom moves back down to the second from last bolt to set up the belay. This way, the tie-in becomes both the top bolt and the second from last. He belays from two knobs.

I bend and stretch the stiffness out of my muscles. The pitch has taken several hours. I am anxious to move. Finally, I am scratching at the rock, straining my eyes in search of crystals. As I arrive at his first bolt, I try to find the footholds he used to place it. I shudder, imagining I'm in the lead. Starting the hard traverse, I stop and stare at it. My rope leads to the side here. I am in love with the idea of swinging fifty feet and inch out on to the traverse, reciting the lyrics of a tune … by The Grateful Dead.

'Three feet and you'll be able to see a pebble for your right foot,' Higgins maintains. I spread-eagle to it. When I arrive up, he hurries me by, clipping on to me the few chunks of hardware we have brought. I picture him speeding along in his Porsche … (he drives a Volks, is obsessed with Porsches).

Higgins: Ament says something to the rock from behind the chalk trapped between his lips. But nothing happens except he drops the chalk. I'm making little curse noises from my belay, thinking we might not make it, and humming. I hum to the rock. A crazy little combo of some blues piece and Erik Satie coming out in little push-breaths.

Ament is both afraid and fearless, working upward on hard moves, complaining that his sunburn is bad and that he expects to faint soon.

Ament: The rock is steeper. I talk to the butterflies in my stomach. Old aspirations. No possible protection. Higgins flicks the rope. It jerks me. I nearly dirty my pants. Tom leans his head against the rock, baking in the sun. I pick out holds.

'Taking plenty of time and making sure I don't fall.'
'Don't blame you. Take all the time you want.'
'If I can just reach that thing up there …'
'Looks like a good hold.'
'I guess I sort of have to commit myself.'
'Go for it.'
'I couldn't climb down that last stretch anyway, so…'
'I'm watching you.'
'There. Got it.'
'The rope's stuck down here. Climb back so I can free it.'
'Huh?!'
'Just kidding.'

Disappearing over the top of a bulge, I find a ledge, which is a relief. Maybe the ledge is a mirage. I bring Higgins up. Our feet are dead from edging. My sunburn is beginning to take the joy out of the climbing. We have reached a point high enough to see over a hill to a glimmering edge of Tenaya Lake. A breeze blows across the wall. I have thoughts, reflecting back through days of climbing. remembering when I am young and it is winter, reverberations of river and pine … in Eldorado Canyon … and Kor. In memory, Eldorado takes on the essence of a supernatural canyon. It is as if I can feel, as I have felt before, the afternoon flight of the shadows up the walls; the higher summits still lit; birds coasting beside the buttresses and landing on ledges. I imagine myself at the end of the tight-wire, looking across it, the ghost of Ivy Baldwin with me. A cable strung over a canyon, challenging me.

'Higgins Skwigglins.'

'You're flipping, Ament. It was all of those avocados you ate on the drive up.'

'Tom Horrendo and Pat Amazing."

'Look at him. *Gone.*'

Tom is leading above me on a vertical corner that arches to the summit. The bottoms of his shoes show. If he comes off, I'll go home with footprints on my face. Now what's he doing? With his foot over his ear …

Higgins: The last lead is short. Still hard, though. The most direct way simply will not go. I am forced right, on to a long sliver of a ledge that feels rotten … What if the ledge stayed but the wall fell off … Friction above the ledge, then the summit of Lamb Dome. I am out of bolts, out of light, out of strength. Sitting down to unlace my shoes, they are already unlaced. Imagine that. As I pull in the rope, Pat holds more chalk between his lips. We are still playing the game, making much of a short and terribly improbable climb. When the climb is finished, we take one another's picture. The camera fixes our images, like those of miners I recall seeing in brown and faded photos, arms slung around the nearest co-worker, companions just up from another day of beating stone, cursing money and fate. Pictures remind me of miners, grandfathers, and death. Pat is caught awkward and smiling … I am relaxed and dazed. In the future I will feel a loss when coming across these photos. Looking down, the sheets and sheets of it are like an endless, aid-bolt job, except the beauty has gone free. We turn toward the cast. Long, dome shadows are on the meadows. We were permitted to pass.

Ament descends the easy slopes of granite before me, camera jostling at his side. I try not to like him too much, but … it is no less than love I feel for Pat, myself, and this day. Much says no to the sense of intimacy: my headlong pursuit of far off personal goals; the shambles of several marriages among friends. Who is Ament? I think. Who is Higgins? Pat thinks. We are two souls moving together from the summit of a dome, wars waging themselves to the east, traffic toiling below, a brief ascent securing within us unexplainable but real joy.

Ament: I am standing in San Francisco International Airport. It is nine o'clock at night. I am gazing at a runway through my reflection in a window. I will have to wait here all night, a new kind of bivouac, having missed my plane. I am duped by a suspicious desk clerk, Susie United, who senses that my youth card is phony.

'What's your date of birth?' she asks.

'1951,' I reply.

'How old are you?'

'Uhhh … sixteen.'

'I'll have to talk to my supervisor about this!'

I'm blushing, be-fuddled, with swirls of blonde hair, black and sleazy trench coat, a bomb in my suitcase.

Put Higgins in this situation. I see him gracing through it … with his fancy footwork, his full, barrel-chested laugh. I don't mesh with the gears of social reality. Quite the contrast: San Francisco International Airport and Tuolumne – our pastoral land of OZ.

I miss the last plane while waiting for the additional money to be sent. A night stranded *here!* Some joke. My parents are waiting to pick me up at the airport in Denver. They'll appreciate it when I don't show. Can't call Peggy. She's deserted me, gone east for a while. Nerve Wrack Point, the climbing, our friendship … The mountains teach us of the joys that are ours. I will be like Higgins: buoyant, never morose.

Voices. Paging *me?* 'Paging Pat Ament, paging Pat Ament, your Rolls Royce is waiting for you out in front…'

Maybe I'll call Higgins and listen to him laugh. Miss him already. Kind of hate going back to Colorado, in some ways. Higgins's routes. He believes in the improbable, 'they will be done.' Our respective climbing teachers are themselves best friends: Rearick and Bob Kamps. We are indeed friends. Though somehow yet alone. Me searching for companionship, living for the day; Higgins, Vista Volunteer, with future, keeping cool. He'll grow old, all right. Higgins has but one fault: he's pernickety. You know, he's never yet lived in Camp 4 because he'd have to share his utensils!

You get the feeling that climbing stories are written in dark, music-filled studies, or on the summits themselves. Words chiselled into granite … in Greek. So, maybe San Francisco International will be some kind of 'first'. Airports seem geared for 1990. People, all different weird kinds, movie stars, lawyers, Cubans, with tickets to Australia and New Jersey. Soldiers. The roar of planes taking off...

Dawn... is time to go, at last. Got the ticket, received my money. I'll see you, Tuolumne, next summer. Higgins, I'll see you.

from SWARAMANDEL *1973*

IN THANKS

TOM HIGGINS

Hey Kamps,

The herds of climbers in Tuolumne have dynamited whatever selfish hope I had for sanctuary in the Meadows. Man, you can't even steal a shower at the Tuolumne Lodge without hearing from the adjoining stall an announcement of the newest line. Bunches of Valley climbers and a frenzy of LA youth have shot through the place... remember seeing them in the Meadows store with hardware on? Vern Clevenger's looseleaf bundle of routes looks like an underground journal, a cauliflower ballooning in the rough. God! As many new routes in two years as in the previous twenty!

Now and then I deride myself for my blatant self-interest. But then I wonder how any climbers – never mind me – can ever again hope to find that rush of loneliness amid the quiet space of high Tuolumne rock.

For all my complaining, only one young lion has homed in on the greatest wall in Tuolumne, the west face of Fairview. Clevenger did the left-facing arch system – remember? – On the right margin of the west face. Get the name – 'Mr. Toad's Wild Ride'.

Now, he and I are going to try to complete the west face route you and I started in 1968, the direct line in the centre of the face. We've been to the high point where you and I retreated, though by three more clean and direct pitches than those you and I originally did. Since then, impatient soul that he is, Clevenger recruited Bob Harrington and together they climbed the sixty-foot smooth headwall above our 1968 highpoint. They took all day, trading leads on ten-foot sections to get the bolts in. Neither Vern nor Bob made all the moves, and at one point a bolt served as aid to get another in. So, we'll see if it all goes free.

If we get the entire route, it will be the finest on Fairview, if not in Tuolumne; better than Mr. Toad's says Clevenger, and better than the other nearby giant, Fairest of All, which hooks too wildly right in the middle to be the grandest west face line.

This will be my finale in the Meadows ... last hurrah ... *pièce de résistance*. There just don't seem to be more good lines between lines between lines between lines in Tuolumne. Pratt steals away some summers to a secret rock palace which leaves his eyes sparkling most of the fall ... got to pry it out of him somehow.

Bob, the years I've spent climbing in Tuolumne were pure nourishment to me. How about you? The Meadows always made the regular, flat world bearable, and the flat world made the meadows a sanctuary. It was the pull between the two which nourished. School and work without the mountains would have been deadly. The mountains without the nervous struggling down below would have been limbo, not heaven.

Well, man, as if you didn't know, you were like a father to me for those summers, modelling a conniving, effortless style, clever protection, and witty love for those soaring virgin walls. So, I'll say thanks and thanks also to Tuolumne for holding us like a mother might between deep blue and granite folds in the warmth of the Meadows sun ... TOM

from ASCENT *1975-76*

A NIGHT OUT

ROB COLLISTER

'Night climbing, sir? No, there's none of that now, sir. It's all demonstrating and smashing things nowadays.' And the elderly porter shook his head regretfully.

David hadn't done King's and it was his last night in Cambridge. Gloomily he remarked that he was 'going out with a whimper'. The remedy was obvious.

David's poncho bulging strangely, we scrunched noisily over the gravel towards the chapel, the din of three May Balls reverberating about us. If only the fifteenth-century sculptor knew how useful the tail of that dog would be! Might be dangerous to swing on it, though. Up the glass, just like a ladder, till half way up there's a tug on the rope. Two voices below. A splashing sound, and one voice remarks that there will be a bare patch in the grass next year. Once before, at that same spot, I had looked through a hole in the glass to see torch-beams flashing inside. Fortunately Saltmarsh mislaid the key to the roof. The voices move away and there is a wide step across into the corner. A stone bracket provides a thread runner. The drainpipe is square, with its sides flush to the wall. Fingertips and friction, but plenty of resting places curious how, in the dark, you feel yourself to be falling backwards even when in balance – and at the top a gorgeous metal jug on which to swing, heave, mantelshelf, before crawling through an embrasure.

David started to climb. The throbbing beat of the Stones would drown anything, I thought. Immediately, the sharp metallic clink of a karabiner rang out like a gunshot. I glared over the edge, but could only make out a vague shape a long way below. The dew on the roof was soaking through my trousers. Too bad. Stars, hold your fires … Where are they, though? Hell, it's getting light already. Come on, David. A head appeared suddenly and David squeezed through the hold, panting.

The pinnacles are easy enough, the spikes no more than a nuisance. Though, pulling up on one crenellation, two foot square, I found that I was clutching it in my arms. Summits can be places for mediation, but there was no time on this one. On the Fellows' lawn the first blackbird was awake. David climbed up and down again, and we prepared to abseil back to the vestry roof. As I started to descend, David touched my sleeve. 'How do you abseil?' he whispered.

Five minutes later we were leaning over Garret Hostel Bridge watching the May Ball couples punting their way to Grantchester. A policeman approached quietly and leant beside us. David hitched his poncho a little closer.

'Morning, officer.'

'Lovely morning,' was the affable reply.

We strolled away. An owl floated down the lane ahead of us. Behind, the archaic rhythms were pulsating still, but in the clear cold morning light, the chapel stood austerely aloof.

from CAMBRIDGE MOUNTAINEERING *1971*

A LONGING FOR WALES

S. GONZALES

He was sick of walking up to Cloggy so I reckoned it was time to tell him about this new line I had seen on Dove Crag in the Lakes. He was derogatory as usual, but I pointed out that we might escape the Whitsun crowds, so he consented to go.

Now whenever I see a line I get really nervous and jittery in case someone else should swipe it and so we expected Oliver and Brown (L) or Ross to come rushing round in the night to steal a march. Even though they didn't come we got up early just in case they crept over from Dunmail.

Flogging up to the crag he kept moaning about the bloody long walks up to Lake District crags, even though this one was only half as far as Cloggy. And then we were there and he was impressed ('Nearly as good as the East') and I was even more impressed because I would get the first pitch since it was my idea. Anyway there was no one else around so I talked him into doing this Dovedale Grooves route which hadn't been repeated for ten years.

So we went over to the climb but the idiot fell off straight away trying to shift a loose block. I swear he's only the clumsiest bloke in all the world. Not to be defeated and determined not to let me have a go he leapt up and pushed the block off and after some more lurching and swearing he crept into this hole under the overhanging chimney and tied onto some cranky chocks. And I tried to look nonchalant on the hard bit, because I never admit that anything he does is hard and vice-versa, but this was hard so I said 'good 'un, youth' and left it at that.

So I grabbed his spare slings and climbed over him and stood on his head. And he started moaning so I said the block above his head was loose to make him moan more. Then I rushed up and grabbed the block and there was this big thrutch and a long step onto a slab on the left. But one of the ropes got jammed so I had to untie it and I was dead chuffed because it's always him that messes the rope up and leaves me in desperates. And he came up the chimney with the rope pulling him off but he didn't fall off, so I was dead sick. There was a lot of spare rock above for a direct finish but we reckoned we would just make a dinner-time pint so we leapt past this raven's nest and rushed off down the valley.

But we couldn't get in for the tourists so we went back to camp and he moaned about drunkard tourists and threatened to smash the loudspeaker which blared out music all day for the spartan campers in their Richard-III-type tents across the river. We could even hear the bloody thing on the crag.

Next morning we got up later but burnt up to the crag in record time determined to smash this new route into the deck. It was my idea so I got first go. A crafty thread and a queer mantelshelf led to the first hard bit. He said traverse right, so I went straight up and nearly fell off and as usual he was right but he got gripped following so that made us even. The stance was a sloping grass ledge that was sliding off, especially with him on as well so I sent him up this steep wall and he lurched round the corner and muttered something sick. But he was at the stance in no time so I let him off, seeing as he hadn't used a peg either. The next bit started off two loose blocks which he kicked off later saying 'that'll sort, 'em out' and they hit the deck like an H bomb and shifted a tree and half a ton of grass and scared the wits out of these two birds who had come up to watch us. I got lost on the bit after and he was jeering so I leapt up this green groove that was hard and unprotected and I was really chuffed when he had a tight rope. Evens again.

The wall above was full of overhanging grooves but he couldn't do any of them so he traversed right and descended to a stance about five feet above me and several feet out and passed the buck. But the overhang was easy for me but I got gripped on this queer slab that would be even harder in normal damp conditions. We looked down the top bit of Extol and I persuaded him to save it for tomorrow and we got down dead on opening time. We decided to call it Hiraeth because we were longing to get back home again to Wales.

Black clouds were rolling over on Monday but we reckoned we might do

Extol before it started raining so we rushed up even faster than ever. The First pitch was a rotten narrow chimney that he couldn't get into so I had to give him a tight rope again. But he got his finger out on the big pitch and was up in under an hour which seemed good going considering its reputation. The last overhang was a bit dicey and he kept the ropes slack to get his own back for Dovedale Grooves. If I had come off I would have ended up in Ullswater but I didn't and we were dead chuffed and got back to camp with the black clouds chasing us hard.

It rained so we went to Keswick and they were all dead sick because we had swiped their routes but they bought us some beer and we bought plenty more for a party. But the clumsy fool dropped the case in Lake Road and broke half the bottles. Still, the empties made good missiles to throw at the tents in the next field.

from THE CLIMBERS' CLUB JOURNAL *1963*

THE DIAMOND – A FREE ASCENT

ROGER BRIGGS and BOB CANDELARIA

Failure on Long's Peak is always costly. I know this from ten years of failures, interspersed with a few successes, and Robert was finding this out in his first summer of climbing on Long's. During July we tried twice to free climb the East Face of Long's … and failed twice.

On our first attempt we hoped to free climb the Diagonal, never before done, then continue up the Diamond Face. This overly ambitious adventure ended quickly about 200ft up the Diagonal. The third pitch had a twenty-foot section running with ice water. We spent hours trying to work around the pitch on the blank wall to its right. Finally, in disappointment, we rappelled off and hiked out, the effort of the previous day's approach seeming wasted. After returning to Boulder it took several days for our bruised egos to recover and for our animas to return.

On our second attempt we hoped to free climb the Shining Slab, a little known lower wall aid route, then continue up the Diamond. Two long aid pitches off Mill's Glacier presented the main difficulties and these went free fairly easily at about 5.10. The second pitch was slimy wet and above that the rock became more broken and low angle. The climbing eased up, but the hauling became proportionately more difficult and took its toll on our bodies. We reached Broadway by noon still feeling up for the Diamond. Timewise we were doing great but the weather looked horrible. We had to make the Yellow Wall bivouac ledge by dark – some 700ft of steep climbing up the Diamond.

> Success …
>   a temptress of the soul …
> Dances naked before your dreams,
> Tries to soothe a restless desire,
> Raping your discretion for a taste of fame …
>   We plunge into her arms.

I was hot to keep moving but just as I started up D-7 it began to drizzle and hail. We sat on Broadway under our cagoules in grim silence wondering if someone up there would give us a break. Then it stopped and I ran out the rope 160ft to a small stance. Robert followed, then ran it out another 160ft past a difficult wet section.

As I followed the weather closed in for its final assault. In the raging hailstorm my hands became numb, making the pitch desperate. We were soaking wet before we could pull on our cagoules. Standing with one foot at a time on a two inch foothold, I looked at Robert and had to laugh: here we were, two pathetic specimens, down and out like a couple of drifters run out of Dodge City for vagrancy. After half an hour the storm was easing and our cagoules were leaking like sieves. Was this a passing storm or a more permanent cold front?

We were still three pitches from the bivouac ledge and it would take an hour before the rock was free-climbable. As it was, every ledge and hold had an inch of slushy hail on it. With heavy hearts we decided to bail out, 1000ft of climbing and hauling having been to no avail. After hours of rappelling we were off the face, standing before the Diamond once again in defeat. The walk-out on the trail was made all the more difficult by all the hikers that would ask.

'What'd ya climb?' What could we say?

'Not much … '

I tried to remind myself that we can learn and grow through pain and defeat but Robert seemed to have no such easy rationalization. Yes, failure on Long's is costly.

Two days later, like two bright-eyed suckers, we were ready again to attempt Long's. We were both sick of hauling from the last two trips so this time we would concentrate on the Diamond only and try to do it in a day by going light. The last 300ft of the Diamond hadn't gone all free yet. A year earlier Goss and Logan had pushed a brilliant free route to Table Ledge, traversing off there, but no one had freed the awesome summit headwall further right. It seemed to us that the entire Diamond had not yet gone free.

We wanted to do it, and in the best possible style as Goss and Logan had. We would go light and fast, cutting every possible corner: one rope only, no hammers, no cagoules, just sweaters tied around our waists and a hat stuffed in a pocket. This would put us out on a limb, high on the wall with a storm, but we both agreed that this was how we wanted to climb it. We would have to rely on ourselves rather than on our equipment, a big step for Western man.

We planned to leave on Monday afternoon but the weather looked frightening. A week earlier one hundred and fifty people were killed in the Big Thompson Canyon, fourteen miles from Long's, when fourteen inches of rain fell in a short time. The weather had been unsettled since then, and we wondered what sort of storms could be brewing. The forecast sounded fifty-fifty, and then we heard that a heavy snowstorm had hit Long's the night before. Things were looking bad for the two drifters with no way to bluff by a storm. This would be the last time the two of us could climb together on Long's for the season. It was now or never so we decided to go for it.

6.00pm Monday, we start hiking from Long's Peak ranger station. Our loads seem light compared with the last two trips. We have one less rope, less food, and very little clothing. We're in better shape but the first half mile is still an ordeal with Broadway seeming infinitely far away. Then we get into a tempo, unplug ourselves from time and float up to Chasm Lake. The view of the East Face from Chasm is magnificent.

> The Diamond leans out over you,
> towers above you,
> strikes you in awe, then
> leaves you with
> an empty feeling of existence.

The weather is clearing but cold, and the mountain is only slightly snowy. In the fading light we see two climbers starting up North Chimney. We wonder if we can make it to Broadway, in the dark, knowing that we have to if we want to get up the Diamond tomorrow.

We gallop around the lake and up to Mill's Glacier. The air feels colder and colder as we try to kick steps with our Adidas in the frozen snow. The snow gets steeper and our fear increases until we reach a nice set of steps made earlier when the snow was soft. Finally we reach the slabs at the base of the East Face. The rock feels like home territory after the snowfield and we scramble quickly upwards. A full moon rises and gives a high energy glow to the Directissima Wall. As we pass the other climbers and reach Broadway, a moonlit panorama of the Diamond unfolds above us. Reaching Broadway is always a relief, and suddenly we feel great. 'Only' the Diamond lies ahead of us now. We get our bivouac set up and settle in for the night, but in our moon crazed excitement we can't sleep for some time.

By first light I'm shivering with the cold. My intent stare at the horizon somewhere out in Nebraska doesn't seem to help the sun up. With its first rays I bravely jump out of my half bag and stumble over to the snowfield to see if we will have water to drink on the climb. I find a few reluctant drops and leave the water bottle to collect as much as possible. I'm ready to start up the Diamond immediately, preferably sooner, but Robert doesn't wake up quite as fast. With my impatient coaxing we eventually get our bivouac gear packed and stashed. I grab the rack of nuts and scramble over to the base of D-7. Robert follows, filling the water bottle as much as possible. We get about a third of a quart, not nearly enough. But at this point it won't stop us.

> The Diamond is engulfed in
>   soft yellow light, being
> caught in the crags of ageless rock.
>
> The wall begins to glow, with
>   gilded scales, that reflect
>   a burning sky.
>
> The crisp air throbs, as
>   the wall begins to breathe and
> writhe like a tortured animal.
>
> Looking into its eyes ... I climb.

Robert quickly runs out 160ft of rope, but needs more to reach a good stance. We climb simultaneously for twenty feet then he reaches a belay. As we embark on the Diamond I try not to think too much about how far out on a limb we could be going. We have prepared ourselves to be warriors and are willing to face the consequences of our decisions. We have only one rope, a rack of nuts, our climbing shoes, our sweaters tied around our waists and a teardrop pack overstuffed with a mostly-empty water bottle, a few nuts and a little chocolate. Our Adidas dangle behind us from our swamis and we feel like we're out for a Sunday climb in Eldorado. We have no hauling to hassle with or tire us out, enabling us to move fast.

I follow the first pitch quickly, stop long enough at the belay to get all the nuts, then take off up the second pitch. The first 130ft goes easily, then a difficult section that is usually wet is dry now due to the cold temperatures, and it goes easier. I need ten more feet to reach anchors and a stance so we climb simultaneously again.

On the third pitch we have to move about fifty feet right to another crack system. Goss and Logan moved right on a ledge some 100 or 120ft up the pitch. I remind Robert to look for an obvious ledge as he moves upward. Some difficult moves and then he reaches a place where he can move right. Twenty-five feet across and he reaches the Black Dagger crack system. We have to move across to one more system to reach the Yellow Wall route, but the next stretch isn't so obvious. He tries several blank looking traverses, then I suggest climbing down the crack and traversing lower. He climbs down five feet then hangs on a move for ten minutes grumbling about how wet and hard it is. Remaining impatient and painfully aware that we can't waste time, I yell to him to go for it.

Leaning against the wall,
    inward and persistent;

Trying desperately to extract moves
    out of cerebral folds,

From the smooth-faced phantom
    who has held our dream
        in demonic confidence.

I relinquish the thought of fighting,
    seek harmony,
        and climb with the rock…

Finally he makes a few moves, crosses twenty-five feet to the next crack system and then goes up a few feet to the belay.

I'm hot to start climbing and attack the first difficult moves. Suddenly a hold breaks and I take a twenty-foot plunge as the rope stretches and I swing across the wall. Great start! I manage to focus my mind enough to get eight feet higher to the start of the traverse. I realise that we are twenty or thirty feet below where Goss and Logan had been. I'm looking at Robert fifty feet across the Diamond with a rope draped limply through one nut halfway between us. I'm scared, even though the first traverse to the Black Dagger crack, isn't too hard. Eventually I rig up an upper belay for the difficult down climb by leaving a nut and karabiner. Then I find out why Robert took so long on it: it's probably 5.11 even when dry. Carefully picking my way across the blank face I reach the cramped stance where Robert is belaying.

I'm anxious to start the fourth pitch and make up for lost time. A horrible looking off-width crack that I quickly decide to face-climb around, then a long fun section, then a thin difficult section, then another off-width section … I'm on a small stance with scary anchors for a belay. I'm starting to feel the creeping fatigue; from here on it will be a test of our endurance. The altitude effects you more and more while the climbing becomes all the more steep and strenuous, taking its toll on arms and legs. Robert follows, then leads a short enjoyable pitch which places us on the Yellow Wall bivouac ledge. I remember reaching that point nine years before, on the second ascent of the Yellow Wall, after a long hard day of nailing. It's now about noon as the sun slips behind the mountain. Times have changed.

We pause for a little food and water, then decide it's best to keep moving. Looking up anxiously at the last 400ft of the Diamond, thirsty, tired, scared of the pitch off Table Ledge, and aware that it's getting much colder with the sun gone, we make our summit bid. It's one pitch to Table Ledge where we could get off, but we know that we won't be satisfied unless we can free the rest of the Yellow Wall.

My hands are numb with the cold as I start up the sixth pitch. After forty feet a difficult section takes me by surprise. I almost fall off when my frozen hands refuse to work. Some exotic stems on tiny crystals save me and then I enter a grungy chimney. The effort of the difficult section has increased my circulation and my hands start to come back to life. I get out of the chimney, pass another touchy section, then I'm on a nice stance at Table Ledge. As Robert follows I study the wall above. We're so close … an all too familiar feeling.

I begin to get hungry for this climb; I've wanted it for five years. When Robert arrives I tell him that I'm psyched to lead the next pitch. He agrees to let me lead it, sensing the sudden energy that's come over me. I am aware that he will have to endure the cold while I climb, and now as never before I sense the feeling of teamwork.

A fifteen-foot traverse to the right, with 800ft of space between me and Broadway, takes me to a faint crack system. The next 120ft took us hours to nail on our earlier ascent. I move up with determination, knowing that every foot I gain brings us that much closer to the top. I get good protection but have to use it sparingly to avoid running out of equipment. I make steady progress, past a wet section, past a sickening loose block, then things seem to blank out. I'm only twenty feet away from the summit overhang and we know we can make it from there. I move left into a wet area and get further and further from good protection. Hanging uncomfortably on slippery sloping holds, I'm unable to piece together the next section. Robert is uneasy and tells me to get moving because a storm is nearly upon us. I look to the north-west and see a wall of white moving our way. As successively closer mountains disappear I know it will be a matter of minutes before we are swallowed whole.

> Running straight towards the Sun,
>   the full moon behind us,
>   No direction but 'Go'…
> Pulse pounding, forcing pupils to undulate;
>   My eyes lost in the sky,
> crystal leaves drift in,
>   tickling the rock monolith.
>
> In the waning sun I share desperation,
>   a parched throat and lactic muscles:
> Afraid to awaken before the dream is finished,
>   I peer into a crystal inclusion,
>   and ponder…
>
> How many hours spent examining my fate
>   a thin fingerhold beyond arms reach?
> How many years in search of a dream,
>   a foothold on life?
>
> Only a thin edge obscurely visible on
>   a painted wall, where fingerprints
>   are left by renegades, and
> Nylon feathers hang in patterns that
>   Mark my future lines…
>   answering my questions in grim silence:
> For we are face-to-face with failure.

New life shoots through my body at the thought. Some slippery jams and wet sloping footholds get me to a belay point. Robert starts up the pitch but his hands are really frozen. I remind him about the storm and somehow he follows the pitch with almost non-functioning hands. As he reaches me a swirling snowstorm engulfs us. Now the only way off is up. Robert's hands are no warmer, so we decide that it will be quickest for me to lead. I take off with nuts hanging all over me – no time for organisation. Robert keeps coaxing me to keep moving. My focus is on one thing only: going up, as quickly as possible. It's a wet, mossy corner with blocks of ice hanging on it. The snow doesn't bother me, it's too cold to make the rock any wetter. Soon I'm breathing like a distance runner in the 14,000ft thin air, my hands are going numb, my arms and legs are screaming with fatigue ... we've got to make it!

The storm rages on but I'm almost up. Then I know we've got it so I pause a moment to relish the absurdity of the whole scene: the two of us dressed like summer tourists and scurrying like ants to escape the wrath of the gods. I laugh to myself because we've squeezed by, our bluff has worked and it no longer matters that it's snowing. As I stretch the rope out 160ft we're up the Diamond, home free. I belay Emilio up and the scene takes on a tranquility with the light fluffy snowflakes embracing us. We're both glowing as we shake hands. There are no words that can be spoken ... I'm eight miles high because I love Bob and I love the Diamond.

As we descend Kiners to pick up our gear on Broadway, we can't really comprehend what we've just done. Had we lost fifteen or twenty minutes anywhere on the climb we would not have made it. I knew that it would take a few days to really believe and understand this adventure. Our bodies are wasted, but the long descent and hike out doesn't bother us. Our minds are still on the Diamond and the energy of our success sustains us. As costly as failure on Long's is, our past failures now seem like a fair price for a free Diamond.

from CLIMBING *September 1976*

'HEAVY' TALKS

IAN McNAUGHT-DAVIS

This interview took place during a short visit to Yosemite Valley, one of the greatest rock climbing areas in the world. We sat round the Californian Redwood log fire and, as 'Heavy' [Regal 'Heavy-Duty' Birdlime] talked, we could hear the bears grunting and the racoons and jackals chattering. Even the elegant jays were enjoying the occasion as the seated group of silent climbers drew on their curiously aromatic cigarettes.

McNaught-Davis: To most British climbers, Yosemite means big overhangs, cracks stuffed with pitons, and six-day routes.

Heavy-Duty: They were the big challenge and the photographs got everyone jerked up, but now you can split the valley into two groups: those who want to do all the big face routes, and those who do one or two, realise how intrinsically boring six days of hammering can be, and promptly relax and enjoy the one-or two-day routes. So far there is only one person in the first group.

Well, I certainly thought that the one-day routes I did gave me some of the best climbing I have ever done.

You should do my latest route: 100ft. of wild stemming up the flare, lie away for fifty feet up the off-width, and past the only horn in the dihedral to the drop-off. I've called it 'Stepping out with Diddly Dick on a Galactic Trip'. 5.12, every move.

Climbing in the valley has created a new language, techniques and equipment. What are the latest advances?

Most recently we have turned our attention to the problem that has existed ever since ropes were first used – the low status of the second man. Leading through is one answer, of course, but with climbers of different abilities we have introduced the Simulated Leader Fall. As the second tries the hard move, the leader lets out enough rope so that when the second comes off he falls as far as the leader would from the same position. Of course it's safer, since the protection won't come out, but even so some seconds don't seem to enjoy it. They are probably prejudiced against innovative technique.

I can see how it would enhance his status, but wouldn't it tempt him to pull up on the pegs?

No way. If he did, he would have to repeat the pitch. As you know, in our grading system, if you pull up on a pin the climb becomes an aid climb. I did one sixty-pitch route and, unknown to me, the second pulled up on a knife-blade. When I found out, we went back and repeated the climb so it wouldn't be degraded to an aid route.

You mention a sixty-pitch climb. Why doesn't the guidebook say how long a route is in feet ?

A guidebook must be subjective, not objective. If it says a route is 1500ft, and it turns out to be 1550ft, the guide is wrong, and everything else in the guide is then suspect. If the guide says it is a six-pitch climb, and you take seven, you just didn't lead out enough rope on each pitch.

That makes sense, nearly. What other ethical problems do you have?

Chalk is the burning issue this season. As the palms sweat, the jams get slippery, and a puff of chalk makes all the difference. This seemed O.K. just before a pitch, but some people are doing it before every move and on some pitches every hold is buried beneath a pile of white chalk. To avoid defacing the cliff, some climbers now paint their hands with tincture of benzoine, rub in plenty of chalk, then spray on a sealer. This gives antiseptic, high-friction hands, more compatible with boot rubber, and they'll last for three or four pitches. It's a breakthrough for technology, but ethically dubious.

What is your position?

I am against it, of course, but I got a thrill doing a second ascent of a Bridwell route, when I found a perfect imprint of his hand as he stemmed on the chicken-head. I placed my hand over it and felt a real pride in following the move exactly as the master had done it.

That must have been a very moving experience. I understand that religion plays a big part in the lives of many climbers in the valley.

Religion has helped in many ways. Faith healing has given immediate cures to hands torn in some 5.10 jam-crack. 'Praise-God', over there, claims that his faith has so lightened his burden that he did fifty one-arm pull-ups on a bashie before leading Stoveleg Cracks free. I personally don't believe it; if so, why was he working out on the parallel bars every day for the past year?

Everyone takes keeping fit very seriously. It's boulder problems every night, jogging round the meadows, and a diet of nut cutlets and alcohol-free beer at fifty cents a glass.

This is old Indian country and we still have traces of ancient and mysterious sicknesses. Jim Domino, for example, sees blue flashes with yellow circles every time he tries to do a 5.11 pitch. He's just not in shape. Even two of your Englishmen, Mo and Benjy, had an attack of the Tuolumne Trembles that caused them to spend all day doing a single 5.9 pitch. They should take things more seriously and get in shape.

> *It's been a real privilege talking to you ...*
> Phew! ... 5.9 ...
> *I spoke to Whillans last week, and ...*
> Phew! ... Heavy Duty ...
> *He said: 'Yosemite – hot and pot'*
> Phew! Far ... out ...

from MOUNTAIN 28 *1973*

EL CAP UPDATE

HUGH BURTON

The Shield ascends the magnificent bulging headwall between the Muir Wall and Magic Mushroom routes. Without doubt it offers the finest eight pitches of nailing on El Capitan. During our ascent we found that the pitch on which Charlie Porter has used forty rurps was an extremely thin, flush face-crack, varying from ¼ to ¾ inch in depth. After using several rurps, I opted for knife blade tips, as I had had problems cleaning buried rurps on the previous pitch. The entire pitch was done on tied-off knife blades and rurps, with two blank sections passed with two bolts apiece. The new Chouinard knife blades of tougher steel made it safe and fairly secure. A magnificent route–mind-blowing, untouchable!

Tangerine Trip is another excellent, highly recommended climb, with lots of wild leads. Steve Sutton and I did the second ascent in four days last June. Charlie Porter took eight days on the first ascent, climbing with a guy who didn't even know how to jumar. For seven days he drilled and nailed away up there in the snow and rain, while his partner got bedsores lying in his hammock. On the second pitch of the old El Cap Tree route you go right, do some weird shenanigans off a bolt, then you're away. You head left, up big flakes and corner systems – sometimes expanding, sometimes thin, then blanking out. On to the headwall, a full pitch of aluminium rivets, really overhanging, then nailing and face-climbing to the top. Royal Robbins did the first seven-and-a-half pitches solo, then rappelled off. It's really amazing he could get down, because the whole wall overhangs up to that point.

I also found myself on the second ascent of Zodiac. Mark Hesse had climbed the first three pitches with Jack Roberts. They came down after one bivi, totally soaked. Hesse didn't have time to wait the weather out, so he split. I returned with Roberts and we made the top six days later. Far from being easy, almost all the sixteen stretched-out pitches are A3+, or harder. Bold, overhanging leads up rurp cracks; expanding flakes and blocks are typical. On several pitches, you have to move into A3+/A4 pins, looking at a probable 60–100ft fall. The A5 rating is hard to pinpoint, and the line being drawn at present is somewhere around a sure sixty feet or more fall. That is, all the pins in the last thirty feet will rip. The Zodiac has several pitches in

this category. The seriousness of the route becomes apparent two-thirds of the way up. In order to get down, the last four pitches would have to be down-nailed, due to their overhanging and traversing nature. It would be just as easy to go up. The always ready rescue team wouldn't have much luck getting to you from above: they would probably be hanging fifty feet out from the wall, unless they were down-nailing. Maybe a rope could be thrown in, but it would be pretty tricky.

True, we found Zodiac easier than expected, but we had been psyching-up for a long time and were prepared to extend our limits. We had been doing practice rurp cracks, but we were still plenty afraid when we stepped off the ground. Our practice paid off, however, and we were technically and psychologically strong enough to handle the nailing. An unfortunate trend recently has resulted in several parties starting up new, difficult, nailing walls, for which they are technically unprepared and psychologically unfit; but they boost themselves with well stocked bolt kits to ensure that they get up the route. Two recent climbs handled in this manner are Mescalito, the new route right of Dawn Wall, and Tis-sa-ack on Half Dome. Mescalito is the biggest, hardest route on El Cap to date. A lot of the aid consists of copper-heads in shallow cracks which you wouldn't stand a chance of nailing with pitons. There is some expanding stuff and a lot of cliff-hanger moves. The second party, finding themselves committed by the overhanging nature of the wall (obvious from the ground), placed bolts to get up several pitches. It may be true that they placed the bolts because their skyhooks were inadequate; I don't know. But it should be pointed out that escape is possible from almost anywhere, once you are above half-height. You can rappel to the Harding/Caldwell bolt ladders and then finish up Dawn Wall, or perhaps go across Porter's bolt ladder to El Cap Tower and rappel down the Nose. The fact is that a climber should be prepared to gauge the desperate nature of a climb before he starts. Topos warn climbers of ensuing difficulties, and you can tell what to expect, just by looking at one. Obviously, it would be stupid to start up such a route without a bolt kit: now and again flakes fall off, placements become impossible in destroyed cracks, and occasionally retreats must be made down blank walls. Still, what counts is the spirit in which the bolt kit is carried: which is more important getting up, or how you get up?

To each his own, and if some bozo wants to bolt a section that previous competent parties have nailed, then that's fine (for him). But the next team that wants to climb the route in impeccable style might be a little pissed off at the degradation. Our cliffs are an unrenewable resource. I know that's been said before, but it's got to be said again and *remembered*, if the climbs are to remain as they are – incredible!

from MOUNTAIN 44 *1975*

THE WALRUS AND THE CARPENTER

BEN CAMPBELL-KELLY and BRIAN WYVILL

Wyvill: The term 'Curry Girl' is not in fact an item taken from the menu of some horrific back-street Bradford restaurant, but a term of endearment describing those poor lasses who have been enticed into the service of the 'Curry Company' of Yosemite Valley. I stared with hungry eyes as the other Camp 4 climbers used their well-tried seductive techniques to cajole from the girls the most valuable of all currencies for man and bear, food. A week had passed since the Nose and the post-route hunger was still not abated.

My reflections were interrupted by the Boss (Ben Campbell-Kelly): 'Come on Patrick, time for the Big Grip.' Another piece of theatre was about to begin.

Saturday: It wouldn't have been so bad if we had managed to scrounge a lift the mile or so to the base of El Capitan, but unfortunately the only available transport was a ripped-off tandem. 'You pedal, I'll steer,' proclaimed the Boss as we made off past the thronging hitch-hikers on our brakeless-rear-wheel-drive-only-tandem. The tourists stared aghast as we cycled along like some comedy duo. Of course not only had I all the pedalling to do, but also the haul bag was strapped to my back, and the pointed Campbell-Kelly dome gave me the just-about-to-take-off look. 'It's currently fashionable amongst we Yosemite climbers,' I cried. Fortunately our journey was terminated by the front wheel dropping off, which left us sprawling in the dirt, fighting off climbing gear and the ferocious Meccano of the bike.

Sweating beneath the nasty side of El Cap, I became sticky with orange as the Boss chased an uncooperative rattlesnake with one of his expensive cameras. Still exuberant from having made the first El Cap start on a tandem we harnessed the 'Bat Sledge' and jumared to our high point of the previous day, two pitches above the naked scree on the 'North America Wall'.

The Boss had won the dubious honour of leading the notorious third pitch and I hung watching in fascination as his neck grew long on poor pegs, until he disappeared from sight and only the cursings filtered through. The adverts had fooled me into thinking Yosemite climbing was always in blazing sunshine, but now I shivered and muttered dark thoughts, sucking on a sweet from my secret store. The rope went tight and I felt the cold inside, but some healthy language from the Boss reassured me of his abilities and after admonishing the pulled peg, he continued on nut and copperhead. Two hours of chewing and the Boss shouted from the safety of bolt and belay seat. I joined him in space to find a tangle of knitting and cameras.

On the fourth pitch I too, praised the ubiquitous copperhead and journeyed up the dead rurp-cracks using a few of the ingenious pieces of ironmongery from our secret factory in North Wales.

Skyhook scraped granite, fingers scraped flakes, and the first bivouac was reached. Royal Robbins must have a good imagination or had a lot of bad bivouacs: the ledge which 'sleeps four' was full of hideous rubble which we avoided by using our hammocks.

Sunday. Campbell-Kelly: From the safety of my suspended sleeper I cast a beady eye over the off-size gash above our heads. 'Nasty,' I muttered, then turned over and put it off for another half-hour. Wide cracks have never been my forte, so I wasn't too keen to get the only one on the route. Halfway up it I realised that this wasn't going to be one of my smoothest leads, in fact I probably wasted more energy squawking than thrutching. 'Blob' sat with the patience of Job, and listened to my bitching without comment. In a last desperate effort I tied my étriers together, lassoed the big chockstone at the top of the crack and clawed my way gratefully into the roof. In my gripped condition the next few A1 pegs seemed like A3, but I was soon sitting on a small ledge basking in the early sun.

Blob took the bolt ladder in style and pendulumed Dervishlike onto Easy Street, a fine bivouac that would have been perfect for the previous night. These pendulums can be quite reasonable and good fun. I find them mildly disturbing, but the Blob takes a positive delight in vertical running... if he lived in Africa he could well put Tarzan out of business. My next pitch also had a small pendulum, but the state of my worn-out boots sent me slithering back to my starting point as the protruding screws on my toes failed to grip the glaciated granite. Blob threatened to increase my daily dose of monkey gland extract and I finally struggled across.

Two pitches later we were on Calaverous Ledge, a huge area of easy-angled rock with a good flat bivvy spot. In comfort we fixed the next pitch and settled down for a leisurely dinner. Both of us were hungry and looking forward to our salami, I carved and shared it out. A few minutes later Blob vomited his portion back up; hastily I gulped mine down before he could get his hands on it.

The thought of having to retreat and then do that wide crack again made us absolutely determined to plough on unless Blob was completely incapacitated. Fortunately he was as fit as a fiddle next day and just hungry.

'Yonder Blob has a lean and hungry look. He should be just about tuned up for the "sling shot",' I thought.

Monday Wyvill: No audience to greet us this cold morning, but I posed as melodramatically as my cramped bat-tent would allow while Ben 'Cecil-Beaton' Kelly went to work with his portable studio. I wasn't at all like a Navajo when it came to piccies. It was too early for sun and I stood cold and stiff trying to put my boots on while they tried to roll down the dirty dolerite slab which was our temporary home. At the Boss's insistence I photographed the bald patches on his boots.

We continued our journey across the map of North America etched in black and white on dolerite and granite, and good mixed climbing brought us on the crest of a wave into the Gulf of California. The Boss cursed his way up a peculiar flake chimney, and I followed losing my cool in that most

awkward mother. The smooth walls were set apart just enough to permit my thin self to gain a few feet, but then the day pack, bulging with our precious lunch, stuck fast in the narrows. I could have thrown out some of the food but that was unthinkable, instead I squirmed, struggled and, like a surfer, pipelined up the chimney and after an immense effort emerged to find the Boss wiped out on the Big Sur, a smashing flat ledge. If only we had reached here last night was my only thought.

We rested in the sun and I dreamed of hot Sunday afternoons at Avon Gorge with tea and pasties. My reverie was broken by the Boss offering me some salami which he had caught trying to lead the next pitch. I declined, remembering last night's gastronomic ordeal.

There were signs of our predecessors: two gallons of water and a piece of old rope which now dangled uselessly, a scar on the almost clinical wall ahead of us. We were both disinclined to get on with the route. Our topo indicated two pendulums and the legend 'Retreat may be impossible after the second pendulum'. A small skull and crossbones had been elegantly pencilled in to emphasise the point. To add to our misery we also gleaned from the topo that the next bivouac was a hanging one in the Black Cave, and that was too many pitches away for an afternoon's climbing.

I moved up grotty flakes and followed a bolt traverse which ended dramatically in the middle of nowhere. Not very far down, but a long way left was a flake. The Boss lowered and I ran fast, very fast. Iron jangled and I, like a hypnotist's bauble, waved about in front of the Boss's photo orientated mind. By some dint of luck on my first real effort, the karabiner I held had clipped itself into an in-situ peg in the flake, and the Boss howled at me to let go so he could get his picture.

'Let go?' I thought, 'Leave my hard earned sanctuary, go through the exhilarating desperate dash from nowhere to somewhere?'

No! I was far too gripped and nailing up the flake was A4.

The Boss grumbled and I fought my way up to the belay ledge, pausing on the way to tie two skyhooks together in order to reach between two of Robbins' bolts which I swear were six feet apart.

It was a roomy stance and the ropes were in a mess as the Boss insisted on leaving them doubled through the bolt I had originally pendulumed from, 'just in case'. I greeted this cowardly action with enthusiasm knowing we could get back if we failed on the next pendulum. On our stance we had only one bolt to belay on and one to pendulum from, thus with trepidation I lowered the Boss for fifty feet using a descendeur and watched him struggle vainly to gain a small ledge at the foot of the Black Dihedral, which was now filling the skyline and casting its evil shadow over our insolent assault. Amused by the boss's antics, I consoled him by taking a few photos.

The wind was snatching at our lifelines, lifting 150ft. of rope as if it were cotton and tying it in knots about any available projection. Fortunately for the Boss the ledge he was trying to gain provided a suitable target for the wind's machinations, and when the haul rope became at one with the ledge the Boss pulled himself across. As I wrestled with the greedy descendeur, the Boss mantelshelved with difficulty and cursed my slowness. Finally I pulled in our escape rope and hopped down to join him. Watching in silence as the final coil was disengaged from the previous stance, we contemplated our total commitment.

Tuesday   Campbell-Kelly: Today the haulbag won. Our trusty bat-tents again saved us from the slow torture of an inadequate ledge, and Brian-I'll-try-anything-once-Wyvill returned to his normal sardine diet while I laid siege to the half-savaged salami. At first light we resumed our vertical safari, and followed the only trail through a desert of bland rope up towards the sheltered oasis of the Black Dihedral.

The pitch leading into the dihedral is typical of the easier sections on the North America Wall. Overhanging and awkward, strenuous and occasionally dirty, but not technically hard. The early morning heat was sapping and moving into the shadow of the dihedral was as good as a cold drink. By some fluke there is a shallow niche where one can just stand in balance, and hauling was easy since the bag hung free in space. As it arrived we fought for the belay site. I thought I was safe when my attention was distracted and the third man suddenly swung into the niche. The next hour and a half were spent alternately trying to lever it out, sitting on it and belaying the Blob.

Jumaring through the overhangs, I too was hit by panic-stricken bats as our repeated hammerings frightened them out of the crevices in the rock. Two pitches and several hours later I traversed out of sight and tiptoed over trembling flakes into the Black Cave. At the very top of the dihedral, this is a stunning bivouac, completely sheltered, the floor a spectacular 1800ft drop to the ground. It was mid-afternoon, so we decided to aim for the Cyclops Eye before dusk.

Blob traversed out of the Cave grimacing and posturing as I shot frame after frame. He disappeared from view and I tried to fathom out how to follow the roof as comfortably as possible.

Gazing out across the valley my view was suddenly ruined by a pair of motley boots thrutching at thin air as Blob traversed the very lip of the roof. It wasn't quite so hilarious when I had to follow on Jumars. Hitens blades in just a fraction of an inch and flexing like razor blades, and then a thirty-foot row of stacked pegs stuck into a diagonal band of quartz. (That band of quartz stretches for hundreds of yards in each direction – who knows, maybe a Californian Dream of White Horses if you can get to the end of it?)

One more meandering lead and suddenly darkness again. Inevitably, we were one pitch short of the Eye. However we had a sloping ledge of sorts and a bolt belay. Blob got the hammock and we tied the haulbag onto the ledge and I was battened down inside. Hardly a two-star bivvy, but at least we slept.

Wednesday Wyvill: The Boss rolled off his narrow sloping platform for the twentieth time and hung in space weeping tears of infuriation. Naturally I was the first target for the voluble expression of his sufferings and, spurred into action, I clumped up a few bolts to the Cyclops Eye, a 200ft high circular depression of dolerite which formed Alaska on our map of North America. Like Hercules I gazed up at the top of the Eye and hoped it would not blink.

Our exit from this Grecian giant was by a difficult seventy-foot traverse and the Boss set off to establish a belay on the far side of the Eye. It was left to me to manhandle the rocket across loose rock and ledges to join him. This procedure provided our audience in the meadows with a hilarious hour of slapstick and the Boss sent me off on the traverse hot and irritated. Rope drag forced me to take a stance and the Boss followed smartly in spite of the difficulties of jumaring the traverse.

We looked up at the next scene, an exotic exercise in loose blocks over a roof: here lay our escape from the one-eyed giant. The Boss disposed of the roof, pausing only to comment:

'If they think this is loose, wait 'til they come to Gordale Scar!'

I winked back knowingly and followed the roof with a lot less panache to join the Boss on the edge of nowhere. Above was a nightmare of blank rock to which were 'Araldited' some enormous and horrible flakes.

The Boss passed me the Bat Sledge and sent me off muttering about difficult route-finding. I traversed right and followed good rock until it became crackless, back left and I was on those flakes that would do credit to Cadbury's.

I reached a long way left and dropped a king pin behind one thin flake of rock and tapped it gently. Gulp! I transferred my weight slowly – and then I was flying, jarring to a halt inches above the Boss's nose.

'Grr!'

'Why don't you chip off the top of the flake and place a skyhook?' inquired the Boss.

'Good idea.'

So I swarmed back up the rope and swung my trusty hammer. There was an almighty hollow thump and the enormous flake vibrated visibly. The Boss below, hatless and vulnerable, squawked:

'Not like that you fool!'

He cowered, and more gently this time I made a nice seating for a skyhook and moved across.

I belayed on the largest flake. It was expanding like the rest and, unable to get more than one peg in, I crossed my fingers and told the Boss to come up gently. Two pitches above was the best bivouac on the climb, a cave called the Igloo, unfortunately it was darkening and still another A4 pitch to climb. The Boss tensioned incautiously from an old sling round the wafer thin point of our belay flake, and disappeared round a corner into the uninviting hands of a soggy thin crack. He re-appeared on a bong traverse and finished off with some super-hard skyhooking to a sloping ledge.

Now it was dark and I spent ages fighting with the bongs, so that when I joined the Boss he had set up a hanging bivouac seventy feet of easy free-climbing below the world's best bivouac. Hungry and frustrated we dangled away the night, surely the hard bits were over by now?

Thursday Campbell-Kelly: I had a bad night; in the dark I'd crossed the tapes on my hammock. We were short of food and I dreamed of the finest there is – cold Christmas pudding. Our staple food on earlier trips, we had been unable to find a supplier in California. Despondently we polished off our little remaining cereal, packed the handicap and Blob moved off up the easy pitch. The bag jammed, but came free when we threatened to throw it off.

Ignoring the Igloo with its fine sandy floor we set out along a spectacular traverse leading to the final two pitches. Blob took the last of the aid, while I blistered in the solar furnace.

Above the next belay bolts, the final slab curved threateningly to the skyline. At least one party has taken a sixty-foot fall here, and I was expecting trauma in my 'nailed' boots. I was not disappointed, but eventually a large angle, stuck in a shallow pocket, protected the last hard free moves. The final obstacle, a series of matted bushes, was an exhausting but delightfully secure struggle, then the summit. Blob followed and I captured him forever on a sheet of celluloid. Jubilant, we drank the last of the water and posed in front of our only observer, the delayed action camera.

Every corner of the bag was searched for food, but the cupboard was bare. Staggering up the summit slopes we stumbled over a tin of chopped ham, and while Blob chanted a quick chorus of 'Spam, Spam, Spam', I opened it up. Manna.

Fortified, it took us three hours to sprint the eight miles to the valley. Having crossed the New World there were other fields to conquer, and on the way down we cast a greedy eye towards the looming bulk of Half Dome. But first we had six days of eating to catch up on.

from MOUNTAIN LIFE *February 1973*

A Letter Received by Steve Roper

LEO F. CORRIGAN
PRESIDENT
EDWARD S. BERNARD
VICE PRESIDENT
MANAGING DIRECTOR
BARON E. BERNARD
MANAGER

MADISON 4-1011

```
Big deal,you God dam ass hole,so you Climbed ElCapitan
what a REAL BIG DEAL THAT WAS. To bad you and your Pals didnt
fall off and cause a lot of people agony.you Pricks should
have your heads examined. You Glen and Layton. GREAT ACHIEVMENT
great work you climbed a hill like a few stupid beatnecks,if
you idiots would shave and look presentable,but you are 3
big slobs.

So you climbed El Capitan..what a great thing to do. It has
a great future for you,you can now rest on your laurels as
the 3 pigs that climbed up a stone steep grade.

                    Get your heads examined.

                    Frank Parckel
```

This is a copy of a letter I received in June 1963 after the third ascent of the Nose. It made tiny mentions in the local papers, and this is probably where the cat got my name and address. For a while I thought it might be from someone I know, but it seems sure now that it is quite real. It was mailed from SF on LA hotel stationery: air mail from SF to Berkeley, with no stamp. Even as I paid the postman I knew what it was – the only time in my life I have ever been prescient.

Steve Roper
from VULGARIAN DIGEST *1970*

MEMO TO R.D. AND TOBY

Subject:
Take off problems we are running into for a successful ascent of The Nose.

Points:
1. We are blowing the social dynamics and the physical dynamics involved in the take off scheduling for a successful ascent of El Cap

2. Our main problem has been operating as if the main problem is the co-ordination of our three schedules. We were in error. That is a secondary problem. The main problem is the weather. We can't do it when we want to but when the weather is permitting. Spring is not here yet and we still have the unstable weather patterns operating.

3. Our secondary problem is co-ordinating our time schedules around periods of weather permitting

4. Summary: re-cap of events so far:
    a. Planned to leave and do climb over Easter.
    b. On Thursday, March 23 we postponed leaving until around April 14 due to unstable weather and hopes that a more stable regime would occur later in spring.
    c. On Sunday, April 2 we rescheduled take-off for Sunday, April 9 at 7am moving off, the desire to get the climb done as soon as possible

5. It becomes obvious upon reviewing the situation that our current take-off strategy and organising/co-ordinating efforts are fossils of our Easter-time schedule, and space. They were appropriate for an Easter ascent and our personal schedules at that time. They are appropriate no longer. Our personal constraints and schedules are now different. We need to formulate a new take off strategy for a successful ascent of El Cap this Spring that revolves around weather permitting climbing time, and our new personal schedules and constraints.

6. Our little group of three was created upon the common purpose of climbing El Cap (the Nose) during Easter. When that bombed out we made the lethal mistake of not recreating our purpose and take-off strategy around the new reality of our current and future time space, its new personal constraints, and what we each are willing to do and not to do. To that end

119

I propose that we meet at my apartment to hash out a new take off strategy and a common purpose and method that we can all agree to (or agree to disagree with and disband) that will result in a successful spring ascent of El Cap. I for one, given our current weather pattern am dubious about success on the week of April 19. If we want a successful ascent we have got to get it together.

Your friend,
Scott

ORIGINAL LETTER 1978

TRUE GRIT

DAVE COOK

To many climbers, enthusiasm for gritstone is regarded at best as a sign of a mis-spent youth, if not a poverty-stricken one. Who now, except old men reliving past excitements over pints of Tetley's bitter, makes claims for hard gritstone that don't evoke yawns from those younger, more mobile and more objective? Last year's Wembley Rock and Roll Festival contained two sorts of people: fat, balding, aged Teds, making ridiculously inflated claims for two-beat stomp – and hip swingers going along for a good leap about. Isn't the Old Grey Gritstone Whistle Test a bit like that? Maybe – but here is a partisan, over-enthusiastic, biased and hopelessly unobjective wallow in climbing's rock 'n' roll festival by one such dotee.

Gritstone is the Pennines. These hills are 'an area of outstanding natural beauty', but it is not their scenery that makes them unique. What does is the fact that on every side a combination of fast-flowing streams, coalfields and industrial revolution have bound a network of industrial towns to their valleys. Only in South Wales, where geology has been less kind to climbers, is there a comparable inter-linking of wildness and conurbation. And where the moors end – and 'civilisation' starts – are the gritstone crags.

Most of the essential ingredients of gritstone climbing stem from this frontier position. Only the remotest edges are natural in the sense of being completely untouched by quarry-men. Some of the most lovely and intriguing areas for the climber owe their charm, and often their ferocity, to industrial ravages which have been retouched and disguised by wind and rain. Marble Wall, at Stanage, comes to mind as an example of the most tasteful plastic surgery of all time.

Although many quarries lurk about on the dingy fringes of some pretty unappetizing towns, most gritstone edges stand as decisively as a Bakewell pudding, in the very grandest of positions. Their uniqueness is usually summed up by the combination of views from their crests: in one direction, industrialisation, or at least its out-runners; in the other, the plateau of black peat and emerald bog, way up the wilderness league.

Almost everything in climbing works to blur the social divisions within the sport – but nowhere in Britain do so many working class people climb as on gritstone. Between the wars, as the dole queues lengthened, more and more turned to rambling and climbing as one of the few sporting activities they could afford, and the tradition has continued. The right to climb on grit has sometimes had to be fought for in earnest, and in 1932 ramblers battled with a private army of gamekeepers on the forbidden crest of Kinder Scout. The ramblers won. The atmosphere of gritstone distils from the various social and regional ingredients of those who swarm upon it – and the mixture is richer and more varied than the weak brew found in most other areas.

All climbing has a pretty rich folklore, a heritage of tasty tales that proliferate as a sort of folk tradition, and this is particularly the case on grit. In men like Dennis Gray and the late Eric Byne, and their scores of equivalents all over the Pennines, this tradition finds its archivists and minstrels who record more (and often less) faithfully the more notable dirty deeds for posterity.

In fact, there was a time in the 1960s when it looked as if the ethos and traditions of gritstone were taking over everywhere. The big jamming fists, and the big jammed mouths of the Rock and Ice, the Alpha, the Black and Tans, the YMC and the Rimmon, proselytised by word and deed all over Britain, brainwashing everyone else into an acceptance of inferiority. This superb public relations exercise still goes on, but not with quite the same success. It was asserted that a gritstone apprenticeship (along with protruding extremities) was the prerequisite for hard climbing; given the self-opinionated conceit of Yorkshiremen, for example, this is no more outrageous than many of the claims they make. What really was amazing was that this preposterous fiction was so widely believed.

All this propaganda has given gritstone a phenomenal power of attraction. The motorways that swirl around the Pennines make the Edges highly accessible from any direction, and at weekends they are devoured by cosmopolitan climbing jet-setters. Summer midweek evenings, see the local boys come out to play, in an irreverent camaraderie that gives the very best of golden gritstone hours. 'From Hell and Hull, and Halifax, good Lord deliver me' goes the old folk song – and deliverance can indeed be swift. Most Pennine towns have a countdown numbered in tens of minutes between workplace and gritstone, and the sudden contrast is as intoxicating as Scotch on an empty stomach.

Each province – the boundaries usually coincide with a section of a guidebook – has its warlords. Allan Austin makes an annual visit to all his West Riding fiefdoms, just to keep an eye on things, and it is rare indeed for a raiding party to steal a crust of a ten-foot variant, let alone a thirty-foot meal. The classic Yorkshire second line of defence reaches its highest point with Dennis Gray's regular answer to claims of new routes in the area: 'No, Pete Cranfield did it in 1949, but we didn't think it worth writing up.' As no one else was around then, and as Pete Cranfield probably emigrated to Australia in 1957, there's not much more to be said. A few thick-skinned geniuses occasionally break through to lay a particularly improbable virgin, and we know what the YMC does to their routes!

To come to the point – the climbing. A few years ago, at Almscliff, Royal Robbins was asked how the climbs there compared with his local skyscrapers. Stereophonic writing would be necessary to catch the aptness of his reply, but his words were: 'Your climbs here are little inlaid jewels'.

In the Stanage guidebook there are 140 climbs of VS grade and above, and at least two thirds of them make substantial use of jamming techniques. The jam is gritstone's trademark – locking, slipping or hurting, accept no imitations. Enthusiasts collect them, swap them and gurgle about them, with an addiction that borders on the obscene and with justification. A gritstone climbing career encompasses every shape of fissure known to man. A jam will boost you when you must go, save you when you are tired, and extricate you when you are foxed. It will give you a love-bite embarrassing in its imprint. Great jams I have known include the following:

The most brutal: halfway up Dead Bay Crack at Curbar.
The most technical: getting out of the top of the Vice at Stanage End.
The most exhausting: starting Freddies Finale at Wimberry.
The most painful: starting Minion's Way at Brimham.
The most repulsive: by definition these cannot be on grit.
The most glorious: all the way up Matinée at the Roches.

In fact, the Roches and Hen Cloud contain the greatest collection anywhere and, along with Wimberry and Tintwhistle Knarr Quarry, would be my gritstone 'Desert Island Jams'.

Gritstone is leading rock. May all who top-rope there be cursed. Protection? Either very good or absent. You can number cracks that cannot be stitched on the fingers of one hand, but move on to the blunt ribs, frugal slabs and over-facing walls and you won't have to queue. Here lie the real boy/man sorters, and most of us are unashamedly juvenile in our choice. Of course, the soft touches tumble fast, and the mean ones repel and thus become meaner. One of the best routes at Stanage is Right Hand Tower (VS) – cruel, keep away. It has been led far fewer times than the Edge's better protected Extremes – and, as a sight lead, it is harder. Getting up most difficult gritstone routes requires a peculiarly combative approach, but most climbers prefer the odds to be heavily tilted in their favour before they will commit themselves to this fighting style. One of the great attractions of gritstone climbing is that a number of factors enable just such an approach to be employed a long way up the grades. The solidity of the rock, its friction, and the sureness of nut protection, generate a verve and confidence that boost achievement and encrust great days on grit with an indulgent layer of self satisfaction.

With apologies to *The Black Cliff*, I finish with an epilogue pinched from it. The passage refers not to Clog, but to Tintwhistle Knarr Quarry, the best unknown gritstone crag in the world:

'We stood for a long time on top of the grass-grown spoil heap. Across the Crowden Valley the shadows lengthened over the brown lines of Bleaklow. In front of us were the seventy-foot corners, in which all day we had been impaled.'

Unlike Messrs. Crew, Soper and Wilson on Clog, we had no need to ask ourselves what 'brought us back time and time again' to grapple with these cracks, and the 'the long drive home' was only thirty miles.

from MOUNTAIN 26 *1973*

A VIEW FROM DEADHORSE POINT

CHUCK PRATT

Embedded in the red earth of an austere and isolated section of America's south-west is a metal plaque commemorating the single point in this country common to four states. The Four Corners Monument, where it is possible to stand in Utah, Arizona, New Mexico and Colorado simultaneously, is the geometric centre of an area that has been frequented for more than twenty years by a subculture of desert-loving rock climbers whose attraction to the alien beauty and legend filled history of the area borders on the obsessive. Why the desert should exert such a fascination on a handful of climbers is a mystery to those who are not attracted to it, for the climbs in Four Corners, with a few remarkable exceptions, have little to recommend them. They are generally short – often requiring less time than the approaches, the rock at its best is brittle and rotten and at its worst is the consistency of wet sugar. Perhaps it is significant that desert climbing presents objective dangers not usually encountered by climbers used to more solid rock. Although the dangers inherent in sandstone climbing are infinitesimal compared to those faced by the mountaineer, it is just these small-scale threats that are more suited to a rock climber's temperament. Among the traits shared by virtually every climber who is active in the desert is the conscientiousness with which they avoid the Expedition Game.

The quality of the climbing however, be it safe or dangerous, cannot by itself fully explain the desert's appeal. There have been too many California Desert Expeditions that have returned home without achieving a single climb, yet judged the trip a complete success. A desert environment is maintained by an irresistible force whose nature cannot be penetrated by superficial efforts. To gain any lasting worth from what the desert has to offer, we had to learn to put our pitons and ropes away and to go exploring in silence, keeping our eyes very open. It wasn't easy. We wasted a lot of time climbing until we got the knack.

Easter 1960
We are walking down a blood-red canyon called de Chelly toward the place where it intersects its twin. Everything around us is a shade of red – the walls, looming above us for a thousand feet; the sand beneath our shoes; the

river, sluggish with its cargo of silt; even the dog that explodes from a nearby hogan to warn the canyon of our presence. His bark, echoing between the canyon walls and amplified by a dozen tributary canyons, becomes deafening and we hurry through his territory to escape the sensation of having climbed over a neighbour's fence into his backyard.

We pass an occasional oasis of colour wherever a natural amphitheatre in the canyon wall protects a grove of luxuriant cotton woods, the bright green of their leaves made almost luminous by the red walls surrounding them like a fortress. Turning a final corner into Monument Canyon, we see Spider Rock for the first time. We already know that it is 800ft high but it is, the proportion that excites us; slender and majestic, it rises from its talus cone like a crimson arrow aimed at the sky. On its summit dwells the Spider Lady, nourishing herself on the flesh of disobedient Navajo children, leaving their bones to bleach in the noonday sun. The Indian legend is a convenient explanation for the pile of white rubble seen on the summit of Spider Rock and the Spider Lady, the Navajo equivalent of the bogeyman, is an equally convenient device for maintaining discipline among rebellious children.

Slowly we circle the spire to see it from every possible angle. We go mad looking at Spider Rock and so we climb it. I have memories of flared chimneys, bolt ladders whose bolts fall out under the rope's weight, Kamps stuck in a mantel position on a piton trying to pull his pantleg from under his foot, and the summit pitch, a lieback over a flake that looks amorous enough to come off in somebody's arms. For a while we stand on the summit, experiencing sensations that are nobody's business but our own and then start down, the first two rappels producing more adrenaline than the ascent.

Retracing our steps out of the canyon we feel, the temporary depression which accompanies an exhilarating experience that belongs to the past.

Returning to the cosmopolitan atmosphere of Chinle, we disguise ourselves as tourists and edge discreetly toward the ranger headquarters to find out how much of a stir we have caused, for we know intuitively that since we feel so happy, we must have done something illegal.

'Are you the boys who climbed Spider Rock?'

We can't tell if the ranger is merely curious or if he is trying to catch two criminals. After a long pause, Bob finally admits to the crime and the ranger invites us into his office for a friendly chat. He informs us that the Indians are infuriated. It seems a conclave of the most powerful medicine men in Navajodom have just completed a three year ritual of removing the curse from Canyon de Chelly that was placed there by the first ascent of Spider Rock; that now they will have to start all over again and the best thing for us to do would be to leave on the next stagecoach or something.

On our way out of town we stop at the local trading post and I go in to look for an ice-cream bar. The place is filled with Navajos and within half a second the conversational hum drops to the point where I could have heard a feather falling. A shadow stirs in a corner and an Indian built like a buffalo looms above me as I lean for the door.

'Did you climb Spider Rock?' he wants to know.

'Why yes,' I answer, reaching for the doorknob, 'now that you mention it, I did. But there's another guy outside who climbed it too.'

Spread the guilt and the punishment might be less severe the logic of Nuremberg.

'What did you find on top?'

Every eye in the trading post is upon us, every ear straining for my reply. It's bad enough to place a curse on the land by climbing Spider but to contradict their cherished myths of the Spider Lady would be going too far. 'We found a pile of bleached bones on the top.'

Now it's so quiet I can hear molecules colliding in mid-air. Slowly I start turning the doorknob but the buffalo takes one step toward me and, demonstrating a remarkable intimacy with the nuances and connotations of a language not even his native tongue, asks:

'What do you take me for – a fool?' and the room erupts into hysterical laughter. I gather the pieces of my patronising ego up off the floor and carry them out the door in my hands.

Not bad for a first desert trip. I get up one climb – the finest in the south-west and I learn a couple of things about Indians. Best of all, I want to come back.

Autumn 1961

Dave Pullin and I are wandering through a graduate course in quicksand trying to find Cleopatra's Needle. We offer our kingdoms for a canoe at the stream crossings but we're stuck with an automobile and have to nurse it cross-country. About noon we find the bloody spire and start up with lucky me getting the second lead. It is very 6.0, the pins going in easily by hand and coming out just as easily under a load about five pounds less than I weigh. How to lighten myself by five pounds? Strip? There is a cruel east wind rising and the sky is growing dark with clouds. I send the hardware down and haul up one pin at a time. I stand on one and count until it pops out. Fifteen seconds. The higher I get the less time I have to place the piton and get off the thing before it grinds out. Halfway up I reach a bolt and retreat, leaving fifteen pitons shivering in a crack. We'll finish it tomorrow.

Christmas City. The snow is everywhere – just crept in during the night and decided to stay. Beneath the howling wind I can hear an occasional dull thud with metallic overtones, as though someone were gently beating Cleo with a hardware loop. I look out of the car window toward the spire, barely able to see it through the snow flurries. I see my rope, slowly swaying from the bolt and at the bottom of the rope is a ten-pound mobile of assorted angle pitons and karabiners. I mention it to Dave.

'Shit, Pullin, every goddamned piton I put in got blown out by the wind during the night. This is no place for an Englishman.'

We retrieve the gear and tranquilising it in a corner of the trunk, drive to the nearest bar.

We are learning that the rocks of the desert are organic. The climbs in Four Corners have a quality of aliveness not usually associated with the inanimate world and for me that quality is becoming a source of increasing attraction. It is fascinating to view erosion as a process rather than an end result, for the wind can visibly alter a spire even as we climb it and a good rainstorm will dissolve the softer sand into mud so that no two parties ever see the same summit.

Dave and I are disappointed about Cleo and we would like to stay in the bar and get blotted, but we leave when an Indian tells Dave, whose beard is rather gnarled and intermittent, that he looks like a paleface werewolf.

Autumn 1963

Shiprock, fabled monument, rises before us in splendour and silence, a tableau from the genesis of the south-west, historical remnant of a unique volcanic violence which has created a collage of mountainous fluted columns, jagged arétes and sheer orange walls that intimidate us into silence. Once on the summit, Roper and I can see for a hundred miles in every direction, but there is nothing to see but a vast plain of sand and sagebrush and a dozen miniature Shiprocks dotting the horizon. Then we hear the tom-toms. Or rather we feel them, a dull sympathetic response in the pit of the stomach that we eventually interpret as a drumbeat. Is this the prelude to a thousand shrieking savages circling Shiprock, launching flaming arrows at us? Are they waiting for us on the ground with their fires and sharpened stakes? We can see nothing stirring on the plain below, yet the drumbeat continues, insistent and sinister. We descend cautiously to be greeted only by silence and an empty desert. The drums are silent now and we joke about it, attributing the whole thing to imagination. Even so, we nearly break an axle driving back to the main road.

Moab is a small community in south-eastern Utah, founded by Mormon pioneers and nurtured in modern times by uranium and potash. North of the town is the Colorado River on whose shore Roper and I decide to camp while climbing Castleton Tower and The Priest. I am just out of the army and Roper is just going in, so this trip will be our only meeting in four years.

Each of us has two years of information and gossip to exchange, so we babble until the moon goes down. We are lulled to sleep by the night sounds – wind murmuring through the willows, the fluttering of a thousand leaves in the cottonwood above our heads, a ring of crickets competing with the frogs down by the river, where the deep currents of the Colorado flow westward to become cataracts.

We are going to try Cleopatra's Needle. Roper has already climbed it so there is little question as to who gets to lead the aid pitch – lucky me again. I am reminded of the last time I was here, with the Englishman, as my pitons fall out from under me, dislodged by the simple action of pulling up five feet of slack. The sandstone, disintegrating with each hammer-blow, rains down into my face so that I have to climb most of the pitch with my eyes closed. When the rain stops, I open my eyes standing on the summit, red from head to toe.

Roper prusiks up, cleaning with his hands, and not bothering to step onto the summit, he jumps into rappel and vanishes. I hardly give him time to get off the rope before I take off too and within seconds we are both on the ground shouting and jumping up and down as though we have just got away with the crime of the century.

A new day arrives and we drive around a corner to try Venus' Needle. We fail and instead of recognising our failure as a sign that our trip is over, we become stubborn and drive vehemently to Canyon de Chelly. The snow catches us on the second pitch of Spider and we can no longer ignore the message. There is a time on every desert expedition when the end of the trip is signified by subtle changes either in our own temperament or in the environment. One morning the sky is somehow different or the sunset will be of such surpassing splendour that no climb can match it. Now that our two failures have brought us to a halt, we pay attention to the wind and migrate west with the clouds.

Spring 1964
TM doesn't want any part of Cleopatra's Needle. He's heard stories about pitons being blown out by the wind so we try Venus' Needle instead. It's the same height as Cleo and the rock is just as soft, but TM hasn't heard any stories about it so that makes it okay. The last time we were here the weather was so cold we couldn't even touch the rock; the closest we could come to a desert experience was sitting in a theatre in Gallup, New Mexico watching Lawrence of Arabia. TM attacks the first pitch vengefully and I can hear his ribs cracking as he tries to force himself through a narrow slot fifty feet up. There is a tumultuous mechanical clatter behind me and a pickup arrives with two Indians aboard. I am paranoid about Indians ever since the incident

in the trading post and now here I am, lashed to an immovable desert spire while some gadget-festooned freak grunts and thrashes above me. One of the Indians gets out of the pickup and strolls nonchalantly over. I untie from my anchor and brace myself for running.

'We're looking for arrowheads,' I volunteer.

His laughter is profuse.

'Well, you won't find any up there. I thought you were just climbing it.'

Then he gets back in his truck, says something to his companion in Athabascan and drives off, both of them laughing hysterically as they bounce away across the dunes. When I climb up to TM he wants to know what the Indians thought was so funny.

'Oh, they thought we were looking for arrowheads.'

And then TM laughs too.

Spider Rock again. It's been three years since the last ascent so the Indians will have to bring the medicine men back for another ceremony. Rock climbers have their religion too, but I doubt that we could explain it to them. We manage it in one day this time but have to rappel in the dark. Two rappels from the ground my mind cracks when an aid sling jams behind a block and I'm left suspended under an overhang trying to cope with a pack, two extra ropes and a camera strap that is strangling me. TM shouts up fatherly advice during the lulls in my gorillarish ravings and I finally struggle back onto a ledge and start again.

This time no one seems aware of the ascent. No council of war from the Indians, no friendly chats in the ranger's office. We remain in the campground for two days and the only visitors we receive are a blind, arthritic donkey and the Chief Ranger's daughter, who is selling Girl Scout cookies. We stock up with enough to last us for the journey home and drive off. If it's this easy to get away with it, I think I'll climb it again.

Spring 1966

We have come directly from Berkeley to Zion, a mistake, for the monstrous walls of Zion Canyon, more intimidating than those of Yosemite, have subjugated us into tourists. We abandon all thoughts of climbing and turn instead to the trails until we once again dare study the walls for routes. But it is useless; we are too small and the lines we have drawn to define the limits of the possible have not been drawn far enough out to include Zion. The place oppresses us and we leave, thinking that someday when we are younger and suction cups are in vogue we will come back and climb the Sentinel.

Remaining tourists, we enter the role with a passion. Southern Utah contains landscapes so alien to anything in our experience that we feel that we are travelling on the moon. Cedar Breaks, Bryce Canyon, Kodachrome Flat areas where ancient varieties of sandstone have congealed like damp soot into formations so grotesque and fragile that climbing is out of the question; much of this country is for the eye only – great reefs of crimson rock, scalloped and capped with foam, stretch across vast areas of the desert plain like waves frozen in time at the instant before breaking. And there is the San Rafael Swell, an oceanic expanse of crumbling sandstone columns, sinuous and baroque, standing in clusters around Gothic arches, the whole merging into a larger pattern of plateaus and mesas which merge again into the timeless design of the desert's evolution. The horizons beyond Four Corners strain the limits of vision and of imagination. The desert can be comprehended only in its detail, for we are dealing with the sea.

Spring 1967
This trip is going to be a strange one. For the first time we are taking a woman along on a desert expedition and I feel that ancient superstition of sea captains. 'But this is a bird of a different hue,' Roper assures me and I take his word for it as we arrive in Zion from Death Valley. The walls seem less intimidating this time, perhaps because we have no climbing plans until we get to Arizona. Still, we don't feel big enough for Zion – maybe next year since we seem to be growing.

One last try at Spider. It will be Roper's first time and my third. We are wary of the Indians and the rangers both so we use a bit of stealth finding the Bat Trail into the canyon. At the start of the trail we find a sign that states, quite unequivocally: No Climbing. 'Balderdash,' I say and 'Bullshit,' says Roper and we turn the sign around so its blank side shows and proceed into the canyon. We will sleep in the canyon tonight, try to get up the climb tomorrow and back up to the rim and the highway without getting caught.

The early morning chill is destroying our resolve and we just about rationalise our way out of the climb when Janet contributes her opinion.

'You guys are not only cowardly, you're soft. It really isn't all that cold and now that you're here you should do the climb.'

'Roper, will you please discipline your woman.'

He makes a fist but cannot look her in the eye. We glance at each other, then at the rock and silently begin to climb. We reach the summit when the sun is close to the horizon, casting Spider's shadow down the canyon into infinity.

Spring and Fall 1969
On the rim of an immense plateau high above the town of Moab, is a newly constructed visitor centre at Deadhorse Point State Park. Like most visitor

centres, it was built on the assumption that a modern building, with picture windows and flush toilets, will somehow attract people to an area of scenic beauty which did not attract them before. Certainly the centre was not built in response to the pressure of an ever-growing population, for very few visitors to the area ever see Deadhorse Point. Not the hunters who each season swarm into Moab to display their trophies and trade deer hearts for elk livers; nor the tourists whose schedules allow only for a trip through the uranium plant; nor do climbers reach Deadhorse Point, for there is nothing there to climb.

The visitor centre houses drawings, graphs, charts and working models all neatly and logically arrayed to explain the view from Deadhorse Point. Some of the tourists who do find their way to the Point wander through the building and then leave, without bothering to look at the reality itself; just as the tourists in Yosemite, content to remain in the security of the lodge, will watch movies of Yosemite Falls rather than walk the one-quarter mile to experience directly the spray from the second highest waterfall on earth. Such is the level of their curiosity.

Approaching the edge of the world, we separate to experience the view in solitude. On the far horizon are the ramparts of a snow-shrouded range of peaks rising above the dark red expanse of Canyon-lands National Park. Across the entire plateau all sounds are hushed and the desert colours, so bright and varied during the day, are subdued by twilight. Directly before us nothing is visible for the earth drops abruptly into an emptiness as vast as the sky. Slowly the view expands as we reach the edge, where a sandstone cliff plunges below us to a sloping plain. We are standing on the summit of an incomprehensible series of steps, separated by sheer cliffs of sandstone. Far below, so distant that we cannot see its motion, is the silver curve of the Colorado River, performing its endless task without regard to night or day, the river and the land living in a unity that will last as long as time.

There was a time when the view from Deadhorse Point was free. Now there is a small fee for the privilege, collected by a ranger dressed not quite in Lincoln green. Someone has to pay for the visitor centre.

from ASCENT *1970*

DENN BLEIBEN IST NIRGENDS*

JIM PERRIN

They say the male menopause occurs in about one's thirtieth year; and thus I feel worried, for here I am, entering my thirtieth year in a hot flush of new-found enthusiasm for climbing. I seem to have spent years in a fruitless attempt to give it up – for as long as I've been climbing almost I've been trying to give it up – yet here I am at the supposed changing point of a man's life, and the symptoms are back with me more strongly than ever. I sit by my fire in the evenings and visions of pieces of rock float past my mind; or I'll leaf idly through old copies of *Wilson's Wonderful World* [aka *Mountain*], and a picture, even just a name will cause my palms to sweat, my fingers to flex and unflex at the touch of each tiny imagined flake.

Yet believe me, I've tried very hard to give it up. Oh yes, so very, very hard. And this stern moral overseer whom I call my malefactor, implanted in me during a Catholic childhood, he whispers to me continually: 'you must choose not to climb, it is mere hedonism, wilful, the self-destructive portion of man, the sin of Lucifer, Godless, and too much on a Sunday'. And if it's not him, it's soft-spoken Belial whispering, counselling, tempting with visions of Sunday mornings spent in slothful ease, toast and marmalade, the Sunday papers, a warm bed and a voluptuous woman, and believe me, that is a style of life which I would not affect to despise.

But still I want to climb these rocks.

Now as my best friends will tell you, I have little consistency, and for this reason I try to give my slightest inference the weight of a moral pronounce-ment – as with a certain heaviness one learns to spell, thus it is on one's Odyssey. I think almost I do not trust consistency; we look for life's essence in its fix or flow, and I would rather, in my own self, live in the flow. I love movement, especially movement on rock; not only my own, though this especially, but also that of others. Have you noticed to what degree you can tell a man's character from the way he moves on rock? Study it, and there it is in essence. Boysen for example; a languorous aesthete possessed of the most devastating polish of phrase a sort of climbing Oscar Wilde, beauty for its own sake in his every move, and effortless as glass. Or Crew, so quick to

*From *The Duino Elegies* of Rainer Maria Rilke that Translates as 'For Staying is Nowhere'

grasp the essentials of a situation, yet with such a tenuous hold on them, such an infinite capacity for falling off. And then there's Wilson, muscle-bound and galumphing, the rock shuddering to his touch and a Rock-Ola jukebox on every stance. You could make a speculative science of it, like palmistry but more liberal. But this is to digress: I wanted to tell you how it came about that I couldn't give climbing up.

You see there are bad Catholics, like Joe Brown, Paul Nunn, and myself, and ours is the climb up to Hell; and there are good Catholics like Achille Ratti – theirs the Kingdom of Heaven. So much is self-obvious; our solemn devils say to us 'you must suffer' and therefore suffer we must, and devilish hard we find it. Joe Brown explained to me once that the routes you did were directly proportionate to the size of your rat, the bigger the rat, the harder the route. I said to him: 'in my church there were no rats, only an Irish priest.' I must tell you here that both he and I come from the poor areas of Manchester, he from Ancoats and I from Hulme; it's a moot point between us which area was the worst, but either way both were bad. Paul Nunn comes from Maccles-field and Cheshire rats are relatively tame; to eat cheese makes one melan-choly is a likely explanation. But to come back to rats, he began to explain:

'The rat is in your belly and it gnaws you into doing the routes.'

'Is it like a wife?' I asked him, but he replied:

'No, because you're the rat who fills her belly and then she nags you not to do the routes.'

I knew what he meant, but it wouldn't do for me; you see Brown's always been rather bellicose, and I've always had this secret desire for the soft and voluptuous life, peppered by the cerebral. Now this is where we tread the path to Heaven, strait is the gate and all that. One of my new climbs in Pembroke I called the Strait Gate, and a very good climb it is too, but of course they began to call it the Straight Gate, which made me irate, so that I had no reply but a string of witless puns. The Strait Gate? Oh yes; well one day it occurred to this implanted adviser, this malefactor of mine, that climbing was something I actually enjoyed. As soon as he knew this he took pains to conceal it from me, and would have it that I was a scared and jaded non-combatant, which like all unfair criticism contained the germ of truth. So he would have me give it up, and deprived me of that sensuous touch of rock, that gross bodily awareness, that awful surrender to movement.

I had to creep back undercover.

On a winter's day I took myself down to Cader Idris and found myself, by chance as it were, beneath the Cyfrwy Arête. Oh shades of Arnold Lunn, the Pearly Gates on ski, package tours to Heaven; there's no getting away from the Malefactor. If you're cursed with a memory like mine it will open up to you its files and memoranda at the most awkward possible moments.

'You and the rock both in body are unsound,' it told me, and proceeded to recount to me in loving detail the fall of that good Catholic, and until finally it tailed off into incoherent ramblings about states of grace.

And I, I wanted the heights and the naked edges and the great plunge of rib and groove, the splintered rock, wind-whistled and myself upon it. So up I went on that shattered hillside in company with a certain fear. It was so beautiful, I was lost. There were pinnacles and great drops; there were moves to be made and lakes far below, mauve horizons and I was unutterably alone; and the mountain did not shake me off, for I am not hubristic. It led me on like the eyes of a woman moving to her recline, and I could not but follow to the green slopes and grey-bouldered crown where I ate my sandwiches and drank my coffee, for I had come well prepared, and watched ravens in the cold air above me. And do you know, those dark birds enjoyed their flights; Oh how they revelled on the wind, upturned and playing, and I thought, it is not a rat has brought me here but a joy, and I shall not listen to you, malefactor, no more shall I listen to you. He replied, of course; told me that my well-being was due to nothing more than the absence of positive ions in the high atmosphere. But I am not a scientist and could give him no credence.

And so I began to climb again, though my muscles ached and it was hard. I called it an epiphany and I was very happy, though climbs that had once seemed easy now seemed hard. There is nothing hard about the average extreme, I told myself, doubtful at the moment of speech, and committed myself to one. I had not remembered that holds could be so exiguous, nor that overhangs could loom so; I struggled, and the muscles twanged across the frets of my bones, the music of pain. But I did not mind, for afterwards I was alive and surely practice will make it easy once more. Where strength has been, strength shall be again, and I shall go to the boulders assiduously.

It chanced one day that I was musing in the sun on top of a crag after the perfect execution of a climb down memory lane when, on a bald wall before me appeared a lithe figure ascending. I'd seen all the best climbers of my years and here was their better. Easy power, and elastic movement; in the years I had been away, climbing had made one of its periodic advances. Note this well, ye elders, an advance has been made. So I went to a climb of this nature, though much shorter, and well-hidden by trees, and tried to emulate this style, though my lax muscles could not cope without the help of the high runner and taut rope. And then to a wall, where I trained most assiduously. Very good. What man has done, men will try to do; we live up to examples, their peaks fire our imagination, and the upward trek goes on.

from THE CLIMBERS' CLUB JOURNAL *1976*

PART 2

THE ALPINE ODYSSEY

With expedition activity and the widening horizons for rock-climbing now demanding so much attention from climbers, the yearly pilgrimage to the Alps, so important in the 1950s and 60s, has tended to lose prominence in recent years. Nevertheless Chamonix still enjoys unrivalled popularity as the premier Alpine centre and it is the base for many aspirant super-alpinists seeking to train themselves for the challenges of the greater ranges. As such the great ice and mixed climbs have formed the major attractions of the last decade, just as previous years saw a predilection for the great rock routes.

The following collection of articles hints at the diversity in the approach to alpine climbing as well as a matching variety of literary styles. The section ends with an account of a major Canadian 'alpine' ascent, representing a region that, with cheaper travel, might well enjoy increasing popularity as an alpine venue in the future.

Note for the 2006 Edition: High-standard alpinism continues to be perfected in the Mont Blanc Range and other challenging locations in the European Alps but areas like Patagonia, the Andes, the Rockies and the coast ranges of Canada and Alaska have also become popular as air travel has become cheaper and access easier. Winter alpinism has increased as equipment, food and clothing have developed.

THE ENGLISH TRAVELLER

RONALD CLARK

'I have frequently observed,' says Thomas Hinchliff, himself one of these later [19th Century] travellers, 'that the best mountain guides look with great suspicion upon everybody except the English and their own countrymen in a mountaineering point of view: they distrust them from the beginning, and always seem maliciously glad when the grounds of their contempt are justified by the subsequent collapse of the luckless foreigner. They seldom take any trouble to cheer his fainting spirits, or offer him any assistance: and take delight in speaking of a difficult mountain as only good for Switzers or Englishmen.'

It would, of course, have been surprising if the English had not played an important part in the exploratory travel of the period. It was, for them, the opening phase of the great Victorian peace, and the world in which they trained and encouraged their guides has today the quality of a long vanished civilisation. It was a world of audacious ventures and expected triumphs, of coaches clattering out from well-servanted hotels, of champagne on the summits and largesse in the valleys, of men going out into a fresh Alpine dawn whose wonder was only then beginning to burst upon their astonished eyes. It was a world of comfortable travel at an equable pace, in which a British passport was the only credential a man needed, and in which the possession of a little wealth was considered a duty to be exercised rather than an achievement to be advertised. And it was a world in which a little wealth went a surprisingly long way.

from THE EARLY ALPINE GUIDES *1949*

THE GRÉPON

C. R. ALLEN

The account which I am about to set forth describes, in effect, a single day spent in Alpine travel; the day concerned was, however, an unusual one and it is my hope that other travellers may find the account amusing and perhaps instructive.

It had been our intention to reach Chamonix early enough to attain the Couvercle Hut, but a certain lassitude delayed us and we found ourselves obliged to pass the night in the dormitory at Montenvers, a noisome place almost wholly devoid of the amenities which civilised beings have come to think necessary. Our party of four consisted of Mr F. D. Smith, Mr D. W. Stembridge, Mr J. Varney and myself, united by the spirit of alpinism and by membership of an excellent and exclusive club rooted in the greatest of England's counties. We were joined in residence by a French party, which seemed to embody all the traditional characteristics of the race. Some sleep was, nonetheless, attained.

We rose at two in the morning and by simple phlegmatic efficiency succeeded in leaving before the Frenchmen. Lack of knowledge, however, resulted in our becoming mazed in a complexity of paths, and we were obliged to await their guidance to the path leading to Plan des Aiguilles. At the foot of the Nantillons Glacier there was light enough to see a selection of dubious looking clouds. A steady ascent of the glacier, including a convenient scaling of its well known Rognon brought us to the foot of the couloir which divides the Grands Charmoz from the Grépon at 6.30am. Here we left all our crampons and two of the axes and climbed the true right wall of the couloir – an enjoyable scramble except for the rubbish dislodged by the French above. At the col we briskly partook of refreshment, contemplating the superb panorama across the Mer de Glace; but some signs of gathering cloud were evident and a bitterly cold south wind was beginning to rise.

A short traverse and climb brought us to a notch beside Mr. Mummery's famous crack. It fell to me, by lot, to lead this section; after a few fitful attempts I did succeed in gaining lodgement in the crack. The wind, owing to local conformations of rock, was blowing, so to speak, from the anatomical south and this I found less than encouraging, especially since it was now

armed with a light hail; while only part way up the crack it became clear
that cold and fatigue would not allow me to continue. After five attempts on
the crux I assumed a pose of insouciance and belayed in it. Smith then
followed me and led through in an effective and forthright manner to the top.
From this point we 'threaded' the ridge, now misted, through the Cannon
Hole and an awkward little chimney, to emerge again on the Nantillons side
of the ridge. I performed a satisfactory penance to St. Mummery by leading
the 'Râteau de Chèvres'; despite my companions' remarks I am disinclined to
believe that any normal goat could have succeeded.

We continued more easily along the ridge, though the wind was
unpleasant; a tight chimney in descent cost me a belt buckle, but a hasty
improvisation saved me from embarrassment and the risk of intimate frostbite. We were soon on top of the Grand Gendarme; roping down from this
was tricky and involved difficulty in retrieving the rope, despite precautions.
Owing to lack of forethought we were then obliged to walk along the 'Route
des Bicyclettes'. Two leads then brought us, outside the rock tunnel known
as the 'Crevasse', to the final crack. My progress up this coincided with the
arrival of a hailstorm, and I sat beside the metal Madonna on the summit
until a lull occurred. It was while Smith was climbing that I noticed that the
Lady beside me had begun to sing in a thin, reedy voice ... while Smith and
I were looking for the route of descent we were both struck a smart blow on
the back; even in the act of mutual remonstration we realised that the
phenomenon was electrical. A vicious crack of thunder on the Blaitière
completed the warning, we roped down very quickly to the Crevasse and
retired into it – clearly for the night, for it was 6pm.

The Crevasse consists of a rock tunnel of roughly rectangular section,
variously eight to twelve feet high and never more than two and one half
feet broad. Smith and Stembridge now set to work as Esquimaux Masons
and quickly built a wall of snow-ice, from the floor, to block up the windward
side of the tunnel. We were all then able to pack ourselves in: Stembridge
sitting by the wall, Smith facing him, myself standing and Varney sitting
below the entrance. No other arrangement was possible.

Foresight had provided us with food, some vessels and one of Mr Bleuet's
ingenious stoves: a meal of hot soup and raisins was laboriously prepared.
The night passed interminably, with the wind roaring outside; we were
all very cold indeed and got but little sleep. At four o'clock we made a hot
drink consisting of hot milk with honey dissolved in it – a wonderful reviver
which I cannot commend too highly; at six o'clock we took a second helping,
extricated Varney from the heap of snow that had surrounded him overnight
and then emerged. The morning was clearing: after an unpleasant session
on ice-glazed holds, with thanks for the rope left hanging, we were on the

summit and in sunshine at 8am. A quick rope-down brought us to the Brèche Balfour, where we basked in the inexpressible glory of the sun and ate the rest of our food.

The descent began with a series of abseils, of which the last was an over-shot into a long ice-gully which had to be reclimbed to a very sharp rock bridge. Smith scored again at this point by devising a method for crossing which was distinguished both by ingenuity and by induced bodily dis-comfort; in this way we arrived back in sunshine on the 'C.P. Platform' at noon. Easy scrambling then brought us to the Col des Nantillons, and we descended the glacier in thick mist to retrieve our deposited equipment. At the foot of the glacier we were again gladdened by sunshine and walked wearily back to Montenvers. I meditated on the horror of discovering that, on the descent of the snow-plastered faces above, any mental attitude but positive alertness would have let me nod off to sleep; on arrival at Mont-envers I was glad to surrender at last to sleep, even in that wretched place.

Of the lessons that might be learned from our tale, the most obvious is the need for speed: be it said with shame that the French party reached the glacier, in descent, before the storm. As to what might have befallen us had the storm continued to rage for another day or two, I prefer not to speculate. I must confess that, except for those contained in the foregoing account, we have no meteorological or glaciological observations to report. Our geo-logical impressions are confined to the conclusion that the rock of Chamonix is among the most abrasive known to science.

from THE YORKSHIRE RAMBLERS JOURNAL *1960–64*

A FACE: A FRIEND

MIKE BAKER

The wind blasted the previous day's snow from the great curve of the Lenzspitze face. It could be heard or imagined even on the sunny patio in Saas Fee where we were enjoying an early, if frugal, Sunday lunch.

'Accuracy?' scoffed Colin as he applied himself to the millimetrically precise apportionment of our meagre cheese ration, 'Accuracy is a concept which no scientists accept today.' He was answering a suggestion that, for all its age, my Negretti and Zambra altimeter was an instrument of great accuracy. Secretly I think he found it slightly disturbing that his own modern plastic-fronted Swiss altimeter did not exude quite the confidence that breathed through the leather and brass of my own. It was inevitable that half an hour later we should find ourselves heading along the Mischabel Hut track. It is a path of unrelenting steepness and does not provide the perfect Sunday afternoon stroll, but it is well suited for the testing of altimeters. Colin's had been set in metres and mine, after some mathematics of such sophistication that the calculation now entirely eludes me, had been wound to the equivalent in feet. For an hour or two while the needles slowly showed our advance, we were able to lose ourselves in reveries of yesterday and tomorrow.

We had set off on Friday afternoon for the Täsch Hut from Zermatt. The Saturday had seen us up the Alphubel by the Westgrat a recommendable route with a crux that is not to be underestimated when the wind is blowing and snow is in the air. The descent to the Alphubeljoch and the Längflue had been at first a cold and blind affair, and then just a wet one. It had snowed high up for twelve hours solid and our plan to return to Zermatt over the North-East Face of the Lenzspitze looked optimistic in the extreme. It seemed more likely that we would have to creep back over the Windjoch and down the Ried Glacier to St. Niklaus, or even, perish the thought, take a bus to the Rhône Valley and go back to Zermatt by train. We reached the hut in good order and in a good time. Over a bowl of lemon tea Colin sat down to disprove the supremacy of my altimeter. It was a puzzled Taylor that reported eventually that his instrument recorded a height of 3321m while mine, when converted, made it 3327m By the map and Guide Book the true height is 3329m I thought it boded well.

Quite contrary to all our expectations, the day being Sunday, the hut began to fill up between five and six o'clock. By 7pm there was no longer any room to sit in the living room. By half past the hallway too was full. Soon all the bed space was taken and the place was undeniably bulging. Against the howling of the wind, which continued all night, the assurance of the Guardian that the North-East Face would be in condition by dawn sounded thin and diffident. From the deepest recess of his sleeping bag Colin muttered that all the wind would probably sweep the face clear of the piled up snow and the ascent would be a doddle. But neither of us believed a word of it. Though we did not know it then we had once again talked ourselves into a route.

It was Colin's theory, one of many, all of which he insisted on putting into practice, that a good alpine day involved at some point an assertion of superiority of his rope over 'the rest'. Deep down I think he felt that this was best done on the hill, but it undoubtedly bolstered up morale to start asserting early. Accordingly at 3am precisely, while others slumbered stertorously on, we gathered our ironmongery, donned our warmest clothes, and crept assertively downstairs, hushing one another as we went. We lifted our warm water from a dormant stove, stuffed our mouths with unwanted rolls spread thick with jam and frozen butter, and shivered as the wind continued its battering of the exposed ridge on which the hut sat. Only as we strapped on our crampons did the first Continentals stumble into the room. The shortness of their axes and the superciliousness of their manner betrayed that they too had designs on the North-East Face. With briefly muttered greetings (not reciprocated) we slipped through the door and, before we had traversed past the hut's ablutions, were in a cold, windblown, steep and inhospitable territory.

For an hour or so we trudged upwards. Each step had to be won from the blown snow. The temperature had not risen sufficiently since the snowfall to form even the merest crust. The snow emitted a high-pitched noise when compacted by our cramponed boots. Soon we could see behind us the lights of the first of the other parties. It was perhaps natural that we should think they were catching up. The ridge flattened out. To our right was the apparently flat Hohbalm glacier leading to the great concave snow face. Above the face was a jagged ridge, then the stars, and everywhere a gigantic wind. We roped up and left the ridge, vainly hoping for refuge from the wind, but we didn't find it. Every pace towards the foot of the route reinforced the feeling that our actions were no more than a performance put on partly for the benefit of those who flaunted the lights behind, and partly to defer for ourselves the moment of facing the truth: namely that the route was not feasible.

The going deteriorated steadily. The wind had piled up enormous and unending drifts leading to the foot of the face. The snow, which had been ankle deep, crept knee-high and further. Simple forward movement became impossible. To make a foot's advance it was necessary to turn half round and sit on the snow, then complete the circle and knee it into a sufficient compactness to create a footstep. Our tracks turned into a furrow, and the furrow into a slowly advancing trench.

It seemed ages before we reached the bergschrund which by then we had openly declared to be the day's objective. Down the maws of this glinting monster there dribbled a continuous stream of windblown snow. We edged our way up, mere warts upon its chin, only feeling bold because we were both convinced that we would come straight down as soon as we had set foot upon the face itself.

Above this bergschrund however the whole situation changed. The snow had been blown from the Face, leaving no more than a rime adhering to the hard compact snow-ice below. Moreover the angle was nowhere near as fierce as it had appeared from below. This is a characteristic of all the Valais snow faces and has doubtless prevented many worthy parties from ever setting foot upon them. So we decided to go on. We climbed on a full 150ft of rope leading through in pitches which we estimated (wrongly) at about 250ft. The distance from bergschrund to summit is 490m expressed vertically but when we had each led five through leads on the full 150ft of rope we did not seem much more than half way. The best line is easy for it follows an aesthetic curve leftwards and up towards the topmost point on the ridge. Yet far below the dots that were the other parties, amalgamated now, seemed to be heading further rightwards. We were, I think, four and a half hours on the face. We did not need to speak. Pitch followed pitch, with a single ice peg to secure the belay. We used Salewa eight inch hollow screws and felt them to provide excellent security. It seemed, no doubt quite falsely, that the final two pitches took almost the total time. They really were, brutes for the wind sweeping from the west had made everything hard as iron and they are steep. But they yielded to Colin, and as he breasted the summit he emitted a most uncharacteristic whoop of triumph and glee which was immediately flung away and dispersed in the greater roar of the wind.

We now had to decide the best means of return. The wind seemed to be coming more from the south and neither of us greatly fancied the long trudge of the route via the Dom Hut. We therefore determined to traverse to the Nadelhorn, descend to the Windjoch to the North East – thus getting out of the wind – and then head north to the Bordier Hut, a pleasantly unknown refuge above the hamlet of Ried.

The traverse was dramatic and was, in Colin's words, 'effected briskly but with circumspection'. Occasional gendarmes would loom out of the mist shredded by the wind which seemed to buffet the very rock bed. Any slack in the rope was immediately whipped in a horizontal curve to the right. There is nothing of any technical difficulty on the ridge, but nevertheless we were both glad to make the summit of the Nadelhorn, and gladder still to find below it some real shelter where it was possible to talk without shouting or fighting for breath, and even to pause for some mint cake and cold tea. It was about midday.

The descent to the Windjoch demanded care but not the complete concentration that the climb had hitherto called for. We were able to look around, particularly to see what had happened to the other party on the face. It had not progressed up our line; we spotted the climbers eventually in a direct line below the Nadeljoch on an unnamed route referred to briefly in the Kurz Guidebook. They did not seem to be making progress. There did not seem to be anyone else on the mountains, although a line of footsteps across the Hohbalm basin showed that quite a large group had tried to reach our col from the hut. From the col it was an arduous plod past the Western bastions of the Balfrin. It is however interesting to tread the Ried Glacier for it gives most interesting views of the Hohberghorn and the Durrenhorn, the continuation peaks of the Nadelgrat. The East Face of the Hohberghorn particularly looks as though it merits more attention than it receives. The peak is, after all, a four-thousander.

It was early evening before we reached the Bordier Hut, a cabin undramatically placed on a moraine above the right bank of the Ried Glacier which falls sharply down at that point. We were both by then fairly tired but had the urge to continue. We had reached the Saas Valley from Zermatt in an afternoon and a day, and the symmetry of our plan required a return to the Zermatt Valley in the same sort of time. Besides, there is something enormously satisfying in walking unhurriedly downhill in the cool evening after a long windy day. We therefore decided to go on.

The going is at first straightforward. The path leads across the glacier and down the left bank to the moraines. It plunges into deep pine woods just below the ruined chalets at Alpja. There we could smell wood smoke and pine and we could hear gentle streams. As the route became more tortuous it very soon became clear that we were not going to reach St Niklaus in daylight. The question then was whether we would reach it at all that evening. Only after we had reached the junction of three paths, and chosen the one which eventually led back uphill, was it clear that we were not. Quite where we came to rest we were unclear. There was a ruined chalet and an irrigation stream which we had followed until it seemed interminable; but there was also a patch of luscious grass and that was enough for both of us. We had some chocolate and some water and some nuts and raisins, and a good measure of whisky. Colin lit his pipe. We both donned duvets, laid down the bivouac sack as a groundsheet and plunged our feet into our rucksacks. We lay back to watch the shooting stars flit across the night sky and silently dowse themselves behind the Weisshorn. We reminisced for a spell. Then we slept. It was not given to us to know that within two days the mountains were to claim Colin's life. We slept, at peace.

from THE CLIMBERS' CLUB JOURNAL *1975*

GOOFY'S LAST CLIMB

ROBIN SMITH

Goofy is a grubby fellow who lives in a sleep. Here is how he climbed the Alps in his sleep.

We drove over to the oberland under little Phraser. We were many and odd and odd, and therefore, smartly, doubleyoked and teamed in twos in furrows into the snows. The sleepy two-timed residue, Goofy plus two, sloped away last and so not least. Phraser and I, that olden team, had boldly struck out white wands well in hand. For ruminant idling little profits, we wander-lustily theorised. But alas describing the circles of the schools we carried each other away and passed a number of days circling base. But at last we opened our eyes and rose through the forests and snows to a desolate hut in a golden silence under the gleaming walls. But herd again from ober the land, here were all the many and odd, Goofy disgruntled with negative plus-two and nobody very positive and each aspiralling sortie come to nothing. Wherewith the well-laid teams of men closed in a scramble and set with the sun.

Out of this confusion Goofy and I turned up our collars and loped into the big night wild with stars. We nosed through moraines and crevasses and looming cliffs of rock and ice away up and round, and sat on the snow as the light came slowly, fumbling into bitter crampons under the long 'schrund of the Fiescherwand.

The North Wall of the Fiescherhorn is snow and ice and bits of rock, miles long by 3000ft of climbing. The spur in the middle looked to be the best (but not the fiercest) line, for all the wall was quite plastered but less so out on the spur, with the angle a little less and the line more defined and less threat of loose stones or avalanches down your neck. Fiercely therefore leaping the 'schrund, we flung ourselves upon the spur. (Only first try, Goofy fell in the 'schrund, for he was half asleep, and so he stayed throughout this insomaniacal sortie.)

From here till the end of the day we were lost in the wrinkled humps of spur, shambling ribs and grooves and shelves, great bulges bald or bristling, sly sidlings round the sides, crusty snow and rubber ice and piles of crumbling rock, axes picking or hacking at almost every step, always threading, thrutching, balancing, bumbling, cunning, where to go, how to save, will it hold, will it go, with always the next bit of hump hiding the spur that lurked above, and awesome gauge of height-not-gained in views to left or right over the sweep of the vast ice walls of the Fiescherwand. And most of all, those slopes of ice too hard and steep to climb without holds, but dotted all over with inset stones from bigger than yourself to the size of your thumb; and saving hours of cutting steps, you plot a course from stone to stone, from tip-toe on one to leap for another, from scarty slab to thumbnail mantel, cutting maybe once or twice to clear the top of a stone, creepy-crawling heart in mouth and trying to push not pull. The ground went down, the day ground on. Huge slow hissing mists coiled around us. Unfit, ill-fed, necks half-wrung, we fluttered up with axe-arms flapping, until at last the spur hardened and reared into one last fearful hump. Sheer rock walls fell away to the right and a grisly couloir swept the left, leaving no ways round, and above the bulges piled out of sight and threatened a full stop; but a questioning scoop curled up and rightwards, and blindly we slow-wormed through its folds, champing and pawing at bits of ice as always the bulges thrust us right, and little white mice of panic whispered round the walls of the brain that the light was beginning to go and the scoop was going nowhere. Then we came out at 300ft at an overhung ledge on the teetering edge of the spur, with no way up, and no way right, and was there, was there, yes there was, a spidery ledge swung back leftwards through the gloom over the bulges under an overhang on to the crest of the spur. By now the sun was buried and the last light going. With seized-up arms and rumbling bellies, we fumbled leftwards under the overhang past the one and only piton we found on all the climb to thirty feet of do or die on knees and elbows up the great hold of an overhanging flake and round the lip of the overhang into a short steep icy groove which twisted up and right to a neck at the top of the last hump of the spur. And there above us a prow of snow soared the last 300ft into the vast luminous cornice booming out of the night.

But here, as we broke the back of the spur, in us, too, something snapped. We hadn't brought any bivouac gear, because we had planned to be down in a day; and now that we were stuck for the night, we could have thrashed on to the cornice and burrowed for ever into the deep snow; but we hadn't eated any goodies all day long, so now all light-headed we just nodded around the neck, Goofy like a totem pole swaying in a dozent trance while I went round about in a mumbling delirium. The neck was a right-angled rock step, six feet horizontally and then four foot vertically, cutting into the profile of the narrow crest of the spur, but filled in with a triangular ridge of crusted powder snow, the shape of one of those crummy one-man tents. Abysmal steepness fell to the right, and the icy groove up which we had climbed twisted back down to the left into the bulges below us. A chill wind blew no good from the right, so starting from the top of the groove we hollowed out the ridge of snow till only the crust was left. There wasn't room for us side by side, so thoughtfully I stood aside for Goofy to sidle in and li lo. Then, classically bridged across the groove, seat on one bump of ice, feet on another, and nothing under my knees, and thinking of Goofy's toes turning black in the night, I took off my crampons and my drooling boots and socks and wrapped my feet in a spare jersey and put them all into my rucksack and knotted the sack into a great club. By now Goofy was asleep, but not for long, for seizing hold of him, heaving and shoving, I struggled by every mounting method to get myself into the one-man tent. But I couldn't get over his great knobbly knees, and all I came near to was demolishing the tent and rolling us over in a stotting clinch back down 3000ft of steps. And so I reverted to the classic bridge, muttering unmentionable spells to hypnotise my knocking knees to lock in animated suspension between my back which slowly gelled to one spine-chilling wall of the groove and my great club-foot planted on the other with crampons, boots, socks, feet and jersey milling about inside. However, I was firmly belayed, to 300ft of rope, lying in fankles under Goofy, sleeping again, grinning like life-in-death, and lashed to an axe thrust to the hilt through the crust of the far wall of the tent. And so the night rolled on, with Goofy like a pupoid grub while I wriggled in the open like an early worm, and all the while vulturous mists wheeled slowly around us, and sometimes, through them, lights, incredible as stars, winked from the lost world of valleys and resorts, and so till the ghoulish shrouded daylight rose again from the grave.

Then for half an hour, while Goofy rubbed his eyes, I chewed four tasty socks and two boots and crampon straps.

When they could bend I battered them on, then we rose all weak and creaking, kicked our happy home to bits, and dragged up three hundred frost-bitten feet of steepening prow of deepening snow to inside the open beak of the biggest bit of the beady-eyed double cornice. We thrashed through the lower cornice, up to our waists in powder snow, folded under the upper cornice curling thirty feet outwards over our heads. But now that it was light of day, we didn't want to burrow for ever, and away to the right a break in the cornice looked like saving time. And so for 100ft of rock-gymnastic nightmare, we bridged, straddled, chimneyed, lay-backed, mantelshelfed and stomach-crawled through convolutions of floating snow friezed by demoniac winds, along the tunnel between the cornices, through the break in the upper cornice, out of the climb and on to the summit ridge.

To the left, the summit of the Fiescherhorn called from swirling clouds on high. So turning right, we widdled off homewards. It was just a walk, but miles around, and mostly in the mist, with fleeting pools of sunshine, into which we belly-flopped for sleeps. Half way down we found another hut, and people, who fed us; and then we stopped for forty winks and hours later staggered on, and then a labyrinthine ice-fall tramelled us for hours and hours, and just one hour from home, night fell, all mist and dripping; and so for hours and hours we huddled in a sodden cave, with that inhuman fellow Goofy sleeping again. But daylight came, and we petered on, and there was the hut, and all the teams, and bits of bread, and down below there were cafes, with chandeliers and tailored waiters and menus as long as your arm, and bars; and as for Goofy, ever since, all he does, he drinks as well as sleeps.

from EDINBURGH UNIVERSITY
MOUNTAINEERING CLUB JOURNAL *1960*

DEUX GRANDES BIERES

IAN McNAUGHT-DAVIS

It is springtime and Snell's Field, which lies hidden in fir trees between Chamonix and Argentière, is looking at its best: the new grass is pushing through the mud, and the winter snows, burned off the glaciers by the warming sun, are swelling the River Arve. It all looks fresh, green and virgin. Suddenly, a rusty mini-van bumps into the field, stops in a patch of sunlight and disgorges its occupants. The latter, bearded and dressed in jeans, place their cassette radio on the roof of the van and, as the tinny rhythms of familiar pop music fill the glade, throw off their worn shirts and expose their white chests to the sun for the first time in eleven months. Soon, climbing equipment, ropes, boxes of supermarket food ('none of this foreign rubbish'), worn-out, porous tents, greasy, well-used sleeping bags, a new pair of boots and a carefully preserved camera are randomly distributed over an area of several hundred square feet. One of the party is busily hammering at the collapsed suspension of the van, another is lighting a smoky Primus stove, and the third, a 'First Season' man, is keenly reading from a thin stock of guide books.
　Who are these people? They are the harbingers of a veritable army of

British climbers who will shortly be battling their way from Dover in worn-out, overloaded vans, fighting for road-space with French salesmen gunning their underpowered Renaults at unbelievable speeds down the Autoroute du Sud. Within the next few weeks the scene will be repeated many times a day. The season has opened and the greatest climbing region in the world is exerting its magnetic pull on every self-respecting climber from Ramsbottom to Rio, from the Shawangunks to Mount Fuji – and all the English-speaking ones will be heading for Snell's Field. Here they will base themselves by courtesy of the Snell family, from whom British climbers have received so much help and friendship over the past twenty-five years.

But back to our three first-comers: the sun has moved off the field now, and the trio are heading for Chamonix, the 'Blackpool of the Alps'. They park the van, not noticing the foreign-looking parking meter, and spend a few minutes discussing whether or not they can face the Nazi prison camp conditions and un-French attendants of the tepid public 'douche'. Deciding that they can't, they acquire some bread, butter and saucisson from the friendly supermarket, following the Chancellor of the Exchequer's instructions to conserve foreign currency by not paying. In the cool evening the streets are full of candyfloss eating tourists flushed from adventures on the Montenvers railway or from a trans-glacier trip in a cage suspended from the wires of the Aiguille du Midi *téléphérique*. The British climbers push their way through to the Post Office, where the plain French postmistress shouts *'rien'* at them as they ask for their *poste restante* mail. Disappointed, they emerge and loiter for a while, looking at the bright tables of the Pontinière cafe across the square. A number of cynical-looking French climbers are holding court, sprawling in their favourite seats in the sun, greeting each new arrival with effusive hugs. As they watch, this dazzling, immaculate group is joined by a swaying bevy of skinny, bronzed girls who sidle up to be kissed and groped in their turn.

The British finally turn away to a shadowy corner where a faded sign announces the 'Bar National'. At last they have arrived at the English-speaking social centre of Chamonix; here they will sit, largely in silence, counting their tiny cash resources and occasionally purchasing glasses of surprisingly strong ale from Maurice Simond, the short-sighted proprietor who, for many years, without speaking any English, has acted as barkeeper, money- lender, confidant and friend to countless young British climbers. He manages to host, with a detached, tolerant style, a group as rowdy and unkempt as can only otherwise be seen en masse in the Padarn Lake on a busy Saturday night. He will be the only Frenchman most of the English climbers will speak to during their four-week stay.

'Eh up, youth. Deux grandes bières, silver plate, mercy blow-through.'

They give him the benefit of all they have learned of French language and culture during the past four Alpine seasons.

Maurice smiles and absent-mindedly operates a complex chromium machine that seems to dribble frothy beer or coffee at random. A group of Germans look in and come to stand by the bar, muttering gutterally. Maurice continues to play with his machine, smiling secretly to himself as the thirty-strong chorus maintains its ceaseless shout of 'Deux grandes bières, youth'. The Germans retreat, baffled.

The atmosphere is that much beloved by today's British climbers: tolerant, cheap and confused, friendly, and possibly even protective.

Here, tales can be told of adventures on the mountain, or, more likely, of the famous Chamonix 'incidents'. Which celebrated climber threw the 'No Parking' sign on to the live rail of the Chamonix railway? How many times has, de Saussure's pointing finger been equipped with flowers, champagne bottles or contraceptives? Which great Himalayan men have spent nights in Chamonix jail, or even been deported? Were you at the great Alpenstock battle, when the Brits and the chuckers-out were locked in combat until all the glasses and plate-glass windows were smashed? And do you remember when, after the baddies had beaten up a lone Canadian in revenge, the fifth cavalry arrived in the nick of time in mini-vans from Snell's Field and extracted a terrible retribution? Or were they too late? Do you recall the Cafe de Paris brawl, when French and British climbers worked out their bad-weather and sexual frustrations by breaking bottles over one another's heads? Don Whillans reputedly came to the rescue this time, and the Great British Press was supposedly responsible for the subsequent, subtly misleading headline: 'English Tourists Attacked on Mont Blanc'.

Yet it could only happen in Chamonix. All the little corners where it was once possible to escape authority have been eliminated from the more organised, bourgeois ski resorts of Switzerland and Austria. Tolerance for schoolboy pranks and ebullient behaviour, if it ever existed, has gone. Except in Chamonix – although, as in the days of the Old West, there comes a time when it is best to be out of town by dawn, perhaps on a climb.

It is easy to say that all this is unimportant, that Chamonix is only neces-sary as a place to buy food and as somewhere to shelter when bad weather interrupts great and glorious climbs on the high, white snows. But every climbing area needs a social centre, where climbers can meet and discuss the latest adventures, and relax and plan new ones; where they can realise, if only by contrast, something of the limitless beauty of the far-away hills, which, due to some curious low-altitude lethargy, often remain far away.

But we may not see Chamonix or Mont Blanc like this for very much longer. Already on any fine day every high-reputation route has more than its fair shares of ropes, all getting in one another's way. The *voies normales* are beset with long queues of novices, each aspirant copying the actions of the man two feet in front. As French Minister of Sport, Pierre Mazeaud, had said, it is not inconceivable that one day on the road from St Gervais to Chamonix there will be a sign: 'Mont Blanc – Complet'. In other words, it's full – every hotel, camp-site, route, foothold and piton.

But until that happens English climbers will still make their annual pilgrimage and, at the end of the season, Snell's Field will be bare of grass and covered in derelict structures of wood and polythene sheeting; the surrounding woods will be ankle deep in bongo, and the police will be there recovering the chairs, tables, glasses and road signs so kindly lent by the accommodating Chamoniards.

The season is finished, the last van has limped its smoking way to the Channel, and I am never going back. At least, if I do, I'll do more climbing and spend less time in Chamonix. Even if the weather's bad. I think.

from MOUNTAIN 43 *1975*

THE DOUCHE: A TALE OF ORIGINAL SIN

RICK SYLVESTER

When I was younger I used to spend a great deal of time thinking about the great questions – the meaning of life, and happiness. Once I came upon a remark supposedly attributed to Aristotle. Upon being asked if he were happy he replied: 'A man can answer that question only on the last day of his life.' For a long time this reply puzzled me. Last summer an experience I suffered caused me to ponder it anew, and wonder if perhaps the same couldn't be said of fortune. Ostensibly an account of an ascent of the North Ridge of the Peigne, what follows will always stand out in my memory as the story of the douche.

I was sitting in camp when they came over. It was a week since the Dru epic, the solo that wasn't supposed to be a solo and wouldn't have been if Andy hadn't dropped out and I hadn't been so headstrong. Five days up there alone instead of a maximum of two, the embarrassment of the helicopter they sent out, the unwanted notoriety in town. Now I'd been putting back the weight I lost, maybe a bit more. Feasting, drinking, lounging on the pleasant grass of Snell's Field, reading in the warm sun, generally over-indulging myself. An idle week. Then it came with some surprise that my interest-in-climbing batteries had recharged. A combination of things alerted me. The first slight pangs of conscience, mixed with mild boredom, over not climbing. The realisation that the idea of climbing no longer seemed unthinkable. The old twitch of panic at having no partner, the last of the Leeds lads a week departed.

'Would you like to do a climb?' That question always massages my ego.

'There're three of us and we'd prefer a fourth for two ropes of two.' So much for ego.

'We're thinking of the North Ridge of the Peigne.'

I wanted to do that route, heard it was a good one, hard enough to feel you've done something but not really serious.

A pure rock climb, not mixed, no snow and ice, no cold, wet and misery. In fact, just the right type of route after the Dru epic. Maybe even enjoy the bugger. 'Sure, great.' What luck. What timing! Just as I was thinking… lamenting… no partner….

They introduced themselves. The one doing most of the talking was Terry, an American from Texas or Alabama or someplace like that. Not too tall, a bit roundish, soft. A Southerner. A Southern climber? Whoever heard of a Southern climber? Alpinism and the American South – talk about conflict of images. I got the feeling he wanted to look like a mountaineer but wasn't quite pulling it off. How could a Southerner anyway? But he seemed a nice enough bloke. Notice this *bloke,* and the *bugger* above, and some of the stuff to come. I was really getting into it. Anglicised. Thank the Leeds guys for that. With Terry was a rough looking fellow, something wild and unkempt about him. Phil. He projected an impression of lanky strength that made me think of Haston. Definitely similar in frame and structure but somehow different. Not so finely moulded, like perhaps a coarser unfinished version, lacking that faint almost feminine prettiness of Dougal. The third was Didier, a French lad, blonde, unblemished, almost too pure in looks to be an Alpinist. I wondered how he climbed, for I gathered we'd be sharing a rope. I'd never had a French partner before and I looked forward to the novelty, even if the composition of the team – American, British, French – seemed more worthy of a cheap climbing novel than reality itself.

'OK, good. Why don't you get your gear together?' Phil and Didier split.

'Didier has to pick up his gear from his camp in the Biolet. Phil and I are going into town to buy food. Oh, and Phil wants to take a douche. Meet us at the Midi *téléphérique* station.'

'Say, isn't it pretty late? Do we have time to catch the last tram up?'

'It's 4.30 now. The last is at 6.00.'

'Are you sure? I thought the last one up was at five.' Four years before I'd had a climb ruined over that very confusion.

A South African and I wanted to do Pointe Lachenal, a short route. Since the Rassemblement paid the hut fees we decided to take the last 'frique up, sleep in the Cosmique Hut, and get an early start the next morning to ensure being on our route ahead of other parties. We arrived in time for the 6pm 'frique only to be told the last had left at five. The next morning we caught the first car and rushed across the glacier only to find three parties ahead of us roping up at the base.

'No, I'm pretty sure they run until six.'

'OK,' not wholly convinced. 'But we should hurry. Your friend isn't really going to take a shower, is he?' A nod of the head yes. 'Why does he want a shower right before a route anyway? He's just going to get all sweaty and dirty again and want another one when he gets down.'

'He's really looking forward to it; he hasn't had one in two weeks.'

I hadn't had one in three weeks – the buggers charge you for them – but I kept that ace up my sleeve.

'OK, but try to convince him to forego the douche. It will be just that much better when we get down.'

I rushed my gear together quickly, proud that I was finally mastering the formula of what to take on alpine routes. Then, thumb out but no real expectations, I started the twenty minute walk to Cham. I hadn't got a ride between Snell's Field and Chamonix the whole summer. Feeling the time pressure. Damn, could really use one now.

Almost into town, steaming with momentum, when suddenly a shout hails and startles me. Terry, sipping a beer in front of *Le Weekend*. That's strange.

'What are you doing here?'

'Waiting for a steak and 'frites,' not at all defensively.

'I thought we were in a big rush. Steak and 'frites?'

'May as well. Phil's upstairs having a douche. You can get one here for two and a half francs.'

So he did take his douche, couldn't wait. Terry's meal arrived. It looked tasty, though I knew it was barely large enough to whet your appetite. Big come-on gyp. Still. Quick figuring. No, no way. Not enough time to order one for myself. I had to be content with a beer. But perhaps I was wrong because by the time it suddenly dawned on both Terry and me that a hell of a lot of time had passed, and where was Phil? Terry ran upstairs and a few minutes later returned, mildly arguing with Phil.

'You should have come up sooner and knocked.'

'Christ, Phil, you were in there forty minutes. You knew it was a long time.'

They were right, there was a 6 o'clock tram. But when we arrived, after town and shopping, it was 6.12.

Sitting on the bench outside the Aiguille du Midi station. Our carton filled with bivy food – yoghurt, chocolate, spaghetti, canned sauce, and other goodies – seems a bit silly and extravagant, considering… What do we do now? And where's Didier? He was to meet us at 5.30 here. Is he even later than us? The whole thing seems pretty haphazard, the type of thing you could expect if I'd organised it. Did he catch the last tram and ride up thinking we'd gone up already? Or is he still in his camp, perhaps returned to it after our no-show. 'Better check,' Phil suggests.

We walk to the Biolet. I'm surprised. It looks very clean, bucolic in fact. The last time I was here it looked bubonic, a polluted garbage dump. Now it's not the pit I remembered. Nature's reclaimed it. Now, only recently reopened, it looks, with only a few tents around, far nicer than Snell's Field. But no Didier. Plenty of climbing odds and ends around his tent but Phil surmises somehow that his main climbing gear isn't here and that means he must have gone up. A fine mess.

If he's gone up and found us not there, what would he do? Spend the night at Plan de l'Aiguille? Hike down? We discuss hiking up, figuring that if Didier is hiking down we'll have to pass each other. Mixed emotions. I don't mind hiking up to the Plan. It's a hard choice at best. On the one hand there are the obvious benefits of physical conditioning and saving the fare. On the other there is the old basic inertia to exertion. But now there are more factors to consider. At this late hour we'll surely have to hike a good portion after dark, perhaps knackering us for the climb. And what's more, it's a bad sign the way things have been going already. We're not even out of Cham yet and I'm getting definite bad vibrations.

The Dru is still, too fresh in mind. I'm just not up for another epic. I want to do the route in good style, everything as it should be for once. For a moment I seriously consider dropping out. I have every reason; it would be the wise thing to do. But my gear's in the sack and I'm up for climbing. The result of all this is predictable: by the time we decide to hike up there isn't a whole lot of daylight left. The only definite decision I come to is that there's no way I'm going to hike up in my too tight boots. Not wanting to waste more of the precious little daylight remaining by running back to camp for my Adidas, I borrow a pair of similar shoes from Didier's tent.

The Blaitière Trail. Loads seem heavy of course. Hope I get in the hiking trance soon: too painful with an overactive mind. Onwards and upwards, the interminably endless switchbacks. Daylight ends. Dizzy and hypnotised from Phil's bobbing body ahead, and from sudden illuminating lightning flashes. Lightning? Then the first raindrops, increasing in frequency, until, inevitably, a real downpour. The tumbledown shepherd's hut can't be far ahead, the unexpected shelter where a month before the Leeds lads and I spent five days waiting for good weather before finally descending back to Snell's. The same story … everytime I try to do an Aiguille … We hurry there.

Late, wet, tired, lucky to have shelter, certainly not going on to the Plan. Need water for cooking and the ten minutes away stream not running. Forty minutes to and from the closest water source discount the heavens and Phil the prince who fetches. But isn't that fair? argues my guilt. We wouldn't have been in this position were it not for him and his douche. A black prince.

Because we're tired from the late trek we don't rise for the traditional early morning start so when we do reach Plan de l'Aiguille there's no Didier and no way to know if he spent the night, then finally gave up on us in the morning and descended. We hurry past men, what? actually raking the mountain paths (perhaps in Holland, maybe in Switzerland). The base of the Peigne, initial off-route meanderings, then the correct line and we find ourselves behind two french parties.

'Monsieur, s'il vous plait, le mousqueton …' Mousqueton? Oh, this karabiner? And I thought karabiner was French. If not universal. Mousquetons, étriers. The girl ahead was leaving everything behind. Sign of a sloppy climber, probably a scared one. Costly too, if we hadn't been here. Slow. We have to pass them, that's definite. Don't want another Piz Badile episode. The perfect day, a great route, in excellent condition, sun and dry rock, spoiled for Andy and me by the slow Spanish party we couldn't pass. With a German party behind us in the unlikely queue. Their leader estimated the Spaniards cost us five hours. 'A record of waiting, ja!' Ja, as we were forced to bivy on the north ridge descent. Ja, as our memory of the Badile became this stupidity rather than the joy of great climbing. Oui, we better pass these French. Oui, with me in the middle simultaneously paying out rope to Phil above, and taking in from Terry below, surely doing justice to neither. Oui, hurried, harried, hassled. The spoiling of another good route. Absurd. The very reason for my being here was to avoid this, this awkwardness of a rope of three. The climb might even have been enjoyable.

Or perhaps not. All that shattered scrambling. What a letdown. Hamlet and the truth about the Alps appearance versus reality. The Alps present the most dramatic forms. The mountains look like mountains; they have peaks the way children draw mountains. But you tiptoe over crumble, vertical jigsaw puzzles, scree fields which have no right to assert themselves into mountains. The shapes keep sucking you in. Aesthetic hangups. Yosemite just the opposite: few sharp towers to stare in awe at, but what rock! What moves! What purity, solidarity, and trust! Sure the Alps are great to gaze upon, when they're not coming down upon your head. Gaze upon, not climb upon. In France the Aiguilles are so perfect, from a distance.

'From thirty feet away she looked like a lot of class.

From ten feet away she looked like something made up to be seen from thirty feet away.'

Raymond Chandler was a climber?

The lead party stops for lunch and we assume the front, free at last. But not for long, for when we reach Pointe 3009, a prominent ledge, Phil and Terry stop to eat. Can we afford the luxury of lunch? Of such a lengthy lunch too, as time drags on, and lo! unbelievably, unquestioned and unchallenged, the French finish first and are again ahead of us. After all the rush and pressure to get in front… Sure I didn't say anything when Phil stopped. Sure I was grateful for the chance to catch my breath and a bite to eat. Sure I knew it was a luxury we couldn't afford. But I was weak, I kept silent and I sold the future down the river for the gratification of the moment, knowing full well the price I'd pay in the end wouldn't be worth it. And knowing I'll do it again. Disappointed with myself and not even any more illusions that I'll change and it will get better.

'History teaches us that man learns nothing from history.' Hegel.

Like not rising in the morning. Like not saying anything as to the other party finish eating and prepare to set off. After all our effort to pass. And now they'd be ahead in the dihedral where we'd never be able to pass.

More shattered useless climbing up to the dihedral's base. Then the dihedral itself, a huge left-facing corner stretching 600ft up to the peak's summit. And it's superb! Smooth planes of rock. Straight cracks. Pure technical climbing. Easily the best thing I've encountered on Mt Blanc. In other words, Yosemite-ish. The guidebook's right: forget about the lower part of the ridge and just get yourself to the dihedral as quickly and directly as possible.

Phil leads a pitch I wish I had, then I get one even better. It continues like this for a while, then rapture recedes as difficulties increase. A large chockstone appears, calling for an overhanging move around it. Another, and the jamming becomes awkward. A third, this time requiring a move of aid.

'Please don't come up here; there's no room.'

Ah, she speaks English. Where am I to stop, in the middle of this move? She can't hog the belay ledge. We're in for it now. If she was so slow before when it was basically scrambling what's going to happen here with real climbing?

Above the belay, a very dicey move around a corner and into a jam. It becomes a chimney and I catch up with Marie-France again. That's her name,

I learn, along with the fact she's studied English for seven years but understands it better than she speaks it, lives in Grenoble, and reads sociology at the University. Ah, something in common.

'Have you read Durkheim?'

Aside from leaving an étrier or the odd occasional piece of gear behind, she's not doing that bad, not really holding us up though the climbing's become severe. Like she's warmed up.

'When the going gets tough the tough get going.'

Hardly likely she's been in an American football team locker room. Of course our rope of three is now climbing one at a time, a far slower more tedious arrangement than even an incompetent twosome. Phil joins us. His French seems quite unhalting, and he's able to speak with her easily. I realise I'm envious.

Above, the pleasant corner suddenly turns vicious. Overhanging sections appear with increasing regularity, and aid begins predominating over free moves. A couple of moves could have gone free if I'd had time to work them out but that last bit was strenuous even with aid, and I find myself glad Marie-France left her étriers hanging behind. Judging from the French expletives drifting down from above, her partner's not overjoyed at having to lead his pitch without them.

With a shock the exact amount of remaining light registers on me. The unthinkable is happening. The nagging possibility I've not allowed myself to seriously consider is becoming reality. Night approaches. The forced bivy on the Badile. The solo Dru fiasco. Now the Peigne! Not another epic, anything but another epic! Not three in a row! Can't I even do an ordinary route like the Peigne in good style, in normal time? An epic on every route this year! No, the possibility's too hard to face, the Dru's still too fresh in mind and body. But as Terry slowly follows Phil's lead up the final pitch and twilight runs its too short span I begin mentally preparing myself for the hardships of an arduous, slow night descent. It's too familiar and too awful, the picking, the feeling by braille of the way down, each move requiring total concentration, every section three times as long as in day, a nightmare of exaggerated care and carefulness. I hold onto a vestige of this fantasy as it becomes my turn to struggle up the pitch, the rope not quite as tight as I would prefer, for it's now pure night. Not even twilight. And on the summit there's no fantasy that can now mask the truth. What had begun as vague premonition, then increased to dim possibility, is now stark reality. Another epic.

For the briefest moment, when I first mounted the summit, before I surveyed the situation, I held onto the human right of choice and decision, the possibility of action. But there's no descent into an inkwell. A chill breeze rakes the summit, and rain and lightning threaten, just to remind us as we have no blessings. What we'll count is seconds, minutes, and hours. Until first light. Very few increments of time will be lost to us. A chill of ice in the wind. A cold night, an awake night. Not like the Badile where we actually slept a good deal, warm in duvet parkas. No duvets tonight. Instead the huddle and shiver game. Another embarrassing cock-up, with no Spaniards to blame this time. A hard night, an exhausting night, a night a bit longer than the dihedral we have just climbed. The descent was long and obviously would have been very hard, even if our lights had worked.

Phil and Terry waited at Plan de l'Aiguille for the 'frique. I hiked to the 'shepherd's hut' to collect the gear we'd left there, including the sleeping bags useless and unused the previous night. We were to meet at Didier's camp. With the strange adrenaline that comes at the end of total exhaustion, and just before two straight days of sleep, I alternately hiked and ran, actually ran, down the trail feeling light, free. Surprisingly I arrived before the others. Didier was there, and I deciphered enough to realise he'd taken the 'frique up, waited two hours, then hiked down reasoning like us that we'd pass on the trail. However, he'd descended the normal route not the more direct but less frequented Blaitière path we'd used. Somehow we'd overlooked that key point. Slightly embarrassed, I returned his shoes. Phil and Terry arrived,

'Do you have my pack?'

'We got a ride to Snell's Field and left the packs there.'

With my boots. The perfect ending. I hobbled back to camp, bone weary, barefoot over the gravelly road, now in a light drizzle, a caricature of the hapless, luckless, down and out mountaineer. Perhaps so much, that even a Peugeot pulled over and gave me a lift, the only one I got that summer. And my thumb wasn't even out.

Snell's Field a couple of days later. A pleasant surprise: Marie-France in Phil's camp. He ran into her in town and invited her over. Nice to know some of the natives. A pleasant, friendly enough girl. That was my first thought. Girl, was my second. Vague, almost forgotten desires flitted through my mind. Not exactly my type, but… a girl! Terry and Phil went for a douche. Marie-France and I drove to the Algerian cafe. Then they joined us and we relived the climb over dinner. The next couple of days I caught the odd glimpse of Marie-France around camp. Then it seemed like everyone disappeared.

Cham a week later. Crowded touristy street scene. A tap on the shoulder.

'Marie-France! I didn't know you were still here, thought you were in Grenoble.'

'No, I've been here. Tonight we're having a *fondue bourguignon* in Argentière. Would you like to join us?'

Us included a petite red haired girl with her whom I hadn't noticed before. 'Is it a lot?' Short consultation between them.

'About fifteen francs each, I believe.'

Hmmm, fifteen francs. That was twice the cost of dinner at the Algerian restaurant, the cheapest cafe in town, and my one infrequent indulgence in that summer of the devalued dollar, that summer when I had only three hundred of those dollars which had to last eighty days. I was just on the verge of declining when I thought:

'I'm all the way here from California ... the first time in four years ... God knows when the next trip will be. The food's hardly any less special than the climbing ... to depart without having had one *fondue*.

'OK. Love to.'

'We'll pick you up in your camp around seven.'

The restaurant's idea of *fondue bourguignon* was a bit unusual. They served it with only one sauce, and when we called this to our waitress's attention she returned with bottles of ketchup and Worcestershire sauce. There was, however, the compensation of two large platters of various vegetable and salad concoctions, and the girls' appetites which proved far more refined than those of the climbing friends with whom I usually shared (competed for) meals. Certainly fifteen francs worth. Yes, certainly. And the wine's beginning to take effect nicely, I was thinking. Yes, I'm really doing all right.

Then all at once a Portnoyish thought struck me. Here I was out to dinner with two, not one, but two French girls. Me, the lonely foreigner, the isolated outsider, cut off and too often trapped within myself, not speaking the language. Me, the perpetual drooler over the suave, thin girls in the streets of Cham, in their tight-fitting blouses, somehow making a little go so much farther than most American girls achieve with a lot. Sure, I'd been able to satisfy certain appetites at the *Payot-Pertin Super Marché* and the Algerian cafe, and certainly tonight here, but deeper ones hadn't even been approached. How long had it been? Months? Years? Lightyears? Not that that was so unusual, or something that happened only in Europe. Only here the problems of language, and knowing scarcely anyone, made contact with the opposite sex a hopeless venture. And that week at the Calanque climbing on Mediterranean sea cliffs hadn't helped much. A solid week of frustrating torture, unable to glance in any direction without gazing on unclad birds. How was I to know the place had become an au *naturel* bathing area since my last visit? This objective danger was formidable, making the Calanque perhaps the most dangerous *klettergarten* in the world. How else to describe trying to climb hard face routes on vertical walls with less than one per cent of your attention on the rock? Wasn't it Bernard, usually so ambitious, who didn't attempt a single route that week? What was it he'd said: 'Climbing is no longer the best thing to do in this area'?

These musings were suddenly interrupted when the other girl, Monique, announced out of a clear blue sky: 'I hate boys.' What was this? For the first time I took notice of her. She was actually quite cute. The more I looked the more I liked. There was something definitely sensual about her. Funny. Why hadn't I noticed her before? Probably because my only attention not directed toward the meal had been to Marie-France, as if she were my date or something. For the first time I saw how drab she was besides Monique.

Despite probings I never distinguished why she hated boys. Could she be a … lesbian? No, at least I hoped not. After dinner we went to a couple of bars. At Monique's suggestion we sampled *Genepi,* the green liqueur of the Haute Savoie. I downed some beer as well, and began feeling better and better. No, there's no denying it. Monique really turns me on. My dim out-of-date notions began to cramp me. Old pre-sixties hang-ups of dates and pairings-off guiltily made me feel that it was Marie-France to whom I owed my loyalty and the lion's share of my attention, that I had little right to be interested in her friend.

Then somehow the conversation turned to the fact that it was September and everyone was leaving and Marie-France's tent was the last standing in her campground and how glad she was to have run into Monique on vacation from Paris to share her tent with, but still they were apprehensive, not really digging being two girls alone and all that. And suddenly this ridiculous idea for a very very uncool, clearly unsubtle, sure to be vetoed suggestion popped into my head, but had I had enough beer and wine and *Genepi* to embolden me to state it? Evidently yes, for all at once it was out.

'I'll stay in the tent with you if you like.'

How can you say these blunt things, but incredibly, incredibly they didn't reject it, they didn't reject immediately and outright this coarse, absurdly-easy-to-see-through idea of mine. They seemed even to consider it, as if it had some merits, consider it, and then, more incredible still, they said they thought it was a good idea, they accepted it! Great Henry Miller! Quiet days in Clichy, old clichés about the French, visions of orgies, *ménages à trois,* to the campground, to the campground! But of course nothing was really going to happen, only a silly tease, two of them and one of me, orgies happen only in books, and me in no condition for an orgy anyway. You need control for that. This was what the analytical, eternally uninebriated spoilsport portion of my mind was saying, when suddenly little Monique dropped the bombshell.

'I'll sleep in the middle.'

I'd just assumed I'd get the middle – democracy, symmetry, and all that.

Now this unexpected setback. Then strike me dead! What can this mean? Does it mean something? Is she cutting me off for herself, which would imply that something will happen...

Now I'm lying there, jammed three abreast in a tent for two, heart beating, mind racing, impossible not to be aware of the warm feminine body right beside me, impossible not to make a thousand and one small brushes and touches at such close contact, through the thin nylon of our two sleeping bags separating us. But do I dare make any gestures? And it's burning off fast, the way I'm burning. So, little toe contacts, and knee pressures, and finger games. Some more overt gestures parried and repulsed, for after all, Marie-France lies not two feet away, perhaps awake, alert, listening, though in the pitch black dark the horny mind can fool itself to believe she's two thousand kilometres away. Oh Marie-France, why don't you go out and take a three hour pee. For perhaps Monique is a well brought-up young lady who must after all think of you lying there so close like an unwanted chaperone to her and this coarse Californian. Repulsed, but in a friendly way, an encouraging way, with finger squeezes and even one unbelievable quick kiss which kept my mind in a fever of excitement, hope, and anticipation, more or less guaranteeing an entire night of sleeplessness. There's a chance, there's a chance, there's a chance! But how? When? Where? Indeed. Then, stupendously, miraculously, Marie-France announced she must return to Grenoble. Oh, such a shame! Already?

Really? Must you? Do you have to? So that night, in Snell's Field, in my tent. Blessed, blessed, blessed.

As were the next few days, before Monique returned to Paris, and I did the Triolet, with another unplanned bivouac, and didn't do the Eiger, but did spend my last three days in Europe with Monique in Paris. Paris finally, the first time and just the right way, as a young lover. The magic of those days and nights with Monique – didn't they make the trip? Without them, wouldn't I have been weighing up the summer, telling myself I didn't do that many routes, hardly enough to justify coming all the way from California, the expense, the bad weather? No. Face it. There's no escaping it: Monique made the summer for me. And next summer too when I'll return, able to look forward to more than a solitary tube tent in Snell's Field.

A sea of clouds with the Atlantic somewhere below. High in a jet, California bound. All at once Phil's douche comes to mind. If Phil hadn't insisted upon his absurd shower we wouldn't have missed the 'frique and we wouldn't have had to hike up and wouldn't have got caught in the rain and stayed at the 'shepherd's hut' and got up late and got started on the climb late and got caught behind the slow French party and met Marie-France... and met Monique... For want of a nail the horse was lost... and the young officer was not able to join his regiment for the Charge of the Light Brigade.

But say, just for speculation's sake, next summer Monique and I are driving from Paris to Cham, and Monique's a crazy little driver, near-sighted with her contact lenses which never seem quite correctly adjusted. Say Monique and I are driving to Cham, perhaps so I can try the Peigne again, perhaps even with the last pitch in daylight, when we get in a terrible accident, French traffic with loss of life, or maybe only limb. A terrible accident … which couldn't have occurred if I'd never met Monique … which couldn't have occurred if I'd never met Marie-France … which couldn't have occurred if we hadn't started the climb late … which couldn't have occurred if … Note: Check to see when showers were invented. As early as ancient Greek times? Aristotle's time?

from LEEDS UNIVERSITY
CLIMBING CLUB JOURNAL 1974

"NOW THE THIRD PITCH IS A FLARING CHIMNEY WHICH ENDS IN A DIFFICULT LIE-BACK! THEN—— /.."

THE SHROUD

TERRY KING

The walk up the Leschaux Glacier to the Leschaux Hut is a long, steep, lung abusing, unrelenting, uphill slog. People with local knowledge will immediately dispute this, it being generally regarded as an easy, one hour walk over flat ground, but to me, whose fitness suffers a severe blow after mounting the steps to the *téléphérique* station, and experiences the infant (going on for junior) effects of altitude before even reaching the glacier, it will forever remain a symbol of extreme human endeavour. Tea, tobacco and ten minutes' rest on the balcony of the hut had barely started to repair the damage caused by this gruelling experience, when the guardian came striding out to see us. All bronzed, rippling muscles and white teeth flashing.

'You sleep in the refuge?' he asked, in English; they can tell, can't they.

'No, we sleep on the balcony.'

'No, you must sleep in the refuge,' he insisted.

'We have no money.'

Quizzical looks all round, and they say money is an international language.

'Pas de sous, pas de l'argent,' explained Gordon, our French expert. I suppose if you can get your tongue around Scottish, you can get it around anything (they do as well, they're not fussy these Scots). Alex and I just grinned, Gordon babbled on a bit and the guardian went into his hut, to emerge several minutes later with bowls of coffee for the three of us, a gesture which earned him a rise of several places in our estimation. Our attitude was suitably altered. Alex and I grinned again and Gordon made some more French noises, of which 'the Shroud' and 'Le Linceul' began to be recognisable. Also, 'We reste dans le hut pour libre?' is fairly straight-forward, isn't it?

The guardian's companion, hitherto silent and not very interested, began to pay us some attention. He was a surly young man, with regulation, outsize, French calf muscles.

'You will climb the Shroud?'

'Er, well, we might have a try.'

'There will be much rock-fall when the sun comes up.'

I must admit that this chilling concept did come as something of a surprise to us, a shock even, foresight not having figured over much in our decision to climb the route because it had such a pretty name. But we tried not to let on and jovially assured him that our horoscopes for the next few days were good. It wasn't long, though, before the brighter ones in our little group were making the inevitable connection between his disturbing prediction and the sound of rattling rocks we could hear on the mountain. Is that lot coming down the Shroud? Apprehension was growing, we fiddled with our coffee cups like schoolboys who'd been caught out by the teacher. The teacher looked on benignly: 'Tomorrow,' he was thinking, 'You will die.' I took to heart his kind consideration for the safety of others, and eventually got to thinking about it myself, at the same time listening to the clattering sounds on the hill, and began to fear he might be on to something.

The evening chill crept in as the stars crept out, and the weather was looking horribly good; where were the rapid, incoming storms that the Grandes Jorasses are so famous for, why must tonight, of all nights, hold out such promise? I lay on a bunk with no hope of sleeping; surely I wasn't the only one having such sickening doubts, didn't the others have any imagination? Surely between three intelligent people a plausible excuse could be formulated. If nothing else, we could sleep too late and, as I had the only watch, I felt confident that it could be fixed fairly easily. A little comforted by this idea, I finally managed a kind of insomniac's doze around about midnight. At 2am I dreamt of golden girls, swinging hips and long blonde hair, Pirelli women smiling through the dark; but the undreamt noise of out-of-bed activity began to invade my private pleasures; alarm clocks and kettles boiling madly, the guardian saying sorry he was late in rising but be quick now and eat the porridge before it went cold. It took a few seconds to take in the full significance of this new situation, a moment or two of blinking eyes and I began to wake up to his game. This mad Frenchman was calling our bluff, trumping our last card and, to set the seal, he blazed a trail for us, in knee deep snow, half-way up the glacier, then he turned back with smiles and wishes of good fortune. I don't know whether he was exercising some kind of grudge or whether he really thought he was doing us a favour, but I felt as though I'd been towed into the middle of the Atlantic and cut adrift, brought face to face with a Bar Nationale drunken day-dream.

We put on the rope, a good ploy in moments of anxiety, but our speed of progress was cut by half at least since the retirement of Mr Powerful. A thick crust of snow would promise to take our weight, then break to let us sink for a foot or more into soggy snow underneath. Time after time, just as we thought it was going to hold, through we'd go. We must have made one of the slowest approaches ever. Alex was the only one who had any success at walking on the crust without breaking it. This was achieved, so he claimed, by pretending to be a fairy; any excuse is better than none, I suppose. I must confess that in desperation I succumbed to the temptation of testing his fantasy treatment of the problem. I didn't half feel bloody silly, too. I mean here was I, a mere apprentice at this big mountain game, approaching one of the mightiest bastions in the Alps, where men do manly things, where folk heroes had gritted their teeth and not surrendered, and I was tripping across the snow trying to become a fairy: real hard man stuff. It didn't work, either; the weight in my sack didn't seem keen to play the game and I was left, knee deep in snow, wondering what I was carrying that Alex wasn't and whether he could walk on water as well; after all, he did go to a Jesuit school.

The Walker Spur, all wintry white still, made an impressive appearance at dawn, and we finally crossed the bergschrund at eight o'clock. The majority of the route consists of a very long, and very steep (60° at the steepest parts), fairly uniform ice-field. I'm not trying to say it's boring or anything, but one move did eventually become a bit reminiscent of the last. However, the access was via 700ft of mixed ground and not nearly so straightforward. We moved together up a none-too-solid snow-slope, trying to relate our surroundings to a rather vague route description: nothing corresponded, but we found a ramp going diagonally left, which appeared to give access to the ice field. The first few pitches, though not hard, were covered in loose snow and gave awkward moves over little rock steps. Gordon and Alex alternated the lead and I soloed up behind, the crucial holds having by then been uncovered. We came across a fixed rope – presumably part of the Desmaison Route – up the West Flank of the Walker. It all seemed to be going well and, having climbed about 600ft, we naturally assumed we must be gaining height. But what no one had noticed was that, as we were making a rising traverse to the left, so was the glacier. We were doing a kind of low-level girdle of the Grandes Jorasses, Gogarth-style. A steep rock ridge separated us from a broad couloir, which ran from the glacier, still only 300ft below, directly on to the main ice-field with no obstructions. It was up to Alex to find an entry to this gully, across the spur which stood between us. He climbed some putrid ice for 30ft above us, to the point where the rock was at its narrowest; Gordon sunbathed; I smoked a cigarette and we both watched the rocks begin to hurtle past. (The guardian's friend had not spoken with forked tongue.) Alex pegged across, more or less doing a series of tension moves using three or four pitons. I was finding it increasingly difficult to remain keen on the whole idea: lots of nasties were coming down, it was already 10.30am, and we were still effectively only 300ft up. Gordon followed and yelled down that he would take the pegs out to save time. I didn't quite understand how I would then get across, so I pretended it meant he was cracking, too, and they were going to abseil down. Much comforted by this show of good sense I wondered what time we would get down to Chamonix.

But it was not to be, and, as my turn to climb approached, the realisation that I might have to pendulum twenty feet or so to join them became a bit too obvious. I climbed up to the traverse line.

'Why did you take the bloody pegs out?' I asked, bitterly.

'To save time.'

'Well what the hell am I supposed to do?'

There was a short silence, saving breath as well; thrifty these Scots. Then: 'Just swing over on the rope.'

Just swing over, just let go, fall off, jump off, close your eyes, be brave, just pendulum.

'Have you got me?'

'Yes.'

'Are you sure?'

'Yes.'

'What are you belayed to?'

'An ice peg.'

'Christ, is that all?'

'Yes.'

I swung like a sack of luggage, grazed every bone on every bit of granite and smashed into the ice like a stunned pig: one of the aesthetically pleasing moments with which alpine climbing is filled. The ice broke up under the impact and I was left dangling underneath a little overhang of my own creation, reaching above it to place 'terrors', scrabbling with my feet below it and shouting for tight. I climbed up to join the others: 'Any more little time-saving tricks?'

The gully widened and we made faster progress up the straightforward ice, but rocks were coming down all the time now. They were being issued from a couloir way above us; a couloir we had vainly hoped might provide a direct finish; how brave we were in Chamonix, how commendably adventurous. In the event, I was far more interested in the abseil slings appearing at regular intervals on the rocks to our right. We continued by a vote of silence and emerged on to the open ice face called the Shroud.

It wasn't hard, but it was exposed, a long way up, a long way down, wide open on either side as well, a kind of three dimensional exposure. It was wet, soaking, sodden wet, springs of water sprouting from the ice, dribbing down in sheets and streams, water in boots, water in breeches and spilling down our sleeves. But we were still making good progress, and by midday we were almost half-way; the climbing was simple and the belays were ice pegs, although they were pretty useless in the slushy ice.

They say that if a bomb has got your number on it, it's going to get you. This wasn't a bomb, it was a brick; but it was coming my way and I knew it long in advance, from the very first noise to the black whirring shape in front of my face. A volley of stones came screaming down, twisting and spinning, racing each other through space, granite bloodhounds bouncing down to bite. I pointed my helmet upwards and tried to streamline myself below it. Bullet noises all around, jagged rocks whining as they passed. My thigh, just above the knee, got hit. The power of a free-falling rock, stopped dead in its tracks, went snapping through my leg, the bone and muscle stiffened with pain, I felt sick and far from happy. Alex led the next pitch and I followed, front-pointing with a limp.

Gordon decided that ropes were an unnecessary luxury on this sort of ground, it being wet, uncomfortable, dangerous and thoroughly (don't want to be here) rather than actually hard. So he set off soloing. Alex and I continued to pitch it, what with my bad leg and all; we alternated the lead, but seemed to make absolutely no impression on the way ahead. It was still very exposed; the whole structure of ice felt like a loose tile resting uneasily on the side of the Grandes Jorasses, holding us, with little enthusiasm, on top of it. We were level with the top of the Petites Jorasses, which appeared to grow as we gained height, for it wouldn't disappear below us. The afternoon was nearly over, we were late; no stopping, no luxurious dreams of descent, the quickest and easiest way to a brew was up; we were, as they say, committed.

Gordon was making better time alone, and it wasn't long before Alex and I dispensed with the formality of silly screws pushed into mush, and began moving together. As we got higher, six inches of wet snow overlaid the ice in big slabs, like lethal toboggans; only fatigue kept the frightening consequences of a ride on one of these from my mind. Across troughs of ice and fluted ribs, we were being funnelled into the rocky summit gully. The Hirondelles Ridge came into view, way above. Six hundred feet: how can 600ft be so far, how can each step measure so little, how can an objective look so near and stay so far away, for so long, so painfully?

Gordon arrived first and set about digging a bivi ledge. Stubbornly, the distance between us submitted; first we were shouting (put on a brew) then we could talk (he said I'd got the stove), and the Shroud gave in shortly before we did. It was over; the sun was dying in a blood-red ball: it looked like my eyes felt. I took off my breeches and wrung out the water, did the same with long john's, socks and shirt, tipped the water out of my boots and, deep down inside, through hardships endured and shared, I felt a stirring in my inner soul: frost. Under a clear black sky, the ice age began, we shivered through the night, three in a bed, wriggling toes to keep them awake and making brews until Alex dropped the pan: expensive mistake. The dawn arrived with a sting in the throat. We elected to skip the summit and descend the Hirondelles Ridge, so we could go down the French side to our friendly coffee-dispensing guardian in the Leschaux Hut. This turned out to be anything but the easy option it was supposed to be. In the first place, the abseil rope kept jamming and, in the second place, it was me who had to keep going back up to unjam it. But worst of all, we found it was impossible to get down the French side, so it was another glacier-bashing session down into Italy. We hitched through the Mont Blanc tunnel, back to Chamonix and, as we got near to the Biolay camp-site (in fact, right by the sign which says: No Camping), we were met by the two Nicky's. This redoubtable pair of scavengers, occupants of a well-appointed plastic home in the up-town district, were on their way to town for a "Mooch" (Midday Offensive On Chamonix Homesteads), and to further Anglo/French relations with their maxim: Biolay Boot Rule O.K.

'Do it?' they enquired.

'Yes.'

'Oh great, well done. Actually, we were going to split up the gear you left tomorrow, but we'll leave it now you're back.'

from MOUNTAIN 50 *1976*

WHY?

ROB FERGUSON

Some places, of course, are malevolent. The day we did the Major I think everyone must have been nervous in the Great Couloir. It was too warm, too still, too dark. My headlamp seemed affected, too: the battery, new at Col Moore, was dead before I reached the avalanche runnel. I could tell I was there, though, by the gentle hiss as snow and ice fragments rolled and jumped their way to the glacier below. The ice, beneath a honey-comb crust, was glassy. It took a long time to start an ice screw, then before it was fully home the ice had fractured. I shouted back to the others, but I think Pete had already started belaying.

I turned to where the shadow was darker. The only time I looked up, the slopes above were long and black against a sky only slightly less dark. My holds filled with spindrift. I felt clumsy, and more nervous than at any time for two years. But how different from '67 – then, it was hot on the south-facing ridge; the snow was soft on the underlying ice. Seven hours from the nearest person, we moved together further into the sunny mystery of the Innominata ...

On the north side of the couloir, the surface changed to powder on dull ice. Progress was slow, and interrupted at intervals as the five people now tied on behind me crossed the runnel in turn. Across to the right, the slopes we had climbed to the Twisting Rib the other day formed an inhospitable ice-field, flecked only here and there with lighter patches, brief snow ribs. We had moved together, eight endless runouts to the doubtful safety of a few boulders on the shallow snow ridge. And that big sérac fall we watched from the hut had completely hidden the Twisting Rib for what felt like minutes.

At last, the arête! One hour only – what's it like being gripped for a whole day? I brought the others up. Behind them other lights bobbed, seemingly in the very centre of the couloir. Suddenly a swishing shadow almost obliterated the pinpricks of light for a neverending minute – spindrift or ice? They seemed to be OK, but it must have scared them.

Three-quarters of an hour later, soon after five Italian time, the sky in the north-east was beginning to colour, though the sun was still well down since the séracs far above were unlit. The length of the doubled rope below me on the Second Arête, Pete was opening his camera case. When it happened he was quicker than the rest of us, but the photograph shows that the ice cloud from the sérac fall was already a ropelength wide by the time his shutter clicked. I didn't really notice, I simply stared numbly at the two lights in the couloir lower down.

Their extinction was quick. The leader, though running very fast, covered less than half a ropelength. It was a strong rope, though, and securely attached to the second man, outside the avalanche track ...

from CAMBRIDGE MOUNTAINEERING *1976*

PINBALL WIZARDS

TORY STEMPF

We have trouble staying in the travelled track. Our little coterie took the back-roads: Lindsrom, Minnesota; St Croix Falls, Rice Lake, Rhinelander, Wisconsin; swept down upon customs at Sault Ste. Marie, at twilight ('... the crack between the worlds...') and hung a huge right. Massey Sudbury – North Bay – a peculiar, exhilarating, uncomfortable collage of familiarity and estrangement, culminating in the Montreal airport. Oh, that rejuvenating lift-off! Alcohol and euphoria, sunset and dawn scant hours apart, and a pin-the-tail-on-the-donkey landing in fog-bound Zurich, *let's get out of here* to Grindelwald we scurry like a pack of junkies to load up on yoghurt, bratwurst and vino.

Now John's an established Eldorado Canyon man and is hard to budge at times. But we had vowed long ago to try our hand at some real alpinism, you know – north face ice climbing, *just what does 'north wall' climbing mean, tory? I'm not sure...*

ice. where's all this ice? well, john, it's under all that snow up there – i mean, i know i saw it up there last year. Yes, John had to acknowledge that there was a lot of snow up there, and *lots coming down, too. Strange there are no other climbers around, john... Well,* perhaps they had found no ice either and had gone home. But we had travelled far and circuitously and could not go home. *john, we should at least go up and have a look for ourselves. okay boss, you know more about this than i do. i do?*

We sized up the grim old Eigerwand, but it was already squatting in its winter coat, looking much less naked and more 'north-wallish' than last year. We sought out further discouragement: then we were advised by an Eiger vet to *forget it* which we happily did. But other fields of glory beckoned. Like *the lauper route – a nice test-piece, john.*

There's not much to say about this effort. With the topos in one hand and an axe in the other, our packs so pregnant we more resembled rookie back-packers, and John confiding that it looked like *a good route for me to learn alpinism on.* Disadvantages soon emerged: the length (it was a jillion-foot monster, and we are still scratching our heads over how this fact eluded us), those strong-but-silent spindrift avalanches, and John's sea-legs which were crying for a wet deck. We wandered all over the place, for when we set our packs in motion we had to follow. Decisions were made – *let's get out of here!* And what was to become the hallmark of our odyssey began: traversing below the final upper slopes, we bee-lined for the Mittileggi Ridge, across 1800ft of uneventful, unsettling ice. *john, what are we doing here? it ain't the beach.* We exited by way of the most innocuous-looking, the most hairy pitch of my recent recollection (to that point, anyway). It should have been an iced-up dihedral, but it was really a wet snow-choked one, awaiting some moron to come along and knock it all down on himself. I came. But I didn't climb it; I swam and waded up it. And I looked under every flake for some ice but found none and then looked for solid rock but found none so I bridged and got John scared so I swam some more. *what's keeping all this shit in place?* At the 160ft level, with more to go, desperately embracing the snow with outstretched arms and head and axe and splayed-wide knees to keep the snow and me up there, John added our extra rope and urged me *let's get up this thing.* I believe my last effort was a breast stroke. I fell into the arms of an old Swiss. *yahoo I'm up, john, come on up!* John-boy got the night-shift. (He said this was a blessing, allowing him to remain ignorant of how bad it really was.) Sometimes John and I don't exactly see eye-to-eye.

Our Lauper variant *was* on the topos; we were in some good company. But we wanted to get to the top of something. The Mönch North Rib looked spectacular. So, a late afternoon jaunt to the Guggi Hut, wine, women and song, a cloudy windier-than-Oklahoma morning and the hum and the haw and the inevitable pussy-out… *let's get out of here.*

We sat in Grindelwald and cried into our beers. *humiliating.* Paying the Jungfrau Railroad good Swiss francs to help us retreat. Perhaps a – cheaper – change of scene. *we can certainly get in trouble just as easily somewhere else for less.*

The Bernese Oberland, from its apices of the Eiger, Mönch and Jungfrau, carves south-west for a ways and gradually turns to the west. Thusly an immense "wall" is formed, 3500ft high and quite long, comprising the peaks of the Gletscherhorn, Mittaghorn, Grosshorn and Breithorn: a most wild-looking assemblage in a very remote setting. The north side of this is a precipice called the Lauterbrunnen Wall, after the village at its base. A place of great adventure and greater history – one climbs with hobnail-booted ghosts here. And it was here that we searched for that one redemptive climb.

Perhaps the Breithorn North Face…

We became obsessed with speed. In August, Messner had done the Eiger in ten hours, and this news juiced us up like our old school rouser. *C'mon man, ditch that parka and bivi sack… stove? hell, we always forget matches anyway, and how about jettisoning some pegs? i don't know how to use them, and you never seem to want to.* The planning: *race for the top and no more of that bivouac jazz, john. We'll climb the damn thing and get back to the hut in one day. yea, man. la dolce vita.*

On Wednesday, September 19, we parted from our ladies-in-waiting, their vigorous exhortations punctuating our plod up the path – *and don't worry about the weather, just think hard and climb!* I wondered if somehow the wrong people were not doing this thing.

It was a steep grunt! One hour up we collapsed on the terrace of the Trachselhauenen Hotel and convalesced on beer and Coke, like any proper country gentlemen on such a day. *it'll be nice coming down here after our climb tomorrow.* And with visions of a sumptuous Friday breakfast obliterating any nagging apprehensions, we chugged the final three hours to the hut.

God, how bleak! The nicely furnished Schmadri Hut deserved better environs than this place. I wish we had had it in Italy. The oppressive humidity was now a mist that chilled right through your underwear. We squinted into the fog for a peek at the Breithorn, but it was in solitary. Anyway, we knew it was out there, *waiting for us.* We thought of the warm bodies we had foolishly left behind, *but now forget this chill and trembling – tomorrow we climb! (thanks, ladies.)* One last run to the privy and we barricaded ourselves in for the night, leaving the fog, weather, mountain, chill and fear outside by the door, to greet us in the wee hours of the morning like a faithful hound…

That diabolical alarm drove us out of the blankets at 3am. I staggered to the door, unlatched it and peered outside… still many clouds and a low ceiling, but they seemed to be moving away to the south and east now, for the Dippers were freed to cast their familiar, perpetual forms. The Breithorn was just a great black vacuity in the low-lying heavens.

Our daily fix of yoghurt, bread, butter and tea. A brisk punctuality quite unlike us. Headlamps locked in place, a final *see you this evening* gander at our hut and out into the 4am gloom.

We became lost immediately, *hey, john, where are ya hey, waaait!* Our lights in the wetness cut about eight foot's worth. Then good old John, known usually for losing his way between cairns, and who had slyly surveyed our path last night, with beginner's luck found the track. Stumbling across scree fields and a few precipitous streambeds, we got lost again and my battery petered out. Mackerel again came through with an extra light and we pointed our beams toward the west, because we at least knew the Breithorn was in that direction.

We eventually bumped into something and recognised the icefall which prostrated itself obscenely before our faces. To left and right it was bound by rock ribs that accompanied it to the more open upper slopes. Our route was the right rock rib. As we stood beneath the icefall it began to lighten in the east. The dawning revealed to us some gruesomely fragile, squeaking séracs squarely above our stance. They're speaking to us. The rock was beckoning, so we wasted no time in renewing our old acquaintance.

It was a bit loose, but easy, and we quickly gained height. Shallow troughs and rotten ramps, good edging and occasional nearly orgiastic jamming. I observed myself climbing feverishly, as if executing an escape. Soon soaked with sweat and finding that I had out-distanced John, I scooped a seat in the snow and perched there, craning to see round the corner of the sérac barrier. It all seemed so familiar, as though I had been there many times, in many lives ... I knew what was round that corner.

I came back as John grunted on to the ledge. We chose to stay unroped and John moved out, me in drag, up the ramp, *tiptoed* past the sérac barrier, weaved, scrambled, scraped, burrowed and bridged. *wow, look out, this shit's loose. i want a rope, are you on a belay? are you kidding – where?*

It was so glorious. Not the weather, but to be moving like that, so one got tired once in a while. *man, i wish we coulda moved like this on the lauper.* Stumbling into the sun, a final hanging ice shield startled us. We moles collectively blinked. Bible in hand. *it says go left. yea, man, where else?* We did this thing.

How to describe it? Like the bear going over the mountain – past the shield everything opened up for a real gripping gander. We were on a face all right. High, ever so high above, the summit cornices winked at us, *the arrogant bastards.* Below them, way too much of that frosting stuff caked all over everything. *hey! Where's that rock rib that's supposedly so prominent? I'm a little confused, john. are ya ? doesn't look like the beach to me.*

But John was digging the ice now (or he was trying to forget the goulash, I'm not sure which), and it's a good thing, for here there was plenty of it: a steep, 600ft ironing board, running up to where our rock rib reportedly dwelt. He used his axe to poke me into the fore and thus began that endless recapitulation of that most basic of ice-climbing themes – *axe in, kick firmly, step up, kick firmly, step up, axe in,* on and on. *anchor. Belay. come on up, john. lord. john, look down. nyaaa! put in another screw, tory.* And on.

The end of this ethereal place marked the beginning of our next deviation. All this snow that had been chucked at the mountain dappled the whole upper face. Here and there, pools of ice twinkled at us, bared naked by the winds; snowbanks (that's right) duned our vision of the top treasures, and always it was that damned rock – not solid stuff as one has a right to expect, but a cairn-like pile of stones, pasted together by some unknown untested cement peering out at us. A chunk here. A small step there. Dark, wicked splotches everywhere. A bewildering collage of all the wrong ingredients. *john, i sure wish we could find something fat to stand on – my ankles hurt. me too.*

The need to canter and the need to crawl cried havoc in my head. *hope that wasn't the glue I just removed … slot a nut now? nope. how about a screw? no ice. by the way where is that ice??* John begged for some protection and I wished I could accommodate. It was no fun any more. Our hunt for that which we had come so far to climb was drawing us left, into that uncharted land bypassed by the topo, always tantalised by the icy runnels which teased us with a peek but turned to powder beneath the foot. Rock just scared the starch out of us; we knew it wasn't really rock. We had caught on to the game.

So it went. Mandatory fourth class. Usually disguised third. But this fooled nobody now, either. The sun accelerated in its course. We hit the base of a short rock step. Right and left looked *verboten,* so I asked John to give me an analysis of the step as he saw it from below. *yaaa. It'll go – not too steep – holds – jugs – you go on. you think?*

I was damn tired of taking off and putting on my crampons every 50ft. They stayed on. I looped a runner on a large *loose flake* and, questioning its stability, mantelshelved up on to it, wheezing *i don't know* all the while. Being in no immediate hurry to leave, I experimentally edged with the side points, then the fronts, and then the sides again, and concluded they were equally murderous; scooped away snow with my mittened paw – *hope i don't have to use these, they seem mighty small.* That awful chalkboard-grating emanating from my claws drove me nuts. I threw in a good jam and fumbled for a nut. And here I began to lose it. *i don't know about this …* Impatience took over. Then spasms. Another fumble and a nut whistled away. *fuck! how sickening. oh john.*

I begrudgingly edged and wheezed up again, cleared the top of the cliff with my head and perused. Beginning at my nose, another ugly ramp scampered up and away. And here I lost it. No possible mantelshelf. No edges. No hands. I felt screwed for the first time in aeons. I yanked out my hammer, swallowing down that Big Grip, and swung mightily at the ramp to get a high hit. Well, that damn hammer may as well have pulverised a plump pillow – right out of sight it went and rebounded off the rock beneath. *oh jesus.* So I began a probe: thunk – thunk – thunk – thunk. *oh jesus!* I stuck the point between two stones and with a twist it seemed to hold all right. *glad john can't see what I'm doing up here – he'd get mad.* My climax – my *lovely* climax – found some ice right off, though a bit lean. Hanging on to these things, I was drawn against the cliff as around a barrel. Here it went. *oh jesus.* I jerked up, hanging by the hammers, heaved my feet up under me, and in my indelicate squat threw one hammer at a straw above me – and it neatly pierced the ice. *jesus, I'm home!* In the twilight (again) I completed the pitch in an utter flap – like all the hundreds before. Fingered a crack and pulled out a pin. *lord. it fits! just one,* And John came up, again having the grace of not being able to see. A compliment from John is a fine thing. I had hung both our asses into the fickle wind on that one. *john, it's so good to see you.*

But now a new urgency. Where shall this night's abode be? Headlamp on, I worked left across a shallow bowl to a rock step and *lo and behold!* a two foot by four foot nookery. *flat.* Honest to God – the only flat spot we saw that day (or were to see again). I kicked off its snowy accoutrements and put home two solid pegs. *voila!* It was a bit small, so we suspended our packs from a pin, stepped in and sat down, back to back. An alpine hemi-hang. I faced north-east, John north-west. Our crampons, helmets and hardware we tacked to the wall. The carelessly folded rope mattress hurt my butt. The wind began to blow out of the north-east. *well, this is okay, because tomorrow we'll finish this puppy and celebrate with our lambrusco in the hut tomorrow night. It's only one night. I'm glad you're with me, old boy – i feel a little shaky.*

That night the storm hit.

It was a doozy. Avalanches poured silently down and picked our rock to fall over. *engulfed.* Snow worked efficiently in between us, and over the hours reproduced with harey speed. Our knees became our involuntary pillows. Standing up to clear it away was awful. Just no room for house-cleaning. *It's okay, tomorrow's gonna be good. damn this constant shivering. I'm glad i feel you against me, john …*

Morning brought only the bother of having to open the eyes and peep at the distastefulness of our position. Our rock was the only rock in the middle of a great bowl. *i seem to recall that the direct misses this spot, john.* And no gentle sweep below us. Oh no – a queasy drop into the bottomless mists. I dropped a glove, just to show how steep it was. All mountains look alike at this point, john …

Let's get out of here!

John kept saying – to himself I think – *well, we can always rappel down. down.* Down? In this? I think he spent all his time counting them – *28 … 29 … 31 … john, you're forgetting about anchors – there aren't any.* Poor John, I thought. I thought a lot about helicopters, rescue bills and Connie. No one was pitying me, though.

Mid-morning, John thought we ought to try and fight our way up. *go round the corner and see how it looks, tor. you think?* John stayed put. The belay rope ran lazily into a sleeve of his inert cagoule. *stand up – oh, I hope ruger's sewing is good – and get on to the ledge. these f— frozen crampons.* I don't like this. I kept wondering about that thing in the cagoule. It was quiet! A traverse left and up a short headwall and my eyeballs met the upper slo – Whooosh! It went behind my glasses and compacted there and I crept back from my mugging with my snowy cataracts, back to our home, undressed, hung it all up and retreated into my lonely den. Something in me was unhappy. *not a good idea, john.* Later the storm abated again and the avalanches stopped. *try again. tory, you think?* Up again, crampons fought again, traverse and up again and the hit smack in the face again. *not a good idea, john.* I felt that I must have killed an albatross a while ago.

john, we may not be able to get up. i hope the girls call a chopper soon – i know they will. It'll come. I'm impatient to get out of this, john. me too – it ain't the beach. I had to surface for air occasionally. The ice-crystalled clove hitch which was keeping me up there greeted my nose and laughed at me. I withdrew. *your backbone's killing me, john, but I'm glad it's yours. i sure wish we could see each other. i love ya, john.*

> and through the drifts the snow clifts
> did send a dismal sheen:
> nor shapes of men nor beasts we ken
> the ice was all between.
> the ice was here the ice was there,
> the ice was all around:
> it cracked and growled, and roared and howled,
> like noises in a swound!

The call came and I stood in my crow's nest, wishing the sewing well, *damn this zipper and all this clothing – are you in there?* It was in full retreat. My whole body was in full retreat. I urinated on myself. *you barbarian.*

I'm getting awfully tired, john – over twenty-four hours here – no sleep since wednesday. you know, john, that chopper's not going to be able to come in this shit – and we can't go down… you think?… so we must go tomorrow, no matter what… yea… tomorrow it is, john – we'll fight like hell, right? you betcha – no one can come for us in this weather, and we can't go down – so tomorrow, right?… right?… right. is what I'm saying makin' any sense, john? i think so… The temperature dropped and it began to clear that night.

Let's get out of here!

We two tin woodsmen stretched out at first light. Clear and cold above. Below us, all of Switzerland slumbered in a fathomless comforter of cloud. The high peaks thrust through to catch the sun. Only the highest. We were as *gods.*

We stumble-stepped the last 700ft to the summit. Moving again after an incredible fatal inertia for forty hours. The mindless recapitulation again… Our hands froze into our mitts… It took both of us to open karabiners. *my hammer's busted!! That's okay, here's mine.* Five leads. Five hours to the *arrogant* cornices and the sun. The same junk snow. *oh, to toboggan in now would be so ignominious.* The steepest I thought that last lead was, and *hello there you miserablelooking things. be cool once more, tory… my hands are in the sun! I'm up, john – yahooo, come on up!!!*

We looked around, and it was cold, white and marvellous. And then we saw the hut longingly awaiting us. *Let's get out of here…* Uncontrollable staggering. *john, i hear italian opera – a baritone. Why, I hear… it's a catholic mass. of course you do – it's sunday. I'm weeping, john…*

That's about all there is to this mighty lengthy tale. We did a great north face under shit conditions, and a new route to boot. A super-direct finish. Only thing is, we didn't mean to. It was a twisting, tortuous path that got us there. I never wanted to do it again. But now we're in Grindelwald, sipping our wine and being consoled by our fine ladies, our yoghurt and our bratwurst. Man forgets easily. A bit longer, a tan on the beach and fighting the Italians in Florence and – *john, let's go to Chamonix. Let's get out of here.*

I don't know how we do it.

from MOUNTAIN 42 *1975*

THE FINAL DAY ON THE EIGER DIRECT

DOUGAL HASTON

Sigi and Roland kept shifting uncomfortably on their stance. They could not even take their crampons off. A vague greyness was the signal of day. Staying on the bivouac hadn't been too easy but preparing to leave it was really unpleasant. My gloves and gaiters were frozen solid. My numb fingers pulled ineffectually on the crampon straps. To add to my troubles, one of the straps broke. I then had painfully to extract a cord from my ice-coated ruck-sack and fix it to the crampons. This simple manoeuvre took over an hour.

Slowly my mind began to face up to the day. I started painfully prusiking up the ropes again. I hadn't thought it possible that the storm could get worse, but somehow nature managed to drag up her last reserves and throw them at the five miserable figures fighting for fulfilment of a dream. Half-way up the first rope my fingers started to freeze. There was nothing I could do to stop it. The hostile forces were insidiously beginning to win. I pulled off my gloves at the stance and was confronted with ten white wooden objects. The only thing to do was to take a super dose of Ronicol. This eventually began to take effect and I waited in agony for half an hour as the blood began to recirculate.

Then it was on with the gloves and up to our high point of the previous night. There was neither sight nor sound of Jörg and Günther. To my surprise, there was a gap of forty feet between the end of one fixed line and the beginning of the next. Also to my surprise, they had taken all the ice-axes and hammers with them. For a long time I contemplated doing this stretch alone but eventually decided to wait for Sigi and Roland and lead it on a rope. It was perhaps fortunate that I did. Though not a very difficult pitch, it was not too easy without an axe.

I scraped up it and fixed the line for Sigi and Roland. The cloud suddenly parted for a few minutes and there were Jörg and Günther a rope's length ahead cutting up a 60° ice slope. This could be the Summit Icefield, I thought, but there was no indication of the summit or neighbouring ridges, so I decided not to be too optimistic and wait and see.

About an hour after we saw Jörg and Günther, the three of us were gathered on a small stance in the centre of the icefield. There was a slight problem ahead – another gap in the fixed ropes. A slightly larger one this time. Around 150ft. The other two were out of sight again. There was nothing else to do but tackle the pitch.

The next hour was one of the most testing of my climbing career. It was 60° water-ice. The steps of the previous rope had been wiped out. I had no axe or hammer. My left crampon was wildly askew on my boot. The right one was loose. Armed with one dagger ice-peg, I moved off the stance. The wind was crashing the snow into my face with such force that it stuck in huge masses on my eyelids, making it impossible to see ahead. My move-ments were cautious and groping. I would search around for traces of a step, scrape it out, then make a breath-holding move up on my wobbly crampons. The pitch went on and on and I became increasingly aware of the extreme-ness of the situation. Sigi and Roland were on a very poor belay. There just could not be any question of falling. Yet in a strange way I was enjoying this test. I knew the odds were stacked with the house, but I felt in perfect control. There was no panic, only well-planned movement.

Fortune favoured me and I reached the top of the pitch. Slight trouble again, though. The rope I was aiming for was twenty feet to my left. I made a few tentative moves left, but came back quickly. There was no chance of doing it without an axe or some protection. A tension traverse was the obvious solution, but on what? I could see only one solution and that was a terrible one to face. Down below I had once or twice tried to knock my ice-dagger into the ice with my Heibler clamp and had only succeeded in getting it in about an inch, which was no use whatsoever for protection. But it might stand the slight pull of a tension traverse. I didn't want to spend the rest of my days at that spot, so I knocked in the piton. It wouldn't go further than an inch. It also wobbled. Swallowing my heart, I tied the piton off, fixed a sling and began the longest thirty seconds of my life. Point by point I edged across the icy slabs. There was no real point in worrying because it was out of my hands anyway. Three lives on an inch of metal. A last long reach and there was the rope. I quickly clipped on a Heibler, then hung, drained of everything by the terrific release of nervous tension. Then I tied off the rope for Sigi and Roland and prusiked on into the mist. I felt that somehow the summit must be near as the wind was now terrific in its intensity. It was almost impossible to breathe, far less see. Suddenly, through the storm I could make out two figures. My first thought was that they were Jörg and Günther; then Chris's voice came floating down. It was finished. The direct existed. There was no elation as I pulled on to the summit. Only a tremendous feeling of gratitude that Chris and Karl Golikow had come up to meet us.

There was no time to linger on the peak of my ambition. Chris led me down towards the snow-hole that he and Mick Burke had dug several hundred feet beneath the summit. The tension was over. I could happily stumble in someone else's footsteps. We cramponed downward in the never-ending storm. Suddenly there was a hole in the snow. I stuck my head inside into a different world. There was a happy chatter. Jörg and Günther were there, along with Mick, Toni Hiebeler, Günter Schnaidt and Rolf Rosenzopf. I lay down in a great daze at the sudden transformation. A brew of coffee came up from the depths of the hole. It was like no drink I had ever tasted. It provided the necessary link and slowly I began to unwind. My hands were blistered and useless, so I stuck them in my pockets while Günter Schnaidt unlaced my crampons.

About an hour later Sigi and Roland arrived with Karli. I hadn't realised how wild we must have looked until I saw them with the eyes of someone who was no longer fully occupied with the problems of the Face. Their clothing was ripped, their eyes sunken and wild. Eyelids, eyelashes, beard and nostrils were completely coated with ice but, incredibly, still smiling. It was a moving moment. The party was complete. Everyone began to relax after their appearance. The cooker hummed away with a never-ending supply of hot drinks. Food was passed round. Eleven people in a hole built for four. No national barriers existed here. We were united by the spirit of extreme climbing.

from EIGER DIRECT 1966

NORTH TWIN, NORTH FACE

CHRIS JONES

Yesterday all was indecision. The north faces above the Columbia Icefields were plastered in ice. Could North Twin be any different? We had gambled on the beginning of August for our attempt, had traded our fear of a rival team for our knowledge of ice conditions. All July we anxiously awaited news from Canada. But now, when all seemed ready, we faltered. Should we give it a few days to clear? Should we go to Robson and come back later? Fear was countered by desire, caution by competition. No matter what alternatives we dreamed up, we could not avoid the basic issue. Were we ready for North Twin, or were we kidding ourselves? We packed our gear.

One foot up, pause, and then the other. It was much like any other uphill grind with a heavy pack. Yet there was a difference. In a few moments we would be at Woolley Shoulder, and I would have my first view of the fabled North Face of North Twin. I became strangely detached. I saw George Lowe and myself as figures in the past. I saw our attempt as something that happened long ago. There was a clear sense that it had some meaning for a future generation, but what it was I could not say. More importantly, I knew this would be a very personal moment. I was intrigued to know my limits, wanted to push myself as never before. I had a feeling that North Twin might provide the answer. When I reached the Shoulder I ducked into the wind and glanced across at our face. I was impressed…

There was no alternative. I chipped away at the ice in the back of the crack, bridged up the groove, and repeated the performance. It was our fifth day on the wall. We had hoped to be up in three days, but the scale and the difficulties were unrelenting. We had equipment for a typical mixed climb, but the 2000ft upper wall was of Dolomitic steepness and severity. One of our Bluet cartridges had been damaged in the haul bag, and without gas there would be no water to drink. The intricate route-finding had necessitated retreats and pendulums, and together with the gear we had simply dropped or failed to remove, we were down to a dozen pitons and nuts.

George put in a lead and called for me to come up. When I arrived he pointed to a ramp that led around a corner. Was this the connection to the ice gully that led through the headwall? Excited and relieved I led upwards; the ramp gave out on a blank wall. I then tried to reach the headwall above me. The rock was poor and I could not get any satisfactory anchors. Thoroughly despondent, I asked George to take over the lead. He worked hard and unearthed a couple of nut placements, then started up the headwall. A knifeblade, a sky-hook, a thin blade. Slowly he inched up. Now he needed a regular angle. The only one was the principal belay anchor; so I tied off the ropes, stood in a sling, and hammered at it. Suddenly the rope jerked upward. 'God, he's off,' I thought as I grabbed for the belay rope. In a flash I saw the last piton pull, saw the tremendous wrench on the remaining belay anchor. Then all was quiet. George bobbed up and down at the end of his rope.

I was tense. I insisted we have a rest, eat lunch, and talk over the situation. Four thousand feet up this wall was no place to start taking leader falls. But George was pissed-off. He wanted to get back on the rock right away. Not up the same crack, he was sure of that, but up a nearby depression. As he started up an even less promising line, it began to snow. He doggedly tried this line, but it was hopeless; another was equally bad. Finally he traversed leftward around the base of the headwall. After an age he returned through the falling snow. It was almost dark, but he had seen the ice gully which led through the headwall. It was 100ft away from his high point and was vertical water ice. Maybe we could pendulum into it, then tie the ropes together and protect the lead by leapfrogging our three ice pitons. Even George could not hide the fact that this was a desperate proposal.

The bivouac was austere. We perched on ice-crusted rocks with our feet thrust into our climbing sacks. After a cup of soup and a mouthful of cheese we settled into the bivouac sack. My mind raced. We were in a hell of a spot. We had almost no climbing gear. With our limited means the headwall appeared impossible. The ice gully seemed like madness. Retreat was out of the question; that option had been closed since the day before. The storm was now serious. Snow covered the rock. Tomorrow we would be overdue, and warden Hans Fuhrer would be concerned. But even if he flew in to look for us, what could he do to help? Did we really imagine that they could pull us off this wall? Besides, how long could we hold out?

George was also awake. He must have been going through the same gyrations. Finally we began to talk. He had come to the same conclusion – the only way out was up. We both had been badly rattled; I, when the hoped-for exit ramp turned to nothing, and George, when he unthinkingly attacked the headwall after his fall. We were near our limit. Well, if this were the real thing, I was damn glad I was with George. He was solid. I told him of my confidence, and he replied that he felt the same way. I might be lousy on 5.10, but he reckoned I had a high survival potential. As we discussed the options, confidence returned. Conversation died out and we fell asleep.

It was the seventh day. I headed into the bleak nothingness of a white-out on the Columbia Ice-fields. Behind me, George kept us on a compass bearing. Yesterday we had lucked out. During a lull in the storm we had made an improbable lead into the ice gully. Fifteen leads of ice climbing in continual storm had brought us to the summit ridge at dusk. Now all we had to do was find the col that gave access to the valley. At mid-afternoon we headed down a dip in the glacier. Just then we heard an unmistakable sound: a helicopter was circling in the valley below. They were looking for us! The noise grew faint and then went away. We crossed a shoulder and plunged into a snow basin; at last we could see where we were going. Suddenly the noise returned; the helicopter shot over the col. We rushed headlong down the slope, oblivious to the crevasses. The pilot spotted us and swung the machine over in our direction. 'You guys OK' came over the loud-hailer. Apparently satisfied by our shouts and waves, the helicopter circled away. As abruptly as they had arrived they were gone.

The emotional impact was devastating. We realised that someone cared about us, that we were not alone. The last few days had been overwhelming. We had crossed the undefinable line. Now the tensions were released. As I walked toward the valley, tears ran down my face.

from ASCENT *1975–76*

PART 3

STYLE AND CHARACTER

This section is devoted to the idea that it is not what you climb, but how you climb that counts. The essays have been chosen as examples of the varying personal styles and approaches that climbers adopt to their sport. Of how they react under the strain of action, of how they interact with each other, of their secret hang-ups and their shouted triumphs. The three articles dealing with the now famous Smith/Marshall week on Ben Nevis in 1960 act as scene-setters. Winter climbing seems to bring out the best in climbers when they are united by fear, discomfort and (for most) an unaccustomed high level of risk. As Robin Campbell wrote:

'Such writing and such climbs remind us that mountaineering is a struggle and winter mountaineering often a desperate one. No dry exercise of logic and skill, but a 'howking of immense jug-handles', a frozen waiting in icy torrents of 'thundering rubbish', a fight with the green rockless wastes of the last 400ft of Scotland while the sinister dark clutches at your ankles, a world where to spend time is maybe to spend your last time and where only the bold stroke will suffice, where victory is celebrated not with a shaming glow of smugness but with great baying whoops of triumph and relief: a world of primitive delight.'

The other articles touch on dramas and personalities no less colourful. Perhaps the message they carry is that climbing is a pursuit as much concerned with people and shared adventure as with mountains.

THE OLD MAN AND THE MOUNTAINS

ROBIN SMITH

Old Man James and I on a Friday night in February went to the hut halfway up the mountain. Stackalee [Ronnie Marshall] and Typhoo [Tiso] came as well because Typhoo has a car and needed someone to climb with. All nine days long the moon grew big and round and all the big black Ben was shining white. On Saturday we had breakfast for lunch and went and climbed the Great Chimney on Tower Ridge. We shambled up soft snow slabs, then I went up a pitch of Chimney with my eyes on the crux, only the rope just sort of stuck when I was just below it, so I made a belay and the Old Man went and fought it out sitting in a sling under an overhanging chockstone and pressed on to the crest of the Ridge below the Little Tower. I dropped my ice axe, so when I reached the top I fixed a sling and abseiled back down the Chimney into the gathering night. I was right at the end of the rope and had to let go with my bottom hand and the ends were just sliding over my shoulder when I came upon my axe. The Old Man, who is very bold, went solo down the crest of the ridge and came upon terrible difficulties in the moonlight, but in the end we got to the hut for a big brew.

On Sunday we made an early start in the wee sma' hours of the afternoon, only I forgot my axe and had to go back for it and we were quite late starting up Minus Three Gully. I was scheming for the crux, so I took a belay and James went up in nice ice grooves into a great ice cave. I climbed halfway up the back of the cave and through a hole in the curtain of ice and out on to the face of a terrible icicle, but here there were great jugs ready to be cut and places to bridge and you went up no bother at all and the next pitch was longer and harder and I had to sit and gnash my teeth while the Old Man led through. We came out on to the North-East Buttress ridge and wandered up to the Plateau and down by diverse routes screeching at the moon.

By then our transport had left for the big city but chosen men of the Mountain Rescue came up to the Hut to train for a week with lots of food. The next day we were really late because I was hunting my ice axe while the Old Man squatted at the foot of Tower Gully hurling oaths at the Hut. In the end I thought, we won't climb two at a time if it gets steep, and I went up the hill without it. We went to Gardyloo Buttress. The top half is split by a couloir which was pouring vast waves of ice down the middle of the steep bottom half. James went up an ice groove on the right and made a peculiar piton belay, and settled down for a real deep freeze. I hacked away up and left over the ice-field for ninety feet till I came upon a bit of rock probably on the line of Kellett's summer route. By then it was going dark and I couldn't think whether to go straight up or go to the right or look for a runner or look for a belay. I tried all four and picked on the last and put in two pitons so that they didn't fall straight out and threaded a sling round a bit of snow in a crack and said I had a belay. But the Old Man is very wise and analysed my tone of noise and decided I was shattered and using a manky belay to pass the buck so he sat tight. Then I dropped the axe. It stuck in the ice on top of an overhang five feet below and I crept down to pick it up in a sweating terror of kicking a bit of snow on it. At least you might say I had a runner now, and so I decided to go up and right across a great barrel of snow-ice strangely shaped and leading nowhere evident. The top six inches were crusted snow and no use to anyone. I had to use our monster ice piton, knocking it in as high as I could and using it for balance while I cut steps and pressing on until it was down about my knees and pulling it out and putting it in again. Then I dropped it at the biggest bulge and it disappeared into the night. That meant I couldn't go back, unless (as it were) out of control. Then I lost my grip of the axe and it started somersaulting in the air with both my arms windmilling trying to grab it and my feet scarting about in crumbly holds. Somehow all was well and I came to an ice arête below where it still cut away into vast overhangs but above the angle fell back one or two degrees and I went up till the rope ran out just as I came into moonlight on the snow at the foot of the couloir. The Old Man was moaning in throes of misery, but he came up on his knees groping for steps in the moon-shade and led through easily to the plateau while I took a piton hammer belay. We shambled down Number Four Gully and I found my axe.

I was still exhausted the next afternoon so we went up a wiggly line of snow and ice grooves on Observatory Buttress for about 600ft until it gets very easy where Good Friday Climb comes in from Tower Gully. Nothing very exciting happened except that Old James got the crux. We slid round into Tower Gully up to our stomachs in powder snow and we got back to the Hut almost in daylight.

On Wednesday we were monstrously early; we were up by half-past eight, but the weather was manky and thawing at the Hut with bits of rain and sleet. But around ten it faired up, so we struggled out of the Hut with stacks of gear and this time wearing duvets and went to Point Five Gully and here conditions were great. The first pitch was a doddle on snow-ice; what took time was finding cracks for piton belays. James led pitch two, an ice wall very steep for twenty feet. Then I went up a groove to a great boss of ice, but here you could stick your hands under the boss and away up behind it and clear the gap running round it on the right and semi-lay-back on the snow above. I pressed on up a chimney full of evil crusted snow and took an axe belay at the side of the gully. Then the spindrift started drooling down, and just as the Old Man spread himself halfway over the boss of ice it grew to a hissing torrent and piled up on his great stomach and pushed him out from the ice while he clawed away for the holds and through the tips of his gloves. It seemed half an hour before it ran dry. The next pitch was beautiful, a long funnel of ice, mostly vertical but just curved enough to let you bridge. Then the gully opened out and we charged on whooping through swirling clouds and pools of moonlight to the plateau.

In the morning there was mist and a big wind. Around mid-day we attacked the slopes of Càrn Mòr Dearg, with lots of pounds in our pockets and no map, whistle or compass. We went into the fangs of the wind over Aonach Beag and all the Grey Corries to Stob Choire Claurigh and round to the Spean Bridge Hotel. Shortly we took a bus to Fort William for fish suppers, only Hell's Kitchen was shut, so we had to turn to drink. They threw us out at nine o'clock and we walked a bit and thumbed a wee car and here it stopped and two great policemen leaped out and arrested us. They took us away to the Station and put us under a bright light for interrogation by a grim circle of sergeants, but it was all a mistake, something about dominoes, and they let us out for the last bus past the Distillery. We beetled up the path and entered the Hut on the stroke of midnight.

The next day it was foul and cold and we were feeling ill, but in so far as it was the Ben it was good weather and about two o'clock in a state of disgust we felt obliged to heave our way up the mountain. We went up Pigott's route on the Comb, from bottom left away up right to the end of a tapering shelf of snow, then up a short fierce chimney and long ice grooves, and along the crenellated crest to the plateau. We tossed a coin for the chimney; Old James won.

Overnight the wind died and Saturday was so fabulous that one o'clock found us under the Orion Face. Between Slav Route and Beta Route a great tumble of ice fell out of the Basin to the foot of Zero Gully. Even the Old Man recognised he had had his share of cruxes, so he offered me the choice and I chose the first because the third looked terrible, but here the second turned quite hard and the third was a wee doddle. It was all fabulous climbing, 500ft of ice to the Basin, then over the snowfield and out on the right by iced slabs, and next thing I found myself belayed below the Second Slab Rib of the Long Climb and the Old Man was turning it by a great pitch on the right. Then I went by iced slabs and he went by iced slabs and I went over a snowfield and we found ourselves into the night with the moon hidden in clouds, below the final towers at the crest of North East Buttress with 1400ft of climbing behind us and the perishing Old Man in the lead again. Above it looked drastic; I just saw murky white overhangy shapes and a shadow sidling very slowly through them. He couldn't really see more than ton feet, and he hadn't a clue what way to go or even if there was a way. First he wandered leftish, but 100ft without any runners he came back right and sent all his rubbish thundering down on my head while I froze from cold and terror and thought about the twenty-four points of his crampons. When he got up I had to follow through a maze of grooves and bulges and icicles groping for holds that had all filled up again and taking double-handed pulls on the rope. We battered up snows to the Plateau and back to the Hut for a final feed.

Late in the Sunday afternoon I ran my pack over the CMD arête and the lowest pass in the Mamores for a lift on the JMCS bus from Glencoe to Edinburgh. James went down the Allt a' Mhuillin and round by the road on his thumb, but then he's getting old.

from EDINBURGH UNIVERSITY
MOUNTAINEERING CLUB JOURNAL *1961*

GARDE DE GLACE

JAMES MARSHALL

Gritty eyes open to the familiar gloom of the CIC; a hopeful glance over to the stove; but no Wheech [Robin Smith]. Hell! What's the weather like outside? Jeez, another good day, back inside; I guess it's my turn to cook; the stove pump clanks, the infuriating pricker pantomime and the explosive roar, then the welcome hiss of the burner – all's well; reddened eyes peer from the pits … An hour later, bellies full of unwelcome food, we collect the gear – what a pile! – and step into the scouring hygiene of a winter morning.

Slowly, crampons rasping, I arrive below Observatory Gully. Where has Wheech gone? From my boulder perch Gardyloo looks great; a sprauchle quits the hut, circles it many times; foul oaths fill the air, eventually it moves up the slope. I trudge on with occasional whoops to beat the ghosts back, things are perfect, what a load of ice about! Wheech arrives minus axe, we have a swearing bout, apparently he left it somewhere last night, we agree that one axe should do, and eventually gain the foot of the buttress; things begin to look possible and we agree and disagree on the chosen line; two great slabs rake the buttress from the lower right to the exit funnel at the top, ice is hanging all over them, and with any luck this will be the way. I get the first run, it's great, hard snow, then plenty ice, easy to cut. I'm told to keep going to a giant belay, I keep going and after 100ft the giant belay isn't. A piton between loose blocks, an attack of nerves, another piton, which sounds better, gradually I begin to feel at home, the stance grows bigger, and Wheech arrives. He's for the overhang, I'm for the line of least resistance, I win but he does the work, a nervous traverse left on steep ice, then a happy announcement that it's a doddle. Two hours later, hoarse with singing and groaning, I'm still watching the movement of the rope. To combat the creeping death I've tramped the equivalent of the Butlin Walk, by now my stance feels like home, the contemplation of retreat brings warmth to the mind; what joy to leave Wheech to his Hell's Wall and whoop down the gully with the blood singing through the veins to swill a big brew in the hut's steamy gloom. A shout of 'Come on!' rakes me back to frigidity; it dawns on me, he's too polite, something is ugly up there besides Wheech; having lived so long for a climber and acquired a cunning commensurate with age, I point out that there is still fifty foot of rope to go; a short exchange of unpleasantries follows, and the rope continues its neurotic advance. I return to the deep freeze, singing, howling and 'Barbara Mooreing' to exist, the ice glints green in the evening light and the cold claws of night creep up the gully. A favourite karabiner and ice-peg rattle past to meet them, little prayers from above take off into the night. I later learned Wheech was playing drum majors with the only axe, but fortune and the axe remained with him. Silhouetted against a starry sky the wee bauchle comes into sight, grunts of 'I'm nearly there' go on for another prolonged spell, then a great whoop sears the night. By now the moon has cleared the arête and the crest of the Tower Ridge gleams superbly in the white light, but we remain in moonshade; this time the call from above bodes well, I come out of my shell, unspiking myself from the mountain and move on, frozen gloves rasping on immense jugs, an ungraceful fumble up the ice, feeling for the holds, round the steep rib, all's well, then the angle relents, the holds are full of snow, and hellish hard to find, a scuffling crawl up the icy roof leads to Wheech's proposed belay. It doesn't look too bad, but one peg lifts out, and the other slips from the first hammer blow; now the holds lead rightward and in the gloom I can make out a white rib, like a giant candle … it's plated with nine inches of sugary snow ice so that great holds had to be hacked out to reach the good ice beneath. I'm real impressed, feeling high and deep into the holds, a thrash with the feet for the lower steps, a quick judgement of soundness, then a queer off-balance swing for the next hole – Wow! that was a false one – hands slip on the glassy ice, the footholds crunch down, I expect to come off then the searching frozen mitt slips comfortingly into one of Wheech's rabbit holes, and balance is established. This is no place to linger, so the struggle continues, and at last the angle eases slightly, it's possible to stand – not hang - the holds get smaller and poorer – signs of a tired lead! – and finally I arrive beside partner Wheech, very much impressed; it was a fantabulous lead, and even though unusual, I tell him so. Then feeling like a relegated ruin, I lead up to the moonlit arête, spirits return, the magnificence of the ascent and wonderful moonlight send us screeching over the plateau by differing routes to filter down the cliffs of the Ben to the cave-like security and comfort of the CIC.

from THE SCOTTISH MOUNTAINEERING
CLUB JOURNAL *1961*

THE ORION FACE

JAMES MARSHALL

Sheets of flame reveal partner Wheech doing a dervish dance round the hut's mangled old stove; his fat-fingered fumble provides an amusing ten minutes of cosy reflection before the soothing hiss and familiar gloom swallow the hut. But thoughts of prolonging the horizontal are rudely thrust aside as his hacked and filthy visage, that could frighten lesser men, peers over the bunk to pronounce the day 'the mostest fantabulous' of the week.

An hour later, bellies filled with rich greasy omelettes and all goodies that happened within reach, we are toiling towards the tall white face of Orion, intent on making a superb *Diretissima* by the great ice fall which pours from the 'Basin' to the foot of Zero Gully.

By the time we have staggered to the base of the wall, the route is dissected into his and mine sections; so Wheech leads off, up a pleasantly fat ice slope, whilst I sort out the many slings, hammers and karabiners from the bag.

At fifty feet Wheech's tour had misled him on to a thinly iced slab, where it was obvious he would either waken up or roll back down to the hut; his bow-legged bumbling at the foot of this great ice wall seemed as out of place as a can-can in the Swan Lake; however, by performing an exciting traverse of crampon scarts to reach thick ice, the rapid progress is resumed and a large ledge reached 150ft higher; joining Wheech after being truly stung by his *mauvais pas*, we searched for a peggable crack with delayed success. The situation was magnificent: above us a great groove, rich with ice, swirled into obscurity; rightwards, Zero Gully took on the air of an escape route, whilst the great iced slabs to the left promised future 'joyous days upon the mountainside'.

Fully whooped up and anxious to reach the key passage to the wall which we both felt was somewhere about 100ft above, I climbed over Wheech into the groove and hacked and whooped the way up over grand bulges, howking immense jug-handles in the ice; an ice column runner gave joy at ninety feet, then a little higher the angle eased, and a small hole under a rock roof forty feet above promised security. Gaining this hole, I hacked away a curtain of icicles and squeezed in like a frightened ostrich, to manufacture a belay on an inverted channel piton in the rock roof, this didn't instil a sense of security so with an incredibly awkward manoeuvre the axe was driven into the floor and a cowardly sprauchle backwards performed to stand secured by slings above the void. Feeling brave once more I took in the rope as Wheech came on, babbling back and forth about character, quality and senility.

We were now at the question point of the route; to the right, the difficulties were obvious and in sight, whilst above nothing could be seen but a steep icy rib and a skyline begging the question; naturally the unknown appealed, so the bold climbing machine hacked away up and round the rib out of sight, but unhappily not of sound. A few minutes after he moved from sight, a horrible flow of oaths seared down the sterile slopes; I thought he was in a cul-de-sac, but no, he had climbed into easy ground, with the way to the Basin clear, and the share of labour too small for a step-hacker of Wheechy's calibre. With an added sense of satisfaction, I watched the rope snake out at an increasing pace and soon the ostrich act was repeated, as I removed our comforting anchorage. The climbing above was delightful and somewhat reminiscent of the slabs of the Crowberry Gully junction, but continuing for greater lengths.

A short wall above Wheech led on to a long snow rake, where a quick, cramponing crawl brought us to the snowfield of the Basin. From a rock belay on the right edge of the depression, Wheech cut up an ice slope for 100ft, then made an icy fifty-foot traverse rightwards to belay at the foot of the Second Slab Rib of the Long Climb. Standing at the belay in the Basin I couldn't help recalling the last visit, when Patey and I had made the girdle traverse of Ben Nevis; there had still been traces of the Smith-Holt rope leading out by the 'V' Traverse to the North-East Buttress, from their ascent of the Long Climb one month earlier which unfortunately, owing to a lack of time, stopped short at the Basin. It was this sense of the unfinished that was partly responsible for our very presence on the face at the moment. However, Wheech was finished with the work above and I hastened to join him, where I was rather disappointed to find the rib above too thinly iced for comfort. An exploratory ten-foot traverse round the corner disclosed a well-iced wall, shining green in the evening light and perched over the now impressive drop of the wall beneath: 130ft higher the hunt for peg cracks failed in the gathering gloom of night and a belay in powder snow brought sharp edges of frost and fear into the struggle: Wheech came and went, swopping wet gloves for dry, trending left and up by shallow grooves, over treacherously difficult breaking snow and verglassed rocks; night was fully launched when the rope ran out, but the moon stayed sly behind a blanket of cloud. Following up was like walking on eggs, the dark pit beneath our heels sufficient warning to take care; a short step of ice above Wheech led on to the high snow slopes which form beneath the terminal towers of the Orion Face. Here the expected respite failed to materialise; knee deep and floury, they whispered evil thoughts, threatening to slide us into the black void and extinguish the winking lights of the CIC Hut. Floundering up this snow, doubts plagued the mind; our original intention to spiral up right-wards round the towers lost its appeal on the face of such threat; perhaps a move left would bring us on to the crest of North-East Buttress? But again the snow. Great shadowy forms confused the issue, so we persisted with the straight-up as being mentally the least trying.

   A yell from above lit the night; Wheech had found a rock belay. A jumble of talk awakened vague morning memories of the face, then by right of sequence I deprived partner Wheech of his dry gloves, leaving him to fight the cold war whilst I tackled the obscurity above. A scrabble up a cone of snow above the belay led to a well-iced groove; it was necessary to feel the angle ahead with the hands, as up here everything was whitened by fog crystals and in the misty gloom distance was incalculable. Up above there appeared to be an immense cornice; the thoughts of an enforced bivouac beneath the icy beak passed absently through the mind as I chopped away at the ice. About forty-foot up, the groove steepened to a bulge; finding the holds with the cramponed feet was extremely awkward at times, and often moves were made hanging from the handholds whilst the crampons scarted about in search of the 'buckets' cut below. Above, the bulge loomed more ominous, so a trouser-filling traverse was made on to the right wall, along a short ledge; then a frightening move, leaning out on an undercut ice hold, to cut holds round a rib on to the slab wall of a parallel groove. The ice here was only about an inch thick and moving into the groove was very difficult; the cat crawl up the thin ice remains imprinted in the memory, for at this 'moment of truth' strains of an awful dirge came up from the Blackfoot ninety feet below, 'Ah kin hear the hammer ringin' on somebody's coffin ...' Other ditties may have followed, but that particular one registered and stimulated progress across the slab to a comforting snow-filled groove, where the calf muscles could recover.

At last things were beginning to take shape; a large cornice at my level closed the top of the first groove, and above me was a steep wall, thick with ice. This looked the way and, having no desire to freeze, a short traverse was made up the thinly iced slab to an accommodating ledge; then the great hacking resumed. Strain on the back of the legs was becoming very trying, and I had to cut a deep step occasionally to stand on to relieve the calf muscles. I began to worry about the length of rope, feeling much more than 140ft had passed; the thought of having to continue without a belay gave further chill to the night; then suddenly there was no more ice to cut, and in front a gentle slope, catching the cold filtered moonlight, shone in a heart-warming scene. Whoops of delight went down to thaw out Wheech, then up a couple of feet to discover the rope was out, a retreating belay from the edge as Wheech came up the snow cone enabled me to take an axe belay ten feet back. It was grand to be able to sit down and relax. A whooping session began as Wheech came up in a series of frozen jumps, purring about quality and character. 'What a climb' was our chorus, then his amorphous shape appeared over the edge, covered in snow, ironmongery clanking, like some armoured beast from the underworld. Gathering up the rope, we rushed up to the plateau, to arrive at the point where the North-East Buttress branches from the summit plateau. Then stowing heaps of rope, slings and snow into the frozen sack we pushed off across the misty plateau making for the hut, heat and the big sweet brew, occasionally stopping to howl into the night what a 'mostest fantabulous' climb we'd had.

from THE SCOTTISH MOUNTAINEERING
CLUB JOURNAL *1961*

THE BLACK CANYON WITH KOR

PAT AMENT

'I ... let myself down rapidly, striving by the vigour of my movements to banish the trepidation which I could overcome in no other manner ... But presently I found my imagination growing terribly excited by thoughts of the vast depths yet to be descended ... It was in vain I endeavoured to banish these reflections and to keep my eyes steadily bent upon the flat surface of the cliff before me. The more earnestly I struggled not to think, the more intensely vivid became my conceptions, and the more horribly distinct. At length arrived that crisis of fancy, so fearful in all similar cases, the crisis in which we begin to anticipate the feelings with which we shall fall – to picture to ourselves the sickness, and dizziness, and the last struggle, and the half swoon, and the final bitterness of the rushing and headlong descent. And now I found these fancies creating their own realities, and all imagined horrors crowding upon me in fact. I felt my knees strike violently together, while my fingers were gradually but certainly relaxing their grasp. And now I was consumed with the irrepressible desire of looking below. I could not, I would not, confine my glances to the cliff; and, with a wild, indefinable emotion, half of horror, half of a relieved oppression, I threw my vision far down into the abyss. For one moment my fingers clutched convulsively upon their hold, while, with the movement, the faintest possible idea of ultimate escape wandered, like a shadow, through my mind – in the next my whole soul was pervaded with a longing to fall.

Edgar Allan Poe

The passage of Poe's from his tale of Arthur Gordon Pym, brings to mind certain feelings which I had the misfortune – or fortune – to experience in the Black Canyon of the Gunnison at age seventeen under the unique guidance of Layton Kor, my climbing partner, who at that time was twenty-five. The adventure was a complete fiasco and has become somewhat of a legend amongst older climbers. The story has undoubtedly been exaggerated and capriciously altered over the years, but it nevertheless retains without error the underlying fact that an extraordinary, absurd, humorous, stupid, and altogether dangerous ordeal took place. It is with partial guilt, partial urging of conscience, and a desire to reveal one perspective of vintage Kor that I give this pseudo-Poe narrative of the unsuccessful trip to, and our preposterous flail upon, the walls of Colorado's Black Canyon.

Layton had recovered instantaneously from an unbelievable, backwards, head-over-heels leader fall off the Bastille Crack in Eldorado. My hands, however, were blistered nearly shut from the serious rope burns I had suffered catching him. I had been warned by a doctor to stay away from rock for at least a month, as the blisters were in danger of becoming infected, but Layton was impatient and wanted to depart immediately for the Black Canyon. He showed me a fuzzy snapshot of a 2000ft, vertical and over-hanging wall called the Chasm View, and reassured me that I was tough. I wanted to be with him, and Layton's wide eyes and warm laugh were very persuasive. Just the thought of such a first ascent was enough to take my mind off the burns and diminish, in my idiocy and immaturity, all pain.

It was the middle of summer, and the three hundred or so mile drive from Boulder was hot. The old, blue Ford had four bald tyres, and Kor gunned it up to eighty miles-an-hour most of the way. His eyes bulged and face contorted as he drove. His huge form leaned over the steering wheel, and he gazed nervously ahead. He held a peanut butter sandwich between his long legs and knobbly knees and shook to the tune of rock 'n' roll which blasted out of the radio. I sat gripping the seat, making peanut butter sand-wiches at Kor's command and, at one point, agreeing to take part in a handshake contest. There were two hundred pounds backing up his grip and about a hundred and thirty behind mine. My blisters burned at the thought, and I was squeezed out like a flame. A poor, hapless chipmunk was flattened while attempting to cross the highway.

The final part of the drive was a fifty-mile dirt road above cliffs and steep drops which were the beginning of the Black Canyon. I was terrorised by this road, its unending, sharp curves, and the drag-racer behind the wheel. I couldn't chew or swallow, and a lump of laughter and peanut butter stayed in my mouth for what seemed like an hour.

We arrived at the north rim of the canyon late in the day, parked, and, after a brief walk, were able to peer down our wall. The eerie, distant roar of the Gunnison River which flowed far below, combined with the peculiar, lonely fragrance of sage, the desert-like silence, and hot wind, began to stir in me a fear of the remote area. My heart sank at the thought of having to catch another Kor fall or of encountering one of the huge, horribly rotten, sickly pink, pegmatite bands which Layton had, during the drive, described with dread and superstition.

Layton snatched me up into his arms, pretending to have gone mad and to want to throw me over the edge. His fun was soon over, for I shot away from the exposed place like a rabbit, desperate to escape his mock chuckles. I endeavoured to console myself, returned, and was from then on pre-pared to bear with personality and fortitude all further absurdity which was destined to occur.

After briefly exploring a steep, alien gully which appeared superficially to be a feasible descent route into the canyon, we spent a bad night on the rim.

It was anticipation of the climb that kept us awake, also hunger. We had practically depleted our supply of bivouac food – the peanut butter – and would have been foolish to break into the small ration of meat which Layton had brought in addition. Kor was immensely energetic and would not be discouraged by heat or hunger. Conspiring to stimulate me in the morning with a cup of boiling tea, he exploded his small stove and nearly burned down a picnic table. This put him in a bad humour, and he stared at me with a look as insidious as a sly sun which rose and began drawing the first beads of sweat from my forehead. We sorted pitons, slings, and karabiners, loaded bivouac gear into a large haul bag, filled a couple of water bottles, stuffed bolts and provisions into an old pack, and headed off to descend the steep gully.

He was obsessed. He wanted to get at it, to purge his soul on rock. He loved to go out on a limb, to be cleansed and dirtied by the deep shade and undiscerning power of his singular, high asylums. A sensation of emptiness, almost anger, flowed through me, as I questioned my role in the game. All doubt, all shadow, fell prey to fear – fear of Kor! He stared at me silently.

My thoughts were with facing the fear, with moving into Layton's world. I needed to discover life, to help find this route, and, if necessary, be led blindly by the master. The descent was hideous! The sultry gully into the canyon was filled with soil and sticker bushes, small whimpers in a fretful, broken voice were my sound of protest. Proceeding down into the expanse of the gully, we found it to be suffocating. It was a treacherous sort of chute, eventually becoming slippery walls on all sides. Layton had loaded on to me what seemed an enormous amount of rope and hardware – plus the old pack. It was not easy to breathe with slings choking me and pack straps tearing at my shoulders. It felt unfair.

The heat was unbearable. An hour into the morning, I was ready to consume our entire two-day supply of water in a sitting. I was anxious, watching Kor climb without a belay. He moved smoothly down the precipitous, slabby walls of the gully. The weight upon my shoulders and around my neck made it impossible to follow without great strain. At one difficult section, a tiny slip would have meant a fall of about 800ft. This took a lot out of me, and I worked up a horrible sweat. My burned hands stung as they scraped across crystals. I listened to the river crashing over boulders below, and the sound slashed at my thoughts. I groped at loose flakes, contemplating the anguish of one coming off in my hand. I wanted to do well, to win respect, to cling successfully to Kor's dream. My muscles quivered, and the moves were hazy before my eyes. Layton lowered himself down bulges, over ledges, and around bizarre heaps of gravel. He descended confidently, having no trouble with his load and ignoring my struggles. He was full of hope. I was a scorpion. Light, grey rock, the blue flame of the sky, and a rainbow of images were the kaleidoscopic fluid of the search. The peculiar, personal release and lunacy of seeking out danger seemed a reward of disputable value.

Layton was for a moment outside his utopianism and thirsty but could not relax for thinking about getting to the base of the route. He carried the bottles of water in the haul bag, and I prayed that he would save a sip. I licked the parched lining of my mouth. Who was this maniac? Why was I permitting myself to go along with him?

At last, we were at the base of the route, dripping with sweat and trying to solve the puzzle of rope and snarl of slings which bound me like a fairy-tale squid. My hands were soft and white, oozing with puss which drained from a couple of broken blisters. Kor allowed me a swallow or two of water which only antagonised my thirst, then tied-in and led upward. A towering illusion, tall as a man, with white T-shirt and pants, long socks, and *kletterschuhe,* hung on an overhang above my head. The jewelled light of the sun scorched my thoughts. I had, above me, a kind of surrealism - a creature whose ability on rock matched my vision Layton Kor, spread-eagled and sihouetted, his senses suspended momentarily but bodily powers frenzied. I squeezed the rope, then fed it out as he led swiftly up a difficult crack. The man was driven, afraid to fall, afraid to fail, tormented, all-powerful in a search for rich experience. He ascended with imagination, inclined to go the hard way when a choice existed, tense, uneasy, jumpy, jittery, critical, happy. He was awesome – more so than the wall – and disappeared up into the lair of an overhang. I sat like a piece of cactus, sweltering, stifled in a furnace of talus, awaiting the restless cry, 'Come on up!' The river was a hundred-and-fifty yards below and glistened even in the shadows. Scrambling down to it for a cold drink was an idea dismissed in view of the uphill hike back.

He was too big for belay ledges and looked uncomfortable hooked into one. As I followed the pitch, attacking strenuous pulls and long reaches, I discovered that my worst opponent was the old pack. While thinking I was in perfect balance, I would start to fall backwards and would expend precious energy recovering. My hands were a mess, and it was difficult even to hold a piton hammer – much less pound out pins. I was unable to retrieve the first piton, although I worked at it to the point of exhaustion. I was convinced that Layton had over-driven the thing and so left it. I began to feel extremely insecure and yelled for tension. I received slack. The lack of communication was frustrating, and my yells were overruled by the superior authority of the river. When I reached Layton, he asked, 'You get that pin out?' I trembled and replied, 'I have it here somewhere.' He complained of aching feet and insisted on doing the next lead. I was too busy contemplating my lie to argue, so belayed. He stemmed over an impressive overhang and vanished into the heights. The route seemed to have been built for Kor, because I found the holds always out of reach. Layton suggested I take the third lead. It was an incentive to forget for a while the sorry state of my palms. The hammer was too painful to hold, but the rock relented momentarily, so I was able to climb unprotected to a stance about 100ft straight up. Kor was impressed with this but irritated when I could not haul the bag. My hands simply couldn't take it. He hurried up the pitch, and we tugged at the clumsy duffel bag together. That was the end of my leading, I was informed.

It was at this point that war began. Suddenly and quite unexpectedly, Kor yelled, 'Where's your hard hat?!' I answered, 'My what?' He thrust a handful of rope against the wall with such force that I thought we would both fall off. He kicked the wall and, looking as if he was going to strangle me, shouted, 'No one climbs in the Black Canyon without a hard hat!' I was so intimidated by this outburst that I failed to notice he was not wearing one either. I indiscreetly let pass, at this moment, a bit of silent although untimely *flatus* of so foul and putrid an odour that all oxygen was removed from the vicinity of our perch. It took but an instant (which seemed an eternity) for the very bad message to reach Kor's nose. Now, I almost unroped with the intention of jumping rather than face the frightful demon who stood gagging so near at hand. He hovered over me, his face puffing with rage. He let out a chilling scream and raced up the wall, not bothering to place pitons where he knew I would need them. I nearly vomited when he thrust himself into a ferocious, dizzy, overhanging crack and forced his way up it with rope and haul-line dangling down to me like cobras.

All flexibility had gone out of my fingers. I removed the pack and set it atop the haul bag which sat comfortably on the stance without an anchor. It was surely a 100°F, and my thirst was intolerable. I forced a hand and arm into the bag and pulled out a bottle. While belaying with one hand, I twisted the top off with my teeth and began to guzzle. The tone of the climb had changed so radically that I felt faint. A muted 'off belay' from above told me that I had best get the bottle back into the bag fast. Stealing water might be punishable by more unprotected leading. As I fumbled with the bottle and bag, the haul line grew tight, and, just as the bottle disappeared into the opening, up went the big bag with my pack teetering, to my horror and dismay, on top where I had set it. The heavy bundle remained intact and was dragged over a bulge and up into a place hidden from my view where, by all indications, Kor was losing his mind with anger. 'Oh my God, my arms are numb,' he raved.

I had to keep my wits about me. A display of skill, I thought, might save me from the wrath of the fiend above. But it was all I could do to gain an

inch on the pitch without tension. I very skilfully wore my voice out bellow-
ing for the tight line. My hands were two blobs of dirt, puss, and shredded
skin. 'Heel and toe,' Kor shrieked. I was encouraged, but slipped several feet
down, trying to figure out what he meant.

At the belay, he had regained his composure, but did not speak to me. We
hung from slings attached to two feebly placed knife blade pitons which
Layton was eager to get away from. A severe chimney became the object of
his study. He would climb it conscientiously, I reasoned, for there was no
desire to die here ... was there? I was delirious and needed water. Adrenaline
flowed and, as I found myself somehow following the obstacle – the 5.10
crack-chimney affair – I was bewildered and inspired by techniques which
I had applied but did not understand. There were expressions of struggle so
deeply found that they would not transpire again. I became confused, drew
upon untapped resources, and stretched my limbs through a hundred variations of divine bumbling. One thing was for sure: the pack and I would not
both fit into the slot at once. Kor advised me to try the 'Yosemite haul'. I was
to hook the pack to a long sling, then the sling to my waist loop, and drag
the pack as it hung well below. I regretted tackling such a scheme, for it was
5.11 just getting the beast off my back. Then the buckles of the straps caught
on every conceivable projection until I was certain that the tension from
above and immovable weight below would tear me in half.

I somehow achieved Kor's position, after pulling and being hauled on the
rope. Kor did not delay in leading up one more unbelievable, overhanging,
obscure pitch. His tremendous skill was absolutely evident. It was easy to
know why he was one of the great climbers of the world.

The pitch was all direct aid, and, jumars (prusik handles) having not yet
been invented, I thought I would die trying to reach from one karabiner to
the next. As usual, Layton could not see me and was unable to determine
whether my winded gripes were from falling, trying to get tension, or just
pain. I would give each piton a half-hearted tap and grimace, before deciding
that it was over-driven and a permanent fixture. I had no hands left, no voice,
no spirit, only hope that we could bivouac, drink the water, and somehow
rejuvenate. All the pitons stayed in, and I was ashamed but kept fighting.

As I drained the last of my will trying to surmount the belay ledge, I caught
sight of my companion. Kor's hair pointed in every direction. His mouth and
eyes were full of dirt. Sweat rolled down his cheeks. His famous buck teeth
were the focus of an inimitable grin. He was a rebel with a bit of a temper,
supremely talented, fuelled by sheer force, set off from other climbers by a
light – an illumination or charisma – and profound competence. He asked,
'Did you get all the pins?' I had none with me but seemed to feel that the
summit was near and that a few of the little iron strips would not be missed.

I was unable to speak but simply nodded my head in the affirmative while reclining and gasping for air. We were seven hundred or more feet above the gully, a little less than half way to the rim. Kor gave me a worried glance and observed, 'You look bad, Ament. You're pale'. He then ventured up on to the next formidable pitch, examining it for its artistic qualities.

What was I to do or say? I regarded life at that instant as an illness for which help was not available. I dreaded the thought of continuing but also feared retreat. Going down would mean Kor finding the pitons still in place. It would mean having to thrash our way back up the horrible gully. To my amazement, Kor returned and, with no explanation whatsoever, made preparations for rappelling. This abrupt decision on his part filled me with disconcerting questions. It was only later that I would know it had been Kor's genuine concern for my condition which turned him back. He placed a bolt, and I watched the small thing bend in its hole as he applied his weight to the rope. I listened to the tinging of metal against metal as he discovered and removed the pitons while on rappel. Small, indistinct curses drifted up to me and, finally, 'Off rappel'. I was sure that I would not be able to hold on to the rope – even with a break bar – but resigned myself to trying. Layton kept guard over the rope ends, in case I decided to pick up speed. In the course of the rappel, my blisters became mangled cuts while sharp throbs pierced my cramped fingers.

Kor detested my lack of candour about the pitons, and so did I. That was half the hurt. His smiles gnawed at me with excruciating clarity. For an instant, he was understanding, and I remembered other sides of him which existed – patient, insightful sides. My wretchedness and misery permeated the desolation of his stare, and my dejected state brought upon Kor an eagerness to escape the Black Canyon of the Gunnison and all of south-western Colorado.

A quick, violent rainstorm gave us relief but was accompanied by several disturbing bolts of lightning, and thunder crashes. After several agonising rappels, we stood at the bottom in darkness. The ominous, forbidding, evil gully rose endlessly above. Melancholy of night and uncertainty filled the gully. Climbing insufficiently expressed, a poignant denouement and dismal disappointment, blameless loss with cruel psychic and emotional meaning, overcame me like the heat. I was unable to see the glorious images and romantic insights which, sometimes, rescue crucified minds from such drudgery and despair.

Kor withdrew upwards into the night, leaving me to the demons of unbearable and unpredictable allusion, as well as with a rack of hardware and heavy, rain-drenched rope which I could barely lift. I had let my heart be moulded by him and, strangely, knew that I would probably do so again. I loved Kor and hated him and in no way could deny either. The gully was a horrid task, and I was alone in it. Kor was somewhere far ahead, maybe almost up to the rim, possibly in pieces below. It was a vexed question, for it was I who had a 'longing to fall'.

I persevered toward a glimmer of sky, up steep slabs, through mud and stickers, over loose boulders, as if steering my bones through the grave, and clawing in the direction of a dim glow – the headlights of the Ford. My exertions became greater, I stumbled through sage, got into the car, shut the door, and fell asleep. Layton was determined to grind-out the drive back to Boulder that night.

I wished not to awaken out of my dream and into the nightmare of his speeding along the scary, dirt road. He was sailing around corners in the wrong lane and demanding that I sing songs to keep him awake. There was only static on the radio. I groaned a few hoarse and sour notes while leaning slowly over on to his nervous lap, falling back to sleep. He tried to wake me several times, and I would sit up, only to slide rigidly back over on to his lap like a corpse, still dutifully humming.

My eyes opened in the town of Gunnison. It was past midnight, we had stopped, and Kor stood outside rapping on the door of an A. & W. Rootbeer stand which was closed. He looked like death and for all practical purposes frightened the janitor into letting him in. The fellow was obliged to fix the apparition a float! I went back to sleep. Was it really happening?

About an hour later, Layton pulled off on to what appeared to be a turn-out, stopped, got out of the car, and threw his sleeping-bag, me, and my sleeping-bag into the dirt. There we slept for the rest of the night. At the crack of dawn, we made a quick dash to the Ford, delivering ourselves from a rancher's perverse sense of humour and two thousand hooves of five hundred cows being herded toward us.

Kor said nothing to me all the way home but, upon arriving in Boulder, reported voluntarily to a number of other climbers. His account of the ordeal was marked by a lack of particulars and was, simply, 'Ament… left all the pins in, so we had to come back'. I recalled saving his life on the Bastille Crack in Eldorado and felt that he was being ungrateful. I began to realise how hard I had actually pushed on the wall of the Chasm View and in the exposed gully. Through young eyes and foolish insecurity, I saw Layton as the dishonest one … but, with a bit of reflection, returned to my senses. He had told the truth, really. I understood and forgave him for his madness. He had shown me the Black Canyon, perplexed me, and tortured my will and ego; but, following our adventure, he made plans to climb with me again in Eldorado, forgot for a while about the Chasm View, laughed, and, after all, was my friend.

from MOUNTAIN 50 *1976*

CLOTHES – A MODE OF COMMUNICATION

T. I. M. LEWIS

I recently had a good opportunity to study a pair of young hard climbers on Dinas Mot. I was struggling on Black Spring, they were progressing far more rapidly up Black Shadow not in itself, you might say, an event which is going to set the climbing world alight. What gave me pause was the deliberately perverse nature of their apparel. In particular, the trousers of one of them were of the type known as 'Loons', frequently seen advertised in the mail order sections of the Sunday papers, next to the cut price long johns and fun lingerie. These might have been expressly designed to frustrate the climber in every way. Cripplingly tight from the buttock to the knee, they balloon fulsomely below, hiding the feet in enough yardage of flapping cloth to get the Cutty Sark under way. Even walking down the high street in them requires a cowboy gait and a sharp lookout for cats and small children caught up in their voluminous folds.

What, I pondered, could motivate a man to handicap himself in such a way? What was behind this defiant, quixotic choice? Did it arise from simple boredom; was he an earnest climber-sociologist, busy inventing new games to play; or was it the existential *acte gratuit* of a cragsman cum philosopher? This led to the reflection that clothes, aside from their relatively insignificant functional aspects, have always been a mode of communication even if their message is not always easy to construe.

In the Golden Age around the turn of the century, merely wishing to climb at all was sufficient to establish one's bona fides as an 'interesting' and idiosyncratic person. No loud gesture was needed, and the climber was able to adopt a tweedy reticence appropriate to that popular Edwardian hero-figure, the eccentric bachelor-recluse. The ideal was a cross between Sherlock Holmes and Richard Hannay. Indeed, Dr Norman Collie, on a visit to Norway with Cecil Slingsby, was mobbed by delirious fans of the famous detective, under the misapprehension that he was the sage of Baker Street himself. (Collie, by the way, as well as being a dab hand with the ice-axe, carried enough mental wattage to put one in mind rather of the enigmatic and surpassingly brilliant Mycroft Holmes.)

In G. Winthrop Young's exhaustive compilation *Mountain Craft* (1920), which at the least equals such modern works as 'Blackshaw' both in thoroughness and tedium, there is a wealth of sartorial information.

'Carry ... a very light woollen muffler, about one foot wide and six feet long at least. In very cold weather or if sleeping out, pass this tight twice round the stomach and fasten with safety pins.'

This startling device, so obviously derived from the cummerbund, demonstrates that a tinkling echo of the gay yet decorous ballroom world of the 'twenties enlivened the grim bivouacs of the Alpine Club hardmen. In the next passage we see the soft underbelly of decadence.

'I prefer as an alternative to a shirt, two or three very light silky-woollen 'Shetlands', opening down the front and sitting close to the body all the way. One at least should come right down to the thighs. The lowest a zephyr or almost silk-web ...'

I don't know about you chaps, but this sort of stuff makes me feel ill-at-ease, like sitting on a warm lavatory seat.

'Grey flannels, tucked inside the stockings below the knees are very comfortable; they also give one the appearance of having enormous calf muscles ...'

He also pontificates futuristically:

'On a hot day climb in shorts by all means. It will do your style a world of good.'

J. M. Edwards, photographed during this period, wears the type of clothing a suburbanite might don to dig the garden. Considering the sort of routes he was pioneering at the time, this is perhaps not surprising.

After the Second War the style was set by the vast quantities of ex-W.D. clothing flooding the market. The prevailing image was of a bunch of low-grade mercenaries who hadn't been paid for six weeks and were about to change sides. In an atmosphere of shortages and austerity, there was nonetheless plenty of room for individual expression. Cut down raincoats sprayed with engine oil, *pakamacs* and cycling capes were pressed into service as waterproofs. Some items such as the Whillans flat hat and Brown's woolly balaclava, attained exalted status as the cult objects of an heroic myth. (Perhaps Drummond's shorts are destined to be transformed in a similar way.) Whillans' headgear, in particular, epitomised all that was hard, aggressive and working-class about the new climbers.

Nowadays the situation is analogous to that in many of the arts. Affluence and ease of communication have presented the climber with an enormous range of established styles. To be different, quirky, individualistic is becoming more and more difficult, and it is, after all, the reason why people take up climbing in the first place. Many resort to a parody of excess. Thus as well as all the historical echoes, we have those who climb in collar and tie, emulating the ultra-respectable façade of the Belgian surrealist master, René

Magritte. At the same time the tramp image has been taken surely as far as it can go, short of loin cloths and begging bowls. There are some who present a Mediterranean playboy image, attired in cut-off Levis, carefully frayed and faded, and T-shirts bearing an inconsequential motif or advertising slogan. Others gain their effects in a striking incongruity between items of clothing unremarkable in themselves; for example, Duvet and jeans, or wool breeches and shirtsleeves, worn with Millarmitts. One sympathises with those who opt out of the game altogether, and climb naked on the Shawangunks.

What of the future? What for the fashion-conscious climber who wants to be one jump ahead? Well, the whole 'skinhead', and 'boots and braces' syndrome has made very little impact on the climbing scene as yet. Perhaps we are in for a period of short hair, 'skinners' with four-inch turn ups, and 'Crombies' instead of Duvets. Who can tell? Your guess is as good as mine.

from ROCKSPORT *November 1973*

A WEEK IN THE HILLS

ROBIN SMITH

In spring, 1960, a party of visiting Russian and English climbers was entertained by the SMC. The Russians were, inevitably, shown Glen Coe and Skye. But there was no bear-leading: they were happy to explore by themselves, enthusing over the mountains and the sea, but not over the weather or the slime. Feasts and lectures followed, in Edinburgh, where the projected film suffered a technical hitch. Though one wonders how much of Scotland as a country, not as a countryside, they did see, the Russians appeared to have enjoyed their stay; their hosts certainly did. The usual distortions were made by the gutter Press; but if what our propaganda tells us about what their propaganda tells them is true, they would expect that.

However, we do not print the following as a mirror of truth, either; it rejoices in its own distortion, a picture of the proceedings seen by one of the thrawnest participants. Allowances must be made here, too! [SMCJ Editor's introduction]:

Sunny Lagangarbh crackled under the brooding Buachaille.

Then 'Hear that clutch?' said Ritchie. And higgledy-piggledy here they were, Dr Slesser and Kenneth in the van, weaseling down the dirt-track, AC evergreens down from the Red Snows, overlapping meets of ladies, six climbers from Russia, and in the rear Tommy Weir, Scotland's greatest chronicler; here to put another page to Annals of the Mountain World.

'Take these chaps to something tough,' said spirited young Wraith Jones.

Ritchie fled with Big Brother. Big Elly, James and I took Eugene, Misha, Tolly and Tommy to Great Gully, Glencoe's grimmest grotto.

Notes on Climbing in Great Gully 1894–1961:

This fine yet frightful line fell direct to N.C. solo (1894). 137th equal in shades of ferocity on this mountain, this line never flags, and yet essays on this line have not been repetitious, while novel lines have broken out on all sides. 1930: A.J. and J.H.B.B. scaled ponderous Cuneiform. Great balance required. 1937: JC.-de-B.N. (and party) plucked Raven's Gully. 1946–1956: CDMC opened ways of some importance over walls on right and also pleasant ways of passing merit over walls on farthest left too. (Black Dan, Snotter Blob and new exciting trends will be cleaned up in a later tissue.)

With then a sense of history, we crept up and down cracks on the far right and up the far left edge of Slimey Wall. Poised on the very Gully bed, Tommy composed and cool as a cooker snapped his jaws. 'Dynamically posed,' said Tommy. The rest of us went to the summit, and lay in the sun, exchanging harmonious pidgin notes on capitalism, dinners and England. Thence we rushed to Lagangarbh, very late for schedule for journey for dinner for Russians for furthering paths to peaces. Ritchie, Elly, James and I went up the Lost Valley, we made a great new route.

Scavaig stravaiged around the beetling Cuillin.

They hove to. Still with this crew, we lent a hearty hand to heave-ho chests and firkins to the Hut. Skye! Mecca to these chaps, all in a froth for Gabbro.

Of an evening we four put an end to the Crack of Dawn to lend that route some matter and form. The Russians tight-roped the razor Ridge, they cut their feet to ribbons. 'At home we haff not such feats,' they said, dismayed. Jones led out the fiery 'Inglish', fishing.

'Now,' said Big Brother, 'there will be Discussion.' With ears for hours on end we witnessed bottling of priceless notes on inseminative education of Scholars of Sport and spotty Outward Bounders.

And so we left this happy Isle, wedding of thrusting rock and sucking sea.

Last Anglo-Russo Goal was Edin Berg. Of natives, Elly and I alone hazarded this expedition. Plotting multiple courses, homaging mighty lamas, swallowing monsoons, led on by gaping snaking gorges, at the last we faced the final dinner.

Elly and I, in the lead, not in tails, swung into the George, and open arms of Dr. Slesser, sheathed in smiles, Kenneth and Tommy, rows of pillars of the Club, and Sir John Hunt who was the conqueror of Everest. Dinners downed, all rose as one, and bubbled up the Mound to the Clubrooms. Crowds had gathered. The excitement was terrific. And here – peak of the week – Red Snows flashed past two hundred goggled eyes, never have we seen such Cinema. 'Here was a Summit made,' declared the great ovation, and another brick was laid for salvation of the nations.

from THE SCOTTISH MOUNTAINEERING
CLUB JOURNAL *1961*

A MEETING WITH DOLPHIN

PETER HARDING

It was rare to meet other climbers or even people at [Black Rocks] Cromford. But one winter's day, early in 1944, I wandered round the North Face to find a huge party of climbers gathered at the foot of Sand Buttress. One of them was engaged in a wrestling match (this was before I had invented the modern hand-jam technique) with the lower part of Stonnis Crack. Remarks about 'the critical eye of the local expert' from one of the party soon demoralised the climber into descent. A friendly leer invited 'the local expert' to show how it was done. I had managed the climb previously, finding it not without difficulty. However, when one is addressed as 'the local expert' one has certain obligations to the home crag. I volunteered to lead a rope, and did so with, fortunately, less apparent difficulty than hidden trepidation. Two or three stalwarts – of the Leeds University Climbing Club, I learned – followed appropriately.

It was whilst standing at the top of Stonnis Arête that I noticed a rather extraordinary-looking character at the foot of the climb – a tall lanky figure in a black overcoat and maroon paratrooper beret who had been a spectator of the antics on Stonnis Crack. He looked blue with cold and was shivering visibly. Under one arm he carried a small attache case; hands thrust deep in pockets and trouser bottoms tucked into stockings. He wore a scruffy-looking pair of ordinary black shoes.

'Are you going to have a go, Arthur?' chorused the LUCC. This clinched my thought that the fellow was the club wag.

Arthur disappeared down the nose of the buttress and reappeared at the foot of Stonnis Crack. He put his attache case carefully down, at which everyone laughed – pulling his leg, I thought. Within the space of time occupied by a couple of grunts the black overcoat and red beret were beside me at the top of Stonnis Arête, hands once again thrust deep in overcoat pockets. He still looked cold.

'That was quick,' I said. 'My name's Peter Harding.'

A typical enigmatic smile creased his face. He extracted a woollen-mitted hand from one coat pocket, extending it towards me.

'Arthur Dolphin,' he said.

from ' A Rock-Climbing Apprenticeship'
RUCKSACK CLUB JOURNAL *1960–1963*

THE ART OF CLIMBING DOWN GRACEFULLY
A compendium of commonly-used Ploys ...

TOM PATEY

Modern climbing is becoming fiercely competitive. Every year marks the fall of another Last Great Problem, or yet another Last Great Problem Climber. Amid this seething anthill, one must not overlook the importance of Staying Alive.

This is why I propose to devote a few lines to 'The Art of Climbing Down Gracefully' – the long, dedicated Decline to Dignified Decrepitude.

I have had another title suggested, viz: 'How to be a top climber without actually climbing.' This is not only misleading – it makes a travesty of this article. One must assume that respect has been earned honourably on the field of battle and not by mere subterfuge. It is in order to maintain this respect, that one employs certain little subtleties that would ill befit a brash impostor.

In short, this is a compendium for Mountaineers – not mountebanks!

1. The 'Off-Form' ploy

This one is as old as the hills but still widely used. Few climbers will admit to being 'on form'. Everyone would feel uneasy if they did. Again, a climber who was 'on form' during the morning can be feeling 'off-form' by early afternoon. If an interval of forty-eight hours or so has elapsed between climbs, he may talk of being 'out of condition'. If the interval is a month or longer, he may justifiably consider himself to be 'out of training'. Unfortunately, so many climbers take their training seriously nowadays (with press-ups, dumb-bells, running up the down-escalators in tube stations, etc.) that it is unwise to be out of training when in the company of dedicated mountaineers. A friendly invitation to Bowles Rocks Mountaineering Gymnasium can be the natural outcome of such a remark.

2. The 'Too Much Like Hard Work' ploy
This is the Englishman's favourite gambit when climbing (or not climbing) north of the border. Many Scottish cliffs are admittedly remote by comparison with Shepherd's Crag, but I have heard such remarks at Glen Coe, where you can scarcely leave the main road without bumping your head against an overhang. No, this simply will not do! Far more effective is the Sassenach's Second Choice Gambit, viz:

3. The 'Chossy Climb' ploy
'Poxy', 'Chossy', 'Spastic' and 'Rubbish' are all terms characteristically used by English and Welsh climbers to denigrate Scottish routes which they have either failed to climb or failed to find (without searching too minutely).

Eyewitness reports could in fact reveal that Spiderman made repeated attempts to overcome the crux, before he was ignominiously repulsed and left hanging in a tangle of slings and étriers. But this is at variance with the official Party Line, which stresses Spiderman's disgust on finding the initial holds cloaked in greenery. His aesthetic senses had been so offended that he had instantly abandoned the climb and spent the day more profitably in a nearby hostelry.

Spiderman's reputation remains untarnished. It is – the luckless pioneers who are singled out for derision just as they were preparing to crow over his downfall – a neat demonstration of how to convert defeat into a moral triumph. A really selective 'route gourmet' like Spiderman can sometimes spend years in a fruitless quest for perfection without ever finding a climb to which he can justifiably commit himself.

4. The 'Ice-Man' ploy
This is the exiled Scotsman's counter-ploy when lured on to English outcrops. 'I'm a Snow and Ice Man myself!' is a fairly safe assertion at Harrison's where it is highly unlikely that you will be given the opportunity to demonstrate your skills.

Oddly enough, the first time I heard this line it was spoken by an Englishman. The scene was the now defunct Chalet Biolay at Chamonix, which at that time (1952) was almost entirely populated by Oxbridge types

– pleasant fellows, although all unmistakably tarred with the same brush, and handicapped by their common background. Amid this select group one particular rank outsider stuck out like a sore thumb. I was captivated by his facility for saying the wrong thing at the wrong time. ('I say! You two lads have got definite promise. If one of you gets himself killed would the other please look me up? I'm looking for a partner for the Brenva.')

This man had swallowed Smythe and Murray piecemeal and could regurgitate selected phrases from either author with gay abandon. His impact on the Establishment was shattering: 'All this talk of VIs and A3s bores me to tears,' he would announce in a loud voice, addressing no one in particular. 'Show me the Englishman – Yes; show me the Englishman, I say – who can stand upright in his steps, square set to the slope, and hit home hard and true, striking from the shoulder! There must be very few of us Ice-Men left around. Ice-Manship may be a forgotten craft but it's still the Cornerstone of Mountaineering. Never forget that! Any fool can monkey about on rock overhangs but *it takes craft and cunning to beat the Brenva!*'

He got away with it too. The 'Great Mixed Routes' are so seldom in condition that a dedicated Ice-man can remain in semi-permanent cold storage without much fear of exposure.

5. The 'Secret Cliff' ploy

This dark horse is seldom seen in the Pass, but makes a belated appearance at closing time. He speaks slowly and reluctantly with a far-away look in his eyes. 'We've been sizing up a new crag,' he eventually admits after much probing, 'amazing why nobody ever spotted it before, but then climbers don't get around much nowadays... We're not giving away any details of course until we've worked it out... Should be good for at least twenty more top-grade routes...'

None of these routes ever appear in print, but this too can be explained away at a later day by the Anti-Guide-Book ploy: 'Why deprive others of the joys of original exploration? We don't want such a superb crag to suffer the fate of Cloggy, and become vulgarised by meaningless variations.'

Evasiveness can be finely pointed.

'What route did you climb today then?'

'Dunno, we haven't named it yet!'

All these ploys find their ideal medium in the 'Solo Man' ploy.

6. The 'Solo Man' ploy

The subtlety of this ploy is that no one, apart from Solo Man, knows how he spent the day. From the moment he disappears at the double over the first

convenient hillock, his movements are shrouded in mystery. H
accomplice, and he holds all the aces.

'Had a look at Vector today... Quite thin.' (Solo Man had inc
at Vector. He did not like what he saw.) Or: 'Forgot the Guidebook
where I was... damn'd good route all the same!... Yes, it probabl
ascent, but I won't be entering it. You can't expect me to remem
one route is just the same as another as far as I'm concerned.' Or.
Tension Traverse pretty tricky.... a rope would have been quite u

7. The 'Responsible Family Man' ploy

This is the most stereotyped of all the non-climbing ploys. How
the marriage altar (halter?) proved the graveyard of a mountaine
tions? The little camp follower who cooked the meals and darned ev
socks is suddenly transformed into an all-demanding, insatiab
whose grim disapproval makes strong men wilt in their *kletterschu*
ing weekends become less and less frequent and, despite well-mea
from climbing friends on the benefits of 'the Pill', it is only a year b
union is blessed with child. In many cases this is the natural end of
but a few die-hards still put in an annual appearance – pale shrunke
who glance nervously over their shoulders before they speak.

'Don't seem to get away much nowadays,' they mutter despe
'Can't take the same risks – unfair on the kids.' So saying, they leap i
Volvos or Mini-Coopers and become power-crazy charioteers,
down crash barriers and terrorising the walking populace. Back ho
scream to a halt in a cloud of dust and shrink back into normal dim

'Sorry you had to wait up for me, Dear – just dropped in for a q
with the lads and got a bit carried away.'

This is very effective because it contains an element of pathos, an
a lump to the throat of the most hardened of Hard-Men. Some
climbers, no longer able to make the grade on the crags, have been
to contemplate matrimony as the only honourable way out.

8. The 'Wrong Gear' ploy

With a little foresight it is always an easy matter to bring the wrong
ment for the day, and then allow everyone to share your vexation.
man will turn up for a winter assault on Point Five Gully, wearing
new PA's.

'Great God! I didn't expect to find snow on the Ben this late. J
luck...'

For a week-end's climbing at Harrison's he will have borrowed a
High Altitude Everest Boots.

e needs no

eed looked
… No idea
was a first
ber details:
'Found the
seful …'

often has
er's ambi-
erybody's
le virago
he. Climb-
nt advice
efore the
all things,
n ghosts,

ndently.
nto their
mowing
me they
ensions.
uick one

d brings
ageing
known

equip-
Such a
brand

st my

pair of

l Thing. Not much use on the small hold
ol.'
ber who survived an entire summer at

her,' we told him.
d, 'and I'm stuck here till my hardware
York three weeks ago and the last I heard

er reached its destination. First it was in
amonix. From Chamonix it was redirected
stake his claim. We left him a month later
the Bar National.
dammed luck,' he complained bitterly.

ty can be a useful handicap, but before it
t must be something immediately obvious.
Ninthrop Young climbed the Grépon with a
al.)
cely worth the discomfort it entails. Everyone
llans used to perform with a whimsical knee-
dislocated every time he turned in his bed,
ed him to Gaurishankar and back, with only
nent. Joe Brown, when not putting up new
l a disc in his back garden. Raymond Lambert,
n better when all his toes had been amputated.
avity nearer the footholds. There are many more
over adversity. Too many, in fact. Extracting
younger generation is like wringing blood from
an old War Wound from the Dardenelles, your
te.

ploy
acture Faulty Alarm-clocks for weekend climbers.
nanimate object for your misfortunes, than to
s …

ine, a Mr X, always made a point of discussing the
before turning in for the night. Companions, who
d to rise and breakfast himself, were dismayed to
ht of an irate Mr X. pointing accusingly towards an
nysteriously appeared at their bedside overnight.

'You promised to waken me when the alarm went off!' he thundered. 'And here I've been, lying awake not knowing the time, and now it's too late to attempt anything worthwhile! Really, this is too bad!' etcetera.

11. Various time-wasting tactics

Let us assume that the climbing party has been roused at an early hour by some misguided fellow whose insomnia rendered the Alarm Clock manoeuvre futile. What additional stratagem may be adopted to delay or divert the party on its way to the crags? There is a wide choice. One of the leading exponents of this art was a certain Captain 'Jungle' of the Royal Marine Commando, whose name will be recalled with affection by several generations of National Servicemen. 'We shall proceed carefully and deliberately, walking in single file,' Jungle would announce in portentous tones. 'I myself will go in front, and I shall be demonstrating what we in the Cliff Assault Wing call 'Commando Pace'. 'Commando Pace' ensures that we arrive Battle-fit at our chosen destination, however distant that may be.'

A close observer would have detected a twitch in the rugged features of the senior NCO instructor. He alone knew that 'Commando Pace' was Jungle's private invention, and that it was designed to ensure that Jungle never reached his chosen destination. Considerable acrobatic skill was required to follow in Jungle's footsteps. Many young recruits fell over as they attempted the slow transfer of body weight from one foot to the other. As Jungle himself once remarked, 'it was like learning to walk all over again'.

Among the various philanthropic diversions, the most praiseworthy and time-consuming is adding stones to wayside cairns ('Somebody must set an example').

Cooking is a very effective form of procrastination, but the all-important meal – breakfast – offers little scope to the culinary expert unless he be a Porridge King. Porridge making is a specialised craft, and great care must be exercised using the traditional wooden 'spirtle' instead of an ordinary spoon. This can easily be mislaid, but is essential to the consistency of the finished product.

Sandwiches take time to prepare; if you are safety conscious enough to refuse to leave for a day on the hill without forty-eight hour's emergency rations, it can well be early afternoon before you can justifiably set out.

12. The 'Föhn Wind' and other Bad Weather Ploys

With spine-chilling candour, René Desmaison wrote: 'I have heard it said that it takes more courage to retreat than to advance. I cannot share these sentiments!' M Desmaison is of course a Frenchman writing for Frenchmen, but he would scarcely get away with this sort of remark in the *Alpine Journal*.

Not by a long chalk. It strikes at the very foundations of British Alpinism and undermines our most deep-rooted traditional ploy – 'Giving the Mountain Best'.

It was during my first Alpine season that I came into contact with the ever popular Zermatt gambit. An elderly gentleman, wearing knickerbockers and armed with an alpenstock, would totter out on to his hotel balcony, raising aloft one pre-moistened, trembling index finger.

'Aha! – I thought as much,' he would chuckle grimly. 'The Föhn wind is in the offing! No climbing for you, young fellow, for a week at least!'

I was a bit frustrated by this and the next time I went up to a hut I determined to follow the advice of local Alpine Guides. If they don't know, who does? Thirty-two Guides slept at the Couvercle Hut that night, and they all got up at 2am like a major volcanic eruption. One Guide, with an attractive female client in tow, walked out, prodded the snow with an ice-axe, sniffed the night air, and without a word retired to his bed. It later transpired that this was the celebrated Armand Charlet. Thirty-one silent Guides looked at each other, shook their heads, and retired likewise. We woke at 8am to find brilliant sunshine.

'Pourquoi?' I demanded wrathfully of one, 'Pourquoi?' (It was one of the few French words at my disposal, so I used it twice.)

'Charlet a dit!' he said reverently, mentally crossing himself, 'C'est trop dangereux!'

'Pourquoi?' I demanded again, not without reason.

'Charlet a dit!' he repeated, waving his arms towards a cloudless horizon, 'Tempête de neige, qui va venir bientôt sans doubt.'

The last time I saw Charlet he was heading for the valley with the attractive blonde in close attendance. It was the first day of what proved to be a ten-day record heat wave. I remembered the time-honoured Victorian advice, 'Follow the Old Guide – he knows best!' There was more than a grain of truth in that statement...

In the hands of a reliable weather-lore expert the Bad Weather ploy can be practically infallible. Such a man can spend an entire Alpine season without setting boot to rock, simply by following the bad weather around, and consistently turning up in the wrong place at the wrong time.

13. *The 'Greater Ranges' ploy*

Historians tell us that Frank Smythe only began to function properly above 20,000ft. This adds up to a pretty considerable handicap, when you consider how much of his life must have been spent at lower altitudes. It is all part of the mystique which surrounds The Men who are expected to Go High.

For this ploy some previous Himalayan experience is essential; it may involve a tourist weekend in Kathmandu, a transcendental meditation with the Maharishi, or merely bribing Chris Briggs to append your signature to the ceiling of the Everest Room at Pen y Gwyrd (he will probably refuse but there is no harm in trying). Once the aura has formed, you can hardly go wrong. You can patrol the foot of Stanage with all the invested authority of an Everester. No one expects you to climb. It is enough that you retain a soft spot for your humble origins.

'This is all very different from the South Col!' you can remark crisply, as you watch bikini-clad girls swarming over the rocks like chameleons. Any off-the-cuff comment of this nature goes down well, and gives them something to talk about after you have moved on. As I said before, nobody really expects a man who has survived the South Col to risk his neck on a paltry outcrop.

'I'm a Gritstone Man myself!' you can admit with pride, and then proceed to qualify the statement, 'But let us keep our sense of proportion, and remember that British crags are not an end in themselves but a Springboard to the Greater Ranges. The Battle of Waterloo was won on the playing fields of Eton! That is something we must all remember ...'

Old Winthrop Young summed it all up in his Valedictory Address to the Alpine Club: 'These armies of young boys and girls practising their wholesome open-air callisthenics, flooding the valleys in hale and hearty chase of pins-and-needles upon which to thread their athletic limbs upside down ... What was their love to ours? ... the pursuit of the distant white Domes ... etc ... etc ... etc.'

14. The 'Base Camp Martyr' ploy

This philanthropic character always contrives to be the Odd Man Out.

'Look here, chaps! Let's be sensible about this. A rope of two makes much faster time than a threesome, and I'm only going to hold you back. It's the team effort that counts, after all. If we get Two Men to the Top we will not have failed! I may be kicking my heels at base camp but I'll be with you in spirit: you both know that. Good Luck and Good Hunting!'

15. The' Weak Member on the Rope' ploy

A Past-President of the Aberdeen University Mountaineering Club used this ploy with such remarkable success that he was never once crag-bound during his entire term of Office. 'No hard climbs for me today, Tom,' he would sigh heavily. 'I'm afraid I've got a weak member on the rope – can't afford to extend myself.'

Where Charlie managed to find his chain-gang of incompetents was an irritating mystery. Even more irritating was the fact that most of them were good-looking, impressionable popsies who venerated Charlie as a natural successor to Sir John Hunt. We threw snowballs and shouted at them from our lofty heights, but only earned their silent contempt. Only on one occasion did we find Charlie unchaperoned by his brood. That was when he pulled his Master Ploy. 'Snow climbing today, Tom? Surely not!' he exclaimed in genuine astonishment. 'I'm going to build an igloo! Perfect snow conditions for Igloo Building. You won't find better conditions for fifty years.'

I commend this to anyone as a useful Winter Ploy, adaptable to all weathers and all conditions. Very few people, apart from Eskimos, know anything at all about igloos.

16. The 'Old Man of the Mountains' ploy

The essence of this ploy is that you cannot teach an Old Dog new tricks, viz:

'Play up, and play the game' – but learn the rules first. Ignore the rules, and the game is no longer worth playing. Present-day rock acrobats don't accept exposure as part of the game. They protect themselves every yard of the way with ridiculous little gadgets of all shapes and sizes. The designations are unimportant – they are un-British in name and un-British in nature! Gone are the days of Kirkus and Edwards, when a leader had sufficient moral conviction to run out 150ft of lightweight hemp before taking a hitch! Who wants to join the clanking Slab-queues to witness the crucifixion of a long-loved friend. I found *this* at Abraham's Ledge on the Crowberry last week!' (unwrapping a rusty piton which he carries around for this purpose). 'Covet it young man at your peril! My race may be run, but never let it be said that I helped beget a generation of Cream-Puff climbers.'

To qualify for the Hob-Nail Brigade the speaker need not have reached the allotted three-score-and-ten, but he should at least cultivate an aura of venerability and familiarise himself with the appropriate vocabulary, viz.:

Acrobats, monkeys, engineers, technicians, and steeple-jacks	the Modern Generation
hare-brained escapade	a new route
Munich mechanisation	artificial climbing
Death-or-Glory fanatics	Hard-men
Dangle-and-Whack merchants	Aid-men
The Golden Age	pre-1930
The Iron Age	post- 1930
A sound climber	an old climber
A cautious climber	a very slow climber

A mature climber	an ageing incompetent
A die-hard traditionalist	a rude old man
Unjustifiable	perhaps quite hard
Utterly unjustifiable	quite hard
A great mixed route	a snow plod
A courageous decision	chickening out
An Alpine Start	the time to leave the *Bar National*

from MOUNTAIN 16 *and*
ONE MAN'S MOUNTAINS 1971

ALL OUR YESTERDAYS

ALLAN MANSON

Bloody creep, who does he think he is? Right Pete, we'll show these bastards. Murdered Almscliff, huh, bloody creeps. Just what right have they got to thrust their way into our domain? What right have they got to be better climbers than us? Murdered Almscliff, more like a sordid mugging, not just a rape but a gang-bang.

God are we sick. Bloody Lancastrians, they should stick to their clog-dancing and tripe quarries. The King and his Court are deeply upset. Revolutionary bastards. No longer are we the hunters. We have become the hunted. No longer will we be able to strut around our roost pouncing upon any unfortunate foreign prey.

'Is he watching, Peter?' Cough, Cough. Ah that's better now just watch and learn. Look at us, look at us, we can do this climb and you can't. Ha, ha ... Oh! what a pity, can't you get up there? Ho ho! Watch me! Put on anaemic look number five. Shuffle up to the rock, reach up for secret hold number one, explode into a frenzy of skill and strength. Move number two, balance on left feet in ridiculous out of balance position (out of balance to you, you sucker – don't try it though, you might do it and call our bluff) take both hands off to scratch arse, pick nose and adjust balls – careful here, at least 5'9" off ground. Some wise guy says:

'Been here before? More like climbing by numbers.'

Oh, so that's how it's going to be is it? Well my fine friend you can't expect to come to the Crag and not get your fingers charred – burn baby burn. Climbing by numbers eh! Right, OK then, odd numbers only and your right hand stuck in your pocket. Follow that then wise guy!

That was in the good old days. Jeez those golden halcyon days. The memories flit back like a recurring dream. What a life it was, Saturday at the Crag, Sunday at the Crag, Monday, Tuesday, Wednesday, Thursday and Friday at the Crag. We were great; the ultimate. Can't wait to get on those Derbyshire crags. Ken says we should murder the place – yes this is true, we'll murder the place.

But who cares about Derbyshire or Lancashire or that nasty white stuff when you've got the Crag, with it's endless opportunities for new additions? Christ just think of all those vast two feet expanses of rock with no routes on them. A brief flurry of activity and there are about ten or eleven succulent new pickings. What makes us do it? Quite simply fear – fear that someone else will sneak in ahead of us. After all Woodsy does pass it every morning going to work.

The van settles into its own well-worn rut and parks itself next to Geoff's limousine. Humm, so Geoff and John are here already. We look up and see Syrup leaping off the crux where Encore will eventually go. (Pasquill isn't the only one who doesn't fall off.) What sort of work-out are we going to have Pete? The five 'Morrells', OK. Hell fire that was harder than I've ever remembered it. Oh that's why. I've forgotten to take off my rucksack, Donkey Jacket, and Onitsukas. 'Bull-shitter,' says Pete as he ploughs his way up The Gypsy. It's going to be a great night. Every day and night at the Crag was like a sparkling diamond, equalled only by the occasional gem at Caley.

Those were the days. The sun always shone at Almscliff. But where does it shine now – out of Pasquill's arse!

We creep up to the Crag. 'Christ Pete there's some strangers on Fluted Columns, keep out of sight we'll go round the back way.' Hell, I wish I knew what *he* looked like. Daren't try Crucifix Arête – haven't done it for two days, might run out of strength, might have forgotten where the holds are. Shit, is that Pasquill or not? We do the unimaginable. We approach *them*.

'How do! Good climb yer on, what else have you done today? Have you? Mmmmm, great climb is Three Chockstones Chimney. Had a good drive over from Lancashire?'

'Lancashire, cor fackin'ell mate, we jast arrived from the Smoke ain't we?'

Thank God for that.

'Right Pete back to work – try this but you mustn't use yer feet!'

Our pride, our reputations survive another day. But one of these days our paths are going to cross. .

Oh God, Oh no, Pete, Pete, over here by these boulders, look on that rucksack, it says H.P. and I don't reckon it means brown sauce!

from LEEDS UNIVERSITY MOUNTAINEERING
CLUB JOURNAL 1974

DESCRIPTIONS OF ROUTES FROM THE TRYFAN AND IDWAL GUIDEBOOKS

JOHN MENLOVE EDWARDS

TABLE CLIMB A fine open climb which tends to be slippery when wet. Then, one may well feel insecure.

ROUTE I A route, scenic and circuitous

ROUTE II Perhaps the only reason to prefer this route to its senior partner is that it starts less far uphill! It seems to have more rock, too.

OLD MAN BUTTRESS 230ft The quantity of rock on this route is negligible, but that twenty feet is interesting.

WHINBERRY ROUTE Interesting enough, mainly up steep vegetation. It is worth doing and may, with use, degenerate into a rock climb!

YEW BUTTRESS A short, severe and good little route, harder than one would expect, more difficult than Cheek, with which it is not comparable.

PROGRESSIVE CRACKS A good strenuous little climb. It is a pity that it is so little! It has sport with the climber, yet is not unsafe.

FLAKE CROSS Two good pitches for nailed boots. With rubbers they lose their point.

GREAT FLAKE CRACK The crack is comparable with the long one on Dinas Mot's Lorraine, but steeper. The grass cannot be politely compared to anything.

SOAPGUT   Hard Severe in nails which are proper, a good deal easier in rubbers, perhaps only Very Difficult. No deviations by desire or apparent possibility. Now it is clean it has become easier but it is still an inspiring line, although only really a drain.

TWISTING GULLY   Not a stereotype route. Only Moderately Difficult as a rule.

TWISTING GULLY BUTTRESS   It slants like a strip of weather bordering. It is steep only for the first few feet and on these the holds are excellent. The rest is sprinkled with grass and very easy, but the left wall saves it from the ruck of the impossibly indefinite.

EAST ARÊTE   The climb starts off well but soon, like the Gully, it degenerates into a semblance of a steep hillside. A worthy route to the summit when alone or meditative.

PIECE BY PIECE CLIMB   The rock is thoroughly rotten in general and in particular, but, though the position is exposed, the technical standard is nowhere considerable.

HOTHOUSE CRACK   The climb is quite interesting and not too energetic. It is neither much exposed nor much enclosed, and the level is kept up. It is full of a large variety of flowering plants which all show the most luxuriant growth.

DEVIL'S DUMP   The resemblance to a Dump is remarkable, and is due to a prevalence of various types of herbage, the projections of agglomerate on the steep section, and to the general melancholy appearance… It will be easier when some of the surface rubbish is discarded.

DEVIL'S KITCHEN   It is more a great type than a good pitch, yet the pitch alone would deserve attention anywhere. Standard: Mild Severe perhaps, due to its character. It is however less hard technically than the start of the Staircase and less confusing than the finish of Hanging Garden Gully.

DEVIL'S APPENDIX   A very airy climb about the most exciting part of the cliff, with bad rock. Ranks definitely with the open air group. There are no large ledges on it.

from CLIMBERS' CLUB GUIDES *1937 and 1940*

STYLE IS THE MAN

JIM PERRIN

Cloggy on a warm Sunday is an abominable place these days; the game's become serious, unreal, the climbers are no longer at play. Perhaps you could have seen the same in the 1950s, those studious men from Oxbridge struggling earnestly with the great climbs of a decade before or more, whilst the Rock and Ice played their stylish games regardless of the anguished decisions being made in the silence below. The Rock and Ice! How they laughed, and how their humour permeated through to the 1960s when the cliff was alive with badinage, good climbing, and the systematic destruction of myth. How different things are today; static leaders and a sullen silence prevail. So many climbers and so little movement; glossy-shelled snails each clinging to their little pieces of wall, tenuously, flicking their antennae over the next few feet, trailing their ropes like slime plastered to the rock by a proliferation of runners, their necks infinitely retractable. There was a time when the situation was better than this.

Climbing is a remarkable sport; it blends the simple and the complex, the humorous and the serious, it is one of the few spheres where physical action can express a full and affirmative response to life (dance is perhaps another such).

Above all it is fun, a thing to be enjoyed, to be experienced to the full. Most climbers nowadays no more give themselves to a situation and live it through than they would if their feet stayed firmly on the ground. By technological expertise they raise themselves to the top of the crag and in doing so seem hardly to move. I don't want to be interpreted as saying not only must you move, you must be seen to be moving, but where's the style gone? Climbing has lost something, and for such loss received no abundant recompense; the activities of a climber like Drummond constitute a travesty of human achievement; a climbing bureaucrat whose productions are so tightly bound by red tape and rehearsal of procedure that they have lost any human validity.

A changed state for which I can give no adequate account. It could stem from the philosophy that any sector of climbing is merely training for a greater one. (Is John Gill any less than brilliant because his horizons end at sixty feet?) It could stem from the fashionable ascendancy of limestone as

Britain's premier outcrop rock; the style of climbing required by limestone is generally one of adjustment rather than a dynamic one. With certain notable exceptions the climbing on limestone is tedious in the extreme, a fact which cannot be levelled against sandstone or gritstone where the emphasis is on dynamism, speed and commitment. But most likely it stems from modern protection allowing many more climbers to venture into realms once the preserve of the most competent and highly motivated. Whatever the cause, the fact remains of a decline in recent years of climbing style.

The story of the tortoise and the hare comes to mind; tortoises are cold-eyed, lumbering, slow, and exceedingly well-protected. They live for a long time and in doing so make the whole process seem rather absurd. Above all they are totally devoid of style. Hares on the other hand, are fast, stylish, and vulnerable; they give the impression of being alive. To make another observation, I take the Eastern meditative religions, Acid and Cannabis in their common usage, the preoccupation with the merely fanciful in literature, and other like outlets from a modern civilisation, as constituting a denial of the life-force within us. I see them as anaesthesia and a renunciation of the fullest instinctual modes of life. Likewise I see climbing devoid of grace and style, where every move made is laboured and pondered over, and infallibly protected, as a denial of the potentialities of the sport. In the story of the tortoise and the hare, the tortoise's winning is made to matter. Of course it doesn't; the tale is a social parable to make us feel that we are getting somewhere within a strictured society that will only move at the pace of its slowest member, and would thus happily make tortoises out of us all. Civilisation inexorably catches up with those anarchic offshoots from it where a degree of free expression can be found, and this is now happening with climbing. The safety-mongers, the educationalists, the organisers, journalists and dogmatists, are structuring climbing and in consequence destroying it. I do not advocate a return to first material principles; we are too far along the road now, the rat-race momentum has become too strong. But if only the emphasis would shift; not the achievement but the act itself is of primary importance, and style is the individual expression of an act. My admiration goes out to what is forceful and brave, vital and gay; my loathing only to those ponderous, grim-faced salesmen who cry their wares to the heavens and themselves remain iron-clad in the mud.

Climbing is to be experienced, it is an existential act; it has no point, it will bear the weight of no consideration beyond an instinctual affirmative to experience. Give me those vital, impassioned, dynamic climbers bred from a situation where climbing, through the risk factor, was felt to be meaningful as experience. An awareness of death presupposes the individual's awareness of his own life; movement expresses that awareness.

In climbing there are pockets of hope: Syrett, Livesey, and Wood in Yorkshire, Myhill in Derbyshire, the Cannings of a few years ago in Cornwall, the mercurial career of Alan Rouse, and the Bacchanalia of Minks and Molyneux; these have produced movements when climbing has been alive. From this I take comfort, and from the potentiality in climbing for self-realisation and self-awareness informed by a vital simplicity of action; that instinctual response of the individual to his situation which gives rise to our concept of style.

from ROCKSPORT *August 1973*

A TIGER'S FLING

ALLAN AUSTIN

This short article is written for all of you who wonder what a first ascent is really like, for those who would like to know what goes on in the mind of the bold and courageous tiger when he's up there on some high and exposed wall, fearlessly pushing on through a maze of overhangs, pausing elegantly now and then to work out the line of his great new classic, before moving up to some fearfully exposed stance with only the merest protuberance to hang his belay sling from. This could be the story of one such ascent, or any first, but it took place on Heron Crag in the English Lakes and it's called Flanker, or is it Spec Crack? It could be either because we got sort of mixed up and lost a bit, and started here and finished over there, and only sorted it all out when we got off the crag back to our boots again.

I went over to Eskdale with Eric Metcalfe (from here on called Matie because he is not) to do these two lines that I had previously espied. The reason we went then instead of waiting till it dried out was because Pat knew all about them. I knew he knew, because in a weak moment I had shown him, and Pat was still on holiday, but would be back next week. So we went and cursed the moss and the wet and our socks which wore out in holes, but most of all we cursed Pat for not taking a longer holiday.

It looked steep. It was steep, so I said I would belay on a ledge about twenty-foot up and Matie could do the first pitch. I messed around chipping spikes and trying to insert chocks, until Matie soloed up and pointed out the tree which he said I might as well use, which I did. Then Matie started out on his pitch. There were two possible ways, straight up a clean, steep sort of scoop, or out onto a moss wall on the right. So thinking in our cunning little minds that the shortest route would be the steepest and therefore the hardest, we tried the roundabout one. Out onto the wall went Matie, only it was steep and hard, so we decided the clean direct way was for us, but it had a lid on it. So once again onto the wall, this time a bit higher up and onto a ledge where Matie loitered and tried to get a runner. Then he announced that it was too steep so he had better have a piton. From my stance on my comfortable ledge I was well placed to administer a stern warning on the degenerate ways of ironmongers, but he ignored me and planted one. It belonged to a well-known variety of pitons, probably the commonest and best known of all. It was a 'Manky Piton'. And there he stayed perched on the wall like a kitehawk. Presently he dropped something, but it was only a threader, deserting like a rat from a sinking ship, to hide away in the bracken at the bottom. Presently he announced his retirement and seconded me for the job, and said he was coming back. At this I got all crafty and thought I would like the piton tested, so I offered to lower him off. But he declined.

Then it was my turn to mess about on the bulge and examine the piton, a poor specimen indeed. It was hammered lengthways along a horizontal crack, and the way it flaunted its vital statistics would have amounted to indecent exposure anywhere else. But I was the only one there and I wasn't impressed. So I chipped, threaded and wedged till I got a single line thread. Our immoral piton pulled out without a blow being struck, a cowardly act. Then I tried and tried again to climb up but I couldn't, so I paused and thought about it. If it had been dry... And why shouldn't it be, when I carried in my pocket those excellent towels known as handkerchiefs. So I mopped and dried the cliff in front, or at least the parts that mattered, lavishing as much care on that bit of rock as a mother on her new born baby. So I got over the bulge and went to nest in a crack on the left.

Above was an obvious line of handsome flakes embedded in moss and grass and leading up to easy ground. I was doubtful. They would have to go, but in spite of all my digging and scraping they refused. They were not loose flakes after all but jugs, great jugs fastened firmly onto mother rock. But still the fear of rock was upon me and I messed about and almost fell off in sheer fright when I recalled that by now I must be at least forty-foot out. But I remembered that today I was a tiger, and not to be afraid. Then the stance arrived and tied me on to three different belays so that I could sit down and enjoy the climb. But Matie arrived and would not let me.

1   Bouldering at Fort Collins, Colorado. John Long tackles Pinch Overhang
on the Mental Block. *Photo: Michael Kennedy*

2, 3 Cerro Torre, Patagonia – one of the world's most challenging peaks. The first ascent in 1974 was made by Casimiro Ferrari, Mario Conti, Giuseppe (Pino) Negri and Daniele Chiappa who took the West Face (right – in the upper picture) and turned the delicate summit encrustations (*inset*) by a rising traverse to the right. The South and East Faces offer a range of very difficult routes. The ice encrusted North Ridge on the left having defeated a number of attempts from the late 1970s (the 1959 claim now considered unreliable) was finally climbed in 2005 by Rolando Garibotti, Ermanno Salvaterra and Alessandro Beltrami. *Photos: Daniele Chiappa*

4 Gritstone climbing on Almscliff, Yorkshire – John Syrett making the first ascent (?) of Encore (E2/5c) in 1973. An earlier ascent by Eric Lillie, with a protection piton, discovered after Syrett's claim, was not given first ascent credit in the guidebook. *Photo: John Harwood*

5   Dale Bard leads Butterballs (5.11) the final pitch of the four-pitch Nabisco Wall, on the Cookie Cliff, Yosemite. This is one of the finest of scores of hard free climbs made on the smaller Yosemite cliffs during the 1970s following the introduction of well-designed nuts and the revolutionary 'Friends'. *Photo: Gene Foley*

6   The Bar National, Chamonix, for years the spiritual European home of english-speaking alpinists. *Photo: John Powell*

7　Tough conditions during an attempt on the North Face of Les Droites in 1964 typify the alpine challenge before major improvements in ice climbing gear in the 1970s. For years this photograph in Snell Sports in Chamonix 'thrilled' ambitious alpinists.　*Photo: Heli Wagner*

8   Bolder expedition tactics began to be employed in the 1970s following improvements in clothing, gear, food and cooking equipment: here Malcolm Howells, Martin Boysen, Joe Brown and Mo Anthoine bivouac during the first ascent of Trango Tower in 1976. *Photo: Tony Riley*

9, 10   Reinhold Messner was the central figure in Himalayan climbing during the 1970s whose emergency traverse of Nanga Parbat (with his brother Günther who, sadly, died) astounded mountaineers. Despite severe frostbite injuries *(below)* Messner made a near alpine-style ascent of Hidden Peak (1974) with Peter Habeler, and two years later the pair (as part of a conventional expedition) made the first ascent of Everest without bottled oxygen. Messner's soloed new routes on Nanga Parbat (1980) and Everest (1982) were similarly ground-breaking. In 1986 he became the first person to climb all fourteen 8000m peaks.

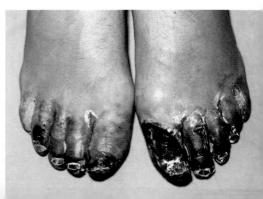

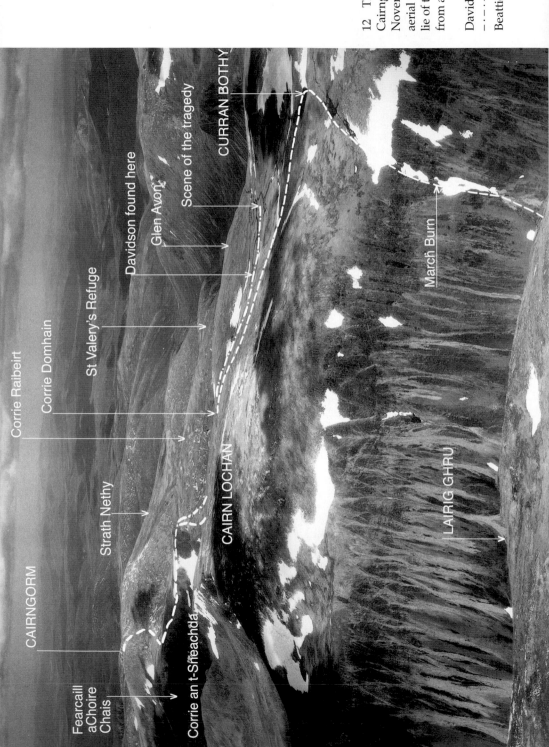

12 The scene of the Cairngorm tragedy of November 1971. This aerial photo shows the lie of the land in summer from above Breariach.

Davidson's route: – ⋅ – ⋅ – ⋅ –

Beattie's route: – – – –

Over there, about twenty feet away across the wall on the left was a steep bulging crack, liberally garnished with grass and choss and things, served with a dash of loose rock. He wanted it. I agreed, he could have it. But he seemed to think that his second's place was over there on that ledge beneath the crack. I could see that his blood was up and he was thirsting for revenge, so I went, rather sourly I admit, because I was thirsting also, and not for the crack. The stance was a sitting one, on some rather damp turf, with the crack rearing up over my head. I inserted a couple of chocks for belays, threw a loop round a block a few feet along the ledge, then spent a long time tying on, delaying the time when Matie would have his fling. Fling being the operative word. Before he set off I pointed out that a large block poised above my head would require care. He agreed to bear it in mind and then he was at it, kicking and shaking the block with gay abandon, sending echoes way down my spine to my boots. Before I had time to tell him what a cad he was, he must have decided that a crushed second was no good, so he took my top belay off, used it for a runner and moved up. I subsided into my pants and took no further interest in him, he was better ignored. There were much nicer things to look at, sheep and such like.

Above me Matie was getting into his stride and down below I was crouched against the rock wondering whether to take shelter under my doubtful block or weather the storm in the open.

'He must be swimming in it,' I thought, 'It's almost as if the cliff is falling down.'

Suddenly there was a commotion up above, and it did. Whilst I was getting my senses back, Matie, who had suddenly appeared alongside me on the stance, explained. The overhang needed gardening, but halfway through the job he decided to have a rest so he had swung down onto a sling. The chockstone round which the sling was threaded had plummeted down, under the combined influence of Matie and gravity until stopped by my head. Then having completed its task it rolled away to join its brothers on the scree below. Matie must have realised I was displeased, for he paused only long enough to accept my offer of an insertable chockstone, a small one this time, before he was back up there sending it down onto my already tender head. Amidst all this muck and manure my last and favourite threader came past, deserting to join its brother below. We were fast losing the necessities of life; things must be hectic up there. As time passed the sounds of toil grew less not so the sods. After a pause he announced that he had reached an area of loose rock. Half an hour of indecision came and went, He would go straight up, but the holds though large and comfortable had a decidedly deciduous air about them. No, the way lay to the right, but that was the way of another climb. To join it was unthinkable.

'It looks sound over to the left, but it's smooth and exposed, no runners either!' Then silence. Suddenly a shout broke the stillness.

'I'm there,' followed after a few minutes with the words, 'but the belays aren't so good.' Thus encouraged I wrung out my trousers and followed.

It was a good effort on Matie's part. (This is the hardman's way of saying that I was hard pressed to follow.) The stance was a small affair, and it was stretching the imagination a bit to call it a stance, but Matie was able to stand there so I suppose it was technically correct. It was obvious from the moment I stood on his foot that I wasn't welcome, and as there was nowhere else to go I stayed just long enough to load myself down with all the slings in Eskdale and started looking for a way on. The top was only thirty feet above and already I could see a runner, so I set off all courageous and bold to finish it off. But it wasn't a runner and it wasn't long before I was wishing I was somewhere else.

I became wedged in a wet greasy crack-cum-niche with my hands on top, or what should have been if it had been more permanent. Laid across the top of my crack like a lid was a stone, a loose one. I began to shake a bit. As the hardmen say, I had got muscle fatigue and started the long involved process leading to a retreat. It begins with some words such as:

'It's a bit loose up here' or It's so slimy it's like trying to catch a frog,' closely followed by 'and it's too steep to rest.'

But there were no encouraging sounds from below, only a stony silence. A hard taskmaster my mate. So I turned back to my stone. Now it's well known that I am a coward so although the stone was only half my size, it will cause no surprise when I say I was frightened. Anyway to cut a long and pitiful story short I girded up my loins and made my summit dash. I got there, after all it was only a matter of three or four feet, and wandered off to find some belays.

Matie's arrival at the top was signalled by a loud crash. 'A super trundle,' he said. It arched right out and landed somewhere amongst the rucksacks. I was annoyed. It should have been mine, I got there first. But there was nothing left to throw down.

from THE YORKSHIRE MOUNTAINEERING
CLUB JOURNAL *1962*

PART 4

ETHICAL DISCUSSIONS

The whole business of analysing and discussing the way we climb, skilfully summarised in Lito's keynote essay, is open to limitless debate. Many articles have been devoted to the subject of the unwritten rules or ethics that, it is said, should guide our actions. This growing concern may be prompted by a feeling that the world is getting smaller and climbers are becoming more skilful and more numerous. There may be a fundamental need for an increasingly tougher code of ethics, not only to protect the mountains from abuse, but also to maintain the exclusivity of the top performance, and thus retain the interest of the sport.

A glance at the pages of the journals and books of yesteryear soon reveals that ethical wrangles are not a new phenomenon. The Victorians who pioneered alpine climbing were just as concerned about the niceties of style as any latter-day purist.

This section contains essays on a number of themes that reveal the ethical conundrums which obsess the present-day climber. Further ethical points will be found in the Expedition section of the book.

The position in 2006: Climbing was largely unified by a common ethos in the late 1970s but that unity has now been fragmented to some degree. Aid climbing, led by Yosemite ethics, utilised nuts and pitons in ever more precarious ways to keep bolting to a minimum. In conventional rock climbing, the great improvements in leader-placed protection equipment in the 1960s and 1970s removed the need to place pitons whenever things got tough.

As a result there was a far more concentrated effort to do climbs completely free (piton placing on difficult sections of steep routes sometimes merging into a semi-aiding style). The result was that a lot of old piton-protected climbs were cleaned up and for a period at the end of the 1970s and the early 80s rock climbers around the world (greatly influenced by events in Yosemite) attempted to climb free, using leader-placed protection.

This brief window of ultra ethical climbing ceased with the invention of the cordless drill that allowed the easy placement of bolts, particularly if placed by abseil. Initially this was employed on very steep crackless cliffs (to allow sport climbing) but its use soon spread to normal climbing areas where there had been no previous tradition of leader-protected free climbing. Its most indulgent form this was practised by the Swiss Plaisir movement – a trend initially developed to generate business for remote huts by turning nearby climbs into climbing versions of Via Ferratas. Here was the response of a nation steeped in the mores of tourist 'development', producing the climbing equivilant of piste skiing, or a modern day version of the fixed ropes on the Matterhorn. The more demanding sport climbing enabled climbers to concentrate solely on technicalities. Great increases in strength, technical skill and athleticism were the result, some of which was brought back to push standards in traditional climbing by climbers like Wolfgang Güllich and Alexander Huber. There were also some areas of high mountain (but sub-alpine) cliffs and areas of blank slab-climbing where sparing bolt placement retained sporting challenge. But the growth in Plaisir type areas that made few risk-demands, often down to the easiest levels of climbing, are clearly far removed from the whole adventurous ethos presented in Lito's thesis. More recently the popularity of bouldering and Deep Water Soloing, have allowed high standard activity without placing bolts and are clearly reaffirmations of the adventure ethos. The long-term sporting threat of Plaisir remains however with its attendant despoilation of covering cliffs with bolts and chains. The future dynamism of the sport is thus far from assured as bolt-placers seek every opportunity to process cliffs to provide their sanitised form of climbing (akin to outdoor climbing walls). The picture is further confused as sport or Plaisir enthusiasts may well indulge in some conventionally challenging form of climbing from time to time – a bit like going to church at Easter and Christmas. Big rock walls in places like Greenland, Baffin and Patagonia form tempting targets for bolt-placers and users and when these are added to bolted climbs in holiday locations like Spain, Mexico and Thailand, and the Plaisir areas of Europe a picture of a steady erosion of the adventure ethos becomes clear.

CLIMBING ETHICS

ROBIN CAMPBELL

I would like to begin by contrasting two ethical decisions – a climber deciding whether or not to place a peg on some crag or other and a doctor deciding whether or not to allow some aged suffering patient to die or to prolong the patient's life against his own wishes. There is no doubt in my mind about which of these two decisions is the one which merits more thought nor about which of them will produce the great mental anguish. I hope there is none in yours.

Ethics is a serious business; I should like to say right at the start that I'm quite sure that climbing should not be a serious business. It is clear, however, that many of you in England regard it in this way – in fact you treat it so seriously that you have built up a powerful national organisation and have even taken to holding National Conferences. The first thing I would like to do is to speculate a little about this sudden attack of gravity. I suspect that a case could be made for the view that a strong interest in mountaineering only arises in countries where the people are denied the opportunity for meaningful work, where they live lives relatively free from personal danger and where they are obliged to live in squalid surroundings in large cities. When mountaineers become excessively serious as well as excessively numerous this, I think, is simply because they wish to invest their mountaineering activities with a significance which their other activities palpably lack. I believe also that this is a factor which has led to the tremendous increase in outdoor education. The mountaineer in charge of children has his fantasies fulfilled – he is now engaged in what we all agree is a serious business, namely, the care of children in dangerous places. In his mountaineering he now has really important decisions to make, decisions which are irreducibly ethical.

The mountaineer who enjoys mountain rescue work is, I believe, another case in point. He enjoys it because his mountaineering has acquired a real significance which it formerly lacked. In these two cases I make a temporary exception of the professional mountaineer, whose case is rather different, since mountaineering is his working life. This line of thought leads me to the following conclusions:

229

1. the serious ethical problems that confront certain abnormal varieties of mountaineer are often welcomed by them (unlike the case of the doctor contemplating euthanasia) and this is surely pathological; *2.* any mountaineer in either of these two abnormal categories who recognises this aberration should immediately cease these activities and direct his energies to the valid tasks of reforming his life-style and the structures of society which encouraged him to adopt it; *3.* the tendency to treat the trivial ethical problems of normal climbing as serious matters may be a manifestation of the same phenomenon. I hope, then, that I have made my own attitude to the present concern with mountaineering ethics perfectly clear: I believe it to be symptomatic of a general desire amongst us to invest our climbing activities with a significance which they do not possess and that this desire, in turn, arises from dissatisfaction with our daily lives. That this desire has in fact achieved its end in the case of the armies of schoolboy-shepherds I regard as quite abominable and I would like to take this opportunity to call upon all of you who are concerned with this enterprise, however indirectly, to ask yourselves the question: 'Who is providing a service to whom?'

Now my arguments so far have put me in a rather odd position, for here I am to talk about climbing ethics at a National Mountaineering Conference, exactly the sort of behaviour I have just called in question. I came here because of an impulsive promise to the BMC National Officer, Dennis Gray, which I now regret. However, I try to keep promises, even to Yorkshire Scotsmen, so I will try to do him and you the courtesy of discussing the problem as helpfully as I can. I would nevertheless re-emphasise my belief that very little depends upon what view we take of the ethical problems that arise in normal mountaineering (short of grotesque rarities like 'Should you eat your climbing partner?'). If mountaineering as we know it turns completely sour, as I think it will, then this will just be one among many things in the Western World which are rapidly turning sour, in which case it will deserve no undue mourning.

I will begin by outlining a minimal set of 'Categorical Imperatives for Ethical Mountaineers'. These are:

1. *Climb the Mountains*
2. *Test Your Skill*
3. *Test Your Nerve*
4. *Love the Mountains*

These, I think, can all be supported without controversy in the sense that most climbers would accept them as minimal conditions for being a Good Mountaineer. *1* is so obvious it is usually overlooked; *2* and *3* have been extensively discussed – they were dealt with by Lito Tejada-Flores in his widely published article, *Games Climbers Play,* and they are much in the minds of all normal mountaineers (though 3 is often rejected by the serious-business brigade); 4 is perhaps the most intriguing and the one about which I shall have most to say. I would like now to discuss each of these in turn.

Climb the Mountains

Nothing much need be said about this except that it is the primary source of ethical conflict since it is often most easily obeyed by disobeying 2, 3 or 4. A good recent example of this is the bolt ascent of Cerro Torre where these three imperatives were all sacrificed in favour of the first.

Test Your Skill

This imperative leads us to put a negative value on the use of mechanical aids of various kinds and to put a positive value on the selection of climbs which will have a level of difficulty at or near our own limits. In *Games Climbers Play* Flores does not distinguish between these values and those which arise from the next imperative. This is, of course, a trivial criticism but one which I think can be sustained.

An interesting question is whether or not a climber who puts a positive value on the selection of climbs grossly beyond his own abilities has dis-obeyed this imperative. Certainly, he has disobeyed some imperative since such behaviour is generally deplored by other mountaineers. However, I shall argue later that this sort of transgression is better thought of as a breach of the Fourth Imperative.

Why do we value this Second Imperative? I think simply because climbing by means of your own limbs and wits at a level difficult enough to be taxing is psychologically satisfying.

Test Your Nerve

There seems to be a growing realisation that this is a very potent imperative. Its message is that climbers value danger and risk-taking as well as difficulty. One can point to Harold Drasdo's interesting article, *Margins of Safety,* as the most explicit argument for the potency of this imperative. Ken Wilson's paper at last year's Safety Conference was also about this. In the actual practice of climbers we can see a recent tendency to frown on mechanical protection as well as mechanical aid.

A useful analogy for examining this imperative is the game of Russian Roulette. Russian Roulette is undoubtedly stimulating, sometimes fatally so. No doubt it is a tremendously exciting pastime while it lasts. However, it would be a dull game when played with no bullets and a short one when played with them all. We can think of the climber *who tests his* nerve as a kind of Russian Roulette player who gives it a whirl every so often. Of course, *how often* is crucial. The professional guide or outdoor instructor must clearly use a very small number of bullets if he hopes to play the game regularly and still survive. On the other hand the amateur climber with exactly the same margin of safety can use more bullets since he plays less often.

This Third Imperative conflicts with a most important general ethical value – the Value of Human Life. I shall argue later that this works against the survival of the imperative in mountaineering enterprises where society at large is involved. It seems reasonable, however, to say that even mountaineers have some limits to what they are prepared to value in this area of danger and risk-taking. One thinks, for example, of the famous campaign of criticism mounted against the early attempts on the Eiger North Face. Currently, there is what seems to me to be a surprising amount of sympathy with the aims of Mountain Safety instruction. Again, I shall argue later that such attitudes are ultimately based on the Fourth Imperative.

Love the Mountains
I suggest that this imperative should be interpreted quite literally, so that we treat the mountains as we would treat a lover. Of course, the conjugal relationship is somewhat promiscuous – there are a lot of us and a lot of them and each of us loves all of them. It is as a result of 'love of mountains' that climbers deplore the acts of defacement and defilement to which our mountains are so often subjected. Defacement by chairlifts, railways, fixed ropes, paintmarks, pegmarks, rubbish, beaten paths – all are acts of assault upon a loved one and are therefore deplorable. Defilement by excessive indiscriminate promiscuity – so-called 'people pollution' – is also deplorable, particularly so when the people concerned do not love mountains. Elitist attitudes of this sort were forged a long time ago. On that celebrated occasion when Moses climbed Mount Sinai to receive those more important Ethical Imperatives, the Lord was very specific with respect to this point about how the mountain should be treated by the rank and file. First of all He informed Moses that He had sanctified the mountain and then warned him of the dire consequences that would befall any of his people who set foot on the mountain. For good measure He ordered Moses to instruct his men-folk not to 'come at their wives' for three days!

A second consequence of this Fourth Imperative is that, like any lover, the mountains should not be treated lightly, should not be taken for granted. And so it is here that we derive our proscriptions against the attempting of the unduly difficult or the unduly dangerous. The mountaineer who takes these liberties is taking them with his life but it is not that that we should care about: it is that he is taking liberties with the mountain.

A final implication of this imperative is that rape is unethical: the mountain must have the chance of turning you down.

I would like now to finish by making two general points about these four imperatives and to try to rationalise the current widespread suspicion of two increasingly important climbing institutions, the Professional Climber and the BMC.

Firstly, the four imperatives appeal to distinct emotional systems, which supports the claim that they are independent.

1 Appeals to an atavistic instinct, the one which the late Tom Patey identified with the climbing instinct of our arboreal ancestors in his article *Apes or Ballerinas* [see page 595].

2 Arises from the pleasure of any purposeful and well-controlled physical activity – the mental harmony which is the semi-mystical goal of all recondite forms of physical exercise, such as Yoga, Karate, Body-Building and so on.

3 Derives its impetus from the catharsis of fear and 4 from love.

Secondly, there seems to be a shift in the relative force of the four imperatives that comes with age and experience. In the beginning 1 is paramount, then 2 and 3 and finally 4. This explains the often troublesome value-conflicts between young and old climbers without requiring us to suppose that they subscribe to different sets of mountaineering values. It is simply that priorities change.

It seems to me that the amateur climber climbs and talks about climbing more or less as if he acknowledges these Ethical Imperatives and that, were he left to his own devices, the value-system I have associated with them would not be seriously threatened. However, he is not being left to his own devices. Educators have been persuaded to involve themselves with mountains in what I believe is a wholly immoral enterprise. Entrepreneurial individuals in the tourist industry offer package holidays which include mountaineering along with other so-called adventure sports. A massive public interest in mountaineering has been stimulated by certain well-managed professional climbers with the help of TV and other mass media. The effect of all this busy work has been to put some of our mountain areas under intolerable pressures so that those climbers who climb because of, if I am right, certain inner compulsions which mountaineering can satisfy become submerged in a polluting flood of sheep. A further and equally pernicious development is the strengthening of mountain rescue facilities in the popular areas. The effect of this has been to introduce a quite extraneous factor into our calculations relating to the Third Imperative. Now to the risks of climbing we must add the probability of being unnecessarily rescued!

A third blow is the introduction to our fragile world of large numbers of climbers trained by the schools or by the 'adventure' industry. Since they are trained by professionals they are inevitably less impressed by the Third Imperative than the traditional young climber: their norms are the crash hat, maximum protection, the peg belay and the roadside crag. Now I do not doubt the good intentions of the professional climber. Nor do I see anything necessarily wrong about his activities. The mountain guide is a quite traditional component of the mountain scene. He provides a valuable service to would-be mountain lovers. However, most of our professionals are not guides: they are teachers. So long as they continue to provide a service (rather than to sell mountaineering) and as long as they do not ignore the Third and Fourth Imperatives in their teaching (as I believe they have a tendency to do) they will not harm mountaineering, nor could they be reasonably regarded as engaged in anything unethical. However, if they try actively to sell mountaineering then the Fourth Imperative says clearly: Do Not Be A Mountain Pimp. As I have said, I do not doubt their good intentions. I don't believe that more than a handful of such professionals reject any of the characteristic values of mountaineering I have mentioned. However, they are employed persons as a rule. I would urge these professionals as a matter of some importance to form themselves into a trade union as soon as possible so as to influence the decisions of their employers more effectively.

The position of the professional climber who is employed to teach school-children is rather different, since the question of responsibility becomes acute here. Moreover, the whole issue is shrouded in muddled and tendentious argument. A nice example of this is the notion that children may be responsibly exposed to *apparent* danger (whereby they experience real fear and enjoy a real feeling of adventure) but that to expose children to *real* danger is irresponsible. If there is some likelihood that such children will continue to climb as a result of this process of education, then such training constitutes a recipe for disaster, since experience will have taught the child that his fears can be safely ignored! The issue of responsibility cannot be dodged in this way. Climbing should be taught properly (so that the child learns what constitutes a dangerous situation) and the children exposed to risk, or it should not be taught at all. The question then becomes one of general ethics: 'Is it right for schools to expose children to unnecessary risks?' Surely the answer is no. On the other hand, if the demand for such instruction comes from the child (with parental consent) and if the child's motivation is genuine (an obviously spurious case is the child who would simply prefer to be at the outdoor centre than be bored in school) then responsibility rests where it should – with parent and child – and the schools can act. It is, however, doubtful whether any education authority acts in so circumspect a manner at present.

The remaining kind of professional climber is the Media Man, and there are several well-known examples of this species. Here again I feel that the Fourth Imperative says clearly: Do Not Be A Mountain Pimp; Do Not Let The Armchaired Millions Come At Me.

Lastly, I should like to say a word or two about the BMC's role as defender of climbing values. Here again its good intentions are not in doubt. It seems plain that the vast changes in the BMC in recent years have come about because those involved have felt it necessary that the BMC should become more active, more political, in order to ensure that the views of mountaineers were adequately represented in areas of public concern such as conservation, access to mountains, the training of climbers and so on. However, I would like to make some cautionary remarks. Firstly, the expense involved in this activity inevitably means close co-operation with the Sports Council and since public funds are now being consumed by mountaineers, that makes us publicly accountable. Recall that a cardinal ethic of our society is to put an absolute value on human life so that we try to save people from the consequences of their own folly. Surely this will mean a good deal of pressure on climbers, through the BMC, *to abandon the Third Imperative*.

Secondly, the time and work involved in the new BMC inevitably means that professional climbers of one sort or another will take on more and more of BMC functions. How happy are we to have professionals to represent our views and our interests? Already, according to a recent issue of *Mountain*, we have what looks like a kind of House of Lords forming within the BMC. I may well be wrong, but I think there is a great danger that, even with the best of intentions, a powerful, active BMC may succeed in hastening the demise of traditional climbing values. Such a happening is described in 'Behold now Behemoth', a chilling little article by Pete Sinclaire, which appeared in *Ascent*, in 1968. In this piece, Sinclaire described how well-intentioned climbers and Park Service bureaucrats in fact *facilitated* certain developments inimical to climbing in the Tetons National Park. In Sinclaire's words, we must make sure that our 'bureaucratic behemoth' is a 'useful beast of burden' and not 'an uncontrollable monster'.

I would like to conclude by reiterating my belief that ethics in climbing as traditionally practised is not a serious business and that the climbing sins which I have suggested we sometimes commit are minor ones when compared with the sins we commit in other walks of life. I have no doubt that Tom Patey's attitude was the correct one – treat such things lightly with a song or with satire. It is perhaps not irrelevant that he lived in beautiful surroundings and had a meaningful occupation: he at least had no need to pretend that climbing was anything other than occasionally exciting fun.

Paper read to the NATIONAL MOUNTAINEERING
CONFERENCE OF THE BMC *1974*

TIS–SA-ACK

ROYAL ROBBINS

First attempted by Royal Robbins. Dennis Hennek and Chuck Pratt in 1968, the previously untouched central section of the great face of Yosemite's Half Dome was completed in October 1969 by Robbins and Don Peterson. In the following account the author has attempted to reconstruct the thoughts and attitudes of his companions. Any resemblance ... [Original *Ascent* preamble]

Hennek: It was Robbins's idea, mainly. It was on a lot of guys' minds. Had been for a long time. I had thought of it, and when I loaned him my glass I figured he was taking a look. Meant more to him than anyone. He already had two routes on the face, and couldn't bear to see anyone else get this one. He wanted to own Half Dome.

Robbins: In the afternoon Marshall – I call him Marshall because Roper started that. Roper likes to call people by their middle names, and such. Like he calls me 'Roy', because he hates the pretentiousness of my first name. And I can't help that. Anyway he likes to call Pratt Marshall, so I will try it for a while. Marshall led a nice pitch up into this huge slanting dihedral of white rock streaked with black lichen: the Zebra. Those black streaks, legend tells us, were made by the tears of the Indian girl for whom I named the route.

Pratt: I belayed in slings at the top of this pitch which wasn't too bad, except at the start where you're thirty feet out with nothing in and then you start aiding with a couple of shitty pins. Royal liked the next pitch because it was loose and gave him an excuse to play around with those damn nuts and feel like they were really doing some good, which I doubt. But I am, it's true, rather conservative. Then we came down on fixed ropes and slept on a big ledge we called the Dormitory.

Hennek: We would have been all right in the Zebra but we didn't have enough big pitons, even though we were carrying two sets of hardware. We needed about ten two-inch and a dozen inch-and-a-half pitons. The reason we had two sets of hardware is so one guy could be climbing all the time while another was cleaning. I led to the top of the Zebra and Pratt came up and started leading around the overhang at the top while Robbins cleaned the last pitch.

Robbins: From Hennek's hanging belay the crack widened to five inches. So Marshall used a four-inch piton, our biggest, endwise. It was weird, driven straight up like that. Then he got in a couple of good pins and used two nuts behind a terrible flake. Pitons would have torn it off. He didn't like it. Marshall hates nuts. He was talking about how it was shifting and then lodging again, just barely. I think he wanted it to come out so he could say, Robbins I told you so. But it held long enough for him to place a bolt, but it wasn't very good because he wanted to get off that nut before the nut got off the flake.

Hennek: We couldn't see Chuck bolting above the overhang, but Glen Denny, who was taking picture from across the way, got some good shots of us hanging there and Pratt working away. About dusk I lowered Royal out to jumar up and then I started cleaning the pitch.

Robbins: When I got up there I saw Marshall had managed to bash three pins into unlikely cracks. There was nothing to stand on. When I pictured the three of us hanging from those pitons I immediately got out the drill. Marshall isn't known as an anti-bolt fanatic – it's true about that thing on Shiprock, but that was mainly Roper – he isn't known as a fanatic, but there is no one slower on the bolt gun draw than Marshall Pratt. I got in a good solid bolt and we settled down for the night.

Hennek: Royal says settled down, but he didn't get settled very fast. He was screwing around and cursing in the blackness, and then I heard this rip. He had put too much weight in one end of his hammock, and he ought to know better having designed the mothers, and then there was this explosion of screeching and shouting and terrible foul language that would have done credit even to Steve Roper. I thought it was funny. It went on and on. Fulminations in the darkness. I was amazed that he so completely lost control because he always seemed like such an iceberg.

Robbins: I had a unique experience the next day: placing sixteen bolts in a row. It was just blank and there was no way around. But it was a route worth bolting for, and after a time I began to take an almost perverse joy in it, or at least in doing a good job. I put them in all the way, so they're good solid reliable bolts, and I put them quite far apart, so I think that it's perhaps the most crafts-man-like ladder of that many bolts in the world. Still, I was really happy to reach with the aid of a skyhook a crack descending from a ledge fifty feet higher. When Marshall came up he was raving. He raved a lot on that wall. He's an outstanding ravist, often shouting at the top of his lungs like Othello in heat. 'Why, why, why,' he shrieked 'Why didn't I re-up? Christ, I could be a sergeant by now, with security and self-respect. Why did I start climbing in the first place? Shit, I could have been a physicist, with a big desk and a secretary. A secretary!' he repeated, brightening, a leer breaking across his face. 'But, no, no, I couldn't do that. I had to drop out of college. Because I… I,' his voice rising in a crescendo, 'I, like Christian

Bonington, chose to climb.' I was convulsed. We were having a good time. Nobody uptight. No ego trips. But we were low on bolts and low on water. We would have to go down the next day. It was late afternoon and …

Hennek: I'll take over here to save all of us from another of Royal's glowing descriptions of how the sun goes down. After a night on the ledge – and a rather long October night at that – we rappeled, placing bolts and dropping from one hanging stance to another. We all wanted to return. It was going to be a good route and we left a lot of hardware at the base, to save carrying it up next time.

Pratt: But when next time came, in June, the summit snowfield was still draining down the face. It had been a heavy winter. So we put it off until the fall and I went to the Tetons, Robbins went to Alaska to stroke his alpine hang-up, and Dennis went fun-climbing in Tuolumne Meadows and re-damaged an old injury so he was out of the running for the year. In October I got a card from Robbins saying he'd be up in a few days for the Dome, and when he didn't arrive it really pissed me off, and when days later he still didn't arrive I said fuck it and made plans to go on El Cap with Tom Bauman. Christ, when Robbins didn't show, people were looking for him on Half Dome, solo. And then when he finally came up several days late his mood really turned me off. He was tense and cold. He said he couldn't wait until Tom and I had done our climb; he was taking the Dome too seriously, so I decided not to go.

Robbins: When Chuck said he wouldn't go I was almost relieved. At least now he couldn't make me feel like I was dirtying the pants of American Mountaineering. I feel guilty with a camera when Pratt is on the rope. It's like asking a Navajo to pose, and I would never do that. Marshall hates cameras as much as he hates my puns and 5.10 psychos. He doesn't want anything to get between him and the climbing experience. He suggested I ask Don Peterson. Peterson had been up the Dihedral Wall and was hot to go on anything as long as it was difficult. Although he had never studied the wall, it didn't take much persuading.

Peterson: We agreed to go up in the morning. Robbins was like a man possessed. He was totally zeroed in on Half Dome. He had a lecture date soon and he had to squeeze it in. It rained like hell that night and looked bad in the morning but Robbins figured we might as well go up because it might not storm. I didn't like it but I didn't say anything and we started walking up expecting to get bombed on any minute.

Robbins: Our loads were murderous. We stopped where the great slabs begin and gazed upward. 'Didn't know what you were getting into, did you?' I asked, facetiously.

'Well,' replied Don, 'it can't be any harder than things I've already done.'

I turned absolutely frigid. The tone of the next eight days was set right there.

Peterson: What I didn't like was his assumption of superiority. Like he figured just because he was Royal Robbins he was the leader. I didn't buy that. Christ, I had done climbs in the Valley as hard as he'd done, and I did the Dihedral faster. Yet when we got up to the base of the wall he sent me to fetch water. I just don't buy that crap.

Robbins: On the way up Don asked if there was anything on the North America Wall harder than the third pitch. I told him no – as hard but not really harder. Well then, he said, we shouldn't have any trouble with the rest of it. Mead Hargis and I have been up the third pitch and it wasn't too bad. Oh, really, I said. Well, it might be a little easier now because Hennek and Lauria had to place a bolt. Oh no, he said, we chopped it. We went right on by.

In a few hours we were at the Dormitory. It was strange climbing with Don. Like many young climbers he was intensely impatient. He was used to great speed and just going. Speed is where it's at. It's not the noblest thing in climbing, but it moves many. Still, I didn't expect to feel the pressure of Don's impatience running up the rope like a continually goading electric current. And I didn't expect a generation gap, but there it was. For eight days we would be locked in sullen conflict, each too arrogant to understand the other's weaknesses.

Peterson: On the second day we reached the top of the Zebra. Royal belayed in slings while I led the pitch over the top. Right away there was the wide crack. Robbins told me Pratt had knocked a four-incher endwise into the five-inch crack. I screwed around for a while, wondering why he hadn't brought a bigger bong this time. I couldn't get it to work so I took three bongs and put them one inside the other and that filled the crack okay, but God was it spooky. Still, I thought it was a pretty clever piece of engineering.

Robbins: After Don made this strange bong manoeuvre, he reached the flake where Marshall had had his wild time with those tiny wired nuts. 'It's been a long time since I've used nuts,' said Don, to cut the power of any criticism I might have on his chocking ability. After he had put his weight on the second one it pulled and he ripped out the other, falling fifteen feet. He didn't like that and this time he nested two pins first. But he still couldn't drive a pin higher as the flake was too loose so he put the nut back in and got on it. It was holding so he started to take in rope and as he was reaching for Pratt's bolt the chock came out and down he came, pulling the pins and falling twenty feet this time. I feared he might be daunted but he swarmed right back up the rope and got the top nut in and got on it and pulled in a lot of rope and got the bolt this time. Fighting spirit, I thought. I reflected how Don was a football player and how he must charge the line the way he charges up those pitches.

Peterson: Robbins was rather proud of his bolt ladder and bragged about it while he was leading it. I passed his belay in slings and led on up to the previous high point which Robbins called Twilight Ledge. In the morning he took a long time leading around several lips of rock. I was getting pretty antsy by the time he finished. Christ, was it all going to be like this?

Robbins: Above us rose a deceptive five-inch crack. Don went up to look at it and said do you want to try it? It won't hurt to try I replied, but when I got up there I wouldn't do it without a bolt, and we had no bolts to spare. So for about an hour I played with bongs driven length-wise, and with four-inch bongs enlarged by one-inch angles driven across their spines. It was distasteful as hell, and if anything came out I'd be right in Don's lap. I was trembling with more than exertion when I finally clawed my way to Sunset Ledge. When Don came up I was gratified to hear him say he didn't think he could have done it. Maybe now the tension would be eased between us. He probably wanted me to say, 'Sure you could,' but I couldn't give up the one point I had won.

Peterson: It was a good ledge. We were halfway or more. It was my lead but Royal had a lot more bolting experience so he led off, placing a bolt ladder diagonally across a blank section. In the morning I finished the ladder, nailed a big loose flake and put in a bolt and belayed in slings. When Robbins came up three or four pins just fell out.

Robbins: The first thing I did was put in another bolt, for above Don's belay rose another of those vile five-inch cracks, too big for our pins and too small to get inside. I launched an all-out effort, struggling and thrashing desperately in the slightly overhanging crack. Four months later I still bear the scars. The top of the flake was like a big stone fence without mortar, but I got across that and placed a few bolts and then nailed a thin horizontal flake. I placed seven pins there and four fell out before I had finished. With two good bolts for a belay and hanging bivouac I was safe and happy with nothing on my mind but the next 800ft. Don wanted to try the jam-crack because I had said it was probably the hardest free climbing I had done on a big wall, but I told him we don't have time man, which we didn't. I was very relieved, for I was afraid he would come up easily and go down and tell the fellows I said it was hard but he didn't find it so. What the hell, that would happen in the next ascent anyway. Let the pitch have a reputation for a year.

Peterson: At about this point I wasn't feeling too happy. Robbins had taken almost a whole day to lead one pitch. I just didn't see how we could make it at this rate. I knew he had to place a lot of bolts, but it about drove me out of my skin waiting for him to finish. I felt I could have gone faster. We were using too many bolts when we still had this big blank section above us. What if we didn't have enough? But the only thing Robbins had to say was 'We can always turn back, or else they can pull us off.' I didn't think we were going to make it. I had never gone so slowly on a climb in my life.

Robbins: I hated drilling those bolts. We had these extra-long drills, that were all we could get at the last minute, and we had a long drill holder too, so I was bending over backwards drilling, and drilling is plenty bad enough without that. Here I was working away and always this mumbling and bitching from below, and finally the shocking ejaculation, 'This is a lot of shit.' From then on I felt I was battling two opponents, the wall and Peterson. I had learned to expect a grumble whenever I made the slightest error, such as not sending up the right pin ('Goddamn it, everything but what I need'), or forgetting the hauling line. I began to feel incompetent. It wasn't really so much what Don said, it was that he said it. It was a new experience climbing with someone who gave his emotions such complete freedom of expression. I was shocked and mildly terrified by Peterson's dark passions bubbling repeatedly to the surface. It probably would have been healthier to have responded in kind every time I felt scorn, real or imagined, coming my way. I didn't lack such feelings. The things I was calling Don were far worse than anything he said, direct or implied. But when I said them I kept my mouth shut.

Peterson: On the fifth morning I had to use up three more bolts because there was another five-inch overhanging crack. I finally got into it and went free for a 100ft completely inside a huge flake for half the way. Then we had three straightforward pitches before some bolting brought us to a great ledge, where a ramp led up to a huge blank area below the summit. That night our water froze. In the morning I led up the ramp to a tight little alcove. The blank wall started about thirty-foot up. It looked awfully big.

Robbins: As I nailed up to the blank area, I thought hard about our remaining thirty bolts. We would place some so they were barely adequate, allowing us to pull and re-use them. We had now traversed too much to descend. Those long drills were murder. I had three Rawl drills and another holder, and I used them to start the holes. They were extremely brittle, but I soon learned that a broken Rawl worked fine, and if they didn't break well, I would re-break them with the hammer. I was saving three short Star drills for the end. I didn't get far that day. It was slow going. I used one drill seven times before discarding it. Don spent the night scrunched in his cave while I bivouacked in a hammock. The weather, which had been threatening, was holding well. The next day was an ordeal. Sometimes it took nearly an hour for one bolt. Whenever I wasn't drilling I had my head against the rock in despair and self-pity. And always that electricity along the rope, that distracting awareness that Peterson must be going mad. Poor Peterson, but poor me too. Besides the hard work, there's something mentally oppressive about being in the middle of a large, totally blank piece of rock. I was sorry I had disdained bat-hooks, believing as I had that if you're going to drill a hole you ought to fill it with a good bolt. I was so far gone now that anything went. I just wanted to get up. But there was nothing to do but what we were doing. When Don came up to my hanging belay the first thing he said was, 'I was sitting down there for twenty-four hours!' That's energetic youth. Don had suffered as much sitting as I had drilling. That afternoon Don placed a few bolts, more quickly than I had, but with no more enthusiasm. The next day I again took over the bolting, inexorably working toward the barely visible lower corner of the dihedral leading to the summit overhangs. That edge of rock was our lodestone, drawing us like a magnet.

Peterson: Robbins had hoped to do the wall in six days, but this was the eighth. We really wanted to get off and thought maybe we could. The bolting was going a little faster now with Robbins using the short drills and not putting the bolts in very far. He would place one fairly well and then two poor ones and then another good one and then come down and take out the two bad ones and re-place them above. He did this about twenty times. Robbins rarely said anything while he was working on a pitch. He was like a beaver working away on a dam, slow and methodical. At times I felt I was going to burst, just sitting in one place doing nothing. I like to climb. This wasn't climbing, it was slogging. But I had to admire Robbins' self-control. He had about as much unmanageable emotion as an IBM machine.

Robbins: We reached our lodestone just as the sun was reaching us. Don eagerly grabbed the lead, nailing up from the last bolt. Thin nailing it was, too. By stretching a long way from a rurp, he drove a knife-blade straight up behind the rottenest flake imaginable. It seemed impossible it could have held. I had vowed that I wasn't going to give Peterson an inch, but I weakened. I told him it was a damn good lead. It would have been too flagrant not to have done so. We were now on a ledge beneath the final overhangs. Above, gently pivoting with grotesque finality in the afternoon breeze dangled a gangly form, mostly arms and legs, with a prophet's head of rusty beard and flowing locks. It was the artist, Glen Denny. He and the rock around him had already taken on a golden hue as I started up in an all-out effort to reach the top before dark. It didn't look far, but using two rurps just to get started was a bad omen. I went as fast as possible, but not fast enough to escape Peterson's urging to a greater speed. The summit tiers overlapped one another, building higher and higher like the ninth wave. On several, reaching the crack separating the folds was barely possible. On one, a hook on the wire of a nut saved a bolt.

Everything happened at once as I neared the top. The cracks became bad, the light went, pulling the rope was like a tug-of-war, and I was running out of pins. I had just gotten in a piton and clipped in when the one I was on popped. As I got onto the next one the piton below dropped out and then I was off the aid and on to a sloping smooth slab in the blackness, realising I was really asking for it and picturing the fall and the pulled pins and hanging in space above Don. I backed down and got into my slings and cleaned the top pin with a pull, then began nailing sideways. Glen Denny is watching silently as I start to crack but I realise I am getting melodramatic and find myself looking at it through Glen's eyes, completely objectively and so cool down and feel with fingers the cracks in the darkness and bash away with the hammer smashing my fingers and pins coming out and me complaining in the darkness putting fear into the heart of my companion and asking him to send up his anchors so I could use them but he refusing and me saying to Glen that's the way it's been all the way up.

from ASCENT *1970*

THE MURDER OF THE IMPOSSIBLE

REINHOLD MESSNER

What have I personally got against 'direttissimas'? Nothing at all; in fact, I think that the 'falling drop of water' route is one of the most logical things that exists. And of course it always has existed – so long as the mountain permits it. But sometimes the line of weakness wanders to the left or the right of this line; and then we see climbers – those on the first ascent, I mean – going straight on up as if it weren't so, striking in bolts of course. Why do they go that way? 'For the sake of freedom,' they say; but they don't realise that they are slaves of the plumbline.

They have a horror of deviations. 'In the face of difficulties, logic commands one not to avoid them, but to overcome them,' declares Paul Claudel. And that's what the 'direttissima' protagonists say too, knowing from the start that the equipment they have will get them over any obstacle. They are therefore talking about problems which no longer exist. Could the mountain stop them with unexpected difficulties? They smile: those times are long past! The impossible in mountaineering has been eliminated, murdered by the direttissima.

Yet direttissimas would not in themselves be so bad were it not for the fact that the spirit that guides them has infiltrated the entire field of climbing. Take a climber on a rock face, iron rungs beneath his feet and all around him only yellow, overhanging rock. Already tired, he bores another hole above the last peg. He won't give up. Stubbornly, bolt by bolt, he goes on. *His* way, and none other, must be forced on the face.

Expansion bolts are taken for granted nowadays; they are kept to hand just in case some difficulty cannot be overcome by ordinary methods. Today's climber doesn't want to cut himself off from the possibility of retreat: he carries his courage in his rucksack, in the form of bolts and equipment. Rock faces are no longer overcome by climbing skill, but are humbled, pitch by pitch, by methodical manual labour; what isn't done today will be done tomorrow. Free-climbing routes are dangerous, so they are protected by pegs. Ambitions are no longer built on skill, but on equipment and the length of time available. The decisive factor isn't courage, but technique; an ascent may take days and days, and the pegs and bolts counted in hundreds. Retreat has become dishonourable, because everyone knows now that a combination of bolts and singlemindedness will get you up anything, even the most repulsive-looking direttissima.

Times change, and with them concepts and values. Faith in equipment has replaced faith in oneself; a team is admired for the number of bivouacs it makes, while the courage of those who still climb 'free' is derided as a manifestation of lack of conscientiousness.

Who has polluted the pure spring of mountaineering?

The innovators perhaps wanted only to get closer to the limits of possibility. Today, however, every single limit has vanished, been erased. In principle, it didn't seem to be a serious matter, but ten years have sufficed to eliminate the word 'impossible' from mountaineering vocabulary.

Progress? Today, ten years from the start of it all, there are a lot of people who don't care where they put bolts, whether on new routes or on classic ones. People are drilling more and more and climbing less and less.

'Impossible': it doesn't exist any more. The dragon is dead, poisoned, and the hero Siegfried is unemployed. Now anyone can work on a rock face, using tools to bend it to his own idea of possibility.

Some people foresaw this a while ago, but they went on drilling, both on direttissimas and on other climbs, until they lost the taste for climbing: why dare, why gamble, when you can proceed in perfect safety? And so they became the prophets of the direttissima: 'Don't waste time on classic routes – learn to drill, learn to use your equipment. Be cunning: If you want to be successful, use every means you can to get round the mountain. The era of the direttissima has barely begun; every peak awaits its plumbline route. There's no rush, for a mountain can't run away – and nor can it defend itself.'

'Done the direttissima yet? And the super direttissima?' These are the criteria by which mountaineering prowess is measured nowadays. And so the young men go off, crawl up the ladder of bolts, and then ask the next ones: 'done the direttissima yet?'

Anyone who doesn't play ball is laughed at for daring to take a stand against current opinion. The plumbline generation has already consolidated itself and has thoughtlessly killed the ideal of the impossible. Anyone who doesn't oppose this makes himself an accomplice of the murderers. When future mountaineers open their eyes and realise what has happened, it will be too late: the impossible (and, with it, risk) will be buried, rotted away, and forgotten forever.

All is not yet lost, however, although 'they' are returning to the attack; and even if it's not always the same people, it'll be other people similar to them. Long before they attack, they'll make a great noise, and once again any warning will be useless. They'll be ambitious and they'll have long holidays – and some new 'last great problem' will be resolved. They'll leave more photographs at the hut, as historical documents, showing a dead straight line of dots running from base to summit – and on the face itself, several hundred bolts. Newspapers, radio and television will once again inform us that 'Man has achieved the impossible'.

If people have already been driven to the idea of establishing a set of rules of conduct, it means that the position is serious; but we young people don't want a mountaineering code. On the contrary, 'up there we want to find long, hard days, days when we don't know in the morning what the evening will bring'. But for how much longer will we be able to have this?

I'm worried about that dead dragon: we should do something before the impossible is finally interred. We have hurled ourselves, in a fury of pegs and bolts, on increasingly savage rock faces: the next generation will have to know how to free itself from all these unnecessary trappings. We have learned from the plumbline routes; our successors will once again have to reach the summits by *other* routes. It's time we repaid our debts and searched again for the *limits of possibility* – for we must have such limits if we are going to use the virtue of courage to approach them. And we must never break them down again, even if it's impossible for us to reach them. Where else will be able to find refuge in our flight from the oppression of everyday humdrum routine? In the Himalaya? In the Andes? Yes, certainly, if we can get there; but for most of us there'll only be these old Alps.

So let's save the dragon; and in the future let's follow the road that past climbers marked out. I'm convinced it's still the right one.

Put on your boots and get going. If you've got a companion, take a rope with you and a couple of pitons for your belays, but nothing else. I'm already on my way, ready for anything – even for retreat, if I meet the impossible. I'm not going to be killing any dragons, but if anyone wants to come with me, we'll go to the top together on the routes we can do without branding ourselves as murderers.

from MOUNTAIN 15 *1971*

COONYARD MOUTHS OFF

YVON CHOUINARD

'Today's climber … carries his courage in his rucksack …
Faith in equipment has replaced faith in oneself.' *Reinhold Messner*

Mountaineering is very much in vogue in America. What was once a way of life that only attracted the oddball individual is now a healthy, upstanding, recreational pastime enjoyed by thousands of average Joes. The climbing scene has become a fad and the common man is bringing the Art down to his own level of values and competence.

Living in California, I can see previews of coming attractions in America. I saw the Peace and Love movement turn to Violence and Hate even before it got to other parts of the country. Now there are bad vibrations in the over-populated surfing scene and even worse vibrations with the climbing craze. The same problems which prevented us from realising the 'Great American Dream' are now facing mountaineering. Just as man continues to disrupt the natural order of things, so mountaineering has become increasingly technical, decreasingly difficult, much too crowded and far less adventuresome. The purity, uncertainty, naturalness and soul of the sport are rapidly being changed.

Having been passionately committed to climbing for seventeen years, and with a business directly related to climbing and its problems, I feel a heavy responsibility to make known my apprehension over what climbing is becoming.

Bolts. After the Wall of the Early Morning Light fiasco, there was a considerable increase in the sale of bolts in the climbing shops in Southern California. A kid buys a bolt kit before he even knows how to use a runner! Yet Reinhold Messner became one of the world's greatest alpinists without ever having drilled a single hole.

It's no longer enough to say that only the expert climbers should be allowed to place bolts. We've said that all along and it's not working! Even the 'Mad Bolter' surely considers himself an expert.

On the big-wall climbs of the 1960s, bolts had their place. They made it possible to ascend the great routes on El Capitan and Half Dome. This era is gone and yet bolts are being used in ever greater numbers to force illogical routes up blank faces. This permits the average Joe to do climbs that are normally over his head and they allow the experts to do incredibly hard climbs without having to stick their necks out. Bolts are even used for no apparent reason, like the one I once saw next to an eight-foot diameter ponderosa pine.

I believe we have reached the point where the only hope is to completely degrade bolting. We must refuse to recognise it as a legitimate means of climbing. If you are in sympathy, you must stop using bolts. Disparage others who do. Moreover, tell your local climbing shop that you are not buying anything from them until they stop selling bolts, or at the very least remove them from the front counter.

Hard Rock Mining. The Lost Arrow Tip is as dead as the Hudson River. It is no longer a climb. The Nose of El Cap up to Sickle Ledge is a disgusting experience. You now use 1½ inch angles where the pioneers used rurps. Bashies have been welded into piton holes, leaving the rock once again smooth and flush, except for the rotten sling sticking out. Cracks are deteriorating, flakes are broken off, trees are being girdled by rappel ropes. Even the quartz-hard Shawangunks in New York are suffering from the onslaught of too many climbers. It can't go on like this. And it won't. The Park Service has already closed three climbs in Yosemite because of deterioration of the rock.

We once thought that America had the highest standard of rock-climbing in the world because we removed our pitons and left the climbs 'clean'. This policy worked fine when there were just a handful of us and it's still a good way to climb a big virgin Alaskan wall. But in the Valley or the 'Gunks, it is now a selfish, destructive ethic.

I'd like to offer a few immediate solutions. Stay off climbs which you don't intend to finish. Don't climb to Sickle Ledge unless you plan to do the entire Nose route. Stay off climbs that are obviously over your head – otherwise you will just be placing more pitons than necessary for protection. Don't use artificial aid on free climbs. These actions would certainly help solve the problem, but the final answer is to leave the *necessary* pitons in place on all climbs, artificial and free.

The fixed-piton idea would appear at first to be a degeneration of artificial climbing standards, and it will probably end up being so. However, we could start playing the chock-and-natural-protection-game instead of the piton game and thus perhaps even *raise* the existing standards. For instance, I believe that it's possible to climb El Cap using only chocks and a few thin pitons (these could be fixed).

The chock solution is dependent on everyone *using* nuts, not just carrying them around for looks, but really trusting them. Nuts and runners can be used in place of pitons on free climbs 95% of the time in Yosemite. I spent five days there last spring, climbing every day, and never placed a piton. I don't even carry a hammer in the Tetons anymore. This system of necessary fixed pitons and using natural protection will only work if the guidebook writers co-operate. The 'all-clean' (no pitons necessary) routes should be mentioned to avoid extra piton placement and removal. The new Shawangunk guide will contain this information, plus the names of the party doing the first clean ascent.

Responsibility. I prefer to climb without wearing a hard hat. I won't argue the safety issue pro or con – it's just that my head feels freer and more receptive to the good things happening all around when I climb. I believe that the wearing of a crash helmet should be a matter of personal choice. However, in some climbing areas, like Devil's Tower, Wyoming, it has become governmental policy. The same thing is true with solo climbing in some National Parks. We have no one other than ourselves to blame for these restrictive policies. We have allowed the overstressing of the safety aspects of crash helmets in the American Alpine Club Accident Reports, which insurance companies read. It won't be long before your life insurance will cover you only when wearing a crash helmet. It already applies to motorcyclists, to gardeners working along freeways, and to students in climbing schools.

We have also allowed the Park Service to feel directly responsible for climbing rescues to the extent that either rangers are on the rescue teams or the Park Service pays your friends to rescue you! Since Big Uncle has become responsible for our safety, he feels the obligation to legislate on matters that should only be a personal choice.

The responsibility for rescues should be with the climbers themselves, and should be handled on a voluntary, non-paying, non-charge basis. Helicopter costs could be paid for by an Alpine Club insurance policy as in France, or by a rescue-fund kitty, as in Britain.

The increasing frequency of rescues on big climbs goes to show that many climbers are showing an irresponsible attitude by attempting big walls before they are really equal to the problems involved. During the spring of 1971, there were over thirty attempts on El Capitan, with only four successful climbs! One of the failures involved climbers who had merely got wet, sat down and waited for a rescue while another party (on another route) continued.

Population. One day last summer sixty-five people stood on the summit of the Grand Teton. These people had camped either on the Lower Saddle or in Garnet Canyon. This means that there were probably 100 persons camping in the area, a timberline environment which is not capable of supporting more than ten groups without suffering severe damage to the fragile meadows, trees and wild flowers.

Already, the State of California is requiring reservations and is limiting the number of people allowed to go into a wilderness area. This will also happen in the Tetons and the climber will be the one to suffer.

The Alps are able to support far greater numbers of climbers than we are because of their hut systems. I agree that huts encourage even more people to go into the mountains, but the huts need not be as elaborate as those in the Alps. In any case, a hut on the Lower Saddle and another in the meadows of Garnet Canyon, plus a ban on open fire and tent camping, is the only way we can preserve the environment and still allow more than a few parties a day to climb in these areas.

Should a hut system be adopted, I only hope that the builder will have more aesthetic sense than to build a wooden A-frame at Boulder Camp in the Bugaboos (as the Canadians intend to do). To build anything but a rock hut there is like putting a Spanish Adobe on the coast of Maine.

Get Back, Jo Jo. A party now starts up El Capitan with the confidence of knowing that if anything happens they can be rescued within a day or so from any point on the wall. The fear of the unknown, the fear of being unequal to the wall, of flaming out 1500ft from nowhere can still be a real fear, but the outcome is now a certainty.

We have our topo to make sure we won't come up against any unforeseen difficulties. Let's take our jumars so that we'll only have to climb every other pitch and thus save our strength for leading because that's where it's at. Don't forget the chalk for that 5.9 friction and a few bolts, mashies, bashies and a space blanket for security. And a hundred Moms and Dads down in the meadow ready to get that rescue going just as soon as you yell for it –

maybe even before! When you come up to the A5 rurp traverse, just smash in a few tied-off 1½ inch angles, plug up that hole with a mashie and you're up. In a bar remember to tell your friends that El Cap is a piece of cake – nothing over A3 and 5.8. Then go back to Iowa and quit climbing because you've done the ultimate.

I'm trying to say that maybe Yosemite and El Capitan are not the Ultimates. It was a spaced-out adventure once, when the odds were more stacked against you, but it's not such a big deal anymore. George Lowe thought that his winter ascent of the North Face of the Grand Teton was a far more difficult climb than the Salathé Wall. If you want to experience the same adventures and the same difficulties that the El Cap pioneers had, then you've got to go somewhere else, where there are virgin walls, where you are going to feel the same loneliness of being five days from the bottom and five days from the top.

The Bavarian climber Willo Welzenbach was the greatest climber of the post-World War 1 period. He was a complete alpinist, equally adept on rock and ice. In 1925 he put up over twenty new routes in the Alps. He made the first ascents of six of the greatest north walls of the Bernese Oberland. His routes were characterised by their logic, audacity and beauty. Objective dangers, foul weather, bad conditions and rotten rock – these were not absolute obstacles for him. Caught on a wall many times by bad weather, he would wait out the storm, then continue to the summit.

All of his climbs were done in impeccable style, without fixed ropes, bolts, crash helmets, topos, radios or even down gear! These were climbs encompassing all the techniques and difficulties of Grand Alpinism: steep ice, hard free-climbing, avalanches, rockfalls, storms... and most of all, fear of the unknown.

This was the golden age of climbing; this was the pinnacle of the art, perhaps never to be equalled again. Since Welzenbach, Gervasutti and Salathé, more difficult climbs have been made, but generally as a direct result of better equipment and consequent use of that equipment.

We are entering a new era of climbing, an era that may well be characterised by incredible advances in equipment, by the overcoming of great difficulties, with even greater technological wizardry, and by the rendering of the mountains to a low, though democratic, mean.

Or it could be the start of more spiritual climbing, where we assault the mountains with less equipment and with more awareness, more experience and more courage.

from ASCENT 1972

A REVIEW OF *DOWNWARD BOUND*

ROYAL ROBBINS

This book is a farce. And in so far as the success of a book is to be judged by the achievement of the author's intentions, *Downward Bound* must be judged a success. Its war cry repeated throughout is: 'Semper farcissmus!' To take a cue from a film advertising cliché. Warren Harding is Downward Bound. And the book is distilled Harding.

Downward Bound was sent to me in galley-proof form by the editors of *Mountain Gazette*. I have reservations about writing a review from a galley proof. It isn't, after all, the finished product. There may be mistakes and absurdities caught by the reviewer which do not appear in the published work. And more than words make a book. The presentation is part of it – the paper size, binding, type, layout, drawings and photographs. I assume that the finished product will be appropriate to the text.

The galleys arrived with the appendix in front. This seemed quite natural, because of what was in the appendix, and also because I wasn't surprised at Harding putting his book together ass-backwards. The appendix is, as a matter of fact, the best part of the book. I hope it remains in the front because it provides a good introduction to what follows.

In this appendix, we are given a hierarchy of climbing levels, from one to ten. The white hats are at level one, and the hats slowly grey, becoming black at level ten, where we find 'those blackguards, who climb for heathen reasons'. Harding, of course, is at level ten. He likes to fancy himself the worst rascal around – no wishy-washy good guy, no second-rate bandit, but Billy the Kid himself. The generalised hierarchy is followed by vignette-like character sketches, as Harding assigns his numerous acquaintances, many of them well-known in the little world of climbing, to their proper niches:

Tim Auger – Zone 8: This mild-mannered little fellow has compiled an impressive list of ascents as a result of his being included on strong American climbing teams as a 'token Canadian'.

Dean Caldwell – Zone 10: An archfiend of alpinism; set standards of despiciosity.

Jim Bridwell – Zone 2: Head Kahuna of Yosemite's Camp 4 and is the founding director of the Jim Bridwell Memorial Rock Climbers' Gymnasium in Camp 4 olympic-training centre.

Kim Schmitz – Zone 2: Similar to Jim Bridwell but not as handsome.

There are many more in the same vein. If Harding knows you, you may be there.

Harding has long been known, and feared, for his ability to see a person's weakness and sum it up savagely, to caricature. By contrast with what I have seen him do, the portraits here are almost loving. Anaiis Nin says in her diary, that it takes great hate to caricature. This book, though angry at times, seems to have been written in a generally benevolent mood.

After the portraits, we are treated to 'Miscellaneous Inconsequential Bits of Climbing Information,' which provide Harding another opportunity for satire, such as:

> Climbing Schools: Rock Craft (sic) – RR and his hairy giants provide rock-climbing instruction at any level that can be imagined and some that can't! and Climbing Journals: *Mountain* – Ken Wilson, the editor, is clearly insane! He is a veritable alpine Elmer Gantry.

Harding likes that last sentence. He used the identical words to refer to me in the 1971 issue of *Ascent,* in an article titled *Reflections of a Broken-Down Climber.*

After the appendix, which provides a good introduction, comes 'Acknow-ledgements', wherein Harding acknowledges lack of any knowledge of writing. 'It may not sound classy, folks, but it's all me!' And so it is. In Harding's own words, the book is about

> ... twenty years of mountain experience, all those great people I've climbed with, eaten and drunk with, loved and hated, the mountains themselves, the good times and the bad.

The format is unusual, quite apart from the appendix. It's a story told as a slide-lecture programme: 'The Last Lecture Show', with an unusual cast of characters, among them Batso (Harding), Beasto – 'a beautiful, talented young lady who, in a lapse of sanity, became romantically and professionally associated with the infamous Batso', a Martian, Dr Sigmund Freud, and Penthouse Pundit (Ken Wilson).

In the preface, Harding promises to 'shed some light on the fun and games known as rock climbing', a hint of his great (and healthy) contempt for all those who take climbing seriously, a contempt expressed again and again here in the form of mockery of the climbing establishment, its organs, and its spokesmen.

The first section is 'Act One – Climbing Information on How to Get Nowhere the Hard Way'. This is a sort of manual explaining what rock climbing is and describing the equipment and how to climb rock. It is direct enough, though with numerous attempts at humour, not all of them successful. And there are a few oddities – for example: the definition of a peak as a summit; the statements that all climbing hammers have heads weighing about 32oz (some are half that), that runners are loops of one-inch nylon webbing (some are); Tahquitz is misspelled, and in discussing the high cost of climbing equipment, Harding quotes ropes at $50. It must have been a long time since Harding bought a climbing rope, as the current price is nearly twice that.

In this same section Harding ventures onto some thin ice without his crampons. He discusses the questions of ethics and morality in climbing and lambasts those who have truck with either. With much of this I am in agreement, especially with the instinct for anarchy (a healthy instinct, but best kept in bounds by 'archy'). In one paragraph, he cleverly likens the 'Puritan aversion to, and fear of, sex' and the 'phobia concerning bolts'; he concludes that the fears of Chouinard and Robbins (that everyone will follow Harding's example of bolting blank walls) are exaggerated, because although everyone has become sex-happy, everyone won't become bolt-happy since 'screwing is more enjoyable than drilling bolt holes!'

Fair enough. But then he says a 'bolt is simply one of the tools, and I attach no moral significance to its use'. And later, 'a climber who places bolts where pitons, or other things would do just as well is simply wasting his time and is something of a fool'. Well… who says A must equal B? Harding says the use of equipment is simply a question of efficiency. But on the Wall of the Early Morning Light, there were many places where the nailing was so difficult that it would have been faster to rivet. At five minutes per rivet (Harding's estimate) why was Harding wasting his time placing marginal pitons? In one case they were so marginal he took a forty-foot fall. Could it be he was playing the game of minimising bolts – and was being 'something of a fool'?

The second part of the book is more interesting. It's a brief history of Harding's climbing career, and a not-so-brief account of his biggest climb, 'The Dawn Wall'. The last is, indeed, the core of the book, and is described with a minimum of raving. It is the story of twenty-seven days on a 2800ft cliff, vertical, or overhanging much of the way. Harding calls it 'the Big Motha Climb'. Harding and Caldwell showed a remarkable tenacity and toughness, more than has been shown by most climbers and by probably all of their detractors and critics. It was, in fact, a formidable effort. When Lauria and I made the second ascent in February, 1971, I was impressed by two things. One was the quality of the aid work. Harding, by his own definition, may have been foolish to have wasted time avoiding rivets when the nailing got sticky, but the route is more challenging and of a higher quality because of it. The other thing was the difficulty of retreat. I had doubted that this was a genuine problem, but when we were about 600ft up, it came home to me with a chill, just how committed we were because of the overhanging nature of the rock. I was very pleased to have been spared the ordeal of fighting our way up through winter storms.

The aftermath has its high moments too. Harding is at his best when talking about other people – he's such a satirical rogue. One night he came to a party at my house, a booze party for climbers. His leg was still in a cast from running in front of a truck. He passed the evening standing on one leg – leaning against our kitchen counter – indulging in his favourite sport, and indeed, we were all drinking freely. He was in a nasty mood, and stood there, picking us off one by one with slashing verbal attacks, startling in their power and trenchancy. I have never been put off by Harding's ravings, but this time the tone was so acid it put a damper on the party (a bit). Most of us were in bed by three, but Harding and Don Lauria argued until dawn.

But as I was saying, Harding is at his best when talking about people. Some of Caldwell's characteristics, which came out on the climb, startled Harding. And he was to be even more startled by some others which evinced themselves in the aftermath. There was a rapid dissolution of their friendship because of Harding's aversion to Caldwell's avarice. Unusual stuff, bringing to mind the suit between Herrligkoffer and Messner.

Then there's the other part of the aftermath – the second ascent by Lauria and me and our ineffectual effort at 'erasing' the route. Along with the applause for Harding's and Caldwell's achievement, there had been dismay on the part of many serious Yosemite climbers – dismay because they judged the route significantly more artificial than any other on El Capitan. This, because of bolts and rivets, accounted for a third of the progress. This seemed to many of us, and to me in particular, to be a foot in the door of a change pointing toward degradation of Yosemite climbing. We felt deeply that the sport of climbing has to have limits, and that these limits had been breached. Whether either of these judgements is true is a topic for a separate discussion. A number of climbers were vociferous in their indignation, but words were cheap compared with the twenty-seven days of action in which Harding lived out his own anarchic instincts. The only effective course was a countervailing action which would make vivid the other side of the story. So I hit upon 'erasing' the route as an expression of where I thought the line should be drawn. Of course, Lauria, and I botched the job. But although Harding, in a sense, won by default, our message did get out, and there have been no more such escapades in Yosemite.

Considering Harding's ability to rage over comparative trifles, and that he was the injured party of our erasure scheme, his reaction, as expressed in his book, is mild and generally fair. He calls me an 'alpine Carrie

Nation', substituting hammer and chisel for hatchet and expansion bolts for whiskey bottles! (That's another of Harding's favourite phrases, culled from his article in *Ascent* for use in this book.) And he's got it nearly right. Unlike one of Harding's defenders (or my attackers), whose hysterical complaints envenomed the pages of *Mountain Gazette* a few issues back, Harding understands that, given his philosophy, we had as much right to remove the bolts as he to place them; and that given my philosophy, there was a temporary setting aside of the precept of leaving established routes alone so a large and pressing question could be battled out. The whole thing is *passé*, and a bit silly, but if one demands the right to place bolts as one pleases, the right to remove bolts as one pleases must be granted as well.

I might add that I am still in favour of leaving bolts in place, the exceptional circumstances of The Dawn Wall notwithstanding. When I was chopping those bolts I felt badly about doing it. It was as if I was hitting Harding with every blow, and I counted Harding among my friends (I still do). Our motives were quite different from those of the ace Yosemite aid man who made a subsequent ascent and chopped bolts he could pass without using. The same chap told me he intended to return and chop quite a few more bolts, the better to remake the route in his own image. Such bolt chopping is merely a way of underlining one's own superiority, and show ruthless contempt for the work of other men.

Aside from occasional flashes of humour, insight and character delineation, there are generalisations that ring true, such as:

I've never really understood what's supposed to be so bad about climbs receiving publicity. I don't believe the majority of climbers feel it is undesirable. It seems to me more of a snob thing among the elite who have come to believe that (presumably, because they climb rocks) they are some sort of superior breed, who should remain above the public view and that climbing must retain a mystical esoteric image.

That's a fair statement.

But a lot of the writing is pretty terrible. And there is some false sentiment (a very hard thing to avoid). Like all passionate climbers, Harding is a romantic. He strives for the impossible. And he fancies himself all bad. He takes pride in wearing the black hat, and he likes to picture himself as drunkenness, gluttony, sloth, cowardice, treachery, lechery and avarice incarnate. Drunken, but he has no claim to other sins. Harding can be demonic, but he is not as much of a devil as he likes to think. He is anything but lazy, (though he may be indolent for brief spells). He is clearly not a coward (he may at times be afraid, but he does things a man paralysed by fear can scarcely imagine). No one has ever suggested that Harding is not loyal to his friends, but his generosity, even under duress, has been commented upon. Most important, Harding is honest. His main aim, his obsessions, has been to climb the Ultimate Rock Wall. Doing big walls gives him a sort of peace. I think he likes the gaze of the public – but so what? I, for one, have had a belly-full of those exquisite moralists who complain constantly about minor human vices. That's certainly not the reason he climbs, even if it is a corollary of his climbing impulse. Harding climbs primarily for the satisfaction of achievement. Everything else is secondary. He doesn't elevate his own importance by talking down the achievements of others. And he would never step on a piton and forget about it and say he had done it free. Because what is most important to him is what he does.

Though not the bad hombre he romantically pictures himself to be, Harding is a hombre. He keeps his integrity and gives the finger to the world. His cussedness and orneriness are virtues. In a climbing world becoming ever more grey and homogenised, Harding stands out as a richly colourful character. We wouldn't want too many Hardings around, but a few more like him would be all to the good.

As an 'insider', I found the book interesting. What others will think is hard to guess, but I doubt if Prentice Hall will sell many copies. I hope I'm wrong, and perhaps I will be. After all, who would have predicted that the doughty dude who climbed the Wall of the Morning Light would have briefly become one of the most sought after celebrities of American climbing history?

from MOUNTAIN GAZETTE *May 1975*

A CLIMB IN CAE COCH QUARRY

HAROLD DRASDO

The amphitheatre proved to be an interesting place. Nature was locked in isometric exercises on the floor with a mob of healthy young birches pressing an assortment of taller conifers. Three sheep and a huge orange dog lay rotting in the trees and we had to steer tortuous lines through these obstacles. Later, with a correct compassion, Swallow removed the dog's collar and read the inscription aloud. I have forgotten what it said. In every sod and behind each loose flake a worm was coiled; the whole place stank of death and rebirth. Evan Roberts was astonished when I described it to him and his old head nodded. He had been working there as a quarryman when operations were abandoned just after the war and there was not a blade of grass to be seen then.

One wet week I persuaded Tony Moulam to come to look at it and so we laid hands on it at last. The first day we broke through the undergrowth and climbed the most cowardly line: Gwydir Gully, not easy in the rain to start or finish. A day or two later we got onto the slabby buttress on the right and climbed it in three pitches: Transect. (He says it happened the other way round and he's usually right.) Next I came back with Jack Soper and Jim Swallow. Jack did well to lead the first pitch which was a bit thin and was further defended from mid-height by a short but menacing shower. I went a fair distance up the second pitch but I could see that the finish was really dangerous so I came back and proposed Jim. Jack seconded and I went third – it seemed a characteristic situation and I believe the words have a familiar ring: but then they made me lead the last pitch. Eventually I found an easy way out though I was told afterwards that at one point Swallow bent his head downwards and slightly sideways and called, 'Speed, speed,' with emphasis but without malice, so showing consideration for everyone's feelings. That route tended rightwards and we called it Tendency. Later I did a more direct route to the same finish with Holroyd: Embargo. There was more excitement in these climbs than this paragraph gives away.

This brings me to the climb we called The Nave. It is the line of the cliff. It is the junction between the main slab on the right – 200ft high, 300ft long, and still unclimbed – and the cracked buttress left of it, giving the routes already named. The line is evidently inescapable: diagonally left up the steep, nearly featureless slab to the corner of the big overlap; along and up beneath the overlap to get into the main fault; and up that Garden of Eden to the top.

We were a party of three. Trevor Jones, full of enthusiasm and drive, kept saying so. Mouly, quietly keen and confident, kept edging Jones on but prepared to step in if things didn't go ahead as intended. The writer, sceptical but fascinated, wanting to combine irreconcilables by climbing a desperate new route without doing anything risky.

Jones led off in fine style but came to a halt after thirty feet just above a shallow niche. Said it was impossible but would only come down if someone else would go up. Mouly went up, put a nut into its proper place, and came down. I went up, stood in the sling in the nut, cleaned out a hole to allow further progress; and came down.

Round two. Jones went up, got onto the hold, lurched upwards, knocked a peg in and came down. While he was up there he reported several times that he was buggered; but when he found himself safely back on the ground his strength and optimism were miraculously restored. A change of order then and I went up to the peg and moved fractionally higher. It was barely fifteen feet to the overlap where a crack with vacancies for every sort of piton had been teasing us for a long time; but there was no wrinkle anywhere in that gap on which hands or feet or hopes might rest. Since no movement in the right direction was possible it was necessary to stand still or descend; since we wanted the climb very badly it was inexcusable to go down; and since standing still for a long time looks foolish I had to find something to do.

Well, what happened was this. Only eighteen inches to my right there was a projecting penny-sized tuft of grass – we wanted to go leftwards. To make the place tidier I pulled it off. And it proved to be securely attached to a perfect core of earth a foot long, revealing a borehole into which the shaft of a hammer slotted perfectly. It was set at just that angle to give confidence and I was surprised to notice then that the weather was magnificent. With tension from a sling round the hammer I was able to precariously lay away and with the reach gained I could inspect a hairline crack marking the back of a small flake.

So I forced the blade of a second hammer into it – a degree of brutality is admitted here – and so split it as barbarously as the last infinitive. This done, a perfect hold for the archetypal steep mantelshelf was produced. It looked good. By this time Jones was extremely excited so I excused myself from a rather committing move, went down, tied him on, and had him hoisted halfway up before he realised I was taking advantage.

Well, he did the pitch. First he got to the overhang and supplied the crack with its peg. Then, with the determination of which he had spoken earlier, he slowly followed the stepped overlap upwards, removing what was temporary and leaving behind a briefly spaced series of runners on which the eye was able to rest with some satisfaction. From time to time he called out that he was finished and at times we feared this might be true. But there was little that we could do to help him and as you know it gets to the point on a long and arduous pitch like this at which going on is desolately exhausting but at which the mere thought of trying to get back without leaving your gear or honour behind drains you completely. Your throat gets so dry. With a 100ft out he reached a sturdy little tree with a neat little ledge underneath it and without stopping to get his breath he lashed himself hard on to every possible point of attachment. Powerful stuff, boy. We tried to encourage him along the remaining thirty feet of overlap but it is impossible to pass a stance like that after such effort.

Mouly went steadily up to join him and set out immediately on the remaining traverse. Again this proved difficult, the sort of irreducibly awkward passage that may be taken by two or three methods but no way easily. It needed cleaning and it was greasy and insecure. Mouly crossed it in his crabbed and painful but unfailingly effective style. Jones and I were both rather unhappy on it. It was a real bit of Moulamite. Coming last I allowed myself the luxury of a back rope round the little tree.

I caught up with them at the foot of the huge corner attached to two much bigger trees. These were ostensibly healthy but I suspected that their roots lay on stony ground. Everything seemed ready to peel off and I was forcibly restrained from setting a magic circle of pegs around the whole party. The corner was filled with grass and other matter for its whole distance and it was steeper than we had expected. It proved deceptive at a couple of points and we thought that not all the decoration was there to stay. You dig your fingers in, make some sort of foothold, move up, and the stuff starts to pull away before your eyes. Gripping. I will show you fear in a handful of dust. But there was no stopping now and a typically gruesome quarry exit was avoided for a pleasant nose on the left.

We were all pleased at this result. Jones, who had led the crucial pitch and had incidentally snatched first place in an eventual list of first ascents; Mouly, who had directed the ascent and had used his authority to allow no one to chicken out; the writer, who had shown the way up a good eight or nine feet of difficult rock but who was easily able to persuade himself that his contribution had been a significant one.

from 'Punch Up at the Padern Lake'
CLIMBERS' CLUB JOURNAL 1962

ARMS LIKE A FLY

PETE LIVESEY

Hell! He's got big arms – and that blue-eyed god-like expression doesn't help either. The object of my scrutiny was John Syrett, who'd just failed to get up Kilnsey's Central Wall on what could have been the first free ascent. Could have been, yes, but would it ever be now that the reincarnation of J.M.E standing over at the bar had turned back on it? The pace was hotting up in Yorkshire now, we'd had it virtually to ourselves for six months, now here were two teams scrapping for Kilnsey's prize. We'd snatched Diedre the week before, lifted it from the same team that were ahead of us in the Central Wall stakes.

The Saturday after, and heavy rain shrouded John and I as we slipped over the edge on a long, airy inspection abseil. The route looked steep but possible from out there in space. Syrett's two aid pegs grinned tantalisingly, though I couldn't see any reason for the second one; but it's alright talking from a floating bath chair. A climber's van pulled up on the road below and two disinterested looking climbers sidled straight towards us. We sorted and resorted our gear, arranged it in rows and piles; anything but look at the rope hanging there thirty feet out from the base of the crag. The lead sidler approached, appearing to ignore the rope, and asked important questions about the weather – which was still deluging outside – and about ten-foot crags down the road. He sidled away backwards to the next dry route where he climbed and reclimbed the section in full view of our rope. I thought about his big arms as we scrambled to the top to retrieve our rope – bigger than Syrett's; hell they must be good. I kept looking at my withered little arms and decided it wasn't fair. That was it for the day; I was demoralised, the climb was steep and they'd all got bigger arms than me. Even Sheard's arms seemed to be bulging Popeye-like under his Ben Sherman shirt – John always climbs in that kind of gear, he's never been the same since he saw Rouse at Stoney in his velvet loons. No, you just couldn't attempt a new route with the cards stacked like that.

We shot off to Loup Scar where we just managed to put up Lapper, an all-weather fun route that should become a classic – it had been waiting a while for suitably wet conditions. Pulling over the final three-foot roof boosted confidence in my demoralised muscles – I was subconciously preparing for the day after. I reckoned if we weren't at Kilnsey on Sunday, Syrett and R.B.J. would have it during the week.

Sunday morning rolled over and it was wet again; this bird kept sticking her foot in my ear so what can you do but get out – I could have hidden for a day in bed. Sheard arrived two hours late – that's good for John so the sod must be keen. John's car pointed inexorably towards Kilnsey, wipers at double speed vainly scraping at the weather. I was getting edgy now, only half confident that the route would be wet. Kilnsey loomed up, a black dripping hulk with a laughing patch of powder dry rock right where Central Wall should have been wet. A finger of wet crossed the route at one point but fate said it had to be done. John said nothing, just handed me his store of slings and crabs. Neither of us said much – I was now engrossed in fright. The start is a vicious little pull over a roof to gain a ramp rising leftwards. Ten feet of climbing and you're committed, but so far the holds were good and I was finding lots of little threads below the guardian overlap I was following. I felt very unhappy up there, I'd used a lot of energy getting over the initial bulge and things were going to get a lot steeper in the next hundred feet. The wall steepened as it merged into the overlap, a high side pull enabling Syrett's first aid peg to be reached. I was just about to swing on it when there was a little hold above it – would it do? I climbed down a few feet for a look. The problem was to get my left hand on the hold and make a huge swing right for a flake, but the move was perfectly protected. I kept thinking – if I fall onto the peg, will it be aid? I was still trying to resolve the problem as I lunged off rightwards and made the flake. It was a case of climbing fast now for twenty feet to a loose block with a resting ledge. I just made the ledge as the familiar finger-fade symptoms crept on. Nearly halfway now with a long steep groove ahead running out in a blank wall. The groove looked obvious but I hadn't a clue about the blank wall – still, limestone being limestone…

You've got to go soon when you're plastered on a blank wall like that, so off I went. The groove went very quickly, a good nut too, but I took a long time working out an exit to the foot of the wall. Eventually I reached a little overhung ledge on the right, heartbeat ledge, and smiling down slit-mouthed from above were a couple of handhold like breaks. Lunge and lunge again? Both were handholds, and I was there, at a peg on Trauma Traverse. For the first time I felt happy, then nearly fell off traversing left over grease squeezed out of cracks by the sheer weight of the crag.

The tree belay grows horizontally out of a crack, forming an airy seat (so I had a peg as well) from which I could gloat down the great overhung wall at John. The slack was up and in came John, powering up on fingers and the occasional toe. He started talking again at about three quarters height; that must be where it eases off – I was too gripped to notice any easing off? John arrived and hung his arms around his ankles for a while. Next was an overhang with a corner above, disappearing as it eased to vertical. This was unseen ground but there looked to be plenty of holds lurking behind the grass. I climbed the tree until it bent too much to be of any further use, got a finger jam and a nut in the same hole and swung off. The steepness of the situation became immediately obvious, and the holds above were jammed full of sods. I gave in, sat in the sling and gardened the groove above. The holds just below the overhang were now apparent, if still muddy, so off we go. I could quite happily fall off now, you know how it feels, nothing can go wrong – the main pitch was done. Above the overhang the climbing eased to VS on large holds and in forty feet it was all over. John joined me in the rain and cold on top but it didn't matter now – we'd done with Kilnsey for the time being. We could just drift euphorically away without looking back; we wouldn't have believed it anyway. It's almost a pleasure going back to work after a route like that – can't wait, give the kids a stack of maths and write up the route for the glossies – hell! my arms look big now ...

from ROCKSPORT December *1972*

IN PRAISE OF CHEATING

HAROLD DRASDO

Though play as such is outside the range of good and bad, the element of tension imparts to it a certain ethical value in so far as it means a testing of the player's prowess: his courage, tenacity, resources, and, last but not least, his spiritual powers – his 'fairness'; because, despite his ardent desire to win, he must still stick to the rules of the game.

The player who trespasses against the rules or ignores them is a 'spoilsport'. The spoilsport is not the same as the false player, the cheat; for the latter pretends to be playing the game and, on the face of it, still acknowledges the magic circle. It is curious to note how much more lenient society is to the cheat than to the spoilsport. This is because the spoilsport shatters the play-world itself. By withdrawing from the game he reveals the relativity and fragility of the play-world in which he had temporarily shut himself with others.'

Johan Huizinga, Homo Ludens

Over the past few years monologues and dialogues on what have come to be called climbing ethics have become a regular feature of climbers' magazines. Tejada-Flores and Robbins have presented intriguing and comprehensive descriptions of how the ethical machinery works or ought to work, and recently Robin Campbell has offered a shorter decalogue. To be sure, Campbell and others have mentioned their discomfort at talking about ethics in this respect – as if climbing had dilemmas as weighty as those of the medical and legal professions. Recall, though, that in a famous essay on conservation written no less than forty years ago Aldo Leopold urged a further extension of ethical concepts: ethics dealt with property and people at first, he said; but ethics ought to consider unimproved land and the life-forms it supports. Clearly there is a sense in which many young climbers agree with him and want to go a step further by protecting the inanimate world of rock.

Ought one to apologise for adding to this literature? If so, I offer two apologies, alternatives if you like. First, climbing and mountaineering have been great fun and very satisfying. But the threats from technology and population pressure in the past are nothing to the threats looming in the immediate future. I find myself reluctant to agree with David Roberts (*Ascent*, 1972) that the sport is probably doomed and may already be in its last throes. But I am sure that if we want to enjoy these pastimes in roughly the same sorts of ways as in the past, it would be wise to ascertain whether and how we ought to protect them. Second, at some time or other I have flouted almost every rule within an English climber's reach. And yet, in the very act of committing each misdemeanour, an utterly plausible excuse has been taking shape in my mind. So perhaps I write with unusual authority and have important new material to contribute?

It makes sense to begin by scanning the entire field of unethical behaviour on mountains, using 'unethical' in our contemporary sense. Some readers may be upset at the inclusion of certain items in this list but all these practices have been complained of by someone at some time. It might be worth adding that less heinous offences, best referred to as breaches of 'climbing manners', can also be identified; some of the prototypes of these peccadilloes were excellently dealt with by Winthrop Young in *Mountain Craft* and more modern forms can be extrapolated.

So we begin, obviously, with the use of a power drill to get up a mountain and of a helicopter to get down; with the use of light aeroplanes to look for or at prospective routes; with the use of helicopters, aeroplanes, skidoos, jeeps, scramble bikes and so on, to get men or material nearer to the climb than other or earlier visitors.

Next we have the use of pegs, bolts, nuts and slings to allow one to stand or hang in comfort where it might otherwise be difficult or impossible; and the abandoning of this or other material on the mountain. Then there is the whittling-away of climbs from below by the use of siege tactics; and the softening-up of climbs from above by inspection or rehearsal by rappel or top-rope and by the placing of useful or displacing of unhelpful material.

Here we might add the dissemination of detailed information about the mountain and its climbs in the form of guidebooks, magazine articles, route descriptions, photos and topos. And then comes the guiding on mountain excursions of people who want to go that way but daren't go there on their own; or of those who might just drift there by chance but who don't understand what the mountain is for; or of people who don't admire the mountain and are scared stiff anyway.

All sorts of other complaints have been lodged: about the presence on mountains of people with uniforms, or with badges and certificates to prove it; about the building of shelters and refuges; about the over-development of rescue facilities; about the use of funny shoes on easy climbs, and so on. But that will do for a start.

Now it is clear to me that matters of right and wrong in climbing involve actions with effects of two quite different categories. First, they involve actions detrimental to the scene in its widest sense: conservation ethics, called here *environment ethics*. Second, they involve actions that threaten the accepted styles of climbing: game ethics, called here *competition ethics* to emphasise the dominant aspect of their nature. Some activities certainly lead to both sorts of damage but it remains possible and important to separate the categories and effects.

We can list the main offences against environment ethics briefly. First, there is damage to the biological life-bank of the cliff or mountain, its plants and bird or animal life. Second, there is damage to the rock itself, considered as something natural and admirable rather than as a climbing problem that might need re-grading after rough treatment. Third, there are the litter nuisances: bog paper on every ledge and bolts in every wall. And, fourth, there is the erosion of the absolute mystery, dignity and privacy of the mountain and the contamination of the local or native culture the mountain stands behind and is coloured by.

There are other problems as well. But in summary these are the sorts of complaints that might be made by non-climbers who love the mountain in an entirely platonic sense. The general type of offence is *disturbance*. One could say a lot about these matters and if it were claimed that they are outside the scope of climbing ethics the reply is, no, absolutely not, the two areas are inseparable in many instances. But it is true that the most heated arguments at present are about the ways in which climbs are carried out.

Competition ethics are based upon a number of factors or desiderata. There is the need to exert oneself; there is the need to scare oneself; there is the need to excel; and there is the example of archetypal climbs. Beyond this, competition ethics respond to change: advances in techniques; advances in technology; increases in wealth and leisure; and the effects of population pressures.

In mentioning the more important of these factors, Tejada-Flores' indispensable description of 'climbing-games' has to be used as a model yet again. One notes that he remarks that the climbing-game hierarchy isn't the only way of thinking about climbing and no doubt he went through a number of alternatives. But an obvious way of describing breaches of competition ethics is by saying that they amount to the use of a handicap-system to assist the climber rather than to defend the climb. The subversive purpose of this essay is to ask how much competition ethics matter; but the question will have to wait a moment.

Having listed offences against environment ethics we can now look at the flouting of competition ethics. And here the cardinal sin is simply the use of too much advantage, especially in support of a pre-emptive strike. To this we can add the leaving of aid in place, a temptation to subsequent parties. Over the past few years remarks about the use of excessive protection have also been voiced from time to time. And then there is the creation of a variation or traverse which, whilst giving a new climb, detracts from the ambience of an existing line, a question of manners possibly. But the general type of offence is that of reducing the personal handicap in relation to other climbers likely to attempt the same route.

It was remarked earlier that some activities offend both ethics and some only one or the other. So, for example, a pure bolt ascent might be held to flout environment ethics (by leaving litter on the wall) and to flout competition ethics (by eliminating the personal handicap). Gardening, on the other hand, violates environment ethics but ratifies competition ethics because it leaves the climb in a more permanent condition; whilst rehearsal by top-rope may be held to offend competition ethics but does not threaten environment ethics in the least.

Excursus on sentiment: The great climbs can stand an ancient victory piton and the odd retreat pegs; even, perhaps, extended peg and bolt ladders in certain situations depending mainly, rightly or wrongly, on how much anxiety the situation arouses in the average climber undertaking the route. Climbing is an art-form, engaging our feelings; and these mementos, speaking of the struggles of our predecessors, of success and failure, arouse emotions in us. Even litter, then, may add to the impact of a climb. So here is the related crunch question for frustrated ethicists. Does an unrecorded bolt ascent of an otherwise unvisited wall breach environment ethics? Or competition ethics? Or both? Or neither?

Another general observation on breaches of ethics centres on the relative permanence of the effect. I began by mentioning the use of a power drill to get up a mountain and of a helicopter to get down. Each of these bits of assistance constitutes a total breach of both ethics. But note that the bolting is a relatively irreversible gesture against both ethics: the use of the helicopter insults the environment ethic only until the echoes have died away; whilst it damages the competition ethic for as long as we say it does.

Here's an odd difference then. Environment ethics can be breached temporarily, with perfect repair, or permanently and irreparably, or something in between. But how competition ethics are breached depends purely on what we say about the matter. And we are influenced by factors that tend to make us change our minds and construct new rules.

One can observe the rules, or one can pretend to observe them, or one can ignore them. And it is those who assume the last two roles who interest me now: the cheat and the spoilsport.

In climbing, a spoilsport is something more than just a climber who takes an advantage one had not thought of oneself. A spoilsport might be described as a cheat who admits, announces or boasts of his cheating; or, retrospectively, a cheat who gets found out. But, to confuse matters, British climbers use the expression 'cheating' in two ways. First, we joke that we are cheating when we use more assistance than is usual; but by this self-accusation we resign from the contest and clear ourselves. Second, we cheat when we don't tell the truth about the aid we've used. The opportunities for this on smaller crags have become less with population pressure. But even on British cliffs there can be few leading climbers who have never found themselves with a foot 'caught in a sling'; 'whilst gardening holds', maybe. And if any essential aid has been admitted to, dispensable aid is less likely to be recorded.

Something can be said in support of both cheat and spoilsport. In defence of the cheat it has to be said that, in contrast to the disturbing practices mentioned earlier, cheating stands alone; it does not really threaten the game of climbing. Hence the title of this article. In defence of the spoilsport one can say what Durkheim said of other criminals. That his existence is inevitable because he is the agent used to clarify and define the edges of permissible behaviour. Perhaps both cheat and spoilsport might be regarded as the guerrillas of the mountaineering world, sabotaging the ethics machine when its workings are causing absurd or undesirable effects.

So here's a health to Mr X*. Half cheat, half spoilsport, ably seconded by his three fantasised companions (how real and individual were their person-alities to him? Who was the best of the three? Where did J. S. Martin spend his August holiday in 1967?) he blazed his way to glory through thirty dream climbs. One has to give credit where it is due. In *The Decay of Lying*, Wilde speculates on the character of the true liar – 'his frank, fearless statements, his superb irresponsibility' – and defines the really breathtaking lie: 'Simply that which is its own evidence'. The genius of Mr X was of a very unusual, very broad and visionary nature, easily damaged by the cynicism of the world. He was able not only to look at cliffs and write up fairly plausible descriptions of impressive lines: but he was also willing and happy to attend climbing club dinners as guest of honour and to make long and stupefyingly boring speeches about his latest achievements and the state of the campaign. There's conviction for you! One hopes that he has not been too distressed at the response the uncovering of his initiatives drew. It would be nice to think that he might one day return to the climbing scene with new ideas.

I will assume now that most of us agree that breaches of environment ethics are matters worth serious thought, even if some alleged abuses need to be looked at rather sceptically. But these are not the main subject of this article

*A climber who was believed to have invented over thirty fictitious routes in North Wales in the late 1960s.

so only one question now remains: do competition ethics matter? There are certainly points to be made for and against them.

Clearly, competition ethics are essential for competitors. They enable them to sort themselves out and to get into order of size, this operation giving great happiness, anguish and excitement. Further, it is surely the case that the better one climbs a route, the closer to the archetypal style, the more pleasure one gets. For the most brilliant climbers, ethical climbing is the only means by which a high enough level of tension can be achieved and that goal becomes more elusive as technique and technology progress. Finally, ethical climbing ensures that some problems are left unsolved; and apart from the fact that this conserves a field of action for the experts of tomorrow it is also claimed that there is an intrinsic virtue in modesty and self-denial.

What, then, can be said against competition ethics? First, that they should only apply to competitors. Might it not seem reasonable for a man to ask to compete, not with other climbers – the collateral competition – but only with the route and his own limits – the vertical competition: and therefore to use whatever assistance he feels to be necessary? This seems fair enough to me. The joy of climbing includes elements other than the pleasure of excelling, including, as claimed already, the catharsis of exertion and fear; and that satisfaction is quite independent of one's performance as compared with the standards agreed by groups. It might be said that unethical climbing is simply a means of avoiding any such catharsis, but this is usually true only for the scornful bystander in a particular situation; the unethical climber is probably finding his unethical solution amply exciting.

The excellence of climbs, given a certain length of route, also depends more upon such aesthetic factors as beauty of position, rock architecture, setting and view, than upon the actual method of achieving the hardest move: and on a fairly long route the experience is not much affected whether the crux has been climbed by layback, by jamming, or by standing in a nut sling. So that sixty-year-olds, I think, ought to insist upon their right to nut the crucial sections of routes climbed free by thirty-year-olds. The fact that this right is derided in Britain at present is lamentable. We have reached the point at which sensitive climbers are having to spend their holidays in Patagonia, where the wind is too loud to permit prolonged discussions on ethics.

But now, unhappily, I reach the problem on which the theorists break themselves: that posed by climbers who, in using extensive aid, reject the competition ethic (since they're achieving a high enough level of tension as it is) but who record their claims to first ascents. Is the First Ascents List a competition? Does it pre-suppose adherence to the competition ethic of a particular time and place? Or is it no more than it calls itself, a historical record? At this point I find myself in a bit of a fix. I cannot help commenting here on how irresistible the sexual metaphor appears to be. Don't rape the mountains, says Campbell; leave a few monuments to Virginity, says Robbins. It is a commonly held opinion nowadays that a false value has often been placed upon virginity; and many readers, no doubt, share Dr Comfort's view that chastity is no more a virtue than malnutrition. Perhaps, then, the metaphor is misleading? And yet, in mountaineering the image of the undespoiled seems to remain central and essential. Even those who imply that too much is made of this legend of purity seem, by the very act of recording their unethical ascents, to shake their own case. (Curious, too, to note how many climbers have put on record the fact that they've made new routes without recording them.) From this point several trains of thought depart and it's not possible to catch all of them at once. So I content myself with saying that metaphors of violation ought to be scrutinised carefully. In fact, I suspect that some interesting understandings of the nature of the wilderness experience might result.

My own predilection, and my practice, is for doing new routes as best one can; and, despite my title, for being reasonably honest about the methods used. It doesn't perturb me in the least if someone has made a new route by using more aid than I find to be necessary on my subsequent ascent. If someone repeats my own climb with less difficulty, I'm suitably impressed; with more, and I'm childishly delighted. I think I know who made the first ascents of the Mont Aiguille, the Devil's Tower, Lost Arrow and whatever, and I know how they succeeded. In a strange way the histories of climbs made outside the competition ethic are often as interesting as those of climbs made within it. So I think that the moderate climber ought to reject the spectatorial role the élite have assigned to him. If I find a desperate crack, accessible to me with two or three nuts and slings, I'm not going to watch it for years until someone arrives who can finger up it. His aching fingers will be his eventual reward as my dry throat was mine. His ethical ascent can be used to underline the advance of the generations or simply my lack of skill. But note that it might also be necessary to record the weather and perhaps other variables; unless it is proposed to forbid the use of aid (or top-roping or gardening *en rappel*) on new routes except in fine weather. Clearly, the freeing of hard British rock-climbs is basically a fine-weather sport for gentlemen of leisure who can wait for perfect conditions; whilst British rock-climbing itself is (surely?) an all-weather sport.

(I must add here, in relation to the use of aid, that the problems of speed and manners are often present. The objection to the use of siege tactics surely stems in part from a response to the arrogance of blocking and claiming a route in an area in which there is a population pressure problem. And when I encourage old men and poor performers to use aid on difficult routes, I beg them to consider whether they have a right to hold up a queue of climbers who are genuinely longing to ascend that particular climb.)

This article has changed shape a dozen times since first I sketched it out. I had a hundred dazzling insights, which I could not accommodate at this length, and I met a hundred baffling problems, which I could only evade or ignore. The general field of environment ethics, the critical problem of people pollution, the intriguing area of the influence of archetypes, and the matter of orders of preference in the use of advantage, have had to be passed by. The basic structure of the article seems to me to be a reasonable way of looking at the practices of climbers. But now I begin to notice a suspicious resemblance between the different pronouncements on the subject, each having a catch clause at the end.

Tejada-Flores' hierarchy of climbing-games allows an ultimate judgement from the concept of good and bad style. Robbins proposes a revolutionary First Ascent Principle and his benevolent ethic allows the moderate climber to have as much fun as he likes; but then he announces a class of actions called Outrages and these cannot be permitted. Campbell outlines three restricted Categorical Imperatives and then comes up with a fourth, Love the Mountain, which can be used to deal with any abuses he may notice. Some readers may think my own suggestions disgustingly permissive; they have probably forgotten my Environment Ethic, which enables me to forbid anything that makes a mark or a noise. Perhaps, from the beginning, I ought to have distinguished more rigorously between clean aid and dirty aid, nut and piton, as the Americans keep doing. At any rate, I write in the certain knowledge that people will let me know where I went wrong.

In the end, especially for those who climb in public, it's a dialogue. It's a good thing that a climber should recognise his capabilities. He should see the world as it is and understand, if he doesn't already, that he may not be the best performer in the game. And it's a good thing also, provided that the environment ethic isn't brutally offended, that a climber should feel free to do his own thing and to reject the rules of others. I take J. E. B. Wright's account of an incident during the German attempt in 1936 on Lliwedd's then unclimbed Central Gully Direct as a model for this dialogue:

> Stöppler had been warned about the Welsh weather and he had a tube fitted to his Bergen Sack which took an umbrella. He was leading with the umbrella open keeping off the rain. Teufel was leading me up Reade's Crack. Along came five climbers. As they arrived at the foot of Central Gully, bang, bang, went Stöppler's hammer. The spokesman of the five shouted, 'What do you think you're doing?' Bang, bang, went the hammer. This question was addressed

several times, in a rising crescendo, to Stöppler and Schneider, neither of whom could speak English. The banging and shouting went on alternately. Finally Stöppler said to Schneider in German, 'if he shouts again, throw a rock at him.' The stone was not thrown but the banging went on and the party of five continued on their way.'

There are some extraordinarily puzzling questions in the field of climb-ing ethics and it's rather amusing to see the young philistines torturing themselves with new forms of the sorts of conundrums that have teased philosophers for centuries. But if matters of environmental damage aren't involved perhaps the really crucifying dilemmas are for very small groups of people – the freakishly talented, the disgustingly rich, and the clinically disturbed: but not for you and me.

from MOUNTAIN 39 *1974*

TWO LETTERS

KEITH MYHILL and ED DRUMMOND

Dear Sir,
    In *Mountain 28* you reported an 'attempt' by Ed Drummond on the wall to the right of Right Eliminate on Curbar.
    This event must surely mark the lowest point in gritstone climbing for a very long time. A hammered nut may seem undesirable to some, and repeated top-rope rehearsals do not impress, but chipping ledges to use two skyhooks for aid and a chipped flake is just too much. When routes like these are recommended, there is every encouragement to Joe Bloggs to bolt up Great Slab or chip holds in Three Pebble Slab. If Ed Drummond continues to peg, bolt, bash and hook his way up gritstone, why shouldn't a more average climber chip a hold when a bit pressed or place a peg to make things easier? There is really no reply to this if leading climbers employ such tech-niques while putting up their routes. The point is that if a climber of lesser ability (and reputation) than Drummond produced a route like Linden, it would be dismissed as pathetic and over-aided. Drummond, however, has the undoubted ability to produce hard routes in good style (e.g. Archangel on Stanage), so the issue becomes a little more confused.

At present, the position of Peak grit as a sanctuary of free climbing is very finely balanced and the outcome is in doubt. Pegs are appearing on Stanage VDiffs, and jammed nuts are becoming more common. It would appear that the example being set by a few leading climbers is beginning to influence more average climbers, to the detriment of the state of the rock. The Swan, Calvary and The Guillotte are all good, hard climbs, apart from the defiling peg on each, but now we have the unhappy Linden – what is to be Drummond's next offering on the altar of his ego?

There must be a few good lines left on grit that would be possible with a peg or two, but is that the way? The bigoted attitudes of some of the Lakeland guidebook writers may seem unpalatable to many, but at least some standards are being defended, which is better than none at all.

Yours etc., Keith Myhill (Sheffield)

Dear Sir,

So Molehill and Myhill have joined forces. Not content with the murder by innuendo of my efforts, Molehill opens its pages to the service of the notorious Peak District landlord.

Oh that picture! And that headline: 'Myhill attacks ...'

What did he use? A piton hammer? (from the look of the picture). Excuse me – of course I mean a toffee hammer; (or was it humbugs that he was trying to swallow that account for his admitted confusion?). How could I climb 'a hard route in good style' and also (although he doesn't see it) an even harder route (The Linden) with impeccable style? If he doesn't think that my ascent of The Linden was impeccable then why didn't he go and climb it first? Why doesn't he go and climb it now? If he knows, or if he wants to know, what he's talking about – which he can't until he's done the route in at least the same style that I did it in (even then there's no guarantee that if he could he'd tell the truth about its magnificence) – he'd realise that Rome wasn't built in a day; nor Cenotaph ascended by Saint Joseph without a pin here and a pin there. And Quietus top-roped first. I'm still learning how to learn. Silly Myhill. It isn't your hill. The route is there for you, too. Go on – open your legs – let's see what you can do. Balancing on those two impeccable skyhooks should keep you quiet. You might even learn to pray; and not prey.

Also, I chipped no flake. Just the two dots for the hooks.

Finally, try to get your facts straight Molehill (and your face will take care of itself). Drummond did not do the South Buttress of El Capitan (popularly known as The Nose) 'mainly on nuts'. He did over half of it free – which means hands and heart and feet. He placed no pitons and used only nuts for protection and aid, except for the occasional fixed points: that is, he studiously avoided using as many fixed pins as possible. And in fact used no more than twenty.

I ought to know as I was with him all the time and I was proud of him. It is himself he beats.

Truly, Edwin Drumstick (Yosemite)
from MOUNTAINS 31 & 35 1974

THE HANDICAP COMMITTEE

RUSSELL TAYLOR

To enable all members to climb on an equal footing (a thing which many climbs lack) it is proposed that the club institutes a handicap committee. Golfers will be aware that a golf club has attached to it a group of sages known as 'the Handicap Committee'. This august body assigns to each member his just and proper handicap, thus ensuring that the race is not always to the swift.

Handicaps shall be used to arrive at the 'True Grade' in accordance with the formula: (True Grade) equals (Grade of climb) plus (Climber's handicap).

The handicap shall be calculated from a median grade of 15 with respect to the grade which each climber is just capable of leading. Table 1 shows some examples.

Climber's Capability	Handicap
15*	0
22	–7
8	+7

There shall be a further proviso that any climber given a handicap of more than +7 shall be entitled to use unlimited aid (direct and for rests) on any

---

*The Australian grade 15 approximates to British 4b and American 5.6

climb. Also anybody climbing at a true grade greater than 15 may use an unlimited amount of runners. Finally there shall be the following overriding provisions:

1. The decisions of the Handicap Committee shall be final and binding – members shall not enter into any correspondence concerning their own handicap but may freely report on any other members; and

2. At its discretion, and without prior notice, the Handicap Committee may vary handicaps and/or alter the handicap formula and conditions so as to ensure that the aims of the handicap system are met.

The advantages of the handicap system are obvious. Unseemly and deplorable public displays of hard climbing and ego-tripping will be curbed. In future the practice of these vices shall be confined to secret, furtive struggles. The gentlemanly art of histrionics shall come into full play on our well frequented cliffs. The 'hard' man will give way to the 'soft' man who can fool the handicap committee with his brilliant simulations of gross ineptitude (e.g. top ropes and regular benightments on grade 8s/V.Diffs), thus upping his handicap. Indeed we can look forward to the restoration of climbing as a pastime for gentlemen, where the robust muscular Christians sit around the roaring fire as the storm outside beats on the window. With stout mugs of ale at their sides and pipes in hand, they go over the day's epic struggle up a classic V.Diff. and recall the glories of departed climbers and the old days gone forever. To them defeat (retreat) does not matter, as long as the game was well played.

A less obvious benefit of the handicap system is the status it will confer on senior (i.e. old men) club members. Although dwindling in energy, and stiffening in the joints, these senior men are long in experience and the wisdom of years (i.e. old fools). This wealth of accumulated wisdom is manifested in the ability of these sages (i.e. climbing bores) to discourse at infinite length on the merits and demerits of climbs and climbers. Such senior men shall be automatically co-opted onto the handicap committee, where they will devote their profound advice (i.e. drivellings) to the secret councils of the committee.

To get the handicap system started it is proposed to call nominations for the Handicap Committee members at the next monthly meeting of the club – so have your names ready.

from THRUTCH *1975*

PART 5

EXPEDITIONS

For some reason this field has failed to produce any mass of worthwhile literature. The odd book and article demand attention, but in general the activities of expeditions have been recorded in a workmanlike but prosaic manner. The chore of writing articles for the main alpine journals fails to inspire climbers to any great creative efforts, and virtually all the recent expedition books have been equally unadventurous. It may be that the tensions that simmer under the surface of even well led expeditions demand a rather bland style of description resulting in books that are diplomatic but predictable. Another contributory factor may be the wearisome demands made on the climbers by the media and the lecture circuits. By the time they come to record their stories in the official accounts, much of the zest for the telling has been spent.

Thus the best writings on expeditions are invariably the first printed accounts by the lead climbers on their return, or the whimsical observations of the support climbers or informed observers. That this can still be said after a decade of intense expedition activity is depressing. We look in vain for an expedition book of real creative worth to match the literary efforts of the other sections of the sport; possibly some of the future biographies could make up the loss.

Note for 2006: The situation changed dramatically in the late 1970s. The demise of the big set-piece expedition in favour of smaller, lightweight ventures led to far more eventful narratives. The list overleaf notes a selection of books of this ilk written since 1977. It gives mainly first-hand accounts of climbs and does not include books of comment, biography, history and other tangential ruminations. The *emboldened books* are those where the climbing involved was essentially done in a lightweight capsule or alpine-style. In this the climber is more active and involved and accounts are thus usually more dramatic and eventful. In recent years conventional expeditions have increasingly become the territory of disparate climbers in guided groups (the Albert Smiths and Henriette d' Angevilles of the 21st Century) making ascents of well trodden routes on the 8000m peaks. This has led to a growth of populist accounts describing their experiences and epics. Everest (in particular) has attracted celebrities, often attempting to climb for charity, to record first national ascents, youth or age records or to promote other causes. A new genre of detective expedition/books linked to investigations about the Mallory/Irvine attempt on Everest in 1924 has been another development. The quality of these accounts is therefore variable – Boardman/Tasker winners* and shortlisted entries** giving some form of quality guidance after 1984 (the date of the first B/T assessment).

Some Mountaineering Expedition Books published since 1977

1977 *The Challenge* Reinhold Messner
1978 *Shining Mountain* Peter Boardman
      Trango: the Nameless Tower Jim Curran
      Everest: Exped. to the Ultimate Reinhold Messner
1980 *Annapurna: A Woman's Place* Arlene Blum
      The Last Step Rick Ridgeway
      Solo Nanga Parbat Reinhold Messner
1981 *White Death* Georges Bettembourg
      Everest the Cruel Way Joe Tasker
      K2 Mountain of Mountains Messner/Gogna
1982 *Sacred Summits* Peter Boardman
      Savage Arena Joe Tasker
      Kongur Chris Bonington
1983 *Everest: the Unclimbed Ridge* Bonington / Clarke
1985 *Summit Fever** Andrew Greig
      *The Shishapangma Expedition** Scott / MacIntyre
      White Limbo Lincoln Hall
1986 *Kingdoms of Experience* Andrew Greig 1986
      *Painted Mountains** Stephen Venables 1986
1987 *Nanda Devi: the Tragic Expedition* John Roskelley
      Living on the Edge Cherie Bremer Kampf
      *K2 Savage Mountain, Savage Summer*** John Barry
1988 *Touching the Void** Joe Simpson 1988
      *K2, Triumph and Tragedy*** Jim Curran
      Thin Air Greg Child 1988
1989 *The Endless Knot*** Kurt Diemberger
      *Everest Kangshung Face*** Stephen Venables
      The Crystal Horizon Reinhold Messner
1990 *Elusive Summits** Victor Saunders
      To the Top of the World Reinhold Messner
      All 14 Eight Thousanders Reinhold Messner
1991 *Coming Through* Andy Fanshawe
      Free Spirit Reinhold Messner
1992 *Last Days* John Roskelley
      My Vertical World Jerzy Kukuczka
1994 *No Place to Fall*** Victor Saunders
      On Top of the World Rebecca Stephens
1995 *Vertical Pleasure*** Mick Fowler
      *Everest Calling*** Lorna Siggins
1997 *Deep Play** Paul Pritchard
      The Climb Anatoli Boukreev
      *Into Thin Air*** Jon Krakauer
      Risking Adventure Jim Haberl
      The Death Zone Matt Dickinson
      Everest: Free to Decide O'Dowd /Woodhall
1999 *Ghosts on Everest*** Hemmleb/Johnson/Simonson
      High Exposure Dave Breashears
2000 *A Slender Thread*** Stephen Venables
2001 *Snow in the Kingdom*** Ed Webster
2002 *Expeditions*** Andrew Linblade
2003 *The Naked Mountain* Reinhold Messner
2005 *Learning to Breathe** Andy Cave
      *On Thin Ice*** Mick Fowler
      *Broad Peak*** Richard Sale

EXPEDIENCY

FRANK SMYTHE*

British climbers may justly consider themselves free from taints of mechanisation and nationalism. For the most part they have always looked upon mountain climbing as a sport in the purest sense of the word, a test of strength and skill in surmounting natural obstacles undertaken in accordance with traditional rules, and governed by a love of the thing for its own sake. At the same time, they cannot be wholly absolved from a charge of expediency. There exists, or has existed, a school of thought that Everest must be climbed, if not by traditional methods legitimately augmented by the best that manufacturers can supply in the way of food, specially suitable clothing and the usual mountaineering equipment, then by the employment of oxygen breathing apparatus. It is true that the diminished oxygen content in the air near the highest summit of the world suggests the use of such an apparatus; there is little enjoyment to be had out of climbing without it at the highest altitudes of the Himalayas; at the same time, there would to my mind, be singularly little satisfaction in reaching the summit of Mount Everest with oxygen apparatus, and any satisfaction in so doing would be offset by the thought that perhaps it might be possible to get there without it. It is certain that were Everest to be climbed with oxygen apparatus, mountaineering tradition – were it worth anything – would very soon demand a non-apparatus ascent. This cult of expediency, as exemplified by the scientific experts, is to my mind one of the evils of the present age. Let us keep mountaineering clean and undebased even on the highest peaks of the Himalayas. Let us win through to the top of Everest for the love of the thing, not because it is expedient to get there. Expediency and good sportsmanship simply do not go together.

If any charge can be preferred against mountaineers as a whole it is that they have taken their achievements too seriously. I have been as guilty as any in that respect. I now realise that it is the joy, the good comradeship, the climbing that matter in mountaineering, not the attainment of the objective.

*Prior to the Messner/Habeler 1978 ascent, Frank Smythe had made the best non bottled-oxgyen bid on Everest in 1933 (reaching about 28,100ft/8567m at 11am while still going strong). His solo completion of the difficult Mana Peak 7272m in 1937 was one of the best pre-war alpine-style ascents in the Himalaya. See *Camp 6* and *Valley of Flowers* collected in *Frank Smythe, the Six Alpine/Himalayan Books*, Baton Wicks 2000.

Mummery was the great apostle of the joy of mountaineering, and it is impossible to associate such a character, bubbling over with irrepressible gaiety, conscious always that it was the game that mattered and not its prizes, with the dour exponent of the expedient in mountaineering today, with his pitons and his oxygen apparatus and, not least, a nationally-minded Press to spur him on to some fresh 'conquest' for the fancied honour and glory of his Fatherland. It is essential to the well-being of mountaineering not to overburden it with mechanical aids but to keep it as simple as possible.

from Mechanised Mountaineering:
FELL AND ROCK CLIMBING CLUB
JOURNAL 1942

OUT WITH THE BOYS AGAIN

MIKE THOMPSON

Our leader had decreed that, in order not to place an intolerable burden upon the Nepalese countryside, we should walk to Base Camp in two parties, one travelling a day behind the other. Perhaps unwisely, he labelled these the A Team and the B Team, and immediately there was much speculation as to the underlying basis for his selection. At first there were fears among the B Team that the choice of summiters had already taken place and that they were travelling with the leader in order that they could plot the fine details of the assault in secrecy. But even the most paranoid could not sustain this belief for long, and a more popular theory was that the 'chaps' were in the A Team and the 'lads' in the B Team. This perhaps was nearer the truth since what had happened was that Chris had, quite understandably, taken with him all the executives: Sirdar Pertemba, Base Camp Manager Mike Cheney, Equipment Office Dave Clarke, Senior Doctor Charles Clarke, and of course the media in the shape of the *Sunday Times* reporter and the television team. These middle managers were, during their fortnight's walk, to have the interesting experience of, in the words of Our Leader, 'being let in on his thinking'. The B Team, gloriously free of logistics, planning, scenarios, computer print-outs, communication set-ups and the like, immediately sank into that form of communal warmth generated by squaddies in a barrack room, that impenetrable bloody-mindedness born of the I-only-work-here mentality of the shop-floor. A series of perfectly sensible decisions led to the emphasis of a division that is always incipiently present in any large expedition. The A team represented the Overground Leadership, the B team the Underground Leadership.

In theory, we, the B team members, were in the tender care of the Deputy Dawg, Hamish MacInnes, but Hamish is never one to assert his authority unduly and even if he had tried to he would have had to cope with that powerfully-built and passionate anarchist, Doug Scott. One of the disadvantages of anarchy concerns decision-making. For myself, I always feel that too much fuss is made about decisions on expeditions. There seems to me to be only one real decision, which is when that letter in unmistakeable scrawl arrives, saying: 'How about coming on the coldest holiday of your life. PS Will you do the food?', and like a fool you write back and say 'Yes'. But on the day the A Team left Kathmandu, Deputy Dawg fell ill. Should we set off the next day as planned, leaving Hamish behind, or should we wait a few days to see if he recovered – a course of action (or, rather, inaction) that might also allow Martin Boysen, who had got his leg stuck in the Trango Tower, to catch up with us? Of course, Hamish himself should have taken the decision, but he, though unable to walk, refused to admit that he was ill. His Scottish stubborness is so highly developed that even if he had a leg amputated he would insist that it was just a slight limp. Not one of us was prepared to take that enormous step from private soldier to lance corporal, and make a decision, so several delightful days were passed in the fleshpots of Kathmandu until very early one morning some land-rovers arrived at the hotel. They seemed to be for us, so we set off.

I suppose that during the approach we should have been organised by the second Sirdar, Ang Phu, but he had been having severe marital problems and was hitting the chang pretty hard, so we just wandered along, stopping where the Sherpas usually stopped, eating what Kancha the cook gave us to eat and generally building up a casual yet strong rapport with the Sherpas, by approving of their choice of camp-sites and menus, and by luring one another into wayside chang-houses.

The members of the A Team had adopted the puritanical regime of getting up in the morning, eating breakfast, and then walking until they got to the next camp-site in the afternoon. We followed the more traditional pattern of just tea and biscuits in bed, followed by two or three hours' walk during the cool of early morning, until, rounding a corner, one came across the kitchen with its alfresco breakfast of pancakes, eggs, chips, cheese, tuna fish, tea and chocolate biscuits, almost ready to serve. After this a little sleep and a gentle run-in through a few chang-houses would bring us to the next camp-site in the early afternoon. Of course there were occasional interruptions to the idyllic progress of this mobile, intensive-care geriatric unit, such as when Doug Scott was waylaid at a chang-house by Ang Phu before the sun had even risen and never even reached the breakfast place, or when I foolishly followed Ned Kelly (who had been there before) and ended up in a trackless jungle and on the wrong side of a monsoon-swollen torrent.

The level of conversation was exceptionally high, by which I mean that we gave full rein to a very childish brand of humour, often in questionable taste. The greatest favourites were Whillans Jokes. One could always tell when one of these was coming as the teller would suddenly screw up his face, narrow his eyes to slits and begin to emit a high-pitched whine. Useful on many occasions, to justify the imbalance between a porter carrying about 70lb and a sahib carrying his Olympus OM1 was: 'No! No! These fellows are used to it – they've done it all their lives'. Happy hours were passed recounting those epics in which Whillans would gradually unfold an account of his rectitude and forbearance in the face of seemingly intolerable chicanery and provocation. Like some Greek tragedy the sequence of events would move inexorably to the inevitable, fateful conclusion. All such tales led to the same final and literal punch-line: 'So I 'it 'im'.

Hamish MacInnes recounted how, during Dr Herrligkoffer's European Expedition to the South-West Face of Everest, Don, apart from nicknaming his leader 'Sterlingscoffer', did in fact behave with astonishing forbearance in the face of almost unendurable provocation and never once stepped out of line – *until the expedition was over.*

Apparently, during the earliest stages of the expedition, when the members were just getting to know one another, they heard on the Base Camp radio that Germany had just beaten England in the World Cup. 'Aha!' cried the dour Felix Kuen (the climbing leader) to Don 'we have beaten you at your national game!' Don paused, looked around, narrowed his eyes to the merest slits, leant forward, paused again and said in a harsh whisper: 'Aye, but we've beaten you at your national game twice now'. No wonder the individualistic, subversive Whillans became the cult hero of the B team. Never was anyone more present by his absence.

The other great approach-march sport, I'm ashamed to say, was 'Boardman-baiting'. Poor Peter had recently been appointed to the post of Permanent Under-Secretary to the President of the National Amalgamated Union of Mountaineers of Great Britain and Bradford. What is more, he alone amongst us was being paid while on the expedition: somewhere, we believed, in the region of £30,000 per year, of our, the taxpayers' money. The reality was barely less infuriating: he was the National Officer of the British Mountaineering Council (the BMC) which as you will all know is run by Dennis Gray who, on several occasions (on the basis of his experience on some very large expeditions to quite small mountains) has attacked modest expeditions (including ours) to very large mountains as being counter to the proletarian ideology of the true heartland and fountain-head of British Mountaineering – Yorkshire.

But perhaps, while on the subject of Yorkshire I can digress for a moment, for we did have with us one Yorkshireman, Mike Rhodes (from Bradford, to boot). Mike had not, until Everest came along, travelled outside Yorkshire. After all, what is there outside Yorkshire worth travelling for? Whenever anything un-Yorkshire-like happened to him, such as being bitten by a leech, being offered curry and rice, spaghetti and Parmesan cheese or chang, or falling through a crevasse in the ice-fall, he would remark in a surprised and slightly pained voice: 'Nothing like this in Bradford' (pronounced 'Bratfud'). As Martin Boysen remarked, when he finally caught us up: 'People are always going on about the dangers of professional mountaineers but what about professional Yorkshiremen?'

But to return to Boardman-baiting: this would usually be initiated by some seemingly innocent enquiry such as, 'What do you do all day in your office on the fiftieth floor of Dennis Gray Tower?' And then we would hear about all sorts of official bodies, such as the UIAA and the MLC Board, about negotiations for access, about grant supports for students writing PHDs on climbing harnesses or crash-hats and reading papers on specialised aspects of their research at international seminars in the Caucasus. All this was a revelation to me: I had been climbing all these years unaware of the existence of this bureaucracy, and it was all I could do to keep up with the initials and the jargon. Crags, I discovered, were 'recreational facilities' and the BMC was empowered, if need be, to acquire these recreational facilities by compulsory purchase (CPO, you know). And all this time I'd thought they were crags!

Recreational Facility of Ages cleft for me
Let me hide myself in Thee.

Usually, by this time, Tut would be writhing on the ground in paroxysms of laughter, gasping: 'PHDs on harness, BSI kite-marked nuts'; and Doug, fists clenched and beads of sweat standing out on his furrowed brow, would be dreaming of the not-too-far-off day when he would lead his first guerilla raid to blow up a National Park Information Centre; or the glorious morning when the newspaper headlines would shriek: 'Stanage Warden Murdered By Inadequately Clad Climber.'

If the baiting was taking place in a chang-house, the chances were that it would really take off at this point, the British Mountaineering Council becoming one with the British Motor Corporation and Dennis Gray merging with Lord Stokes and being blamed for the state of the economy and for mini-vans breaking down on the M1. And then, in a desperate conciliatory gesture Peter would deliver the final stunning blow: 'But we're doing all this *on your behalf'*.

At Kunde, we momentarily met up with the A Team. Though we were forced to attend an expedition meeting ('Welcome aboard' said Our Leader, adopting the terminology of the only one of the armed services of which he has not been a member) and to perform the more menial tasks of equipment-issue and crampon-adjustment, we did have the rare pleasure of watching Dave Clarke as he presided over the most depressing thing that can happen to any shopkeeper – the distribution of his entire stock without receiving a penny in exchange. There was a brief respite when we split again into A and B Teams for the walk to Base Camp, but once there the Underground Leadership was totally submerged as The Logistic Machine swung into action – and very impressive action it was too! We got our kicks in the Ice-Fall – up at two in the morning and glissade down in time for breakfast – and did penance trying to break down the MacInnes boxes into 30lb loads: all the sections of the incredibly complicated aluminium frames were threaded together with elastic string and, just as one coaxed the last bit into a large cardboard box, another bit would escape and the whole frame would re-erect itself like a monstrous Jack-in-the-box. It was more than even Boysen's legendary patience could stand and the Old Fox of Glencoe's ears must have been burning as, far above us in the Western Cwm, he indulged himself constructing the highest truss-girder bridge in the world.

The Sherpas built a shrine to placate whatever it was that lived in the Icefall and consecrated it with McVitie's chocolate wholemeal biscuits and John Haig Whisky; and Mr and Mrs Boardman (Dim Juff, the Duff Doctor) excavated outside their tent a patio-cum-sun-terrace which, with its genteel folding chairs and sun-shaded table, might have passed unremarked on the Algarve, but had a certain incongruity at eighteen-and-a-half thousand feet on the Khumbu Glacier.

At this early stage of the climb there were far too many Chiefs and far too many Indians, and this, coupled with the fact that there was only one camp and that all the action took place within full view of it, meant that the traditional avenues whereby the Underground Leadership could assert its devious influence were firmly closed. Usually, on such expeditions, the Overground Leadership can be contained by witchcraft accusations, of which the most feared (and therefore most effective) are 'secret-eating' and 'equipment-hoarding'. 'Unnatural sexual practices' is, by comparison, surprisingly ineffective. On the positive side, the Underground can, once the expedition is strung out over a number of camps and communications are strained, influence the course of events by withholding information. In this way the Overground still makes all the decisions, but on the basis of grossly inadequate information, and this means that, skilfully handled, the Overground without realising it simply okays the wishes of the Underground. When communications are really stretched it may be possible to ignore the Overground competely and present them with, in Mick Burke's phrase, 'a fait accompli, as they say in Spain'. For this kind of action to be constructive in the long-run, one needs a leader who changes his mind a lot and has difficulty in remembering from one day to the next what he has decided. We were fortunate in having such a leader.

Once on the face itself, the situation suddenly changed. It was like Annapurna again: all at once the expedition was quite small; there weren't enough people to do everything that had to be done and one's own contributions and omissions were immediately evident to one's fellows. At last, this was what we had come for!

The fulfilment of long-cherished desires can take some curious forms at high altitude. As a 'support climber', I was aware that I was fortunate to have got as far as becoming the Camp 4 Commandant, responsible, in theory, for five face boxes, an equipment dump, nine Sherpas, and a variable number of 'lead climbers' in transit. I became obsessed with actually becoming a Sherpa and increasingly I resented the lead climbers who passed through on oxygen carrying just their personal equipment. I was quite ridiculously touched when, having managed to drag myself and my load up to Camp 5 without oxygen, Pertemba said, with what I now suspect was heavy sarcasm: 'You are a real Sherpa now'.

Camp 5, perched in its little notch, was filled with slightly unbalanced euphoria. Our Leader, doing his usual thing of shooting up to the front (and rightly so), had now entered his Mad Madhi phase, running out drums of fixed rope in the wrong direction, ranting on at Ang Phurpa about 'really good Sherpa food', working out logistics on his porridge-encrusted electronic calculator, and communicating his befuddled instructions to the outside world on a broken walkie-talkie that had been persuaded to work again by jamming a ballpoint pen into its circuitry.

A few days later I, too, became a transit passenger and moved up to Camp 5 along with Dougal Haston who was being whisked on oxygen from Camp 2 to Camp 5, like Lenin in his sealed train, to join Doug (who was resting on oxygen) for the first summit attempt. Still playing the Sherpa, I stopped off at the old Camp 4 site and spent a happy couple of hours excavating the Japanese peg-store (we had in fact run out of rock pitons). As I clanked into Camp 5, the triumphant Rock-Banders, Nick and Tut, came leaping down the fixed ropes (cries of 'aye, aye, aye...' etc.) and there was Doug, the angst-ridden giant, happily sorting out the food and equipment for the summit bid. A changed man, he explained to me that, at the very moment when success was within our grasp, the impossible had happened: the Underground and the Overground had merged into a single upward-thrusting force. Miraculously free, for the moment, of Sandhurst-trained leaders and trades-unionised bureaucrats, at peace with the world, he could direct his all towards what Whillans would call: 'T' job we've come 'ere for'. He was his own man at last.

And he was right about the Leadership: Bonington and his image were now clearly separate, and all the logistics of climbing Everest were condensed into just six heavy loads which just six of us would have to carry through the Rock Band the next day to establish Camp 6. In the jargon of the sociologist, success on Everest requires massive redundancy, duplication and overlap, but this was just what we didn't have. If just one of us didn't make it up the fixed ropes, then the summit bid would be off. What was more, the route through the Rock Band was not complete nor had a site for Camp 6 been found. Doug and Dougal would have to set off before us, complete the route, fix 300ft of rope, and find and excavate the site for their Summit Box. In consequence, it was a happy little non-redundant, unduplicated, non-overlapping group that sat enjoying the view and the sunshine that afternoon in the little crow's nest that was Camp 6.

As is the way on such momentous occasions, the conversation was quite spectacularly inane: me getting at the technologically illiterate Dougal who the evening before had omitted to turn on the oxygen bottle, with the result that we spent the whole night sucking the thin outside air through saliva-filled masks; Mick Burke remarking 'What a lovely spot for a bungalow'; and then Chris, after much deliberation, announcing: 'You know, we must be the highest people on earth'. Since the Americans had just failed on K2, since there was no one on Kangchenjunga, and since we could see that there was no one on Lhotse, I suppose he was right and we *were* the highest people on earth – but not for long! For, as we wished Dougal and Doug good luck and set off down the fixed ropes in the evening sunlight, I knew that for me Everest was over. Still, I consoled myself with the words of the great Maurice Herzog: 'There are other recreational facilities in the lives of men'.*

from MOUNTAIN 50 *1976*

---

*I quote, of course, from the official translation of *Annapurna*, by P. Boardman, published by The Closed Shop Press, Bradford.

A BIVOUAC ON EVEREST

DOUG SCOTT

After a fitful sleep, we stirred into action, excited by the prospects ahead. We fried up the last of the corned beef and packed our sacks. I decided to travel light, and left my feathered suit behind, relying on my jumpers and ventile/ nylon wind-suit. However, I packed a stove and billy for hot water, and Dougal put in his duvet boots and bivi sheet. We had two dead-men each, four pegs and one hammer. Lastly, we connected up our oxygen bottles and set the flow at the second of the five positions. We needed to conserve the oxygen as we were not sure if two bottles each would get us up and down again from the top of Everest.

We set off, battling with the wind, nursing aching muscles and dulled minds. I always lack confidence early in the morning and am prone to nervousness until my body and mind warm to the tasks ahead. I stumbled along the ropes in the half-light and was soon absorbed in tackling the new ground. We swung leads up to the South Summit Couloir. After 1200ft, Dougal began to falter. His oxygen set had packed up and all our doubts about our chances returned. He said that we were in trouble – as if I didn't know it – now that thirteen of the expedition's total of eighteen sets had broken down. I worked up a hatred for Dougal's mask that fortunately stopped short of hurling it over the Rock Band. I drew out my penknife for drastic surgery, but found the bottle opener most use in prising off a jubilee clip around the pipe at the mask. With the release of pressure, a mass of ice broke off inside the rubber pipe, and Dougal could breathe again. We were back in with a chance. The wind had dropped and Dougal belayed while I went up a steep step at the foot of the couloir. This was another unknown problem, but it turned out to be only thirty-foot of 65° rock, covered slightly with powder snow, and thereafter 60° rock and increasingly thicker snow leading finally to a belay point.

I put in three pegs for protection, taking ages to scrape away the snow and unearth a crack in the amorphous yellow rock. I fixed one of the ropes off to a fourth peg, and Dougal jumared up. I had emptied one cylinder of oxygen half way up this step, and therefore changed to my second bottle on the belay. We left the rope there for our return, and carried on up into the couloir. The snow was manky and getting worse, and on one 200ft, 60°

286

section it was chest deep; we had to sweep away the top layer of snow and form each step before carefully moving up on it. We reached the South Summit at 3.30pm, five hours after Dougal's oxygen failure.

After all those months on the south side of Everest, in the course of three expeditions, at last we could look down the north side. There was Makalu, Kangchenjunga and the endless Tibetan plateau. The South-West Face had been climbed. That wasn't enough and so my true nature revealed itself. Chris had at one stage told me that he wanted me in the Rock Band team, and not in the first summit party. Down below I had been convincing myself that it was the climbing that mattered, and not the summit; but now, faced with the reality of going down or going along the known ground of the summit ridge, I wanted to carry on.

Dougal wanted to push on, too, but not immediately. He suggested bivouacking and going out at about 3am, when the soft snow might be more consolidated. We mulled over this while Dougal boiled a pan of hot water inside his bivi sheet. Meanwhile I scraped a hole out of the snow to find shelter from the wind which was whipping over the South Summit Col at about 40mph.

We drank the hot water neat, as we had nothing to put in it and no food. I gradually brought my dulled mind to bear on the problem. One thing stood out sharp to me, and that was how awful I feel at 3am. I mumbled something to Dougal about trying the ridge now, just to see how bad the snow was. I led out a rope-length, and it was reasonable. I waved him on and he started towards me, leaving behind the stove and other bits and pieces at the brewing place. He led on through and up and over a 'whipped cream roll' of a cornice hanging over Tibet. We moved along the frontier ridge, until my lead ended below the Hillary Chimney. But there was no chimney, only a 40ft bank of snow which Dougal led while I photographed him. Unfortunately, I had only one frame left in my camera, and I'd left the spare film at the South Summit with the gear. In the hope that a cassette had been brought, I rummaged around in my sack, praying that Dougal's steps would not collapse under his weight. I found one roll of twenty exposures of high-speed Ektachrome, which I fitted into the camera with difficulty. Meanwhile, Dougal worked his way up the Hillary Step, knocking off slabs of snow which fell down the Nepal side, broke into bits and were promptly caught by the wind and blown over into Tibet. The Step took him about half-an-hour. In the meantime the sun was rapidly going down, and it looked as though night would be on us before we reached the summit. But that did not seem any reason to stop and return, for we knew from previous experience that we could always escape the wind by digging a snow cave, even on the top itself, providing the snow was deep enough.

Just as I was preparing to follow, I noticed a tiny smudge of red on a distant bump on the ridge. I yelled the information to Dougal, but we would both have to wait to see what it was. I took over the lead, walking well to the left of the cornice, stumbling every third step or so as I broke through the crust into deep powder. Dougal walked behind, but a bit to my side. I was aware of a confident presence that seemed an extension of myself. Whenever I walked too far to the right, it urged me back left, and when I tripped through the crust it suggested slowing the pace. It was as if part of my reasoning was outside my head. It seems odd, now, but was a quite natural happening at the time.

Dougal took over the trail-breaking up towards the mysterious red object. As he approached, he slowed down to let me come alongside, and after a few more paces we arrived at the top together. The red object was a tripod, festooned with red ribbons and crowned with a rosary – like a Maypole. It turned out to be a Chinese construction put there in the spring by nine climbers who came from the north. Here at last was proof to the doubters that the Chinese had climbed Everest.

We took off our masks and I could see Dougal's face lit up in the setting sun and filled with happiness. This usually reticent man became expansive, and we thumped each other's backs and congratulated each other. The wind had dropped to nothing as we stood up there in wonder at the scene before us. It was everything and more than we had dared to hope for. Beyond the Rongbuk Glacier silver threads meandered out north and west across the brown land of Tibet. Peak after peak in all directions. We tried to name them, and also spent time looking down the north side, picking out features from the history books. The sun filtered down behind layers of cloud, occasionally breaking through in an explosion of light. We watched this happen several times – one sunset after another – until we had only about half-an-hour left before it got dark. We gathered up the rope, and prepared to move back down our tracks. We left nothing on top, because we had nothing to leave – except the tripod and flag already there.

We moved down rapidly, hoping to follow our tracks down to Camp 6. We abseiled down the Hillary Step from a dead-man and left a 40ft piece of rope hanging there, as it jammed when we tried to pull it down. As we blundered on, lightning flickered through the sky, all the way from Kangchenjunga to Ama Dablam. It was pitch dark when we reached the South Summit. Dougal searched for the tracks going down the Nepal side, but they were blown over with snow, so we set about bivouacking at the South Summit Col, at 28,700ft. Dougal heated some more water, while I enlarged my previous hole into a cave. We soon had a home, and the primitive fear of a night in the open was assuaged. We would survive, but it was the quality of the survival that mattered. With so many other mountains and crags to climb, we were determined not to lose any fingers and toes on Everest, so we set to work massaging. I now regretted leaving my down clothing, as I had only the gear I climbed in to keep me warm. The oxygen ran out at 8.30pm, and the stove was finished at midnight. To keep warm, I hacked away at the cave with my axe, until it was so large that it could have housed five people. It was essential to stay awake and concentrate on survival. I carefully took off my socks and stuffed them under my armpits, while I rubbed my toes and tried to ensure that snow did not get on my rucksack – which was my seat. Mostly I shivered and cursed, telling Dougal how desperately cold it was, as if he didn't know. Once, when I was massaging my feet, I left a sock out in the open and found it frozen stiff as a board when I came to put it on again. Dougal must have thought me a right softy when I accepted a place for my feet inside his down clothing, one foot at his crutch, the other under his armpit. But still the cold seeped into our backs, into our kidneys, and seemingly into our very bones. We began to wander in our thoughts: Dougal had short conversations with Dave Clarke, our Equipment Manager, perhaps hoping euphemistically, that he would arrive with our sleeping bags. I kept on chattering away to my presence and to my feet. It was a long nine hours.

At 5.30am, we crawled out of our hole and went over the ridge into Nepal, for we had spent an illicit night out in China. The wind grew stronger, and clouds were gathering all around, as we plunged down rapidly, hoping to gain more oxygen and warmth. We reached the tent and safety at 9am, got into our sleeping bags, put a brew on, and lay back breathing oxygen; then we radioed Chris with the news. We knew that we weren't going to lose any digits as the warmth seeped back into our bodies and out to our extremities.

I came down with ambition fulfilled, and an empty space for noble thoughts and feelings; but I knew that space would soon be swamped back in the city – it had happened before. We had taken a big breath of fresh air, and now it was back to the valley and people, to breath it out ready for the next breath, perhaps in Alaska, the Andes, or even back here again in the Himalayas.

from MOUNTAIN 47 *1976*

EVEREST IS NOT A PRIVATE AFFAIR

PETE BOARDMAN

Is there no-one, no-one in the whole swirling chaos, no-one in the abyss, and no-one in
heaven? A soul can go then, so unspeakably poor, back into nothing, in the grey mist.
Peer Gynt – Ibsen

All the winds of Asia seemed to be trying to blow us from the ridge. A decision was needed. It was four in the afternoon and the skies were already darkening around the South Summit of Everest. I threw my iced and useless snow goggles away into the whiteness and tried, clumsily mitted, to clear the ice from my eyelashes. Bowing my head into the spindrift I tried to peer along the ridge. Mick should have met us at least three quarters of an hour before. Something must have happened to him. We had been waiting for nearly one and a half hours. There was no sign of Doug's and Dougal's bivouac site. The sky and cornices and whirling snow merged together, visibility was reduced to ten feet and all tracks were obliterated. Pertemba and I huddled next to the rock of the South Summit where Mick had asked us to wait for him. Pertemba said he could not feel his toes or fingers and mine too were nailed with cold. I thought of Mick wearing his glasses and blinded by spindrift, negotiating the fixed rope on the Hillary step, the fragile one foot windslab on the Nepal side and the cornices on the Tibetan side of the ridge. I thought of our own predicament, with the 800ft of the South Summit Gully – guarded by a 60ft rockstep halfway – to descend, and then half of the 2000ft great traverse above the Rock Band to cross before reaching the end of the fixed ropes that extended across from Camp 6. It had taken Doug and Dougal three hours in the dawn sunshine after their bivouac to reach Camp 6 – but we now had only an hour of light left. At 28,700ft the boundary between a controlled and an uncontrolled situation is narrow and we had crossed that boundary within minutes – a strong wind and sun shining through clouds had turned into a violent blizzard of driving snow, the early afternoon had drifted into approaching night and our success was turning into tragedy.

A mountaineer when he is climbing is doing, seeing and feeling and yet on his return home from the hill he often baulks at recollection in public of these experiences because he treasures the privacy and intensity of his

memories. And yet, as Hornbein remarked after being asked to write about
his ascent of the West Ridge:

> I soon learned, Everest was not a private affair. It belonged to many men.

The stories of man's adventures on Everest have almost reached the stature
of myth in the popular imaginations of the twentieth century. The full record
of our expedition will eventually appear to add to these stories. I do not
aspire here to document the planning and events of the expedition, nor to
presume to evaluate its achievements, nor to predict the future of climbing
on Everest. I fear that at such a cold touch, the pains and charms that are
my memories of Everest will fly.

My memories are of a keen apprehension that turned into a living nightmare. Even on the leech-infested walk-in we dreamt about the climb to come
– one morning Tut and Doug confessed, with gallows humour. 'I keep
getting stranded above the Rock Band' and, 'Dougal got severe frostbite last
night.'

Whilst Nick and Tut were tackling the Rock Band I wrote:

> Everyone is very optimistic that we'll crack it soon, but it's still early days.
> We've been lucky with the weather and there could easily be a storm at any
> time to curtail or even set back all movement.

'Think upwards' always seems to be a good dictum for success in climbing,
and the Everest summit was in my mind night and day all the time I was
moving up the Face into position for the second attempt. Aside from the
physical effort and practical judgement and worry, there is a dream-like
quality in the climbing on Everest. At Camp 5 I wrote:

> The Face is a strange unreal world. All dressed up in one piece oversuits and
> six layers on the feet, oxygen mask and goggles, one seems distanced from
> where one is and what one is doing, like a sort of moonwalk.

This half-glimpsed quality was preserved far back in my mind. As a child I
used to day-dream over a painting in a big picture book *Adventure of the World*
which depicted the tiny bold figures of Hillary and Tensing on the top of a
summit that thrust out of a sea of clouds.

As Pertemba and I crossed the traverse above the Rock Band in the early
dawn of our summit day it felt as if we were on that highest peak above the
clouds, as if the sight of the endless cloud sea was joining hands with the
dreamland of the past. The weather was changing and the cloud layer was
up to 27,000ft, covering Nuptse and everything beyond it. Only the top of
Lhotse peeped out below us, whereas above us the sun sparkled through the
snow smoking over the summit ridge. For three days I had been jumaring up

fixed ropes, counting steps and trying to keep in front of some Sherpas coming up to Camp 4, gasping up to Camp 5, and then following Nick and Tut's intricate route through the Rock Band. But now I felt free and untrammelled, and exhilarated as if I had just become committed on the start of a climb in the Alps. Pertemba and I moved, unroped, steadily away from the end of the fixed line and kicked away the spindrift from the tracks that Doug and Dougal had made two days before. Everest, the myth, with its magic and history, seemed to make me feel strong, thinking upwards. Invincible together.

The snow was only a few feet deep on top of the rocks and the route wavered around spurs and over rock steps. The South Summit gully was steep but there was a fixed line hanging over the rock step half way up it. As I reached the South Summit, Pertemba dropped behind and I waited for him. His oxygen mask had stopped working. One-and-a-half hours and several cold fingers later we had slit open the tube and cleared the two inches of ice that were blocking the airway, and patched the mask back into working order. We changed to fresh oxygen cylinders and moved, roped now, along the ridge towards the summit of Everest. Its red ribbons were fading in the strong light and fluttering prayers from the other side of the mountain. The Chinese tripod was catching drifting snow and leaning defiantly in the wind. Its presence was strangely reassuring. Pertemba attached a Nepalese flag to it and I hung a Dead-man snow anchor from it. We ate some chocolate and mint cake and I burbled into a tape recorder 'Where's the local bank branch?' Then we started down.

We were amazed to see him through the mist. Mick was sitting on the snow only a few hundred yards down an easy angled snow slope from the summit. He congratulated us and said he wanted to film us on a bump on the ridge and pretend it was the summit, but I told him about the Chinese maypole. Then he asked us to go back to the summit with him. I agreed reluctantly and he, sensing my reluctance, changed his mind and said he'd go up and film it and then come straight down after us. He borrowed Pertemba's camera to take some stills on the top and we walked back 50ft and then walked past him whilst he filmed us. I took a couple of pictures of him. He had the 'Blue Peter' flag and an auto-load camera with him. He asked us to wait for him by the big rock on the South Summit where Pertemba and I had dumped our first oxygen cylinders and some rope and film on the way up. I told him that Pertemba was wanting to move roped with me – so he should catch us up fairly quickly. I said 'See you soon' and we moved back down the ridge to the South Summit. Shortly after we had left him the weather began to deteriorate.

A decision was needed. I pointed at my watch and said 'We'll wait ten more minutes'. Pertemba agreed. That helped us – it gave some responsibility to the watch. I fumbled in my sack and pulled out our stove to leave behind. The time was up. At first we went the wrong way – too far towards the South Col. About 150ft down we girdled back until we found what we thought was the South Summit Gully. There was a momentary lessening in the blizzard, and I looked up to see the rock of the South Summit. There was still no sign of Mick and it was now about half-past four. The decision had been made and now we had to fight for our own lives and think downwards.

Pertemba is not a technical climber, not used to moving away from fixed ropes or in bad conditions. At first he was slow. For three pitches I kicked down furiously, placed a dead-man and virtually pulled him down in the sliding, blowing powder snow. But Pertemba was strong and adaptable – he began to move faster and soon we were able to move together. Were we in the gully? I felt panic surge inside. Then I saw twin rocks in the snow that I recognised from the morning. We descended diagonally from there and in the dusk saw Dougal's oxygen cylinder that marked the top of the fixed rope over the rock step.

We abseiled down to the end of the rope and tied a spare rope we had to the end and descended the other 150ft. From there we descended down and across for 1000ft towards the end of the fixed ropes. During our traverse we were covered by two powder snow avalanches from the summit slopes. Fortunately our oxygen cylinders were still functioning and we could breathe. It was a miracle that we found the end of the fixed ropes in the dark, marked by two oxygen cylinders sticking out of the snow. On the fixed rope Pertemba slowed down again and I pulled him mercilessly until he shouted that one of his crampons had fallen off. The rope between us snagged and in flicking it free I tumbled over a fifteen-foot rock step to be held on the fixed rope. At one point a section of the fixed rope had been swept away. At half-past seven we stumbled into the 'summit boxes' at Camp 6. Martin was there and I burst into tears.

The storm pinned the three of us to Camp 6 at 27,600ft for thirty-six hours. Pertemba and I shared one of the two boxes and were competely dependent on Martin. Pertemba was snow-blinded and I was worried about my feet. Luckily we had a good supply of gas for making brews and oxygen cylinders. Our box was becoming buried in snow every four hours and Martin kept on dragging himself out to clear them, damaging his fingers from frostbite in doing so. It was miserable inside the box, the snow was pressing the walls inwards and it felt like that medieval dungeon 'the little ease – maddeningly too short to stretch out, too low to sit up'. Pertemba lay back, his eyes closed and lips moving in silent incantation. I felt isolated from my friends lower down the mountain by a decision and an experience I could not share.

During the second night the wind and snow ceased but their noise was replaced by the roar of avalanches sweeping past either side of the snowy crest on which we were perched and plunging over the edge of the Rock Band. Dawn came – clear and cold, sad and silvery. We looked across the traverse and up the gully to the south summit but there was no sign of Mick. We turned and began the descent, that long repetitive ritual of clipping and unclipping the piton brake and safety loop and abseiling, rope-length after rope-length, 6000ft down to the Western Cwm.

As we emerged from the foot of the gully through the Rock Band we could see tiny figures outside the three boxes of Camp 5, 1,000ft below us. It took a long time to reach them, for many of the anchors on the fixed ropes had been swept away. Ronnie, Nick, Tut and Ang Phurba were waiting for us and helped us down into the living air and warmth of the Western Cwm and the reassuring faces of Camp 2.

Everest is not a private affair; it belongs to many men.

That afternoon I was in front of a camera, explaining what had happened. But now friends were all around me. Dougal, usually so distant and undemonstrative, had walked out in the midday heat of the Western Cwm to meet me, Doug had tenderly taken off my boots, Chris had reassured me. It was good to hear about other people's experiences, and all the individual traits I had noticed in others in the last few months seemed refreshingly evident – Tut, strutting about like a starved turkey, Ronnie hoovering the table, Doug his hair still at half-mast, Charlie dressed in his red silk underwear and Dave still fretting about organising everything to perfection and stirring into action anyone loitering within tent. Nick, the excitable eccentric from Eastbourne, had been followed up the ropes to Camp 5 by a ghost (all the nice ghouls love a sailor). Adrian had been stranded in the dark during the evacuation of Camp 4. Ned was nursing a black eye and bruised ribs as a result of the draught from an avalanche from Nuptse which that morning had demolished half the tents at Camp 2 and thrown the 'superbox' containing the BBC crew into the air and on top of another 'superbox'. For thirty days a lucky truce had been maintained with the mountain, but now it was time to retreat. The next day a long line of heavily laden climbers and sherpas stretched down the Western Cwm. Within three days the entire expedition was back at Base Camp.

The Sherpa's involvement with the expedition and its success was total and euphoric. No sherpas had been killed, the route through the icefall had been made as safe as could be hoped, and a sherpa had reached the summit. Pay had been good and they had been given good equipment, the climb was over early while there was still money to be made in the trekking season and they had been treated in a relaxed and trusting way as human beings and equals. Mutual respect and friendship resulted. As we tottered out of the icefall the two Base Camp cooks stood before a shrine of burning juniper and greeted us with scarves of welcome, drinks of rakshi and orange juice, and happy smiles. The following night everyone gathered around a fire and the shuffle thump of the sherpas' dance and the ringing tones of their trance-like songs rose up with the sparks from the fire towards the stars.

Next day we started down towards the lamasery of Thyangboche. After a month of sensory deprivation in the Western Cwm the chatter of the streams and the mellow reds and browns of autumn seemed magical. Our leg muscles stiffened, unused to walking on hard ground.

At Thyangboche we had an audience in a building of mutterings, chants and drums with the Head Lama. The sherpas were wearing sheepish grins, for them it must have been like one of us taking twenty sherpas round to bounce teacups with our local vicar. The Head Lama was quiet, thoughtful and wise.

> Now you have reached the top of the mountain, and you have achieved your success. But on reaching a summit you must descend and on descending you must go on living. So it is in the west of the world – there man has achieved the heights of material comfort, but from there he must descend to find an inner peace. A sherpa has reached the summit. Twenty-five years ago Tenzing made my people famous. This has changed them greatly. But more important, respect for the inner peace and happiness they have achieved has spread out into the world.

The mountaineer returns to his hills because he remembers always that he has forgotten so much.

from MOUNTAIN LIFE 1975

ANNAPURNA HIGH LIFE

MIKE THOMPSON

Base Camp, with its green grass and gurgling streams, its superb food and casual efficiency, was a wonderful convalescent home for exhausted climbers returning from the face. It is probably safe to say that in Base Camp we lived better than any previous Himalayan expedition. Our closest rival in this respect may well have been the 1922 Everest expedition, which took crates of champagne and chickens in aspic. Tukte Sherpa, our cook, built a magnificent kitchen by stretching some large tarpaulins over several conveniently placed boulders. The gaps between the boulders were filled with makeshift shelving for the rations. From this kitchen there issued an almost continuous stream of excellent meals – breakfast, morning coffee, lunch, afternoon tea, dinner and finally a bedtime brew. So efficient was the catering that a pint mug of tea always reached climbers returning from the face before the television cameras did.

The great thing about base was that we were able to supplement the menu with fresh meat in the form of two buffaloes, half a dozen goats and innumerable chickens. The buffaloes were slaughtered in spectacular Ghurka style by having their heads lopped off with one blow of the kukri. Ready-cooked chickens were an occasional delicacy at Camps 1 and 2, and fresh meat even reached Camp 3. One cockerel survived as an alarm clock until the very last day at Base Camp.

Food was the all-consuming passion of the expedition. If members were not actually engaged in eating it or getting rid of it from one end or the other, they would be talking or dreaming of it. Hour after hour was passed in ecstatically recalling past meals and contemplating those that lay ahead. At Base Camp, recipes and tips were continually being swopped as if it were some remote branch of the Womens' Institute. Some items became more popular as new ways of cooking them were devised. At first, the Christmas puddings did not get eaten except by Tom Frost, who regularly ate two at a sitting, and Dougal, who made himself ill. But then, more ingenuity was applied to their preparation. 'Christmas Pudding Boysen', for example, a thinly sliced pudding, fried, drenched in whisky and served flambante with cream, was universally appreciated (except by Tom – a Mormon – who disapproved of the whisky on religious grounds and was anyway quite content to chew his way through any pudding, even when it was frozen into a solid brick). 'Christmas Pudding Bonington', a thin gruel made by stewing the pudding with melted snow, sugar and whisky, was really only appreciated by its inventor, who nevertheless forced it on anyone unfortunate enough to share his tent.

Passionate arguments often raged over the merits of chips in 'trannies' and 'chippers' along the length and breadth of the British Isles. With glazed eyes and drooling lips, one would recall the trannie at Beattock summit where 'steak pie and two veg' announced over the loudspeaker meant steak pie, chips and mash; another would invoke an 'egg in dry cake' in Dot's Cafe in Craven Street, Hull, and a third the 'sausage toad and double bubble, bread pudding and custard' at the Double L in the Liverpool Road, Islington. Even sleep did not bring release and the night air was often rent by Mick

Burke's anguished cries for the meat and potato pies of his native Wigan. Burke was perhaps the most deeply afflicted of us all and at times it seemed that, like the Knights of the Round Table, his whole life was a ceaseless quest, not for the Holy Grail, but for the Perfect Chip. A soul in torment, it seemed that he would only find peace (and the Perfect Chip) on that far-off day when he finally pulled his clapped-out artic of life into the lorry park of the Great Trannie* in the Sky.

from MOUNTAIN 12 *1970*

*British transport cafés – the best ones prized for their cheapness and ability to fill the bellies of impecunious and hungry climbers with well cooked basic food.

MAC THE BELLY TALKS TO CASSIUS BONAFIDE

The problems facing expedition leaders grow more acute every year as budgets soar and commercial pressures increase. Here a bloated climbing commentator and TV star, discusses the difficulties with a successful expedition leader.

Mac: How did it all start, Cass?

Cassius: Well, you see, Mac, I wanted to lead an expedition to the hardest small peak in the world. A new trial to test my developing personality.

You'd need a strong team for that.

Yes. I chose three of my very closest friends and we formed the hardest team of climbers in the world.

Sounds good.

Ah. That's when the problems start. Low peak – low box office. Nobody buys lousy routes on small peaks. We really needed a bigger scene. That's when I thought about Annaplus, the biggest and hardest face in the world.

But that would cost real money.

We estimated about £500,000 including oxygen and larks' tongues for the porters. A hundred thousand of rope and twenty thousand man days of margarine.

A hundred thousand feet, that's impressive.

Yards, old boy, yards.

Where did you get the cash?

Nobody is interested in cheap, trashy peaks. Annaplus isn't the highest but its face is the hardest in the world and by the time we were finished we believed it was the highest. You see it's a marketing problem, old boy. In the professional climbing world we call it creative mountaineering marketing. You find the mountain, create the image, sell like hell and then go out and climb it. If you get all this right, money falls on you like snow on the north face of Annaplus. We created the hardest route in the world on Annaplus, and who can resist that?

But it would take more than four of you?

Yes, that was a problem. In fact we ended up with 86

That includes the porters?

No. There were 16,000 of them, in fact the whole of the working population of the country. We had ten cameramen, four announcers, six producers, eight sound men, six lighting specialists, six camp managers, one for each camp, my English, American and European agents and forty-one climbers and a partridge in a pear tree.

That seems quite a change from four close friends.

Yes I agree, but we were the hardest group of climbers ever to leave Britain, in fact none were left. They were all close loyal friends. We did have one American who's the hardest climber in the States and also the most religious. The idea came from my agent and it guaranteed the American sales of my book and implicitly got God into the team at the same time.

I'm impressed, Cass. How did the climb go?

We were fantastically successful. It took nine months to climb the first 500ft. Harder than the North face of the Eiger. Then two of the hardest men pushed through the next 8000ft to the summit. Artificial climbing all the way on overhanging ice with constant avalanches. It took them nearly all day. On the summit their anoraks were whipped by 200 mile-an-hour winds as they ate their margarine sandwiches.

You must have felt proud. Did the other thirty-nine go up as well?

No. They crapped out lower down but don't quote me on that or I'll get my agent on to you.

Didn't they set everything up for the two you had chosen to go to the top?

We couldn't get all forty to the top and if we hadn't got anybody we would have had no film, book or road-show. Think what that would have meant. So I think my plan was justified.

Don't you think in the future everyone will want a chance to go to the top?

Ha! ha! A few weeks carrying 80lb at 24,000ft soon cools their enthusiasm and lets the hard men get through. Anyway it would be too expensive and bad box office. How can it be the hardest climb in the world if everybody gets up it? They'll think it's a scramble like Everest.

Tell me about your reputed craving for margarine at high altitude.

That's a bit below the belt, old boy. Marvellous stuff, spreads in ninety below and tastes like butter. We didn't take any. At least I don't think we did. You see I can't tell the difference.

What's next? Anything must seem dull after your last tremendous achievement.

This year's hardest climb in the world is the South face of Everest. Great box office. An international team from 90 countries, 200 climbers. It's the Grand Slam. They are going to climb it by every route and they've got world wide rights for film, books and this time it's covered by the BBC not crummy old ITV who didn't like to move out of base camp. It's fantastic.

Are you going, Cass?

I was asked but decided not to go. You see, old man, the whole thing is getting a bit too commercialised for me.

from MOUNTAIN 15 *1971*

THE CLIMB OF CLIMBS

GARY BOCARDE

THE CLIMB

Off in the heart of the mysterious land of enormous mountains and great challenge lies one of the greatest mountaineering problems of all time: Peak 18,217ft the 102nd highest peak in the world. The summit of this magnificent Himalayan peak has never felt the footprints of man, and its eleven attempts attest to its extreme difficulty. Massive ice falls, constant avalanching on all possible routes, and numerous rock-bands (mostly rotten rock) are just a few of the difficulties on this great peak.

The first attempt came in 1909 by a French team of explorers, who got lost for forty-five days on the treacherous approach march before finally giving up. And then just one year later a strong German team fought their way to the base of Peak 18,217ft and then disaster struck: a massive avalanche swept down on Base Camp burying everything. Only a few lived to tell about it! Most of the other attempts on this mountain have met with similar fates. Except in 1960 when a large group of Japanese climbers (forty-two climbers in the team) reached the 16,500ft level, before their luck ran out. During a spell of bad weather their high camps were completely destroyed by vandals. This was the last serious attempt on this fantastic mountain.

This is the challenge the strong team of American climbers will face in the spring of 1976. Their route will go up the untried and very impressive north-west ridge. This route will be an extreme challenge for this six man and one woman team, with only their vast experience and superb equipment to help them up one of the most sought after peaks in the world!

THE CLIMBERS

The climbing team consists of some of the toughest climbers in the United States. In the coming months they will be training together in some of the more rugged mountain ranges in North America (including Mt Washington and Mt Hood).

Tim Nitwiter, 48, is the leader of the expedition, and the most experienced member, with numerous years of climbing behind him. His record includes such greats as 143 ascents of Mt Hood, a solo ascent of Mt Whitney, and an unplanned rescue off the West Buttress route on Mt McKinley. He also runs a hardware store called Rebuilding Equipment and Ideas.

Sammy Steadfast, 39, is deputy leader. He is one of the most versatile climbers on the expedition. In his seven years of climbing his most notable ascents are the Lion's Head Spur on Mt Washington and Tuckerman's Ravine, Lake of the Clouds start. His rock and snow experience will be invaluable! He is a part time climber for Alaska Airlines (a Seattle company).

Julie Lovelace, 22, will be the Expedition Photographer and Recreation director. She will help the climbers relax after their struggles with the mountain. She has never climbed before, but she is a fast learner and enjoys rappelling.

Gaylord Foul, 33, (who has become a household word because of his articles in *Ladies' Home Journal* and TV *Guide*) will be Julie's assistant photographer. He has climbed in the numerous mountain ranges in California, with his solo ascent of the Anderson route on Half Dome his most outstanding achievement.

Frank Hardbod, 17, will be in charge of supplies. He is the youngest, but strongest member of the team. He can do 31 one-arm pull ups, 195 push-ups, 327 sit-ups and more. He has no mountaineering experience, but he is determined to learn. He works at Nitwiter's Hardware store.

Dr James L. Hartwekk, Jr, 51, will be the expedition doctor. His record includes ascents of Mt Washington (La Carriage Route) and Mt Jefferson. He is on the AAC Board of Directors.

John B. Good, 29, hasn't been assigned a job as yet. He was the last climber to be added to the expedition team and is the only non-AAC member. And he will have to prove himself worthy of this team. His record includes a few good peaks Logan, Hunter, St. Elias, McKinley; an assortment of climbs in Europe and South America; plus numerous wall climbs in Yosemite and Colorado.

Your help and contributions are needed now! Large, serious expeditions are expensive ($65,000 for equipment alone), but by getting the support of the nation everyone can be a part of this great expedition. Anyone who loves the outdoors, loves to climb mountains, loves adventure, loves the AAC and loves to help his fellow man should help. All contributions may be considered tax deductible.

This expedition wants to give the contributors more for their money than just a five per cent postcard. The more your contribute to this expedition, the greater will be your reward.

The peak, which is unnamed, will be named after the person or company that is the most generous (Metropolitan Life Insurance has already donated $25,000). The 'Thank You' for the second highest contribution will be the naming of the route and various landmarks along the way after you and your family. Base Camp will be named after the next highest. And fourth to tenth will get to name anything that is left after them: including rivers, special equipment used on the climb (remember the Whillans Box?) towns, animals... What a deal, and you can write it all off on your next tax form.

For those generous people who can't afford large donations, we have something for you. For just $25 you can get an autographed photo of the climber of your choice (photo of Julie is $10 extra). And for a mere $10 you can get an equipment list, with special comments by each member of the expedition. (Why wait for the book?) And for the down and out climber who can barely afford to buy a copy of this magazine, they offer a postcard from their 15,905ft Base Camp for anything over fifty cents (to cover postage and handling).

So join the Fun! Sit down tonight, and send whatever you can afford. Call a friend too! Think about it: A Mountain named after you.

from CLIMBING *July 1975*

SOME COMMENTS ON AN EVEREST BOOK*

DAVID COX

Like the leaders of past Everest expeditions, Chris Bonington was presumably committed to writing a book about the 1972, post-monsoon, British attempt on Everest's South-West Face, whether or not the expedition succeeded. Naturally, it makes his story to some extent anticlimactic that his party was forced to abandon the climb at about the same point as had been reached by earlier expeditions – and particularly because this point, the foot of the Rock Band, marks only the beginning of the route's serious technical difficulties. But much the same thing is also true of pre-war attempts from the Tibetan side, which were so often defeated at, or below, the point reached as early as 1924.

So Bonington's book is a worthwhile addition to the literature of Everest in the same way as was, say, Ruttledge's *Everest, 1933*. If the decision was

*An excerpt from a book review of *Everest South-West Face*.

right to try the South-West Face with a, relatively large party, rather than the South Col route with a very small one, it seems difficult to fault in any major way either the planning or the execution of the British 1972 attempt, which was clearly forced to give up in conditions of wind and cold which made it impossible to go any higher.

Notably, too, the expedition avoided dividing its objectives (a mistake made by two of the earlier expeditions) and also remained free of internal splits (which largely ruined the third). This made it the most single-minded and coherent attempt on the face to date. All this is well described; and the book incidentally contains chapters on the Japanese, International and European expeditions, not to mention the usual appendices of an official expedition account.

In his chapter of conclusions, Bonington writes: 'And so the siege goes on. Is it worth it?' This, of course, is the central question raised by the book itself, and it is the old question of whether the end justifies the means. Is the climbing of Everest by the South-West Face so overriding a mountaineering challenge as to justify the cost, both material and intangible, which is involved if anyone is to have any chance at all of getting up the route?

The British 1972 expedition cost £60,000, and was probably considerably cheaper than any of its three forerunners. It was a good deal criticised at the time – mainly on grounds which seem illogical if the South-West Face is indeed such a supremely important immediate objective. It was said that £60,000 might have supported a dozen expeditions to less ambitious areas; but in fact only Everest could ever have produced that sort of money. Sponsorship and the drumming up of publicity are unattractive to most mountaineers (Bonington himself refers to 'all the ballyhoo'); but if big money has to be raised such things have to be accepted – nor, incidentally, were the media as much in evidence on this expedition as on some others. These points, and others of the same sort, are perhaps really secondary.

What it all comes back to is the importance of the end itself as an objective in the early 1970s.

The South-West Face is, of course, a route that must be climbed one day. Clearly it has come to be thought of by leading mountaineers in many countries as the greatest unpicked plum of Himalayan climbing, an objective comparable to the summit of Everest itself when that was still unclimbed. It is a pity that this has happened, simply because it seems premature. Even Chris Bonington doubts whether standards of equipment, notably as regards oxygen, are yet sufficient for tackling 'what, in effect, is a high-standard Alpine problem at an altitude of over 27,000ft.' At the moment, only siege tactics can hope to succeed; how vulnerable these are has been demonstrated by each successive attempt.

Five expeditions have now failed in three years. For political reasons, attempts from the Tibetan side before the war did not come so thick and fast, the first actual attempt being in 1922 and the fourth in 1936. At that stage people began to question the whole concept of the cumbersome, costly expedition and its pattern of repeated gallant failure. It was like a breath of fresh air when in 1938 Tilman's party, on a budget of less than £2,500, climbed to 27,200ft and had two pairs of climbers in a position to go higher if conditions had permitted. Whether or not, in a good year, they could have reached the top, no one can say; and it would be silly to suggest that at present similar methods would have any chance of success on the South-West Face. But in ten years perhaps they might; if it was twenty years, or even thirty, perhaps that would not matter.

For there are certain indefinable costs involved in all this, as Tilman saw; and what they boil down to is the simple, old-fashioned proposition that the ascent itself does not matter so much as the way in which it is made. Publicity and commercialism are not in themselves good things in a mountaineering context, and the worthwhileness of an ascent is in inverse proportion to how much it costs, i.e. to how far it is necessary to use the massive expedition approach. If one thing is more certain than another, it is that developments of technique and, especially, equipment, will make it possible to tackle the South-West Face of Everest in a more modern idiom in the not very distant future. It will then seem a pity that the face had to be climbed by the siege methods of the 1970s. But this may be wrong: as *Mountain* said just after the expedition, 'for decades the mountain (Everest) has exerted a compelling fascination over some of the leading climbers of the day. That such men should find it worthy of their continued attention seems to point to a more subtle challenge than is immediately obvious ...'

from MOUNTAIN 30 *1973*

THE DHAULAGIRI AVALANCHE

AL READ and LOU REICHARDT

Read: Death is not uncommon in mountaineering. Its cold fingers follow you into the rotten couloir. You see it above as you traverse below the cornice. And there it is below your line of shifting pins. Most certainly it stalks in the incessant animation of an active Himalayan glacier. But is this not part of the satisfaction and ultimate splendour of the climber, perched on the abyss, daring the early intrusion of the inevitable, while denying the Black Caress through cunning, skill and often incredible luck? And all this in the most beautiful surroundings. This is adventure – life. But what of annihilation? A climber seldom contemplates this realistically. Even more rarely does it actually occur. He calculates the risk in pursuit of the essence of being.

A cliff of blue ice thrust forward by the East Dhaulagiri Glacier fell just as five skilled mountaineers and two Nepali Sherpas, on a carefully judged schedule, stood below it. The wall collapsed, sending a thunder of tumbling death into half the American Dhaulagiri Expedition, crushing and burying, wrenching off to bare ice the deep snow from the glacier, plunging over a 500ft cliff and, far below, finally resting and refreezing.

This was annihilation.

Reichardt: Boyd Everett, Dave Seidman and Bill Ross were occupying our old camp. They had been working hard with the others carrying loads to this height. Now they wanted to see the route. Boyd thought it might be easier to leave the glacier immediately and gain our elevation on the ridge. We decided to spend the night together – an evening transformed by the many taped symphonies Boyd had brought with him. Our camp became 'base camp', a psychological change that seemed destined to be repeated as we moved up the mountain.

Bill Ross and I had to wait in the morning for Mingma to bring the logs from below. Then, with them balanced on top of my Kelty, we set out after the others. Sunshine and companionship conspired to make a relaxing morning. The pace was slow, and friendships were being renewed in this first large sortie on alpine terrain. Still, the twelve-foot logs made a strange load, frequently threatening my balance, on what already seemed a curious day, one in which we were carrying loads up a route that might be abandoned. I, at least, knew that the logs could be abandoned with the route. After mentioning this to Bill, he replied, 'I think we are committed to something up here.'

'Quick! Let's get the logs across so Boyd can cross without taking off his pack.' Bill and I reached the crevasse a few minutes before the others but it took time to rig the ropes properly. Everyone had time to arrive and unload. They stayed to inspect the proposed route. Encouraged, they remained to kibbitz. Then an afternoon fog descended upon us. A few minutes later, just as Bill and Vin were finishing the delicate pivoting of the timbers to the crevasse's far rim, a roar entered our consciousnesses. Neutral for a moment, it quickly posed a threat. We had only an instant to seek shelter before it consumed our world.

I found only a change of slope in the glacier for shelter and was repeatedly struck on my back with debris – all glancing blows which did not dislodge my hands. When it was finally over, assuming that it was snow that had been unable to bury us, I stood up fully expecting to be surrounded by the same seven companions. Instead, everything that was familiar – friends, equipment, even the snow on which we had been standing – was gone. There was only dirty, hard glacial ice with dozens of fresh gouges and scattered huge ice blocks, the grit of the avalanche. It was a scene of indescribable violence, reminiscent of the first eons of creation, when a still molten earth was forged; and at the same time it was uncannily silent and peaceful on a warm, misty afternoon. A triangular cliff of ice, thrust out of the glacier by some invisible band of rock, had collapsed and the resulting debris had cut a 100ft wide swath across the broad basin, filled the crevasse, and overwhelmed us.

Yells of reassurance became expressions of my disbelief. A systematic search down the slopes revealed little above a high cliff and convinced me that everything had been carried over it. I spent an hour in this search and in a less thorough one of the debris below – a period of time allotted as a compromise between the conflicting demands for immediate rescue and for summoning people and equipment to help. Then I made the loneliest of trips down the glacier and rock to the 12,000ft acclimatisation camp, shedding crampons, overboots, and finally even disbelief on the way. I returned with equipment and people to make a more thorough search of debris, but with no success. Probes were useless; even ice-axes could not penetrate the huge ice mass, roughly the size of a football field and twenty feet deep. We had no rational basis for hope. The avalanche was ice, not snow. The few items of equipment found were completely shredded. No man could have survived a ride in such debris.

We spent another week on the mountain retrieving equipment, not so much for its value but because of our reluctance to sever bonds with the past.

Much in each of us died that day, and time spent alone with memories of past hopes, exertions and companionship seemed necessary then and appropriate later. I remember them now as my closest climbing companions – men who believed in testing their own limits and who enriched the lives of their friends by sharing their experiences and motives, men who died enjoying their avocation in a place they might have chosen.

from THE AMERICAN ALPINE JOURNAL 1970

A SECOND TALK WITH MESSNER

REINHOLD MESSNER

Mountain: How do you think your Nanga Parbat climb – the descent that is – will feature in the history of Himalayan climbing?

It won't really be important historically, because it wasn't a planned thing. It wasn't like climbing the South-West Face of Everest and bivouacking on the descent, or traversing Everest as they did in 1963, and descending. It wasn't a planned climb; it was forced on us by events: we had to do it, because it was an emergency. So it doesn't really have a place in the development of Himalayan climbing; it was merely an arbitrary incident.

But it happened. Buhl climbed Nanga Parbat in a pretty exceptional way. Wasn't your climb rather like that?

Not really. Buhl planned to go to the top and descend the same route. My idea was also to go to the top and then descend our route, the Rupal Face. But when my brother arrived, we got into a new situation: we were forced to go down the Diamir Face, and this was not planned. Minute after minute, I had to make decisions during that descent; not every hour, but from minute to minute.

Were you frightened?

It was perhaps the only time I have been in a situation in which for, two or three days I was always at my limit – physically and mentally. We were close to going crazy, because we were worried not only about not finding the correct route, but also about the ever-present possibility of dying, because of cold or avalanche. I had, of course, experienced short periods of this sort of tension on other expeditions, and on climbs in the Alps. There are moments when you think that now you are going to fall, fall down for ever; during solo climbs, for instance, when you are in a very difficult situation and maybe haven't got the right piton, or when you have to do a very difficult move without protection. On Manaslu, I was perhaps at my limit for one or two hours, but not for days. On Nanga Parbat, it was for days: sleeping without a tent, just surviving.

Since then you have written nine books. From your writing it is clear that you are interested in the historical side of climbing, and in assessing future trends. During the last ten years, we have seen some very exciting expedition climbing. How do you view that particular period?

To me, it is fairly clear: expedition climbing seems to be developing in the same way as alpinism. There appear to have been three periods of development in the Alps: we have had the alpinism of conquest and the alpinism of difficulty, and today we have the alpinism of style, or sporting alpinism. In the Himalayas, it is the same thing, although the cycle has been greatly compressed. A hundred years after the exploration of the Alps, we had the big expeditions of conquest in the Himalayas: Annapurna in 1950, Everest and Nanga Parbat in 1953, Kangchenjunga in 1955, Makalu, Dhaulagiri, and so on. After that came the period of difficulty. Bonington's expedition to the South Face of Annapurna perhaps marked the beginning of this period: now, after years, it has reached its climax and is really a declining force.

What would you regard as the highpoints of that period?

Annapurna South Face and the Rupal Face of Nanga Parbat in the same year, and the West Pillar of Makalu in the next year. Manaslu South-Face was in the same period, but it was not so important, as it was neither as difficult nor as steep as the others. After that, there were the big face climbs on Everest and Makalu in 1975, and maybe they were the most important.

All big expeditions.

Yes, all big expeditions, all adopting more or less the same style and tactics. Perhaps some had a little more gear and some had a little less, but there were always ten to fifteen climbers and a lot of Sherpas. After that, it was logical that the next period should be marked by a more sporting style of expedition, and that is what we were trying on Hidden Peak [Gasherbrum I].

What developments do you predict in the next ten years? The big expeditions are clearly going to continue, aren't they?

Surely. There will be more big expeditions to big faces in the old style, but these will really only be interesting to the people involved. It is impossible to make any advance now with the type of big expedition that was mounted to the South-West Face of Everest. That was the most difficult face on the highest mountain, and it was valid to make every effort to climb it. But now we must move on to new styles. We must climb with less equipment, fewer people and less money: that is the only logical way to progress.

What sort of problems do you have in mind?

There are six or seven great problems left on the highest mountains: the Eigerwands and the Walker Spurs of the Himalayas. After that, we will see the advent of routes like the Eiger Direct and the Cima Grande Direct: routes without logic, but part and parcel of the search for difficulty. The logical problems that remain include all the ridges on K2, the South Faces of Dhaulagiri and Cho Oyu, the North Spur of Kangchenjunga, the two remaining lines on the South Face of Annapurna, and the East Spurs of Manaslu.

In climbing, we frequently refer to the ethical or stylish way of doing something. How do you see this criterion being applied to the problems you have mentioned?

Two groups of climbers will develop. Some will join big expeditions, in the hope of making a new route on a big mountain. Others will try, with perhaps less chance of success, to climb difficult routes on 8000m peaks, in groups of two, three or four, and a maximum of five.

And you consider that problems like the South Faces of Dhaulagiri and Cho Oyu should be climbed by such groups?

Yes. Look, in the 'fifties, mountains like Annapurna, Everest and Nanga Parbat were climbed by big expeditions, involving a lot of money and a lot of people. But in 1954, Tichy climbed Cho Oyu, admittedly by an easy route. As far as I was concerned, that was a big step forward, because everyone could see that it was possible to climb an 8000m peak with a small expedition. But the next year there was a French expedition to Makalu and a British one to Kangchenjunga, and they were put together like they were on Annapurna and Everest, because people had learned that with these techniques they would succeed. But those expeditions didn't constitute any real development. So, when I consider this period historically, it is clear that Annapurna was a new thing. So was Everest, because although it was still climbed in the same way, it is much higher. Nanga Parbat was a new thing, too, because Buhl went up alone. After that, Cho Oyu was a development but Makalu and Kangchenjunga were not. The next real development was perhaps Broad Peak.

The problem, of course, is that the sheer cost of big expeditions encourages leaders to make every effort to ensure success. If that means taking two or three more people and a bit more gear, then they are likely to do so, rather than fret about ethics and style.

That's true, but I feel that the chances of success are largely the same, whether an expedition is big or small. It doesn't matter if there are two climbers or ten climbers: they must still be very good, or the climb will not be possible. But, providing there is good weather and no sickness, the party should be able to succeed, and it is much easier to finance a'small expedition of, say, four people.

But what about K2, for example? Last year there was a big American expedition on it, and this year the Poles are there. Then it's going to be the Japanese, and probably the British. Surely it is naive to expect these expeditions to be small?

They can take a hundred climbers, if they wish; but, as far as I am concerned, success achieved in that way would be of minor importance. I'm not saying it would be nothing, but it wouldn't really be big alpinism.

What, then, do you see as the ideal K2 expedition in the late '70s?

I am sure it would be possible to climb K2 by the original route with two climbers. For a classic new route, four to six people should be enough. It ought to be possible to climb K2 like this, because, although it has a difficult approach, it doesn't have a big icefall at the start like Everest. Perhaps we will get permission for the mountain in the early 'eighties; if so, we will take a maximum of four climbers. There might be a TV team to finance the project, but the actual climbing team should be no more than four. And there will be no high-altitude porters, either. Otherwise K2 is not a problem: if an expedition is so big that the leader can confidently predict success from the outset – assuming no bad weather or illness – then this is not really a challenge for me. It is only when there is some doubt about the outcome that such a climb becomes interesting.

A four-man expedition on K2 will clearly have to be composed of very experienced and able climbers who go well at altitude. Where would you find such a party?

Put together Haston, Seigneur, Habeler and Scott, and they will do it.

International parties don't have a very good record for harmony.

In small groups it is possible. I may try to set up an international expedition on Dhaulagiri, if only to raise the finance. Small groups don't really need a leader. The leader is, or should be, only important for obtaining permission, and for dealing with formalities in Kathmandu or Rawalpindi. After that, you don't need a leader. Whenever I have done a climb with a small group, we have never had leadership problems.

But, when four people are climbing a mountain, they aren't always climbing together; once they become separated, unless there is a clear understanding between the climbers, funny things can happen. You saw that on Manaslu, for instance.

Yes, but the really important thing is that everyone is going well and climbing about the same. It's not good when one is much stronger than the others. Everyone must be able to climb alone up to 7000m. There is no place for alpine 'kids' on this type of project. So it is important to have a really able group.

Do you think that a long Himalayan apprenticeship is necessary as a basis for this type of expedition?

After you have made two or three visits to high altitude, you will know a little about yourself – not everything, but enough.

The same sort of thing is true in the Alps: when a man has done the Eigerwand, the Matterhorn, the Grandes Jorasses and maybe the Dru, he knows he can do most things in the Alps. But only one of these climbs is not enough: it could have been a fluke, or just a matter of luck. Only when you have succeeded three or four times do you know that luck isn't really a factor. And that applies in the Himalayas. There are all sorts of things that are different at high altitude: the light is different, for instance, and that plays havoc with scale; things seem so close when really they are far away.

It must also help to have a fair idea of your own capabilities. Scott's and Haston's bivouac on Everest and your descent of the Diamir, must both have been very testing experiences. Things like that must give you tremendous confidence.

Yes. Although that can also be a little dangerous, because you may think: 'Well, I bivouacked at 28,000ft on Everest without oxygen, so I can do everything.' For me, it was a good thing we failed on Makalu and Lhotse, after succeeding on Nanga Parbat and Manaslu; otherwise we would not have succeeded on Hidden Peak.

Why is that?

Because I had a big respect for Hidden Peak. Also, Makalu and Lhotse made me realize that it is very difficult to succeed on an 8000m peak. Perhaps I had built up too much confidence after Nanga Parbat and Manaslu. So, on Hidden Peak, I was more careful and left nothing to chance.

The evidence suggests that there is no guarantee of a consistently good performance at high altitude. Hillary for instance, failed on Makalu, eight years after his success on Everest. How confident are you that you will be able to spot something like that coming, so that you don't get ill in the middle of a big climb?

I think I can feel it. I seem to have developed a sense about my body, so that I know when it is performing well on a big expedition. For instance, I have a troublesome zone around 6000m, where I always feel bad. So I avoid putting camps at that height now, because it's not good for me.

You were slower than Habeler on Hidden Peak – your second expedition that year.

Yes, I was carrying the cine-camera and spare cassettes and our rucksack on the last day. It was the strain of filming that really slowed me up.

Were you at all worried about Habeler, about how he would perform at altitude?

Not really. I had seen him on Yerupaja, and I was pretty confident that he would go well. He has a slow pulse, he is thin and small, and he has a low blood pressure; all that is very important.

You obviously feel that we are on the threshold of an exciting new phase in Himalayan climbing. What do you think will be the ultimate climb of the new era? A solo attempt on Everest?

I'm sure it would be possible, but I think it would be a little bit crazy. The icefall and that long glacier would have to be negotiated, and it would be very difficult to solo there with any degree of safety [here Messner was talking about the Western Cwm approach – the Tibetan side was still restricted].

So what is the ultimate? In Alpine climbing it is a winter solo of a new route on a very difficult face. What is the Himalayan equivalent?

Perhaps to solo a new route on an 8000m peak that has few of the glacier and icefall problems that really do call for the presence of a companion. Ideally, there would be no porters and no support. Someone else could be in the base camp, but on the face the climber must be alone.

Presumbly you are thinking of peaks like K2, or perhaps Cho Oyu South Face: peaks with a reasonable descent.

Yes, the descent is an important factor. But I don't think you should seek out such a route specifically in order to do it in winter, as Bonatti speculated in one of his books. That wouldn't be logical, in my opinion. It's logical to do the climb solo, but not to stack up the difficulties artificially by doing it in poor or colder weather.

Who would you think was capable of such a performance?

There are a few people who could do it, but I doubt if anyone would succeed on the first attempt. The problems, of course, are not merely technical; there are also psychological difficulties attached to being alone for perhaps fifteen days, carrying all your equipment and food.

Looking back, do you think now that you could have soloed Hidden Peak?

No. You need to have somebody near you: it gives you tremendous extra confidence. Anyway, Hidden Peak is not a good mountain for soloing. The normal route is OK, but our route has a dangerous crevassed glacier, and it would be crazy to solo that. You might make it once, but not twice. Really, there are only a few routes in the Himalayas that are suitable for this sort of climbing. But the big problem facing anyone envisaging the type of climb we have been discussing is the matter of obtaining permission. In Nepal and Pakistan, they are selling the permits, and they are interested in getting big expeditions. I have been trying to get permission for a two-man expedition to an 8000m peak, in both Pakistan and Nepal, since 1972, and it took three years to get permission for Hidden Peak. Our next project, Dhaulagiri South Face, is also going to be small, and the Nepalese don't like it. 'Why do you want to come with only four or five men?' they ask. 'Why not bring ten men – it's better for us." Luckily I persuaded them to agree to five for this trip.

So what is the answer in the long term?

Knowing the authorities in these countries, I think it will be very difficult to get a one-man expedition lined up. Of course you can climb in a clandestine way, but you will be in trouble if they find out. We will just have to wait for the authorities to get used to the idea that climbers are interested in a new type of alpinism. In my view our generation has the chance to take part in the most fascinating period of Himalayan climbing; the situation there is similar to the great periods of the Alps and Yosemite, but now we are looking for logical problems on the highest walls in the world.

Note for 2006: Reinhold Messner climbed Everest in 1978 (with Peter Habeler) – the first ascent to be made without using bottled oxygen. He then soloed new routes on the Diamir Face of Nanga Parbat and the North Flank of Everest (1980 and 1982) and became the first person to climb all the 8000m peaks in 1986. In 2004/5 controversy over the circumstances surrounding his 1970 traverse of Nanga Parbat resurfaced in Germany and his comments here, plus those in the earlier *Mountain* interview in 1971, may have value as early debriefs of events during that tragic descent. In 2005 relics found at the foot of the glacier below the Mummery Rib appear to confirm the broad outline of what he reported about the emergency descent of the Diamir Face.

from MOUNTAIN 51 *1976*

JOE BEIGE MEETS GODZILLA

IAN McNAUGHT-DAVIS

Mountain has just received video-tapes made for LWBS (Lost World Broadcasting Services), featuring the final moments of the Human Flies Expedition, to the Lost World Crag. The following is a transcript:

Joe Beige climbs elegantly into view. Casually adopting his secret, world famous hand-jam to overcome difficulties, he uses his other hand to brush away the waves of snapping, mandible-waving, poisonous insects that threaten to overwhelm him. The LWBS News Reporter, Ramon Godzilla, comes into shot carrying a microphone.

Joe Beige: It's a bloody dinosaur.

Godzilla: Hello, old chap. Welcome to LWBS. I'm Ramon Godzilla but my chums call me God. How did you like the climb?

Beige: Are you from the BBC?

Godzilla belches; a stream of fire from his left nostril instantly grills a low-flying pterodactyl.

Godzilla: Really, old man. Started with Challoner, don't you know, and all those other clever chaps. They walked up the back way; it's a lot easier than the way you came.

Beige: We do it for the fun and a bit of excitement.

Godzilla: Just like old King Kong. He used to love it. Graded your route HVS and A3, used a lot of aid. Got killed roof climbing with a woman in the States some years back. Nice chap, but a bit too randy. Tell us about your climb.

Beige: It was hell. The first 200ft were overhanging, until we got to the niche. This turned out to be a nest of the dreaded *Bullshitmaster* snakes, twenty-foot long with huge dripping fangs. They were terrifying...

Godzilla: I know, I know. Had one for breakfast this morning. Damned indigestible too.

Beige: Then we did some more overhangs to the cabbage patch... odd that...

Godzilla: Council allotments, old chap. Hope you didn't do any damage.

Beige: Then another two hundred feet of overhanging rock to the Tarantula Terrace. They were knee-deep and crawled everywhere…

Godzilla: Scrumptious covered in chocolate…

Beige: Then it was overhanging all the way up Africa Flake, only one foothold in hundreds of feet, and it took us a whole week to get over one overhang. All the time we were being attacked by the evil vampire bats that suck your blood and carry rabies.

Godzilla: So that's where the little devils are hiding. When the bat-shooting season opened on August 12th the bags were pretty poor. They're very good grilled, wrapped up in their own wings and stuffed with camel dung…

Beige. Where do you get the camel dung?

Godzilla: Africa Flake, old boy.

Beige: Then we climbed the Wet Chimney. It was a solid waterfall and full of snapping man-eating piranha swimming up to spawn.

Godzilla: Yum, yum – just like kippers.

At that moment the immaculately dressed, robust figure of Sir Donald 'Sup-Up' Williams comes into view, jumaring up the rope hanging from Joe Beige's waist.

Sir Donald: It's bloody Brasher in fancy dress.

Beige: You're on telly.

Godzilla: Welcome to Lost World Television, Sir Donald. How did you enjoy your climb?

Sir Donald: Oh aye. I've just jumared up from Base Camp to see how the lads are getting on. We're paid to do a job of work and I'm here to see they do it.

Godzilla: We would like to watch you lead the last pitch so we can study your elegant technique.

Sir Donald: Aye, well, I'm having a bit of trouble with my special outsize harness, so I'll come back when it's fixed.

He abseils out of shot to be replaced by a perspiring Hamish McPiton, hung about with cine-cameras, bagpipes, haggis and deer-stalker hat, and trying to look as if he should be somewhere else.

McPiton: Och aye and what's this queer beastie that looks like Brasher in fancy dress?

Beige: It's telly, so get those blank contracts out of your sporran; it's another chance to establish our position in the Hall of The Greats.

McPiton: I'm just going to get a shot of Sir Donald abseiling past that big nest.

Beige: We've got enough stuff on abseiling and prussiking. Get set up next to God over there and we'll get a good shot of Moses Antheap leading the last pitch.

McPiton: Och weel, perhaps we can spare a few feet on Sir Donald fighting yon birdie.

The camera pans to show rotund Sir Donald, bottle in hand, flying low over the steaming jungle in the mouth of a pterodactyl.

Beige: I don't give that thing much of a chance; one bite and it'll go off like a rocket on high-octane fuel...

With an incredibly athletic, double-handed flip, muscular Yosemite climber Moses Antheap springs into view. A cult figure for middle-aged, anti-establishment climbers, he has remained unknown by refusing all pleas to write or even to broadcast. Despite his shy, self-disciplined, frugal personality, he is obviously enraged to find himself appearing before television cameras.

Antheap: What's Brasher doing here?

Beige: It's LWBS and Hamish has got a contract under his kilt, so get climbing.

Antheap: What's he doing with that snake?

Beige: It's a kind of interview technique; it ate his sporran.

Antheap, with forty-three slings round his neck; ninety-three pitons and eighty-two wire nuts on his waist, and his Hilti.45 semi-automatic bolt gun in his hand, swings up the overhangs on the Green Tower, the quadruple rope slowly unfurling behind him.

Godzilla: That's all today folks from me, Ramon Godzilla. Next time we hope to bring you SIR DONALD MEETS THE ICEMAN, direct from the snowy wilderness of Patagonia, THE RETURN OF JOE BEIGE from the sheep pens of North Wales, and the ever mysterious BRIDE OF ANTHEAP. So, till next time, it's good-bye from Godzilla and the team from The Lost World of Sport.

from MOUNTAIN 31 *1974*

CLIMB TO THE LOST WORLD*

ROBIN CAMPBELL

Another plastic expedition; but at least this one only beats about the bush in a literal sense. MacInnes is no metaphysician: they are there to make a film for the BBC, to tell a story for the *Observer*, to establish a territorial claim for the Guyana Government – no old-fashioned hypocrisy about 'exploration', or 'accepting a challenge', or 'because it's there'.

The cast of this outdoor melodrama is headed by MacInnes, Whillans, Brown and Anthoine, who play the leading roles (at least, Anthoine, and occasionally MacInnes, play leading roles, while Brown and Whillans do a lot of jumaring). Minor parts are played by Adrian Thompson (a sort of Guyanan Jimmy Roberts) and Neil McCallum of the BBC. Extras consist of Guyanan natives, Indians, snakes, vampire bats, orifice fish, scorpions, tarantulas, and so on. The script is classical English Kitchen Sink. For example:

Act II, Scene III. In El *Dorado Swamp*.

Hamish: (striking his foot against rock) Bugger it!

Hamish: (shouting to Mo, who is swimming) What about the perai and caimen?

Mo: Fuck them!

Neil: (throwing down his stick) Jesus Christ! What about the fucking film?

Mo: Mike and I have been charging around like farts in a phone booth. Neil would have got all his crap and piss shots then.

All this coruscating dialogue has been faithfully preserved by MacInnes and/or Miss E. Whittome (who 'so competently drafted the Ms'), and practically every page sparkles with well-aimed farts, fucks, snots, craps and pisses. Nor is this mere verbal virtuosity; our heroes' sphincters wink

*Originally published as a book review of Hamish MacInnes's book of the same name.

roguishly in several tasty scenes: 'MacInnes Drinks Brown's Piss', 'Whillans builds a Shithouse', 'The BBC Dirty Underpants Competition', 'Joe Struggles with the Giant Snot' are perhaps the choicest of many buttock-splitting adventures.

In the last act, 'The Ascent of the Great Prow of Roriama', the author's control seems to lapse momentarily, for some of the principal characters are seen to display outmoded 'virtues' such as fortitude, endurance and altruism. But this is merely a temporary aberration; in the epilogue, 'Return to Civilisation', the author regains control and our heroes return to their former state of grace with an evening of native-brewed rum and a visit to a Georgetown brothel.

In the past, MacInnes has shown himself to be a master of two quite different theatrical *genres*, the historical farce *(Scottish Climbs)* and the soap opera *(Call-Out)*. *Climb to the Lost World* now establishes him in the first rank of outdoor *avant-gardyloo* dramatists.

from MOUNTAIN 38 *1974*

A SHORT SIESTA ON THE UPPER SLOPES

ANON

What do we do now? called Ulf the Unwashed. *Njal's Saga*

A report on the Keele 1965 Peruvian Andean Expedition in the previous issue of the Journal included reference to 'a new route on Chichiccapac made by B. Chase, A. Tomlinson and G. Bonney,' adding 'the latter took a short siesta on the upper slopes while the other two pressed on to the summit'. Such reports are liable to give false impressions, and I feel it my duty to record the facts in fairness to Bonney, who is, alas, still with us.

It is no longer possible to discover with certainty who first suggested that he should join the expedition. Attempts to recall the days when we were selecting personnel produce instant violence and recriminations:

'So you thought he could carry the kit?'

'He could if he didn't eat so much.'

'I always said a woman would have been more use.'

Each insists that he was the first to devise the schemes to get rid of Bonney (known by the code-name GROB). It is not that he is unusually revolting, but when it comes to organising an expedition he is the very antithesis of Major Pingle. I shall say no more.

It is most probable that GROB was initiated by Bonny himself. When we were still unpacking deliveries, he announced that he would not go unless we took an adequate supply of Dr Gritte's *Muesli*. Almost simultaneously Webster and Gallagher leapt out of their crates to suggest that he should go to Germany to negotiate directly with the *Deutsche Muesli Gesellschaft*. He left the following afternoon and we found to our surprise that although he hadn't actually done anything while he was present everything was much easier in his absence.

So we progressed rapidly during the winter of 1964, and the months passed without news from Germany. Then, without warning, a letter arrived in which he not only claimed to be gainfully employed, but proposed that one of us should join him for a skiing holiday in Austria. This was a disappointment, but we decided to send Tomlinson to see what could be done, with instructions to survive the Alpine Tragedy himself. He did a good job. He met Bonney at Landeck and helped him to hire a pair of ski-boots. They then drove

321

into the Omaler. After a few days Tomlinson arranged a hard day's skiing which took them, towards nightfall, to the top of the shortest, steepest and most twisted descent in the district. When Tomlinson was about half-way down he heard a howl of agony above him, and was overtaken by a pair of skis carrying only the soles of the pair of boots. He then returned to England.

Our programme for the expedition work in Peru was comprehensive. Not content merely to climb our mountains, we were to make a map to find them with, and then to transport lumps of them complete with adhering vegetation, back to England. When finally assembled, the equipment weighed about three tons and it became clear that the five of us could no longer rely upon wearing it all at the airport baggage check. To this problem was added the return of Bonney, which made poor Webster quite ill for some time. The solution, however, was simple. Baggage and Bonney were taken to Liverpool and put on the next cargo boat to Lima. We told the First Mate that if he could induce Bonney to leap overboard in the course of a game of deck quoits, he would not go unrewarded. As a failsafe we included among his personal luggage an ex-army bazooka which we told him was a range finder. We were confident that this would ensure his prompt arrest and execution on arrival in Lima.

The rest of us flew out in June, and immediately set about finding the equipment. We found, instead, Bonney, living on a roof in the suburbs, still clutching the bazooka. Our difficulties of living in and leaving Lima are recorded elsewhere, but we eventually became incorporated in the load of a lorry bound for Arequipa.

At Arequipa we caught a train which hauled us slowly up onto the *altiplano,* and we became intrigued by the spectacle of odd Indians dismounting at unlikely spots, and walking slowly off towards the distant horizon. The idea made an immediate appeal, and at the next stop, we told Bonney that we had arranged for him to meet here a man called Gonzales Gonzales who was to accompany us to our base camp. Without question (not even 'Where is the base camp?') he climbed down and standing like an uncomfortable cactus, watched the train grind slowly out of sight.

We were sitting in the back room of an inconspicuous cafe in Juliaca eating *Guisco de pansa* (stewed paunch) when his dishevelled figure appeared in the doorway surrounded by small children. We retreated to the station waiting room to spend the night, though poor Webster, distraught at Bonney's ubiquity, spent it being sick on the platform, to the utter delight of the small children.

At Tirapata we dropped him again, but despite being savaged by a plano-wolf, he caught us up at Ayaviri and stuck with us all the way to Base Camp. It was clear that we should have to stage an Andean Tragedy.

We actually staged two. Neither was successful, but it might be worth relating them for the benefit of others (other expeditions to the Carabaya have taken one llama too many).

The first was planned with great care and executed without a hitch. We climbed Huayaccapac (5500m), by a gully on the N.E. Face, arranging things so that Bonney was the last to arrive (not difficult). The summit was a steep pointed snow pyramid, and as he climbed the last ten feet we placed an opened sardine tin on the slope above. The tin slid off down the slope with gathering momentum, and passed him at speed. Then, with a blush of fulfilment, the kamakaze sardines, still in perfect order, disappeared over the edge. We had by then untied his rope, and cannot understand to this day why he did not jump after them.

We paid dearly for our miscalculation. Back in Base Camp he built an automatic coffee grinder with two tins, an ice-peg and a twenty pound boulder, which got out of control and plunged into the egg powder. Then he made a bath, and Floyd was nearly carried off by a condor while bathing naked. Then he built a raft with our air-tight packing drums, sailed it to the far end of a lake and ran it aground. Finally, he set fire to his sleeping-bag in the middle of the night and Chase, five inches longer than his tent, straightened out in alarm.

Tomlinson spoke for all of us: 'Let's face it, as a human being you are a complete write-off. There is no point in taking you home. We have decided that you should be exposed on the mountain.' We very nearly lost him in the camp below Chichiccapac when he became trapped under two inflated air-beds in a two-man tent. We managed to coax him to the upper slopes however, and we abandoned him while he was admiring the view. Let's not waste words on euphemisms.

Anyway, he caught us up at Miami as we were settling down for the night on the airport roof.

from THE CLIMBERS' CLUB JOURNAL *1967*

'ADVANCE TO BASE, WE HAVE ENCOUNTERED UNFORESEEN DIFFICULTIES ON THE SUMMIT RIDGE'

A CRAWL DOWN THE OGRE

DOUG SCOTT

Chris was feeling the effects of his previous attempt. He was moving well enough, but suggested that I led the rocks ahead, as I should be faster, being fitter. I greedily accepted and soon 'lost' myself climbing two 150ft pitches up a pinnacle and down its far side to a snow patch on the north side of the summit rocks. From the snow we followed a diagonal break right up to a seemingly blank wall. This turned out to be the crux of the climb, for a crack I eventually found and followed for eighty feet suddenly ended. From a wire chock wedged into the crack, I got Chris to lower me some forty-foot so that I could make a pendulum swing across the granite wall. I swung first to one side then to the other, gradually increasing the arc by a sort of gallop against the rock, until I could reach over to another crack that looked climbable. I was just placing a chock when my feet slipped off and away I clattered across the rock. Chris continued to hold his end of the rope firm and, after another session of galloping about, I regained the crack, banged a piton into it, clipped my étrier to that and stood up from the peg, gasping for air after these exertions. Chris let out the tension in the rope and, by leap-frogging the aid up the crack, I was able to reach a point higher than before. Here, the wall relented and I was able to free climb to a point fifteen feet above the pendulum swing, to where a crack went through an overhang to the top of the wall. I climbed this using direct aid from chocks and the odd piton and, just as the 150ft length of rope joining us together had all been run out, I arrived at the top of the wall. Chris then jumared up the rope to join me, and from there we traversed down seventy feet and climbed an overhanging corner into the summit gully.

This final 100ft took up the last hour of the day, for when Chris arrived on the top of the Ogre the sun had gone down over the Hunza. As he had my camera, I had been able to sit on the top and take in the new perspective of Snow Lake and the hundreds of snowy peaks stretching off in all directions, without, for once, having to riddle with camera stops and speeds.

Not having any bivouac equipment, Chris and I were very anxious to get down to the snow-cave. However, it had been a good climb, at least above the fixed rope. There had been so much variation – a veritable magical

325

mystery tour of a route, taking in steep rock and ice, a climb over the West Summit and then a traverse across and up to the Main Summit.

We worked our way down a ridge of soft snow to a block of rock. We put a nylon sling round it, threaded our two climbing ropes behind that, and threw both down in the direction of the 150ft wall. To regain the peg crack, I had to push myself well over to the left as I abseiled, but eventually I got to the crack, just as I was reaching the end of the double rope. I leaned across to fix myself on to a peg, pressing myself over with my feet. I stepped my right foot up against the wall, but, in the gathering darkness, unwittingly placed it on a veneer of water ice. Suddenly my foot shot off and I found myself swinging away into the gloom, clutching the end of the rope. I couldn't imagine why the swing was going on and on.

I had not realised how far left of the abseil sling I was. And all the time I was swinging, a little exclamation of awe, surprise and fear was coming out from inside me, audible to Mo some 2000ft away at the snow-cave. And then the swing and the cry ended as I slammed into the opposite side of the gully, 100ft away. Splat! Glasses gone and every bone shaken. A quick examination revealed head and trunk OK, femurs and knees OK, but – Oh! Oh! – my ankles cracked whenever I moved them. The right one felt very peculiar: Potts' fracture, I diagnosed, without much real idea – left one, too, but perhaps it's just the tendons. So that was how it was going to be: a whole new game with new restrictions on winning – it was curious to observe my own reactions. I had no fear then, there was too much to do: I banged a peg in, put a couple of wire nuts in, tied off direct from my harness and hung off them while Chris came down the abseil rope.

'What ho!' he said, cheerily.

'I've broken my right leg and smashed the left ankle,' I said.

'We'll just work at getting you down,' he replied, airily. 'Don't worry, you're a long way from death.'

Too true! – the thought that I might have major problems of that kind had not then entered my head. I felt extremely rational, remarkably clear about what to do.

We continued our descent as far as we could that night. Chris abseiled down to a large patch of snow on a rock slab. By the time I reached him, he'd hacked a step out in the snow and, for the first time, I put my body weight on my legs and ankles. They both collapsed, the right leg cracking horribly. So I got on my knees, with my lower legs stuck out behind, and kneed across the ledge with no trouble at all.

'So that's how it's done,' I thought. And that's how it was done over the next seven days, with a little help from my friends – Chris, Clive and Mo.

Chris and I hacked away at the snow patch, producing a passable ledge on which we could lounge back in a half-lying, half-sitting position. Most of the time we sat facing each other with our bare feet stuck into each other's crutch. Every half hour or so we would reach down and rub a bit of life into each other's feet, a lesson learnt whilst bivouacking on Everest two years before. Mainly I cursed the night away, moaning and groaning at the cold, afraid that internal bleeding might cut off the blood going to my toes. That thought kept me grabbing at Chris's toes which I would rub furiously, hoping that he would take the hint and rub mine, which he did with gentle pressure. The night passed in these little flurries of action. At 5.30 next morning we abseiled four more rope-lengths down to the snow basin of the South-East Face. Chris kicked steps up towards the snow-cave to wake Mo and Clive. I followed as best I could, but it was slow going, as Chris had left only toe-holds in places. Mo came down and took our gear and kicked out bigger steps, and I was able to go at more or less normal speed for those altitudes.

We spent that night in the snow-cave and ate the last freeze-dried meal, leaving ourselves with only soup and tea. It was with some concern, therefore, that we found a howling blizzard raging outside the snow-cave the next morning. We had to get down to Advance Base to get food, and even lower to escape the debilitating effect of the lack of oxygen. But first we had to climb up 500ft to gain the West Summit. Mo and Clive went out to try it, but after an hour or so returned to the warmth of the cave. There had been so much snow in the air it had become impossible to see, and the wind made it difficult to stand up, let alone climb steep snow.

The next day, July 15, there was less wind and we all set off out into the heavy snowfall. Clive took the lead, slowly kicking his way up desperately deep powder snow, angled in places at 60°. Mo went next up Clive's rope, then me, then Chris. It took all day for us to move across the West Summit, abseil down the other side and traverse over steep ice to the snow-cave we had used on the night of the 11th. The weather was terrible – cold and violent. We had to dig out snow that had drifted into the cave, but as it was dark when we arrived no one felt like waiting around in the storm whilst the digging took place. So we ended up with cramped quarters and an inadequate entrance. Mo and Clive already had damp sleeping bags, and these became quite wet during the night with snow drifting in on to them. It was the worst night of all: no food, wet, still above 23,000ft, and me slowing them all down with the 1000ft Pillar still to come. There was only one way for me to tackle a big, complex problem like that, and that was one day at a time, keeping the broad idea hovering around in my mind that I'd got to get to Base Camp, but each day thinking no further than that day's objective, confident that if each day's climbing was competently executed then the whole problem would eventually be solved.

Next morning, Mo stuck his, head out of the cave and announced that the storm was now, if anything, worse. He went off, followed by Clive, then me, then Chris – all of us bent on reaching the tents, for there we had left a pound of sugar, which was something we had not had for two days. That seemed to be a number one priority. But also there was no real resting place between the snow-cave and the tents – so we had to make it. It was a nightmare descent. Whenever there was a ridge of level ground, I found crawling painful, seeming always to be catching my legs on protruding rocks. Only on steep, snowed-up rocks did I feel comfortable, for then Mo would have fixed up the abseil ropes and I could slide down with my body making contact with the snow and rock, whilst my feet stuck out, out of the way of obstacles. In this fashion I started to descend the 1000ft Pillar.

Unfortunately, on the way down, Chris abseiled off the end of one of the double ropes. Luckily, Clive had tied the other off to a rock, so Chris fell only about twenty feet or so, but he still broke two ribs and painfully damaged his right hand. Cold and getting colder, he had no alternative but to continue the descent. Mercifully, he did not at once start to experience the pain in his thorax that was to dog him later. It was a sorry little band that made the tents. Mo was the first and he had to re-erect them, as they were both flattened under three feet of snow.

The rest of us were happy to crawl straight in out of the tearing wind and into our sleeping bags. For me, it was a long and painful process removing gaiters, boots, inner boots and socks. But it had to be done so that I could rub my frozen toes back to life, for circulation was somewhat restricted by having my legs permanently bent at the knee. More serious, though, were my frozen finger ends. Crawling about so much I had no opportunity to keep my gloves dry, and not much time to stop and warm my hands when they started to lose sensation. I hoped that things would improve now that we were losing height, and we all kept thinking that the storm could not go on for many more days.

Mo came into the same tent as Clive and me, to warm up, as his sleeping bag was now reduced to a useless clump of wet, soggy feathers. We played cards, hoping the storm would finally blow itself out during the morning, so that we could move the tents down to the West Col later in the day. Chris was now in a bad way – coughing his throat hoarse, his voice down to a whisper, and every cough increasing the pain under his ribs. He burst into our tent during the morning, announcing that he really must go down as he thought that he had pulmonary oedema. We discussed this with him, but he did not seem to have any of the gurgling noises one hears about.

It was probable that he bad mild pneumonia which wouldn't have been helped by spending the day out in the swirling spindrift. Neither did the three of us fancy the sub-zero temperature and harsh wind, for Mo announced that he had not felt his toes for nearly a week and Clive's digits were also numb. Despite it being our fourth day without food, we decided to give it one more day. At least now we had enough sugar for the next dozen brews of tea. We had been taking tea without milk or sugar for breakfast, and half a curried meat stock cube for dinner, and we were lacking in energy but now noticed a slight change for the better with the sugar.

It was still blowing hard the next morning as we roped down to the South-West Col. By now I had become quite expert at knee-climbing. I found that being on my hands and knees was actually an advantage in particularly deep snow, and I did a bit of trail-breaking. Mo unearthed some old Japanese ropes, and we slid down the first 500ft to the West Col. We went across to our former camp-site and dug around until we uncovered a waste bag, in the bottom of which was some boiled rice mixed with cigarette ash, which we ate. We rummaged around some more and found an ounce of milk powder and, in another bag, three packets of fruit sweets and two packets of cough sweets. We shared them out when Clive and Chris arrived.

We moved off to the top of the fixed ropes that would take us to Advance Base the following day. I carried Clive's sack as he had to go and recover a tent that had fallen off his sack higher up. There was now about a mile to go across soft snow, but at last the clouds were rolling back to reveal the mountains all around covered in fresh, sparkling snow down to the glaciers. My arms kept sinking down into the snow with the weight of Clive's sack pressing down over my neck. Despite following Mo's footsteps, I took many rests, flopping down flat out in the snow. Expeditions are usually good times to sort out a few things in the head – times to drop down a level or two – but it occurred to me then that since my accident I had brought such an iron will to bear on every moment of the day that I had not given such matters a thought. But there had been some compensations, for whenever I shut my eyes I went off into a hallucinatory world of lilac and purple colouring, incredible shapes and forms, caricature people and stylised views of distant times and places. It did not make a lot of sense, but it was one way to while away a few minutes and recover enough to take a further twenty or so crawling paces through the snow.

Mo, and I dug out tent platforms, put up one of the tents and then the other when Clive arrived with it. Chris came in very slowly, coughing up a rich yellow fluid from his lungs.

Chris and Mo set off at first light for Advance Base. Clive and I followed four hours later, for by then the sun would be up to warm our frostbitten hands and feet. Also, Chris and Mo would have had time to cut out big steps at various key places.

Abseiling down fixed ropes was no real problem for me, so I was able to descend 2500ft in four hours. Crawling over soft snow down to 17,000ft was also relatively easy, but after that the snow became thin, and I had to crawl over hard, sharp glacier ice.

We arrived at last to find that Advance Base was no more – either blown away or taken away by Nick and Tut – so there was nothing for it but to follow Mo and Clive down to Base Camp. The next section was the most painful of the whole retreat. The distance was about four-and-a-half miles from the end of the fixed ropes. About one mile was on soft snow, two and a half on ice and one on moraine. At 10.30 that night (July 20), I crawled over the last of the moraine rocks. My legs were very swollen from knocking them countless times. I stopped to examine them and was horrified to find that I had worn right through four layers of clothing and that my knees were numb, bloody and swollen.

One last bank and I was on the triangle of moraine that surrounded the thick green grass of Base Camp – a little oasis amongst the chaos of shifting rock and ice. I crawled to the old kitchen site to find that Mo had gone off in hot pursuit of Nick, who had that same morning given us up for dead. 'If you get as far as reading this, then it presumably means that at least one of you is alive,' he wrote in his note, adding that he was going down to fetch Tut from Askole and form a search party.

They obviously did think us dead from the meagre supplies that were left. However, it was good to eat Purdy Cake with a cup of milky tea and then to fall asleep on that little meadow.

Next morning the sun shone on to our wet sleeping bags – you could feel the warmth come right through into the murky interior. Pulling open the draw-cord from inside, poking my head out to see the grass, the flowers and the stream running across; then getting out, brewing a mug of tea, eating a powdered egg omelette and feeling the sun burning my skin: beautiful memories these.

from MOUNTAIN 57 *1977*

PART 6

SOME PART-TIME GAMES

Climbing is not all about Climbing. There are countless peripheral diversions to occupy us when we are not doing battle with mountain or crag. These range from the current underground pursuit of 'grossing' (which encompasses the whole gamut of degenerate behaviour patterns) to the elevated highbrow pursuits of literature, poetry, glittering formal dinners, science, politics and conservation.

This group of articles covers a range of obscure pursuits from testing the depth of quagmires, seeing which brands of whisky float in baths, observing the mating patterns of snails on Snowdon, discussing the various styles of after-dinner-speaking, to confronting the challenge posed by women in a hitherto male-dominated sport.

The position in 2006: Post '60s bacchanalia declined as the novelty wore off. Perhaps the most notable developments since 1977 have been the growth of film and book festivals building on the lead set by the still very popular Trento Film Festival. In Britain the TV climb spectacular, also very fashionable in the 1960s and 1970s (and lampooned in the previous section), virtually disappeared leaving only periodic documentaries and a handful of risible (from a climbing standpoint) mainstream feature films (*K2, Cliffhanger*). Then the film *Touching the Void* stunned both filmgoers and mountaineers as a fine example of a real climbing epic being depicted in a commercial film. Its success may well encourage further developments in that area.

Although a form of climbing, albeit still a curiously unsatisfactory hybrid, the proliferation of bigger climbing walls (or gyms) should be noted. These in turn led to climbing competitions, eagerly adopted by those more at ease amidst conventional sporting mores. One wonders what Tom Patey and Sheridan Anderson would have made of competition circuits especially as other noted satirists became closely involved in their organisation. If literary activity is a measure of their appeal, these events are of transient interest.

In less contentious areas the already mentioned Deep Water Soloing (a growth from earlier sea level girdling) joins Free Fall Parachuting (from places like El Capitan, Mount Asgard and the Trango Towers) and snowboarding or skiing down vertiginous couloirs and north faces as further examples of the eclectic extra-mural tastes of climbers. Rick Silvester's James Bond ski jump and long free fall from Mount Asgard being the most amusing public demonstration of the genre (especially as an American pulls the rip cord of a Union Jack parachute) – Sheridan would have enjoyed that.

BOULDER TRUNDLING*

S. F. FORRESTER

Boulder Trundling may be defined as the propulsion of fragments of the Earth's crust down mountain slopes of suitable inclination sooner than would occur from the interaction of natural forces.

Like other sports and pastimes it has different phases and degrees. No one could object to pushing a stone weighing (say) two ounces down a two yard slope to drop two feet into two fathoms of water; while even I should draw the line at sending some tons of rock down High Tor Gully into a train full of widows and orphans on their way to Buxton Well-Dressing. The sport, then, as I understand it, lies somewhere between these two extremes, and is one calculated to afford pleasure and profit to many right-minded persons and offence to few; that is, if practised reasonably, with due regard to time and place.

I may mention one particular spot where I have spent many profitable hours in moving some tons of rock downhill a little before it was due to go in the course of nature. This is a gully on the right of the Alport, some little distance below the waterfall. Surely there could be no valid objection to this: no one should get hurt; and although it leaves some marks, they seem

---

*This essay is the outcome of an argument between its author and the [Rucksack) Club Treasurer on the ethics of boulder trundling, in the course of which the former averred that this practice had received the sanction of many reputable mountaineers, and had, in particular, been mentioned with approval by Leslie Stephen in *The Playground of Europe*. Wilding threw doubt on the former statement and categorically denied the latter. On further examination he withdrew this denial but maintained that Stephen's remarks were not meant seriously. It was finally decided that the two disputants should argue their respective cases before a gathering at the Club Hut and that the decision should he left to a single arbitrator. The parties agreed on Pryor as the judge, and that the following three questions should be submitted for his decision:

    1. Is it possible to justify Boulder Trundling?

    2. Is there reasonable evidence that any mountaineer of repute consistently practised Boulder Trundling?

    3. Was Leslie Stephen serious in this passage from *The Playground of Europe* regarding Boulder Trundling?

    The cases were duly pleaded by their respective advocates before a large and enthusiastic audience (fortified by one of Burton's brews of rum punch in which spirit could be distinctly smelt).

    At the end Pryor gave judgement for Wilding on the first two counts and for Forrester on the third. It had been agreed that all bets were to be settled by the Judge's ruling; but afterwards Pryor himself asked the jury for their opinion as a matter of interest, and found that they disagreed with his judgement on the second count, while agreeing with the other two.

    This is substantially the plaintiffs case, cut down and also slightly modified to suit the new circumstances of presentation. This explanation has been deemed necessary in order to make clear the general form of the essay. It has not been found possible to persuade Wilding to publish his counter-arguments. – Editor, *Rucksack Club Journal*.

without desecration. Another charming boulder shoot is a Bowfell gully above Angle Tarn; the remembrance of a crowded half-hour of life in this gully is very sweet, and the marks left here are less obvious than on the gritstone.

In any case it is quite arguable that the marks made look more natural than the nail scratches of rock climbers. The latter, of course, are inveterate Boulder Trundlers. How often, in reading the account of a new climb, do we not come across something like this:

> The leader carefully examined a large slab on the left which would have been of great help in this difficult pitch, but it looked unsafe and moved slightly when tested. The leader and second therefore gave it a wide berth, while the last man, after being anchored from above, managed to send this dangerous rock hurtling down the gully.

All this however is beside the point. Boulder Trundling as I understand it is done for the sheer joy of the sport: there is no thought of the future – the present suffices.

Consider a long slope, up which you have painfully toiled in the wake of a hardened grough-hound. At the bottom maybe is a vertical drop or a mass of jumbled rocks, and at the top there is a stone of inviting appearance and precarious tenure. You sit down above it, and after a necessary rest the feet are pressed against the rock. It moves perceptibly, but you can do no more from that point. You shift your ground and try again; still no luck! You excavate a little on the underside and heave some more. You are not strong enough: some help is wanted and you shout for your companion. The force is now sufficient, and with the expenditure of a few buttons or perhaps some part of your braces the rock is moved from its bed and makes a revolution. It gathers momentum ... soon it is going really fast, and no matter what its shape it elects to travel on the longest axis. Speed increases rapidly now; sometimes the boulder will take great bounds and at other times scuttle close to the ground like a rabbit.

The zenith of Boulder Trundling is attained if it now meets solid rock in full face: the crash does one good to hear; the rock breaks into shivers, while part of it is ground absolutely into smoke. Favourable winds bring the scent of this smoke to you ... and what an indescribably beautiful scent it is. Chesterton must have known of this delectable odour when he wrote of 'The brilliant smell of water, the brave smell of a stone.'

Or there is Boulder Trundling in a rock gully with great slabs – lots of them together walloping down in a confined space. A tarn on the Rhinogs has a steep face of bare rock on one side where you may trundle straight into deep water. Time was short on the only occasion I was there, so that I hope to go again to work out the course properly. I cannot analyse the delight of Boulder Trundling, nor say why it pleases – better men than myself have tried and failed. I can only say that it affords perhaps the purest joy we can expect in this terrestrial life.

The first Boulder Trundler of whom we have any record is Sisyphus, who was so addicted to the sport – in fact he seems to have spent his whole life at it – that we really know nothing else about him, so that for our first instance of a well-known mountaineer who practised the art we must turn to Moses. Moses was the most celebrated climber of his time and has at least three first ascents to his credit, namely Mounts Horeb, Sinai, and Pisgah. In addition, he led a very difficult traverse of the Red Sea, which was effected without mishap despite the unusual size of his party. The magnitude of this achievement can be gauged from the fact that another party which attempted to repeat the traverse suffered total disaster. The Red Sea by Moses's Route is now considered unjustifiable and has not since been attempted.

As regards Boulder Trundling by this great pioneer, it is recorded that on his way down after the first ascent of Mt Sinai he came upon a slope of surpassing excellence, on viewing which he had but one idea in mind – to push the handiest rock down it. This rock unfortunately bore most important inscriptions, and Moses got into serious trouble for giving rein to his inclinations. I have always felt the greatest sympathy for him on this account.

Before passing on to recent times let us take one glimpse at a medieval devotee of our sport. I quote from Arnold Lunn's book *The Alps* (pp. 30-31):

> The Stockhorn is a modest peak some 7000ft in height. Simler tells us that its ascent was a commonplace achievement. ... Its ascent by Müller, a Berne professor, in 1536, is only remarkable for the joyous poem in hexameters which records his delight in all the accompaniments of a mountain expedition. Müller has the true feelings for the simpler pleasures of picnicking on the heights. Everything delights him, from the humble fare washed down with a draught from a mountain stream, to the primitive joy of hurling big rocks down a mountain side. The last confession endears him to all who have practised this simple, if dangerous, amusement.

I now come to modern mountaineering, and the first case I will cite is the behaviour of Whymper on the occasion of the first ascent of the Matterhorn. It will be remembered that there was a race between the Italian and English parties. On getting to the top and finding that the Italians had not yet arrived Whymper looked down the mountain side to see where they were, and on finding them wished to attract their attention. He writes in *Scrambles Amongst the Alps*.

'Croz! Croz! come here!' 'Where are they, Monsieur?' 'There – don't you see them – down there!' 'Ah! the *coquins*, they are low down.' 'Croz, we must make those fellows hear us.' We yelled until we were hoarse. The Italians seemed to regard us – we could not be certain. 'Croz, we *must* make them hear us; they *shall* hear us!' I seized a block of rock and hurled it down, and called upon my companion, in the name of friendship, to do the same. We drove our sticks in, and prized away the crags, and soon a torrent of stones poured down the cliffs. There was no mistake about it this time. The Italians turned and fled.

Boulder Trundling in the dark sounds attractive, to judge by an incident during the ascent of Mont Pelvoux, as described in the same book.

This night we fixed our camp high above the tree-line, and indulged ourselves in the healthy employment of carrying our fuel up to it. The present rock was not so comfortable as the first, and, before we could settle down, we were obliged to turn out a large mass which was in the way. It was very obstinate, but moved at length; slowly and gently at first, then faster and faster, at last taking great jumps in the air, striking a stream of fire at every touch, which shone out brightly as it entered the gloomy valley below, and long after it was out of sight we heard it bounding downwards, and then settle with a subdued crash on the glacier beneath.

Another mountaineer of repute who practised the noble sport was Sir Martin Conway, who says quite casually during his account in *The Alps from End to End* of an ascent of the Wilde Kreuz Spitze: 'We amused ourselves by throwing stones down the slope we had come up and watching them vanish in the fog.'

It might be thought that although the sport was practised by amateurs, no reputable guide would ever have anything to do with it; but this is not the case. One of the most celebrated, perhaps the most justly renowned of all Alpine guides, is not found wanting. I refer to Jean Antoine Carrel. I quote once again from Arnold Lunn's *The Alps*, where, describing an early attempt on the Matterhorn by Carrel, his brother, and Gorret, he says: 'They mistook the way; and, reaching a spot that pleased them, they wasted hours in hurling rocks down a cliff – a fascinating pursuit.'

I think it is not straining matters too far to suggest that 'wasted' is here used in the Shakespearian sense, as when Portia speaks of '... companions. That do converse and waste the time together', no sense of reprobation being implied. The following passage is of supreme interest:

We waited patiently a long cold hour for the views that did not appear, and our geologist had ample opportunity to indulge in the innocent pastime of stone-breaking. We had plenty of fun too in heaving great rocks over the giant precipice. This is a sport the fascination of which few members of the Alpine Club can resist, and I for one must in my time have rolled hundreds of tons from the tops of mountains.

It might have been thought that I had invented this quotation especially for use on this occasion. Not at all! It is the work of a very eminent mountaineer, of whom I may safely say that there are few men whose words would carry more weight in the mountaineering world. The author is the late Mr Slingsby, and the words occur on page 106 of his book on Norway. Later on page 379 in the same work we come across the following:

> A small cairn was hastily raised, and we hurried along a saddle to the south-western or highest peak. Loud were our hurrahs and many were the rocks which we threw over the gaunt precipices. Most new ascents are commemorated in this manner.

I strongly recommend this book of Slingsby's to the youthful Boulder Trundler, as it contains several references to the sport.

One more quotation before we pass to our last point. This time it is from an article on Skye in an early number of this Journal.

> We started at 10 o'clock and walked up the north branch of the corrie, stopping to inspect a very deeply cut gorge, into which we hurled boulders, which struck the pool at the bottom with a resounding 'pomph'.

And now for Leslie Stephen!

The passage in *The Playground of Europe* occurs during Stephen's discussion of Rousseau, and I must give it at some length as the context is important to my argument. It seems clear to me that the author is here engaged in a perfectly serious attempt to show that Rousseau was a mountaineer at heart; and the reference to Boulder Trundling is a definite link in his reasoning. To suppose that his intention is merely flippant here is to suppose that his whole attempt to make out Rousseau a mountaineer is just a joke, and that would be too pointless a joke for a man of Leslie Stephen's wit.

> Rousseau's sentiments must be gathered rather from the general tone of his writings than from any definite passages. In the *Confessions* indeed there is an explicit avowal of his hatred for the plains and his love of torrents, rocks, pines, black woods, rough paths to climb and descend, and precipices to cause a delicious terror; and he describes two amusements so characteristic of the genuine mountaineer that we feel at once that he is on the right track. One is gazing for hours over a parapet at the foam-spotted waters of a torrent and listening to the cry of ravens and birds of prey that wheel from rock to rock a hundred fathoms beneath him. The other is a sport whose charms are as unspeakable as they are difficult of analysis. It is described somewhere (if I remember rightly) by Sir Walter Scott, and consists in rolling big stones down a cliff to dash themselves to pieces at its foot. No one who cannot contentedly spend hours in that fascinating though simple sport really loves a mountain.

No words of mine can emphasise this eloquent simplicity. When I go to Heaven, may my spirit join the spirits of Leslie Stephen, Slingsby, and the illustrious Boulder Trundlers of the past, present, and future, to spend eternity rolling asteroids and comets down the infinite abyss of interstellar space to meet in cosmic collision the multitudinous celestial bodies of the Milky Way; that in gorgeous impact all may be resolved into the imponderable protons and electrons of ultimate matter.

from THE RUCKSACK CLUB JOURNAL *1931*

INTRODUCTION TO SAUSSOIS

ALLAN AUSTIN

The skies above were grey and storm-tossed, weeping curtains of rain that drove across the great plains of Northern France. I looked out. I was ready to go home. We had just arrived in all this drenching downpour and had pitched camp. I was wet, very wet. We had driven 1500 miles to see those scruffy little limestone cliffs, the ones we could see peeping over the tree-tops just beyond the river, urged on by Claude's 'It is always fine at the Saussois.'

We wandered over to the crag and watched a young French incompetent playing about in étriers. Disconsolately we turned towards the camp – when again the heavens opened, and it rained. It would have been unpleasant if the café had not been at hand – the first lucky break of the holiday. It was a black day for Yorkshire however, as I was the only one with money; and beer at three shillings a glass.

The following day dawned bright and clear and we made the most of it. We loafed and lazed and made a late start. When eventually we arrived at the crags climbing was in full swing. I must admit, the place looked attractive. We stood in the shade of some tall trees and leaned against Claude's car which we'd parked just off the road. The crag was a mere ten yards away. It was glowing yellow and white in the sun. Some of the things these lads were on looked good. I felt a bit better, maybe even a little impressed.

'Looks quite good,' I remarked, speaking to a silent Claude. 'That line up there looks particularly impressive.'

Still no answer. I cleared my throat and prepared to start again, when I noticed his face. It was all hot and flushed. Beads of sweat were standing on his forehead. 'Must be the sun,' I thought: though that didn't account for the way his eyes were bulging. I turned my attention back to the crag.

'By Jove!' I thought, 'I haven't seen that before.' 'She's wearing a bikini,' I ventured.

A particularly futile remark. It was obvious that he'd already noticed. I glanced about. 'There's another over there!' I passed the information on to a hard-breathing Claude. The eyeballs moved. Attention was transferred from the red to the blue ...

Eventually the passage of time (and the bikinis) saw us roped up on a little climb well to one side. There were no spectators, and so, naturally, no climbers. I found myself on the sharp end doing some particularly bold laybacking, in what I thought was a very thin crack. I was impressed! I passed the information on to Claude.

'Mac said it was good,' he replied.

I warmed to it. 'It's steep and remarkably sound. You'll like it Claude.'

'He may have been referring to the climbing,' he continued. His thoughts were obviously elsewhere.

We collected our gear and scrambled back down to the road. Claude was already engaging the Red Bikini in small talk. She was worth engaging in anything! I rushed down, and was just in time to meet a young blond giant, magnificently muscled, clad in swimming trunks and climbing boots. He looked familiar. I racked my brains – and then I remembered. He was the front end of the Red Bikini's rope.

'Er, how do you do?' I quavered, hurriedly stepping away from the Red Bikini and giving Claude a nudge on the way. 'We were just asking about the routes.'

'He doesn't understand,' came a tinkling laugh from behind.

I was not so sure. English maybe: but Claude?

Explanations were difficult, but with a bit of intelligence on the other side, and determination on ours we got out the information that we had done that little crack up there. We stood back waiting for the applause. A raised eyebrow maybe, or a sharp intake of breath.

The Red Bikini looked at the Blond Giant with an unspoken question. It was answered with an avalanche of French. I understood nothing, but managed to pick out the word *'facile'* which cropped up once or twice.

We hurried away, crestfallen, to start on the next climb. It was her choice; La Rech. It was the one the Blue Bikini had just rushed up – on the sharp end. It looked good, even though it did look easy. Yet another well-filled costume was climbing in front. She was being hauled up by some tall young

Frenchman. Obviously incompetent, and equally obviously, she never lacked climbing partners.

I started out (Claude had done it before with Mac).

'It's probably the easiest pitch on the cliff,' said Claude as I teetered my way up the easy slabby ridges on slabby sloping holds. 'It gets harder higher up.'

The second pitch was a deep thrutchy crack and I was able to hide my shame deep inside. It wasn't often that the French were treated to the sight of a genuine Yorkshireman, complete with baggy ex-army trousers, sweating his way up a thrutchy crack. They probably laughed their sunburnt sides sore.

The third pitch was a pleasant open slab. 'At last,' I remarked, 'this is something like it.' I came to a full stop hanging on a peg, about ten feet short of the next stance. It seemed hard. There were only bits of nicks for finger holds and the thing had steepened up abominably.

'It's only five inf.,' Claude's reassuring voice came up from the rear. 'It's the classic of the crag.' I had another go.

'That's the place where we saw the Blue Bikini; she didn't have any difficulty.'

Claude took the rope in tight as I flopped back onto the peg.

I simply couldn't let all these bits of French fluff beat me. I wiped my sweating palms on the seat of my steaming trousers and made a desperate last attempt.

'I think the peg's only for protection,' the voice from the rear tuned in as I managed, at last, to get a trembling foot on it.

'You're not climbing so well today,' announced Claude on arrival, and deftly lifted the slings from my neck. 'I think I'd better lead the rest.'

It was a delightful pitch, slabby, juggy and with a peg where it looked as if it might get hard – but didn't. He was no mug, this Claude chap. He'd been here before.

On the top, and sharing the same stance with Claude was the Blond Giant. I gave him a nervous smile and looked over the edge at his route. Gad, it was impressive. A long thin curving groove, without as far as I could see, any runners. The Red Bikini came up quickly and easily. When she arrived I strode forward, crashing into Claude's back as he smoothly stepped in front. It was the Blond Giant for me again.

'Er, how do you do?' I said again as I listened to the smooth flow of talk from over my shoulder '… not easy like the one you've just done… but not too hard … only a few steps of six…'

We wandered back to the campsite in thoughtful mood.

'Can you imagine that lot in Briggs' joint?' remarked Claude.

'By gum,' I thought, suddenly struck with the vision of a PYG* filled with all these Bikinis. 'Even Doug [Verity] would take up climbing again.'

I was enthusiastic on my return to the tent. I waxed lyrical on the impressive local scenery and the ability of the locals. Jennie was not impressed. I almost lost my dinner. So did Claude.

It was a rather sad pair of climbers who wandered over to the crags that evening for a last look; before rushing off back to Paris.

from THE CLIMBERS' CLUB JOURNAL *1966*

*Pen y Gwyrd Hotel, North Wales – whose landlord at the time was Chris Briggs.

THE CRAGGIE

G. J. F. DUTTON

Just on the corner, the wheel came off. Fortunately, it was a right-hand corner and an off-side wheel. I was sitting in the front and saw it appear in the headlamp beams, skipping joyfully in its new freedom. Speechless, I grabbed the Doctor's shoulder, and pointed.

'Ah, a wheel,' he said.

I curled myself up in the old nylon sling which served as safety belt, and watched fascinatedly through the fingers shielding my face.

Imperturbably, we slowed down, bumped along the grass verge and clomped to a halt. The wheel waved us goodbye and leapt into a sitka plantation. The Doctor opened his door and got out.

'Extraordinary. Rear wheel. Never happened before. Handled very well, considering it's i.r.s.' He rummaged in a door pocket, then he went off by torchlight to retrieve the errant accessory.

In grateful obscenity from the back seat the Apprentice voiced his admiration. We both agreed the Doctor was no more nerve-wracking to his passengers on three wheels than on four.

Before he returned, bowling his wheel, we had confirmed that the threads had stripped. We were stuck on a wet Saturday night in late October, halfway to our goal.

Our goal was a kindred club hut below a well-known and easy ridge. We were to scramble up the ridge and down again; a mere excuse for a spirituous weekend to celebrate the Doctor's achievement and our own survival – for the previous weekend we had taken him up his first VS. An experience cathartic for us – even for the iron-nerved Apprentice, who as usual led – but apparently much enjoyed by our medical companion. I need not describe it here.

We were stuck. We had no tent, and even the Doctor's old Mercedes could not sleep three when one of them was his own six feet two. We inspected the map.

'Here's the road, the plantation. Ah!' He gave a glad cry, thumped his thigh with the torch. The light went out. 'We're just by Kindraiglet! What luck!'

The luck turned out to be that Kindraiglet was a cottage on his brother-in-law's estate. It was occupied by his brother-in-law's shepherd. 'An excellent man, MacPhedran. He'll be delighted to put us up. Remarkable luck. And – yes – I'll give you a treat tomorrow.' He chuckled ominously as he wrestled out his rucksack.

Two hours later we were admitted by a jovial MacPhedran. 'Car broke down, just on the road below,' explained the Doctor, dismissing our purgatorial sojourn in drenching twenty-foot sitka spruce – the prickliest stage of growth – looking for the Kindraiglet track. ('Can't be far off; know it well; pity these trees are so high; otherwise my torch would easily pick it out.')

We dried, feasted, drank and sang. MacPhedran fiddled with gusto. When I fell asleep the Doctor and he were trying to explain to each other what went wrong with Scott Skinner.

The morning was fine, though cold and dripping. After cooking a late breakfast (MacPhedran was long on the hill) the Doctor referred again to his Treat.

'It was damn good of you to take me up 'Constipation' last weekend. I'd never have cared to go alone. Wouldn't have missed it for the world. Remarkable how straightforward those routes are when you rub noses on 'em. Well, here's one for you two. Used to stay here years ago. Always went on The Craggie, as we called it. A jolly nice little climb, quite different from 'Constipation'. You'll like the change.'

So it was to be The Craggie. We had brought the minimum of equipment – only a sixty-foot line and the odd assortment of ironware inseparable from the Apprentice (he clinked perceptibly even in Daddy McKay's). But we were assured The Craggie would require none of it. 'Used to go on The Craggie by myself – just boots. Balance is all you need – and an eye for a good line.'

He led out of the door. The Apprentice and I, heavy-headed, tried to imagine the amorous rugosities of warm gabbro. We splashed up through the birches.

Disconcertingly soon, he stopped. 'There she is!' he announced. We peered past him at a clearing in the scrub. Out there, moss and slime, so long beneath our feet, reared themselves up to a sheer three hundred evil feet. The upper rim was fanged in black, and black rock gleamed hungrily at us through a thousand green and dripping moustachios.

'Wonderful view from the top,' he said. Then: 'Good Lord, there *she* is!'

'Who, now?' asked the Apprentice, sourly. His pallor, I noted, was not all attributable to the night before.

'Why, Aggie. Aggie McHattie. Up there, on the left. The old girl in tweeds. See her? Just by that big wet slab. I *thought* I heard a car early on.'

I found the Apprentice's expression interesting. Then I turned again to the extraordinary sight. The Doctor lowered his Leitz Trinovids and lent them to me. I saw, bang in the middle of the face, a square figure in tweed jacket and skirt, thick socks, nailed shoes, frizzy grey hair and gold spectacles. I saw it standing on a line of slime prising out something from the oozing slab. I saw it lift up the something, examine it, and throw it away. I swore I could hear the 'Pshaw!'

'Hallo' roared the Doctor. 'Allo, allo, allo,' roared back The Craggie, moistily and throatily. The figure looked round, surveyed us. A clear precise voice.

'Good morning, Doctor. I shan't be long. There's not very much here.' Then it returned to its prising, further along the line of slime.

'Miss Agnes McHattie,' explained the Doctor. 'Remarkable woman. Famous lichenologist and moss-classifier; not really Ferns, but does take a look or two at the *Ophioglossaccae*. Used to be my leader on lots of expeditions.'

The Apprentice declined the binoculars. Also, he seemed to be having difficulty in swallowing.

We squelched up to the foot of The Craggie. We stopped below a vertical pillar of green treacle. It wet my elbow.

'Central Buttress Direct' said the Doctor. 'A good line on to the Main Face. I'll lead and show you the way at first; although it's obvious enough. Glad I brought trikes; there's a slippery bit near the top.'

He crouched, adopted a curious kind of dog-paddle, and levitated uncannily. He paused and settled on a heap of watercress or similar vegetation twenty feet up. 'Great to be back again. Lost youth and all that. Come on up, there's acres on this stance.' As he spoke, a large plateful of cress smacked down wetly at my feet. Politely, the Apprentice waved me on. Kindly, he gave me the rope.

'Yes, we may need the rope later on,' the Doctor advised. 'It gets harder in places if you're in vibrams. They're jolly treacherous anywhere off those Trade Routes of yours.'

I agreed. It was impossible even to leave the ground with them. I only succeeded by locking each knee alternately in the soaking groove and spooning heaps of green porridge with both hands to keep me upright. I was not ashamed to take the Doctor's bony grip. I was dragged up, and thankfully clutched a long green stem.

'Ho! Watch that! It's *Lycopodium inundatum*, a mere club moss. No root at all. Dangerous. *Cryptogamma crispa's* a good handhold. Here's one. Ah, there's *Luzula* – even better. You've got to know your mountains, in a place like this!'

I was in terror lest I should have to offer the Apprentice the rope. But up he came, seaweed in his hair.

The watercress was definitely crowded, and raring to go. So the Doctor continued. I instructed my companion in the deficiencies of *Lycopodium* and the relative security of *Cryptogamma*. He muttered darkly, still clutching the piton with which he had clawed his way up.

The cress hiccupped vertiginously. I grabbed several stems, pressed knee-caps into a Gorgon's head of bryophytes. The Apprentice said he was getting the hell out of here and boldly struck off leftward into a succession of roofs, mere vertical or overhanging rock relatively free of photosynthetic organisms and their less ambitious brethren. He panted and swore. Roots and frag-ments fell. I patted and reassured my cress.

A clear voice rang out from below and further left.

'What's that boy doing up there? He'll fall off. Quite pointless. There's nothing but *Hylocomium squarrosum* in that groove. I looked very carefully this morning.'

The Doctor was above me. I glimpsed his toothed toes projecting from an upper moustache. They dripped past my face.

'It's all right, Aggie,' he said. 'We're just up enjoying ourselves. But can we help you at all?'

Silence. Then: 'Ah, Doctor, if you would be good enough to send your Boy down here (mercifully inarticulate splutters from the left) I could use him very well just now.'

'My companions are both gentlemen.' The Doctor continued gazing at the view. The Apprentice clambered and slithered down to Miss McHattie's line of slime.

She nodded, and beckoned him. 'Carefully, now. Just stand here. Oh, you've got boots. *Rubber boots*. How foolish. Should be nailed. And should be shoes – for proper flexion on small ledges. But I expect you've Weak

Ankles. That's why most people have to wear boots. You should walk more. Now stand carefully there, and hold on to this loose piece of rock here and this clump of *Cystopteris*. CYSTOPTERIS! Not *Cephalozia*! That's right. Bend a little, for I'm going to have to step on to your back, I'm afraid. We'll never reach that *Stereocaulon* otherwise. Very glad you've come. I have a meeting tonight in Edinburgh, and I really must go down after this.'

The Apprentice described graphically afterwards the weight of the old battleship, and displayed the variegated indentations of triple hobs and muggers trodden across his vertebrae.

She poked away at a shiny clump with her trowel, fretting with annoyance. The Apprentice gingerly let go *Cystopteris*, tapped her shoe and offered up his piton. She tried it. Her comments were punctuated by chipping.

'H'm, useful tool. Better than anything I've brought, for this job, I must say. Where did you get it? *Who*? A most curious name. Never heard of him. A great number of ... (continuous chipping) ... odd persons have taken advantage of the recent interest in lichenology. Especially since Toshpatrick-Gilchrist cleaned up all the *Lecidea alpestris* variants on Ben A'an. Winter forms, too. *Thul* made headlines. Curious name, Fifo. An immigrant, no doubt. An opportunist. He won't last, poor fellow. I get all my ironware from Pflanzhanger of Munich. Still, it's very useful ... (renewed chipping) ... I particularly like the hole in the handle; one could string them on to one's belt. Very handy. I'll write old Pflanzhanger himself about it. Quite time these continentals caught up on Edinburgh firms.'

Miss McHattie scraped down her spoil, lifted her spectacles, examined it, and nodded approvingly. She handed the Apprentice a mucilaginous clot. 'Hold this, young fellow,' she said '*Stereocaulon* AND *Cerania vermicularis*, an aberrant type.' She hauled at a cord, and a haversack rose from the depths behind her. The Apprentice backed in astonishment. She eyed him severely. 'Be careful, or you'll slip. That would never do. It's the first record west of Clova at this height.' She stuffed the desirable morsels into a small tube, clapped it into her haversack, and began to shuffle rapidly towards a grassy rake. Then she stopped, smiled meaningly, pulled a small flask from a voluminous pocket, poured out a generous capful of spirit and bade the Apprentice quaff. He quaffed, appreciatively. He rubbed his eyes. She screwed the flask back into her tweeds.

'Well, thank you. I expect the Doctor is teaching you to climb. A dangerous pastime, I always think. But the Doctor is an incurable Romantic. He indulges a veritable passion for the more vascular plants. I confess I outgrew the Angiosperms when I was a mere girl; we were positively stuffed with them at school. The Doctor, I fear, is more Byzantine. However, mind you listen to what he tells you, and don't fall off. Goodbye.' And rapidly she handed herself downwards out of sight. Before vanishing, she paused and looked up. 'Goodbye, Doctor,' she roared; and the cress trembled.

'Remarkable woman,' mused the Doctor, turning again to the wall. 'Had an entire liverwort subspecies named after her – *Dicronodontium uncinatum Mchattii*, should have been a genus – *Agnesia.*' He appeared greatly amused by this, and chucklings punctuated the falling moss.

We assembled beneath the final pitch, a quite vertical watermeadow. Our stance was the usual loose-stoppered and quavering cold-water-bottle. 'This is tricky. We could go down, if you like.' Below us the cliff dropped its 250ft to the bottom boulders – which, characteristically, were the only bare rocks at The Craggie. They leered knowingly. Chorally, we shuddered and said no. 'The rock's quite smooth underneath, but the vegetation's sound as a bell, provided you use the insides of your arms and legs. Don't of course use your feet, or try to kick. A pity you don't wear tweed. Nylon slides off everything. Most unsatisfactory.'

He smiled paternally, dived upwards and swam rapidly out of sight. We had persuaded him to take the sixty-foot line, just in case. When it was my turn I got no further than halfway. I trod water breathlessly. Below me a great sodden wig of *Plagiothecium* peeled off and smacked on the anxious upturned face of the Apprentice. He reappeared, spluttering, but still adherent.

'Ha, I told you it was safer than Constipation,' cried the Doctor encouragingly, as from a boat, 'if that had been rock, all your helmets wouldn't have stopped it!'

Meanwhile, the current was washing me backwards. Towards the new black shiny rock. I called, almost for help. The Doctor swiftly knotted the line to a stem and threw me down the loose end.

'Might need a fixed rope, first time up' he agreed.

By grabbing and changing from crawl to butterfly, I reached him on his mouldering rugosity. As I looked up, a wet jelly licked my face. I spat it out.

'Ha, *Hirneola aüricular-judae* – Jew's-ear fungus.' It encircled my stem. The Doctor calmed me.

'No, it doesn't attack the roots. The stem's quite sound low down where the rope is. It's rowan – fine strong safe rooting system – pliable cortex. Now if it had been ash – ' he shook his head expressively. 'Many a good climber's been let down badly by young ash. Fine in an ice-axe. But not on the hoof.'

Above us a fairly dry ten feet led to the top. It was bulging with good holds such as wild rose, broom and birch seedlings.

'Never trust heather,' admonished the Doctor, as we turned to go, 'all right in ropes, but ...'

'Hi,' from below. We had forgotten the Apprentice. The Doctor gave me a pebble. I placed it under my boot as support, leaned out from my root and looked down.

The Apprentice was in trouble. My last swim had kicked away every hypnaceous deception. Between us lay a black slab, wrinkling only with water.

The Doctor looked. 'No go in vibrams,' he said. 'Try it in socks. One pair only, mind. Tie your boots round your neck, out of the way. Or to the end of the rope; but they'll get wet there.'

Bitterly, the Apprentice, on his foot-square bath-mat, removed his boots and socks. Foolishly, he slung them round his neck (he always loathed walking down in wet boots). He hauled, unashamedly upon the line. The Doctor, myself, and the root, resisted manfully.

I need not recount the inevitable. The slip on one sodden toe, the twist, the grab on the line with both hands, the clatter of falling boots, the flutter of socks. The appalling and – considering his uncertain position – imprudently blasphemous oaths from the sufferer. We landed him at last. The Doctor, in some ways quite sensitive, moved up to let him on. I inculcated the botanical rudiments necessary for the last few feet.

The Doctor sat on the cliff top, smoking his pipe.

'Pity about the boots' he said. 'Rather a lot of scree on the way down to them – Damned uncomfortable. Could go back the same way, but I don't like taking two inexperienced chaps down, and we'd better stick together. It's not hard, but it's not easy. Although I grant you it's not a stiff climb like Constipation. Just as well, when you go losing your boots. Bad technique that; hope Aggie didn't see us.'

His soliloquy was interrupted by the Apprentice vividly explaining why, in his judgment, our present route should be termed 'Diarrhoea'.

'No, it's Central Buttress Direct,' said the Doctor. 'A good classical name. Not in the least subjective. And look at that view. There's Schiehallion – unusual from this side.

'We'll get you down all right. Piggyback, if necessary. Might even meet with old MacPhedran. He humphs yowes about all day. Remarkably tough. He's docked and castrated 300 lambs in a morning. He'll take care of you all right. And there – look over there – there's Lancet Edge. Wonderful in the sun.'

from THE SCOTTISH MOUNTAINEERING
CLUB JOURNAL *1975*

SONG OF AN UNFIT CLIMBER

DOUGLAS FRASER

I've been sick on Beinn Alligin's summit,
I've puked on the slopes of Beinn Eighe
And Slioch is crowned with my vomit
For such is the tribute I pay.

As, retching and wretched, I've stumbled
On Liathach's pinnacled crest,
I've proved, though my body is humbled,
My spirit is up with the best.

The agile and confident tiger
May cover a group of Munros
While planning a route on the Eiger
To spotlight that anything goes.

But who is the keener I question,
The hardened athlete in his prime
Or the man with the failing digestion
Who conquers both it and his climb.

OF BOGS AND SWAMPS AND QUAGMIRES

S. F. FORRESTER

Differences of opinion have arisen from time to time regarding the qualities of bogs in various localities. R. D. Blackmore for example registers considerable respect for some in Devonshire, while Conan Doyle plumps for Grimpen Mire. But I have come across men who scouted the idea of danger in Cranmere Pool – said there was not enough gravy to silence the Talking Mongoose, never mind to cover a body the size of Carver Doone's. Maybe even during his own lifetime the author of *Lorna Doone* met folk who said he talked through his hat, but first-hand knowledge was then much more difficult to acquire and no doubt that was why he got away with it.

I have met those in Hayfield and vicinity who have *seen* places where a ten-foot pole would not touch bottom – argument is not possible with such as these. Again, a man was leading a bull over the moors and at an awkward moment the animal set off at speed. This being a roped party, each member had to maintain the same speed and it is reported that the man's legs were moving like bees' wings. A halt was made only when the leader floundered into some black ooze and stayed there for quite a time. I heard that it was coming to a case of fetching ropes, horses, blocks and tackle, but after all the bull managed to work his own way out.

Having had a long experience with Pennine bogs I thought I possessed all the information about such things that was to be had and considered there was no danger in any bogs, till a sight of something near Portree gave other ideas. It was an area of at least 100 square yards showing an extra juicy surface: Pennine stuff has mostly a grass basis, but this had a long-staple moss basis and looked really horrid. It may not have been as dangerous as it appeared, but being on honeymoon at the time I made no attempt to find its depth and did not give the place the attention it deserved. Certainly comparison is needed between moss bog and grass bog, but this must be the subject of future investigation. I have been told of some of the former not far from where I live, but Wild's removal to Wales has upset things and prevented a report on it.

The Crumlyn bog near Swansea is a great place, which is said to have engulfed the ancient city of Swansea. There is no present evidence of that city so it surely made a comprehensive job. The bog is about three miles long by three-quarters of a mile in width at the broadest place, where I attacked. I had admired the bog for some months before an opportunity came for closer acquaintance, but it was only a half-hearted attempt – conditions were unfavourable, being February it naturally rained and furthermore I was returning from Swansea in town clothes, alone. To begin with things went too easily – good firm ground with a small percentage of water patches: by and by, about half way across, the percentages were more like fifty-fifty, with the water area percentage rapidly increasing, besides which the water depth was getting greater. When another fifty yards had been traversed it was necessary to jump from one Turk's head to another, with water about a yard wide and a yard deep between them. Also it was not feasible to keep a straight line as I had to work a passage along such Turk's heads as were within jumping distance of each other. About this time I discovered that the traverse would not be made that day as there was unmistakable evidence of an old canal running across my course; it had no clearly defined banks but there was a minimum width of two yards and a depth of x feet. I thereupon called it a day, and regret never having made another attempt. The water was beautifully clean and sweet, there was no mud to speak of, and it would be a priceless do for a hot afternoon in such clothing as would allow short spells of swimming.

However, to return to local matters: I am prepared to maintain that there is no dangerous bog on the Derbyshire heather moors. A friend of mine held diametrically opposite views and a heated discussion took place resulting in the betting of a quart of bitter, followed by a rather sporting event of which the conditions were:

1. He should select the juiciest spot he could find.
2. This should not be the red iron stuff owing to the stink and general mess which would result therefrom.
3. I should take a running jump into his choice at a marked spot.

It was some months before the event came off, owing to the difficulty of his final selection; and even when he had me on the ground he was not certain which of the two remaining on his short list he would take. We examined them together; both places had the usual emerald-green turf covering a mystery. When you cross such it is like walking on somebody's stomach – you know the stuff I mean.

Lot one had firm ground at one side; lot two had not, but looked a bit more succulent. This last fact appealed to him and he voted for lot two. I said I had no objection but pointed out the impossibility of complying with condition 3 above. He saw the force of this observation and said he would be content with lot one. He threw a match-stalk onto the exact spot where he wished me to alight; it was about six feet from the edge, and the edge was about one foot above the green skin. He expressed doubts as to whether I should go through the skin but thought it likely; so he exhorted me to jump high and shook hands with me for what he said might be the last time. Everything being now in order I took a five-yard run, made a charming take-off, hit the match beautifully, went successfully through the skin, and sank slowly to equilibrium. This resulted in immersion to just above the knees – rather deeper than I expected but legs, body, and head less than he hoped. I was able to get out without help, so there must have been some sort of bottom, although I cannot recollect it. Then in order to give full measure a trial was made of lot two by walking into it. Results were to all intents and purposes identical with lot one.

The bet was duly liquidated (to my satisfaction) at a place provided for the purpose, but if the mud had been say eight feet deep one wonders at what point equilibrium would take place. Would the suspended matter cause the water to support the body more or less than pure water would? Opinions from more experienced readers are invited.

A rather different matter put the wind up me more than anything else wet ever did. A certain path in olden days crossed a valley. Then some works wanted a reservoir and made a dam below. When the reservoir filled, the path had to be diverted round the standing water which had come up the valley. This diversion added 440yds onto the length of the path. Years later occasion arose on a hot morning when it was preferable, if anyone would carry my clothes, to swim twenty yards across the reservoir rather than walk 460yds round the path. A kind friend was pressed into service and I entered the water.

It *was* water all right to begin with, but when half way across I found that there was very little water – there might have been two inches or there might have been four inches in a place which I knew must have been ten feet deep at least; the balance of about nine feet was the finest peat sludge, brought down by the stream and deposited in the stiller water of the reservoir. Nothing went wrong, as it happened, but I have often pondered on the particular state of viscosity of mud which would render swimming impossible.

A report came to me that Sowerbutts had some inside information about a dangerous bog, but when at last I found opportunity to ask him for it the result was disappointing. It appeared that one of his party (a lady) had walked into some swamp in Loch Nevis district. He considered that she could have got out herself, but that the aroma of the stuff was beyond anything in the experience of the party.

The different aromas and bouquets of various swamps is a subject worthy of study. There must be some remarkable stuff around, to judge, for instance, from the liquid they draw off one of them and drink in Harrogate.

Shuttleworth told me that the first time he went on the Pennine moors he jumped into a grough and stuck in the peat about up to the waist. His friends pulled him out with such difficulty that his arms and shoulders were sore for a fortnight. It is a disappointment to learn that though he has since tried frequently to find the spot he has had no success, nor has he ever discovered another where he could stick.

I have never had the fortune to see will-o'-the-wisp, but two of us were once messing about in gross darkness within a mile of the Club Hut when, in attempting to get over a peat-hag, my foot slipped and scraped down the face of the peat; immediately about twenty pin-points of light showed up and then gradually died away. Forthwith we both set to, and with all our might started scraping and kicking like horses in a hovel till we had about 6 x 3ft of the face lit up with hundreds of pin-points. I believe a very small worm is responsible for the effect; the light shows as soon as the beast is exposed but it does not like fresh air and immediately makes for cover, taking the light with it. The light is white and nothing like the green signal of a glow-worm.

from THE RUCKSACK CLUB JOURNAL *1932-34*

THE PEAK OF ACHIEVEMENT

MICHAEL PARKIN

Two men with an altimeter will search Snowdon (3560ft) this weekend to find out how far snails have climbed up the mountain.

Mr Peter Dance, of the National Museum of Wales at Cardiff, and Mr Adrian Norris, of the City Museum of Leeds, are collecting information for the survey of molluscs being carried out by the conchological society.

Snails on Snowdon are rather like leopards on Kilimanjaro: people cannot help wondering what they are doing up there. Perhaps, like mountaineers, they climb their peaks 'because they are there'.

At any rate, the brown-lipped snail, *cepaca nemoralis,* has already been recorded on Snowdon at 3000ft, sharing his chilly habitat with a slug who was apparently no sluggard. Mr Norris hopes this time to find a mollusc even higher, perhaps one carried up by the mountain railway and living on rubbish dumped by tourists on the summit.

With luck, Mr Dance and Mr Norris could catch the Snowdon snails at the beginning of their loveplay. Two snails raise the soles on which they creep, lock them together and rock their bodies to and fro in blissful union, caressing each other at the same time with the horn-like projections on their heads.

The snails follow this with a love duel, shooting at each other a calcium carbonate love-dart:

'A stimulating process,' said Mr Norris, 'rather like flinging a carving knife at the wife.' (Some snails have love-darts shaped like boomerangs, but the darts are not returned to sender.)

The snails interlock again, and remain thus for a long time before mating. They are hermaphrodites and impregnate each other.

Snail love, even in the colder climate of Snowdon, has been brought to a high pitch of refinery. And so it should. Snails have been making love for about four hundred million years – ten thousand times longer than man.

from THE GUARDIAN

WOLFINGER MOVES

SHERIDAN ANDERSON

Dear Ones

Would have 'gotten' back to you sooner but wuz off in the down-timber winding up details on a house in Oregon, $5,500 complete with pines and assorted small mammals in the rafters, four blocks from the confluence of the Williamson and Sprague rivers, thirty miles south-east of Crater Lake National Park. I can see McLaughlin from the slope in the back of my hovel. Klamath Lake, the headwaters of the Klamath River is just beyond the low hills to the west of this funky little burg. Eagles and wolves about, or so I am told, waterfowl by the thousands including the White Pelican and Sandhill Cranes, lousy with Canadian Honkers and of course the loggers stir their coffee with their thumbs; Indians, with the loggers ...

Various infestations of the liver, bronchial complications and urban blight mandate this exodus; however I'd prefer to consider Chiloquin as merely the northernmost gate to the City. I couldn't abandon the insanity without losing essential qualities of spirit.

I'm sending a couple of little ditties that I cranked out for *Off Belay*.

Best from the patroon of the Chocktoot Heights flugelhorn refurbishment and unspeakable practices research centre.

Sheridan
Chiloquin, Oregon

MAINTAINING THE SPIRIT

IAIN H. OGILVIE

> … usquebaugh, at first taste affects all the members of the body, two spoonfuls of this liquor is a sufficient dose; and if any man exceed this, it will presently stop his breath, and endanger his life.?[1]
>
> He walks into the sea up to his middle with his clothes on, and immediately after goes to bed in his wet clothes, and then laying the bedclothes over him proceeds to sweat …[2]

Yes! They were a tough lot! But modern technology has improved both the whisky and the bathwater, and our lot is a much easier one.

Unfortunately, our national habit of sinking whisky as if it was beer has led to technological research being largely devoted to production, with the result that some of the finer points of consumption have been overlooked. I am therefore encouraged to hope that this note may usefully fill a gap.

It cannot be disputed that nothing is nicer, when one comes off the hill, than a dram and a hot bath; preferably both; preferably both together; in fact, preferably a dram in your bath. There are, however, snags. For example, the older types of bath, commonly found in Highland hotels so often used for New Year and Easter meets, have curved tops to their parapets, and even modern ones, though flat on top, have a ridge round the edge, so that a whisky glass placed there may get upset. Some people have recourse to putting a glass on the floor beside the bath, but this is also unsatisfactory. The glass is difficult to locate and water is liable to trickle down the arm and dilute the whisky. In extreme cases, when the bather has actually decided to wash and not just to soak, the whisky may even be polluted by soap suds. This not only spoils the whisky but may result afterwards in a general looseness of the bowels.

Original experiment[3] indicates, however, that, provided you don't propose to make a pig of yourself and that the bottle isn't quite full, it will be buoyant and can be conveniently floated in the bath. It is however important to ensure that there is not too much whisky in the bottle, as buoyancy will be close to zero and, with the top off, there will again be a danger of dilution.[4] This can be guarded against by having a stiff dram before getting into the bath.

As the level of the whisky drops, some bottles will be seen to keel over at an alarming angle, but research has shown[5] that, with the exception of Dimple Haig, Antiquary and one or two other types, which become unstable, the bottle will not coup[6] even when empty.

The procedure described above ensures not only that whisky is conveniently to hand at all times, but also that you can have a hot toddy without all this nonsense of having to dilute it with boiling water.

Specific gravity is also important. For absolute alcohol it is 0.792, and the percentage of absolute alcohol in proof alcohol is 57.06, both at 60°F. Therefore, by simple arithmetic, the specific gravity of proof alcohol must be 0.881. Distillers state that it is 0.920 and explain this away by a supposed loss of volume when alcohol and water are mixed. There is no scientific justification for this and it should be ignored as being merely a blind to conceal normal sampling losses.

For easy reference, since not all bathers have a slide rule conveniently at hand, I append a table giving typical characteristics of a few significant indicator brands.

A warning must be given at this point about the introduction of a chilled bottle into hot water. Senior (members will remember all too well an unfortunate incident some years ago, when, during an early research programme,

BRAND	ORIGIN	PROOF	SP. GR.	C[7]
Glenmorangie	Tain	70°	0.917	.99
Glenfiddich	Dufftown	80°	0.905	.75
Smith's Glenlivet	Tomintoul	100°	0.881	.50
Talisker	Skye	175°	0.792	.25
Auchtermuchty	Not known	0°	1.000	0
Laphroaig	Islay	200°	N.A.[8]	±

a bottle of Talisker had been left[9] on the window sill of an unheated bedroom. Returning late and cold from the hill, the researcher seized it and jumped straight into his bath. The bottle at once shattered and, as the bath was already full, the whisky became so severely diluted as to be virtually unpalatable and the programme had to be abandoned.

A more recent researcher[10] may have had this incident in mind when he started work on the development of the 'Bather's Liquid Comforter'. This is reported to be a bicompartmented container, one half of which is vacuum insulated and can hold a bottle embedded in crushed ice. The other contains a bottle exposed to hot bath water. The whole clamps on to the side of the bath by means of ingenious rubber clips. The bather can indulge in the luxury of alternate drams of hot malt and cold blend.[11] The present author can conceive of no valid reason for drinking cold whisky but this may be a refinement to the self-inflicted agonies ritually performed in the latter stages of a Sauna bath.

Research continues.

from THE SCOTTISH MOUNTAINEERING
CLUB JOURNAL *1976*

1. 'A description of the Western islands of Scotland.' Martin Martin. Gent. 1703.
2. Ibid.
3. Archimedes. He was a Greek, poor chap, and must have had to use Retsina or Ouzo.
4. There is little danger of pollution at this early stage.
5. The stability of a floating body is a function of the draught (Tippler's Law).
6. Tech: = Go arse over tip, with consequent loss of contents.
7. Credibility factor.
8. But ref. Martin Martin above.
9. Levison-Smith – Crianlarich – New Year 1923.
10. Unidentified but reported to be a senior member of the club.
11. 'Bugger up the Blend but don't muck about with the Malt' – Confucius.

'DAMMIT, SCHLEIF, I THOUGHT YOU BROUGHT THE HARDWARE!'

THE YOUNG SHAVERS
Recollections of an Alpine Club Member

SIR DOUGLAS BUSK

By 1936 a group of younger members [of the Alpine Club] had begun to form. Their community of thought was not devoted entirely to climbing together or climbing better than the Old Stagers. Unlike the GHM or the ACG the group was not exclusively composed of hard men and the objective was different: to reform the AC from within as far as was reasonable and possible, and to unite the Old Stagers (including some of the greatest names in mountaineering, in the Alps or far beyond) with the 'impatient young know-alls with filthy habits'. The object of the Group, which now began to assume a capital letter, was contact – what would now be called 'bridging the generation gap'.

We owed much to Frank Smythe and to Bentley Beauman, who of an older generation (he had gained his pilot's licence before the first war) was able to suggest fruitful contacts with the Old Stagers. Bentley, an enterprising mountaineer at all seasons, on foot and ski in many parts of the world, was admirably placed to use his tact and unobtrusive persistence in being what the French call a *trait d'union* (pronounced 'trade union', but far from that) – a hyphen or link in this case between generations. He found a useful forum at Bradley's parties at Capel Curig, while others of us talked in London and under the aegis of Geoffrey Winthrop Young at Pen y Pass. The Group owed much to the enthusiasm of Scott Russell. He recalls that he had been inspired to action by a conversation with Geoffrey Young and Geoffrey Bartrum, who developed the view that the AC depended for its survival on tradition being reasonably harmonised with the changing attitudes of successive generations. Periodic 'revolutions' by the young had been, and would continue to be, necessary for this balance to be maintained. Geoffrey Young had inspired an AC revolution early in the century (as he tried to do throughout his long life, not always with success, in the wider fields of mountaineering, particularly in Britain). Scott therefore wished to ascertain if, now I was back in England, I would play a part in obtaining the backing of my generation and those younger, on the basis that we were opposed *not* to the personal attitudes of older individuals as such, many of whom we liked and admired, but to their conservatism in the Club and on the mountains. These views coincided perfectly with those I had long mulled over – with the addition that I felt that the initiative must come from the young, since older members seemed unlikely to move. The alternative was back-biting and the formation of splinter groups within or in addition to the AC. With the example of the CAF/GHM imbroglio in mind, this seemed an unspeakable alternative. We decided on cautious but persistent action.

It was Frank Smythe who phoned me one morning: 'All my best ideas come to me in my bath and I've just had one. Let us call ourselves The Young Shavers.' At that date several older members of the AC sported beards, while the young did not. Now conditions are reversed, so that if the Group still existed as such, we should have to call ourselves 'The Old Shavers' and the *double entendre* would be lost. Beards loomed large in our youth. Some may recall the Ancient Order of Froth Blowers, to which I was introduced in the early 'twenties by Kenneth Irvine, then treasurer of the Oxford University Mountaineering Club. This admirable, though short-lived Institution raised considerable sums for medical charities. As its name suggests, its members drank beer and, as a sport, 'collected' beards. The highest prize was 'a red beaver on a green bicycle', which entitled the spotter to free pints from all present. Frank Smythe regretted loudly that there were no red beards in the AC, and anyhow none of any age came on bicycles of any colour.

The Young Shavers (YS) wished to dine together before AC meetings and, after some considerable prowling, I found that the Red Lion, very close to South Audley Street, had an upstairs room where an adequate and cheap meal could be provided for up to fifteen hungry men. The menu was almost always soup, steak, a baked potato and cheese, washed down with pints of beer. The more affluent (over £200 a year annual salary) could afford a sherry first. Sometimes, when I knew Ferdie Crawford was coming, I arranged for curry. Though it was quite hot enough for most of us, he used to lace his portion so generously with tabasco sauce that it would have excoriated the hide of a rhino. Thus fortified, he would hold forth at length on the glories of climbing and the malevolence of his seniors in the AC, many of whom were in fact younger than he.

The YS were happy in having no rules, no qualifications, no committee and no subscription, but I suppose I could have been called the secretary, until I was posted abroad in the autumn of 1938, when Scott Russell took over the light burden. The YS ceased to exist as such on the outbreak of war, but happily many survive and some are still active on rock and ice. We had only one foreign member, the unforgettable Jean Morin, then temporarily resident in London. He was killed in the war, but his widow (née Nea Barnard) is now in the ranks of the AC.

The main purpose of the dinners, as planned at the outset by Frank

Smythe and myself, with much drive supplied by Scott Russell, was not
merely to enjoy our own congenial company, but to make contact with older
members, paying particular attention to those whom we regarded as likely
to block the progress we hoped for in the AC and whose views on mountaineering methods seemed to us retrograde. Our 'targets' were accustomed
to dine with the Alpine Dining Club in more luxurious surroundings, but
many could be enticed to accept our invitation. Some shook us with requests
for *apéritifs* not included in our menu, such as a gin and french. George Finch
demanded, and got, a gin and sherry, and supported the YS vigorously.
At almost every dinner we had one such 'old' guest and the chill thawed,
so that by the time we all moved to the AC for the meeting, understanding
and even cordiality had been established. We had our failures, or comparative failures. Strutt, for instance, could hardly be expected to relish the
plebeian atmosphere of a pub and was rigidly set in his views. Mateyness
was beyond him, but he came and I know he was flattered by the invitation
to share a new outlook and surroundings, however essentially repugnant
they remained to him. He may have writhed on his seat on Olympus when
news reached the Gods that the sacred ADC had been forced by financial
stringency to quit the Travellers' Club and dine at the Red Lion.

Other oldsters were so obviously indurated against anything novel in the
AC or on mountains that we did not waste time on them. Tom Longstaff,
whom we all revered, was far from easy to handle. His vast experience
entitled him to strongly held views on many subjects, but he came far to
meeting ours. An eminent ex-YS has described Tomstaff as 'invincibly
idiosyncratic and conceited', in contrast with some other Old Stagers who
were merely vain. To the YS preoccupied with internal AC affairs Tomstaff
remained a problem, possibly because he disliked Geoffrey Young and all
about him: but it was more important that, as regards mountaineering (for
example, over the Everest expeditions 1933-38 and other Himalayan
ventures), he was the staunchest ally of a 'young' approach. His coevals,
Strutt and Kenneth Mason among others, never forgave him for this.

Apart from the perennially young, like Ned Porter, Leslie Shadbolt and
Claude Elliot, who had the knack of treating those much younger than
themselves as contemporaries, there were successes. One obdurate 'case'
that delighted us was the redoubtable R. W. Lloyd, who bore no resemblance
to any YS. (In a recent article in *Mountain*, McNaught-Davis asked: 'Who was
R. W. Lloyd for that matter?' Obviously he has never stayed at Ynys Ettws.
He can now read on.) He was a millionaire and an exceedingly shrewd
businessman, deeply suspicious of any approach unless he saw the
possibility of financial profit. Yet he had done some fine guided climbs (e.g.
the first ascent of the North Face of the Col du Bionnassay and the first

descent of the Old Brenva Route, a formidable task in 1912 without crampons). His gallantry later in life, when he had to have a leg amputated because of phlebitis, was an example to all. He attended AC meetings in his wheel-chair, from which he would observe and talk with friends young and old. Nor must it be forgotten that while he gave nothing financially to the AC he served devotedly (and parsimoniously) as Hon. Treasurer and, above all, in the same capacity for the joint AC/RGS Mount Everest Committee ('Umbrellas, never heard such nonsense. If they want them they can take their own. I won't pay.'). Climbers' Club members will also recall that he gave them a hut.

It was Bentley Beauman who engineered Lloyd's introduction to the YS. Wylie Lloyd had certainly the finest collection of eighteenth and nineteenth century alpine prints in the world. As a director of Christies he was well informed and he bought ruthlessly from every available source. Though he haggled ferociously price was ultimately immaterial and of all but the rarest prints he had up to ten copies. It could be said that his wealth enabled him to corner this market for nearly fifty years. He left his collection to the British Museum and it is sad that he would neither give nor bequeath a single print to the Alpine Club. Greatly daring, I once asked him if he could not add from his surplus to the meagre AC collection. 'The AC has never done me honour', he snarled. This was a reference to the fact that he was never offered the Presidency. This was indeed mooted, but the Committee unanimously decided against and it was left to the outgoing President, Tom Longstaff, to break the news alone to Wylie Lloyd in the anteroom, while we sat with bated breath in the inner room. Tomstaff was physically and morally a most courageous man, but even he was shaken when he returned. 'I have never had such a talk, but the deed is done, let us now proceed with the agenda.' Scott Russell and I rejoiced secretly to see the dictatorial Tomstaff shaken, because we had just had a brush with him. I had been elected to the committee and, when another place suddenly fell vacant, Scott was chosen to fill it. We stoutly maintained YS views and, after one meeting, Tomstaff took us aside. 'One of you must resign,' he said, 'You nag.' We firmly refused and I fear that Tomstaff continued to regard us as a pair of ill-bred terriers forever yapping at his heels.

Wylie Lloyd also had splendid collections of English silver, samurai swords, lacquer and porcelain, in his castle in Wales.

I never visited it, but Bentley Beauman recalls that he and his host dined off gold plate, waited on by two footmen supervised by the butler. In London, RWL, delighted in a collection of beetles – every beetle in the world except two, he once told me, as he displayed the pinned corpses in drawer upon drawer. What he would have thought of the latter day 'Beatles' is easy to imagine: he would have skewered them with Japanese daggers to the wall of his castle. One of the missing coleoptera dwelled in Ethiopia and, years later when I was posted to that country, I at once received a letter from Lloyd, accompanied by a detailed and illustrated description of the minute insect, with instructions to find a specimen for him at once. This missive was delivered by hand by a representative of Drage & Co., the purveyors of cheap furniture ('Delivered in a Plain Van'), another concern of which RWL was Chairman. 'You must get to know the Emperor and tell him we will furnish his palace', ran the instructions. I did not even look for the beetle; I forbore from telling RWL that the Lion of Judah went to Aspreys for his household equipment, but I did help Drages to win a contract to supply cheap furniture to a hotel the Emperor wanted to build near Addis Ababa. I regret that I did not ask RWL for a commission on the deal; his reply would have been memorable.

In addition to all these hoards RWL had, in the three sets he occupied in Albany, probably the finest private collection of Turner watercolours of the time (also bequeathed to the British Museum, under conditions so stringent that the Trustees hesitated to accept the bequest). My wife was anxious to see the Turners and I the alpine prints, and it was here that Bentley Beauman came in. He arranged an invitation from Lloyd. After we had inspected his treasures a diverting incident occurred. Wylie Lloyd remarked that at a recent AC meeting 'some young scallawag' had been put up for the AC Committee against the official candidates and had been, of course, defeated. 'That was me, I said.' 'If I had known that, I would have voted for you,' grunted RWL. It was then I asked him to dine with the YS and he accepted. He enjoyed himself and praised the simple fare. Quite typically he asked how much it cost. I cannot say that we converted him to modern ideas, but thereafter he was always amenable to argument and did not use his influence with die-hard older members to rally them against the progressives.

from MOUNTAIN 54 *1977*

AFTER DINNER SPEAKING MADE EASY

IAN McNAUGHT-DAVIS

'Your Club Secretary, Harold Griper...' (subdued claps, almost drowned by drunken cheering)... 'rang me only two days ago to ask me to speak at this dinner, and I have had very little time to prepare anything.'

The speaker pauses to peer at a thick pad of neatly typewritten postcards, and a scarcely muffled groan passes through the audience. It is the annual dinner, and the ritual of after-dinner speeches has begun.

Ever since Brasher, as his idea of a practical joke, ran an advertisement in his magazine offering my services as an after-dinner speaker, I have received a regular flow of requests to speak at dinners throughout the country. Whilst it is gratifying to receive these kind invitations and astonishing that there are people who actually read *Mountain Life*, a speech at a club dinner every weekend from September to April is more than even my robust and well-nurtured constitution can bear.

During the winter season, when the old men can safely come out of hiding without running the risk of being asked to climb, there are six or seven club dinners every available weekend. Each calls for the services of from one to four speakers, in an attempt to provide some meagre entertainment for the club members. Every tolerant hostelry, from the Erw Fair in Llanberis to the Royal Oak in Keswick, from the Llarregub Arms in the Rhondda to the Banks and Braes Hotel in Bonnie Doon, is thronged with climbers, normally interested in more solitary pursuits, trying to enjoy themselves in communal jollity.

This curiously British tradition has intrigued me for many years. I have eaten with small, humble, but friendly clubs and with the giant assembly of that famous Lakeland club, spreading over several hotels. I have eaten at all but four of the Climbers' Club annual dinners, and have been entertained at the Alpine Dining Club, which exists, or used to, for the sole purpose of eating, and has no pretensions towards climbing at all. So, having carried out all this research, I felt that I should share my findings. How do you spot a good dinner? Which are the clubs to avoid?

Firstly, and above all else, refuse all invitations that do not come from a climbing area. To find yourself at 11pm in the middle of Norwich, faced with the prospect of spending the night with some octogenarian member, is intimidating. An offer of a room in a hotel is a good sign, providing you are not expected to share it with the rest of the club. It may be an indication that they intend to entertain you until you are incapable of surmounting the short three-mile walk up the hillside to their club bothie.

Avoid all single-sex clubs (except for the Pinnacle Club, last of the freaky all-women clubs), unless you expect to speak, with utter tedium, for at least an hour – they deserve it.

Refuse all university dinners, unless you are capable of consuming huge quantities of alcohol, and are prepared to participate in some bizarre activities. For example, at Cambridge, there was a period when it became very popular to eat strange concoctions. Bottles of 'Daddies Sauce' and spoonfuls of curry powder were consumed with delight by Nick Estcourt and other gourmets, but that was only the thin end of the wedge. On one occasion, the current eating champion, Bob Keates, approached Don Whillans, the master of rhetoric.

'I've eaten three daffodils and a tulip,' he squeaked, appealing for recognition.

'Aye, well – carry on lad, you're doing a grand job,' said Whillans.

This particular blind-alley of entertainment came to an end after one guest squatted on the table, defaecated, laid a five pound note alongside the resultant turd, and challenged anyone in the room to eat it.

On another occasion, at Sheffield Univerisity, a famous and distinguished mountaineer, who had just given his very proper and rigorously dull speech, was amazed when the Club Secretary, standing up to reply, vomited a shaft of absolute alcohol and orange squash right across the table, and then sank out of sight without saying one single word. In general, university climbers are very disappointed if you can't put up a similar performance, but if you do they will applaud loudly.

Beware of regional clubs. The atmosphere of Midlands clubs, such as the MAM or the Oread, is more redolent of wife-swapping than of climbing, and if you have nothing to trade you will be disappointed. North of the border, the Scottish Mountaineering Club, true to tradition, doesn't like inviting guests at all. Members turn out in skirts, air their nationalist and sexual prejudices, sing a few stale, sentimental ballads from a bygone age, buy their own drinks and stagger home drunk down Sauchiehall Street.

The best dinners are highly organised affairs, and probably the most outstanding is the Rock and Ice annual do. You will be offered a room in an unusual hotel in the hills, there will be drinking, eating, dancing, and finally a series of games that are played by the members and their spouses through the night. Although it seems that something a little more sensual would be appreciated by some, these games are of the violent, bisexual, body-contact kind, such as 'musical chairs' and a variant of 'ring-a-ring-of-roses'. They are enjoyed as much by the drunken onlookers as by the participants. The only thing that mars the evening is the club's insistence on having four speeches which, even with the high quality of speakers they usually manage to field, is carrying conformity too far.

So, as President of the Altrincham Allstars Club, you have accepted an invitation to speak at the annual dinner of the Llanberis Llayabouts Club, in Wendy's Cafe. How do you write your speech?

In the first place, don't do any research, as this can easily cause confusion and sap your confidence. Most 'club' types are uninteresting and lead completely mundane lives, so you can rely on invention to bring them to life. If you are toasting the guests, don't bother with their names – get them from the menu at the last minute. And if there isn't a menu, invent them, their clubs and their records. The chances are that only the guests themselves will notice, and they'll get their revenge by not inviting you to *their* club dinner, so that's one more off the list. It is, of course, important not to go through this phase too obviously, and you should look as though you really have done a lot of preparation; a handful of toilet paper can look like a carefully prepared brief from only ten feet away.

There are four classical speeches. The most popular, known as the 'fancy asking me' speech, is an apologia for being such a poor entertainer/climber/ Club President, or whatever. Then there is the 'I remember, many years ago ...' speech, which consists solely of a series of tall tales. These can go on for ever, and were a speciality of one distinguished Alpine Club President who could bore from New Zealand to the Himalayas, via the Alps, for many hours, and frequently did. Once, at the Yorkshire Ramblers' Club, he droned on for two hours. Ten years later, when they again had an AC representative, they produced a huge hand bell, and threatened to ring it if the speech lasted for more than ten minutes. A very commendable technique.

A familiar university speech is the 'have you heard this one?' where the speaker tells a disjointed sequence of dirty jokes to a willing audience. But for sheer tedium, nothing beats the 'and next to him (we have Albert Gripwhistle from the Birmingham Bumblies Association)' speech, which is a catalogue of the deeds and misdeeds of the 'top table' guests. The only one of these that I enjoyed was given by an aged vice-president, proposing the health of the guests. He rambled on about his 'old friend' sitting at the top table, '... now President of a distinguished club ...' Ignoring whispers from both sides, he went through several unfunny anecdotes, then asked his friend to stand up. To everyone's delight he had got the wrong man and the wrong club. Personally I admired his inventiveness.

But why is it done? How can anyone expect unfunny men suddenly to become joky? How can the elder statesman shed his lifetime as a bank clerk in Bootle and sparkle as a great raconteur and wit? It is part of the ritual, it is what is expected and, occasionally, like finding a good climb in East Anglia, the unexpected happens and a speech is brilliant. But despite it all, I enjoy going to club dinners. I like meeting members and I like the difference in atmosphere, character, or whatever it is that a group of climbers generates. But I don't enjoy speech-making, and one day I will give my last speech:

'Ladies and Gentlemen, there are four types of speech – mildly boring, boring, deeply boring and utterly boring. I have just given a mildly boring speech. Thank you for the meal, your company, and for listening to me.'

from MOUNTAIN 41 *1975*

STOGAMS OPAPE INTERVIEWS ZEKE BOTTOMLEY

The relentless choreographer always alive in my mind's eye started seeing dances along the sides and fronts of buildings with small human forms in moving imposition against these colossal architectural phenomena, so symbolically denotative of our places in the revolutionary cosmos. *Barbara Salz*

Deah Mista Edita

These are my impressions intoviewed in the last couple of minutes befaw I stat up on what I tink will be my last climb. I entrusted my toughts to my good friend Stogams Opape, the garbage collecta, who showed me yaw magazine ant made me tink I could pick up some free publicity from it.

Zeke Bottomley

When did you first decide to climb the Empire State Building, Zeke?

Escapin from a frantic vacation in the rurals into the more familia glass canyon of the Rockiefella Centa where I am a denizen and part-time winda warsha I set about preparin for a long awaited scale up the Empiah State Building.

Even though the Empire State Building isn't in Rockefeller Centre?

No, of course not, Stogams, that's where my fav'rite bah is located.

Which is how you prepare?

I tell ya from the start, it's a hell of a lot o' windas to warsh. An the foist most obvious facta is the perilocity of the venture. The slightest false step you know ant your nothin' but a man in the street … wit no overtime for bariul. An it is of a constant risk, let me tellya, not because of bad equipment but because they keep changin the buildins with less brick an more steel, less ledges an more windas – now how in the hell d'ya hang onto a winda?

Did you have any trouble preparing for this climb?

Trubble? Gevalt! Getting on the subway with my ropes and buckets, my squeegee and my ammonia bottles in my imported Italian galoshes wit Japanese buckles in da middle o' rush owa is moida. An then I got mugged three times, twice by a panhandler and once by a boy scout, on my way down from the bah. I hear they're tryin ta clean the town up – just wouldn't be the same adventure no maw.

Is this going to be your hardest climb?

I am reminded of the hardest climb I eva done. Especially of all the buildins spindly that range extends along 6th Ave, the Time-Life for instance is one of the least climbed because of many false reasons. These are chintzy tips ya get at Christmas time, and there is a rumor going around that unwarshed windas is part of their foggy view of the woild.

But what do you consider to be the real reason, Zeke?

Well, Stogams, the inside story, the real doit, is that wit all the glass there's no place ta rope inta. Now this is what they call the architectural byooti of the buildin' and so the winda warsha has to figya new ways of doin his pitches and travoisds witout marrin the byooti o' the facade. That is why if you ever catch one of us bent ova in a bah mutterin somethin in a low chant, he is singin to himself the very movin 'Bruddahood Song'.

> Proud is the Brudda
> And his glory is sweet
> When he earns his bread and Budda
> Hangin by his nails
> With his winda warshin pail
> Danglin from his feet
> Chorus
> 0 21 stories
> & 34 more
> Tell yer kids the glories
> If ya live til a ¼ to 4

That was very moving, Zeke. Tell us a little about the brotherhood you belong to.

The Bruddahood, oh yeh, heh, well the Bruddahood is just ar nickie-nomer for old Local 846 of the Amalgamated Salt Picklers and Winda Warshers Union where we all hang togedda. It pravides us wit jobs and badul benefits.

I don't think I'm familiar with it.

Well it ain't poifeck, nuttin is, An occasionally they'll send a guy up a buildin without axin if he's a salt pickier or a winda man. But it don' happin awffin. An it's woise besides when they send a winda warsha out to pickle cause that's when ev'rythin begins tastin like soap.

At night the bruddahoods crown togedda in the Joe McMealy Memorial Bah'n Grill.

Joe McMealy what tried ta warsh the windas of the Empiah State in the middle of a soot and smog storm. When ya can't tell the diff 'twixt the windas an the bricks. McMealy had weak lungs, you know. Well, Stogams, he sniffled on the 34th story, coughed on the 67th, wheezed on the 68th – an though he was losin strength, McMealy never quit! But on the 69th, soz as not to sneeze all over his windas freshly warshed he turned and kachoo'd into the wind and before his partner could say 'gazoonheit' and wish him luck, he was following his sneeze at, in abidance with natural law, the same rate of fall as his spew.

At a somberly drunken orgy that night it was decided to change the name of the bah 'n grill from Feeney's (as old Feeney had been dead long enough) to McMealy's Memorial Bah 'n Grill an it was decided to sent another up the grimy bricks to avenge the death of our fallen comrade. A vote was taken but I was too drunk to vote ay or nay, so I was elected on the first ballot.

That's a very heart warming story Zeke, and I don't want to keep you any longer from your appointed task. Let me ask you this one final question: What makes you, Zeke, or any of the other window washers risk the danger and the anonymity and the lousy pay just to wash the windows of these skyscrapers? Are you some kind of special breed?

We're Americans, Stogams. And America is a great country. When ya tink about it, it stretches from east Saigon aroun the woild to west Saigon, from Ford in Canada to Ford in Argentina. It's a regula empiah, and its grandyoor is reflected in its skyscrapers. When yoor way up there, clingin to the home offices of the empiah you have a real feelin' of yoor destiny. Special breed? Yes – yoore an American!!!!

from CLIMBING July *1974*

'CERTAINLY GETS LONESOME OUT ON THESE BIVOUACS, DOESN'T IT?...'

CLIMBING AS ART

HAROLD DRASDO

Now to say that climbing is a creative act is one thing; but to say that a climb is like a work of art is quite another. To some it will seem that the comparison is good only within a very limited area of overlap. But I want to claim that the likeness is extensive and important and so I represent the suggestion one step at a time.

First, it surely has to be agreed that mountains and cliffs often impress us in the same ways as the great achievements of such arts as sculpture and architecture. In fact we often have no choice in describing them but to resort to comparison with these arts or achievements. This tendency is very evident in the early records of mountaineering in the form of conscious analogies. Modern writers are more likely to use these metaphors unconsciously but even today we find, for instance, A. D. M. Cox having to liken the two great buttresses of Clogwyn du'r Arddu to medieval fortress and cathedral in order to try to capture their fascinating antithesis of form. For every unnamed mountain which becomes Someone's Peak, another becomes Somebody's Tower or Spire or Dome or Pyramid. Its features are described and named as buttresses or pillars or ridges or walls or columns. These tectonic metaphors are the natural expression of our process of thought.

Or, instead of seeing the present shape of the mountain as resembling a type or feature of building we are struck by the way it has been carved from a greater form. We do not have to anthropomorphise a titanic sculptor to see the sculptural qualities of mountains. We think of the forces of wind, water, ice and lightning as tools because there is evidence everywhere of how the rock is being ground down, split, hammered, washed and crushed – nature's process which man appropriates and forgets where they came from.

But there is a limit to the reach of these metaphors. In fact it might be claimed that cliffs and mountains are façades without shape or dimension until they are floodlit by human effort. Just as the Prince wakes the Sleeping Beauty so the climber's touch brings the cliff to life. The more it is worked over, the more aspects are revealed and the more secrets suggested. And this mystery is never diminished. Every storm, every change in the weather resurrects and reasserts it.

To see the extent to which climbing invests mountains with significance, consider a hypothetical problem: how to write a symphony using as inspiration the North Face of the Eiger. Before the nineteen-thirties this proposition would have seemed an intangible and hollow exercise. But one can imagine that today a piece of music might easily utilise as theme the 1938 route and would not strike many composers, especially those working in cinema, as too daunting an undertaking – the chief artistic problem might well be the avoidance of cliches, Wagnerian passages, a spacious exit, and so forth.

Climbs interpret mountain faces. A climb is the most human relationship possible with a mountain face. Climbs amplify the persona of a mountain. The more effort has been expended, the more increment to the mountain's character. The Hörnli Ridge is not desecrated by those half million climbers who have ascended it. It is hallowed. The mountain might indeed be considered a holy place, as in many cultures it has been. The climber reveres each detail, he knows it as a monk knows his abbey or as the curator of an historic monument knows the parts of his building. Even on the meanest gritstone escarpment on the darkest, foggiest winter afternoon he tells off the buttresses, corners and gullies one after the other, name by name or presence by presence as he passes underneath them. And every feature is charged with meaning.

In descending the easy slopes below a great cliff or mountain many of us cannot help but turn again and again to review its structures even when we know these structures like the backs of our hands. Or we trace the line we have just climbed upwards and upwards, over and over again, trying to grasp that line in its integrity and to establish its relationship to the cliff. Some of us find it impossible to make an uninterrupted descent however much the circumstances might advise this. We could look for ever and we make a fine art of walking backwards.

If we turn our attention to the climb now, rather than to the cliff, we see that it cannot be considered apart from its setting and that it can sometimes hardly be separated from its story. The world's most classic and celebrated routes – say, the Grandes Jorasses by the Walker Spur, or the Nose of El Capitan – are pre-eminent because in addition to the technical merit of their climbing problems they are enlarged by their dramatic histories and, above all, they are superbly placed.

Look at the excellences of climbs such as these for a moment. We can conveniently use the first-named as our subject taking advantage of some remarks made recently by the man who first climbed it, Riccardo Cassin. The Walker is regarded as an incomparable route, Cassin rightly says, 'for its continuous difficulties and for the grandeur of its development, as well as for its setting'.

'The grandeur of its development.' The expression stops us dead. Then we speculate on whatever nuances may have been gained or lost in translation. But next we wonder to what province of human activity an allusion is being made. Surely an aesthetic or intellectual metaphor is hidden here? The remark suggests an elevation of design and experience to disallow its use to describe a mere game. Does the idea come from music or drama? Is it as though there are identical processes involved when, say, a great symphony or tragedy involves and possesses the listener; and when the climber follows his route or, relativistically, the wall's huge structures unfold around him? (Each part distinct in character and fixed in sequence; the serial nature of the whole, once established, as irreversible as that of any familiar piece of music; themes hinted at, then taken up and developed: the thirty-metre dièdre, the traverse of the ice bands, the seventy-five-metre dièdre, the pendule, the Black Slabs, the Grey Tower, the Red Tower.)

Or does it come from the epic novel? 'The grandeur of its development.' A surprising thought, might we share it with an epochal game of chess or even with a superb mathematical proof? As though, going step by step beyond what had previously been imagined, there has been an extension of possibility to expand the consciousness once and for all time.

The Eperon Walker is one of the greatest climbs. But the very shortest routes on outcrops are tested to exactly similar specifications. At one time an absurd dialogue between British hillwalkers and rock climbers persisted and echoes of the argument are heard to the present day. It was alleged that the really fanatical climbers – 'rock gymnasts' - were utterly indifferent to the beauty of mountains. Whilst in fact no climb, however short, is agreed to have value and importance unless it satisfies certain uncodified but stringent aesthetic criteria – it must be difficult, it must be separate, it must be unique, it must not change, it must not incorporate the irrelevant.

Difficulty, because the experience should not be cheaply available. Separation, because the experience should be inescapable. Individuality, because the experience should be distinguishable. Permanence, because the experience should remain on offer to others. Unity, because the experience should not be subject to interruption by other experiences.

In summing up these remarks on the attributes of good climbs it seems to me to be incontrovertible that climbs offer rewards very like those of works of art. The great routes expand the consciousness, each one enlarges us. They live on in our minds for the rest of our lives. The very memory of these adventures can evoke powerful feelings. Our imaginations can recreate and perhaps surpass these experiences but first our senses must acquaint themselves with them. Only those who believe that true art is always moral or didactic will be able to reject this view on principle.

But if the climb is like a work of art, is the climber, then, a sort of artist?

Yes, I say: though more often in an interpretative than in a constructive sense. In climbing, as claimed already, the two roles almost merge. But in either of these senses, why not? In movement, as though in dance? Certainly. I can imagine the brief orgy of tomfoolery and amusement the suggestion will inspire amongst some of my friends. It pleases me to entertain them for a moment. But no-one who has seen something of the range of style and attack displayed by those who lead the hardest rock-climbs could doubt for a minute that these experts exist on just the same plane as the greatest performers in the world of dance. Pavlova or Nureyev would stand anonymous amongst this company. In dramatic confrontation as though in the writing or staging of theatre? But of course. What else is climbing about? In a reach of the imagination like that of the novelist? No doubt. Every new route makes real an unexplored possibility and the epochal routes are made by those who have seen that a generally accepted or even unnoticed boundary can be crossed.

Perhaps this excursus on the nature of climbing has now become tedious and circular but certainly all sorts of speculations continue to suggest themselves. I have compared the art of climbing with that of dance. Yeats asks himself, in a famous poem, how can we know the dancer from the dance? When the room is cleared, however, all that remains is the idea of dance. To separate the climb, the climbing and the climber may be more rewarding. For the climb has a physical existence independent of climbing and the climber; and it is capable of almost infinitely extendable description, both objectively and in terms of value, utterly different in degree to any description of golf course or dart board, also existing independently of the player. I am sure that an analysis of both recreational and artistic activities along these lines would raise some interesting questions. But whatever their place in human activity, climbs and climbing exist uniquely and whether they are best thought of as a kind of art-form or as a pastime almost dominated by its aesthetic components, they remain irreducibly fascinating and rich.

from ASCENT *1974*

THE MOUNTAINEER AND SOCIETY

DAVE COOK

The first task I have in opening this session of the Conference is to attempt to justify its inclusion on the agenda. Is it part of some 'Red plot'* to transform climbing into a front line in the class struggle? Is it to add a dressing of academic respectability to what might possibly be described as a weekend of wanking? Could it be a move in some inner BMC power struggle, about to be 'exposed' by certain fearlessly campaigning editors in the mountaineering press? It is here for none of these worthy reasons

I'm puzzled myself as to why I'm here; there seem to be two justifications only. Firstly, a central part of the sport, indeed to many, *the* central part of the sport, is talking about it. Usually climbing is spoken about as an enclosed world. I hope to show that to a large extent climbing is like it is because of its connections with the world around it. At first sight this may seem strange. Many people define the attraction of climbing in terms of its separateness from the rest of their lives – for the total contrast it offers to their daily routine. Climbers have been compared to the weekend hippies who used to descend on downtown San Francisco to live as freaked-out ravers every Friday night, and then return to bourgeois respectability at work on Monday morning.

The second justification is that our ability to climb seems increasingly to face obstacles that can only be overcome by understanding the connections between the sport and society – and acting on the implications of that understanding. If the discussion that I hope will follow contributes towards this understanding, it will be justified.

Changes in Social Background
I believe that we can understand much about the development of our sport if we examine the social backgrounds from which climbers are drawn, and the impact exerted by changes in social background over the years. There are almost no statistics that I have seen to guide such an analysis, and all I have to go on are my own estimates and those of my friends. As a result, the assertions that I'm going to make must be regarded as tentative in the extreme.

*Cook, an experienced climber, is also a leading figure in the Communist Party of Great Britain.

I think it is fairly widely agreed that the majority of climbers in the so-called 'Golden Ages', up to and including the 1930s, were from the wealthier sections of society; almost exclusively men, they came predominantly from a public school and university background, with the professions, especially teaching, very strongly represented. The very fact that they had the resources in time and money to get away to the hills, differentiated them from the majority of the population. Their life-style peers at us from a thousand murky photographs of moustachioed pipe smokers, dressed in tweed jackets and stout breeches, and grouped around blazing fires, their faces exuding a determined 'muscular Christianity' that is a thousand light years distant from the studied coolness of the 'moderns'.

Although climbers were then few in number, this period of the sport has exerted an enormous influence. They were the first, so traditions were shaped by them. A highly literate band of men, they produced books and journals which left an indelible stamp on the whole way we look at rock. They established powerful clubs through which their sometimes baleful influence lingers on.

In the 1930s, the first significant changes in the social composition of the climbing world began to be felt. In the areas close to the Pennines there appeared a new breed of climber – one who worked on the shop floor. Eric Byne's and Geoff Sutton's book, *High Peak,* is full of references to these new arrivals – men who climbed in overalls, the same clothes they wore to work. But they were still a minority.

Why was it around the Pennines that working-class people first began to climb? A unique feature of the gritstone edges and moorlands of those hills is the extent to which they are enmeshed with the industrial towns that flank them. Poverty and unemployment also played an important part: moorland walking, and to a lesser extent rock-climbing, were amongst the few sporting activities that working-class people could afford. Socialist-inspired organisations, such as the Clarion Cycling Club and the British Workers' Sports Federation, regarded rambling as an activity that would expand the morale, consciousness and combativeness of their primarily working-class members. Such organisations provided the leadership and manpower for the battles over access to the Peakland moors which were fought in 1932/33 – battles which generated a scale of mobilisation among walkers and climbers unequalled before or since.

The Second World War loosened social barriers in all fields, including climbing. Many men had trained in the mountains in the Forces, and although most of them probably developed a bitter dislike for the hills they slogged, a few became brilliant climbers. Routes like Sheaf and Suicide Wall testify to this.

By 1950, the trickle of climbers from working-class backgrounds had grown; it was still not sufficient to shift the overall public school image, but in certain areas, such as Sheffield, the West Riding, Northumberland, Glen Coe and Arrochar, the effect was marked. An interesting article in *Rocksport*, by Charlie Vigano, a Creagh Dhu member, described the prickly reaction from the SMC that greeted the Clydeside influx at the end of the 1940s.

The great turning point in British climbing is often linked with those groups of climbers associated with the Rock and Ice and the Pennine cliffs around 1950. I realise that regional controversy rages strong here. Yorkshiremen, and in particular Dennis Gray, strongly contest the view that the breakthrough began in Lancashire. The Scots, too, often get annoyed at our assumption that there were no hard routes in Scotland until Brown and Whillans climbed Sassenach. Be that as it may, the important point for my argument is that during this period, wherever there was rock in abundance relatively close to large centres of population, standards rocketed. The question is, why?

It is at this point that the weaknesses of regarding climbing as a little enclosed world become apparent. In the past these advances have been attributed to the alleged presence in the Rock and Ice of large numbers of short men with long arms and big fists, or to a sort of climbing industrial revolution deriving from the invention of a new technique – jamming. These explanations are ridiculous; obviously a number of factors arising out of changes in society as a whole must be taken into account: expanding horizons as young people spent longer at school; the opportunities that the ending of war time austerity opened up; the impact of the publicity received by the attempts on and eventual ascent of Everest. As a result of these changes, more and more people took up climbing, and new recruits to the sport were drawn increasingly from working-class backgrounds.

It is surprising that a generation of climbers so acutely conscious of, and indeed dependent upon, modern protection methods should not sufficiently recognise the important part played by new equipment in the breakthrough in standard in the early '50s. These were the years when nylon ropes, vibram soles, and the carrying of more than one or two karabiners and slings became widespread. All these equipment changes were the result of spin-off from military research and usage. Nylon ropes, for example were first used in parachutes. In fact, the average working-class climber in 1952 would almost certainly have been kitted out in ex-WD gear. His university brother would have worn equipment purchased in Chamonix or Zermatt.

In sport, as indeed in all areas of life, each generation revolutionises the achievements of its predecessors. There was an increase in the numbers of climbers in this period, so it was inevitable that standards would rise.

However, it is also important that working-class climbers formed a large part of this increase.

According to popular legend, the members of clubs like the Rock and Ice were not inhibited by prevailing attitudes about what was possible and appropriate. Existing clubs, like the CC, the FRCC and the SMC, were not only the preserve of a certain type of climber, but also of a certain type of attitude – an attitude that in an important way was not competitive. The very exclusiveness of the established clubs led the new working-class climbers to form their own clubs and groups, and unconsciously to assert their own attitudes. In complete contrast to the old middle-class clubs, the new ones were most definitely competitive. Let me be clear: I'm not talking about competitiveness between clubs, but within them. After 1950, when climbers became good they became good in relatively big groups – not in very small ones as had previously been the case. The new sort of competitive, primarily working-class club, coming to the sport disrespectful of the accepted way of doing things, acted as a type of hothouse, forcing the growth of those within it. And obviously it was not only internal competition that was at work here; mutual reinforcement also played an important part. Anyone who has been a member of such a group, be it the Rock and Ice, the Black and Tans, the Creagh Dhu, the Alpha, the Wolverhampton crowd or the Wallasey, has seen this process at work. At times, as in the case of the Cioch Club at Stoney Middleton, all the competitive vigour exploded out on one cliff, resulting in achievements of almost freakish difficulty.

Of course we must recognise that what may have been true in 1950 is not necessarily true today. There have certainly been changes in the Rock and Ice. Their once 'proletarian' militants have now become company directors or international superstars.

Having said all this, it is equally important to recognise that there is much in climbing that blurs the social divisions in the sport. Even in the early 1950s, ethnic proletarian Don Whillans was a friend and partner of academic Bob Downes. Quite obviously what unites climbers is far greater than that which divides them.

Nevertheless, this working-class element in the climbing population has left an indelible, perhaps a determining influence on the 'style' of the sport in Britain. The life-style, more often imagined than real, of the men who achieved the breakthrough in standard at the start of the '50s has been given enormous prestige by virtue of the feats achieved. For years, many climbers measured themselves, modelled themselves, defined themselves against what they imagined were the characteristics of this small, predominantly working-class group of men. If you had wanted to compose an identikit advertisement-style prototype of your aspiring hardman in, say, 1963, you would have included the following: First, the 'h' on 'hard' would have been dropped; certain insignia, ranging from flat 'ats to Morris 1000 vans, would have been adopted; in the Alps it would have been compulsory to be very dirty, and in bars everywhere to drink loud and long. An intensely chauvinistic attitude towards British climbing was essential. By definition, the continentals were unable to free-climb hard rock, while the Americans only got up cliffs because of the power drills on their backs. The most essential ingredient of this style was a sort of exaggerated 'workerism', and throughout the 1950s this grew until eventually it replaced the public image that had gone before.

Now the period from 1950 to 1960 was very important with regard to the development of popular culture in Britain. For the first time, 'youth' achieved a separate identity. Before the '50s, young people's lives were not markedly different from those of older people; but sometime in the mid-'50s, concurrent with the rise in popularity of rock 'n' roll, there emerged a distinctive and separate way of life for young people. This change itself was the result of political and social developments, the most important of which was the improvement in standards of living that derived from the relative boom conditions in the last half of the decade.

The 'old days' are now legendary in climbing. When did they end? Well, everyone now wants to extend them to cover the period when *they* began to climb, so that they can bask in the glow and claim the right to bullshit about them. I can state quite categorically that the 'old days' ended in 1959; which just lets me in! In the magnificent summer of that year, many of the old Rock and Ice routes received early ascents, and a new generation of first ascensionists began to put up important routes. Modern footwear and nut protection (not purpose built, but actual nuts bored out and slung on slings) became widespread. 1959 also saw the end of the rock 'n' roll era, and the beginning of what Nick Cohn called the 'interregnum': that is, the period between the 'sell-out' of Elvis Presley and the advent of the Beatles. These were also the years of the Robbins Report, which transformed post-school education in Britain. In the ten years since 1964, the number of students in full-time higher education has more than doubled.

Youth Culture
It is my impression that in the period since 1964 the majority of recruits to the sport have come from colleges. Of course the expansion of education has meant that a greater proportion of these were from working-class backgrounds. But this infusion is notable for reasons other than its impact in class terms; that breakthrough had already been made. It seems to me that the really significant elements in the climbing scene since 1964 have been

associated with the *'youth culture'* which this student influx brought with it. By 'youth culture' I mean the startling succession of social/cultural phenomena which have found their most typical expression in the colleges.

Much of this has been grafted on to the climbing scene. Read through the historical sections of guidebooks up to 1966: most climbs are named after rock features, or the climbers associated with them. Since then, there has been a complete change. Names since 1966 have often been drawn from a mind-expanding collage of obscure musical, literary or narcotic references. The discerning guidebook reader can sometimes trace the first ascensionist of his or her choice by looking at the names. It is interesting that Leeds University and Cioch Club climbers have left a trail of depravity behind them, encompassing lust, necrophilia, bestiality and debauchery, as well as some new favourites from the pages of medical dictionaries, if not from actual experience. It is interesting to note that at Avon Gorge the richest proliferation of names drawn from youth culture are to be found in an area where climbers from university backgrounds have been particularly active.

I have argued that for a long time climbers affected the super-proletarian style which they imagined characterised the Rock and Ice hardmen. In recent years, Wendy's Cafe has sparkled with all the bizarre glory of a college refectory. Climbers staggering back at night are not only drunk; some are stoned as well. Once, when I was climbing on Cyrn Las, a well-known climber on an adjacent route remarked that he was going to Nepal. 'Oh, which peak have you got in mind?' was my innocent question. Great was his scorn: 'I'm going for the grass, man,' he replied.

And there are many more girls. The 'muscular Christianity' of Menlove Edwards and Wilfred Noyce would freak at the healthy heterosexual debauchery that characterises the climbing community today. Women are not yet on the scene on their own terms: Women's Lib cannot count many converts among climbers. But there are now women who are defined as climbers and not just as 'so-and-so's-bird' – and their numbers are growing. 'Right on Sisters.' An element of this youth culture is concerned with the validity of the experience, above all else. Personally and politically, I am at odds with this attitude, but probably such views are very beneficial to climbing morality. An obsession with the meaning of the experience is unlikely to go hand-in-hand with a tendency to sully that experience with artificial aids.

The inclination amongst modern climbers actually to go and live in the mountains, strikingly illustrated by the growing colony of English climbers and ex-climbers who live in Llanberis, was strongly boosted by 'drop-out' attitudes amongst young people – especially those who were, or had recently been, students. Such attitudes became prominent in 1968, and it is since the late 1960s that the search for old cottages has preoccupied many climbers as much as the search for new cliffs.

Expansion of Numbers
The dual impact, first of the working-class climbers, then of those who had been at college, did much to change the climbing scene after 1950. A second great cause of change was the enormous expansion in the numbers of people climbing. There are few reliable figures: a recent rough estimate suggested that 50,000 climbers own their own gear; the circulation of *Mountain* is 11,000; there are approximately 160 climbing clubs. In terms of participants, climbing must be one of the biggest sports in Britain. Increasing numbers of people have gained some experience of the sport in school or college, where it is widely used as an educational medium.

This growth in scale has had obvious and far-reaching effects. The cliffs have become crowded; the roads, parking spaces and camp-sites have filled up; powerful economic forces have moved in; climbers have become a big market, for we are addicts and must have regular injections to survive. The 'rip-off' by the equipment manufacturers and sellers is in the best traditions of monopoly exploitation of an inelastic demand curve. As the sport grows, so do the professionals within it: those who teach it, talk about it, write about it and broadcast about it.

Magazines begin to create attitudes, as well as reflecting them. Government organisations are set up to plan the sport, and a small bureaucracy is established, characterised we are told by power struggles of Watergatean, or rather Audleygatean, intensity.

It is pointless and ridiculous to adopt an ostrich-like attitude to these developments, or to regret some lost age of innocence, real or imagined. That there must be car parks, camping places, equipment, planning boards and bureaucrats is beyond dispute. Increased numbers will increase still more, and the hills will remain the same size.

What is required is that climbers themselves develop those organisations and attitudes that will enable them to determine the necessary changes. The alternative is that others will determine the direction and nature of these changes, and they will do so in their own interests, not ours.

Obstacles to Our Ability to Climb
It seems to me that climbing in Britain is entering a period in which limits will increasingly be imposed on our right and ability to climb. In the past, most notably in the early 1930s, climbers and ramblers had to fight big battles to gain access to cliff and mountain. Access is always an issue somewhere. There are probably few climbers who have not been confronted with the

problem at some time. In my climbing career, I've been prevented from climbing on Kilnsey Crag, Bamford Edge, Simon's Seat, Yellow Slacks (this last was actually blown up by an irate landowner), Huncote Quarry and a number of small quarries in the West Riding. The S.E. England Guide contains a tantalising description of idyllic rocks hidden away on what it calls 'exceedingly private land'. Such barriers are outrageous wherever they occur, but they are very much the exception – at the moment. By and large we are able to climb and walk where we wish.

However, there are developments which could threaten that freedom. Firstly there is a threat that stems from changes in the mineral requirements of modern industry. Most of our big cliffs are composed of the geologically ancient rock of the north and west, and it is here that deposits of a number of vital 'trace' minerals have recently been discovered. But these deposits are characterised by the fact that it will be necessary to remove a very large amount of rock to obtain a very small quantity of mineral. Several important mountain areas are already threatened.

The significance of the threat from firms like Rio Tinto is that we face not just an idiosyncratic landowner, as in the past, but a vast, monopolistic complex with enormous resources at its disposal and all manner of friends in high places. The whole logic of their role in society compels giants like Rio Tinto to devour mountainsides, in their search for profit. This is a new form of 'landlordism', infinitely more dangerous than anything climbers have faced in the past.

Similarly, in the Highlands, restrictions on access during the shooting season have undergone a qualitative change. In place of a landowner excluding walkers for his own purposes, big firms now exclude them for wealthy clients. Bulldozed pathways are driven into the heart of unspoiled wilderness to make access easier for these clients.

The third threat comes from probably well-intentioned attempts by local government officials, National Park authorities, Sports Councils and so on, to try and solve the problems caused by the growth in numbers of climbers. Everyone agrees that a car park is necessary at Harrison's Rocks, and that Avon and Cheddar Gorges must be safe for cars and pedestrians. The crucial questions are whether climbers are going to be involved in the decision-making processes, and whether those processes will enable us to wield appropriate influence.

I would argue that the threat posed by this heavy-handed bureaucracy is of a different nature to that which derives from the new form of landlordism. With all their weaknesses, local government and planning bodies do allow some avenues for presentation and pressure. The giant monopolies do not.

The obstacles I have described are more of a potential than an actual threat. But they seem likely to loom larger in the future, and it is important that we identify them as the enemy.

How do we fight them? Well, I won't make the speech I would have made in Clydebank over the last fortnight campaigning for Jimmy Reid, but I will say this: I have argued that one of the main reasons that climbing is like it is derives from the crucial influx of working-class people and young people during the early '50s and late '60s; their numbers are still on the increase, and they now make up the majority of the climbing population. Climbing is now a mass sport, and the response we make to threats against our freedom must involve harnessing the combativeness and creativity of those that make up our ranks.

The Rio Tintos of this world will not be stopped by polite lobbying, or by sporadic acts of individual protest like overturning drilling rigs. Only the massive involvement of climbers, in alliance with those forces in society which confront the same monopolies in other ways, will do that. I have a feeling that actions like the mass trespass on Kinder Scout may have to take place again.

NATIONAL MOUNTAINEERING CONFERENCE *1974*

CHINESE WOMEN CLIMBERS

At 14:30 hours (Peking time) on May 27, 1975, Phanthog, deputy leader of the Chinese Mountaineering Expedition, triumphantly reached the top of Qomolangma together with eight men climbers and thus became the first woman alpinist in the world to scale the highest peak of the globe from its north slope. Her feat clearly demonstrated the new outlook of Chinese women steeled in the Great Proletarian Cultural Revolution and the movement to criticise Lin Piao and Confucius, and showed that with their revolutionary courage they can scale the greatest heights and storm the most formidable fortresses.

One may well recall the wretched life of the working women of China, particularly those in Tibet, who were at the bottom rung of the social ladder before liberation. Phanthog, daughter of a serf, had been subjected to brutal oppression by the serf-owners since childhood, when she had to go begging with her mother. After new China was born in 1949, an event of earthshaking significance, the Communist Party delivered China's working women from the abyss of misery. When she grew up Phanthog got a job at the 'July First' State Farm in Lhasa and became one of the first women farm workers among the Tibetans. In 1959, she was one of the first Tibetan women selected to train as mountaineers.

The Great Proletarian Cultural Revolution and the movement to criticize Lin Piao and Confucius swept away the reactionary and decadent doctrines of Confucius and Mencius, and all the old traditional ideas of contempt for women were repudiated, thus further freeing the minds of the masses of Chinese women.

> Times have changed, and today men and women are equal.
> Whatever men comrades can accomplish, women comrades can too.

Living up to this teaching of Chairman Mao the women members of the Chinese Mountaineering Expedition plunged into the battle for the conquest of the world's highest peak, displaying peerless courage worthy of the proletariat.

Among the thirty-six women who took part in the expedition were workers, commune members, People's Liberation Army soldiers, cadres and students of Tibetan, Hui, Evenki and Han nationalities. With the exception of thirty-seven-year-old Phanthog, who had twice broken the women's world alpine record in 1959 and 1961, all were newcomers in mountaineering, their ages ranging from seventeen to twenty-three. For many of them this was their very first expedition.

Throughout the ascent these heroines proved themselves as staunch as the men in standing up to trials and tribulations. Not a word of complaint was heard from them in spite of the afflictions caused by violent winds, heavy snows, bitter cold, oxygen deficiency, hunger and hazardous climbs. Carrying their considerable share of the equipment and supplies, they tackled névé, crevasses and ice walls in excellent form. In addition to Phanthog who reached the summit, three of them (Chamco, Gunsang and Zhasang) climbed to 8600m; three others (Cering Balzhon, Wangmo and Gaylo) to 8200m; two (Pasang and Balzhan) to 7800m and seven (Cedan Zhoma, Cering Yangjan, Chou Huai-mei, Hsing Ling-ling, Migma Zhoma, Dasang and Zhogar) to 7600m. All broke the national women's altitude record of 7595m. This is yet another convincing proof that women of the new China, guided by Mao Tse-tung Thought, are a great force in building up our socialist country.

from ANOTHER ASCENT OF THE
WORLD'S HIGHEST PEAK *1976*

DOING IT FOR THE PERKS

IAN McNAUGHT-DAVIS

Now that that bastion of male chauvinist piggery, the Alpine Club, has opened its doors to women (not, I might add, as the result of a determined feminist attack, but from the forces of liberalism in the distinguished hands of Lord Hunt), we can take a searching look at other clubs from which good climbers are excluded simply because they happen to have been born the wrong sex.

The Climbers' Club has struggled with the opposite sex for the past seven years; again, I suppose, it has had as many women wishing to join as the Pinnacle Club, bastion of female chauvinist sowery, has had men kicking in the door of its Gwynant hut. In fact, a strong and well organised opposition persuaded a number of ancient members, noted for their inactivity in climbing but with highly active prejudices, to kick the motion out. But at least the prejudices were questioned.

Farther north, no such doubts arise and misogynist clubs proliferate. Those two once proud Lancashire clubs, the Rucksack and the Wayfarer's, now sunk into private, moribund obscurity, still maintain their rarely used, men-only huts to recount tales of past glories, rather like the pensioners in the Royal Chelsea Hospital, weary and broken from long forgotten battles.

And what can be said about that nationalistic, inward-looking oddity, the Scottish Mountaineering Club – other than to hope that any female Highland tiger (if they exist) would have more self-respect than to wish to join if she could, which she can't? But this curious prejudice against the opposite sex is not an exclusively male prerogative. The Pinnacle Club and the Ladies' Alpine Club (which, as far as I can make out, have more or less identical membership) don't have any qualms; they reject men absolutely. As it was explained to me, the tweedy, leather-belt and brogue brigade don't like the competition, and the lace and frills group feel that there are enough 'chaps' in the club anyway. So can it really be said that there is a genuine prejudice against women climbers, or does it all simply stem from the fact that, with few exceptions, they are so useless (at climbing, that is)?

When I did a bit of research into this question, the only sensible explanation came from one fairly active woman climber: 'Men don't want to climb

with women, but they like the perks.' But is that really what it's all about? I am sure that many of my friends have enjoyed taking some nubile female athlete up a sun-baked Severe, steep enough to simulate a real climb and with enough holds to make it easy, and then, as the flushed, excited lass pulls out over the finishing holds, hustling her away to spend the long, hot afternoon tumbling in the heather. But there must be more to it than that.

In France, Germany, Switzerland and the USA, there are women climbers who habitually lead climbs at the highest level of difficulty. During the recent Spring holiday, for example, Simone Badier returned to Wales, with Ron James's book of selected climbs clasped in her delicate, thirty-eight-year-old hand. In a few days she led routes that included Vector, Central Wall on Castell Cidwm, Big Groove and Winking Crack and, after a futile visit to a wet Cloggy, filled in an afternoon by leading Diagonal, Cenotaph Corner and Cemetery Gates. So really, there is no reason, physical or mental, why women should not attain the upper echelons of our sport and lead climbs of the highest order of difficulty.

Why, then, have British women climbers contributed so little for so long?

I am going to stick my neck out and propose a couple of hypotheses. The first, as I have already implied, is that female climbers in this country lead at a significantly lower standard than do their contemporaries in most other important climbing countries. The second hypothesis accounts for the first, by blaming British female climbing mediocrity on the attitudes adopted by British male climbers towards any female who shows any climbing promise.

Probably the most powerful disincentive for women is what I would call the 'gentle bullshit' (or the 'pat-on-the-head', as it is called in the USA). It goes like this:

CC Member: 'Hello, had a good day?'

Nubile Female Climber: 'Yes, I led Gashed Crag today.'

CC Member (thinking, 'Well it's only a Diff, but it was a cold day and she is a woman'): 'That's an extraordinary achievement! Well done! Jolly Good!'

The NFC preens and rushes off to write an article about it for the Pinnacle Journal. Normally, if it was worth discussing the matter at all, the conversation between two men would have gone as follows:

'What did you do today?'

'Nothing, took a bird up Gashed Crag.'

'Christ! You missed the best day for months.'

So they get deceived into thinking that their minor achievements have some significance. I am sure that the motivation is basically kind, the idea being to stimulate more interest, so that, after years of struggle, she can confidently lead some crummy Lakeland V. Diff. on a sunny day. But is there any real excuse for this patronising dishonesty?

There is also the problem of pure male chauvinism. The man takes the girl climbing (for the perks), gradually she becomes his accepted partner, his leading standard falls (either because of too many perks or too little ambition) and she is cast, irrevocably, into the role of second. Eventually their standards, his on the way down, hers on the way up, meet. They both become dissatisfied, and they part, he to marry a short-sighted teacher from Heckmondwike, she to join the warm, mothering embrace of the Pinnacle Club where she becomes a star ('She leads Severes').

Of course, what that basically means is that they opt out of any competitive scene. The only way to measure how good you are is to measure yourself against your peers. Once women accept that they cannot climb at the same standard as men, they fall into the Pinnacle/LAC maw of benevolent 'gentle bullshit'; they measure themselves on a totally feeble, outdated scale.*

Finally, there is the fact that there are anyway far fewer female than male climbers. Once again, the reason for this lies with the selfish male. The climbing may be great, but the attractions of furtive sex in stinking sleeping bags, huddled in leaking tents, quickly fade even when measured against that exquisite alternative, the 'drink in the pub'. This involves three hours of standing shoulder-to-shoulder with sweating male climbers dressed in rags, watching that ultimately tedious and endless game of darts, while pint after pint of beer is swilled and the conversation, what there is of it, is restricted to discussing unknown climbs on unknown crags. It is surprising that there are any women there at all. But perhaps they, too, are there for the perks, whatever they may be.

from MOUNTAIN 36 1974

---

*1974 saw the first ascent of Right Wall of Dinas Cromlech – a climb generally acknowledged as the main UK test piece of the period. Ten years later Jill Lawrence, Rosie Andrews, Catherine Destivelle and Christine Gambert each led the climb during an international women's meet. Later Louise Shepherd led Lord of the Flies and Glenda Huxter led The Bells, The Bells – both harder and more committing climbs. In the United States, Lynn Hill's free ascent of the Nose in 1993 was a rock climb of the highest standards. During the same period high-level performances by women were recorded in alpinism by Catherine Destivelle, Allison Hargreaves and others. These and a range of other top performances by women have effectively answered the questions raised in this section.

FOR ENGLAND READ MIDDLESEX

IAIN SMART

As the domino theory would predict another English mountaineering club has gone hermaphrodite. We quote below a comment extracted from a recent Alpine Club circular.

> Members who have not already heard will be interested to learn that the Climbers' Club decided at a meeting in Derbyshire to admit women to membership. The vote was overwhelmingly in favour, and the place of women in Mountaineering Clubs in this country seems to be resolved.

These goings-on at the anglo-saxon fringe are of peripheral interest to us. We mention the matter only to provide an opportunity of expressing our admiration for the dignity and self-restraint of the various ladies' clubs. The quoted paragraph manages to imply with typical patronising male chauvinism that the existing ladies' mountaineering clubs are not Mountaineering Clubs. We trust the Pinnacle Club and the rump of the Ladies' Alpine Club will keep their grip on their tempers and their standards and continue to bar the porcine male from membership. The fall of the first Ladies' Club will be far more unfortunate than the present slitherings of their more feckless and emotionally unstable brother clubs.

from THE SCOTTISH MOUNTAINEERING
CLUB JOURNAL *1975*

HANDS

ANNE MARIE RIZZI

I hadn't seen him since Half Dome. Oh, maybe once in the Lodge bar when we pointedly ignored each other. And, yes, a few weeks later we did confront each other over a bottle of burgundy, trying at least to understand our differences, mellowing our bitter feelings into half-hearted laughter. Now, he is sitting with me again, flipping through the slides, the four days in thirty frames: 'Over-exposed ... Sandy Ledges? ... This one of your hands is OK.' Nine months ago we became strangers; now, we maintain our distance with gay repartee. We carefully avoid discussing the climb.

The top! Oh God, at last. Hurry, untie. At last, I'm free of him. Never again.
'You can have my 'biners ... Yes, I'm sure ... Take them, dammit!'
Careful now, don't lose control. Just repack the haul-bag and you'll be done with this. Try to be civil. Remember how well you used to get along with him.
'How 'bout a picture of my hands?' Good, to remember this by, to remind me how each cut ... Never ... What's with him? He won't even let me coil the rope I'm going to carry, I've got to get out of here.
'I'll start down for the pack and meet you at the saddle.' No?! He hates me as much as I hate him. Of course.
'Well then, I'll be down tomorrow. We'll celebrate.' Ha! Watch your manner, lady. Find the cables. I've never come up these cables, now down them twice. Should I wait to help him? He's got most of the load. He asked for it. Don't think about him. Get away from him ...
Ahhh ... the saddle, the sheltering tree. The snowplant – of course it's still there – you've only been gone four days Silly; seems longer. How soon to the snowbank? God, I'm thirsty. Gone. What a masochist you are child. Look at your hands, your self-esteem, your mind. I hate climbing. You never did before. I hate walls. You liked the Column. I hate Half Dome. It's a beautiful rock. The route is screwed. Was it? Never again.
... There's my pack. The snow cave has melted down. Mmm, sweet, sweet water. I was thirsty up there. C'mon now, look up, face it. Ladies and horridmen, above you stretches the vertical desert of the mighty Half Dome ... my God, it's *big*. Did I climb *that*? No. He did. I shouldn't have backed off that lead. That was when he started blaming me for ... That was

where he took over. 'If you can't lead this fast, I'll take it.' Damn! He was slow too. I should have asserted myself; especially when he yelled at me – blamed me. I should have strangled him with a runner and left him to rot on Thank God Ledge. He was so unhappy. Four days instead of two-and-a-half. Enough water: 'enough' is always too little. I should have…

I can see the whole route from here: half rubble. That low-angle section that I couldn't haul without his reluctant help. How long before my scars heal from those hauling blisters? I've got to start work next week. How long before I forget his accusing glares?

And that broken section: must be where we slept one night – how many nights ago? – the night he finally yelled at me. I should have screamed at him then instead of maintaining diplomatic silence.

Traverse – up – pendulum – up – traverse. It takes up the whole damn face. But we were always hidden round corners, in chimneys, with only ourselves to look at. I don't want to see him again. Should I keep my aid slings as souvenirs? I won't use them any more.

And the summit overhang: I suppose that was sort of funny. Below its shade: 'Goddamned motherfucker cocksucker, eat shit' A bellow, touched with high-pitched hysteria. Then, from the overhang: 'Hello down there. I've been photographing you all day. I'll send you the pictures.' Not a friend's voice.

I suppose the voice got one of me taking a dump. We were almost off – my pitch, but I didn't protest when he took the rack. He'd have yelled at me more if I'd asserted myself – I think.

… Oh stop thinking, lady. Half Dome's a rock, not a bad time. Think about the Valley, being there tomorrow. How quiet it seems from here. A clamour tomorrow. They'll congratulate me and expect details: idyllic dancing up the Zig-Zags; romantic bivies; poetry. How to reply? 'Yes, I read Burnt Norton on Sandy Ledges,' and he said shut up and just belay me. How to explain? They want a 'good and bad, but more good' climbing tale.

… A long nightmare… Go to sleep now, tomorrow you'll forget. I'm so alone. I'm never going to tear my hands on a nightmare again. Don't blame the rock. Oh, good night, Half Dome! I think – to be free – I'll… Yes, I'll take up hiking – alone.

He's up now, walking towards the door.

'Well, we'll have to get together again soon. No, I don't want any of the slides.'

Yes, stranger, I know you hated it too – we've talked our share about it. My glance goes to his hands and then to mine. I give him a brief hug instead.

'Sure, see ya later alligator.'

from MOUNTAIN 36 *1974*

CORRESPONDENCE ON VULGARITY

Dear Editor,

Much as I enjoy and appreciate most features of your magazine, I regret that I shall not again renew my subscription unless the magazine ceases to acquiesce in the encouragement of vulgarity.

The most striking example was the article 'Hands'. I find your reply to Mr Langdon's letter about this is quite unsatisfactory. The phrase 'creative relevance', which you use to justify the printing of an extraordinarily blasphemous and obscene expletive of eleven syllables, seems to me on a par with the sociological jargon in vogue today, which is used to justify anything which anybody wants to do. However, I assume that you are sincere in what you say, but I fail to see that the expletive contributes anything worthwhile to the article in question.

I also find it amazing that you should describe the role of your magazine in terms reminiscent of those often used of publications devoted to the seamy aspects of sex: '... aimed solely at an adult and hopefully mature audience.' (Incidentally, are those who object to the printing of extreme obscenities 'immature', by definition?) Even if the magazine is directed at adults, are you really happy that many parents will not care to leave it lying about?

The issue of 'creative relevance' can hardly be said to apply to the use of a four-letter word in *Mountain 32*, page fifteen, penultimate line of right-hand column. Its use there is gratuitous. (I am puzzled by the fact that the appearance of obscenities in *Mountain* is often connected with women, particularly Americans.)

A further fine example, or set of examples actually appears opposite Mr Langdon's letter on page forty of *Mountain 38*. I refer to Mr Campbell's review of Hamish MacInnes's latest book [see page 392]. I do not normally care for highly sarcastic book reviews, since one often suspects the motives of the reviewer, but in this case it would appear that there is a great deal to take exception to in the book. Was it really necessary, however, for Mr Campbell to detail all the four-letter words and mention some of them two or three times?

You publish so much that is of great interest and value. It seems a pity not to uphold reasonable standards of propriety throughout the magazine.

Yours sincerely,
John Shorter (Hull)

Dear Sir

... John Shorter and Peter Langdon, seem to imbue common expletives with an almost mystical power. The words themselves are nothing; indeed they are in most current editions of dictionaries, for all to see. Do Messrs. Shorter and Langdon refuse to subscribe to *Chambers Dictionary* (1972 Edition), for example, because these words appear in it? Do they hide dictionaries from their children?

Climbers are people, Mr Shorter, with varying degrees of fluency. In moments of stress or excitement, or sometimes to emphasise a point, a number of them, even females, use expletives. Contributors to *Mountain*, if they want honestly to recreate the emotion and stress of a particular situation, use them in turn. On Half Dome, Anne Marie Rizzi was at odds with her companion, with the climb, with climbing itself; she then had the honesty to tell the truth about the experience in an article which came close to brilliance – no wasted words (not even those!) – taut punctuation – tight, evocative writing – what more do you want, Mr. Shorter? Shall we have a nostalgic return to the third person incomprehensible of a century ago: '... Mr Slingsby/Collie/Mummery/Hastings cogently expressed his dissatisfaction with the topography of the crag with a well-chosen epithet...' What in heaven's name do you think he said – was it 'Bother!'?

Mountain has an obligation to readers and contributors to respect the style of an author and to accept his (or her) method of creating atmosphere. In 'Hands', the pain of the experience has been given form by disjointed prose and the use of ugly (in the aesthetic, not the moral, sense) expletives. Isn't this 'creative relevance'? Does Mr Shorter keep a file of the four-letter words in *Mountain*? He harks back to a quote from a letter from Ellie Hawkins in *Mountain 32*, in an attempt to shout down the 'creative relevance' idea. If Mrs Hawkins wrote that, then she wrote it. *Mountain* quoted it as part of a girl's reaction to a great climb. Should the editor have left it out? Should he have rephrased it in diplomatic jargon? – '... consequent upon my involvement with the rewarding experience of extreme rock-climbing, I have decided to relinquish the artificial stimulus of amphetamines...'!

Finally, I would like to ask Mr Shorter two questions. On the crux of a climb at the top of his standard, when he is tired, and the conditions are poor, what does he mutter to himself? Does he really want a climbing magazine of world class to carry out editorial censorship, so that every report becomes a dull succession of guidebook information?

Mountain deserves great literary style: it deserves more than a Noddy approach to artistic licence.

Yours faithfully,
David Hewlett (Uttoxeter)

Dear Sir

Regarding Peter Langdon's (and friends') repugnance at my coarse language in 'Hands': I am thankful that he (and they) at least read as far as the offending passage. My intention was not to shock or offend your readers; rather I wished to impart a true account of a horribly bad time on a climb that such as Mr Langdon regard with reverence and idyllic promise. Whether he would, in a similar situation, say 'Gosh, darn, jeez, fudge,' etc. is irrelevant. The language is a minor but truthful part of my story. Thank you for your editorial comment in my defence. Yosemite cohorts laughed uproariously; I was touched.

Cheerfully, as always,
Anne Marie Rizzi (Berkeley)

from MOUNTAINS 41 & 42 *1975*

A BEAR HUNT ON THE BLOSSEVILLE COAST

ANDREW ROSS

A Warning: The trouble with Greenland is that once you have been there you forget all about mountaineering. The place is riddled with superb mountains, but most of them, especially those on the spiky East Coast, can only be reached by means of a major expedition and therein lies the catch.

Once you have felt the thunder of the dog sledge runners on the skinny sea-ice, and been there when the bear turns towards you, it's like discovering the clue to the crux on Main Wall, or the trick in doing a somersault on skiis – in short the effect can be shattering.

Since an expedition three years previously to East Greenland, I had been thinking about another mountain we had seen on the way, the Rigny's Bjerge. It was not particularly high, about 8800ft, but encircled by green glaciers, its peak towered straight from sea-level, above all the surrounding mountains. I'd been thinking about it ever since.

Anyway, I needed an excuse to go back. Spending every penny I had I went to Scoresbysund, the nearest settlement to the mountain, 600 miles inside the Arctic Circle, bought eight dogs and a sledge and began to think it out.

I sat on the newly acquired sledge for a while pondering on how to feed eight hungry dogs. The Eskimo I bought the dogs from had said, when he gave me some seal meat the day before, like handing over the log book to a new car:

'Do not give thanks for your meat, it is your right. In Greenland every man is an individual, we are *inuit* the human beings, giving food is not a favour. No one gives or receives gifts of food, sharing is the law.'

Well, you have to begin somewhere, I thought. I was getting pretty hungry too. I went back to the Eskimo, Sanimouinak, and suggested a hunting trip together.

'Perhaps next week,' he said, with a glint in his eye.

'Not now?'

He laughed and pulled on his jacket.

As the only person to get off the plane that lands on skiis in the springtime on the iced-up fjord, people wanted to know where I was going with my new dog-team. Many had never met an Englishman before. 'Oh, just a short hunting trip,' I said, to hoots of laughter.

Sanimouinak's sledge bounded off down the slope and out onto the sea-ice. 'Well, here goes.' I thought and pulled the rope that tied the sledge. The dogs rushed along the track, children leapt out of the way and old women waved from their houses. By the store, as the sledge took off over a steep snow bank, and it and I parted company, I dimly heard a roar of applause as everything overturned and plunged into a snow bank.

I had so much to learn, perhaps too much, I wondered, digging snow from my neck, for me to leave tomorrow on a 400-mile sledge journey over the sea-ice of the Denmark Strait, on ice that often shifted above strong and dangerous currents, with storms, polar bears and a degree of cold that froze hot coffee solid.

But I asked all the questions I could think of, and when they saw I really wanted to learn, the Eskimoes told me everything. Things became much easier when the girls in the town decided who would scrub my back in the bath on Sunday. Sanimouinak's daughter, Augustina, was chosen. I had no idea there was still an area of the world where being British could be such a delicious sensation. Sanimouinak, the hard man locally, disapproved of baths. He gave me an Eskimo name – *duluit* – soap-skin stranger.

During the summer he and I caught salmon in the rivers and geese on the lakes. Then in August we built a hut on Steward Island, 100 miles south of the town on the edge of the best Polar Bear hunting area in Greenland, the Blosseville Coast, and went down there to live the winter.

By the spring of the following year my dogs were strong and fast enough for me to be invited on the bear hunt with Iarikai, Barsiliasne, Arke and Sanimouinak.

We set off in March.

The sun rose over the horizon on the 5th and on that day Iarikai shot a bear. At midday as the red sun hovered between sunset and sunrise we had the 'sunshine breakfast – *kirinak nererk*', an Eskimo festival for the first day of sunshine after the long winter. We had a splendid feast; seal soup, bear paw steaks. Chocolate biscuits and brandy. Not a cornflake in sight.

It was to be a three-month journey in March, it was really cold. The other four sledges were strung out ahead of me eight or ten miles down the fjord. The breath from the dogs hung in the air and the sunshine filtered through it and reflected from it the colour of gold-dust.

We drove out onto the pack-ice and by then, in the dusk, I could barely see the tracks on the snow. The dogs followed them unerringly through the dark starlit night. I stopped the sledge to have a piss. As I stood under the vast canopy of stars with the Pole star almost over my head, thinking my thoughts, the dogs decided to run for it. I saw the blur of the sledge and dived after it, missed, and landed flat in the snow. I ran, stumbled, after the sledge fast disappearing into the dark to God knew where and my heart thumped with worry. I clutched my trousers and ran harder than I've run in my life, made a two-handed goalkeeper's dive for the handlebar, caught it and the dogs promptly lay down panting in the snow with the fun of it all. I lay gasping. Hours of boredom, sudden crisis. Rather go climbing.

I met the others out on the ice-edge at about midnight. The sea stretched away solidly black from the grey, moonlit snow. They had the tents up and a pot of seal meat bubbled on the Primus. I told the story about the dogs and they all laughed with glee. Accidents are fun.

Clouds were driving up quickly from the south. We tethered the dogs and tied the tents between the sledges.

'Seela ayupok the sky is bad,' they muttered, but I went to bed, glad at the prospect of a long day's rest.

The dawn came with a welter of snow and a howling gale. The dogs buried their noses in their tails and Sanimouinak and I sat with our backs against the tent poles. It was impossible to sleep, we just sat in the sleeping bags listening to the storm.

A sudden crack woke me up. There was a terrible noise and it was quite black. I checked desperately through my memory to remember where I was. The pack ice. The storm. I called to Sanimouinak. Another crack! And on the darkness of the floor there was a darker line and through that there was water. That was the sea. The pack was breaking up!

Sanimouinak struggled out of the tent to warn the others. He came back plastered in snow to say the crack divided us from the others. They knew of the danger but no one could say which of us was on the main pack-ice. We could all be drifting down to the North Atlantic. There was nothing to do. In the storm it would be madness to begin sledging in to the land. We packed everything ready to move when the storm dropped a little.

It was eighteen hours before the wind let us go. Snow writhed over the ground but up above there were glimpses of clear skies. No one carries a compass that far north in the Arctic and when we set off, still in the storm, I was really scared about losing the others and the sledge in front of me was just a blur. I trusted the dogs. The others did because they knew them. I just did.

The wind dropped enough to let the snow settle and the visibility improved rapidly. The ice had broken badly in all directions but we could see the dim outline of the coast. We sledged from flow to floe over a shattered mosaic of ice. The dogs hopped over the gaps and by the time the sledge was on the edge, and bridging the gap, the floe we were leaving was sinking slowly under water. Some floes were so isolated we used them as a raft, slinging a leaded shark-hook to tow the floe over the open water. The journey took all day but when we reached the shore, and I was last, as usual, the others were laughing and shouting happily. It had been a narrow escape.

'Oh, how worried he was,' said Sanimouinak, pointing at me. He jumped around wiping tears from his eyes. I stoutly denied it and that made the joke even better.

On the next morning we found the cold during the night had frozen over the areas of open water and the others took the opportunity of returning north. Sanimouinak and I sledged on south. No one had sledged this far south before, except 'Angakok' the magician (and the others always looked at Sanimouinak strangely when he told the story), who travelled with the souls of dead men in the glaciers and the mountains and gave them birth again in the form of weird icebergs.

As the sledges rumbled over the thin ice of the night the runners scored through it and water oozed up in the tracks. It was important to keep the sledge moving fast to spread out the weight; if the sledge stopped…! Following Sanimouinak's sledge the ice heaved, and a bulge, like the stern wave from a boat, flowed from it. At times, undulating over the ice, as the sledge rose and dipped, I thought he had gone through. New sea-ice is very elastic and slippery and we drove very fast for the dogs were scared too. Souls of the dead, giant icebergs at forty-five million tons at a time, some 300ft high, gathered in this area where strong currents spun them in slow circles of destruction. Every so often one would pick up its skirts and run with the current, devastating a tract of pack-ice leaving in its wake a bobbing, ticking, crush of ice, a path a mile wide and ten miles long.

We drove all day through this still, silent group on grey, paper-thin ice, then, at last, onto strong white ice.

We were then in the heart of the Blosseville Coast.

'This is where the bears are,' said Sanimouinak and I would have been happy to leave them to it but for the prospect of re-crossing that thin ice again.

'Can we get back?' I enquired.

'Maybe,' he said. That word, in Greenland, is not so much a reply as a philosophy.

We spent some time seal hunting. At that time of year they come up on the ice to sleep and using a white hunting screen it is possible to creep up to within twenty feet for a rifle shot. We fed the dogs on seal meat and it was a matter of expertise, that I acquired slowly, to know which parts of the seal could be fed to them that produced neither a run of diarrhoea spurting over the dog-lines or a barrage of farts first thing in the morning. Greenland dogs also have an insatiable love for human excrement. One or the other of us had to stand guard with a whip before a snarling pack of dogs. They can un-nerve that essential sense of relaxation in even the most resolute Eskimo.

Four days after crossing the thin ice we stood at the foot of the mountains I had come to see. They were like the Chamonix Aiguilles moved into the sea, turreted spires rising into a pale blue sky.

No one had ever seen these mountains except from far at sea in the summer-time when one or two boats have wriggled this far through the pack-ice. Standing in their shadow, our whole world, two sledges, some sixteen dogs and a baby bear-cub we had found lost on the ice and had strapped in the sledge-bag to take back to Scoresbysund, all seemed very small in front of these majestic mountains.

Sanimouinak lowered his binoculars.

'There is a bear.'

'Where?'

'On the mountain, two bears,' he said with a grin.

And sure enough, high on the mountain, on a long, wide snowfield was a dark furrow, a chute. And poised above it a bear, who, with a jump and a tumble came glissading down on his bottom spraying the snow with his hind legs. He rolled in the snow, throwing the stuff in the air, showing off to a female at the foot of the slide.

'Why is he doing that?'

'It's April,' said Sanimouinak slyly. 'Pumpimik!' (No translation.) Then he added:

'Is it like that in Scotland?'

'Well, maybe.' I said, wistfully.

It had taken me a year and a half to get to this mountain and not only was it far too big to attempt, but there was someone else on it. It seemed I had been to an awful lot of trouble for very little mountaineering. And but for the sense of living dangerously and the company, among the Eskimos, of people who had both real humour and a contempt for incompetence, I was glad to leave the mountain to whoever wanted it.

We turned to go and I caught sight of a dog tugging at a reindeer skin on the sledge.

'Mountain! (the dog's name) Damn you!'

'WOW! GET A LOAD OF THAT BEAUTIFUL DIHEDRAL!'

PART 7

EPICS, RISK, FALLING, DEATH, OBITUARY AND RETIREMENT

An unavoidable reality in mountaineering is the ever-present risk of injury or sudden death. Climbing is a dangerous sport, and however much climbers try to play down this factor, it returns time and again to remind us – with the unexpected demise of a close friend or the wipe-out of a party or expedition. It may be that mountaineering is the most pointless and irresponsible of all sports, analogous (in Himalayan climbing at least) to Russian Roulette.

Some climbers try to ignore this. Others seem to gain inner satisfaction from the risk of the sport, toying with danger, joking about close escapes, making fun out of death whenever it is impersonal and well removed from them.

Conversely there are those who contend that the precious talismans of 'skill', 'prudence' and 'good judgement' will keep them safe, and that those who court risk are hooked on some dangerously subversive creed. This might be taken seriously if it were not for the numbers of *skilful* and *prudent* climbers of impeccable *judgement* who have pranged over the years.

Not surprisingly this undercurrent of risk and danger has made its mark in mountain writing. For the most part the literature on the subject has been light-hearted – a form of whistling to keep our spirits up – but serious comment can sometimes be found, often in obituary notes.

Perhaps those who are capable of facing this matter with any semblance of sanity have ceased to be climbers anyway. Another explanation, possibly too glib for present tastes, is that 'life without risk is not worth living'. Such a *credo* would certainly invest a few historical events with greater clarity.

A note for 2006: While ice climbing, alpinism and expedition climbing remain very risky activities, rock climbing (with its better equipment) has, in some respects, become safer. We no longer have the two or three fatal accidents on rock every bank holiday as was certainly the case in the '50s and '60s. On the other hand, with rock climbers learning much of their trade on climbing walls (a bit like learning how to drive on grand prix circuits), once they get out onto proper crags and inevitably leapfrog the old apprenticeship training of the easier grades, they can be more at risk for the lack of the essential crag and belaying 'savvy'. This readjustment must be taking place however as there are definitely fewer accidents (on rock at least) than in the past. That said, at the top end, traditional rock climbers, edge ever closer to the mysteries of what is possible – our new front cover giving a graphic illustration of such quests into the sea of the unknown.

SCENERY FOR A MURDER

JOHN MENLOVE EDWARDS

I did start by trying to write an essay, but it was soon clear that it was not an essay I wanted to write but the facts, the plain facts as they happened. What do I mean? You will see what I mean. The fact is, there has been murder done, a murder, done under their noses, and the fools can't spot the murderer. So I will set it all out; but I will have to be a little careful, for the murderer is a gentleman and very well connected; one is supposed to talk of him carefully so to speak, as if he wasn't there or didn't do anything.

But the story.

This is what happened. I opened the paper one morning at home and saw that an accident had happened; a well-known climber killed in the Alps; one of the most notorious slices of cliff in the world; frozen to death on it; three nights out; now trying to get the body; and it was he, my friend. But that is the barest summary. I can tell you more than that. For I was there when it was done.

The first time I saw him was nothing to do with climbing. It was in the Albert Hall. In fact, strictly, I didn't see him; heard him over the wireless. Eight of them; they walked down the centre of the Hall on to the platform, and I didn't notice him, naturally, during that part of the business; but then, what they had come for, they sang, a dozen or so of the folk-songs of their country; and then I couldn't help it, for a really fine voice does not need careful comparison or notice to pick it out, it stands out of itself, and this was a young voice, one in a million, high, sung full out, accurate, but a wild voice. What a voice! The Albert Hall faded out in two seconds: he stood still, head thrown back a little; you could see that, though he stood in line amongst the others.

And even then you could see it was tragedy.

Of course that was years ago. Then one of those strange things happened. I met him. Got talking with a German boy in Berne: was leaning up against the railings watching the sky over the roof-tops, and I saw him, quite suddenly, walking past, and you couldn't miss it, the same look, the same attitude; didn't even have to ask his name: it stood out all over him: power, courage; love, honour; the heroes, fame, God, the Devil; no, I can't phrase it, but you can take it from me it was not the boy so much as the scenery.

401

I've never seen such wild scenery; it stood out a mile. So I got in tow. He was a tall young fellow, could obviously climb as well as any man, but as I say, I was in luck that day, and I got in tow.

Skip a few days, and the two of us, Toni and I, enormous rucksacks on our backs, walked slowly out of an hotel, together, sweating we were, brown, in the heat of the sun, out of the village, past the few last houses, beside the hay plots, and up, leaving the fir-trees one by one, along the scorched dry bed of the valley, the hills sloping high on either side, up the track towards the thin, far-away line of the mountains. I think I have never known a hut walk go so well. Toni looked around contentedly enough, but he seemed not to notice much; yet he transformed the land, he gave it an atmosphere, a scenery, a hauteur, that made the bare places and the vivid sky seem beautiful. Noticeable with me, for in myself I am dull. Like most people, perhaps, the things that happen to me come, pass over me, then they travel on; but as they go I go also, with them, into the past; and if I walk out, for instance, I am often behind-hand and cannot catch up, cannot produce in time the right attitude with which to appreciate a scenery. So to me the effect on the valley was remarkable. He spoke a fair amount, but that was nothing. It was his atmosphere, in which the features of the country became more beautiful than I had known them.

We got to the hut in good time, had a meal and sat over it, and my mind was still running over the same subject so, as we were well fed and he seemed not to mind my talking, I held forth. Now you are all right, I said, I'm not a fool and I know the genuine article – phrase we have in England – when I see it, but I think there's nothing I've hated so much in my time and so reasonably as the love of the mountains. And as I talked I got enthusiastic. Now follow me, I said; take a chestnut, cover it with sugar. He was a shy fellow and looked quickly round, but I make no difficulty of an incident like that and I carried straight on. No, no, I said, cover it with sugar, more, boil it in sugar, say that you are a bad cook, five, six, ten, twenty times its own weight of sugar, boil it for two days, no, two years, and you get my meaning, you have a fine piece of sugar left, but not a chestnut; after two years it would be a tragedy to go on calling a thing like that a chestnut. And a man's feelings are more tender than that, surely. So when a fellow produces thick syrup whenever he sees a hill, he may protest any fine origin for it that he likes, but most of us consider it simply sickening. We are right? Yes, he said. So I went on talking; for he did not understand: he had had less experience of having other people's feelings himself than a child of ten.

We went to bed; at least, we didn't go to bed, we lay on the floor that night, for the hut was crowded out and the breathing was terrible. But who cares; throw off the cloak, make no pretence to be beautiful, cuddle down a bit, all fully dressed, all close together, and it's pleasant enough. No, I had forgotten; funny how one's mind goes on. He must have such feelings, but not the same I suppose; they'd get a different sort of reception in him; try to find out tomorrow; what a hope. So I lay on my back that night, Spartan. But next morning, early breakfast, it was just the same as the day before, the crowd did not count, we were in the heights again, miles away, and man's desires rose up over the sweat over the earth and chased madly away, out of sight, in the air, where they dallied.

We went up one side of a mountain that day, down the other, over a fine snow col, and stood at about two o'clock in the afternoon by the front of a small tin cabane, miles away high up on the side of the mountains, difficult to get at, used ten or a dozen times a year perhaps, not more, at the top of the small steep armchair valley beneath our cliff, not a valley, a ledge, a slight relenting of the main sweep, existing for no good reason. I was excited. Toni went to bed and I was alone. I became a little frightened inside me, and I stood at the door of the hut. The sun streamed in at the window; the stones shone white before me; the little cabane dwarfed, crouching away; nothing moved; down on the left there was a faint sound of running water, but none visible; then the slope dropped steeply over into cliffs, then beyond that, far below, the valley, a little river in it, with trees and a few pastures, and beyond that the hills, the trees rose steeply up their side in dark patches and then the deep green of the high Alp pastures, cool, dry, in the distance, then more hills, grey-green hills. But up here there was not much green. And the boy still slept. And I couldn't get it out of my mind. Then after a time I got some water in the bucket and made some tea for him. Woke him up. He was quiet now; enjoyed the drink, and he even accepted my attention. Then there was nothing else to do, and we stood at the door of the hut again. The valley shimmered still in the warm sun of the late afternoon, but up here the shadow of the great ridge opposite was coming over us, and there was a slight cold breeze. And, up on the right, dominating the whole, part white in the sun, part black, hard and scintillating, stood the shape of the mountain. He gazed at it carefully, so did I. Then we went in, and went to bed early in preparation for the morrow. Toni looked a little tired. Well, we were here now; and I didn't like it.

Why we got up at that hour of the night I don't know. To miss the avalanches perhaps, the stone falls, but so far as I could see we couldn't miss them anyhow on this route, so what was the use? I expect Toni liked getting up: it was all right for him; he could take it. And as I laced up my boots in the early morning I cursed, and as I ate I was angry, and all the while under the warm shirt my muscles shivered slightly in the cold, and the shiver flitted on and over my mind, so that my heart beat quicker than it should do before a climb. Then Toni got up, ready; I am always in a bit of a scramble with my things on an early start, and I went out after him. God, it was black. I am a rabbit at heart, I said. He said nothing. We set off along a tiny track. Panting and unhappy, I said, I yet shall do it. I shall follow this boy until I drop, nor will I ask for sympathy; though with his massive limbs he has no pity for me, me small, following after. Here, where a slight temporary difficulty on this patch of rock makes it impossible for me to keep to his heels, I will make a clatter with my ice-axe, rather louder than the ordinary, and attract his attention so that he will notice the labour of my breathing and go a little slower. No. Now I shall have to run a few paces to catch up with him. No. He has a heart of stone, this boy, he cannot respond. All my kindness, my special treatment is to no purpose. Panting and unhappy. And we picked our way along the head of the valley, crawled up a small rock slope, stumbled over the stones across the tongue of a short moraine; ach; then we stepped off on to the snow of the glacier. Ah, now my friend, now let me not be angry. In the cold morning air I can forget. Well? You take no notice? You do not understand? My hatred and my forgiveness have nowhere to go? You have come here welded, set into something, I believe, and your weldedness, your one object, is to climb, apparently, this mountain. But aloud I said, do you think we might rest a minute? And he assented.

So we turned and stood, looking outward over the valley, and we were high up and it was dark, and in the cold I shivered and was excited again, and Toni took off his hat, loosened his hair with his hands, and looked out over the dark beneath, over to the north far horizon, with me for a minute, then we went on; and the cliff rose before us, as we turned, bare and dark, standing like a ghost over the glacier. We went steadily up, not difficult, over the grey snow, crisp to tread upon, bending slightly, winding in and out, making our way. We were playing the part now and no mistake. An hour passed and another hour, the glacier steepened, we trod carefully in on the edge of our boots, now and then kicking slightly; the snow was perfect; if all would go like this – then the glacier stopped and the bergschrund lay before us, eight to ten feet wide, uniform, curving, the far side steep, so we stopped too, sat down in a dip on the top edge of the glacier and ate a little. It was lighter now. Then we unhooked our sacks, drew up our legs, strapped on the crampons and pulled them tight round the instep; and then we stood up again and felt strong like conquerors; but there was this damned bergschrund yet. Would it go? So I made myself firm while Toni scouted, and he walked along the edge of the bergschrund to the right a little and said I will try here, and he got on to a little bridge, looked at the wall above split by a vertical crack, thin, the right size, jammed his ice-axe at chest height into it, put a foot high up and lay back on it, then he pulled in a bit, slipped his right arm into the crack up to the elbow, held on so, and with his left hand, a twist, got the ice-axe out, jammed it in higher and so proceeded, ten feet or more; then the angle eased slightly and the crack was not so good and the ice gave way to brittle snow, but the crack widened also with a thinner crack at the back, and he stood up, jammed himself, cut a wide foothold out on the right, and at last, about quarter of an hour I should say, got on to it. And the snow sloped steeply up before him towards the rocks, but could we stand there? and he rested a minute, then cut big steps hand- and foothold upwards in good hard snow. It was eighty-foot before he took me up and I needed aid. There was no doubt he could climb. But the cliff looked steep up ahead. A groove and rib structure, the groove going up wide, open and parallel and about fifty yards between. From a distance it had looked as if, when you got fed up with one groove, you would climb into the next on either side, but now you could see it better, this was none of your Chamonix stuff and the rock had no holds on it, nasty. The grooves were backed with a runnel of ice or snow mostly and the ribs with verglas. If you came off you wouldn't hit up against anything outstanding by the look of it either, but shooting the bergschrund you would skate for miles; the odds are, I think, you would not stop on the glacier going at that speed, but would follow it to the mouth of the little valley, tip up over the end over the cliff edge and die.

The dawn had risen unnoticed away on the left, but it was still cold here. Toni was off again and it looked bad. Our groove was rather bare at first, but he kept his crampons on and as there didn't seem to be much in the way of holds, he was using a pressure technique, pressing against the little grooves sideways to keep the snow up, and with hands pressing sideways also to keep himself up, and the method was slow, and produced much scraping sometimes, and now and then it took convulsions for a moment or two when a position became untenable. I can watch a climber and tell what he is doing exactly. Poor old Toni, he didn't like it any more than I did; but luckily in those days he didn't know how much he didn't like it. Then at last, it seemed hours, at 100ft he got a stance for his feet, stuck in a piton and took me up. Then it looked as if it might get better, but it got worse instead. And so it went on; some patches of ice were more good than bad, though needing hacked handholds all the way, and it took a time. I led one or two bits of that, but was not safe on the rest. At midday we had done 800ft or so; several times he stood on my shoulders; then it got worse and we were getting tired, and towards evening we were not much above 1200ft from the foot of the rocks still, but there was the best ledge we had met; carefully roping we might both lie down; so we ate a good meal and felt better, and decided to stay there for the night. Stones had been dropping a bit all day, but it was cold and you hardly noticed them, and what could you do, anyhow? And now the sun appeared on the right, and at last unexpectedly we were warmed, and he sat and watched it set, and I began to think again of what we were doing for the first time that day. Why should he be noticing the sunset? But he was noticing it, watching about the weather maybe, the chances for the night; no, he wasn't looking like that; it was those other things, he could drag those same thoughts out of me still. What a sky it was! Restless, slowly moving; and gathered now, far away, she stopped, lifted her head and spread her arms out towards us while the sun went down. Look at her. Ha! Red. Light. Straight. A vision. For the faithful a sign. Truth, naked, looking over the mountains. Toni, come down again, come down. But I said nothing. Toni. It was all he knew. It was so he had been taught. And when he was young, early, he had looked out of the window. How do I know that? How? I know it. I was there, I tell you, I was there at the time. The ascension to heaven. I couldn't get it out of my mind. And I knew perfectly what was going to happen. We were going to go straight up into the clouds, he and I, then we might or might not get down again.

We had arranged ourselves on the ledge and, close together, we would be able to sleep. We were well off, but I did not compose myself at once. His chances of survival for the next two years, I thought, are about fifty-fifty: as for me, I have fitted in nobly, have played my part, fool, and have even applauded. I couldn't get it out of my mind. I couldn't get the Alps out either. Then I dozed off.

We slept fitfully through the night, waited for the dawn, a lot of cloud about, then we set out. There was little snow on the next bit. I want to get on. All this is by the way. I think we both braced ourselves up; we were cold, and there was more cloud drifting around than we liked. The next bit was not too bad either. Three hundred to four hundred feet quite quickly, three pitons and they only for safety; perhaps we were over the worst; then a tiny ledge and the groove went on under snow, and we stood on the ledge leaning back against the last rocks to put on our crampons; and that heartened us; I think it would hearten a cow, that particular manoeuvre. Not? You think? With your back against the rock, bent slightly, putting on crampons? Oh, but you know it would! It increases a man's virility, any man's, tenfold. But it did not last. It never does. The snow was ice. The next eighty feet took hours, and then it didn't look too good up above. You know what it is when a cliff is too steep to start with and then the whole structure gets steeper, a little bulge. The steepest part was 120ft or so above us, and a big drop now below; the ice gave out in little runnels forty-foot up, couldn't hold on any longer, north face though it was. He got up forty, sixty, seventy feet, in about half an hour, scraped for a quarter of an hour, and at last, thank God, managed to get down again, found a crack to stick a piton in at forty feet and had a rest. I was shivering hard all that time, watching, and I too was tied on to a piton. What to do now? But his blood was up, a light in his eyes, no talk of surrender, he got down ten feet, traversed out right, quite quickly, on next to nothing, got a piton in I don't know how, let himself down on a long loop and swung out for the edge of the groove, got the rib by the nails of his fingers, more gymnastics, stuck in another piton, and rested. The other side sounded harder; I couldn't see; it took a long time; I didn't go that way myself, either; there was a sureness about hanging on to a rope and swinging, even a long swing, that was preferable in my mind to the longer drawn agony of trying to climb a traverse that you couldn't. I don't know why I'm going into all this, it's not the point, but it sticks in my memory, all this detail. I landed up bump in the next groove, jammed, breathless, into a shallow, square, little, overhang crack, quite a rarity, that crack; and I was surprised; I doubt if there's another crack good enough to jam in on this side of the mountain, and I struggled a bit, I can do that on the rope, got a sort of hold near the top, something stuck, but I gave a grunt of joy, pulled like hell, I am a man with great reserves of strength, though I seldom if ever get the chance to use them, and something snapped and up I went. I was exultant, I felt a lighter man, and it must have been a full second before it dawned on me; my rucksack; the sound of falling; my poor benighted rucksack. Yes, it was making tracks for home. In the wigwam of her fathers she would repose. Now she must be nearing the glacier. There she would burst and her contents would fly from her; separate, they would make their way each to their resting-place. The food; birds might have it. A pair of *kletterschuhe*; by luck a man might find them, some time. The camera; there would be no use for that now, not in this world. The sleeping things. Oh, the devil. What have I done, Toni? And as I came up towards him I almost began to speak to him of my feelings; but I stopped half-way, he was thinking already more of the cliff again than of me, and that was as it should be; for this groove we were in looked difficult and we were short of time, short of everything now.

We got up a bit, and another bit, or rather he did, then the mists came. Like the words of the prophet they stole over, among the ribs of the cliff, and covered us. Then the snow came. What a mess. We put on all that was wearable in Toni's sack, ate, tied on to a piton – we had pitons anyhow – and we scraped in the snow and went on. That did not mean much, but we did what we could. So at the end of the second day we were getting tired and we had got nowhere. We got a scrap of a ledge and anchored ourselves, up against each other, ropes crossed. There was a wind up now, and the snow swirled round us, coming in gusts, eddying very beautifully but appallingly cold. What sort of a job was this? Is there any way out of it? Hell. I for one would be frozen in two hours at this rate. No, I said, slow up; don't let your thoughts run away silly. Do you know, I've just got it, I have been wondering why I was here. My function is that I am the barometer of this party; I go up and down. Oh no, I had forgotten. As regards pressure, that boy doesn't oscillate; if you put him in space he wouldn't alter to speak of, he doesn't know how. Screwed up to a certain pitch throughout his conscious existence, for the last ten years or so, he has had no experience of any variation. If he had a barometer it would not move, unless it had burst perhaps, or unless, protesting, it had begun to vary like me on its own account. My going up and down, then, serves no purpose. My being here is no good. Toni. Then I looked at him more closely. One thing was certain. The boy was about done. There was nothing one could say.

The wind was cold but not very strong. We had a tiny bit of food. I had arranged his ropes very carefully, and mine, and we put our feet in the sack and settled down. We had two balaclavas, four good gloves. The snow coated over them and froze. We rubbed each other at intervals. I did not think at all that night. It was too cold. That's all I remember about it. Our hands and our feet froze; later on it became difficult to move arms and legs, and the cold went right through our bodies. But we did it, we lasted the night, and the next morning we took our feet out of the sack, pulled our-selves up into a standing position, creaking, leaning on the stiff cold rope, and trod about as best we could, painful and cold, to get moving. It must have been nearly two hours before we felt fit to go on, and the groove above looked hopeless; but you never know on a cliff, and as we went up foot by foot, using plenty of pitons, leading alternately, clearing masses of snow, it seemed not impossible. We kept to very short pitches, he did the harder bits. Once, close above me, he was swept clean off by a small snowslide. I fielded him. He gasped, got a footing, and held on. Are you hurt? he said. Me, no, me? Not me, no, I said. He said nothing. His face was rigid and he did not look quite full at me. We went on again. The wind hardened and set round more to the north, blowing right into the groove, colder than ever. Climbing at this rate we didn't get on much, we didn't even keep warm. But we went on steadily, rather desperate. The details of it will not come to my mind now; I doubt if they were ever taken into it. At about five o'clock it looked as if things were getting easier, but the weather was worse than ever, blowing really hard now. We hadn't a chance, though we must be getting near the summit. I looked at Toni and suggested a rest. The storm increased in violence. It might blow itself out any time, but meanwhile it was not possible. Toni was not breathing properly, damn it. I supported his head. He looked at me but could not speak. Toni, Toni, I thought; Toni, why did you listen always to the sounds of the mountains and to those things; and if you had listened some time to me also, and to my voice. Then his eyes went wild a little, they were a little wild always, and then he cried, sobbed out aloud on my shoulder. Not long after that he died.

But murder, you say. There was no one else present, you say, no murderer. So? Nobody else? Have you forgotten the singing, have you forgotten the scenery, the wild scenery? And how are you here to tell the tale, you ask? How! Do you not understand?

But the boy himself, Toni, my friend? Did he die? Was he killed? Or I, or was I alone? Well, those are quite different matters, and really I must confess I don't know. But take it which way you like, that does not alter the facts; and make no mistake about it: that does not justify that very wild scenery; nor does it justify murder.

from THE CLIMBERS' CLUB JOURNAL *1939*

TWENTY-FOUR HOURS

ROBIN SMITH

Whereas a lot of Robin Smith lies undeniably on 'some Russian mountain,' the rest of him goes on as strong as ever. *Editor – SMC Journal**

In the morning the three of us climbed Route I on Nevis. This was Ian's third climb, he had climbed a Difficult, a Very Difficult and now a Severe, and so we thought we should go and climb a Very Severe. Down and round the corner we came to the foot of Raeburn's Buttress. A long scramble leads to a sudden steep buttress which falls back and narrows to a shattered arête running up to the summit plateau, and the buttress in the middle is the bit that gives the trouble. There, the other routes sneak round the side, as the front of the buttress is too steep, but the Crack goes up the front. From below the climb looks deceptively easy; the first pitch just looks steep, and the rest vertical.

*Robin Smith and Wilfrid Noyce were killed in a fall from the West Ridge of Pik Garmo in the Pamirs in 1962

There are four main pitches, a wall leading to the base of the Crack and
three crack pitches. You think all is well, you will scramble up to the base of
the Crack and if it looks nasty come down; the wall looks like eighty feet of
three foot steps, but the wall is a winking monster. You rush off upwards,
but as you rush you feel the wall swing smoothly up through 30°, and then
you aren't rushing any more but are strung up on nasty little overhangs
topped by littler sloping ledges with the odd little crack in the back which
will take a few fingers once you scrape out the mud and the ooze and the
moss. At fifty feet you fix a wretched runner, which at least gives Ted something to do, for you are feeling him muttering up the rope, and then you
climb another thirty feet to reach the stance which slopes at round about 30°
and you look for a belay. You throw off several boulders, big ones, until there
are only small ones left, and then you get fed up and hope you've thrown
off all the loose ones and take a belay on a small one.

Then you are Ted, and you climb up quicker because you know the way
to go, but you find it just as nasty and the rope doesn't go straight up but is
bent and if you let go you're in for a swing but you don't let go. You reach
the stance but there's no room for two, so you find some more boulders to
the right, big ones, and you squat on top of the biggest and probably loosest.

And then you are both Ian and depressed. This wall has depressed all
three of you, but now the first two are on top and don't want to come down,
the third is at the bottom, and doesn't want to climb up. Anyway it is getting
on and the first two have been slow and there is hardly time for a party of ·
three to get up. You take a step or two, prod the rock here and there, take a
step or two down, untie and elect to watch.

You aren't surprised that there follows a chaos of ropes. This is sometimes
found with Smith around, and here, standing on sloping slime and balancing
boulders, with two ropes and a thumbnail belay, they take some time to swap
stances. The first Crack pitch is fifty feet long and is really a chimney. It
overhangs and is undercut and the entry is rotten, and so it is awkward to
enter, but the rest is alright and they get up it alright; then they go to the
right and seem to hang around on the overhanging wall, but they will tell
you later that a ledge runs right for ten feet from the top of the chimney and
they dig out a belay down the back of a block on the right.

And now they are thus. Wise is tied to the right end of the ledge. Smith
stands ten feet left. The ledge is two or three feet wide, slopes, is heaped
with rubble, cuts out of the overhanging wall in profile like the centre stroke
of a streak of lightning. The wall below then cuts back under them, above it
hangs over them thrusting them outwards. The Crack swings up and over
to the left from the left edge of the ledge. For twenty feet it overhangs,
overhanging walls on either side, but then the left wall falls back as a steep

slant, while the right wall still overhangs and hides the rest of the crack from Smith and Wise on the ledge to the right. From the bottom you can see that the crack continues in the corner between the slab and the overhang, and once they are on the slab the crux will be past, but by now the light is going, you can hardly see them, and so the rest of the story is my own unbiased version. It took me about five grunting attempts, blowing myself up to jam in the crack, wriggling up and hissing down, deflated, until at last I could twist up and over the final bulge and get on to the slab on the left. The way was now clear to the third and last overhang fifty feet above, the crack was still steep, but the holds were great and good. I went up twenty feet or so, and tied on to a belay, but it wasn't a very good one. I went a bit higher and took a better belay; then I hauled up our spare food and clothes in the rucksack; then Ted joined the two ropes and tied on to the lower one, so that I had a great pile of slack to pull in; and this was all to the good.

By now Ted had been crouched on the ledge for a long cold time, and his stomach was sinking with the sun, but he came straight away, and from my belay I could see vertically down the crack, and through the overhang, and I made out bits of Ted blocking the light as he climbed to the left, then I saw his head coming up from under the overhang, and then he had wrapped himself over the bulge, and his hands were above the bulge, one hand in the crack, and one hand on the slab, he was very nearly there with only one more move to make, but there he came off. He was on a tight rope, but with the stretch of the nylon he went down about two feet and swung away from the overhang. His fingers were too tired to pull him back, he was hanging on the rope, slowly spinning, with nothing below him for about 150ft but a few slight bulges near the bottom. Now I hadn't a clue as to what was going on, he shouted to be lowered, so I just lowered away, chortling the while. He told me later that the ledge he had started from was too far to the right, he was wanting to pendulum in to a smaller ledge sticking out of the overhang thirty feet below, so he began to swing himself towards and away from the face, but when he first reached the rock he was above the ledge, as he swung away, I was lowering him past it, and when he swung in again he was too low down. A little lower he swung in to something else, but it wasn't much good and he was spinning round and before he could land he had pendulumed back and further down into space. Halfway down the angle eased a bit, and from there the face was just a little less than vertical and Ted went spiralling down here and there brushing a bulge until at last he landed on the easy rocks at the foot of the first pitch.

So Ian and Ted were safe at the bottom, they were all right Jack but I was not. I couldn't climb down and I wasn't going to abseil, because we might have lost our ropes and I didn't like abseils. They offered to go away around by the Castle Ridge to the summit plateau, then down the arête of Raeburn's Buttress to give me a top rope on twenty feet of overhang, but that would have taken a month, already they could see me only when I moved as a darker blur against the darkness, and those last twenty feet didn't look so bad. The face was a great leaning overhang, but the Crack cut up through the middle looking deep enough and wide enough to let me get right inside and wriggle safely up. I told them below, it would go quite easily; they could go back to the hut and I'd join them in a couple of hours.

So they beetled off and I pulled up our 220ft of rope and draped it in a shambles round my neck, then with the rucksack on my back I climbed up to the foot of the overhang. Just there, there was a good ledge, going left, and I thought, this is a good thing because I can stand on it while I look at the overhang. But the overhang didn't look so good now, it looked as though it might not be deep enough to climb as a straight chimney. Moreover my arms were getting fed-up and my stomach and back were all cramped after lowering and laughing at Ted. I tried the first few feet, then came down and dumped the ropes and the rucksack on the ledge, then tried them again and came down. I tied on to one end of the rope and allowed enough slack to reach the top of the pitch, then I tied the rest of the rope and the rucksack together in a bundle so that I could pull them up after me when I got up.

The Crack was at first about a foot wide, which was wide enough, and although it started shallow it soon cut back deeply enough to let me get right inside, but just before the end of the overhang the recess was blocked by a roof. So from under the roof I had to wriggle sideways to the edge of the Crack, and leaning out, fumble for the guidebook's good holds over the overhang, then swing out of the Crack and swarm over the top. When I reached the roof at wriggle level I was facing the right wall of the Crack. Just at head level throughout the wriggle the Crack was too narrow to let my head turn, it had to face sideways, either into the recess or out towards space. I set off on the wriggle, at first facing the recess, but I went too high and my head got stuck, so I came back and I thought, if I face the recess then I can't see where I'm going. I set off again, facing space, and I got to the end of the wriggle and finished up leaning out of the Crack. From here I began to fumble and before long I found the good holds, but I thought, rot the guide-book, these are obviously poor. I had no qualms about the swing, it was just that having swung I might not make the swarm, and I might not manage to swing back, and around this time I looked down through my feet and I was looking straight over the overlay below and if it had not been so dark I would have looked straight down to the bottom of the climb and I shrank up into the Crack like a scared slug's horns. Then I began to reverse the wriggle, but I was still facing space and I soon got stuck and I thought, like this I can't find my footholds. So I wriggled out again to the edge of the Crack and I leaned away out and I turned my head, then I came back along the wriggle facing the recess and this time I got to the back of the Crack. From here I had just to go down about eighteen feet, but going down in my state was still quite hard. I struggled and hung and scraped and finally jumped to the left and landed on the ledge that was to be a good thing because it was going to let me look at the overhang.

There I sat for a while and blew and waited for a bit of strength, and I knew it must be getting very late. The sun was way down on the other side of the Ben and had see-sawed the shadows from the Allt a'Mhuillin up the screes of Càrn Mòr Dearg to cover up the redness. I cursed and stamped about a bit and then went back to the Crack which was really rather stupid because already it was so dark I could hardly see the holds. I got up the Crack to wriggle level, but only just, and I wedged myself away up in the back and refused to wriggle out and couldn't see how to get down. I had already been getting resigned to a night on the ledge, but unless I could find my way down I would have to pass the night trying to stay stuck in an overhanging crack.

All was well, however, and with a lot of luck and a fiendish scrabbling I finally got back to the ledge before I had fallen off, and by then it was sure that I wasn't going to get any further, but relative to an overhanging crack it seemed a very desirable sort of place. The ledge was about eight feet long and only slightly sloping. The right end was quite a bit higher than the left, and so I had to lie with my head at the right end, but unfortunately this was also the narrow end; the left was about one-and-a-half feet wide but the right end was less than a foot. Below the ledge the face went down for about twenty feet as the sort of steep slab that you can just about sit on without any holds, and then it heeled over into the overhangs. There was a thick moss growing all over the ledge and the slab, and I thought, this will be a good thing because it will be soft to lie on. Then I opened the rucksack and I found a spare anorak and jersey of Ted's and a jersey of my own. I pulled a jersey over my trousers and put the rest on in the normal fashion; then I found chocolate and raisins and an orange, and so I was really having it easy. I threaded a sling behind a chockstone in the Crack above my head, and I tied on to one end of the rope and threaded it through the karabiner in the sling and fixed it as a belay. Then I bundled up the rest of the rope as a pillow, and put my feet in the rucksack as all the best books recommend, and lay on my back all buckled up on the ledge. The belay could have stopped me from falling right off but still I couldn't relax because then my head slipped off the narrow end of the ledge. So I fixed the belay rope from my waist under my left arm to come out at my left shoulder and from there to the chockstone. My left hand could keep it taut between my shoulder and the chockstone, and so my head could lean out against the rope which kept it from slipping off the ledge. In this position and after a fashion I was able to relax, and so for an hour or two, but the night was very clear and I began to get cold, and only then it occurred to me that I could make more use of the moss than as a mattress. I tore away great lumps of moss and earth from the ledge, and when I had scraped it clean I started scraping the slab below as far as I could scrape. Then I arranged myself on the ledge again and piled all the vegetation on top and beat it into a great mud pie that covered me all but my head and I passed the rest of the night in comparative warmth.

Sometimes I dozed a little, and now and again I bawled at the night with great bursts of skiffle all about a worried man and long-lost John and Stewball and the like until the stars began to disappear and a vague sort of lightness began to come up from behind the back of Càrn Mòr Dearg. Then it was all red with sunrise and I could see everything clearly and I realised that it would be a good thing to extricate myself before search parties began to appear. I threw off the moss and scraped off some of the filth that stuck to me. I stamped about and beat myself for warmth and arranged the ropes and the rucksack and then struggled up the Crack to the roof and wriggled out to the edge. But everything was cold and I was stiff and I dithered about for a long time until I heard distant shoutings from below. I looked around and I saw four figures coming up from the CIC to pick up my body from the foot of the climb. I shouted back but they could not see me in the Crack, and so, glad of an excuse to go down, I struggled back to the ledge and waved things till they saw me. As they came a little nearer our shouting became a little more intelligible, but still we could hardly understand each other and it was only when I saw them making for Castle Ridge that I realised they were coming round to rescue me. With horrid visions of top ropes and tight ropes and ignominy and the like I felt the need to do something to save the situation, but then as I was bullying myself to go back and wriggle in the nasty overhang. I noticed below me, twenty feet lower down the Crack from the ledge, a line of weakness crossing the face to the right. It had been too dark to see it the night before, but now it looked very promising. I left everything on the ledge and went down to have a look. I traversed well out to the right and it was not at all hard, and from there it was easy to go right round the bulge and back to the Crack above the stupid overhang that had stopped me for so long. By now the rescue party was well up Castle Ridge. I bawled to them to stop and so they stopped to see what I was up to. I went back to the ledge to gather all the gear around me, then down and out along the easy traverse and up and round to the top of the overhang. The rest was simple and I scrambled up the Crack till it disappeared at the terrace below the final arête of the buttress. The arête looked very good in the sun, but I thought I should get down as soon as I could as my rescuers were coming down and across to the foot of the rocks. I found a narrow shelf cutting down across the right wall and into the corrie between Raeburn's Buttress and the Castle Ridge. I rushed along this to the rumble of slabs in the corrie and I slithered down these in a great haste and a great shambles of ropes and rucksack and coated with filth and moss to make my peace on the screes at the foot of the rocks.

from EDINBURGH UNIVERSITY MOUNTAINEERING
CLUB JOURNAL *1957*

SOMETIMES YOU KNOW –
SOMETIMES YOU DON'T

JIM SINCLAIR

I knew it was the crux. It had taken two days to get here, in some ways much longer. I was sixty feet out from Chris, between us was a tied-off knife blade, a small part of it in the incipient crack. The rest of its length protruded out and down, but it would have to do. It was like walking down Granville Street with every neon sign selling the same message ...

'It won't hold a fall.'

I tried to calculate it. I'd drop twenty-five feet if the pin held, and I could extricate myself easily enough. But if it didn't, I'd go 120ft, probably hit the ledge thirty feet below Chris and at best be seriously hurt. Perhaps fifteen minutes had gone by and I hadn't moved; nineteen years of rock climbing was working in my head – I just didn't know if I could get over this last bit or not. There was no bolt kit, no crack – not even a cliff hanger helped. It was free it or go down. Going down was tricky but no major problem. But could we go up?

There seemed to be a microflake at knee level on the steep wall. Was that another six foot above it? Eyes inches from the rock, the hand caresses over it. Yes! A ripple perhaps $\frac{1}{32}$nd of an inch ... but a ripple! Somewhere in the deepest being the pros and cons of justification are being weighed.

'You've stood on as small things before,' the pros say.

'I know,' you tell your other self. 'But this could lead nowhere. I wasn't facing death then, or may be I was. I don't know. But that was then, this is now. World do I love life! Why do I come up here anyway? There stupid, up there, above the right hand.'

The demon pros never let go. The judgement must be exact, precise, infinite. I stood on tip-toe feeling very secure on the inch ledge I was standing on. Strange, when I'd first reached it I was apprehensive about stepping onto it. Now, twenty minutes later, it felt like a ballroom floor. I was safe, if only I didn't try to use the microflake.

Yes! Yes! It was there – a little fingerhold. I wouldn't quite reach it from the ledge but it was there, inches above my reach. The years of climbing, worn out *kletterschuhe,* discarded ropes and the voice of judgement convinced me it was there. But I couldn't quite reach it.

This was no boulder problem, no jump off and try again game. It was the ability to move up and judgement of whether you can or not. You get one chance in the game. You judge right the first time or you don't play again. The left foot went to the microflake and immediately skidded off.

'Howya doing up there, man?' said Chris, secure on his ledge, two comfortable pitons for a station, basking in the sunshine.

'It's hairy buddy, I just don't know about this.'

No answer, then: 'How's that pin?'

'The shits,' I call down ... no answer.

Again, for reasons unknown, the left foot creeps toward the microflake. Slowly ease my weight to it and even get a few pounds off the right foot before retreating back to the ballroom floor. It had held! My left foot had held!

I lit a smoke, trying to get the green taste out of my mouth and waiting for it to happen. What a beautiful thing, a horrible thing like a cigarette was at a time like this. Far down in the valley a crow glided. Below him little toy cars weaved their way through the forest following a white line that never ended. The cigarette finished, with no conviction to do or die, but rather attracted as to a magnet, I again brushed off the little hold. The left foot went up, weight eased over just right, right hand reaching for the sky. I touched it, tips of fingers deep into its ripples. The right foot is ten inches from the ballroom floor ... fifteen inches! Don't come off now, left foot. Please don't come off now. The neon signs are exploding in the head and you know, absolutely, that the piton will not hold a fall. You're committed, it's only fifteen inches to the ballroom floor but there was no getting back.

To the onlooker you suspend there, climbing to nothing, defying gravity to the extreme. Perhaps a suicidal maniac with a death wish, at best a misled youth surely to die. The tricouni set would call you an engineer, safe on your ladder of pitons and hardly climbing at all. You reach a state of near total fusion with what you're doing. Every fibre of the body is instinctively controlled to place the fingers a few inches higher to the hold that must be there. To breed your left foot with the microflake, to seduce it and so to be a part of it. No longer is anything done consciously. The years of training have taken over. The instincts are in control of your body, mind, nerves and soul. They creep your fingers upward even as you know you're moving off, you're on the brink. There is no time but the minute part of the second difference in which will be first, the left foot coming off or the fingers touching the ripple above. There is no distance but the fifteen inches back to the ballroom floor. There is no problem in life greater than the placing of a finger an inch higher. Then it's there, the left hand goes out, a good hold, mantel up ... it's over.

We were on easy terrain, moving fast to the top and I wondered. What if we'd climbed to the crux and retreated off? Did we climb to the crux or were we leading up to the climb? Did we do a two day route? A 200ft wall? Or did we do a one hour climb, fifteen inches high?

from THE CANADIAN ALPINE JOURNAL 1974

DROP, PLOP, FLY OR DIE

IAN McNAUGHT-DAVIS

Last year I was invited to the Annual Dinner of the London section of the Fell and Rock Climbing Club of the English Lake District – how's about that for being in touch with where it's at? Far from being 'Harrison's on Wednesday evening, up the M1 to Derbyshire grit or limestone for a quick Sunday, and the Lake District every other weekend in a Ford Cortina types', they turned out to be your original aged ramblers planning mass walks across the 'Downs' or the 'Chilterns'.

I was scheduled to give one of my normally high-octane boring speeches, which have kept me fed throughout the past few winters.

Having arrived rather late, I hadn't been able to absorb either atmosphere or alcohol and felt coldly analytical as I toyed with my prawn cocktail or whatever concoction the catering profession was passing as sumptuous fare that week. I looked round at an incredible cross-section of the British climbing scene and reflected on what the hell I was going to talk about as soon as I had drunk the tepid coffee served by the usual grumpy waitresses anxious to be off to their bed-sits in Balham.

Well, I thought, they must have climbed at one time so why weren't they climbing now? It couldn't have been simply a matter of age – there are as many men over sixty leading hard climbs as there are women of any age. So what was the core pleasure of climbing that they had stopped enjoying? According to Les Holliwell, real climbers enjoy one thing above all else, and that is seizing two good holds made of warm, sunlit granite and pulling up on them, possibly over and over again. And of course he's absolutely right. But there is more to it than that; just as football is about kicking people, cricket about throwing or hitting balls at people, and car-racing about crashing cars, so climbing is about falling off.

Taking advantage of my total-recall mind, I quickly scanned the pundits on this particular issue. Blackshaw doesn't mention it, Winthrop Young ignores it; but Whymper records it, boasts about it, revels in it. And there it stood plain, the pleasure centre of climbing – falling off.

In the old days, before chocks, wires, nuts, hexcentrics and other modern protection hardware, climbers who fell off usually died. The few that survived became hero figures. As in the case of VC winners, tales of how they won their manhood became distorted and linked with courage and bravery, instead of stupidity and folly. It was difficult to obtain a true opinion when the results were so often so terminal.

Nowadays, of course, the true importance of falling off has been fully recognised, and hardware and techniques have been developed to prolong and intensify the pleasure, so we are in a better position to analyse its significance.

As the number of survivors has increased, it has become clear that there is a wide methodology in the art of falling off, and a whole vocabulary has been developed to describe the numerous advanced techniques. (I believe this is the first time these have been catalogued. I must, however, warn any inexperienced climbers that the following procedures should only be adopted when no other alternative is available.)

To Bomb Off: to make an uncontrolled free fall, usually associated with fingers or holds giving out unexpectedly.

To Flirt Off: to undergo slow, semi-controlled loss of contact with the rock, usually on a slab or easy snow. Can quickly be converted to a 'bomb' (see above).

To Flash Off: to display rapid, showy, non-serious loss of control, usually on an outcrop.

To Plop Off: to fall into water. Alternatively, according to certain authoritative Northern (UK) sources, to fall whilst making it.

To Crater (US): to fall and hit the ground.

To Total (US): to bomb and subsequently crater from anything over 100ft (not recommended).*

A Birdman: a prolonged free fall, where advanced techniques such as shouting 'I'm off' or flapping the arms can be used to prolong the experience.

To Slip: to make a technical error. Can develop into a birdman-crater-total sequence on the part of beginners, but intermediate and advanced students can usually limit the consequences unless tired.

To Fall Off: to undergo a careless, non-technical fall. Usually done by advanced climbers on easy routes when bored or tired.

A Lob: a dynamic leap for a non-existent hold. Rapidly converted by non-experts into a bomb.

Early attempts were made by several distinguished climbers, and groups of climbers, to develop the techniques of falling. Particularly important in this respect were the following.

Alf Bridge: Worked on the theory that falls could be a series of controlled jumps from minute hold to minute hold. He was successful in proving this by making unbelievable controlled falls without injury. Unfortunately this line of development seems to have lost momentum with the development of better protection techniques on which most climbers rely to reduce falling distances. It is useful on slabs, but of limited use on walls and, as I can testify, no use at all on overhangs.

Hamish Nicol: President of the Climbers' Club. Made a considerable number of high velocity experiments and, as a founder of the Alpine Climbing Group, was one of the first people to break the stigma attached to falling off. Reputed to have over thirty falls, totalling over 4000ft, to his credit, with only a fractured skull and jaw to show for it.

Lord Hunt: Doyen of the falling fraternity, and once known as 'The Tumbling Knight'. His contributions to the art have only been released to a select few friends.

Cambridge University: Educational establishment that made considerable early contributions to the art, particularly on beginners' meets. At the height of their gravitational phase the President – one of their most prolific exponents – was reputed to keep a weekly 'lob book' of his falls.

I reflected on how many fallers I had known, the unknown diver from

---

*To this could be added 'Pine Boxing' (US orig. Shawangunks, c.1970s).

some sea-cliff crux, the 'giggling glider' who laughed his way down many a crag – they were all real contributors to the essence of our sport. Waking with a start, I looked round the room and immediately realised why the London Fell and Rockers had lost interest in climbing and were now content with tedious pastoral strolls. So my speech began:

'Ladies and Gentlemen, it appears that many of you have lost interest in climbing, and perhaps tonight you will take time to think why. The real reason is that you have forgotten that climbing is about falling off, and you have built up a resistance to enjoying this key element of your sport. I am going to bring back the thrill of the first fall, the sensation of the summer wind blowing through your hair as you do a birdman with the smell of ivy in your nostrils…'

And so it went on, lyrical, revealing and brilliant. I have never been invited again.

from MOUNTAIN 39 *1974*

IN THE GROOVE

JAMES MARSHALL

Nevis, the most massive, malevolent, most elevated lump of rock on these islands, is itself an island, humping hideous flanks from endless bogs, hard to equal for hidden depths of character.

Years of visitation, pursuing obscure ways traced by obscure men, less obscure men or obviously insane men had led inevitably to the conclusion that the hardest route on the mountain is the Allt a'Mhuillin track to the hut…

Countless proud ambitious men have broken on that evil thrash, to spend ensuing days gazing vacuously from the door of the hut. Drained of all spunk and harrowed by the vision of a return bout with black clutching bogs. The Marquis de Sade must have sited that damned hut!

However, as the saying goes, it's an ill bog… and doubtless the trials of the track made contribution to the exploration of the craggy Ben. Only hardened men survive its noxious cruxes and so emerge anaesthetised from mental anguish, climbers capable of accepting intolerable conditions, cataracts of snow, rock, ice, rain or bodies; endowed with an ability to explore a myriad unclimbed crannies with a seemingly callous indifference.

But that's what it's all about, a state of mind, induced indifference to discomfort and danger within and without the hut. Much deliberation and endeavour left me convinced the best Guide to the mountain was an immense notice at the roadside – DANGER KEEP OFF. Obviously my motives would have been misconstrued, therefore a guidebook eventually appeared; but it is still a confirmed opinion and one unlikely to be withdrawn. With any luck, debilities of old age will arrive to preclude over-frequent participation in the horrors of that track and exposure to the fearful crags above.

In review, it's hard to isolate events sufficiently singular or dramatic to justify inclusion in a journal; after all one story of a climb ends much like another and a collection of such produces yet another boringly familiar *Journal*. However, from a kaleidoscope of 'joyous days' and harrowing times a few occasions provide enough colour to justify the risk of further boring a sanguine few.

There's the story of the gentle giant and dwarf working away on the summit plateau hacking lead from the old observatory, packing it into sacks and toiling down and up the Ben for a week to earn a miserable £20. To improve turnover a muckle great load was rammed into a rucksack on the giant's back, but the bottom fell out! Empty oil drums were then carried up from the CIC, packed with lead and rolled towards Glen Nevis for a 4000ft trundle. A disaster for workers and sheep! The drums were lost, never to be found again; presumably carried off by motorists, or the motorists carried off by the drums. Anyone ascending this slope in future should beware the rolling of distant drums.

Another time, a small group of horrible SMC men, strolling under the N.E. Buttress, scattered in fright as a great boulder plummeted 1500ft from the summit. Closer encounter proved it to be the body of a now deceased 'instructor', which was duly carted down and deposited in the long stretcher box behind the hut, to await police collection. Later, a wee chancer looked into the hut to scrounge a bed for the night and was told he could sleep in the box behind the hut. His ensuing retches had the stags roaring for miles around.

Then there's the Groove Climb on South Trident Buttress. Stenhouse and I, checking out Kellett climbs, looked for a groove in the middle tier. Well there is one, a huge great one, so we climbed it. It matched the description OK but for the exit, where Kellett said a choice of routes led to the top; our only choice proved to go back down the groove or, as was done, to climb a vertical wall of unbelievable looseness.

We rationalised the disparity by assuming that a great rockfall had occurred since the passing of the pioneer, and at the same time we noted the groove could provide a good winter climb.

Years passed before the chance arose to try it. Accompanied by Elly the gentle giant I spent the first day on the lower cliffs of North-East Buttress delicately cramponing up brittle ice, wondering when the whole lot would crackle off the face and us along with it. A worrying thought with such a big lad on the other end of the rope! ... but it never did and the next day saw us under The Trident. It was snowing and blowing as I pointed out the groove. Elly gave me an old-fashioned look but, being gentle, acquiesced and we shuffled out along a ledge until the slopes buffed our noses, where we roped and belayed right under the groove. To those who don't know the scene, we were now in the middle of a two-tiered buttress which looks like a petit, Petit Dru with us perched in the *niche*.

The groove looked thin and hard, the forty-foot entry wall glazed and awkward, with spurts of powder drifting down, so I bashed a peg between loose flakes and offered the toil to Elly. Up he went, showing the soles of his boots, forty feet to a string runner, then leftward a little into the groove and out of sight. Winter's worries assailed me, the axe belay was useless, the peg doubtful, but at least it would save me extruding through snaplinks above! Muffled mumblings and excuses filtered down the rope; brittle ice, glazed bulges etc.; the gut began to tighten, he's an enormous bloke, must get a grip and think happy thoughts. Och, he'll be all right, he's so tall he's over most problems before they start, the happy thoughts prevail and I peer into the grim corrie below. The rope moves up, good, that's the bulge over, and then – a great rasping, rumbling, thrashing, tumbling offends my ear. I race the rope back through the string runner, Jesus Christ! there isn't a higher runner. Elly streaks out off the groove head down like a 225lb torpedo, my eyes are on stalks as he smashes a crater from the ledge and bounces out into orbit. I wrap the rope tight and think of the 500ft drop below – Whang he comes on the rope, I'm up in the air. If you've got to go ... he's got his, now for mine. From a funk cocoon, I hear the peg creaking and crackling, feel the fat gut being severed by a searing rope, how to get rid of that great weighty cadaver, we seem all set to tumble down the cliff. I slip the rope a wee bit to get back on my feet, then a yelp comes up from the other end of the rope and a blood-covered face peers over the edge of the lip. Elly, get on your feet you big bastard, miraculously he does, reeling about like he never does drunk, what a relief to get the weight off! Remorseful now, I ask him to shamble off along the ledge and I follow, get him on a short rope and with gaze averted from the great bloodstained visage usher him on to the slopes of the corrie, to thankfully, plank our butts in the snow.

Our shakes subside and gingerly we examine the extent of damage; incredibly, that cranium is as solid as ever! Then scrubbing off the gore with snow we discover the only damage (apart from pride) to be a tiny quarter-inch cut on the bridge of the nose. However, we're too shattered to push our luck any further and decide to descend.

A party of English, timorously pushing upward, meet enormous blood-stained Elly looming through the drifting snows, to have their awed enquiries treated with traditional disdain in his reply 'Never mind, but dinnae go up there, the whole bloody corrie's avalanchin'.*

Frights come and go, though some don't go too easy, so winters later, salved by an absence of like trauma, the groove was elected as a climb sufficiently possible to our degenerated competence.

The omens looked right, dark gloomy day, equally gloomy team, snarling winds building up for a storm; so with brother Ronnie and Robin Campbell the ledge was traversed to forge strong belays beneath the groove.

In no mood to relive the agonies of another wait, I left the others grumbling and clambered up the wall, sticking runners on every available nobble in sight. Then into the groove to hack away over variable bulges, past the one which had collapsed under Elly. From here it seemed impossible to survive such a nose dive. However the ice was better this time so on I went to belay above, subsequently to be joined by the others.

We were at the foot of an open bay, from which the exit was an overhanging chimney, spume belched over it now and again, so Robin was elected to force the way. He wasn't keen and complained all the way up but we jeered him on to fumble above the bulge, lying about the big holds supposedly there: but Campbell's no daft, and a fine ledge beckoned him away to the right. Despite our vile curses, he took the opportunity, suitably hidden by the now healthy blizzard, to disappear along the ledge out of our sight. A faraway hail took brother away and I hung about, engulfed every now and again by spume avalanches, freezing stiff and cursing Campbell for piking out of the direct; mind you, I disliked its look enough not to try it personally ...

At last the call came to move and moved by curiosity I hurried to examine his escape route. It led along the edge of a flake into a chimney crack perched on the outer edge of the groove. Hell, the man must have been frightened thin to get through there; above, I could hear the two of them laughing away. 'Did you pair squeeze through this bloody hole?' 'Yes' they chorused with

---

*Elly Moriarty, a Darth Vader-like presence in the Edinburgh group of climbers and, with Dougal Haston, one of the developers of the Currie Walls, died of natural causes in October 2005.

malicious glee. So I pushed, squeezed, snarled, swore and stuck; I thought I'd never escape, at least not till the fat starved off. Eventually I managed to extricate downwards, relieved at the release.

More swearing, then I asked the now hilarious pair above to throw the rope out over the face. Decently they did so; after all, they could just as well have abandoned me to the crows. The rope hung clear of the face, I hooked it in with the axe, tied on, then they heaved and I heaved, eventually to be landed like a flaying salmon on a snowy ledge. Ten minutes deriding the cowardly nature of their rabbiting, then off up the arête, blasted by storm eventually, to amaze them with a maze of obscure ledgeways spiralling downward to the peace of the corrie below.

All in all, a good day, somewhat negative but still an entertaining day and sufficiently satisfying to eliminate a return bout with that awful groove.

Months later during a balmy spring walk around the corrie the whole scene clicked into place. Our route was not Kellett's Groove Climb after all. That climb lay tucked in a corner well to the left, a tiny little chimney, ours loomed and leered in splendid scale above, a classic Nevis joke.

from THE SCOTTISH MOUNTAINEERING
CLUB JOURNAL *1971*

BREAKING THROUGH

BOB BARTON

It's always the same. Pulling tight your waist knot and looking up, optimistically keen, but nervous, and then away, but awkwardly, not yet adjusted to the way it is; hollow and shaky. Then the barriers drift away and you're in touch, happier now, enjoying thinking out the moves and balancing up in a kind of stuttering, bubbling flow.

A good feeling. Like chess or fast driving, but with more involvement, importance. More expansive.

You reach a tiny ledge on the edge of a groove. A small runner and then you look up the columns of blank rock to the peg, almost hidden in the shadowed groove.

Perhaps not.

But the ego won't let you think about going back, so up you go, bridging delicately. Two diagonal lines of stress with you tensed at the centre, concentrating – acutely aware of your equilibrium, almost afraid to move, but shifting and leaning up and across and away above it all.

The ledge is small but welcome. You're going well and know it, and can really enjoy the wait at the stance. It's strange how quickly the time passes when you're absorbed in the route; it was damp and cloudy when I started, but now the sun has appeared, and just beyond the wall of my corner the rock dazzles and gleams, with a razor-sharp boundary between the shadow and the hard light.

It's warmer now too and John soon arrives at the stance. We swap around and then I'm off again into the light and across the wall towards the big crack. It looks steep and hard and the exposure is menacing, but a good runner overcomes the second thoughts and inertia and I quickly make a couple of awkward pulls into a niche with a big chock. The rock here is quartzy with large purple-pink lozenges so that when I finally get the sling around the chock I have cut myself, and the red smears spread on the grey rock. I can feel my push evaporating. I'm hanging around too much. No aggression in me. Pull your bloody finger out.

Eventually, I convince myself to go on, but after a few feet the holds begin to fade. The Crux.

I can hang here on this jam but it's steep and I keep having to get a poorer jam for the left hand to rest the right; when I change back my right hand fits perfectly in the crack, but there's a brutality in tensing the muscles against the sharp quartz which turns on my aggression. I keep going up and down up and down the first few feet but each time something is missing. This is the thing that terrifies me, having to force myself at the crux without having sorted it out; I'm still not willing to go and I'm beginning to think perhaps I can't do it after all.

I look down and across at John and when he looks back his eyes are cold and empty. No encouragement there, but I can't really blame him, the time I'm spending hanging about.

One more go. Up or down. Do or die. I get to my familiar high point quickly, but this time I use my momentum to carry me up a little bit higher, so that I can lever myself up on the jam instead of pulling outwards, and I can stretch and reach a small pocket with the other hand.

I am arched and tensed but this could be my apogee and there's a flash of indecision before I commit myself, and *suddenly everything clicks* and I begin to go and swing up and out and irresistibly on and up and the concentration is blinding and ecstatic and the light screams on and up into the heart of it all, burning tomorrow's stars into extinction and I'm outside too and can look across at how I move and sway and it is clean and hard and beautiful till I overflow with screams of fullness and my mind is still.

O Jesus Christ no. No, no, no, not…

As the boy falls he wheels gently and slowly in the air, black and haloed against the low sun, and moves downwards, down further and faster until the slim rope through the runner comes up tight while the other rope snakes wildly and futilely. But the chock pulls out and arcs across the path of the boy, whose slow spirals continue, and you see the inevitability of it all as he arrows silently towards the stones in the gully. The first runner offers no resistance and you close your eyes helplessly, for the inevitable is never pleasant to watch, and listen to the threatening murmur of the hills.

As the boy's head touches the rocks time crystallises for this is the Time of his Time, and he lives another lifetime while the crisp, hard white skull implodes, extinguishing the cold light of existence in his eyes and spilling his brain down the rough slopes of the lonely cwm.

What a beautiful way to die.

from CAMBRIDGE MOUNTAINEERING *1970*

THE LEADER

The leader, to restore his phlegm,
Designs an artful stratagem,
Aware that, with the rope below,
Should fate disturb the status quo,
Then twice the distance of the rope
He'd drop at speed, without much hope
(Acceleration, unimpaired,
Thirty-two feet per second squared).
He threads his rope through loops of line,
Running belays his anodyne! –
From fear alone; from harm no shield
When there's a deadly flaw concealed,
Producing from this scheme, though shrewd,
An undesired vicissitude.
He slips, and from above is heard
A very rude four-letter word;
Then screams, as he perceives too late
His unpremeditated fate:
The loops were thin, a masquerade
Of safety, and have snapped; betrayed,
He drops spreadeagled through the void,
An unprehensile anthropoid.
But from this lack of commonsense
Results no fatal consequence.
Our ignoramus is not dead:
You see, he landed on his head.

Keith McDonald 1961

FALLING

MIKE QUIGLEY

What would your innermost feelings be if confronted by imminent death? What is it like to fall off a cliff, or to be struck by bullets in wartime?

Through the years much has been discussed in literature, in biographical experiences and in story-telling about these intensely personal experiences. Yet little has been done within the scientific community to explain, for the benefit of self understanding, what it is like to face death, suddenly and without warning.

The entertainment industry has traditionally portrayed luckless catastrophe victims as undergoing their final moments on earth in screams of anguish, fear and desperation. We have come to accept this as a normal reaction to mortal incidents.

What really happens, in most cases, is just the opposite.

One of the few and perhaps most objective and thorough studies on actual near-death experiences took place before the turn of the century by a noted Swiss geologist, Albert von St Gallen Heim. His findings were reported in a 3800-word treatise entitled *Notizem uber dem Tod durch Absturz* (*Remarks on Fatal Falls*), which was published in the Yearbook of the Swiss Alpine Club in 1892.

Heim's research remains a basis from which further studies of this phenomena have begun.

Heim gathered his material from experiences of survivors of falls in the Alps. These he compared with the experiences of other catastrophe survivors such as soldiers wounded in battle, drowning victims, survivors of railroad accidents and persons who survived death while performing their jobs.

He concluded from his research that all final experiences are nearly the same irrespective of the type of catastrophe faced by the victim. He wrote:

> In nearly 95 percent of the victims there occurred, independent of the degree of education, thoroughly similar phenomena experienced with only slight differences. In practically all individuals who faced death through accidental falls a similar mental state developed. It represented quite a different state than that experienced in the face of less suddenly occurring mortal dangers.
>
> It may be briefly characterised by the following way: no grief was felt nor was there paralysing fright of the sort that can happen in instances of lesser

danger. There was no anxiety, no trace of despair, no pain; but rather a calm seriousness, profound acceptance and a dominant mental quickness and sense of surety. Mental activity became enormous, rising to a hundredfold velocity or intensity. The relationship of events and their probable outcomes were over-viewed with objective clarity. No confusion entered at all. Time became greatly expanded. The individual acted with lightning quickness in accord with accu-rate judgement of his situation. In many cases there followed a sudden review of the individual's past. And finally, the person falling often heard beautiful music and fell in a superbly blue heaven containing roseate cloudlets. Then consciousness was painlessly extinguished, usually at the moment of impact. And the impact was, at the most, heard but never painfully felt. Apparently hearing is the last of the senses to be extinguished.

Heim emphasised that in all instances there was no pain. Victims of falls could hear, but not feel, their bones breaking upon impact. Men struck by bullets had not felt the bullet's entry. He attributes this phenomenon to:

> Great mental excitement which causes a hypnosis that forces out pain sensations.

Shock, in present day terminology. Also, contrary to popular belief, a faller nearly always remains quiet during a fall. A scream is seldom heard and most fallers are totally conscious until the moment of violent impact. Another phenomenon reported was the often superhuman and methodical attempts to save oneself, even by children as young as two years old. Heim presented an accident involving himself as an example of how precise and logical mental planning takes place within a time span of a few seconds:

> In the summer of 1881 I fell between the front and rear wheels of a wagon travelling between Aosta and St. Remy and, for a fleeting moment, I was still able to hold on the edge of the wagon. The following series of thoughts went through my mind:
>
> I cannot manage to hold on until the horse comes to a stop. I must let go. I will fall on my back and the wheel will be unavoidable. I must fall upon my stomach and the wheel will pass over the backs of my legs. If I will tense the muscles, they will be a protective cushion for the bones. The pressure of the street will be somewhat less likely to break a bone than the pressure of the wheel. If I am able to turn myself to the left, then perhaps I can sufficiently draw back my left leg. On the other hand, turning to the right would, by the dimensions of the wagon, result in both legs being broken under it.
>
> Thereupon, through a jerk of my arm, I turned myself to the left, swung my left leg powerfully outward and simultaneously tensed my leg muscles to the limit of their strength. The wheel passed over my right ham, and I came out of it with a slight bruise.
>
> I know quite clearly that I let myself fall only after these lightning fast, wholly precise reflections, which seemed to imprint themselves upon my brain.

In one case, an eight-year-old child who plunged off a precipitous seventy-foot cliff thought only about whether he might lose the pocket knife that his father had given him as a present. A climber who fell from the Karpfstock, and survived, reported that during his fall he objectively surveyed his situation, the future of his family and the arrangements which he had provided for their security 'with a rapidity of which I had never before been capable'.

Heim avoided attempting to explain the results of his findings and, instead, offered them as a consolation to the families of accident victims. One of his greatest satisfactions was when he imparted his observations to a mother whose two sons had recently lost their lives in falls. He wrote:

> They fell in a blue and roseate, magnificent heaven. Then everything was suddenly still. Unconsciousness occurred suddenly and without agony, and in this condition a few seconds and a millennium are just as long and just as short.
>
> My words were a comfort to her, … then she knew that death for them had been very pleasant.

from OFF BELAY October *1975*

IN MEMORIAM

IAN McNAUGHT-DAVIS

The first time I attended an evening at the Alpine Club, I expected to meet muscled gents, ruddy from an epic ascent of the Winklestock – risk-takers shortly to end their days in some desperate feat of frozen, high-altitude heroism. One by one the members arrived, stooped from the burden of carrying too many rucksacks up to too many huts, limping from old Boer War wounds, eyes watering from too much exposure to high-altitude winds. They greeted each other with respect, and paid a shilling to a grumpy and aged retainer, for a glass of tepid bottled beer. It was about as exciting as a Darby and Joan Club without Joan. At last it was time for the lecture. Making myself invisible at the back of the room, I looked down over the nodding grey heads as the President took the chair. On the left, on a curious velvet bench set parallel to the wall, sat the most venerated, ancient and respected members, all of whom sported walking sticks.

The President stood and, after some muttered ritual, stared his audience right between the eyes.

'I very much regret to have to tell you of the death of our fellow member, Claude Fforde, at the age of ninety-four. Would anyone care to say a few words?'

He sat down abruptly and continued his stare. Everyone seemed acutely embarrassed, concentrating on the polished toes of their lace-up shoes as they shuffled nervously. Suddenly, as the silence became unbearable, an incredibly frail member staggered to his feet.

'Well, I never actually met Claude, or "Bunty" as I believe he was known to his chums, but I recall that he did some excellent climbs in the Plopsteinberge Alps in that very good season in '08, or was it '09 ...?'

A reassuring chorus of "08' was shouted from the white heads at the front. Four members on the ancients' bench, already fast asleep and snoring gently, stirred and muttered 'Hear! Hear!'

The speaker went on: 'I did correspond with him for a time, and I can say what a splendid fellow he was and what a sad loss it is for the Club.'

He sank back into his chair and an audible sigh of relief ran through the room as the President removed his special solemn expression and introduced the fun part of the evening.

Of course this is the real bonus you get for being a member of the Alpine Club: as you hang on to that icy hold, 1000ft above the glacier, you can reflect on who will speak your eulogy and how many brave friends will break down and soak the tattered AC carpets with their tears.

But the repercussions of a death in the climbing community go much further than that. Firstly, your name will be removed from the list of Active or Retired Members of the Alpine Climbing Group, or GHM, and be transferred to the Dead Members Section, presumably for ever. Then there is that moment of high drama – the funeral. These ceremonies can be graded in terms of turn-out, location, tears shed and, if you are very important, by whether or not there is a memorial service. Each great climbing burial is remembered for its incidents, not in themselves of real interest, but which, in the context of high grief, acquire a humour of their own. There was, for example, the vicar who couldn't find the grave; after a careful search of the cemetery in pouring rain, and followed by a retinue of mourners and bearers, he finally approached the hole from the wrong side over a pile of rubble. The bearers slipped, and for an incredible moment it looked as if the coffin was going to be hurled to the ground and its grizzly contents thrown without ceremony into the muddy hole. Only a swift and skilful bridging move saved the day. Then there is the poignant memory of the bearded gravedigger leaning on his shovel, silhouetted against the setting sun, at the side of the hole he had dug right at the top of what he called 'Boot Hill'.

You might imagine, once the box has been lowered into its hole and the last handful of soil has followed it, or after the electric motor has buzzed weirdly, dragging the coffin to the gas ovens behind the tiny swing doors, that it's all over. Not on your life! We have only got through the Mourning Phase; we still have a whole new scene to go at:

'What a great man he was ...'

'... and a great climber ...'

'What a character ...'

'We must remember him. Let's have a collection and build a Climbing University in his honour, or put a brass plaque somewhere. We must do something.'

By this time everyone is deliriously happy about the fact that it is someone else who is in the grave or being grilled in the ovens, and not them. Drink has brought on a mood of euphoria in the survivors, and already we are deep in the Remembrance Phase.

It is very important whilst you are still alive to establish your claim to something significant, or you will end up with a one-minute silence at a BMC sub-committee meeting, or perhaps a bench overlooking your greatest first ascent in Doverstones Quarry. And if you leave that to your friends you will end up with one of those incredibly uncomfortable and largely unused benches carved by some rural craftsman in a remote Lakeland dale; it will never wear out, and younger generations will stare at it, curse its discomfort, and maybe wonder who the hell you were. A suitably inscribed stone set in the Club hut's dry-stone fireplace is popular in certain circles, but this comes fairly low in the pecking order of Remembrance – the ultimate being to have a whole hut named after you. But that has its drawbacks, too. As time goes by, only the names are remembered, and few of the feats or character traits. Who was Charles Inglis Clarke, or R. O. Downes, or R. W. Lloyd for that matter?

In the mountains themselves we discover plaques, stones and shrines,where now long-forgotten climbers fell, and we will no doubt soon see the titanium plate pinned to the actual hold last used before Joe Bloggs fell to his doom.

You may well sneer at all these memorabilia from the monumental mason's stock, and say that they are converting the hills into giant graveyards (or 'marble orchards', as I believe they are now called) and the huts into hushed Chapels of Remembrance for the brave dead, but you will still be unable to escape those mourners who wish to convert you into an eccentric cult figure like Menlove Edwards, to be studied and written about by every budding admirer. Who can suspect their motives?

I used to think that the ultimate embarrassment would be to have a friend whose last pathetic request was to have his ashes scattered from the summit of Ben McDoodle, in the middle of winter. It is sad that reality would not be a few swirls of white dust being blown into a blue sky over shimmering snowfields, but a handful of charred bones flopping into the slush on a rain-driven day, with everyone soaked to the skin and thinking more of hot fires than of the now-departed loved one.

Perhaps the final stroke for remembrance is the intended last request of a good friend (happily still climbing) whose ambition is to die at the age of eighty-seven, shot by a jealous husband, and to have his ashes ceremonially flushed down the famous echoing toilet at the Alpine Club.

from MOUNTAIN 40 *1974*

OBITUARY NOTES FOR
J. M. ARCHER THOMSON

GEOFFREY WINTHROP YOUNG
and PROFESSOR ORTON

... J.M.A.T. was more than the most consistent rock-climber of his time. He was a man of wide and cultivated interests, and, as his writing revealed, of considerable literary gifts. He was familiar with every legend that related to his peculiar hills; he perfected his climbing skill primarily as a means to reach the most intimate recesses, and he loved every stone, bird and flower with an artistic absorption as silent as it was profound. Its presence was only discoverable in the sudden lightening of his eyes at some sympathetic reference to his beloved precipices and valleys. Many of us knew him only as a recluse and a poet, a romantic and occasional appearance, with an unrivalled skill in performance and a generous sympathy and store of knowledge always ready for younger climbers. He led the era of exploration in North Wales from start to finish, and he did not long survive its completion. It is difficult to imagine the district without his presence or without the opportunity of reference to his appreciative judgement. For a number of us the cliffs of Snowdon, and more especially the incomparable precipices of Lliwedd, of which he knew every ledge and cranny, will be haunted, and almost consecrated, by the memory of a figure, solitary and smoking, crouched on some picturesque and inaccessible shelf, or moving with extraordinary lightness of foot along the screes, the grey curls drifting from the Rossetti-like head, or, most characteristic of all, leaning easily outward, with half his body free, in the middle of some gaunt and holdless slab, his feet and knees attached to the rock on some principle of balance all his own, and gazing upward with a smiling intentness that seemed half critical examination and half remote and contemplative pleasure.

Geoffrey Winthrop Young

Thomson was not a prolific writer. He contributed some twelve papers to this Journal and one to the Alpine Club and to the Scottish Mountaineering Club Journals, in the two latter describing his climbs on the Coolin. In earlier days a book of Cambrian climbs was planned and several chapters were written; but, as is shown by a letter still extant, his sense that the mountains deserve appropriate literary treatment, and should not merely act as pegs whereon to hang stories of rollicking adventures, led him to give up the task. The two books which he wrote, several years later, for the Editorial Committee, of the Climbers' Club, *The Climbs on Lliwedd*, with A. W. Andrews (1909), and *Climbing in the Ogwen District* (1910), have been universally judged as of outstanding quality. As concise and accurate guides to climbs they are unsurpassed, although the details of topography did not come easily to him. His writings have a highly individualised style. His phrasing arrests attention; his descriptive expressions remain in the memory. His sentences are suggestive rather than explanatory, and bring the reader to the clearer, cleaner atmosphere of the mountains. At times a cryptic sentence may puzzle one who wishes to read at a glance. He often falls back on a classical quotation to attain a subtle distinction or fuller meaning. It has been suggested that the rhythm of his writings was an echo of his gait, which was highly characteristic. He took great pains to find appropriate names for new climbs and for the prominent 'sancta' of the crags. The Welsh place-names of the mountains and cwms interested him. His suggestion that the name 'Glydr' is merely a Welsh spelling of the local English 'glidder' has been confirmed by the discovery that the mountains did not bear that name a century and a half ago.

... He was reticent, and belonged to the more silent half of humanity; rarely anecdotal himself, he was always a sympathetic and stimulating listener, endowed with the faculty of bringing out the conversational powers of others. The real Thomson was perhaps only seen on some summit or ledge reached after a severe effort by a new and delectable route, when he 'rejoiced in an environment of boldly sculptured crags, and inhaled the influences of rare and beautiful mountain scenery'. Then one saw how largely in the 'element of romance', of 'the glory and gloom of the mountains', lay the attraction.

Professor Orton

from THE CLIMBERS' CLUB JOURNAL *1913*

DOUGAL HASTON – CUMHA DUGHAL

ROBIN CAMPBELL

So, mighty Haston, the painter of Lagangarbh, has gone now, too: killed in some meaningless skiing accident. It's worst when they die abroad. Remember the aching disbelief when Smith went, the dreams from which you couldn't bear to wake, the feeling that you'd turn a corner, somewhere near the High Street, and there he would be – tatty raincoat, grinning suedes, wicked schoolboy smile – and the feeling that came after?

At least they found Haston's body and somebody, Moriarty, saw him buried. You thought it didn't matter about Haston – he'd none of the innocence of Smith, he'd been away from the High Street too long, he'd spent too much time with the worshippers of money and fame – but then you saw the newsreel of Moriarty carrying the coffin through the snow and then it mattered. The indomitable giant, his great head bowed, shuffling up through the drifts with the front end of the stretcher and the black coffin swaying past the camera made you crack.

Now you wish you'd gone, don't you? You wish you'd mortgaged your meaningless house a bit more and gone. Well, it's too late. Sometime soon you'll be walking in the City and there he'll be – loping along in his big boots, long hands slotted in pockets, shoulders hunched, the big wolf grin and the North Wall eyes, ready for anything. But he won't really, Will he?

You remember that time when you both hitched to the Ben, you got there first and he had the key? You kipped in the shithouse, threw the Elsan outside and cursed him. Four o'clock in the morning, a big blue shiny morning, the door burst open and there he was, stripped to the waist cracking that huge grin and waving the key in front of you. Or that other time when you stood all the way from Paris in a train to Chamonix, stumbled out of the station and didn't know a soul? You turned a corner and he was coming towards you like a golden greyhound, sunglassed and sandaled, just back from the Eiger and who could mistake that smile?! Or the time you tried that horrible route of his on the Tannery Bridge, 'grade six sustained' he said, and you quivering on the final miserable finger hold while he grinned down the parapet and held out a merciful hand? Well these times are all gone now, for you and for him, and won't be again. Except, once in a while you'll get that kick in the guts that tells you it's a dream and you're going to wake up and whenever you go moping about the old wynds and closes there'll be the feeling at corners and the feeling that comes after.

Remember Scott, sitting in some dreary single-end of a studio staring at the camera like a pole axed bull while the blathering BBC imbecile asked if he ever really knew him? What does knowing matter (you felt like screaming)! He's gone and, with him, a long loping stride, narrow hips, wide shoulders, a lipless grin and bright blue bivouacked eyes.

from THE SCOTTISH MOUNTAINEERING
CLUB JOURNAL *1977*

THE FISSURE BOYSEN

MARTIN BOYSEN

The snow patch [on Trango Tower] provided the first and only campsite on the face – a tiny ice grotto. Above, the beautiful red granite, as good as the best in Chamonix, leaned over us ominously. Huge sweeps of rock were split only occasionally by cracks and grooves, and it was obvious that the climbing was going to be as hard as anything in the Alps.

Any ideas about climbing rapidly were quickly dispelled. Although we climbed as fast as we could without a load, each and every pitch demanded an incredible amount of energy. We could never manage more than three full pitches a day. Ledges were absent or minimal. The easiest way to make progress was to fix ropes and go up every day from our snow-cave.

Mo [Anthoine], Will [Barker] and I climbed steadily; three pitches a day for three days, the climbing becoming steeper and harder all the time. We were approaching an obvious crux pitch: a gently overhanging crack, with no way round it. We were getting pressed for time. Our only chance was to climb the crack, reach a ledge system above, and then try to get up the huge summit chimneys in a single push.

On the fourth day above the snow-patch camp, Mo and I set out to climb the crack and reach the ledges. We had practically run out of food and had only three ropes left. Unaccountably, the others had not come up; the odds seemed stacked against us. I climbed that day with the urge of desperation.

Two magnificent and frightening pitches were rapidly overcome, and I found myself swept along by a surge of optimism. The horrid crack leered above, but I was sure I could do it.

I led off on our last rope, armed with a single five-inch bong, and slowly fought my way up. Americans would call it an off-width crack: I called it something else. I was conscious of the total lack of protection, yet I had to keep the bong until it was absolutely essential. At eighty feet it was: the rock bulged, but the angle eased above, and all I had to do was climb the next ten feet. Thankfully, I smashed in the bong. Shouting down to Mo to watch the rope, I eased my knee gently into the crack, flexed it and moved up. But then, when I tried to repeat the move, I found that my knee was stuck.

I was merely irritated at first – I hadn't enough energy to waste wriggling my knee about. I slumped down on it and felt the grip tighten, and the first wave of panic began to lap inside my skull. I was very much alone. Mo could hardly jumar up with only a jammed knee for support, even though it would have held him! I struggled furiously, trying to tear the material of my breeches, but to no effect. I was rapidly tiring, becoming more fearful as the time sped by.

Mo shouted up: he had an emergency bolt kit; perhaps a loop of rope would reach him? It did, but then came the problem of getting the bolt in. 'What the hell do I do with all these bits and pieces?' I asked in desperation. The explanation seemed simple enough, but there are no short cuts to bolting. I carved out a hole of sorts, pounded a piece of metal in it and watched it drop out. I banged away again, and down tinkled the drill as my hand opened up in a spasm of cramp. I collapsed, limp and defeated, and slowly sank into a trance-like, painless oblivion. My mind wandered aimlessly, picking out memories, seizing on trivia, until the anguish inside me welled up uncontrollably and forced itself into my unwilling conscious-ness. I choked out a single sob, the distillation of my despair. I would never again see my daughter Katie, my wife Maggie; never smell the warmth of love and life. I would miss everything, utterly. How futile my wasted life seemed; how precarious the balance between my passion for climbing and my passion for life. Three hours slipped by and, as the sun moved lower, I was certain of my coming death.

Mo shouted up again. I had completely forgotten about him. He was going down to get help, to bring up some drink, a rope – to prolong my dying? I still clung on to life; surely there had to be a way out? And then I remembered: I had a knife blade in my pocket. I found it and started trying to cut my breeches. But the blade wouldn't bite, so I pounded it with my hammer and produced a wicked saw edge. With this, I cut and gouged the thick material within the crack with my last strength. Blood began to ooze thickly from my thigh, my fingers and knuckles were skinned, but I continued cutting without regard. At last, I felt the material give: I had cut it through, and now? All my hopes were pinned on my next few moves – I hardly dared to start easing at my knee. I tried, gently at first, then harder. But it would not budge, and all hope drained away. My body sagged, and then – I could hardly believe it – my knee slipped out, and I half fell, half slid, to the bong – which held. I shouted to Mo, and with a great effort worked out how to descend. Mo waited. When I reached him, bloody and wrecked, but alive, I burst into the sweetest tears.

from 'Last Trango'
MOUNTAIN 52 *1976*

THE ICE CLIMBER

JEFF LONG

In their midst was that boy, the enormous climber with wind harrowed hair and severe cheeks, his T-shirt pink with blood and crampons like weapons on his boots, barking hoarse shock, amazed. At his feet lay a head. And like a foetus crouched the body, his friend, rags and joints curled down in a green dimple of ragged river ice. A bald cop bent to touch the shaggy head whispering life away.

'He could have got killed,' yelled the climber to the cop. He yelled to the sky, to the ice. 'Damned ice. See where we fell there.' He pointed sobbing, while they huddled on the frozen river beneath a frozen waterfall, the unstirring corpse beneath them with wet rope tangling its limbs. The cluster of grave men waited in the shadows, waiting with the half-wild climber loudly shouting how his friend should be dead… should be dead. They hugged themselves in their wind-breakers, cautiously shuffling for warmth where there was none. They were stunned by the surreal tragedy, the splintered icefall and blood. Finally, the cop rose among the cold canyon shadows and flipped the limp tip of rope onto the ivory river ice, a gesture of obituary. The man bent to the bald ground again.

'Now he's died, boy.'

But the climber shook his head, unsure who was dead or what it was they'd said. There'd been the rope cracking, snapping ice, and the screws had spat a single black pop as they rattled in sharp flight down. They both had fallen, both slapped the ground and slid heaping down the icy slide onto the frozen river. Now one was bruised and one was dead.

Only one had crawled from their freezing embrace on the river, the other had inexplicably stayed on the ice, in the ice, sibilant and with eyes like fists.

They closed the eyes.

The tall climber hushed himself with a blink. He grinned. His fingers were broken and now they hurt, crooked little sticks. And Jack was dead, when just before Jack had trembled, Jack clinging to the bare ice with his hammer points and crampons. There'd been that ridiculous fart to punctuate the strain of climbing, a nervous giggle, and Jack wigging the rope with his hips, a grotesque farce of copulation and vertigo. Perched below the sweating clown they'd seemed so deliriously invulnerable that they could parody fragility, teasing more mortality. The delirium was gone through. Jack lay coiled in the pocket of river-ice, no longer Jack. The tall climber grimaced as the cops and ambulance men levered at those legs and arms, as they flinched at the face, draped, strapped and lorried Jack away, though Jack was already gone, slipped away.

'Where's Jack gone?' mumbled the boy to the shadows. It was only a Saturday morning, bland and unextraordinary. He turned around with a slow sweep. Had Jack seeped among the swells in the icefall or flowed with the river? Fingers draped a blanket across the grey Mask. Had Jack raced away with the gusts of spindrift on the highway … between what things, underneath what fabric of the plain day was Jack still being as he'd been? The broken body was mute and empty, its vitality, its Jack-ness was gone.

A feeling of dispersal blew all around the tall climber. He felt light and raw, sick with relief, and yet he sensed a dark hole, a pit in his heart as if there was no certainty to the Saturday morning he'd survived. Someone unbuckled his crampon straps.

At the hospital the climber began tentatively to reassert himself to himself. It was a mechanical chore, prodding the stitches and tape on his arm, flexing his swollen fingers. There was pain, real enough. There was reality, but he still addressed the nurses as if they were barely ghosts in a fiction, filaments surfacing and sinking, murmuring, all wafting on through the dark noon. Words circled and died wordlessly. Images quailed into impressions. Through a window the climber watched lacklustre shapes edge between tall and vague trees then the trees fused into shadow, the world slowly wheeling visions drifting and recomposing. At last he was left staring numbly at the marbled reflection of his own face in the dark window. A glassy figure entered, uttered, smoothed his wild hair. He felt his limbs dressed, his joints aching. Beyond that ache in his arms and thighs, the afternoon was only a tone of flickering animation. Everything seemed remote and temporary.

The boy drove home on the snowy spine of the highway, past road signs and road shops, between half built houses and half housed shadows. He heard tyre chains slapping asphalt and the bleating of a car horn, the skeleton of Saturday afternoon. There was a bad smell, sulphur decaying or a dead skunk. Here and there he noticed a patch of tar and fur on the highway, a dead dog, a flattened rabbit, animals stuck into things, things breeding things. He passed a damp pile of guts. He passed a dry pile of bones. Passing and passed by rapid cars, the rapid landscape, the rapid air skirled into a false and rapid wind, the boy steered his way home.

On the vinyl seat where Jack had sat a thin string of karabiners and a few ice screws, a hammer, a wool hat. On the snowy walk where Jack had walked the footprints had pooled and refrozen. The door opened to him. The couch groaned. In the house where Jack had ambled … shadows.

When the sun dipped low a dog was still barking far away. The room turned grey and then dark. All the details of the furniture were gradually effaced. A photograph on the wall no longer cast colours or portraits; it became a flat plaque on the flat wall, then the wall itself was swallowed. Dusk ate everything. His legs sprawled in front of him, calves still cased in gaiters, his boots two dense hooves. They slipped fluidly into darkness too. The telephone rang dimly elsewhere and stopped, began again and stopped. He sat in the black echoes, still as a bone.

Knuckles came clapping on wood. Words flattened through the glass. The screen door squeaked and a woman stepped in cautiously, her face pale with the dusk. From the doorway she stared into the dark room and after a moment found the boy. He sat soundlessly. He noticed a single star glittering behind her shoulder, then looked away. Her voice quavered, betraying a knowledge of Jack, exposing her tears and questions. But he shrugged, fiercely disclaiming all riddles and pity.

At first she stammered, husky and sad, piercing the dark room with her noise. Then very slowly she affirmed his silence with her own silence, and her arms circled the leonine head. Slower still he raised a hand to touch the lines of her unseen face. By the bed she was soft, unbanding her body, cloth dropping, her nude gently assembled piece by piece. The night softened. Later she fed him soup and bread, brought wine and crawled back into bed. Her long hair was a familiar veil on her chest and shoulders, silver in the stray moonlight.

Sleep was difficult. The woman was warm, but his fingers throbbed in their splints and now and then an image would displace the drowsing boy.

It was an image like Jack, which would lie as the boy was lying, curled, an image quiet like the boy was quiet. The boy snipped awake each time, afraid he was dead, that he was the ghost and not Jack. But it wasn't Jack. The face of the image was changed enough to look like many faces. Jack was gone, his face was vague. Each time the image dissipated the boy lay shivering and speechless in the moonlight. Something was missing inside him. He drew in a breath, beyond melancholy or fear, and felt the empty thing inside him, a wordless confusion. Benighted things set all around him, inarticulate and staid: a table, a black mirror, his bound hand. The woman warmed him in her sleep. It wasn't a cold emptiness or a physical one. It was a breathless cavity. Something was gone.

Before the trees became brief stalks in the east the boy edged from bed, aching and sleepless. The woman slept on as he hobbled from the room. Morning, cold and purple, was still too young to illuminate the room. The woman disappeared into the lingering night. The bed, the bottle of wine, her crouched clothing all sank into the blackness. He eased the willowy screen door shut and limped to the car. Frost starred the windshield. The tyres crackled as they rolled from their shoes of brittle ice. There was no traffic in the canyon, it was very early. There was little light. The climber parked and picked his way down from the road, here and there pausing to gingerly warm his bare, taped hands beneath his parka. The river was animal beneath its sturdy shell.

And the icefall still loomed, steepled coldly, a glycerine monolith. The climber approached carefully and pressed his hands to the ice. He peered into its dark, watery bulk. There was no chamber back in there; there were no cells in the ice, no place for ghosts to hide. It was a cold and sterile massif. Nothing had changed in a day and a night. It was still murky and full, as thick and depthless as yesterday. And yet when he tried to retrace the tiny scars of their crampons on the ice he couldn't find them. The lesions had melted and refrozen. Something had changed.

The ice had absorbed the memory of them. The climber frowned. He tried to recall the path of their ascent, but couldn't. It was gone, lost into yesterday. The climber closed his eyes and tried to see again the faces of the bald cop and the nurses and doctors who'd drifted through his Saturday, but he couldn't, not exactly, almost not at all. They were gone. And the breakfast yesterday, the radio, their jokes, gestures, the colour of rope, the hat he'd forgotten on the car seat … he forgot. He couldn't recall them as they'd been, the rope red or the rope blue, the yoghurt and bran, the radio yammering, tea sweet, trees hiding snow, upturned stones, a scurvy deer bounding back into the forest, and them lashing tight their crampons, the worried-on straps, sharp hammers hefted, taped shafts shifted hand to hand and slammed in ice, the hard spring ice green, clean, unriddled, and though it was smooth it was fractured, the memory was fractured. Something had changed. Something was lost. The climber grunted. He couldn't recover the exact details of the memory, there were too many and they were too fast. Yesterday's morning had spun on, passed forward and bred the memory of another morning, this morning, the frosty windshield, this old down parka, fingers stiffly splintered, palms numb against the ice, and Jack melting, Saturday fading, while the ice climber shivered unwillingly. High above the icefall's flank a blue star greyed into day. A slight chinook wind exhaled with the dawn, a whisper of incoherent warmth that would thaw the canyon and purge the shadows, a wind that would melt the ice, scourging the brief immortal.

from CLIMBING *March 1976*

A VALEDICTION

JIM PERRIN

School ends; there are more phases to a man's life than just one, though each phase as it progresses brings a clearer realisation of its own nature, or a firmer grasp on the security it seems to offer. I have been climbing intensively now for twelve years, and I have more or less had enough. I have come to see the nature of the sport; it is not a creative act and it has little left to give me. I expect to give offence or be criticised for what I have to say, and would thus like to define the conditions which lead me to say it. I am not referring to the mountain environment, or to the quiet pleasures of days in the hills, not referring to the huge range of interest encompassed in this scene, not referring to the sheer bodily and sensual pleasure of movement on rock, although all these things impinge upon the central experience about which I write. The experience to which I am referring is the intense neurotic urge to seek out the limits of subjective possibility on rock, the desire to push oneself to the extremes of endurance, adhesion, physical and mental control. I shall be making value judgements upon this experience; whether or not the reader feels intuitions of sympathy towards these is of little account. I have searched myself and found them valid to my situation.

I have heard people claim that climbing is an art form, a creative act. I have read the same statement in essays, such as Harold Drasdo's *Education and the Mountain Centres,* the people who make these statements have neither sufficiently considered the nature of a creative act, nor the nature of climbing. They are talking nonsense at a dangerously inflated level; there is an element of the mystical about climbing, but the climbers are lost not in God but in themselves.[1] This is not invalid at a certain stage in life, but it is a lesson which must not be allowed to harden into a habit. In a sense it represents a shaking off of the last egocentricities of childhood, and a coming-to-terms at last with the external world. The act revokes its own motivation.

Commitment to a series of extreme moves on rock is a tenuous expression of belief in one's personal omnipotence; by its very nature it is an illusion, and one bolstered so often by the mean little tricks and dishonesties of the climbing world as to lose the integrity upon which its validity must rest. No one is omnipotent and on rock we all strive to be so. The ego and the will are the driving forces in climbing, the philosophy behind it is one of despair. Consider us and what we are: we are not well-balanced individuals, as long as we climb, because we have committed ourselves to a pure sphere of self-assertion and will.[2] We turn from a world of which we cannot be the centre, to an experience so intense that we cannot but see ourselves at the centre of it. Every new trip up Sisyphus' Hill hardens the ego a little by proving to us that we can do it.[3] Ego and will by no means lead to happiness; the times when I have been best at my climbing have been the least happy times of my life. Yes, there have been moments of desperate laughter and utter relief, even some warmth of companionship from time to time from an experience shared. But this continual focusing inwards of the climber's mind, this sifting and weighing of every fine weakness of response, endless preparation for mental masturbation, the sudden explosion of the assertive will, this is a path to restraint and not freedom of response. It is a lesson to be learnt, not one always to be lived by, and its repetition becomes not only absurd, for this element was present in its nature from the beginning but also negative and destructive, and a denial of the potentialities of life.[4] Obsessive climbing is a reprisal against nature for making self so small within it.

The toying with death (any arguments that this is not so are utterly spurious) that represents so strong a part of the attraction of climbing adds yet another facet to the basic negativity of the sport. Each new death is a reiteration of the question 'is it worth it', from the answering of which we always shy away. At Lawrie Holliwell's funeral every face was haunted by the realisation of a death that could as easily have been theirs. Is it worth it? Yes, for those who are weak, aimless, discontented, strong and directionless, childless, unhappily married, unresolved or in despair. For all who fit these categories the activity is eminently worthwhile in that it brings them close to ridding themselves of an existence that could so easily become a burden to them, and by the proximity of that negation increases the attractiveness of life.

> 'I balanced all, brought all to mind,
> The years to come seemed waste of breath,
> A waste of breath the years behind;
> In balance with this life, this death'.[5]

Well; all cannot be brought to mind; there is body and soul, there are feelings, intuitions of beauty and wholeness, softness, fullness, warmth. These things climbing alone cannot fulfil; the hard, cold world of intellect and will seeks to destroy the whole man.

I have learnt things from climbing; that the seemingly impossible can be achieved by precise, co-ordinated movement, by direction of energy and conservation and timed application of resources. That things are easier than they seem to be, that falling off is not the thing to do until every last possible scrap of resource has failed you, that a sufficiency of commitment will usually see one through, that a real and authentic desire is the only worthwhile spring of action. But these are lessons to be applied now to the creative act of living, in conjunction with the more warm, full and human values of love, feeling, knowledge, compassion; no longer to be squandered in the negative sphere of rock. One passes from one lesson to another, armed with a new strength of knowledge, and one should be glad that it is so.

In writing this piece I am not unaware of its emphatically one-sided nature. Some of its statements are obviously suspect and require of more careful definition to retain their validity beneath a detailed scrutiny. Despite this, they seem to me justified in their context, and I hope that those whose minds are open to the general direction of the article will see their particular application in this. I would certainly be prepared to argue any of them out at length in a fuller exposition of this view.

from THE CLIMBERS' CLUB JOURNAL *1973-74*

---

[1] This seems to me the basic reason why climbing is incapable of producing anything resembling a worthwhile literature. Whereas literature is a statement of the variousness of life, climbing works the other way and is of its nature a 'turning-off' activity, to which the external world means virtually nothing.

[2] One notes with some alarm the penchant amongst climbing 'intellectuals' for that part of Nietzsche's work, which rests upon fallacy and subversion.

[3] We cannot imagine that Sisyphus would choose his burden.

[4] The absurd is rescued from being a nihilistic view of life because existence is accepted despite its seeming meaninglessness. The absurd is a starting point rather than a conclusion.

[5] W. B. Yeats: *An Irish Airman Foresees His Death.*

PART 8

MOUNTAIN RESCUE
and ACCESS PROBLEMS

The past decade – the third since the social disruption of the last World War – has seen a growing concern for safety and paternal care in society at large. In mountaineering this has been manifested by calls for more safety regulations and mountain-rescue precautions. In Britain the emphasis has been on mountain rescue, where nowadays the most trivial incident can cause major reverberations in the media. In America, with its complex mesh of legal responsibilities, a host of preposterous regulations have been developed designed to prevent or inhibit climbing. Clearly great vigilance will be needed if such pressures are to be resisted, and even greater energy will have to be generated to achieve the abolition of unwelcome regulations. A general sharing of knowledge can only be valuable, and this section makes a small contribution to that end.

The position in 2006: Official desire to regulate climbing and mountain walking developed in the 1970s, much of it in response to the Cairngorm Accident. Since then a variety of instructional qualifications have replaced cruder attempts to regulate. At present ordinary climbers remain free from regulation whereas those providing any sort of formalised instruction, however modest, have become increasing hemmed in with certificates and awards and insurance pressures. In recent years Health and Safety regulations regarding roped access, aimed primarily at the building trade, threatened to inhibit conventional climbing instruction. Another concern is the steady pressure on University and College clubs to refrain from undertaking basic instruction. The 2004 enactment in Britain of the Countryside and Rights of Way (CRoW) Act *appeared* to bring new freedoms to roam and climb but also came close to proscribing night-time activity. Harmonisation of climbing with the very militant and active ornithology lobby is another area demanding constant attention. Climbing walls (gyms), with their development from smaller soloing structures to larger leading and top-roping edifices, form another area where vigilance to maintain freedoms is of growing importance. The freedom to climb, (and mountain-walk) uncertificated and uninsured, is a priceless liberty needing ever-vigilant defence.

A GOOD CLEAN BREAK

G. J. F. DUTTON

We coiled the rope. It had been a good route. Warm eastern granite, and now sunburnt heather. The Doctor arranged himself elaborately at full length, head pillowed on arms.

'It is a shout,' confirmed the Apprentice, looking up from his last coils.

We listened. A feeble cry, which might once have been 'Help', wandered up from the other, easier, side of the crag. I peered, but saw nothing.

The Doctor reassembled his full height, climbed a convenient protuberance, and inspected the heathery hollow below.

'There! It is somebody. Chap lying on a ledge. Some ass fallen off.'

This was one of the Apprentice's best days. He was in excellent form, and swiftly led me down a steep series of slabs to the victim. The Doctor, irritatingly, arrived there first, having walked down a heathery rake neither of us had seen.

'Well, and who are you?' asked the Doctor pleasantly, as he took off his jacket, knelt, and rolled up his sleeves.

'I'm the Casualty,' announced the figure, not altogether surprisingly.

'So it seems. Now,' said the Doctor, frisking him professionally, 'have you any pain? Back or limbs?'

'I'm bloody stiff,' remarked the Casualty. 'Been here hours.'

'Of course you'll be stiff. But have you any pain?'

'Only when you poke me like that. Who are you anyway?'

We all raised eyebrows. The Doctor adopted his blandest bedside approach, suitable for dealing with irate landowners, lunatics, or the concussed.

'Never mind, laddie. We're here to help. We'll soon get you down.'

'Get me down?' remarked the Casualty sarcastically. 'I think you'd better get them down.' And he stood up, yawned, hobbled stiffly to one side and, most disconcertingly, proceeded to empty his bladder over the edge of the cliff.

The Doctor was as near nonplussed as I have seen him. His fingers stroked the air, his cuffs – now loose again – fluttered uncertainly. 'Them? Who are they?'

'The Rescue Team,' remarked the Casualty, turning and adjusting his dress. 'They're all stuck. Up there,' he added, jerking his head towards the cliff behind us.

We turned. Some eighty feet up, a collection of cagouled figures fluoresced ashamedly from various unlikely positions. One was clearly upside down, resting on his elbows. All (fortunately) were tied together by a welter of ropes. In reply to our gaze, they mewed in chorus a feeble and obviously highly embarrassed – 'Aaa … help.'

The Casualty sat on an outcrop and lit a fag. 'I suppose we'll have to go and sort 'em out,' he said. When pressed to describe the nature of his accident, he explained that it was no accident, but just his turn to be Casualty. It was, he further explained, and somewhat belatedly, an Exercise. Training. This was the Pitfoulie Mountain Rescue Team. They came out every weekend, if the weather was fine. A sort of a club. Good fun, and useful.

The Doctor, cheated of his prey, was reluctant to believe all this. 'Concussion,' he confided to us, 'has curious effects. Now I've – '

'Concussion?' broke in the Casualty. 'He got that all right. Same as last time. Always gets it. That's why they're in that mess.' He jerked his fag towards the now silent tableau.

'So there is a real casualty, after all!' exclaimed the Doctor, brightening and rising to his feet. He brushed down his breeches and slipped on his jacket. 'The sooner we fix him up the better.'

'Och, he's all right now, Eck is,' said the Casualty, inhaling and blowing the smoke out again in neat little rings. 'We just drove him back to town. He'll get home in a day or two, like last time. They usually do, with mild concussion,' he informed the Doctor.

Eck, it turned out, was Leader of the Pitfoulie team. He had started it, having apparently discovered a passion for rescue when a mere boy. His absence accounted for the failure of this particular exercise. The rest of the team – apart from the Casualty, who was experienced enough but, as he explained, had to take his turn as Casualty like anyone else – the rest were not too familiar with complex rope manoeuvres and had gradually fankled themselves into complete stasis.

'But how did Eck get concussion?' demanded the Doctor, still obsessed.

'He fell out of our Land Rover. He always does. He's that eager. He leans out, directing us, as soon as we drive on to the hill. It holds things up. We didn't get started again till 11 o'clock – though we were a lot quicker this time than last.'

So the question resolved itself simply into the four of us releasing the rescue team. We turned ourselves towards the cliff, the Casualty nipping out his fag-end with some regret. Just as we were about to plunge down the heather to the foot of the crag, a line of figures appeared above our bowl, twittering.

'Careful, now! It's an EDGE!' boomed out a rich contralto voice, with more than a brush of five o'clock shadow in it. 'Stop where you are!'

One figure, that of a long thin man in a flapping raincoat, did not stop. He slipped, sat down on his raincoat and began, inexorably, to slither towards the edge of the crag. Our eyes popped. The Doctor smelt game.

'I said STOP, Mr Pilchard! I SAID STOP!'

Mr Pilchard slowed down and, obediently, stopped. A large female figure made towards him and plucked him, raincoat fluttering, back to safety. The excited buzz of conversation resumed.

'It's Mrs Cairnwhapple,' said the Doctor. 'Ursula Major. And that's her ornithological party. A breeding pair was reported here last week."

Mrs Cairnwhapple, no mean woman, took in the scene at a glance. 'Just as well we STOPPED, friends. There are four foolish people down there who did not stop and who are now In Trouble. They are waiting to be rescued by the experienced mountaineers you see below you.' (Agonised twitchings from the web.) 'A real Rescue Team. We must sit and watch, and pick up some Useful Hints.' She plumped herself down in the heather, her chicks snuggling likewise. She kept a sharp eye on Mr Pilchard, who still exhibited suicidal tendencies.

We may imagine the next hour or so. Sufficient to say that by the time we disentangled the rescue team and took them down to the foot of the crag, a late June sun had mellowed into early evening. And Mrs Cairnwhapple, with a bittern-like boom of delight, had recognised the Doctor and had trodden heavily and decisively down heather and ledge to join us. Her wheepling brood accompanied her, Pilchard suffering minor mishaps on the way. The Apprentice, who had performed daring deeds over the past two hours, was particularly helpful to one admiring and attractive young lady ornithologist. 'That's Ann Scarsoch,' said the Doctor, rejoining me after wearily separating once again two entwined and fluorescent rope-coilers. 'Old Poltivet's daughter. Only one line of triple hobs on her shoes. Flighty piece.'

Mrs Cairnwhapple had caused baskets to be produced and opened; we munched in satisfaction. The Pitfoulie team, though still somewhat subdued, finished first and, with a commendable sense of duty, stretched out their casualty once more and began trussing him up for the carry-down. The Doctor was suggesting we should examine their knots. 'After all, they're doing it on purpose this time.' Behind us in the heather, the Apprentice was teaching La Scarsoch the technique of pressure grips.

Suddenly we froze. Beneath us, up the long slopes of the evening glen, the sunlight heaved with an army of people. Crowd after crowd. The Doctor snatched up his binoculars. He paled. 'Rescue Teams. Walkie-talkies. Army. Air Force. Police. Navy. Shepherds. Civilians. Dogs. Schoolboys.' We listened. Yes … and helicopters.

We hurried over to the Casualty. (The Apprentice was too much engaged to notice.) We asked him what he knew of this invasion. Was it another, but mammoth, Exercise?

The Casualty, with disarming ease, freed his left arm from a splint, and pulled the bandages from his mouth. He sat up and grinned.

'No, it'll be a real one this time. We'll have to join it. They *still* mustn't have come back to that car. Two whole days away, no notification, no sketch of route taken. Must be lost. That lot'll find 'em. Not that they'll want to be found, when they tot up the cost of this little trip.' He complacently stripped off his dressings, rose, and assumed command.

The Doctor and I felt the earth wither. Why, oh why *had* he parked in that car park? Why *had* he bought a parking ticket? Against all our rules. Yet there was still hope. What sort of car was it, what number? Did anyone know?

The Casualty frowned. The occasion was rather too important for trivial curiosity. 'A big old German crate. Yes, a Merc.' Number? He had, of course, noted that. He pulled out a grubby bit of paper and read off the Doctor's registration number ...

That was that. We would share his costs certainly, despite his protestations, but nothing could lessen the blow from the Accident Report in the next *Journal*. Hummel Doddie wrote these Accident Reports, it was rumoured (by all except Hummel Doddie). Hummel Doddie, whose active pen flayed the tomfools that caused unnecessary searches, that caused vast and growing inconvenience to vast and growing mountainfuls of rescuers (the helicopters nosed above us, attracted by the carrion-beetle orange of the Pitfoulie cagoules); Hummel Doddie would certainly not spare – and rightly not spare – the Doctor, whose views (like those of the Apprentice) on these matters were not the views of the establishment ...

'Blast it,' said the Doctor. He bravely stood and watched the attackers close in. His pipe remained unlit.

At that moment there was a crack, followed by a scream. We all sprang round. Miss Scarsoch sat up in the heather, white, and holding her wrist. The Apprentice stood beside her, rumpled and red. He had been trying to teach the Layback, but clumsy-like ...

With a glad cry, the Doctor leapt forward and knelt down.

He felt the wrist nimbly. He looked up. His eyes brimmed with happiness.

'A Colles, by the Lord. We're saved. A good clean break!'

He issued orders in all directions. The Pitfoulie team, led by their casualty, marched towards him. Behind them rose the dust of advancing myriads, the barking of dogs. The air grew thick with engines and whirring metal, with cries and commands. Miss Scarsoch would doubtless have fainted, had not Mrs Cairnwhapple bellowed encouragement in her ear.

'Stick it, Ann! A little thing like that!'

As the impis approached their aerials glittering in the setting sun, the Apprentice gloomily held Miss Scarsoch's other hand and thought, like me, of our small brown tents alone in the Upper Corrie. The Doctor thought of them, too, but also of a large empty Mercedes surrounded by cameramen and police officers; and blessed the animal spirits of the young human male.

I could imagine his conversation when he at last got back to his car. The saluting police officers. Himself breezily nonchalant. 'Aye, a nasty business, officer, but could have been worse, could have been worse.' 'Werra fortunate you were up there, Doctor.' 'Aye, we're often called upon to render assistance wherever we may be. Inconvenient, but must be done. The Oath, you know, officer, the Oath ...' 'Aye, sir, the Oath.' 'Inconvenient to you, too, officer – I expect, ah, I expect you thought I'd got lost or something with my car here so long?' 'Och, no, sir, no (deprecatingly). 'One never knows when one may be delayed on this sort of business. One always has to be ready.' 'Oo aye, sir, ye cannae tell, ye cannae tell.' 'Why, I've still some Glen Houlet ... I'll not risk any more, driving. But yourself – must be fairly tired and cold, officer ... eh?' 'Och ...' Mutual exchange of understanding. We would be saved.

That night, as we packed up our tents, the Doctor showed us the piece of paper he had been scribbling on by torchlight. 'I'm sending it to Hummel Doddie,' he said. 'Old Doddie likes his reports in early, and from those first on the scene. Later on, you know, there could be all sorts of confusion.' His eyes gleamed beneath the midnight sun. The paper read:

30th June – Ann Scarsoch (19), Scottish, fairly experienced, practising layback with more experienced companion at foot of corrie below Grouse Shoot, Lochnager, fell her length. Fractured wrist, shock, some exposure. Found and brought down by Pitfoulie MR team (acting leader Alec Sprachle). Injuries dressed on spot by doctor climbing nearby. Invaluable assistance given by Army, RAF and RN teams, shepherds, police and civilians. Dogs used, Large bodies out, including Mrs Ursula Cairnwhapple, MBOU. Two helicopters broke down but crews rescued by Army, RAF and RN teams, shepherds, police and civilians; dogs used. One policeman bitten by dog; injuries dressed on spot by doctor climbing nearby. One civilian, T. Pilchard (41), English, lost on way down; found in hotel bar later.

A considerably shortened version appeared in the subsequent *Journal*.

from THE SCOTTISH MOUNTAINEERING
CLUB JOURNAL *1974*

INVOLUNTARY RESCUE:
THE NEW HAZARD?

LESLEY and ED FULTON

Dear Sir,

We are writing to relate an incident which touches upon fundamental issues; we do not wish to imply criticism of individuals involved.

We recently spent a weekend walking in the mountains, camping high on the fell. Conditions were poor, but not particularly bad – we have enjoyed more extreme weather on many occasions, being mountaineers of many years' experience, and were fully equipped for the walk in every sense. We have spent weekends in this way for years.

On return to our car we found a large-scale Mountain Rescue search about to commence; we were supposedly lost. The sole evidence for this supposition was our car, parked overnight in a public car park. The issue is clear. Is our society so 'caring' that one must inform other people as to one's everyday comings and goings? There is a possible criticism of our habit – namely, that we should leave word of our proposed routes. We reject this. First, as a fundamental issue, mentioned above; second, as our routes vary according to prevailing conditions and our inclination at the time; and third, as total self-reliance is to most keen mountaineers an underlying principle of the sport. There are many places, even in Britain, where rescue is very difficult, and many of us seek them out. Novices may be advised otherwise, but telling people where you are going is not a good psychological preparation for more serious expeditions.

As a postscript, we would add that thousands of climbers regularly camp high throughout the year, in all weathers. Will we need certificates of competence signed by an 'authority' in a few year's time? The whole incident, and the broader issue, fill us with incredulity.

Yours Sincerely
Lesley and Ed Fulton

from MOUNTAIN 60 *1978*

SAFETY LAST

IAN McNAUGHT-DAVIS

It seems to me that climbing is about creating a situation of risk and allowing this to escalate in a controlled way until either your physical resources or your nerves give out. If we accept that climbing is about risk-taking, and that the function of most equipment is to enable increasingly difficult climbs to be undertaken, rather than to reduce the element of absolute risk, where does safety come in?

Four main groups of people concern themselves with, or influence, attitudes towards safety. They are the mountain centre instructors, the rescue organisation enthusiasts, the equipment moguls and the gear testers. All four groups mainly comprise climbers who have moved out of the front line into low-risk activities.

The instructor is in a difficult position. He really has to convince the poor parents that climbing done the right way – and his is the right way – is a risk-free sport. You can hardly expect him to say: 'Get your mother's washing line (Joe B. did), an old sports jacket (as worn on Everest in the Good Old Days) and some cheap plimsolls (as worn by Whillans in 1950), and then go out in the rain and get gripped. This sport is about risk and you might as well learn the same way as yesterday's tigers did'. Oh no. These establishments have been set up to broaden character, not to extinguish it, and if little Willie so much as stubs his toe on the path all hell will be let loose. So they teach them to obey the rules and above all not to take a risk. But what sort of climber does this produce? Are the Boningtons of tomorrow being drilled not to take any risks? And without risk where does all the fun come from?

Of course the mountain rescue man is beyond criticism. What a selfless fellow he is: he doesn't take risks for the fun of it, but only to save another man's life. To judge from some of the statements made in coroners' courts, he sees the accident as a consequence of the victim's folly and rationalises it in a practical sense: 'Smooth-soled boots, no ice-axe, inexperienced, and anyway he shouldn't have been climbing in that weather.' So why was he?

The rescue man knows more about mountain safety than anyone else: he knows how to rescue climbers from the most impossible situations and how to make succinct statements to the press and to coroners' courts. In fact, he knows so much about it that he avoids taking any risks at all. When he eventually gets into the lead, the runners behind him lie like a line of white feathers as tokens to his safety consciousness.

The equipment seller plays a more dubious role. I love the advertisement that shows some climber leaving an equipment shop to step out into the streets of Newcastle fully equipped with duvet, crash-hat, sac, crampons, hammer, rope, pegs, and even a snow dead man: the equipment mogul's dream customer. I like to think that he only dropped in for a compass to do a walk across some sunny moor and left equipped for the Eiger. These are the enemies of the washing-line and Woolworth rubbers school:

> Don't forget that your life may depend on it – so nothing but the best. This is our latest platinum piton it comes to you in perfect condition in a presentation plastic case. Only £99 (or $199.9), but as you're a member of the YHA/Boy Scouts/ American Alpine Club/Neasden Bird-Watching Society, we'll give you 2% off.

I'd always suspected that the equipment testers were in league with the moguls, but this just isn't true. You can now use a nylon rope for more than one climb, with reasonable security; but beware of nasty cheap karabiners or pegs – use only nice expensive chromemoly jobs. If you don't, you will die a horrible death, instantly. I have never really been interested in gear, believing that there are many advantages in keeping it to a minimum. Firstly, there is less to go wrong; secondly, you can afford the best, which usually (though not always) means the most expensive; and, finally, it reduces those mysterious equipment losses that seem to occur even when you are climbing with your best friend (who is known to have built an extension on his home to store his karabiner collection).

So there we have it. The instructors say: 'Follow my rules and you'll be safe; break them and you are going to have an accident.' Indeed, but if this were the norm the sport would long ago have foundered in boredom or been so set around with regulations, as in Russia, that its essence of freedom would have been destroyed.

The rescuers say: 'It was your fault, you damned fool.'

'True. But I was only thrusting my climbing limit to a new level, and I know now that I can't get up a 100ft wall on Band-Aids (anyway I've decided they're unethical).'

'You should have bought them from me,' says the equipment mogul. 'Our new ones are fantastic – British Standards – and you get 1% off if you come back.'

'I've tested them,' says the scientist, 'and they stick like shit to a blanket, but only in humid climates.'

I've just realised how the problem has been solved in Europe. The ultimate experts, the Alpine Guides, never have accidents. If they die in the mountains in France, it is put down to a 'crise cardiaque'; in Switzerland they are invariably struck by lightning. But even that wouldn't satisfy the English coroner: 'He shouldn't have gone out in such bad weather. We've banned accidents in our hills.'

from MOUNTAIN 26 *1973*

THE FLESH EATERS

GEOFFREY CHILDS

The Monk sits on a pink high stool of granite, his legs spread apart and his arms hanging down at his side, palms up. Spindrift is gathering like dust on his thighs and in the folds of his jacket. His large head is back and up, his eyes open sightlessly, no longer even blinking away the flakes that land between the grey lids. The oval of his face is colourless. There are several long lines of ice dangling in broken chains from his moustache. Only his bottom lip is visible beneath it, a black scrawl drawn back into his mouth like rubber. Vomit glistens on his chin until it is absorbed by his beard. In back where his helmet is propped against the rock, his brains are seeping out of his broken skull and collecting in a wet sack in the hood of his cagoule. Lafferty has pulled the hood tight to the back of the Monk's head and wrapped it with an elastic bandage. It is as close to medicine as his wooden fingers would allow him to get.

Lafferty had invented the climb. It was his confidence that had brought the Monk here and placed him beneath the rock. But there is no blame, only coincidence; only the providence that saves one and sacrifices another. They had been standing side by side, Lafferty had heard the rock first and screamed but the Monk had moved in the wrong direction. The small boulder struck the back of his helmet and dumped him unconscious down on the ledge. Lafferty could tell by the sound of the impact – like a softball, hitting a mattress – that there would be little he could do, but he had not understood the worst of it until he had placed his hand on back of his friend's head to give him water. He had felt the splintered edges of the hole with his fingers then and his hand had come away wet. His stomach had shrunk and turned over with horror and yet something, whether curiosity or concern, he did not know which, had made him slip a finger inside the Monk's balacava and pull it away from the side of his head.

Brain mixed with bits of blue wool, black hair and pieces of white shining skull had slithered around the Monk's neck towards his ear. Lafferty had then pressed the cap back against his friend's head and bandaged it. As he worked it occurred to him that they would both die on the ledge: The Monk very soon, possibly not until early morning for him. He accepted this calmly and finished his business, then coiled up the rope and made a seat out of it. Now that the excitement is over the cold is beginning to settle on him. He no longer looks over at his friend's crushed head but pulls in close to him, drawing his feet up underneath his coat, leaning against him to absorb the heat. They tilt together like children away from the void.

By dawn the suspicion in the valley that they are in trouble has been confirmed. The excitement is almost tangible. Young men walk through the fog to Grant's shop where they stand around the stove in knickers and patched wind jackets, wearing boots half tied and talking quietly, intently. There is a rumour of a rescue attempt going around and they are volunteering by their presence. Not that they will all be able to go on the operation, what is important is that they will be close enough to it to later say they had been *there*. Coffee cups form them into small huddles and outside there is the smell of early morning marijuana. Jarold Grant, who runs the climbing school, is on the phone with Tasker who runs the park. 'Fish and Game,' Jarold is telling him, 'is just not up to something like this.' The heads in the room nod and smile knowingly. But Tasker is unmoveable. He has the bills, he replies, for having had his men trained by Jarold to be up to it. It is a hard line to argue and Grant is quiet as Tasker establishes his paper proof. Jarold's unusual silence spreads disappointment in the room behind him. It has been a slow winter and everyone wants very much to be in on this one. When he has his chance again, Jarold explains to Tasker in his most amicable voice that the weather is the unforeseen factor for which 'experience is the only preparation.' Tasker agrees to this that, yes, his men need this rescue for the experience. A *sotto voce* slur from the back of the shop mentions that lives are more important than the rangers getting 'experience'. Jarold is already pursuing the same point, only with greater subtlety, and eventually Tasker gives in to the possibility of bad press if something goes wrong. He agrees to two teams: four rangers and four local climbers, one group being lowered to the ledge and the other approaching by the ice fall. Arrangements are quickly made for the airlift, team leaders (Jarold, of course, and an ex-Yellowstone ranger named Ferthe), food, equipment and camera teams. The local television station has asked permission to send along a crew and Tasker has attached them to the rangers. Jarold is too anxious to care about that now and quickly closes the conversation. He turns smiling to the climbers filling the room. No one claps but there is applause in the air. Anticipation spreads like fervour as his face again turns serious. Almost as a single body the climbers seem to lean forward towards him.

'Fine tune, goddammit!' Lafferty mumbles, his head jerking slightly. 'I can't see a bloody thing for chrissakes! Got to tune this damn thing in!' He searches the rock around him for the dials with his bare hands. His mittens have fallen off unnoticed and lie in the snow at the base of the ledge. He is not aware of any discomfort; his arms are dead now to above his elbows. He searches over the Monk who is dead, too, and frozen hard. Lafferty does not know this. He no longer has any accurate memory of the Monk or the climb. He has entered the limbus, gone crazy with the cold and the slow work of dying, shrinking like pastic wrapping in a fire from the torment on the surface and drawing down to what little of the process there is left. Timeless grey light is on him. He sees images lurking in shadows, sees them moving, even recognises a few, he thinks, and calls out to them, but they shrink back into the mist the closer he comes. 'Fine tune, goddammit,' he grunts again.

The rescuers are flown to the top of the mountain and lowered to the dead on a winch. Lines are attached to the bodies and they are lifted up the face like freight. An arm is lost. At the summit Lafferty and the Monk are packed in bags and taken away, nothing very dramatic. The team crossing the glacier is called back before they have even reached the base. Later, Jarold refuses Tasker's offer to come to the press conference and instead goes to Collin's tavern with the others and gets very drunk. They drink 'boilermakers' in silence as more people enter and gather a respectful distance to form a ring of small whispering groups. The four climbers do not talk between themselves or to anyone else. They do not need to. The knowledge has already spread that they were the four who reached the bodies, the four who touched the dead. To discuss the event now would be to limit its proportions. At 6.15 the end comes when they all turn to watch Tasker on the news. He is dressed in his climbing clothes, he is very sombre, he chooses his words carefully, almost wearily, seeming to think out the tangents before answering. It gives his statements a philosophical, climberly effect. He closes with a postscript on safety, his arms folded on the table and his mouth very near the microphones. When the television is snapped off Jarold leans back into single view from the table and shakes his head ironically. 'What the hell does that son-of-a-bitch know?' he asks no one and everyone. 'Hell, he wasn't there. He didn't know them. He didn't have to stuff them in bags for godsakes.' Respect flows towards him like a river.

Time has passed. On the mountain it is a year now and snow has piled up in the Monk's corner until all that is left of his ever having been there is a red smudge on the rock where his helmet had scraped against it. The two pitons planted by Lafferty still remain. They are referred to in Jarold's updated guidebook of the region as the 'death belay'. No one needs to ask why. Everyone has read his story of the rescue, watched him on television and seen the prize-winning photograph of him, his face grim and drawn, his hands in his pockets, his head down and the two bodies wrapped in black plastic shrouds lying in the snow behind him. The same photo that now hangs in a wooden frame over the ice-axe display in his shop. The photographer had given him a copy at Tasker's request. Perhaps to avoid any unkindness, Tasker's name had been left out of the article, but his television appearance had done him all the good he needed, anyway. In the spring he was transferred to Washington, DC, and placed in charge of a study formulating policy on climbing safety in the national parks. Tasker wears climbing boots to work these days and is known to have seen the dead. For this he is greatly respected in the nation's capital.

from CLIMBING November 1975

GRAND CANYON CLIMB

PAT LITTLEJOHN

Dawn: an eye opens reluctantly and registers light filtering through a half-inch breathing-hole in the top of the sleeping-bag cocoon. The bag is just the last defence against the cold, being backed up by long johns, trousers, T-shirt, wool shirt, pullover, polar jacket, balaclava and two pairs of socks. And still I am freezing. Not for a week now have night temperatures on the South Rim exceeded 10°F. It seems miraculous that in a few hours the desert sun will push the temperatures up into the sixties.

I release the drawcord and take a stinging breath of neat air. Thirty yards to the bog – sorry, 'rest room' – a centrally-heated paradise. Step into pumps and run.

Movement causes eyes to stream, nose to run, and then a coughing fit. This cold or influenza or whatever it is has become a way of life. I've been in its grip for two weeks – too long. Time, perhaps, to pay attention to those anxious little voices inside my head, saying: you're asking for it, pneumonia, sleeping out sub-zero every night. What would mother say? I'm emptying my passages into reams of toilet-paper as John bursts in, blue face set in red duvet. He's a sufferer of a couple of days' standing and joins the morning ritual. When the worst has been expelled and we're left with just a dull head-ache, we prepare for the next move, a hop to the cafeteria.

Two hours pass in a studied, drawn-out breakfast. We are slowly sipping our *fifth* coffee and peering outside, trying to guess the temperature. Don't be fooled by the dazzling sun. It actually matters today, as we're committed to breaking our Grand Canyon invalids' routine of lounging, reading, sunning and strolling; for today we have a 'Permit' – to climb. It had taken some getting.

'There is no rock-climbing here,' said the crisply-dressed rangerette. 'The rock's too crumbly. If you want to climb you ought to go to Granite Mountain. That's a hundred and fifty miles south.'

I told her I'd closely inspected one particular band of cliffs and, on the basis of ten years' experience, judged them excellent for climbing.

'Well, I can't authorise it. You'll have to apply to our Head Ranger, he's an expert climber.'

Two miles to the Ranger Station. Far enough for your enthusiasm for climbing to wane, if you're feeling rough. However, just getting the permit seemed a worthwhile challenge, so we pressed on.

On the wall of the office was a huge picture of Half Dome's North-West Face, which seemed encouraging. The Head Ranger got straight to the point.

'What climbing experience have you had in the United States?'

'I've done that,' I said, pointing to the picture.

'Uh-huh, what else?'

'A few other Yosemite classics: Nose of El Cap, Lost Arrow Chimney, lots of shorter stuff.'

'Hmm.' He looked unimpressed. Christ! – did one have to be Royal Robbins to climb this scruffy little crag? I was just wondering what else I could throw at him – things I'd heard of like the Longs Peak Diamond and the Painted Wall in Colorado – when he asked to see our equipment. We emptied our two sacks, and it made a pile two feet high. This must be it, I thought. Still no comment from the chief.

We followed him inside and our group seemed quite naturally to arrange itself into an interview situation: the Head Ranger behind his big desk, and us on little chairs in front of it.

'Our problem is,' he began, 'that we have no real facilities for cliff rescue in the Park.'

I told him I'd done most of my climbing on remote sea cliffs, where there was even less possibility of rescue.

'So where did you want to make your climb?'

I described to him a chimney line in the Cocconino sandstone band of cliffs, about a thousand feet down the canyon. The line is right beside the main Bright Angel Trail, a point in its favour, I thought.

'Can't allow that. People will watch you, try to imitate, and next thing we'll have a dozen accidents or rescues on our hands.'

'Another line we looked at,' I interposed swiftly, 'was a big corner about half-a-mile along the cliff.' His eyes brightened.

'I've seen that line. Always thought it would be an incredible route.'

From that moment, things took a new turn. A message securing our permit began its passage along the pipe-line to the aforementioned rangerette, while the Head Ranger, Ernie, told us of his own quite eventful climbing career. Among other things he had been on an early ascent of The Diamond.

At midday we emerge from the Lodge, blinking in the sun's glare. To be honest, neither of us feel too bad now, as our germs usually give a few hours' respite in the middle of the day. Gear is sorted then we're off down Bright Angel.

'Say, are you guys going rappelling?'

The questioner is one of a pair of scrawny youths. To be suspected of participating in such an activity is an insult to any self-respecting climber, and we ignore him. 'Rappellers' are a novel phenomenon to British climbers visiting the US. They have built a whole sport around abseiling and get their kicks from roping down different cliffs, as climbers get theirs from doing different routes. Apparently you haven't really rappelled a crag unless you've done it on a double rope, a single rope, and both with and without top-rope protection. A van-load of rappellers rolled up at a bouldering crag in Tuscon while we were there, and spent all day roping down a twelve-foot precipice, amid a continuous barrage of instructions and commands from their associates. Our reaction ranged from amusement to total mystification. You could dismiss rappellers as loonies, were it not for the fact that Yvon Chouinard began his career as one.

We round a bend and ahead of us lies the chimney line we had originally hoped to climb. How nice it looks: 500ft of sustained VS climbing, on hard, weathered sandstone. It must remain inviolate, however, as its ascent would have incited hordes of tourists to hurl themselves, lemming-like, at the cliffs, scrabbling upwards until they became stuck or dropped off. Strange this doesn't happen in Yosemite.

Once off the trail, the desert terrain is hard going, not designed for the passage of man. Unstable, sandy slopes, boulders shifting underfoot, every plant thick with spiny weapons. The odd lizard scuttles out of sight; otherwise there is no movement and no sound. The great Colorado River is more than five miles away and can barely be seen, let alone heard, and Bright Angel will be silent until the mule trains whoop and jangle their way up around evening time.

I am freshly stunned by the grandeur of the line we have come to attempt, and at the same time reminded of the reason I opted for the chimney in preference to it. The corner is capped by an overhang at least forty feet across. However, with the exception of this final hurdle, the route couldn't be more compelling and we waste no time in roping up.

It's mid-afternoon by now, but conditions are perfect. I don my sun hat and begin climbing, assimilating through fingertips the characteristics of the rock. Harder, certainly, than the Navajo sandstone at Zion, where we climbed a week ago. A difficult groove, then a swing left into a tight, narrow corner. My brimmed hat scrapes the rock, so I flick it off and watch it circle down into the bush from whence it came. 5.9 eases to 5.8 and fifty feet of perfect jamming gets me to a stance on a pile of sandstone pancakes. While John is following, the sun rounds the canyon rim and the temperature drop is instantaneous. Fortunately, the air is absolutely still. On go the pullovers, in creeps a sense of urgency.

The corner crack has been widening imperceptibly with height gained, and at the stance it is fist-jam width. Twenty feet above is a nasty-looking roof, and I'm hoping the crack won't go off-width before I get over that. It very nearly does, and I hang out on the lip on a lousy little-finger/thumb-knuckle jam, wondering if it will slide out when I go for the swing round. I launch, it holds, and soon I'm running it out in an off-vertical off-width, a long way from protection, and cursing my lack of big hexentrics. On the theory that nothing can be as hard as the Arrow Chimney, I keep cool and keep going. A neat stance arrives but I have nothing wide enough to jam in the crack. Ten minutes are spent in chipping a loose rock to size, then John follows, taking a swing at the roof, 5.10, that one.

Chimneys: are they enigmas to everyone, or just me? I've been scrutinising the specimen above for twenty minutes and still can't decide whether it's going to be easy or insane. Presumably it will be easier facing one way than the other, but how do you decide? I've only one nut big enough for the crack, so don't like the idea of fancy revolving antics. Twenty-five feet of off-width, then I bid goodbye to my hex eleven and enter the flared chute. Try it facing left. Inelegant progress is made before I fall prey to spasms of fear and pain, as the runner recedes into uselessness and knee injuries sustained in Lost Arrow Chimney are reactivated. I'm a no-kneepad freak, as well as a chalkless freak, but the former principle may well have to be sacrificed if I'm not to become a wheelchair freak.

'Watch me, I'm coming down.'

A grinding, sliding motion ensues, arrested at intervals by the panicky wedging of any available appendage. Fortunately, descending chimneys is rarely as hard as ascending them. At the base, I swivel round and begin again the random actions which comprise my chimneying technique. This time I succeed without too much of a struggle, but my elation wilts as I approach the obstacle ahead: an overhanging, off-width crack, forty-feet long and set in a smooth, rusty-coloured wall of softer sandstone. The grimmest-looking thing I've seen in the US, outside of downtown Houston. For five minutes I bridge motionless across the top of the chimney, staring. John's voice eases my solitude.

'How does it look?'

'Gruesome.'

'Do you want to go on?'

We have less than an hour of daylight. The decision to rope off has got to be made some time, why not now? But I'm quite sure I want to do this line, and would rather not face this thing lead-bellied after morning hot-cakes.

'I'll just take a look.'

Jams lead up to the wide crack and, hanging from the last of them, I rearrange my gear on to a shoulder-sling, to keep it outside the crack. I'm keyed-up for the fight of my life, but fate grants a brief reprieve as my left hand sinks into a sharp-edged crack inside the off-width. This God-given feature speeds me on for twenty feet, then it begins to snake away inside the mountain. One more move and I can only reach it with my fingertips; next move, it's gone, and I'm reliant on pure off-width techniques. Not English off-width tactics either – there are no chockstones to lasso – this has to be American style. Just ten feet higher the crack widens to a chimney and easier ground. John's advice would be: if you don't fancy this bit, why not miss it out? Ten paltry feet. I could tell you of the body-racking struggle, with its curses, prayers, anger and howls of despair. But skip to the chimney (it's possible in print), where I'm groaning and gasping like one who has just run a marathon. I fumble with a runner and push on against the gathering dark. The corner becomes much more recessed, accentuating the failing light. I reach a big sloping ledge, strewn with loose blocks, and work on fixing anchors, hardly daring to look up. It's much as I expected. The corner crack, fist-jam width or a little wider, overhangs steadily for sixty feet before reaching a visor of stepped overhangs thirty feet across. Good nightmare material, I think, as I rope off into the gloom.

The rocks ring with curses as we stumble back to the trail. Joined ropes just reached the ground; gear was shed quickly and left where it lay. Not many climbers pass this spot. Our first duty is to report our well-being to Ernie. We meet him later in the bar, drink the evening away, and enjoy the live music which is a nightly feature. While Grand Canyon's social scene is not fantastic, it's many times better than Yosemite's.

Night takes its toll. An hour after waking it's obvious that yesterday's respite is being paid for by today's relapse. John also feels worse than ever. We make the cafe by 8.30 and meet Ernie, as arranged, to borrow a couple of bongs for use in the wide crack above our high-point. They are Dolt originals, squat and heavy, but better than carrying rocks up under your pullover.

'What time do you guys expect to be on the route?'

'Give us an hour or so.'

'We'll be watching through the observation telescope. Good luck.'

An hour slips by, but we can't bring ourselves to move. I sit by the lodge fire, buried in down clothing, withdrawn from the world like a sick animal. John sits opposite me, nodding off to sleep between violent bursts of nose blowing. Around noon we shuffle out to the car and are sitting inside, eating, when Ernie approaches, accompanied by another uniformed ranger.

'Goddamn, aren't you guys on the climb yet? We've been looking through the 'scope for the last two hours, trying to pick you out.'

Our excuses sound lame in this land of health and dynamism. We know we have to get on the route, if only to retrieve our ropes, as we are scheduled to move on south today or early tomorrow. More promises are made: watch for us in a couple of hours.

Another beautiful day; ninety-five per cent of them are, in Arizona. Everything is just as we left it: slings strewn around beneath a fragile-looking pink strand which soars up for 100ft or more, before being swallowed up by the corner crack. Nearly twenty minutes to reach the knot, and I'd made the 500ft to Sickle Ledge in that time a month ago. I slump back in my slings, sweating, throat parched, and feeling feverish. The lower rope is secured so that John can follow, then I continue upwards like a run-down automaton. On the stance in the recess I get myself belayed in a position of armchair comfort, then take in the rope so that John can climb the pitch below. A newcomer to the States, it's his first off-width experience and not a nice initiation. I can tell where he's at by the noise he makes: a whoop of elation as he feels the edge inside the crack; curses when it runs out; grunts, gasps and raves as he fights the inch-by-inch battle to get established in the chimney. He arrives and looks up.

'God, how are you going to do that?'

'Oh, it's nothing. You should see some of the crack lines in North Cornwall.'

A standing joke between us is that every bit of rock we see over here has a super counterpart in North Cornwall, an area John has never visited. Though feeling far from up to scratch, there are some theories I'd like to test on the pitch above.

The gently overhanging fist-jam crack above the stance feels like it's lined with broken glass and I leave a lot of blood and skin behind. It's tough being a tapeless freak. Surprisingly good holds lead up and out: chockstones, jugs on top of semi-detached blocks, perfect hand-jams. Then the rock stops playing games and overhangs twice as sharply, forcing me to use my novel stratagem. Hanging from jams, I swing into a chimneying position, using eye-level footholds between the tiers of the overhang. Each move is wilder than the last, but some of the strain can be taken off my arms till the tiers run out, still more than fifteen feet from the lip. Then there is just the roof crack and nothing for it but to hang, sloth-like, from fist and foot-jams. Six feet from the lip I know I'm not going to make it. My only big hex is about knee-level and I'd need the split-second placement of another to carry on free-climbing. All I've got are Ernie's bongs, clanging like cowbells somewhere in the air behind my back, and not another pair of hands to place them. I yell for a tight rope and plummet back to the sling. With a lot of fiddling I manage to place the bongs as nuts, getting away with a light hammer tap. Hanging from the second one, I'm within reach of the lip and try several times to move around. My reluctance is due more to leaden arms than difficulties, and soon I find myself in a sinew-searing bridge position from which the only way is up. The 5.7 groove above seems like level ground by contrast, and is in fact about perpendicular to the climbing below.

The day is drawing swiftly to a close. I belay in time to watch the last flicker of sun touch the North Rim and the intervening summits. Perhaps for the first time, I'm seeing Grand Canyon with a kind of comprehension, without being blinded by the spectacle. Awareness of it as one of the world's natural wonders comes suddenly and fully. My gaze rests on the spire-like Zoroaster Pinnacle, most attractive of all the canyon's summits to a rock climber and the only place, according to Ernie, where serious climbing had been done prior to our visit. With the sun's quietus the sky becomes metallic and the canyon is filled with shadow. A chill wind sweeps the cliff. John's speedy arrival is imperative as there is a pitch to go and we're not dead sure of the way off. He climbs half the pitch and jumars the rest, taking a pendule as each protection point is removed. Reaching me, he dumps excess gear and leads through without a pause. Contracting into the groove as far as possible to avoid rock-fall and the piercing wind, I watch as the features of the cliff dissolve into a uniform dark mass. A shout tells me John has made it, then it's my turn to grope blindly upwards.

What can be the sense in doing a 500ft rock climb in a canyon 5000ft deep? Did we just create a British climb overseas? Most people come to look, or to walk down the trail and look, but Grand Canyon is a vast area of wild country full of opportunities for adventure. To experience adventure is to heighten perception, and if you find your adventure in climbing, try exploring Grand Canyon through its most basic element – rock. Do our route, do another. The cliff is hundreds of miles long and presents a striking line every hundred yards. That way, perhaps your experience of Grand Canyon will crystallise into something richer and more memorable than if you simply arrive, and depart, as a regular tourist.

from MOUNTAIN 56 *1977*

WARNING RECORD

LAURA JASCH

Dear Editor:

This is the beginning of the end. There is no doubt that a gun-packing 'conservation' officer is a frightening omen. But why, I asked? This is a State Conservation Area. Did the citizens of Indiana vote to prohibit climbing here? Did you vote to limit the driving speed to 55mph, he replied? Somebody makes the rules, and other people enforce them.

I have been informed that my second offence of climbing at Portland Arch, Indiana, will bring me to court. If I plead guilty, the fine will probably be $1.00 and $25.00 court costs. If I plead innocent, may the bondsmen of the earth bail me out if my friends leave me to rot in a Southern Indiana County Jail.

I have decided there is only one thing left to do. Climb during the week, at night, in the nude, so as to be inconspicuous. After all, if the American Alpine Club cannot come to my rescue, I must take matters into my own hands.

Yours Sincerely
Laura Jasch

from CLIMBING 1976

MT. KATAHDIN: TIME FOR A CHANGE

GUY and LAURA WATERMAN

Many Eastern climbers regard Mount Katahdin as their greatest mountain. Its glacial cirques are ringed by 2000ft walls that afford many challenging rock routes, with numerous first-ascent opportunities available. In winter it's an ice-climbing arena without parallel in the east. Its isolated location in the north woods of Maine adds to the feeling of wilderness and challenge.

Yet state park management's safety consciousness has produced a set of rules and regulations that stifle the 'freedom of the hills' so successfully that many climbers simply avoid Katahdin, rather than submit.

Paul Petzoldt said of his one trip to Katahdin: 'It was like a prison camp to me.'

The Appalachian Mountain Club's Winter Mountaineering School ceased operating its Advanced Section there, in part because of cumbersome regulations.

Regulations include a provision that no one may start up the mountain after a certain hour in the morning – e.g., no leaving Abol Campground after 11am in July, no leaving Roaring Brook Campground after 9.30am in October. Also you may not leave before 7am unless weather is perfect, because at 7am the rangers decide whether they'll allow anyone to go up the mountain at all!

On a recent trip there we found the mountain 'closed' because of 'cloud cover'. On the next day everyone milled around the ranger's porch until 7am when the decree came down that we could go up that day.

Sometimes hikers make the long drive to Katahdin only to be told politely that the mountain is 'closed'. If bad weather hangs in for several days, the entire trip may prove fruitless.

Katahdin's trails are rugged and exposed, but no more so than many in neighbouring New Hampshire's Presidentials, not to mention the west. Many hikers and climbers enjoy the challenge of bad weather in an alpine zone like Katahdin. However, the idea that climbers and hikers should make their own judgements on when to go up or not is alien to Baxter State Park management.

If Messner and Habeler came to Katahdin they could not leave before 7am or after 11am – if at all – for an ascent that would probably not take them two hours.

In winter, rules are even stricter. Parties must register far in advance, show proof of competence, obtain a medical exam, provide a back-up rescue team, camp only at one location (next to a ranger cabin, occupied by a park ranger in radio contact with the outside world), obtain clearance to climb each day, specify which route, no bivouacs, no alternate camps, and bring in a long list of equipment that includes such items as a two-pound woodsman's axe.

from OFF BELAY *October 1977*

CLIMBING RESTRICTIONS IN THE MIDWEST

LAURA JASCH

It is with vivid purple outrage that I have been following letters concerning the closure of Indiana State Parks, Nature Preserves, etc., to climbing.

Who climbs in Indiana? I for one climbed there for a long time. Exactly why have the parks been closed to climbing? That remains a mystery.

I personally addressed this issue while face to face with a gun-packing ranger at the base of the crumbling sandstone cliffs of Portland Arch, Indiana. I was being awarded a citation for 'Climbing in a No Climbing Zone' (see page 468)... I could not believe it, but unfortunately I moved out of the Midwest and lost my opportunity to test the case.

My experiences of this nature in the Midwest are not isolated. Returning from an afternoon of ice-climbing in the canyons of Starved Rock State Park in Illinois, we mistakenly crossed paths with a ranger, who noticed our ropes. There is no rappelling here, he said. (It should be made clear that rappelling is a new sport. Grab a six pack, a bottle of cheap wine, and a few impressionable teeny-bopper girls and head for the cliffs to rap ...) Ah, I responded with an air of confidence, I know there is no rappelling and no rock-climbing. (The fear exists that climbing the rotten sandstone would reduce it to sand dunes. This is entirely possible since rock in that neighbourhood can be reduced to sand in your hand.) But we were ice-climbing! Unfortunately this was fuel for his fire, because if anything ice-climbing was the worse offence. Rangers take groups out in the winter to admire the frozen water falls. Most unfortunately, one unwary ranger rounded a corner one day, with a photography club in tow, when to their amazement and the ranger's embarrassment they found some climbers polluting the picture.

The rangers subsequently made their own rule that ice-climbing was not allowed in the park and we were expected to obey the rules. I argued that they must be joking if they thought they themselves could dictate laws in a public park. I was shown some fine print in a Rules brochure that essentially said Rangers could indeed make special rules in their individual parks for various ambiguous reasons. Needless to say I asked what would happen when I returned. The young ranger who understood the argument kindly said we would just be thrown out again. He did not go so far as to say we would be fined or end up in jail.

So, Indiana, Illinois, and would you believe Ohio have restrictions on climbing. Shortly after my letter to *Climbing* I received a phone call from a boy in Ohio wanting to know if I were starting a movement to save climbing in the Midwest. Climbing had just been outlawed in Ohio.

The letter from the Governor of the State of Indiana published in *Off Belay* 34 does not solve the dilemma of why the parks have been closed to climbing. Dr Bowen states that accidents and lawsuits have forced lawyers for the State to suggest closing parks to new and non-traditional activities.

The first and most obvious question is who has been initiating the lawsuits? I have the overwhelming suspicion that it has not been climbers. It is not uncommon for tourists to injure themselves at the parks by overestimating their abilities and exercising poor sense of judgement. A non-climber dropped a watch over the bluffs at one of the Midwest parks. In an outrageous attempt to retrieve it, the man sustained a serious fall. He was thinking about suing the park to pay the bills which resulted from his own error.

This incredible kind of logic has resulted in lawsuits at parks in Wisconsin also, where fortunately the climbers have not yet been made the scapegoats. As Dave Slinger mentioned in the same issue of Off *Belay*, in his twenty-five years of climbing at Devil's Lake two climbers have been killed, but not while climbing. I myself do not know of any deaths which resulted from climbing in the Midwest. And although I know a number of serious climbing accidents, I know no climber who has sued a park.

In addition, it is my opinion that climbers do not set a bad example for the tourists. People have a natural tendency toward scrambling on rock faces. They'll do it whether or not there are climbers to imitate. On the contrary, climbers frequently find themselves helping out tourists in an uncompromising position. The most significant case in point is in Wisconsin, where the Chicago Mountaineering Club teaches rescue techniques to the rangers at Devil's Lake, and all climbers go instantly to help if a rescue is needed.

With regard to damaging flora, there is little doubt that climbers who walk along the top of a cliff setting up top ropes will damage the flora there, just as much as the tourists walking along the bottom will create a dusty trail. At Portland Arch, before the climbing ban, there was concern that delicate moss and ferns which grew on the cliffs up Bear Creek would be damaged by climbers. A unique arrangement was made with the ranger that the only climbing would be down stream where the cliffs were overhung and bare already. We thought everyone was happy. In the past climbers were blamed for the trash heaps of broken bottles and cans at the base of the cliffs, but when it was pointed out that the tourists supplied the trash, and the climbing clubs from the University of Illinois and University of Indiana actually habitually hauled it out in big plastic sacks, we thought the issue was dropped.

Lastly, if the lawyers for the State of Indiana believe that climbing is a new and non-traditional activity, I suggest we send them a copy of Chris Jones' book *Climbing in North America* so they can see who came before us.

The problem as we see it in the State of Indiana is only part of the basic problem that is surfacing throughout the country. How should public lands be used and how should they be regulated?

It appears that the farce of allowing people to sue a government for maintaining a natural park must stop. Because there are no elevators, escalators, guard rails, paved walks, and bodyguards, a natural park could indeed be a hazard. That is because people for the most part gave up moccasins, bows and arrows, and loin cloths, to live in worlds of concrete. They have forgotten the smell of wild onions, the sound of wind in the pines, and the dangers of fast water, thin ice and steep cliffs. It seems that by establishing parks in the first place, the consensus of opinion was that nature should not be allowed to die. If someone by wilful choice enters the park and gets hurt, that is a consequence he should be prepared to sustain.

If a government faces a lawsuit because it maintains a park, it has several options. Pave the trails and allow only guided tours. Remove potential thrill seekers to save them from themselves, and thus save the government from them. How can you blame them? It is survival of the fittest even today.

In 1974 I lost a brand new tent to a bear that leaped in a great arch out of nowhere to attack the sardines he thought were living there. It was a late spring. The bears were starving. This particular bear at Whatcom Pass in the Cascades was desperate and had even torn a Kelty pack to shreds, in search of booty. On the way down from the pass we met a man who asked us if we had had trouble with the bears. Trouble! Let me tell you. When I finished, he asked if I was going to sue the park. You must be a ranger, I said. And why should I sue the park for giving the bear a place to live? It was painfully obvious that the park was too small for both of us, and that the bear was in for bigger troubles than he imagined. This was outrageous enough. If I had known I was talking to a ranger and if I had known what happens to problem bears, I would have kept my tales of woe to myself. But sue the park? I'd have to be crazy. Some people are, the ranger revealed.

The fact that parks do exist, that people enter them, get hurt, and occasionally require rescue is yet another problem. To me it seems obvious that the natural course of events is to let people make their own choices about what they do, if they get hurt put out whatever resources are available to help them out. As Terry Pearce (*Off Belay 34*) has pointed out, adventurers should be aware of existing capabilities to bail them out, and do their best not to stretch the resources. Since universal education is virtually impossible, however, we will face yet another ethical problem. Can we, and should we, pick out and send home high-risk, potential-disaster cases?

I most seriously suggest that a sign be placed at the entrance to every park in the country.

> This park is for your enjoyment. We encourage you to use it wisely. Preserve it for those who follow. Travel safely, because you enter at your own risk. As your representative, the government has set aside the park for your use, as you have wished. But we cannot protect you from yourself. You must understand your own abilities, testing them cautiously and not irreversibly.

I implore the American Alpine Club to take a stand. Climbing has been banned in a significant number of places in the Midwest. There is yet no logical explanation for this type of government control. It appears to be a case of misdirected aggression. Regardless of the reasons for establishing it, you can be certain this precedent will spread. With regard to the future of climbing in North America, this is the most insidious, dangerous precedent I have ever seen.

from OFF BELAY *October 1977*

IT'S A 5.10 MANTEL
INTO HEAVEN, BROTHER

LARRY KUZNIAR

We had come to challenge nature and ourselves. The morning sun was warm upon my shoulders and I experienced an intense happiness as I stepped from the automobile, Redwings crunching the parking area gravel, exposing my existence for all to hear. I could not help but think, 'What a fine day!' as I wrestled my sack from the back seat. The Monk showed that amazing telepathy that develops between friends who have shared an existence in the mountains, when he voiced my exact thoughts.

'What a fine day!' he said.

The sack gave and was free. I opened it and was greeted by the heady aroma of EBs. Oh heavenly smell, halitosis of Aphrodite herself. Fondling slings, perlon and cool chocks, we sorted gear, lost in pre-climb fears, doubts, expectations. Birds sang, and wispy clouds on the horizon only hinted at what this day would bring.

The approach was horrendous, wending our way through the milling herds of climbers, numbered tickets in hand. All waiting to be next to challenge nature and themselves.

'Number seventeen,' the public address horns squawked, in an electrified, authority-vested, nasal, Ranger voice.

The Monk said that this was a bunch of shit. I had to agree. We decided to go round the corner and put up a new line.

The Monk shouldered the rack and led off on some mediocre 5.9 slabs. I belayed from a stout juniper in a style the Monk likened to a reclining tourist. When he had reached the end of his rope, he asked if I could move up ten feet or so, so that he could reach the two spacious nubbins above for his belay. I did, and quick as a wink he was up and belaying.

'I'm coming,' I squeaked and began moving. Muscles flexed and relaxed as the familiar rock greeted me. Up I moved, overjoyed at not having to clean anything, only paste lichen back on the rock where our careless shoes had scraped it clean. Joining the Ascetic Monk on the nubbins, I commented on the intricate patterns the clouds were forming above our humble heads. We were struck with awe and suddenly became aware of our part in the great cosmic circle. We realised then that we were two men on our way to destiny. After only one pitch! What a great revealing day lay ahead of us.

I took the rack and made my way up. It was more slab-climbing. All in all not too exciting, but done in good style. I made the belay below an over-hanging, smooth, crackless wall. It looked difficult. While the Monk was coming up, I stared at the exfoliation flakes near the toe of my left boot. I was aware of the likeness my life had with the tenuous existence of this insignificant flake of rock. My boot came to represent fate. I was lost in deep, profound thought when my partner joined me.

From below, a voice wafted up: 'Hey, there's a new route going up over here!' Then the growing thunder of PA and EB-clad feet coming around the corner. The Park Rangers were in the lead. A Mobile Command Unit was trundled in and immediately they began organising lines and handing out numbered tickets. Another crew of Rangers poured from two trucks and busied themselves erecting the enormous nets. A party began coming up our route while two other parties pushed variations.

The Monk smiled a faint smile, inserted a Number Two Stopper between two rugosities off to the left, and began frictioning the overhanging wall. I paid out the rope as he worked, quickly and coolly. Twenty, thirty, forty feet: almost to the lip of the wall. I looked down. The first party had reached the top of the first pitch, and another party was starting up. The nets were almost completed and a concrete truck was pouring a foundation for a permanent headquarters to co-ordinate use.

Below us we heard a soft 'Jesus Christ!' from the second ascent party. Then silence. We watched the two men, roped together, tumbling through space for what seemed an eternity, then bouncing harmlessly on the nets. The courageous but obviously incompetent lads lined up for another try.

The Monk fished from his pocket a roll of Lifesavers, the only indulgence he allows himself, and offered me one. We sat contentedly munching Life-savers and discussed what a fall like that would have meant several years ago: death, to be sure. But now, with the assurance of a soft landing, climbers are attempting things way beyond their abilities. The Monk and I vowed that should we peel we would do our best to miss the nets.

After our short rest I started jamming up the finger-crack. About seventy feet of hard but enjoyable 5.10 climbing brought me to the roof. Clinging to a large knob with my right hand, I adjusted my briefs with my left and inspected the roof. A hairline crack was its only fault. I pondered for long moments, until I was struck by the realisation that most assuredly aid was the only way. The Monk queried as to what the difficulty was.

'Aid,' I whispered, but the crowd at the bottom still heard somehow, and their murmuring turned to angry cries: 'They're going to use aid!' As one, they began shaking indignant fists and hurling white cubes and little bags streaming white clouds.

'Let me have a look,' said the Monk. I began looking for some way of making a belay. It was one of those classic times that you have all experienced when not one of those chocks that you have about your body will work, I decided that it was time to test the Monk's latest development in climbing paraphernalia:* the inflatable chock (trade name 'Pneumanut', shortly to be available at all fine mountaineering retail outlets for the paltry sum of five dollars; compressed-air cartridges extra). I simply inserted it in the troublesome crack and inflated. Bombproof.

'Come ahead.' I called.

The Monk scampered up to look at the awesome roof as the leader of the formerly third, now second, ascent party came over the edge of the overhanging wall, breathing heavily and looking wild in the eyes.

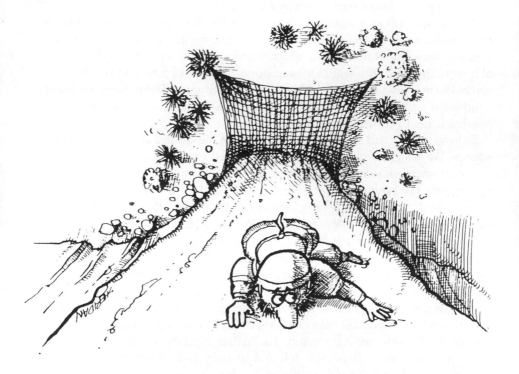

*See the complete catalogue for other items of the Ascetic Monk's equipment, including the fabulous Razor Blade Piton, the now legendary Double-Gated Karabiner, the inventive Roach Line (for those hanging bivouacs) and its accompanying Wind Tube (you can even talk through it). The catalogue has full details on equipment and its uses, in an easy to read text which uses primarily one syllable words. The Monk has also shared his Twelve Doctrines of Climbing Ethics in this full colour extravaganza. Included, too, are articles and attitudes by some of the top names, giving helpful hints on how to.

I turned my eyes back to the Monk. He was quietly contemplating the difficulty, assessing its every feature, fixing the image on the bulletin board of his mind. Clearing an obstruction from the right nostril of his bulbous nose, he mumbled something about showing me a new technique, stepped from the rugosities on which he had been resting and levitated beneath the roof, pushing himself along with his fingertips. In a very short while he was calling for me to follow.

'Must be that clean living,' I thought. Then I, the lowly sloth, dull of wit and slow in action, saw the evil in my life: the self-indulgent foolishness of wine, song and the sensual pleasures of the flesh in the arms of beautiful women. All of this unfolded itself, and I embraced the knowledge. A wonderful enlightenment filled to the very brim the tumbler of my consciousness. I could truly see, hear, feel. Life, precious life was mine.

I studied the roof, fixing every feature of it in my mind. Then the meditation: I became a part of the rock, a part of the air. I knew all, I was all. I knew nothing, I was nothing. Then, in a state of total non-reality, reality came rushing up to embrace me in her fat pink thighs; I began an orgasm of cosmic intensity and stepped into space.

I joined my partner on the grassy ledge above. He was sitting, a blade of grass between his lips, in calm reverie, having achieved an ultimate experience in his young life. All I could muster was a short, breathless 'Wow', as I plopped my body beside his and lay staring at the clouds above. Suddenly, they took on new meaning and, unbelievably, THE ANSWER was in them. I looked at my partner, who was smiling benevolently, and I thought I saw a faint aura about his head. We moved on.

It was an easy scramble to the summit. The Monk was coiling the rope and I was carrying on a conversation with a small ponderosa pine growing from a crack. The pine related the story of his existence, which had been rather difficult in the small amount of soil. We discussed the life of any being that chooses the fringes of civilisation for its existence. The storm-torn skeletons of countless others surrounded us. We were akin, this fragile being and I, forced to be tough by a tough existence. We bore the scars of that existence. Not for us the soft life of the valley, with its straight symmetrical forest. No, we loved the storms, the howling wind, the not knowing whether we should live tomorrow.

A puffing, middle-aged Ranger, carrying a bulging briefcase, appeared from behind a boulder. My back was towards him, but the tree alerted me to his presence. I whirled about, just as he made his cheerful greeting: 'Hello, boys. Fine route that, fine route. Now, I'd like you boys to fill out these route-description forms, in triplicate. And then I'll need some information for our use-management files. Now then, your individual numbers and party number.'

I looked on dumbly. The Monk muttered: 'Number?'

'Yes. You know, the number on the five-by-seven card that is to be affixed at no less than three, no more than seven, points to your back or rucksack. It's the same number that appears in our files, telling us where you are climbing, rating your ability, and giving the number of sit-ups done in an impartial test by a local agency with no connection whatsoever with the Park Service or government at any level,' (he paused for a breath) 'the colour of your foul weather gear, names of relatives, girlfriends, pets, and furniture. You mean you don't have one?' he finished incredulously.

I shook my head in a vigorous negative, trying to be co-operative. The Monk had withdrawn.

'Well then,' the ranger said, ceremoniously extracting an ominous-looking booklet from the aforementioned bulging briefcase, 'That's a twenty-five dollar fine apiece.' His voice rose an octave-and-a-half higher on the 'apiece'. We were ticketed.

Moving numbly down the trail, we were accosted by the local guidebook author, interrogating us about the route. He hurried off with the information securely under his arm, hoping to make the deadline for this week's supplement.

Back in the meadows we elbowed our way through the crowd to the Whataburger concession. Sitting about a lavish concrete picnic table and belching over the Deluxe Whataburger, large fries, and large ice-cold cokes, we surveyed with satisfaction where we had been. Six parties were on the route, following the white line to the summit. We mused how long the guidebook business would be profitable, pushed off for the parking lot, paid the attendant his two dollars, and motored home.

from MOUNTAIN 51 *1976*

PART 9

MOUNTAIN EDUCATION

The Educational Debate is a peculiarly British phenomenon, but it could easily spread to the rest of the mountaineering world. In the 1950s it became fashionable to use mild mountaineering pursuits as tools in education. The impact of the Everest ascent, with a widespread feeling that those involved were worthy of emulation, coupled with the educational connection of many leading British climbers, led to a view that mountaineering was a 'good thing' for young people. As a result a broadly based national policy of taking teenagers to the mountains developed. From this emerged a system of certification to ensure that the teachers had a basis of training.

The national preoccupation about safety (see previous section), which developed in the late 1960s, found an ideal expression in the mountain education field and what had started as a worthwhile idea threatened to degenerate into an over-regulated nightmare. The Cairngorm Tragedy in 1971 brought to a head the concerns of both the climbers and the authorities. Not surprisingly they came to different conclusions about what needed to be done, and the resulting arguments have enlivened the pages of magazines and journals ever since. What has been written has often been both articulate and interesting and it seems valuable to gather together some of the better articles to form the final section of this book.

The position in 2006: Much of the heat seems to have drained from this debate as modern education seems to have little time for extra mural activities. The Duke of Edinburgh's Award Scheme (in Britain) tends to cover this area. Education authorities are now so preoccupied with academic results that give clear work or university opportunities, that outdoor education and sport has been increasingly marginalized. In the 1960s and 1970s, a nation that had just abandoned conscription and doubled university intake, had not yet geared up for today's fiercely competitive trading world. It therefore happily diverted its young people into efficacious fringe activities. The 1980s saw the decline of the old industries (many of which were very physical) and the rise of the new technologies. The changes in world politics at the end of the 1980s may also have contributed to the change in priorities.

Thus national preoccupations now seem very different. There is a clear emphasis on preparing young people for technology, commerce and consumption rather than more vigorous activities – possibly the final manifestations of a 'swords into plowshares' mentality. The only hint of any official rethink in this area is the recent concern about obesity ... with the attendant dim perception that regular exercise may now be worth encouraging.

APES OR BALLERINAS?

TOM PATEY

Man with all his noble qualities ... still bears in his bodily frame the
indelible stamp of his lowly origin. *Darwin*

If everyone made a point of remembering that, we might be spared a lot of
mountain philosophy and psychoanalysis. And Mallory would have been
better informed. 'Why do you climb?' The answer should be apparent to the
veriest moron. 'Because it is the natural thing to do.' Climbers are the only
genuine primordial humanoids, heirs to a family tradition inherited from
hairy arboreal ancestors.

Recently, of course, the scene has altered. All the interesting trees have
been cut down by the Forestry Commission and replaced with elementary
stereotyped firs, which any fool can climb. Bird's-nesting is illegal. That
removes the only obvious reason for climbing trees. Nowadays, if you
decided to take up residence in a tree, somebody would immediately call out
the fire brigade. Admittedly the Queen lives in a Treetops Hotel when she
goes to Kenya to unwind, but then the Queen, as someone remarked, is a
special case. As far as the average citizen is concerned, a man up a tree is
assuredly up to no good, and he must be speedily charged or certified.

So what other outlet is there? Mountains are the obvious choice. We can
discount university types who climb College buildings, because you need a
pretty elastic imagination to be satisfied with a substitute twice removed. As
regards potholers, they are mere troglodytes ... pale, anaemic offspring of
the Cave Age.

This then is the reason ... pure and simple ... why we climb mountains.
But what I am leading up to is this business of 'style', by which every
mountaineer seems to set great store. Nothing annoys me quite so much as
to hear someone described as a 'stylish' climber (largely because my own
climbing technique has never been noticeably so graced).

Everyone knows what is meant by a 'stylish' climber. He features in all
the best climbing obituaries, viz: 'I never saw x ... make a false or hurried
move. He would stand motionless, sometimes for half an hour or more, on
the tiniest of rugosities, lightly caressing the rock with sensitive finger-tips
as he deliberated his next move. Movement, when it came, was a fluid ripple

481

of conscious style executed with the lithe grace of a ballet dancer'. History usually fails to record how he met his end.

The French, as might be expected, are the supreme stylists. If you don't know what I mean, have a look at the illustrations in Rébuffat's book *On Snow and Rock*. Every picture shows the author examining himself in some graceful and quite unbelievable posture ... like something out of *Swan Lake*. Even the captions carry a note of smug satisfaction: 'Climbing means the pleasure of communicating with the mountain as a craftsman communicates with the wood or the stone or the iron upon which he is working' (portrait of Rébuffat, standing on air, studiously regarding his left forearm, hands caressing smooth granite). 'On monte comme une echelle' (inset photograph of Rébuffat self-consciously climbing a ladder).

It all looks so effortless. In fact, by the time you've finished the book and found a smooth 70° slab to practise on, you're feeling light as thistledown and lithe as Nureyev.

Now to the test. Open the book of instructions and begin. The finger-tips brush the rock like sensitive antennae; the arms are not above shoulder level; the knees are retracted to avoid possible contact with the rock; the stomach is tucked in, the head held high; the features are composed, relaxed and earnest ... you are prepared to 'communicate'.

Stage One: with infinite delicacy the right foot is elevated eighteen inches and the boot tip placed deliberately on a tiny wrinkle.

Stage Two: the left boot is aligned with the right boot by stepping up smoothly and deliberately. Any effort is imperceptible ...

Strange! You're lying flat on the ground with a squashed nose. Another attempt; another failure. Time passes, along with your faith in Rébuffat.

Suddenly and inexplicably you succeed.

Why?

Simple really. You lost your temper and became uninhibited. Ancient primitive reflexes took over. The old jungle juice started throbbing through your veins. If you had two hands to spare, you would beat your chest with pride. Intellectually you may have retreated a couple of million years ... physically you're thriving.

Heave, clutch, thrutch, grunt! Up you go, defying gravity with your own impetus. So what, if it looks ungraceful? Joe Brown doesn't look much like a ballet dancer. Primeval? ... possibly.

Now you can appreciate why the chimpanzees are the happiest-looking animals in the zoo ... hurling themselves about and swinging joyfully from bar to bar. Who ever heard of a maladjusted chimpanzee?

Stripped down to fundamentals, this is what mountaineering is all about. A regressive metamorphosis, if you like. Nobody should have to learn how to climb. In fact most people spend a lifetime unlearning. The most competent climbers I ever saw were some city kids on a bomb-site. They were swarming all over the place like monkeys. They were masters of every technique known to man or Rébuffat... chimneying, straddling, hand traversing, and many other manoeuvres quite outside the scope of the average climbing manual.

It all proves that no one needs to be taught to climb; one merely needs reminding of something one knew even before going to school.

Reverting to nature is generally satisfying... physically and psychologically. It may not be ethical, it may not be moral, but it is usually agreeable. Normally you draw the line, if only for social reasons. In the mountains you can afford to be completely uninhibited. Here, man can act in the manner born, using whatever physical talents nature has bestowed on him. He needs no instruction manuals, no rules and no regulations.

Where does style come into this? Every climber has his own natural 'style', to use the word in its proper context. He inherits it. Climbing instruction, to be of any value, must foster natural style. Try to curb it and you land up in trouble. Try to impose your own style on a 'learner' and you double his difficulties.

The sort of climber I like to watch is the man who knows where he's going, and wastes no time getting there. A latent power and driving force carries him up pitches where no amount of dynamic posturing would do any good.

An efficient mountaineer, by this reckoning, need fulfil only three criteria. He must not fall off. He must not lose the route. He must not waste time. Time may be endless on an English outcrop; in the Alps it can mean the difference between life and death.

These are accomplishments to be learnt neither from books nor from other climbers. Although we are all differently proportioned, we all have some natural ability derived from our primitive ancestors, and that's what we need to develop.

Which takes us back to the apes. Climbers are conceited characters when you pause to think about it. They liken themselves in prints to Gods, Goddesses, and Gladiators; tigers, eagles, and chamois; craftsmen, gardeners and ballet dancers; and even, in one case at least, to computers! One seldom reads of climbers who resemble apes, chimps, or orang-outangs. Comparisons are only odious when too near the bone.

You don't teach children to walk... they teach themselves. Why, then, teach the descendants of the apes to climb? They can also be left to teach themselves. But don't expect them to resemble ballet dancers.

So, next time you see a jaded climber at the foot of a cliff, dangle a bunch of bananas from the top. You may be surprised at the energetic response. Why? Because it's there, of course.

from MOUNTAIN 3 *1969*

SKILLS AND SAFETY

ROBIN HODGKIN

> At times during the climb [the Central Pillar of Frêney]... our one ambition had been to get off alive... but having completed it successfully we quickly forgot the discomfort... We remembered only the pleasure of climbing warm, rough granite in magnificent situations, the beauty of the view and the intense excitement of searching for a route where no one had been before. *Christian Bonington*

Here one of the most skilful and daring mountaineers speaks in words which would be echoed by any other adventurous traveller. Millions of people, especially in urban, industrial society choose to undergo hardship and danger for the joy it brings: joys associated with elemental things, rock, snow, speed and sea. The origins of this urge are obscure. It springs probably from instincts as deep as those of sex and survival, but it has been given its modern direction by the easing and dulling of social and economic conditions. The gradual extension of monotony and security in the centres of civilisation drives people out to the edge, where they find outlets for this force.

Certainly some qualities of health and character will be brought back from these adventures, but a price is paid in terms of death and injury. Some price perhaps is inevitable, but mountaineers would agree that far too many accidents stem from personal failure in men of moderate skill and should therefore be avoidable. This is a serious problem, especially to anyone concerned with teaching boys or girls to live adventurously. This article is an attempt to analyse part of the problem and to suggest ways in which it can be met. My main contention is that a greater emphasis on craftsmanship and a proper understanding of the psychology of skills are the keys which make safety compatible with danger.

Unconscious Skills
A skill is the ability to perform a difficult action correctly, not by virtue of consciously held precepts but by unconscious knowledge of innumerable earlier performances and attempts.

A skill can best be understood therefore as a focussed phenomenon – one act in the present deriving from innumerable past sources. This may be diagrammatically shown thus:

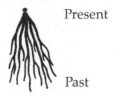

Present

Past

The dot represents a precise act made possible by profound and extensive past experience. One can develop this diagram in various suggestive ways, though like all diagrams it needs regarding with due scepticism. It may be usefully completed by indicating that the skill, as well as having roots in the past, opens up a limited field of freedom in the future:

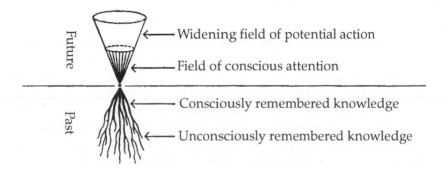

Future

Past

Widening field of potential action

Field of conscious attention

Consciously remembered knowledge

Unconsciously remembered knowledge

If I am the user of the skill my immediate attention is on the horizontal line. The field of potential action stretches ahead into the future. The near part of this is shaded to indicate the field of my immediate attention, where I know, more or less, what is going to happen. But my skill runs not merely through a temporal dimension, it also has a psychological dimension, its roots running back into the past but also 'down' into the unconscious storage circuits of my mind.

These facts can also be conveniently indicated on the other side of the diagram.

It has often been observed that any skilful performer needs to have a relaxed attention fully focused on his acts. At any moment the performer will have a focal awareness of one part of what he is doing or about to do; the rest is left to unconscious control. This matter is fully discussed by Polanyi in his *Personal Knowledge*:

When we use a hammer to drive in a nail, we attend to both nail and hammer, *but in a different way.* We *watch* the effect of our strokes on the nail and try to wield the hammer so as to hit the nail effectively. When we bring down the hammer we do not feel that its handle has struck our palm but that its head has struck the nail. Yet in a sense we are certainly alert to the feelings in our palm... These feelings are not watched in themselves; we watch something else while keeping intensely aware of them. I have a *subsidiary awareness* of the feeling in the palm of my hand which is merged into my *focal awareness* of my driving in the nail.

Polanyi then turns to a common cause of failure:

Subsidiary awareness and focal awareness are mutually exclusive. If a pianist shifts his attention from the piece he is playing to the observation of what he is doing with his fingers while playing it, he gets confused and may have to stop. This happens generally if we switch our attention to particulars of which we had previously been aware only in their subsidiary role.*

Stephen Potter, at a rather different level of scholarship, has commented on such phenomena in his observation of Gamesmanship. 'Analyse your opponent's putting', he advocates, if you want to undermine his morale.

A self-conscious analysis of a skill may have its value in developing or teaching the skill once it has been mastered; but if self-conscious analysis creeps into the execution of a skill it will effectively block its expression. The effect of ill-timed self-consciousness can be observed in such relatively simple skills as boulder-hopping in rough country or in driving a car. An unspoken word of self-approbation or self-analysis is often the precursor of a slip or miscalculation.

These are simple illustrations of the way in which psychological factors can influence skill and safety. Not only does the whole mental 'set' of a person have bearing on whether he is accident prone or otherwise, but the degree and manner in which his self-consciousness intervenes in a skilful act is of considerable importance. The competitive element so evident in many games should have no place in dangerous sports, for this too builds up self-conscious tensions and assertiveness which may be fatal. One wonders how many drivers work themselves into an accident-prone frame of mind by meditating on Grand Prix Champions. (Cf. Thurber's *Walter Mitty.*)

---

*For the kind of knowledge which we have, but cannot fully explain in words, Polanyi uses the term 'tacit knowing' – preferring the present participle, as this suggests that knowledge is a process not a commodity. The importance of Michael Polanyi's thought for education, with his stress on freedom and discipline, risk and responsibility, is still largely unrecognised; though he has received more response in the United States than in Britain. His major work *Personal Knowledge* was published in 1958 by Routledge and Kegan Paul. He gives a more succinct account of his philosophy of discovery in *The Tacit Dimension* (Doubleday, New York, 1966) and more recently Polanyi and Prosch, *Meaning* (University of Chicago Press, 1975).

An inexperienced climber sometimes entertains ambitions which are not far from fantasy. The safest climbers are probably those in whom a high measure of skill is allied to moderate ambition. But this is not the whole story, for it has often been observed that accidents rarely happen to a climber when he is undertaking a really taxing ascent. It is not uncommon for mountaineers who are aware of this fact to utter a word of warning after a difficult ascent has been completed and an easy descent begun. It is not merely fatigue that makes this a dangerous time. Over-confidence and a condescending attitude to the terrain may make climbers succumb to the less impressive dangers of easier ground.

Intellectual Decisions

Polanyi's insistence that maximum awareness is necessary to the execution of a skill can be extended. The 'safe' mountaineer must certainly be capable of channelling much skill and energy into the overcoming of a physical difficulty; but he must also be capable of dealing with another kind of crisis, that which is involved in the making of intellectual decisions. The total time taken in coming to such decisions may be small but a choice of route or objective, the assessment of a party's diminishing resources of energy, or a decision to continue or abandon a climb, often affect life and death. It is important to realise that the exercise of such intellectual decisions involves a distinct break with the predominantly unconscious skills of physical effort.

Before considering these crucial moments it may be useful to note a primarily physiological experience which demands a similar decisive change in mode of apprehension. If a climber is making steady progress over broken ground he needs to keep his visual attention within the cone of sight available to him by the movement of his eyes alone without any independent head movement. If he moves his head to see beyond this cone he will set up a disturbance, presumably in the semicircular canals, which may seriously interfere with his balance. If therefore he needs to turn his head to admire the view or to take stock of the more distant parts of his route, he should stop. The important point here is that he needs to be aware of the limits of his unconscious mechanisms, relying on them fully when they can serve but changing into an entirely different mode of conscious perception and balance when they will not.

On a small scale this illustrates a more general principle which will affect many decisive moments in the life of a mountaineer. During a long expedition the largely unconscious rhythms and skills may have been carrying him upwards for hours. It is possible while this is in progress to turn his mind periodically to other matters without danger. These matters may include problems and decisions affecting the climb. But I rather doubt if this is the best way of making such a decision. Probably the best procedure in such a case is to say 'yes, we will stop and think about this.' The halt may be brief but it will demand a special effort to summon all the available data. Map, compass and watch will be consulted. The fatigue of the party, its resources for a bivouac, and the known and unknown aspects of the route ahead will be allowed for. Opinions will be shared and food will be consumed. To an experienced climber this will all seem very obvious, but I believe that many people find it difficult to make a decisive break in their physical rhythms and to change gear, as it were, into the intellectual effort which such situations demand. Here too, of course, the quality of the decision will depend on the climber's power to exclude irrelevant considerations such as saving face, getting 'value' from a brief ration of mountain days or doing better than the other party, as well as his power to marshal the relevant facts quickly.

Teaching Safety
Teaching methods range widely in the degree to which they involve precept and analysis on the one hand and example and experience on the other. Manual crafts and physical skills like games or mountaineering rely much more heavily on experiential methods. Much of contemporary thinking about teaching is concerned with communicating intellectual skills. But if we are to advance our methods of teaching mountain skills and mountain safety we must learn from the methods of craft teaching, and consider the learner more as an apprentice than a pupil and the teacher as an exponent first and as an explainer only second.

Polanyi points out that the passing on of traditional craft skills can only take place effectively where there is a close personal relationship between master and apprentice (the training of Alpine guides is still largely based on apprenticeship which lasts for at least three years):

> To learn by example is to submit to authority. You follow your master because you trust his manner of doing things even when you cannot analyse and account in detail for its effectiveness. By watching the master and emulating his efforts ... the apprentice unconsciously picks up the rules of his art, including those which are not explicitly known to the master himself. These hidden rules can be assimilated only by a person who surrenders himself to that extent uncritically to the imitation of another.

The rate at which young climbers develop today is often alarming, and parents or teachers who can prolong any one stage of the learning process will help the development of safe skills. It is not a question of saying 'don't do it' but rather of saying 'do more of it' – at the appropriate standard.

Various general conclusions emerge from this dual conception of skills, as things which make possible difficult acts and, additionally, as things which shape the personality of the actor in ways which can increase his propensity for safety. One suggestion concerns a person's attitude to his craft, another concerns his attitude to goals and a third concerns his frame of mind in a crisis.

Pride in the craft, not pride in the achievement, should always be encouraged in the young climber. Interest in equipment in all its aspects, in the history of the craft and in its multifarious background is not merely useful for the practical knowledge that it gives but also because it helps to form the widespread unconscious network which is the essential for any broadly based skill.

Secondly, it is important to use any means which help to relate ambition to the appropriate level of skill. In a school or training course any well-graded system of achievement tests, each one leading to greater opportunities, will help to make young mountaineers conscious of the vital relationship between skill and objective. Further, wherever such hurdles encourage the amassing of experience of 'easy' climbs and expeditions they will help to build up the broad unconscious base on the practical side, just as knowledge builds up the informational base for the skill. The comparison with flying is helpful. Pilots under training always have to amass a lengthy period of flying hours which often seems irksome to the precocious young student but is very necessary to his later safety.

A person's behaviour in a crisis is notoriously unpredictable. But here again the ground can be prepared. Practise with rescue equipment has obvious, direct value. It also has value in encouraging people to explore possible lines of emergency action in imagination before this may be called for in practice. But the kind of crisis that I have in mind is the small *crisis of decision* that we discussed above, not the accident which may result from wrong decision. How can we heighten the habit of cool and effective decision-making?

Something may be done on Outward Bound schemes and in CCF* operations to encourage leaders to write down a retrospective analysis assessing as many factors as possible in a crucial decision. But I think more is needed than this. If a ship in the Navy is damaged as a result of some human error there will always be an official enquiry. This is not merely a deterrent to gross negligence but it must also have a strong psychological effect in bringing home to the man who wields responsibility the grave and complex nature of small decisions. It will help to form a habit of full appraisal

---

*Combined Cadet Force (military training in Britain for teenage school pupils – common in certain schools up to the end of the 1950s when conscription ended).

which can be brought into action even when fear and fatigue make it difficult. One should, I think, consider whether perhaps the public is not too kind to people who make silly or muddled decisions in mountains. The police and the coroner may know little of the special circumstances. The survivors are probably nice and rather pathetic; and anyway the damage has been done. I am not suggesting that any drastic measures should be taken against people who have made such 'human' errors, but rather that more should be done to establish the truth of what happened in an accident and that such truth should be disseminated, in the press and in the climbing journals. It is not fear of consequence but *sustained consciousness of responsibility* that needs heightening.

There is a final point which some people will feel to be irrelevant but which for others will be of central importance. One might discuss it in psychological terms but the words of religion are more apt. How can one consciously become unselfconscious? A man cannot step outside himself in a moment of crisis and attune himself to its demands. And yet the very act of letting go of fear and launching out with one's whole being on a dangerous but skilfully chosen act is akin to both art and prayer. 'Not in my strength alone!' 'Into thy hands, oh Lord!' Acts of commitment are doubtless commonly performed without any conscious religious thought and many mountaineers will admit little or no relationship between these two fields of action. But the Christian who utters a prayer in the midst of danger is not asking for any miraculous help; he is asking (willing?) that whatever power and wisdom is available throughout his limited but complex being may be free to flow into his action, unimpeded by fear, self-consciousness or any other irrelevance. Any mountaineer who has explored even the shallow margins of prayer will see the connection between spiritual and physical effort; but he will also recognise that here is a frontier zone where few have travelled far and that experience, not verbal description, is the only effective guide.

In all our thinking about safety we are right to be concerned with externals, with equipment, with rescue apparatus, with safety codes and standards, but the biggest problems are psychological and internal. The attraction of dangerous situations lies in the demands they make on a man's whole being, and his safety depends on the total response of body, mind and spirit, all harmoniously attuned.

from THE CLIMBERS' CLUB JOURNAL *1962*

MARGINS OF SAFETY

HAROLD DRASDO

In theory they were sound on Expectation
Had there been situations to be in.
Unluckily they were their situation ... *W. H. Auden*

The name of the game is consequences

This is a discursive essay on staying alive. You have to be pretty bold to advise others on avoiding accidents in the hills, if only because subsequent injury to yourself would seem to discredit your recommendations. For that reason, it is tempting to hold in reserve the possibility of 'pure bad luck', as a posthumous pardon for yourself or for deceased experts or friends. But it is just that possibility that we want to avoid. To say that a man can know the answers, but that to err is human, is an unsatisfactory defence, for it suggests that there is a limit to the value of theoretical and experiential knowledge of the matter.

The lavishly-equipped expedition of Auden's poem marched to its disasters because its members believed that all hazards spring from external origins. This opinion characterises present day teaching on mountain safety, which tends to deal with causal relationships in an entirely mechanistic manner, the personal element being largely ignored. Indeed, it might even be said that this approach blocks enquiry about that element, having at its disposal only a handful of premature ultimates – error in judgement, inadequate safety margin, accident-proneness, and so on – with which to deal with it.

Certainly, the advice which is handed out so freely is addressed mainly to beginners; and, of course, it is possible to offer a range of recommendations about equipment, time and distance calculations, navigational skills, and so forth, which will give fairly positive protection to a simple expedition. This is especially true of straightforward hillwalking in Britain. However, it is almost everywhere implied that the same approach – a thorough knowledge of equipment and technique together with the steady development of a sense of judgement (so indefinable a quality that only its particular applications can be examined) – satisfies all safety considerations through all stages of a climber's progress. I think that this is untrue and that there are

491

other aspects of the safety problem which deserve more attention. I think, too, that we should feel an obligation to tell beginners a great deal more about the risks of the game.

It seems to me to be more correct to see advances in technique and equipment as being supports to improvements in performance, rather than as determinants of the margin of safety. Motoring offers an obvious analogy. When a man buys a car with better braking power, he tends to put the brakes on later; when he gets a car with a higher cruising speed, he drives it faster; when he thinks he can handle skids on snowy roads, he toys with this technique. We have a built-in tendency to look for our limits, unless special factors like inhibition or senility supervene. And what is true of drivers is also true of climbers.

Consider a variety of situations in which a man's foot slips and he falls. In one case, he is walking along a steep, wet, grassy hillside, wearing ordinary shoes. The safety experts say: you have to have the right equipment for the job – if you'd been wearing good mountain boots this might never have happened. In a second case, a climber slips on a slab move on a wet but easy rock climb. He is wearing a good pair of boots. The experts say: well, this is often climbed in similar or worse conditions; perhaps you haven't yet learned the right style of balance movement; your technique needs improvement. In a third case, a climber falls off a bone-dry XS. He is wearing PAs and is known to be a highly competent and successful climber. The experts have to say: well, your gear is all right and you say you were in excellent form; you must have been pushing it; you made *a mistake in judgement*. In fact, a very large number of climbing accidents have to be put down to 'mistakes in judgement'. These accidents pose the most interesting and baffling of safety problems. Once a climber has reached the point at which he can be said to have 'found his standard', he usually begins to climb fairly close to that standard, and matters of equipment and technique come to have a different sort of relevance. Allowances are made for shortcomings in one matter and improvements in the other: the climber exercises his judgement. In this context, any light we can shed on the factors influencing judgement will be valuable – not only in relation to the third example given above, but also to the two earlier ones. So, from this point of view, it seems more appropriate to think of the safety-margin as a constant in the climber's head, rather than as a variable on the soles of his boots.

The above argument, which has been telescoped dangerously, has also been set out, although rather differently, by Lito Tejada-Flores in his article *Games Climbers Play*. (In passing, the title of the article, presumably relates to the book *Games People Play* by Eric Berne; Tejada-Flores owes no debt to the book, which deals with interpersonal situations, but Dr Berne's approach might well be developed to touch on one or two aspects of modern climbing.) Tejada-Flores divides climbing and mountaineering into a number of classes or 'climbing games' – the Boulder Game, the Crag Game, the Big Wall Game, the Alpine Game, the Expedition Game, and so on. He shows that each game has generally accepted rules ('ethics'), and he explains their purpose: 'a handicap system has evolved to equalise the inherent challenge and maintain the climber's feeling of achievement at a high level in each of these differing situations'. The rules 'are designed to conserve the climber's feeling of personal (moral) accomplishment against the meaninglessness of a success which represents merely technological victory'. So, the less the objective danger and the less the duration of effort required, the more rigorous are the rules: you can use a ladder to cross a crevasse on Everest, but not to get up Harrison's Rocks. The principle, he says, is 'to maintain a degree of uncertainty as to the eventual outcome'.

I will return to what uncertainty of outcome means or might mean. But, for the moment, the inescapable conclusion is that whenever a significant step forward is made in equipment or technique, the average climber makes a compensation. He does not want to widen his safety-margin indefinitely; he wants to hold it to a satisfactorily narrow measure. And he does this by climbing harder routes within the same climbing game or, if circumstances allow, by moving into a higher or more serious game. His safety-margin has to seem as marginal as ever.

Now, if a climber's safety-margin is adjusted to some internal need, do climbers in fact become safer as they grow older and gain experience? Accident statistics are not yet of any assistance here, as they show nothing of the proportional background of safe climbing – though Kim Meldrum has recently used them to show that climbers *as a whole* do not have fewer accidents when they start using better gear and safer methods, supporting what is said above. For the moment, I am simply going to say that climbers do not necessarily become safer – no matter how excellent their equipment or sophisticated their techniques and, possibly, no matter how many years they have spent developing their judgement – unless they adopt, deliberately or unconsciously, what we might call a *risk-free role,* about which I will say something presently. It seems to me that climbers who do not take up such a position may become more likely to hurt themselves as time goes on, especially if they keep on moving up the hierarchy of climbing games. I think it probable that the fatality-rate, in relation to the time at risk, increases steadily through hill-walking, rock-climbing, Alpine climbing and expeditions. Some people disagree with this view, and it is certainly possible to cite anomalies in particular geographical areas and in specialised aspects of climbing; but I am sure that, other things being equal, the accident-rate rises with the seriousness of the terrain, and that a given injury, say a broken ankle, which might be a minor incident on a British crag, could have major consequences on an Alpine peak and might mean worse again on bigger mountains. At the end, according to Michael Ward, the mortality-rate amongst those who have ventured on to the world's ten highest mountains is seven percent – and this excludes porters, who for some reason aren't counted or don't count. (Dr Berne would classify Greater Mountaineering as a Third Degree Game; that is, one 'which is played for keeps and which ends in the surgery, the courtroom or the morgue'.)

If this line of reasoning is valid, and bearing in mind the tendency to progress always towards more difficult undertakings, a number of serious questions follow. Ought we to encourage young people to start climbing at all, if they don't already feel a compulsion? Must we burn the Mountain Centres? And so on. I'm going to pass over these questions here for two reasons: firstly, they are inextricably tied to a lengthy educational or social argument; and, secondly, I think it might be possible to do something about the safety problem, if we wished.

The gratification-safety dilemma: risk free roles
Before saying something about those climbers who have accidents, I want to say something about those who don't – about climbers who have settled the gratification-safety dilemma. I have said that it is a natural process for many climbers to keep the safety-margin satisfyingly narrow. Some climbers hold this position for many years, but it is quite impossible to say what they have in common. However, when I said that the safety-margin is a constant in the head, I was exaggerating. Climbers often widen their safety-margins, sometimes deliberately and from a specific moment, sometimes slowly and without conscious knowledge. Some rather obvious groups of causes initiate this process. In the most direct, a climber who survives a big fall or a series of falls or misadventures may begin to allow himself a broader safety-margin: this is a dangerous way of learning, although in some aspects of climbing it has recently been made less dangerous but also less effective. Alternatively, a climber may be influenced by having seen injuries or fatalities on the hills, or by having had these happen to friends or acquaintances: this is highly effective, but there are moral objections to human sacrifice as an adjunct to teaching. Again, it may happen that a man's climbing is affected by personal matters, even when these do not restrict his time on the hills – by a sense of responsibility to wife or children, by a loss of energy or drive due to the exigencies of earning a living, by the discovery of values or interests which modify the importance of some of the rewards previously obtained from climbing, and so on.

There are, of course, climbers whose manner, style and drive are not in the least affected by any of these circumstances; indeed, in the last situation at least, the process may occasionally work in reverse. We call some of these climbers 'the hard men', but we ought to have some such phrase to cover all those who climb consistently to their limits at lower as well as at higher standards. On the other hand, many climbers find that their climbing is adversely affected by these factors, and they assume one or other of our 'risk-free roles'. It is worth looking at the ways in which such men organise their activities in order to gain maximum gratification at minimum risk.

The first and most obvious solution in ordinary rock-climbing is the traditional one: to sign on permanently as a second. No immediate drop in the standard of climbing is necessarily involved, but as the climber regresses further he wants to climb on cliffs with sizeable ledges and impressive belays; then he becomes unhappy on routes with overhangs and traverses and, typically, wants to climb second in parties of three. This sort of manoeuvring can be quite rewarding, because a reasonable talent scout will have the background experience to enable him to continue to indulge in difficult climbing, including first ascents, for a long time.

A second role, which may cause argument or resentment by its positioning in this scheme, is that of leader on climbs where the risk is reduced to the possibility of very short falls – artificial climbing or free climbing which can be protected continuously. At this stage, it is worth returning to Tejada-Flores' remark that we try to maintain 'a degree of uncertainty as to the eventual outcome'. Uncertainty of outcome suggests, first of all, success or failure, though these terms sometimes seem inappropriate in climbing; but it also suggests a dalliance with risk and hence the likelihood of injury. Now, at one time, the threat of a fall was a very serious one and almost always involved a risk to life; but, with the development of pegs, nuts and tape for aid in one type of climbing, and for protection in another, there are now many climbs in which the chance of falling means no more than the chance of a short and harmless drop. At the same time, such climbing offers the satisfaction of the most dramatic situations in which a man can find himself. And, since even the shortest and most painless fall is an exhilarating and stimulating experience, these routes can purge the 'worry-potential' of a climber perfectly. So a sort of substitute has been invented to replace the climber's historical exposure to real risks, although he may, of course, still carry out climbs of great technical difficulty. (Perhaps it would be simpler to say that equipment and technique have made a real contribution to safety. But, again, this is only true within the context of the 'risk-free role'. In other circumstances, the climber will start pegging on more dubious rock, or will try to cut down on aid or protection pitons; he may even start soloing.

However, it may be that routes of the type described here are now representative of the mainstream development of British rock-climbing.)

A third role is that of an instructor at a Mountain Centre, or of a guide who only accepts fairly simple undertakings, or of a member of a climbing club who looks after the beginners. His climbing in other situations may well be inhibited by the fact that he dares not risk getting himself into hazardous positions, since he spends a good deal of his time in teaching others to climb safely. He has the reward of being regarded as an expert by novices who have no way of assessing his ability or achievements. Some climbers become so preoccupied with this role that they fail to notice that they have virtually given up serious climbing altogether.

A fourth role is that of the obsessive rescuer. This is an unassailable position. Few climbers dare make fun of those who would as soon stand by for a possible rescue as go out for a climb. Furthermore, the rescuer has every ethical consideration removed, in that he knows that he will be criticised unless he protects his every action to its comfortable maximum rather than to its bearable minimum. So on crag rescues he can get into exciting positions for free, and he can involve himself in the most dramatic events. If he were to make a mistake and hurt himself, what would be a disgrace in other circumstances might be seen as gallantry here. He can say, quite rightly, that he is doing a public service. As a bonus, he gets an obscure emotional pay off of a kind not easy to describe but which many of us find impossible to resist.

A number of other roles for the 'tame tiger' might be enumerated. There are climbers who concentrate upon high but comparatively safe and easy Alpine ascents; with the height advantage, they can feel that they are still part of the world of serious climbing. Again, there are climbers who direct their energies into the opening-up of remote but minor mountain areas, where the difficulties of access join with the mountain objectives to give some sense of commitment. All these roles might be defined more clearly and the list might be extended. However, it seems to me that the best and most direct advice to be given to a climber who worries about survival is to tell him that he should deliberately fit his activities into one of these roles or into a happy combination of them.

Adventitious and Sequential Accidents

Let us now consider those experienced climbers who have accidents. I am sure that it is interesting and valuable to try to look at the safety problem in new ways: to ignore the mechanical concomitants of accidents – or, at least, to ask 'why?' again, after the mechanical answer has been supplied – and to try to find methods by which accidents, or the climbers who have them, may be typified. I have to admit here that, from some intriguing beginnings, my own attempts at comprehensive analysis have led me into difficult positions with unverifiable and tenuous conclusions, and I have thought it best to abandon the exercise; but I am sure that such analyses are possible and I would like to provoke attempts by those equipped to deal with the matter.

For analogy, however, and for entertainment, I will offer what may seem at first glance to be a rather absurd approach to the problem. But I use it for two reasons: firstly, it is a method which cannot be carried much further in its direction and so, at least, cannot confuse a promising line of development; secondly, it does separate two sorts of accidents which are of importance – in the one case because all thinking about them seems to be finally abortive, and in the other because they form a characteristic but rarely discussed category. The approach divides accidents according to their style of development. To avoid trespass upon more likely vocabularies, I have called them *adventitious and sequential* accidents.

By an *adventitious* accident I do not simply mean an accidental accident, though such a type might be possible – one hypothetical limit of the extremes of accidentality of accidents. I mean an accident which the climber arranges without any external assistance, one which occurs when he is not under pressure, when choices of action are open to him, when an accident often looks like an adventitious piece of carelessness or bad luck. Consider a characteristic form: a climber sets up an abseil on a small outcrop, purely for amusement; he uses a rounded anchor and the rope rides off.

Why did he do it? The circumstances exclude the possibility of fatigue having impaired his judgement of having caused him to take risks in order to conserve energy. He seems to be of more than average intelligence and not lacking in mechanical sense. What can we possibly say about this situation?

The only obvious advice is in the traditional manner. We might say: in setting up an abseil you must estimate the direction of strain and check the response of the ropes to a pull at (say) thirty degrees to either side of the abseil path. But the climber must have known this already. We might offer a more general solution by encouraging all climbers to consider a grounding in artificial climbing to be an essential part of mountaineering, since this is a safe and effective way of imprinting a good knowledge of practical mechanics. But the climber might well have had this knowledge, or believed he had it, already. A better understanding might be gained by studying the growing literature on accident-proneness in other activities; but attempts to sort mountaineers into psychological types in the technical or clinical senses would probably be thought distasteful, and it is hard to see what practical good would come of it for a freely-recruited pastime. So, in cases like this, we seem to reach an impasse.

By a *sequential* accident I mean the end point in a chain of events, an accident which happens under pressure and which is any one of a random range of accidents available in the situation the climber has constructed, or which follows the only choice of action he has left himself. The chain of events may appear to have lasted five minutes or five hours; but it may also be seen to have extended for five years or longer, and this extreme case is worth thinking about.

Climbers in this category may be described as being too committed to survive. One has to avoid direct illustration here, but from observation and reading it is perfectly clear that the literature and folklore of disaster exert a powerful influence on some climbers. Psychologists have described a characteristic type of fantasy in which a child invents a catastrophe – a bus crash, for example – from which it is the only survivor. It is possible to see the survivor-stories with which mountaineering is so well provided – Cassin on the Badile, Bonatti on the Frêney Pillar, and countless others – as offering real-life archetypes of these fantasies. The charge of feeling in such tragedies is so strong that, however painfully it is expressed, the reader or listener cannot avoid a response. The drama is almost always accompanied by all the atmospherics at Nature's disposal. And, in contrast to this back-cloth, the onward drive and inflexibility of purpose which carries the protagonist safety through appears as the essential quality which distinguishes the great mountaineer from the good mountaineer and which tilts the scales in favour of survival.

This is an utterly false conclusion, but the voices of survivors impress us more than inscriptions on tombstones. Abstracting from these stories, it is easy to form a specific image of the great climber and a concept of an extreme relationship between man and mountain: the serious climber is always a 'hard man'; the climb is a life-or-death struggle; and the technical difficulty of one route, or the beauty of line of another, come to have less significance than the tragedies a third has witnessed – the Eigerwand weaves a greater spell than the Walker Spur, Nanga Parbat than Everest, and so on. Unfortunately, the notorious routes are naturally those with the greatest objective dangers, and on them the climber is forced to accept extended periods of risk. If he has unconsciously identified himself with the image of a survivor-figure, he is simply carried along by his resolution until, at a time thrown up by chance, the sum of his calculated risks exceeds his calculations. The tendency to select onward drive and audacity as supremely valuable qualities is not only dangerous on Alpine climbs or in relation to objective hazards. It may be equally misleading on a long unprotected run-out in the course of a Lakeland rock-climb, or in pressing on with a preconceived plan through a Cairngorm white-out.

It may be thought that, in cases such as these, we are talking about personality factors. To some extent, this is true but there is also involved a response to a particular conception of mountaineering which may have some proportional relationship with the influence of the mass media. This influence perpetuates a tendency found within mountaineering itself – in the compilation of records in guide books and climbing journals – although the intention in this case has not been to excite the general public. In recent years, however, journalists, publishers and television producers have vastly exaggerated the issue. In Britain, the change of atmosphere came about quite recently, and a single example will serve as an illustration. When, in the years between the wars, the acknowledged authorities of British mountaineering passed comment on the activities of German and Italian climbers, the most damning criticism they could make was to find – to their own satisfaction, at any rate – evidence of exchanges with the State which seemed to them to indicate a false direction for mountaineering. But when, after the ascent of Everest, John Hunt and Edmund Hillary were knighted, the parallel disturbed no-one; and when the news of success was used, through its fortuitous coincidence with the Coronation, as a symbol of national resurgence, there were few attempts by climbers to insist upon mountaineering's independence of, and indifference to, sport and society. In fact, there is a temptation to take 1953 as the year in which British climbing began to come to terms with the mass media and with the implications of public recognition. In some quarters this coming-together has been accepted with tremendous enthusiasm, and it is leading to a reshaping of the structure of British climbing.

Since this development is overwhelmingly dependent on communications, it would seem obvious that the same means might be used to redress the balance. Ironically, in the decade which produced the anti-hero in the novel and cinema, mountaineering literature has reached its worst excesses (culminating, to my mind, in *Straight Up*, the Harlin biography). Certainly, a start might be made in dealing more critically with these offerings, by drawing attention to naive attitudes and sentimentalism and by looking scrupulously at motives. It would be quite possible to adopt entirely new conventions. We might, for instance, exclude from guidebooks any record of first ascents on which there was a fatality or even an injury, on the grounds that the climb was not properly achieved. This would allow us, for example, to look forward to the first winter *direttissima* on the Eiger. We ought to try to give praise where it is really due: for every hundred who knows the details of Heckmair's ascent of the Eigerwand, it is hard to find one who has heard of his ascent of the Walker Spur thirteen years later – a success by which Kollensberger and Heckmair showed clearly that reason and imperturbability are as useful as 'push'. We ought to moderate our language, begging the Character Builders not to use the word 'courage' in talking to young people about climbing; this word is best saved for situations which have not been entered for fun, and in a climbing context 'persistence' might be more appropriate. We ought, above all, to try to assess the effects of the interest shown in mountaineering by outside bodies, and the effects, especially, of their promotion of awards and certificates.

How safe do we want to make it?
In conclusion, it seems to me that a climber's career falls into either two or three phases: first, a noviciate, during which advice on equipment and technique is valuable and may increase the margin of safety widely; second, a 'climbing-game' phase, during which accumulated knowledge is used to support performance rather than to guarantee safety; and, third, the possibility of opting-out into a 'risk-free role'. There is scope for a great deal of thought upon the subject, but at present, considering the pattern of climbing in Britain compared, for example, with Soviet mountaineering, our advice on safety seems necessarily to be of a temporising nature. It recalls Wilde's remark about some of the reforms of his day: 'They try to solve the problem of poverty by keeping the poor alive'. We try to help climbers who are falling off V. Diffs. by showing them how to climb Severes: then we find them falling off VS's. The problem of poverty was lessened by modifying the structure of society rather than by maintaining soup kitchens in the streets. Similarly, we might change the structure and ethos of mountaineering, but we have to ask ourselves what sorts of changes would be acceptable – most of us, I imagine, would not care for the Soviet solution to the safety problem. In any case, whether we do anything or not, British climbing is already being reshaped by the influence of four pressure groups outside its traditionally spontaneous pattern of clubs and individuals. These pressure groups comprise firstly the training organisations, secondly the equipment dealers and manufacturers, and thirdly the climber-journalists and photographers, all of whom have slightly different interests in safety matters; the fourth group is the British Mountaineering Council itself, whose developing influence is as yet unpredictable.

The only possible way of ending this article seems to be by asking some questions which await answers. Exactly how safe do we want mountaineering to be? Is there any consensus on this amongst British climbers? How do we fit into the international pattern in these matters? Is there any permissible level of injury in mountaineering? What would you give to climb this year's 'Worst Mountain in the World?' A finger? A finger-joint? A finger-nail?

from THE ALPINE JOURNAL *1969*

THE CAIRNGORM TRAGEDY

A *MOUNTAIN* REPORT

The enquiry into the deaths of the six teenagers on the Cairngorm Plateau has now finished: the jury, the advocates, the witnesses and the Sheriff Principal have performed their public duty. What, then, are the conclusions that have emerged to help us avoid such disasters in the future?

The jury behaved with commendable level-headedness, sensibly resisting the temptation to find a scapegoat. Throughout the six days of the enquiry, the judicial process systematically cut through the tangled undergrowth of charge and counter-charge. What finally emerged was an undramatic cata-logue of human errors leading up to that ghastly climax when six children died, buried under snowdrifts high on a hostile mountain side. There was no evidence of gross negligence, crass stupidity or incompetence: merely a story of human beings pitting themselves against the ravages of nature, and losing.

Let us trace the story from its origins.

The Edinburgh Education background
For several years the Edinburgh Education Authority, under the influence of its Depute Education Officer, John Cook, has regarded Outdoor Pursuits as an important part of its school curricula. The Authority is generally con-sidered the most advanced in this field. Its faith in this type of education has led to some bold expeditions to foreign countries, including one in which a group of teenage canoeists successfully navigated sections of the River Inn in Austria and another that climbed in the High Tatra mountains in Poland. Outdoor Activities Instructors, experienced in one or more aspects of the subject, had been placed in a number of the City's schools. Ben Beattie was the Outdoor Activities master at Ainslie Park School in Edinburgh. A pro-ficient mountaineer, holding the Mountain Instructors' Certificate, he was a popular master who inspired the enthusiasm of his pupils. Basic instruction had led to greater keenness: under his guidance a school Mountaineering Club had been formed. Every month, under Beattie's leadership, its mem-bers visited a mountain area for hill walking or rock climbing. By November 1971 they had gathered a substantial fund of experience. Some quite difficult rock climbs and a number of demanding hill walks had been successfully

completed, the most notable achievement being a winter ascent of Bidean nam Bian, in Glen Coe, where the group became familiar with crampon and ice axe technique.

For their next expedition Beattie planned a tough Cairngorm itinerary that would combine experience in a number of related fields: navigation in difficult terrain, a rigorous bivouac in a high-level bothy, and, hopefully, the ascent of the four highest Cairngorm summits. But the abilities of his party varied somewhat: half were tough and proven, while the others were rather less able and experienced. He therefore planned to let his girl-friend, Cathy Davidson, take the weaker group, and placed in it one of his best pupils – Billy Kerr – for additional strength. The intention was for Beattie to go ahead with the strong group, in the hope of completing the circuit of Cairngorm, Ben Macdui, Cairn Toul and Breariach, while Cathy Davidson followed with the more modest objectives of Cairngorm and Ben Macdui. The two parties were to reunite at the Corrour Bothy and march back together along the Lairig Ghru on Sunday night. The ambitious nature of the plan indicates the morale and momentum that the club had achieved under Beattie's guidance. Perhaps in perfect conditions the complete itinerary would have been achieved, but it was certainly unlikely; in fact it had only been achieved a few times before, and always by experienced climbers. Like the plans of a group of ambitious alpinists anticipating a good season, Beattie's hopes should not be taken too seriously. A glance at the map reveals that he always had a number of ways of modifying his plan if conditions demanded. Even so there were a number of places on the planned route that could have presented some difficulty, and if any of the party had tired or had an accident, say on the Cairn Toul/Breariach traverse, the situation would have been grave. Beattie discussed the plan with a climbing colleague, Terry Nicholls, now Edinburgh Education Authority's Official responsible for co-ordinating the activities of the instructors. He also informed the school authorities, indicating that he wanted Cathy Davidson to help him. He failed to specify, however, that she would lead a separate party on the mountain. As both the Headmaster and the Headmistress knew that Cathy Davidson had formerly helped Beattie and was fairly competent, they included her as an official assistant instructor on the documents authorising Beattie to lead the group. The parents were formally requested to allow their children to go on the trip, and it was made clear that they would be doing a two-day hill walk and spending a night out in a hut. The party was to be based at the Edinburgh Outdoor Centre, Lagganlia, near Kincraig, where it would spend Friday night, receive special equipment from the Centre's stores, and be provided with transport to and from the mountain.

After several weeks of planning, Ben Beattie, Cathy Davidson and their

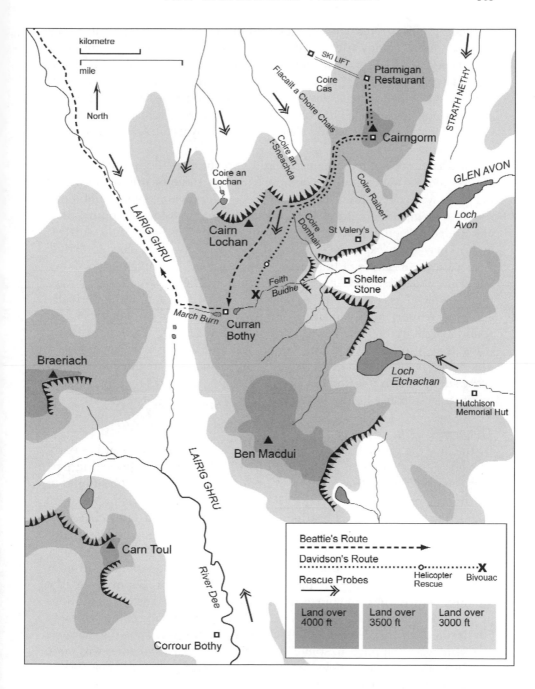

kilometre

mile

North

SKI LIFT

Fiacaill a Choire Chais

Coire Cas

Ptarmigan Restaurant

STRATH NETHY

Coire an t-Sneachda

Cairngorm

GLEN AVON

Coire Raibert

Coire an Lochan

Coire Domhain

St Valery's

Loch Avon

Cairn Lochan

LAIRIG GHRU

Feith Buidhe

Shelter Stone

March Burn

Curran Bothy

Braeriach

Loch Etchachan

Hutchison Memorial Hut

Ben Macdui

LAIRIG GHRU

Carn Toul

River Dee

Corrour Bothy

Beattie's Route

Davidson's Route

Rescue Probes

Helicopter Rescue

Bivouac

Land over 4000 ft

Land over 3500 ft

Land over 3000 ft

fourteen pupils arrived late on Friday night at the Lagganlia Centre. The Warden, John Paisley, discussed the expedition with Beattie and also talked about Cathy Davidson's role. He understood that she was to be given separate control of half the group on the hill, and that the whole expedition would be conducted sensibly by Beattie, the parties reuniting in the event of poor weather. Route cards were completed – a formal procedure ensuring that the Centre would always have a fairly clear idea of the party's whereabouts.

Saturday morning had dawned bright and sunny, although the weather reports forecast deteriorating conditions. At this stage Beattie realised that his plans were over-optimistic: he would have to revert to a less ambitious route, stopping overnight at the Curran Bothy. He told the enquiry that although the weather reports were discouraging he was not unduly worried, as he knew from experience that bad weather was often slow to arrive. Perhaps it was because of this revision of plan that the party started rather late. After breakfast they spent nearly two hours being issued with equipment – which has since been the subject of some discussion. By all normally accepted winter mountaineering standards they were well-equipped to spend a night in the Cairngorms. Although some of the party were wearing jeans, they also had warm long underwear and waterproof over-trousers. The fact that, despite the bitterly cold conditions, two of the beleaguered party survived two freezing bivouacs in the open indicates that their equipment, at least, could hardly be faulted.

The progress of the expedition
By the time the group reached the ski lift it was 11.15am, and Beattie's party arrived at the Ptarmigan Restaurant just before midday. After eating part of their packed lunch there, they set out on the 400ft climb to the summit of Cairngorm, crossing it between 12.30 and 12.45pm. While his pupils were taking their first compass bearing, Beattie stopped for a brief chat with Steve Mitchell, a full-time instructor from Glenmore Lodge, who was mending radio equipment in a hut near the summit. Cathy Davidson's party arrived at the summit at around 1.20pm – about three-quarters of an hour behind Beattie – having left the Ptarmigan at about 12.30pm. From the summit, both parties set course for the Curran Bothy. Weather conditions at this time were: wind – westerly, 30-40 knots; low cloud ceiling; visibility 50–100 yards. It was difficult to tell whether or not it was snowing, because the wind was whipping up spindrift. In other words, the weather was poor, but far from bad. It was, however, expected to deteriorate further, as Beattie had been reminded when he passed the weather report board at the foot of the ski lift.

Beattie's party was next seen by a group of Stirling Venture Scouts who were lunching near the top of the Fiarcaill a Choire Chais. They had walked up Cairngorm from the Sheiling car-park, traversed the summit and had intended to traverse the top of the Northern Corries to the summit of Cairn Lochan. However, the Scoutmaster, John Simpson, thought that the weather looked too threatening and decided to descend into Corrie an t-Sneachda instead. His party, unlike Beattie's, was not equipped for a night out, and he had to reach the campsite near Glenmore Lodge before dark. Beattie's party passed the scouts at about 1.30. Continuing, they met the bad weather as they climbed out of Corrie Domhain. At this point a straight course to the Curran Bothy involves a very slightly ascending traverse. It was here that the party encountered its first continuous deep soft snow which, coupled with the storm and the deteriorating visibility, made the going arduous and slowed progress considerably. Nevertheless, by taking careful line bearings, and using one walker to sight another, they reached the Curran Bothy at 3.45pm, tired but not exhausted. It was just beginning to get dark. Meanwhile Cathy Davidson and her party had run into the bad weather as they started to descend into Corrie Domhain on a line slightly to the south of that taken by Beattie's party. By the time they reached the soft snow that had slowed Beattie's progress, the weather had grown considerably worse, and the wind stronger. In these poor conditions they veered slightly downhill to a more sheltered route intending to locate the Feith Buidhe and follow it up to the Lochan Buidhe where the Curran Bothy was situated. It began to get dark. The tough conditions were tiring the party rapidly and Cathy Davidson grew increasingly worried about the possibility of one of them collapsing with exhaustion. Knowing that the textbook course is to stop and dig in before exhaustion is reached, she decided to bivouac. By then the group was near the Feith Buidhe (concealed under snow), at map reference 988014. The snow was powdery and they could not dig snow holes. After trying to construct a snow wall, the children got into their sleeping bags and polythene bivouac sacs to sit out the night. Beattie, safe in the Curran Bothy less than a third of a mile away, calculated that the second party had either retreated to the north or sought shelter in the St Valery's Refuge, which he knew Cathy Davidson had visited previously.

The following morning conditions had grown worse: there was virtually a white-out. Beattie's team left the Curran Bothy at 9am and set course for the top of the March Burn. During the descent of the burn, there was one rather harrowing passage where the party had to use rope and crampons on some steep ice. When they gained the Lairig Ghru, the weather was predictably better; a stiff walk took them back to their planned pick-up point at the end of Loch Morlich, where John Paisley waited with transport.

The rescue attempts

Not until Beattie and Paisley met was it realised that Cathy Davidson's party had not returned. The gravity of the situation was clear, but it was 6.30pm before the group managed to reach Glenmore Lodge and raise the alarm. Fred Harper, the Warden of Glenmore Lodge, immediately sent three two-man teams out on to the mountain, in atrocious conditions, in a desperate attempt to find the stricken party during the night. It was a forlorn hope. The six climbers could do virtually nothing: their planned sweeps of the key areas in which the Davidson party might be found rapidly turned into personal battles of survival. Eventually all of them reached safety. One of the pairs, having failed to find the St Valery's Refuge, descended Corrie Domhain into Glen Avon, passing within half a mile of the beleaguered party, before reaching the Shelter Stone, exhausted, at about 1.30am. The second party reached the Shelter Stone via Corrie Raibiert, and the third made a probe up Strath Nethy and returned to the Lodge.

During Sunday, Cathy Davidson's party could do very little. Cathy went round digging the children out, and then, with Billy Kerr, tried to force a route out to safety. But conditions were so bad that they only managed to cover a few yards in the soft snow. The weakening party was forced to spend another gruelling night in the open.

At first light on Monday morning, the rescue teams assembled at Glenmore Lodge set out. Finally, Brian Hall, in an RAF helicopter, spotted Cathy Davidson staggering through the snow at map reference 989017. The helicopter landed a few yards from her. As Hall reached her, she collapsed, gasping the three vital words: 'Burn – Lochan – buried.' It was not much, but it was enough to give the rescue parties an idea of where to search. Hall radioed the position back to Glenmore Lodge, and then made a quick search of the immediate area; but the weather was deteriorating rapidly, and it was obvious that Cathy Davidson would have to be rushed to hospital, so the helicopter took off again. Eventually, a small rescue group led by John Cunningham and accompanied by Ben Beattie and John Paisley, found the rest of the party buried in the snow. Only, Raymond Leslie was still alive.

Evidence at the enquiry

It took six days of public enquiry, eight barristers, the Sheriff Principal of Banffshire, a jury and countless witnesses to establish the facts behind this story. Every detail was pursued with zeal. The three lawyers for the Crown sought to establish the basic facts of the case, while those representing the parents of the dead children, Miss Davidson, Mr Beattie and the Edinburgh Corporation, cross-examined each witness in an attempt to reveal further facts, judgements, interpretations or background information useful to their clients, no doubt with an eye on possible future proceedings. John Paisley was not represented by Counsel. The witnesses fell into four main groups: those directly involved with the incident – Cathy Davidson, Ben Beattie, John Paisley and other members of the expedition; those partially involved – eye witnesses, the Headmaster of Ainslie Park School, John Cook (Depute Education Officer for Edinburgh), parents and rescuers; those offering technical information – mainly weather experts; and finally witnesses offering expert technical appraisal and comment on the affair – Fred Harper, Eric Langmuir and Adam Watson.

The most important cross-examinations were aimed at the three main participants.

Davidson's evidence

Cathy Davidson was questioned on a number of issues. Why didn't she turn back while there was still time? What did she do to look after the children in the bivouac? Why did she not press on to reach the Curran Bothy?

The enquiry concluded that she had done her best in difficult circumstances, but it was also agreed that she should never have had charge of the party separately from Beattie. Both Watson and Harper pointed to her error in not turning back while there was still time. Given what did occur, however, Harper's view was that although Cathy Davidson's action in digging in when her party became tired was understandable he felt that in similar circumstances he would have pressed on and tried to find the Curran Bothy. Nevertheless, despite strong cross-examination, he was unwilling to describe Davidson's action as a grave error. Adam Watson, on the other hand, thought that Davidson did not display sufficient commonsense in searching for a bivouac site that was better than the open powder snow slope. It transpired that both the mini-flares and the pair of snowshoes that the party had, were lost in the confusion of the bivouac. Both might have made a marginal difference if they had been used.

General discussion outside the court by the various experts revealed that a better technique with the polythene bags and the grouping of the party might have prevented them from becoming buried and demoralised.

But these were all errors laid against Miss Davidson's lack of experience: nobody in the court seemed to consider that they added up to serious fault.

Beattie's evidence

Ben Beattie was questioned in detail for many hours. With hindsight, it was easy to find evidence of error in Beattie's actions, but no one could bring a charge of serious neglect. Beattie (who holds a Mountain Instructor's Certificate – a qualification which demands a high level of competence and which is held by only about 160 climbers) emerged as a keen and able climber, and a good teacher. His ability to instil enthusiasm into his pupils was clear from the evidence, and Fred Harper openly admitted that Beattie's qualifications would have made him an ideal choice for a post at Glenmore Lodge.

The most serious charge to emerge against Beattie concerned his under-estimation of the Cairngorms as a dangerous mountain group, and his naïvety in taking children into the area in winter. Harper, Watson and Duff (the police witness) were clearly not in favour of using the Cairngorms for youth training in winter. Under questioning, however, Harper admitted that there were a few areas (those with easy escapes to civilisation) that might be suitable. Eric Langmuir also said (outside the court) that he did not consider the Cairngorm to Curran Bothy itinerary to be unreasonable for a trained and fit school party, given good weather conditions.

It was pointed out that Beattie had not made it clear, either to the school authorities or to John Paisley, that he intended Cathy Davidson to have full and separate charge over the second party. He was criticised for starting his expedition so late in the day, and also for not paying due attention to the weather reports. He was also considered by some to have erred in not reuniting the two groups when the weather started to deteriorate.

Another serious error concerned his reaction to the non-appearance of the second party at the Curran Bothy. He claimed not to have entertained the idea that the party might have been benighted close to the Bothy, and so had made no attempt – either on Saturday night or Sunday morning – to retrace the route for a short distance. In the end, despite some doubts about the feasibility of the assumptions he *did* make, the court accepted that Beattie's conclusions had been fair but short-sighted.

Finally, he was criticised for having delegated full authority to Miss David-son in the first place. It was suggested that she was too young, insufficiently qualified, and not experienced enough to take charge of parties of school children. Beattie refuted this by claiming that Miss Davidson was in fact quite experienced, having previously led children on a number of expedi-tions (though always in his sight). Discussion outside the court also revealed that she was a determined climber, with leads such as Hammer on the Etive Slabs to her credit, and alpine courses like the Forbes Arête and the East Face of the Grépon, all with companions of similar experience as herself.

Paisley's evidence

The third crucial witness was John Paisley, the official who finally allowed Beattie to proceed with his plans. Paisley had taken up his post at Lagganlia early in 1970. In the interim he had only dealt with one similar mountaineering expedition, for it transpired that the Centre's activities were mainly directed towards modest projects such as orienteering, skiing, and the walking of nature trails. Paisley, whose qualifications comprised a teaching degree, four years' experience as a full-time instructor at Plas y Brenin in North Wales, and two years in the Arctic, could hardly be described as a Cairngorm expert. It was clear that he delegated much of the responsibility for this expedition to Beattie, who he regarded as very experienced. He also seemed fairly impressed with Cathy Davidson's degree of experience. His judgement of the project can best be summed up by his own comments:

> I had a firm belief in Beattie's ability to assess all the conditions and vary his plan accordingly…
> I understood the children were a specialist group and that they had camped and climbed with both Beattie and Davidson…
> I had Beattie's assurance that he would reunite the party if conditions deteriorated…
> I considered the route was an ambitious one but not beyond their abilities.

Paisley admitted that the weather reports were bad, but that he had left detailed appraisal in the field to Beattie. As far as his endorsement of Miss Davidson's position was concerned, it must be recalled that she was officially listed on the school forms as an assistant instructor, and this, together with Beattie's remarks about her experience, could hardly be expected to give Paisley any grounds for doubting her ability. Much more questionable was his suggestion that Shelagh Sunderland should be included in the party. It transpired that Miss Sunderland had applied to Paisley for a Voluntary Instructor's job, to improve her knowledge of Outdoor Activities. Her experience included some walking with the Girl Guides movement, some scrambling in the Lakes, and two rock climbing courses in Wales. She had only just arrived at Lagganlia, and Paisley judged that her inclusion in Cathy Davidson's party would not only be beneficial to the party itself, but would also give Miss Sunderland some useful experience. Having made sure that she was well-equipped, he therefore allocated her to the party. The fact that he made this decision, even though Miss Sunderland was clearly far less experienced than many of the children, indicates that he considered the expedition to be none too serious.

The court appeared to accept that Paisley was an authority on hill walking in the Cairngorms and to view his evidence in this light. Discussion among experts outside the court, however, revealed that this was far from the case. So it was that in this respect the normal chain of command contained a weak link: Beattie's enthusiastic plans were given full rein, instead of being subjected to close scrutiny by a wiser, more experienced climber who, as hindsight shows, should have counselled greater restraint in the face of such weather conditions. It seems doubtful however whether the Edinburgh authorities ever intended Paisley to vet expeditions such as this, in a serious way.

Technical and expert considerations

The wisdom of taking children on the Cairngorms in winter seems never to have been questioned by Beattie, Paisley, or their superiors in Edinburgh, even though many mountaineers have denounced the practice. In the enquiry a number of witnesses asserted that they considered the area too dangerous for such trips, particularly because of the likelihood of savage weather conditions in featureless terrain from which retreat is difficult. It was stated that these mountains in bad weather provide a stern test for seasoned mountaineers, let alone young climbers gaining experience.

Fred Harper was asked to define in detail those areas in the region of the Cairngorms that he considered suitable for young parties in winter. Qualifying his answer by saying that he thought all such expeditions fairly questionable, he stated that only routes with constant easy escapes to the north should be considered. Thus he believed that Beattie's expedition should have proceeded no further than the high ground at the head of Corrie an t-Sneachda, so that a downhill retreat to the Fiarcaill a Corrie Chais would always have been available if needed. He went on to say that similar expeditions to any of the summits above the Northern Corries might be justifiable providing that escapes never involved uphill sections. The real point at issue, however, was just how much more risk Beattie was taking in pressing on into hostile country, downhill, for a mere 1½ miles to the haven of the Curran Bothy, instead of retreating at Harper's postulated *fail safe* point. The experience of Cathy Davidson's party, of course, shows how much can go wrong in only a short stretch of ground – but how many mountaineers can honestly claim that they wouldn't have tried to cover that downhill stretch, given a party in front and a keen, fairly fresh and well-equipped team of their own? It was certainly not a clear-cut decision and, though some more experienced Cairngorm hands might have retreated at the first signs of bad weather, others would have taken a chance on the downhill stretch. Having reached the Curran Bothy, of course, there is still the matter of further retreat to consider. The latter problem is not easy to solve in bad conditions, for the available routes can rapidly prove treacherous, particularly the descents into the Lairig Ghru. It needs little imagination to envisage the desperate plight of any party that failed to find the Curran Bothy in a white-out. Indeed, a side issue that arose during the enquiry was whether the high-level bothies did more harm than good, by enticing parties to undertake more ambitious expeditions than they would otherwise consider. The findings of the jury clearly placed the responsibility on the mountaineering world to consider this matter with some urgency.

The mood of the court
These, then, were the crucial questions, and the general conclusions that seemed to emerge from the enquiry:

• *Should the Ainslie Park party have been on the Cairngorms at all?*
On the whole, the Cairngorms, in winter, were considered unsuitable for school parties. There are some areas, however, that might be justifiable.

• *Did this party start out too late?*
Yes, although there was enough time to complete the route in good conditions, there was insufficient margin for error.

• *Should the party have turned back at any stage after leaving Cairngorm?*
Beattie should have reunited the two groups at the first sign of really bad weather, and then possibly retreated. Cathy Davidson was generally not considered to have miscalculated in this respect – she was merely following Beattie's instructions without question.

• *Was the party well-equipped?*
By all normal winter mountaineering standards, it undoubtedly was.

• *Should Cathy Davidson have tried to reach the Bothy when her party grew tired?*
Opinion was divided.

• *Was Beattie in error in not suspecting Miss Davidson's plight, and in not trying to retrace the route to locate her?*
He was certainly somewhat unimaginative and over-confident in this respect, though his first concern was for his own party.

• *Should Paisley have vetted the plans more carefully?*
He could have given more thought to the potential pitfalls of the plan, particularly in view of the deteriorating weather situation.

Other evidence
The subsidiary witnesses appeared merely to establish peripheral facts. The weather experts confirmed the poor forecasts for the Saturday evening. The parents of the victims, with one exception, claimed that they had not realised that the expedition was to be so serious, and that, had they known, they would not have allowed their children to take part. Mr Chalmers, the Headmaster of the school, endorsed Beattie's reputation as a good teacher and confirmed that Cathy Davidson was recognised as Beattie's regular

helper on these trips. The police witness, Sergeant Duff, took a stronger line about the sins of visiting the Cairngorms with groups of children. One sometimes gets the impression that if it were up to the police we should all stay safely in our beds, never venturing near such dangerous things as mountains – but perhaps that is an overstatement. Certainly the police seemed to have missed the more subtle points at issue here, while these were fully understood by such experts as Harper and Langmuir, whose evidence was correspondingly less extreme.

Questions for Edinburgh to answer

Although John Cook, the top man in the whole administrative chain of command that led eventually to Beattie, was also questioned, he was not subjected to any serious cross-examination.

We feel, however, that Cook, in so far as he represents the Edinburgh Outdoor Activities Authorities, should have been asked to clear up the following points:

1. Why, if the Cairngorms are such a dangerous mountain group for school children, was the Lagganlia Centre ever established in the region?

2. Had a clear procedure been laid down to direct Paisley in his relationships with visiting parties such as Beattie's? Although the Centre has mainly been devoted to the pursuit of low-level activities and skiing, the question still remains as to why guidelines for mountaineering on the Cairngorm plateau were not established at an early stage in the Centre's existence.

3. How far should instructors go in training schoolchildren in such high risk sports as mountaineering? Where, if at all, should they stop, perhaps jeopardising the effectiveness of their early instruction, but leaving the child to carry on himself if he so desires? This question might profitably be considered by all instructors.

Perhaps it is the officials of the Edinburgh organisation (John Cook and his subordinate, Terry Nicholls) who must give the most serious thought to the rationale behind their whole policy of taking keen pupils on to more ambitious training.

The Jury's findings

At the end of these six hard days the jury retired, returned and, ignoring the entreaties of the Counsel for the parents to censure Beattie and Paisley, brought formal verdicts for the deaths of the six children (listed below). Implicit in their findings was the clear understanding that there was no one area of serious negligence, and that the accident had resulted from the cumulative effect of a number of miscalculations. Their recommendations were mild, to say the least, and mountaineers' fears that they would advocate yet more badges, rules and certificates proved unfounded. If any quality emerged as the supreme mountaineering virtue, it was that of experience; and clearly there is only one way to acquire that.

Findings and Recommendations of the Jury

The Jury recorded the formal verdict that the five schoolchildren and the student teacher had died from cold and exposure near the Feith Buidhe between November 21st and 22nd 1971. They stated that they did not want to discourage the spirit of adventure in children's Outdoor Pursuit activities but they added seven recommendations to their verdict. These were:

1. More care should be exercised in the organisation of parties of young children in outdoor activities with special regard to fitness and training.

2. Fuller information regarding activities should be given to parents and acknowledged by them.

3. Certified Teachers should accompany their pupils to outdoor centres like Lagganlia and that expeditions be led thereafter by fully qualified and long-experienced instructors.

4. Certain areas of the countryside should be designated as suitable for children's expeditions in summer and winter. These areas should be decided after consultation with the Scottish Mountain Leadership Training Board, the mountain-rescue organisations, and those with local knowledge.

5. In the matter of high-level bothies, advice as to their removal should be left to the experts.

6. The jury endorsed the praise given to the mountain-rescue operations in this instance and suggested that thought be given to furthering, financially and otherwise, the good work done by them.

7. In the event of a disaster closer liaison should be kept between the authorities and the parents concerned.

Possible repercussions

One outcome of this tragedy will certainly be that increased pressure will be brought to bear on Outdoor Centre leaders – many of whom are already over-cautious – to *make climbing safe*. The cry now is for young novices to be taught in situations of 'apparent' and not 'real risk'. The result, no doubt, will be a greater concentration on orienteering and similar pursuits. But one thing is certain: if Education Authorities continue to include mountaineering in their outdoor curricula they can no longer be under any illusions as to its dangers.

Many climbers believe that mountaineering should not be used as an educational subject at all, and that if young people want to climb they should learn to do so through more traditional channels. Others believe that the mountaineering world should at least offer schoolchildren the opportunity to experience a fine sport. But the question remains as to how far instruction should go. What is to happen when an instructor has taken children on a few big walks and easy rock climbs? Should he go on to greater things, or should be abandon the training just when it is beginning to take effect? Perhaps Beattie's mistake was that he, with the approval of his superiors, encouraged the children's interest a little too much; perhaps he should have left them to continue climbing under their own steam, without his stimulating leadership. For how far into the Cairngorms would Alan Davidson, Raymond Leslie and Billy Kerr and the others have ventured without Beattie? Not far, one suspects. They would have progressed more slowly and gained experience at their own pace, without the extra stimulus their instructor provided. The members of the second party should clearly never have been in such an exposed situation in the first place. If any conclusion has emerged from this sad affair therefore, it is that we need to probe much further than the errors of two young instructors in order to draw lessons for the future. Perhaps it is the whole educational basis from which they worked that needs the most searching scrutiny.

Personnel and Experience
First group:
BEN BEATTIE* 23 Competent all-rounder. Three alpine seasons (Badile, N. Ridge; Frendo Spur). Exp. to Hindu Kush. Rock climber (VS-HVS). Instructed on many expeditions including several Cairngorm winter trips. Special knowledge of native Irish mountains. Holder of MIC Had taken pupils up grade 3 winter ice climbs. Familiar with the region of the tragedy.
ALAN DAVIDSON 18 Keen mountaineer with expeditions in the main British groups and the Tatra (grade 4). Led VS climbs with other pupils (Gimmer Crack and Gordion Knot). Over twenty tough hill walks – winter and summer (Buachaille and Bidean in winter).
JOHN BLAIKIE 16 Keen walker with both school and parents (Liathach in winter). Won orienteering championship.
TOM BISHOP 15 Regular weekend rock-climber (led Severes).
BILL JEFFREY 15 Regular weekend hill-walker. Winter ascents of Bidean nam Bian and Buachaille Etive Mor (led through on North Buttress).
BERNARD McLAFFERTY 15 Keen rock-climber (led Amen Corner and other Severes). Good rugby player.
CATHERINE CAMPBELL 15 Regular hill-walker with parents and school . Seconded VDs. Led through with Jeffrey on North Buttress of Buachaille in winter.
ALEX FARRELL 14 Weekend rock-climber and walker. Buachaille and Great Gable in winter.
PAT McGOVERN 15 Basic Outdoor Pursuits course and a follow-up course at Lagganlia.
Note: All (except McGovern) were fairly competent at map and compass work, and had also practised basic ice axe and crampon techniques.

Second group:
CATHY DAVIDSON 21 Very experienced for her age and sex. Exempted from MLC and planned to take MIC. Two Alpine seasons: Matterhorn (Hörnli) and Badile (North Ridge) with

*Ben Beattie died in a fall from high on Nanda Devi East in 1978

Beattie, and Aig.du Chardonnet (Forbes Arête) and Grépon (East Face) with another girl. Had led Hammer and other VS routes. Led students up Severes. Experienced in summer and winter walking (15 Cairngorm winter trips). Familiar with the region of the tragedy, in winter.
WILLIAM KERRt 16 Walker and rock-climber (led Sev.). Expeditions to Buachaille and Bidean in winter.
RAYMOND LESLIE 15 Canoeist and mountain walker (Lakes/Wales/Glen Coe/Trossachs).
SUSAN BYRNEt 15 DIANE DUDGEONt 15 CAROL BERTRAMt 15 All had been on the Basic Outdoor Pursuits course run by the school, and had also been on follow-up courses at Benmore and Lagganlia (up Cairngorm, down Corrie Cas). All had practised ice-axe technique. Byrne and Bertram good Orienteers.
LORRAINE DICKt 15 Canoeist (skilled and very fit). Basic Outdoor course, weekend in Lakes.
SHELAGH SUNDERLANDt 18 Student Teacher and Voluntary Instructor at Lagganlia. Two basic rock courses and walking in Lakes. Girl Guide experience.

Equipment worn or carried by each pupil: 3 Sweaters, Corduroy Jeans or Breeches, Pyjamas or Ski-Pants, Scarf, 2 pairs of Gloves, Axe, Crampons, Balaclava, Waterproof Cagoule and Overtrousers, Boots, Gaiters, Rucksack, Sleeping Bag, Poly Bivouac Bag, Karrimat. *General equipment among the party:* Food, Cooking Gear, Stoves, 2 pairs of Snowshoes, Flares, Whistles, Torches, Compasses, Maps.

from MOUNTAIN 20 *1972*

BRIDGING THE GAP

TOM PRICE

I hope you won't be disappointed in what I have to say. With a title like 'Bridging the Gap' you may be expecting something like 'How to Set Up a Tirolean Traverse or The Employment of the Schermuly Line-Shooting Pistol in Climbing'. In fact, I have been instructed to say something about two kinds of gap, which may actually turn out to be two aspects of the same gap.

Firstly, there is the gap that is felt to exist between the person who has taken up mountain leadership as another teaching skill, and the ordinary sporting mountaineer and club member; and secondly, the gap which actually exists between the numbers of youngsters introduced to mountaineering by education, and the comparatively few who continue the interest and join mountaineering clubs.

The first thing I asked myself was: 'Is the teaching mountaineer really any different from the sporting mountaineer?' And my first cautious reply was:

'He doesn't have to be.' I can think of people from courses of training who have become devotees of mountaineering indistinguishable in their outlook from those whose introduction was a keen personal interest leading to membership of a club. Like members of the Establishment, it's often surprising where they have come from. I suppose the truth is that once the spark is kindled, it matters little how it was first ignited; the result is a mountaineer, an enthusiast.

Nevertheless, all too often one can see a difference, and when one does it is basically a difference of attitude. I can well recall the time when I myself became a teaching mountaineer, after many years of private climbing and fell-walking and club membership. It was when I became Warden of a Mountain Centre. My friends were very generous about it, they made allowances, they conceded that everyone has to earn a living somehow, and that no one could be blamed for wanting to go and live in Eskdale; but few of them really approved of what I was doing, and one or two said as much. I felt they had the same kind of reservations that the contemporaries of the Abraham brothers must have had when the brothers went into the postcard business. I was no longer quite pure.

So perhaps there is a gap. And if there is it is one of outlook. Crudely stated, the difference is that educators care about people, while climbers care about mountains. I don't mean, of course, that mountaineers, by caring for mountains, do not care for people, nor do I suggest that the educator, by caring for people, is thereby indifferent to mountains. They are not incompatibles: on the contrary, most mountaineers are highly gregarious and, for many, good companionship is one of the greatest joys of the hills. It is simply that the teacher-mountaineer and the mountaineer *per se* have different preoccupations and often a quite different outlook. For example, the mountaineer does not climb for the good of his health. That mountaineering is, on the whole, a health-giving pursuit is a mere fringe benefit. In fact, the mountaineer is likely to persist with his sport to the *detriment* of his health, laying up for himself who knows what stores of arthritis, haemorrhoids and the like. The educator, on the other hand, does tend to climb for his health, or rather his pupils' health. He deliberately uses the mountain environment to improve the physical, mental and spiritual condition of his pupils. Contrast this with the mountaineer who will sell his soul to the Devil so long as he is not kept off the hills.

One can pursue this difference of outlook into the realms of safety. Sporting mountaineers, one cannot but admit, are on the whole a bit dangerous. It is only when they turn professional that they become concerned and preoccupied about safety. What keeps them alive is a certain sensitivity to danger, and an element of unconscious judgement, born of a long succession of near-misses. For in a sense all mountaineers are survivors.

The difference of approach to safety is illustrated for me by the recollection that as an experienced private climber my idea of introducing four sixteen-year-old novices to rock-climbing was to take them up Scafell Pinnacle by Slingsby's Chimney on a greasy November day. Later, as a teacher-climber, I would have objected to this on at least two important counts: firstly, four novices were too many for one instructor, and secondly, the instructor had no colleague in the vicinity to help him in an emergency. The sporting mountaineer is certainly much more inclined to travel hopefully than the teacher-mountaineer. I would like to bet, for example, that if you made a raid into the hills one Sunday, and pulled in two or three hundred club mountaineers, and frisked them, it would be a scandal how few orange survival bags you would find on them.

The fact is that the sporting mountaineer sees climbing as a slightly anti-authoritarian activity, or at the very least as an assertion of personal idiosyncrasy. It was particularly so when I was first taking to climbing, for at that time the general public saw it as a perverse and irresponsible activity. People were hostile to the sight of a rope, and would tell you off on railway stations. The teacher-mountaineer, on the other hand, is necessarily a responsible chap, on the side of society rather than against it or outside it. Joining a University Climbing Club, therefore, is quite a different thing from doing mountain-leadership as part of a main PE course.

It might be worth pursuing this thought further, as it may shed some light on the second 'gap' of my title – the question being asked by some members of the BMC committee: 'What happens to all the young people who are introduced to climbing at school? Why do they not appear in greater numbers in the climbing clubs?'

Well, it may be that the inclusion of climbing as a school subject has the effect of putting them off. Education has in the past done a magnificent job in putting people off poetry, for example.

It is too simple, however, to blame this kind of thing on the schools and the teachers. It is really an aspect of the fundamental distinction we make in our society between work and play. There was a time when work was man's chief concern and chief fulfilment. For some, this is still the case, notably for the old hill-farmer who looks without full comprehension at the weekend climbers. And of course the same applies for people with a vocation. But for the majority work is dull, necessary and repetitive, its chief justification being the fact that it earns money. And school counts as work.

This is one of the reasons why many people feel so uneasy at the thought of children enjoying themselves at school, and so inclined to place the onus for disciplining children upon the schools rather than upon themselves.

Ideas about the severity of work and education are frequently attributed to puritanical attitudes in our culture, unjustly in my view. The puritans were in fact much concerned with human happiness, the word 'joy' was prominent in their vocabulary, and at their best they showed a keen appreciation of the privilege of being alive and a readiness to praise the Lord for it. What makes education sometimes such a dreary business is not puritanism but something much more recent, what Matthew Arnold, the first Inspector of Schools, called middle-class philistinism. It is the attitude that insists that pleasure shall always be frivolous, and serious enterprises always dull. It is inveterately status-seeking, and has given a new and deplorable meaning to the word 'respectable'. It has turned education into a device for claiming superiority, and this in its turn has led to an insincerity that has estranged poetry and art and devalued popular culture. Whatever it embraces becomes solemn, pretentious, exclusive and dull.

I think many mountaineers are intuitively aware of the menace of philistinism. Perhaps that is what makes some top climbers feel compelled to be gratuitously coarse and anti-heroic in their public lectures. And there is a long British tradition of not training for mountaineering feats. Foreign mountaineers prepare for a major ascent in the gym, British mountaineers in the pub. Or so they pretend. So it may be that the best way for a school to produce future members of the *Groupe de Haute Montagne* would be to construct a climbing wall on one side of the building, and then forbid anyone to go near it.

The teacher-mountaineer is likely to be, and certainly ought to be, a mature, well-balanced person fully aware of his aims and fully aware of his responsibilities. The sporting mountaineer, on the other hand, is inclined to be determinedly immature. After all, climbing, even the climbing of Everest, is fundamentally a boyish prank writ large. Mallory's random remark, 'Because it is there', has been given undue prominence in our explanations of why we climb. I'm pretty sure Mallory said it only in order to close the tiresome subject. A more carefully considered explanation was given by André Roch at a club dinner just after the Swiss attempt on Everest. He said – apropos of the nationalism which was so apt to creep into the sport – that the only reason for climbing was that it was 'fun'. He was speaking in English, in which he had no great facility, and it was clear that by 'fun' he implied a good deal more than he was able to put into words. He was suggesting, I believe, what the Archbishop of Dublin was suggesting when he said: 'Happiness is no laughing matter'. I think that by the simple unassuming word 'fun' he was even perhaps asserting the primacy of the things of the spirit. And that is, surely, where the educator and the mountaineer can be reconciled, where the spirit of joyous independence and

personal fulfilment can be linked with the spirit of purposeful and responsible concern for young people's development.

With these reflections in mind I would make, for discussion, the following
suggestions about the way in which mountain education might move.
Firstly, a greater element of voluntariness should be introduced. Secondly,
the 'closed shop' attitude to qualifications should be discouraged in some
way. Thirdly, there should be a move away from the concept of the Outdoor
Pursuits Centre, with its once-only offer of a week or two's training; instead,
informal work should be encouraged in schools and youth services, with the
Centres offering guidance. Fourthly, we should avoid establishing a methodology, avoid laying down the law, avoid rules and deal chiefly in terms of
general principles. Finally, and most important by far, we should look more
closely and thoughtfully at our educational aims, and be prepared, in doing
so, to turn for guidance to the sporting mountaineer while retaining the
degree of responsibility and concern for safety vital when looking after other
people's children.

MOUNTAIN SAFETY CONFERENCE 1973

CLIMB ONLY WHEN YOU'RE READY

IAN McNAUGHT-DAVIS

During the extraordinary spell of fine weather before Easter, I found myself
sitting in the sun at the foot of the Napes. Overall this is a fairly boring little
crag with no real route for my sports plan, and really I should have been
doing a carefully selected 'golden oldie' on Scafell; but I'd forgotten its name
and where it went and, what was more frustrating, I'd left the Scafell guide,
shiny in its new plastic covers, in the lavatory where it is essential reading.

The Needle was being attacked by several parties, each equipped with
enough harnesses, double ropes, chocks and runners to meet every possible
need. The whole scene was a thousand chrome-moly pegs removed from
W. P. Haskett Smith, who broke all the rules of the modern climbing school
by soloing the Needle on sight, eighty-eight years ago. The groups I was
watching had doubtless signed out with the Mountain Rescue, ingratiated

themselves with the National Park Warden and registered with the local police, so that, if their ventures went astray, immediate rescue was ensured, with minimum trouble and inconvenience for everyone.

I lay back and watched the performance with interest.

'I'm there,' the leader cried, as he floundered on to the top, as if after all the huffing and puffing he could be anywhere else.

'Taking in.' Perhaps he thought the second might imagine he was trying to steal the rope.

'Climb when you're ready.' This I found totally baffling. I suppose there really are people who climb when they are not ready and, before they have a chance to put it away, they spring on to the crag in the sycophantic hope of pleasing their leader. At this point, to my total amazement, there came a shout from the second:

'Climbing.'

What else did he really expect the leader to think he was doing? Golfing? Swimming? I lay back and listened to the music of the cliff.

'Taking in.'

'Climbing.'

'I'm there.'

'Take in.'

Suddenly I realised what I was seeing. It was the new generation of climbers bred from the educational machine, drilled into a routine xerox-copy, one of the other. The crag was a bedlam of shouts and cries, accompanied by the clatter and clangour of pegs, chocks, wires and other bread-and-butter products of the equipment moguls who, hand-in-glove with the educationalists, indoctrinate every beginner with the urge to equip himself for every climb, however easy, however trivial, with enough gear to storm a Dolomite North Wall. Indeed at some schools, on rainy days, they even go so far as to take the pupils on guided tours of the local chock factory and neighbouring equipment shops. No kick-backs, of course.

A few weeks later, I was climbing on that incredible crag and much-loved venue of New York climbers, the Shawangunks. The equipment moguls here are not satisfied with only three cars, night clubs and a life of permanent pleasure-seeking. They fly around in their private aeroplanes, watching the multitude of New Englanders heaving over holdless overhangs, each carrying more equipment than is stocked in all the equipment shops in North Wales. Not that they have opted out of climbing to fish, ski or fool about in fast cars like their English counterparts; on the contrary, they are dedicated to putting up harder and harder routes that call for the use of even more of their varied products. But to get back to the point: I was sitting in the sun at the bottom of the crag (as usual), when I suddenly found myself tuning in to the mysterious calls which were emanating from the cliff and which, despite frequent explanations, I still fail to comprehend. There was, for example, 'Leon!' I'm not sure whether this was someone's name or an instruction to the second to carry on doing what he had been doing. It was shouted frequently in the *basso profundo* voice so often adopted by American climbers. The response was generally 'Lay off', which I think means, 'Let go', but whether this refers to the rope or the rock is not clear. The most innovative cry was, 'Up rope!' This could be shouted by the second ('Up, up, damned rope.') or by the leader, perhaps in the vain hope of obtaining some assistance from his second.

In comparison to English, of course, American is a very precise language. What other country would go 'horseback riding', as if there was any other place to ride a horse; or endure 'back-packing', presumably as opposed to 'front-packing'? There was one Americanism, however, whose meaning I had never quite grasped, and that was 'psyched'. But that afternoon on the Shawangunks I learnt more about it.

To be 'psyched by a move' means to have fallen off that move.

To be 'psyched by a climb' means to have fallen off that climb.

To be 'psyched out' means to have fallen into the ground, or 'cratered', and is used as an excuse by the climber who has accepted the permanent role of second.

I couldn't resist the temptation. A few words of explanation to our rope of three and we joined the throng.

'I'm there.' (Where?)

'Leon.'

'Up rope.'

'Climbing.' (What else?)

'Are you there?'

'Lay off!'

It was great, but after a few climbs the black flies psyched us, so we logged off and encapsulated a few buds at what laughingly passes for a boozer, as we deconceived the day.

Of course, some communication between leader and second could be considered essential. I seem to have spent much of my time on cliffs with small phlegmatic northerners who positively discourage conversation and totally ignore polite code messages. Communication has generally been as follows:

'Pull, for Christ's sake! Pull!'

A weird giggling can just be heard from above and a mass of loose coils spiral down the crag.

'I'm off!'

'No you're not. Just get that finger jug above yer 'ed, get yer bloody feet up and go for the jam.'

'Slack, you're pulling me off, slack!'

Again that insane, frenetic laugh, as the rope twangs hawser-tight.

'Didn't you hear me shouting?'

'Aye, but I couldn't 'ear yer. That's what t'ropes for – communication. I felt yer all the way up, just like a bloody frisky whale.'

So why should I grumble, just because the crags sound like passing-out parade at some highly-disciplined Outdoor Pursuits Centre where, to make the instructor's life as easy as possible, every move, shout and presumably, fall, is standardised? Let's have more individuality, more eccentricity, more colour and more variety in our climbing; let's hold up to derision the cliché-shouting instructors who are making our hills sound like mindless Bingo Halls.

'I'm there.' 'I'm off … '

from MOUNTAIN 37 1974

ADVENTURE BY NUMBERS

TOM PRICE

The idea of adventure is now widely accepted in education, yet when one comes to think of it, it is extraordinary that something that is by its very nature so fortuitous and uncertain of outcome should be harnessed and brought into the service of educational programmes. I sometimes wonder, indeed, how adventurous adventure courses really are, for as soon as one becomes a deliberate purveyor of adventure, one is in danger of losing much that is fundamental to it. It becomes a package deal, with something false about it, like the packages described by Jeremy Sandford and Roger Law in their book, *Synthetic Fun:* 'Synthetic fun is the smile on the face of the holiday camp fun people, this Friday and every Friday, as they are ritually thrown into the blue, blue swimming pool.'

Synthetic fun is for people who are too tired, or too busy, or too timid or too pusillanimous to go in for real fun. Similarly, painting by numbers is for people who are unwilling to take on the agony and ecstasy of original com-position. And it is all too easy, I should think, to deal in synthetic adventure, or adventure by numbers: in other words to methodise it out of existence.

We are, of course, inclined to want to have our cake and eat it. We say: 'give our children thrilling adventures and make absolutely certain nothing untoward happens.' This suggests a curious misuse of the word adventure, and I prefer the thinking of the Army commander, who said, in briefing a party for a landing by canoe on the enemy coast, to be followed by the surprise abduction of a senior officer from a heavily guarded headquarters: 'And, remember, men, we want no adventures.'

There is no need to pursue tediously the meaning of the word. It is a common one that everybody knows. But it is worthwhile making the obser-vation that how people use it reflects their outlook and is as variable as people's outlooks are.

Anyone who has been mixed up in outdoor activities in the hills has come across ill-experienced and naïvely adventurous individuals leading parties of youngsters. We have all seen the difficulty with which they conceal their elation at having the rescue teams out, and the peculiarly injured way they receive their chastisement. I've always had a soft spot for such fellows, exasperating though they are at the time, for, however inept they may be, they are genuine adventurers, with something pure and quixotic about them that the MIC holders lack.

I think there is no question that much of what we describe as adventure is not adventure at all, and it is my view that if that is the case we should stop calling it adventure. Young people find adult thought processes con-fusing enough as it is, and we only add to the confusion when we describe walking on an empty, rounded hill, laden with emergency equipment, as an adventure (whereas, for example, making gunpowder, or cycling two feet behind a bus to take advantage of its slipstream, is condemned as irresponsible). We pay lip-service to adventure, but what we mostly teach is prudence, and the importance of being comprehensively insured. As a middle-aged family man I find nothing much wrong with this, but why can't we acknowledge it?

But, of course, it is too narrow a view of adventure to equate it simply with taking risks. After all, those who make their living by dangerous jobs don't find them adventurous, except perhaps at first. Once they have mastered the work, they find it demanding and exacting, perhaps, but not adventurous. In fact, dangerous work is frequently described as tedious, because it demands such endless painstaking routines and precautions.

Many a lad goes to sea in expectation of a life of adventure, but pretty soon finds himself tied to the interminable tasks of watch-keeping, log-reading, safety-checking, measuring, recording and dead-reckoning. People who climb for a living have much the same experience. Though they may derive some satisfaction from the awareness that other people regard their job as adventurous, to them it is just work. The only difference between it and more ordinary work is that it demands perpetual care and discipline.

Nor is the scale of an adventure so significant. I have heard an ascent of the Old West Route on Pillar Rock represented as the ultimate in cliff-hanging, and who is to say that, in truth, it was less of an adventure than, say, an Extreme done by a party of experts? The truth is that in one important sense, adventure, however much it may be concerned with physical conflict and danger, is really of the mind. What is an adventure to some, may be, to others of more prosaic nature, an ordeal, or an imposition, or a nuisance, or a calamity, or even simply a bore. For just as beauty is in the eye of the beholder, adventure is in the mind and spirit of the adventurer. It is not risks and desperate situations that make adventure, so much as adventurousness.

It makes more sense, therefore, to consider the spirit of adventure, rather than adventure. Some people have it in greater measure than others. Some appear not to have it at all, and that, perhaps, is the mark of complete maturity. For adventurousness is a peculiarly youthful quality. Maturity is held up as a desirable educational goal, and it is often claimed that outdoor pursuits bring young people to maturity. It might equally be claimed, however, that they keep people young. Certainly one of the most attractive things about outdoor pursuits instructors or teachers is their youthfulness, their refusal completely to grow up and abandon 'the heaven that lies about us in our infancy.' It is odd the esteem in which maturity is held, considering how close it can be to over-ripeness. The truth is, of course, and in education we neglect it at our peril, that each stage of life is equally valuable *for its own sake*. The practice of regarding any one stage as nothing more than a training ground for a later one leads to a squandering of the precious gift of life. Furthermore it is cruel and untrue to suggest, by valuing maturity too much, that the old and doddering are of no account. We can turn to R. L. Stevenson, whose essay on Crabbed Age and Youth has much to say on this subject, for a wise and kindly comment on the process of maturing: 'To love playthings well as a child, to lead an adventurous and honourable youth, and to settle when the time arrives to a green and smiling age, is to be a good artist in life, and deserve well of yourself and your neighbour.'

That word 'honourable' reminds us that adventure is strongly linked to romance. Now romanticism has two sides to it. It may be condemned as illusory and false, but on the other hand it has its noble side, visionary and idealistic, raising man from the commonplace and trivial to the heights of aspiration, transcending his finite nature and looking towards the infinite and the sublime, 'the eternal spirit of the chainless mind'. It is romantic aspiration and vision that can turn a long hard plod over the Pennine Way into a real adventure. There is a kind of poeticism, shared by all who love the hills, which is expressed not in words but in physical effort, in technical competence, and in good companionship.

What is so valuable and formative in an adventure is the commitment it invariably calls for in one way or another. There is always, somewhere, a point for girding up one's loins, taking a deep breath, and making a step into the unknown. It is a giving of oneself, a spending of oneself without which, paradoxically, there can be no personal adventure. Really hazardous activities call for close control and discipline and the decisions cannot be left to the pupil. Yet there is considerable pressure, in all sorts of ways, to proceed as though the more advanced and technical the activity, and the more costly to equip it and provide for it, the greater the adventure, and the greater the educational pay-off. It is simply not so. If it were, the upper Himalaya would be a better place for a centre than the Lake District.

Perhaps the real truth of the matter is that we make too much of the adventure idea when that is not the essence of what we are about at all in outdoor education. The real core of the business is the enrichment through exposure to experiences and through various feasts of the senses, not least the kinaesthetic sense. That great and unpopular poet Wordsworth who knew hardly anything about nature study and even less about climbing, (though he did walk over 100,000 miles, so they say) has, nevertheless, more to say for outdoor education than any writer I know, and as recommended reading I would give him higher priority even than *Safety on Mountains*.

> The eye it cannot choose but see
> We cannot bid the ear be still
> Our bodies feel, where'er they be
> Against or with our will.
> Think you midst all this mighty sum
> of things for ever speaking
> That nothing of itself will come
> But we must still be seeking.

You cannot plan adventures. The best one can do is allow them to happen.

from MOUNTAIN 38 *1974*

THREE LETTERS ON
EDUCATIONAL CLIMBING

SIR JACK LONGLAND, PETER WOOD
and ROBIN HODGKIN

Dear Sir,

I am appalled by the selfish arrogance of Rod Bulcock's letter, 'Educational Climbing: a Contradiction in Terms' *(Mountain 51)*. Hills and mountains are frequented by a variety of people, for a variety of purposes: by shepherds and farmers, who contribute a great deal more to the community than any modest climber would dare to claim; by family parties, probably not straying far from their cars, but glad to get a glimpse of the wildness which they are too timid to penetrate; by naturalists, geologists and other scientists, who pursue their researches there; and by parties of adult-led youngsters who, under wise or incompetent leadership, are getting their first experience of mountain country and its possible attractions.

It is the invincible ignorance displayed by most of the critics of 'educational climbing' that I find so frightening. Looking back over mountaineering history, how have people become climbers? A few (and good luck to them, because they certainly needed it) took the legendary path of borrowing mum's clothes line and learning rocks the hard way. But that was not, at least until recently, considered the high road to becoming a mountaineer. Fathers and uncles taught sons and nephews (nieces too): others sought out qualified guides; schoolmasters – Irving, Mallory, Noyce and Pettigrew among them – thought it an obvious duty to introduce to their favourite sport of climbing those pupils who might possibly become mountaineers; university climbing clubs developed programmes for turning novices into leaders. Nearly all of those training methods started with raw, young human material which didn't even know whether it wanted to go near the mountains, much less climb amongst them. All of these training methods were more or less organised ventures in 'educational climbing'. What, for instance, was Geoffrey Winthrop Young trying to do? For nearly forty years, he arranged his Pen-y-Pass parties as an inspired blend of experienced mountaineers and youngsters who, but for him, might never have visited the mountains at all. What was that but 'educational climbing'? How many of today's distinguished climbers, have not been guilty of trying to introduce to climbing offspring who were sometimes bored, sometimes frightened or just plain uninterested? What was that except 'educational climbing'?

More recently, even before but more particularly after the last war, some of us have been trying to further the beliefs of Geoffrey Young and of Kurt Hahn, the inspirer of those Outward Bound Schools, which, amongst others, nurtured Doug Scott, in opening the love and adventurous use of the mountains to many more than the lucky and privileged few who earlier made the mountaineering scene. We tried hard to persuade the established climbing clubs to open wide their gates to youngsters, and in general we failed; we backed the Duke of Edinburgh's Award Scheme, which showed promise of introducing to wild country thousands of young who might otherwise never have escaped from the local disco; and when, in their unpaid spare time, many teachers followed our lead and, because of their own love of the mountains, began to take parties of pupils walking and climbing, and ignorant accidents followed, we invented and developed the structure of Mountain Leadership Training and Certification, which has, in twelve years, dramatically reduced the toll of accidents, near-accidents and searches throughout our mountain districts. Was this wrong? Should we have left them to their own unskilled devices or should we, as we did, endorse Kurt Hahn's view that it is the birthright of the normal child to be taught to run, to throw, to jump, to swim and to climb, in order to complement the acquisition of equally essential academic skills?

I repeat, I am appalled by the selfishness of those climbers who assert that the mountains are theirs, that mum's clothes line is the only passport to the 'true' use of the mountains, and that all except their own peculiar sect of Seventh Day Adventists should be kept out.

Yours faithfully,
Jack Longland (Bakewell)

Dear Sir,
Sir Jack Longland's defence of 'educational climbing' is a specious one. He simply calls every well-tried, traditionally familiar introduction to climbing a form of 'educational climbing', thus emptying the term of any specific meaning. Citing the examples of schoolmasters taking lads out on the hills and the activity of university clubs, Sir Jack telescopes them all together and says 'all of these training methods were more or less organised ventures in educational climbing'. But were they? And surely the degree of organisation is precisely the point at issue in the minds of Sir Jack's critics? First, many of those who start climbing at school would hardly maintain they had undergone 'training methods' or anything so pretentious. It is equally doubt-

ful whether university clubs, even when Sir Jack was an actively climbing member, ever 'developed' anything so formal as 'programmes for turning novices into leaders'. Finally, he equates the public school and Oxbridge reading and climbing parties led by Young and others at Pen-y-Pass with today's outdoor activity 'programmes'. Such a feat of abstraction is unreal.

For someone who believes, in a freedom-loving way, that the hills are for everyone from shepherds to schoolboys, Sir Jack shows an odd preoccupation in his vocabulary with methods, programmes, organisation, training, certification and, presumably, with the inevitable loss of freedom that submission to these entails. The explanation lies, perhaps, in his avowed admiration for the great Kurt Hahn. Dr Hahn developed the Outward Bound idea – as he himself explained some years ago – because of what he felt was the inadequacy of young lives in peacetime conditions.

He felt that those youngsters unfortunate enough to be denied the educational experience of living through stirring times of war and crisis could get a comparable experience fighting the mountains and the waves, rescuing people and performing bold deeds. Dr Hahn called this sport of outdoor activity 'the moral equivalent of war'. Sir Jack should perhaps explain to the untutored amongst us whether he thinks that to reject such ideas as these is arrogant? He is not only in strange company, but for an enlightened member of the educational establishment he uses a strange logic.

Perhaps we simpler climbers ought not to trust what he is telling us after all?

Yours faithfully,
Peter Wood (Penrith)

Dear Sir,
All that Sir Jack Longland says [in his] letter in *Mountain 52* about how we learned to climb is true, but he does not touch the central, contemporary issue. This is to do with individuals in an open society and the choice which we all face between more rules and more responsibility. Here is a typical case: children who go to the Welsh hills from the ILEA centres are not allowed to leave the tarmac unless they are accompanied by a teacher with a ... you know what [MLC]. I happened to meet the senior official concerned with this ruling in County Hall recently and he said: 'But of course, we must have something to fall back on in case anything should go wrong.'

Under Geoffrey Young's eye we were influenced not to take foolish risks and in more positive ways too. But there was nothing resembling the absurdity of rules about who went where. There were a few customs and minor rituals but it was skill, judgement and achievement that we were after

– all part of our initiation into a tradition, at the centre of which were a few people whom we admired and who seemed to have been particularly successful in holding the balance between daring and good judgement (Jack was eminently one of these). We willingly, almost passionately, accepted (and criticised) the mountain way of life. In the ILEA case, however, and in many others like it, there is a crucial contradiction –the admission of a public demand for 'safe adventure' – a false notion which soon contaminates mountain activities in education. The falsehood, note well, is not spoken by a person but is implicit in the system. But the young get the message.

The wider issue, so often ignored, is the creeping influence of bureaucracy and one of its manifestations – 'the diploma disease' – as it gradually encroaches on our lives and lays its fat hands on our schools. Mercifully there are many individuals who resist, but nevertheless our institutions are becoming less personal, less free and, at the same time, more standardised and *safe*. Of course some aspects of our lives must be safe – bound by rules and procedures. Railway lines and chemists' shops would not be much good if they weren't, nor, though in lesser degree, would road transport; so we certainly need reliable bureaucrats and quantifiers. But all true cultural activity, all enlargement of vision involves skill, responsible judgement and risk – risk of error, of foolishness and even of death. Such innovation and discovery take place in the spaces which 'they' leave open.

I enjoyed Rod Bullock's *cri de coeur (Mountain 51)*, but he was mistaken to say that teachers must 'remove all possible danger'. There is a place for limited risk-taking even in primary schools; while for adolescents some challenge and stress and risk are essential if education is to generate value and vitality. We need more Outward Bound Schools and White Halls and better public understanding of their task. Whenever adventure is sought, whether in an original dramatic production at school, on a weekend expedition, or on Mount McKinley, the judging of risks must be, and must be seen to be in the hands of responsible individuals whose actions speak louder than any words, rules or certification schemes. Such individuals thrive in, and are judged by, the small groups with whom they work and that is how standards are raised; not by tightening up some test or selection procedures. It is all part of a big national and post-industrial problem: do we want adventure constrained by responsibility; or safe thrills?

Yours etc.,

Robin Hodgkin (Oxford)

from MOUNTAINS 52 & 53 *1976 and 1977*

Editor's: Note: At the time of writing Sir Jack Longland was Chairman of the Mountain Training Board and Robin Hodgkin was Lecturer in Educational Studies at the University of Oxford.

THE PHILOSOPHY OF ADVENTURE EDUCATION

COLIN MORTLOCK

To begin to understand the real need for the development of Adventure Education it is necessary to look closely at my opening remark, 'There is no more potentially dynamic form of education than Outdoor Pursuits'. What I meant was, 'There is no more potentially dynamic form of education than adventure'. The justification for this remark is from watching all types of adolescents in different adventure situations, and trying to both understand and evaluate what I have seen. I have come to the following tentative conclusions:

1. The adventure situation demands the best from the person concerned. This is extremely important as the human being, especially in our present society, generally has an option. He may adopt a very positive approach, of really trying hard at something and giving of his best, or alternatively presenting a negative approach to the problem and getting by with the minimum – or just not bothering. It is a sad reflection on the human race that if given the choice the human being will tend to take the easy way out. In an adventure situation with the skilled teacher there is no easy option for the pupil.

William James posed the question, 'The problem of man is to find a moral substitute for war'. In other words the human being needs challenge but it must not be destructive of fellow human beings. Adventure provides a moral substitute. The war is an internal one between the positive and negative sides of the individual. Should he try to overcome his fear and tackle the problem, or not bother? The positive approach will lead to personal satisfaction. The negative approach will bring feelings of failure and inadequacy.

2. The obvious criticism that this type of challenge is only relevant to some physically gifted boys, and even less to girls, is untrue. There is an instinct for adventure. Virtually all young people can find satisfaction from adventure, regardless of their physical, mental, or emotional limitations. Such a remark must be very difficult for many readers to accept. It took six years of full time adventure work with thousands of adolescents of both sexes with great diversity of limitations, including a seventeen stone girl and

a girl with a hole in her heart, before I realised that it must be an instinct. Now I have no doubts that one can take a complete class from practically any school in the country into a wild area and provide adventure in safety and consequent pupil satisfaction for each one of them.

The likelihood that the urge for adventure is instinctive in part is what makes this form of education so potentially powerful. The whole class can succeed. Individual pupils may well find a form of adventure in many other aspects of education as in one sense adventure may be construed as an emotional involvement in a new experience that ends with feelings akin to those of satisfaction. Nuffield Science for example is an adventurous approach, and the time may come when this approach is the normal approach in education. What makes adventure through Outdoor Pursuits so important is that it is instinctive, and therefore can emotionally involve each pupil for the most positive of educational reasons. It can point the way forward for him, as to how he should tackle any problems he will meet during his life.

Research might well indicate that not only is the urge for adventure instinctive, but that unless society provides socially acceptable forms of adventure in physically expressed terms, then the younger generation will seek it in anti-social forms. They are at an age when their desire for adventure must be expressed through the use of their bodies. Modern developments in anti-social forms of adventure – delinquent crime, rave-ups, vandalism, for example – are already serious problems in our society.

3. The validity of this form of education will obviously depend on the educational objectives of the relevant administrators. There is a vast range of activities that can be available to young people as part of their education. If one accepts that one of the most important aims of education is to create in the pupil a desire to go on learning through discovery, then Adventure Education has great validity. This desire for learning is created by the pupil obtaining enjoyment and satisfaction from an activity. Adventure guarantees these feelings.

4. There is no validity for the view that adventure is perhaps acceptable as an extra-curricular activity, but not to be compared in educational importance with conventional school subjects. The truth of the matter is probably the reverse. Adventure provides one of those unique educational situations that is direct experience of that overall educational aim of *mens corpore in sano*. In adventure the dominating aspect would appear to be a strenuous physical exercise and therefore educationally not very important. This is a fallacy. The pupil is involved not only physically but mentally and emotionally. The emotional involvement is that of fear initially, followed ultimately by – satisfaction. The physical involvement is obvious. Less obvious but

crucial to the whole psychological process, is the use of the brain. This is involved in two ways. First of all the brain must control the fear – a very demanding task – and failure to do so will lead to panic and misadventure. At the same time the brain has to work out how to overcome the problem. On a rock climb for example, a wide variety of possible holds may surround the pupil, but only certain holds used in a certain combination may provide the right answer. The brain may well be working overtime controlling the fear, calmly thinking out the moves ahead, and then translating them into physical action.

A comparison in the school environment might be the examination, but it is a poor comparison. In the latter the pupil may well feel fear initially and have to use his brain in both senses. On the other hand he does not have to translate his thoughts into demanding physical action; and neither is he generally likely to feel enjoyment and satisfaction immediately after the experience. The adventure situation, on the other hand, demands the use of three fundamental aspects of his personality, and that he must obtain the right balance in the sense of his brain controlling his emotions and bodily actions; and at the same time gives him ample psychological reward for his efforts.

from ADVENTURE EDUCATION AND
OUTDOOR PURSUITS *1973*

HAS OUTDOOR EDUCATION ANY FUTURE?

HAROLD DRASDO

Has outdoor education any future? In one sense of course it has. The remarkable development of the last few years is only the beginning. There will be more and more Mountain Centres, more and more schools and colleges with properties of their own in the hills, more and more courses for students and teachers, more and more Advisers advising and Organisers organising; more and more certificates. In the idiomatic sense I am less certain that outdoor education has a future. Ten or fifteen years ago it felt like the most promising experiment in British education. There was a degree of freedom about it which made it more progressive than the Progressive Schools. But an unimaginative pressure for standardisation ('in the interests of consistency' – why?) has exercised a repressive influence upon the experiment.

In the outdoor pursuits approach, in order to take the fullest advantage of all possibilities we must arrange first that the teachers are not processed. We must restructure the various outdoor pursuits qualifications to encourage variety and experiment rather than to secure uniformity of approach.

We must abandon any qualification system which is becoming insubordinate to the experiences it attempts to measure. We must take steps to ensure that Centre Wardens and Instructors are drawn from as many different fields of teaching as possible and that we do not suffer from a preponderance of scientists and physical educationists. It is high time that, to keep the balance, Colleges of Art begin to run outdoor education courses.

If the teachers are not processed it will be easier to ensure that the students are not processed. We must diversify the programmes and arrange, with adequate safeguards, that young people are able to spend a little time alone without any project whatsoever: no difficult map and compass scheme, no huge sack filled with survival gear, no insulation by the company of others from the personal confrontation with Nature. We should try to arrange that they see a particular area at different seasons, even if only briefly, rather than see it only once for a longer spell. We must always try to prevent our programmes from turning what should be natural, direct and immediate into a contrived experience.

We should try to retain at least that degree of autonomy that already exists in Mountain Centres. Above all, we should turn for our interpretation of the values of outdoor activities to men and women who have enjoyed and are enjoying wild country outside any teaching context – to those who have written about it in the past and to the climbers, sailors and naturalists of today.

from EDUCATION AND THE MOUNTAIN CENTRES *1972*

HUNT REPORT – ANNEXE A

THE HUNT COMMITTEE

The pursuit of mountaineering should imply a certain feeling for the mountain scene, as well as a sensitivity in regard to other people who wish to enjoy the mountains.

Mountaineering in all its aspects should be pursued as a matter of personal choice for its own sake, whether from a sense of adventure, or from a desire to acquire knowledge or fresh experience. The essence of motivation to engage in activities in the mountains is that the decision should be that of the individual, acting spontaneously rather than under impulsion.

A basic element in mountaineering is the presence of serious risk in varying degrees. Without this element it would lose something as vital as is competition in organised games. The attraction for some people lies in discovering where the risks lie and in developing skills and gaining the experience to measure up to them.

Those who go to the mountains of their own free will must be free to court these risks. Those who are being introduced to mountaineering must be safeguarded against accidents arising from exposure to risks that are beyond their experience to cope with. At the same time, they should not be taught attitudes or practices which, by overplaying safety, may stultify enjoyment and restrict their ability to progress in climbing with all its attendant challenges and opportunities. By becoming prevalent, such attitudes and practices deprive mountaineering of its unique characteristics and charm.

Mountaineering is a pastime that most people like to enjoy with a few friends, or occasionally alone. Some are more gregarious. But whether they go alone or in smaller or larger groups, all would wish to preserve a sense of remoteness and an element of wilderness in the mountains.

from THE HUNT REPORT ON
MOUNTAIN TRAINING *1975*

BEGINNINGS

COLIN KIRKUS

Mountains have always been in my blood. Some people have a passion for the sea, but for me it was the mountains that called. Luckily my parents have similar tastes, so that I did not have to endure the all too usual seaside holiday; horrible pictures of crowded beaches and bathing tents and gaudy ice-cream stalls come into my mind. I am afraid that in certain ways I was a wretched little snob in those days, looking down with scorn on all who were content with a normal holiday. I conveniently ignored the fact that young children and old people might not be able to disport themselves among the hills, and of course it never entered my head that anyone who had no desire to climb a mountain was worthy of the slightest attention. I am more tolerant now and thankful that people do go to the seaside and leave the mountains free.

I ascended my first mountain at the age of seven – a rocky 2000ft lump called Manod, near Ffestiniog (in Wales, it is hardly necessary to add). That was a great day in my life, and ever afterwards I gazed at all mountains with longing. I was not content to laze about in the valleys; I was itching to be on the summits. I can still remember my tears of rage and disappointment when my father refused to take me up Moelwyn because there was cloud on the top. I thought he showed a very poor and unadventurous spirit.

Then came the great day when I made the ascent of Snowdon, at the age of nine. We went up by Glaslyn, and I was thrilled beyond words. It was very hot and I can remember the cold crystal-clear springs that I felt certain had saved my life on the laborious but, to me, entrancing zigzags. It was wonderful to be at last actually on a slope composed entirely of rocks, surrounded by terrific precipices that exceeded my wildest expectations. I had provided myself with a stout and knobbly stick, which I had cut myself with loving care; it had rather the appearance of a petrified snake or a giant corkscrew. But in my eyes it was an indispensable companion, and I decided that some young men we saw coming down at breakneck speed without sticks of any kind must be very ignorant of mountain-craft. The whole day was one orgy of continuous rapture which I have never since been able quite to recall.

Two years later there was another thrill, when with great trepidation we crossed the knife-edge ridge of Crib Goch. I must have presented a queer spectacle, with a canvas tea-bag in one hand – for we could not dream of doing without our 4 o'clock tea – and a walking-stick in the other.

We used to spend our summer holidays at Carrog, in the Vale of Llangollen, and before I was twelve years of age I was allowed to wander over the mountains on my own. This shows the value of training one's parents from the very earliest age. I found that, properly managed, they gave very little trouble.

I walked over the Berwyns in all weather and learnt to find my way in mist by map and compass. I even tried some rock-climbing. There is a broken slatey cliff on the eastern side of the highest summits of the Berwyn range, and I lured my two younger brothers there on a stormy day of cloud and wind and hail. I had thoughtfully provided myself with a clothes-line, for which I had paid the large sum of eight-pence. (It broke later when I was trying to pull my brother up a haystack.)

We traversed across the slope to the foot of the steepest-looking buttress of rock I could find. My brothers naturally objected – one was only eleven years old – but I assured them that this was the easiest and in fact the only route, and that they had better follow me if they wished to escape with their lives. Luckily the cloud hid the simple gullies on either side from view. So up they had to come, wet and cold and thoroughly miserable, up the loose muddy rock, with the cloud swirling round. Fortunately the clothes-line – we had only thirty feet for the three of us – did not choose this occasion to break. And when we reached the top, blue with cold, I took out a wet and battered thermometer and solemnly informed them that the temperature was 38°F. This item of news was received with no great enthusiasm.

The following Christmas I was given *British Mountain Climbs*, a climbing guidebook, and this fired me with enthusiasm to do some real rock-climbing. So I purchased a proper climbing-rope, or rather line, guaranteed to hold nearly three-quarters of a ton and not to break on haystacks. And I nailed my boots with hobnails, putting them close together round the edge to make them look as much as possible like real climbing-boots.

Next summer a school friend was staying at Cynwyd, about five miles away from Carrog, and we used to cycle together to the Arans, which involved fifty miles cycling, apart from the walking and climbing. We found some nice, wet strenuous gullies, which had probably only been climbed a few times before, and enjoyed ourselves immensely. The Arans are nearly 3000ft in height and very wild and lonely; we usually did not see a soul the whole day. But I was not very popular with my friend's parents, since he used to arrive back at all hours of the night. Unfortunately they were not such well-trained parents as mine; he had not taken them in hand early enough.

When I was nearly seventeen, and had just left school, I managed to persuade the family to vary their usual routine and go to Betws-y-coed – a special concession because it was to be my last holiday before going to business. It seemed like heaven to me – only ten miles away from Snowdon and the Carnedds and the Glyders – on the doorstep of all the best climbing in Wales, in fact.

I spent practically the whole of this holiday in continuously breaking a rule that is being constantly hammered into beginners – climbing alone while still a novice. But what else could I do? I did not know any climbers, and it was only occasionally that I could get my father or brothers to accompany me. There was only one alternative – not to climb – and that was unthinkable. The ambition of my life at that time was to do some recognised rock-climbs; not just casual little scrambles, but real routes that had names and were described in the guidebook.

Though wrong as a policy, this early solo climbing taught me an immense amount. I knew that if I made a mistake I had no one to help me; I had to rely entirely on my own skill and my own judgement. Thus, after a few sobering adventures which I shall presently relate, I learnt to climb carefully and safely, even when I knew I had a good second man behind me.

British Mountain Climbs was my climbing Bible. But it had been written in the days when gullies were in fashion, when cragsmen were still afraid to venture on steep exposed faces. Therefore gullies at first took up rather more than a fair share of my climbing, and it was in one of these clefts that I had my first fall.

Now you will first of all want to know exactly what is a gully. Imagine you are looking at a large precipice. The face of it is not flat; it is seamed by deep rifts, running the whole height of the crag. These rifts are called gullies, while the jutting masses of rock that separate the gullies from one another are known as buttresses. Now you will notice that the gullies are not nearly as steep as the buttresses, and you may think you can walk up quite simply. Let us imagine you decide to do this. You pick out a likely-looking gully and begin walking up. The walls of the ravine are very steep, but the bed of the gully is set at quite a gentle angle, probably with a little stream running down.

All goes well for a time, and you imagine you are in for an easy scramble. Then, a little way ahead, you notice a great boulder jammed across the gully, but imagine that you will get round it easily enough. You scramble up to it and begin to feel a little doubtful. You are standing in a cave some thirty feet high, the roof of which is formed by the boulder, fully twenty feet across, which completely spans the cleft. In a situation like this there are three possibilities: sometimes you can climb up the back of the cave and find a tunnel behind the boulder – it is usually a strenuous job squirming through; sometimes it is possible to climb one of the walls or work out from the back of the cave on to the outside of the chockstone, as this type of boulder is called; or if both these methods fail you may have to try to find a way round on one side or the other. But in any case it has not proved to be the easy job you expected.

On the occasion in question I had cycled the ten miles from Betws and then slogged for an hour-and-a-half across the grassy slopes of the Carnedds, over the saddle below Pen Helig, and down to the grand precipice of Craig yr Ysfa. My objective was the Arch Gully, which was classified as difficult, so I was all keyed-up for a great struggle. The lower pitches – pitches are the stretches of actual climbing between the easier sections – went quite easily, and I arrived at the foot of the fifty-foot chief obstacle. This was a vertical, three-sided cleft, about a yard across and had scarcely any holds, or so it seemed to me. The only way to get up is to put the back against the right wall and the feet against the left. Then you have to raise one foot a few inches, then press with the palms of your hands on the wall behind until your back goes up a bit. This type of problem is known as a chimney; it is strenuous but usually safe, since you are firmly wedged. You can quite easily practise this technique in an ordinary doorway at home.

It was drizzling and the chimney was streaming with water and made more slippery by a coating of thick green moss. However, I arrived quite safely underneath the small chockstones which closed up the top of the chimney and overhung a little. I reached up cautiously with one hand and felt about until I found a fine sharp hold. One hard arm-pull and a struggle, and with a gasp of triumph I landed at the top of my first difficult rock-climb. It was a very small triumph really, for there are three harder standards, but it seemed a notable victory to me.

I descended a moderate gully into the Amphitheatre, a magnificent hollow in the centre of the cliff. Nothing easy would do for me in my exultant state of mind, so I made a bee-line for B Gully. This has one very awkward pitch, a steep slimy crack overhung by a smooth chockstone. It was raining heavily now, and muddy water was dripping down dismally on every side.

I climbed the crack with a good deal of difficulty and felt for holds on the boulder above, hanging backwards from one hand. It all seemed as smooth as glass and my fingers were so cold that I had lost all feeling in them. My supporting hand was getting tired and I felt I must do something quickly. I did. I scraped the mud out of a slight crevice on top of the overhanging boulder and decided to make it do. I let go with my left hand, my right hand slipped numbly from the boulder, and before I had time to think I found myself lying in the bed of the gully.

My first feeling was one of pained surprise that it should have been possible for me to have fallen off. Then I wondered how many bones I had broken, and found that I was completely uninjured. Finally I was overcome by such a feeling of baffled rage at being thus ingloriously beaten that I rushed at the pitch again, like a mad bull at a gate.

The same thing happened again, only this time I fell and slid about thirty feet and stopped dangerously near the edge of the pitch below. I decided it was time to stop.

It was a very chastened and rather shaky climber that made his way back to Betws that evening. Needless to say I did not breathe a word of the affair to any one. It was a disgraceful secret, to remain locked in my guilty bosom.

It is very easy to discover the causes for this little mishap – over-confidence, inexperience, and complete lack of judgement. It was bad enough to fall off once, but to go and do it again in a spirit of reckless petulance was sheer madness and showed that I was not really fit to be a climber. In climbing, everything should be considered calmly, and each move carefully thought out beforehand. Still, the whole thing did me a great deal of good. It showed me my limitations, made me think a lot, and made me much more careful in future. It was lucky for me that the fates picked on a nice safe place to teach me a lesson.

Youthful spirits soon recover, and the buttresses of Tryfan made my spirits rise again. Instead of gloomy wet gullies I was climbing on beautiful silvery-grey rock, warm and dry, and very rough. Tryfan is a superb mountain, three-peaked and very grand and rugged. And the climbing, too, is ideal for novices. You can taste the joy of being in exposed places with good holds; you can look down quite calmly over a drop of a few hundred feet if you have an arm round a rock as big as a milestone. The rough rock feels wonderfully safe and comforting under your fingers and your boots seem to grip anywhere. But the best feature of Tryfan is that the climbs finish on the summit; you feel that you have really climbed a mountain. And at the summit are two fifteen-foot stones known as Adam and Eve. These are quite close together, and people sometimes jump across. I have done it once or twice, but I feel that you would look rather silly if you slipped and broke a leg here after safely doing a difficult climb.

My next adventure was on Idwal Slabs. These lie at the south end of Llyn Idwal, on the Glyders, and are quite unique in their way. Imagine a flat slab of rough rock, 400ft long and about 300ft wide. Then imagine the whole thing tilted up at an angle of 45 or 50 degrees, and you have the Idwal Slabs. There are no large ledges and the holds are very small. Yet the climbing is not difficult on the whole, because of the easy angle.

I went up the easiest route, the only way described in my guide book, and found it very simple. This lies up a groove, well marked by the scratches of thousands of nailed boots, and it would really be quite difficult to fall down, though you would have a long slide if you did. In fact some friends of mine, becoming bored with ordinary methods, once descended the lower part of the climb head-first. The mountains were rather crowded that day, and the spectacle caused quite a lot of excitement. Seeing two climbers apparently hanging upside-down on the Slabs, people naturally thought there had been some very unusual type of accident and rushed to the spot from all sides. They then had the disappointment of seeing the two human caterpillars arrive at the bottom safely, though very red in the face. Others have descended the Slabs head-first – but not purposely.

At the top of the Slabs is a 200ft wall of steep rock, which provides climbing of a much higher standard. At this point I should have made my escape either to the left or to the right, on to easier ground; but I did not realise this and tried to climb directly upwards. I got into a recess called the Javelin Gully, though I did not know what it was at the time; in fact I had never heard of it. The rocks became steeper, and soon I reached a completely perpendicular section. I could just touch a flat ledge with my hands, but there were no footholds at all. I was standing in a little recess like a sentry-box and wondering what to do next. I had quite a good ledge for my feet, but as soon as I left it I felt horribly insecure.

I got my hands on to the ledge above and tried to pull up, scraping feverishly with my feet against the rock. I made the effort several times, but could get no farther. My arms were feeling tired and it needed more and more courage each time to leave the safety of my foothold.

I remembered my fall on the Carnedds, and decided to return. It is lucky that I did, because the Javelin Gully is a severe climb that needs a good deal of strength as well as skill. In 1937 two climbers were killed here; they fell, roped, to the bottom of the Slabs, 500ft below. How it happened remains a mystery; there must have been some mismanagement of the rope. Probably the second was giving the leader a shoulder, instead of remaining safely tied on to the rock a little lower down.

I came down a little and saw a line of slightly nail-marked holds leading diagonally out to the left. The holds got smaller and smaller, and finally I seemed to have reached the end of all things. Here, to my surprise, I found a piton (an iron spike) driven into a crack. So some one had been here before!

This was the first time I had been in a really exposed situation, and I was very impressed. I was standing on a narrow foothold and below me the rock dropped nearly vertically for over 100ft. Below that again were the 400ft of the Slabs.

I realised that I was in a tight corner and would have to keep a cool head.

I had the horrible feeling of being like a fly on a wall, without, unfortunately, being provided with a fly's wings. I would have given anything to have been able to float gently off into space.

The rock above looked terrifying. It was obviously far beyond my standard. Then I saw a spike of rock about twelve feet above me. If I could reach that, I thought, I might manage to get up; it looked easier above.

Luckily I always carried my eighty-foot length of climbing-line about with me. I uncoiled it now, and after several attempts managed to lasso the spike, cowboy-fashion, taking care not to swing myself off into space whilst I was doing so. Then I tied myself on to the end of the rope, so that I could not fall beyond the little ledge. So far, so good!

Then I climbed up the rope and managed to reach the spike. It was large and comforting and I grasped it thankfully. But the next section above was still difficult; the holds were very small and I funked it without the security of having the rope above me. So down the rope I slid. Then up and down again, several times. I swung the rope off the spike in disgust and decided to double it round the piton and slide down the face of the cliff. I was beginning to get a little desperate now. But the rope jammed behind the piton and would not run, besides not being long enough to reach easy ground. So I gave up that idea as well. I was growing really tired of this spot; I seemed to have spent half my life on a two-inch foothold.

More lassoing, and I got the spike again. Now for a do-or-die attempt. I climbed quickly up the rope and attacked the rocks above before I had time to change my mind. The holds seemed minute but I did not dare to hesitate, and almost before I had time to realise it I was above the difficulty and safe at last. What a relief I had never before felt so thankful for anything. The whole experience was worthwhile just for the sheer elation I felt at that moment.

There is no moral to this story. I made no real mistake; I avoided running into actual danger; and I succeeded in escaping safely from a difficult situation. And I had a glorious day of climbing adventure.

The following winter I managed to join a well-known club, and the next summer, while staying at the club cottage in the Ogwen Valley, I ran into real danger through my habit of climbing solo.

I now had no difficulty in obtaining climbing companions, but this time it happened that I was on my own. I had an urge for exploration, and probably also wished to make a name for myself, so I decided to have a look at Craig Lloer, a crag above Ffynnon Lloer, a lonely little lake set deep in one of the wild hollows of Carnedd Dafydd. I picked on the West Buttress, the shortest but steepest of the three sections of the cliff. It was about 200ft high and had never been climbed.

The main feature of the route I had planned was a sinister-looking crack, some eighty feet up. So the first thing to do was to find a way to the foot of this crack. Things started quite easily but grew much more difficult when I reached the airy crest of the buttress, overlooking the vertical wall that dropped dizzily into the depths of the gully on the left. I climbed straight up the steep edge and gained the sloping ledge at the bottom of the crack by a very awkward movement.

The crack was about forty feet high and overhung at the top. It looked very difficult. I tied the rope round my waist, with the other end hanging free, and started up. The crack was just about wide enough to fit a boot, and I progressed chiefly by jamming my hands and feet. In places there were small chockstones jammed in the crack and these were a great help, though I had first to test them very carefully to make sure that they were firm.

After an exhausting struggle I arrived at the overhang. I felt tired, because when you are climbing a pitch that is really vertical the arms get no rest at all. And now I had the overhang to tackle, where my whole weight would come on my hands. There was a convenient little stone here, jammed firmly in the crack, and I threaded the whole length of my rope down behind it, hanging on meanwhile with my left hand only. Then I tied myself on to the chockstone and was able to rest my arms, hanging more or less bodily on the rope.

Before I started off again I untied the rope from the chockstone but still left it hanging down behind, hoping that it might jam and hold me if I did happen to fall off the next section. Then I started up the overhang. It was very strenuous, and I struggled frantically. Then, just at a crucial moment, my rucksack jammed in the crack. With a despairing effort I worked it off my shoulder and abandoned it, precious camera and all. Another blind struggle and I was up, surprised and relieved to find the rucksack still hanging over the other shoulder.

Conditions looked much easier above and I continued gaily. There was an innocent-looking bulge ahead, and I got halfway up without thinking very much about it. Then I realised that it was much more difficult than it had seemed. I could see a good handhold a little higher and made rather a grab for it. That was all very well, but there were no footholds, so that I was hanging from my hands alone. There were no holds above and I could not descend. My arms were getting tired. I looked down and saw a sheer drop of nearly 200ft below me. My arms were aching now and I felt that I could not hold on much longer. I just hung there and waited for the end. Then I got into a panic and made a sudden convulsive spring round the corner on the left, where my hands mercifully landed on a hold.

I count that as one of my narrowest escapes. It was a foolish affair, because

I don't think it was really such a very difficult place. I made the mistake of acting first and thinking afterwards. Always remember that the strongest man cannot hang for long on his arms alone. So when you make an arm-pull, be sure that it will land you on a foothold where you can rest.

You will probably have noticed that in spite of all these narrow escapes I did not suffer any injury. You may think that the risks cannot have been so great as I have made them appear. Well, you are probably right. The danger seemed real enough, but that is one of the most noticeable points about climbing; you have all kinds of narrow squeaks, and yet nothing serious happens. You get all the thrilling sensations of danger without much real risk.

Still, inexperience does lead to more than half the nasty smashes that do occur, so I am going to try and show you how you can take up climbing without having any similar disturbing adventures. When I began I had no one to help or advise me, and I did not even know of any books that would tell me how to make a start.

Since those days I have taken many a novice up his first climb, so I can realise the difficulties of almost every type of beginner, from the ultra-adventurous to the super-cautious. I have always taken a kind of showman's delight in introducing the marvels of the mountains to my friends, and it has given me the most intense pleasure to see their enthusiasm increase by leaps and bounds. Now I want to do the same for you. I want to take you through the whole field of mountaineering, from the very beginning, so that you can share all the glorious experiences which have meant so much to me. It won't be tedious; there is very little book-work to be learnt. You can just go as far as you like with it, until you have found your own level. And when you have found that level – whether it be modest fell-walking or the most difficult rock-and-ice work – you will never regret having become a mountaineer.

from LET'S GO CLIMBING *1941*

ACKNOWLEDGEMENTS

The following authors and publishers are thanked and acknowledged for use of © copyright material:

To Lito Tejada-Flores and Sierra Club Books (Ascent) for *Games Climbers Play*;

To Ed Drummond and Sierra Club Books (Ascent) for *Mirror, Mirror*;

To the Edinburgh University Mountaineering Club Journal and Mrs Smith for *The Bat and the Wicked, Goofy's Last Climb, Twentyfour Hours* and *The Old Man and the Mountains*;

To Bernard Amy and Mountain for *The Greatest Climber in the World*;

To John Long and Climbing for *Pumping Sandstone*;

To Pete Livesey and Crags and Rocksport respectively for *I Feel Rock* and *Arms Like a Fly*;

To Kevin Fitzgerald and The Climbers' Club Journal for *Surely We're Off the Route?*;

To Douglas Fraser and The Scottish Mountaineering Club Journal for *Song of an Unfit Climber*;

To Allan Austin and The Climbers' Club Journal for *Lazy Men's Ways* (excerpt) and *A Visit to Saussois*;

To Cambridge Mountaineering and John Cardy and Keith McDonald for *Summertime* and *The Leader* respectively;

To Ed Drummond for his poems *Snowdon, Whitsuntide* and *Llyn du'r Arddu, the Black Lake*; also to Hart-Davis MacGibbon for *The Great Wall* from 'Hard Rock';

To Pat Ament, Tom Higgins and Vitaar Publishing for *Nerve Wrack Point*;

To Tom Higgins and Sierra Club Books (Ascent) for *In Thanks*;

To Rob Collister and Cambridge Mountaineering for *A Night Out*;

To Pete Crew, Barry Ingle and The Climbers' Club Journal for *A Longing for Wales*;

To Climbing and Roger Briggs and Bob Candaleria for *The Diamond – A Free Ascent* (originally – *Escape from the Prism*);

To Ian McNaught-Davis & Mountain for *Heavy Talks, Deux Grandes Bieres, Joe Beige Meets Godzilla, Doing it for the Perks, After Dinner Speaking Made Easy, In Memoriam, Safety Last, Climb Only When You're Ready* and *Drop, Plop, Fly or Die*;

To Hugh Burton and Mountain for *El Cap Update*;

To Ben Campbell Kelly, Brian Wyvill and Mountain Life (Holmes McDougall) for *The Walrus and the Carpenter*;

To Dave Cook and Mountain for *True Grit* and *The Mountaineer and Society*;

To Chuck Pratt and Sierra Club Books (Ascent) for *A View From Deadhorse Point*;

To Jim Perrin and The Climbers' Club Journal for *Denn Bleiben ist Nirgends* and *A Valediction*;

To Ronald Clark for *The English Traveller*;

To C. R. Allen and The Yorkshire Ramblers' Club Journal for *The Grépon*;

To Mike Baker and The Climbers' Club Journal for *A Face. A Friend*;

To Rick Sylvester and The Leeds University Mountaineering Club Journal for *The Douche, A Tale of Original Sin*;

To Terry King and Mountain for *The Shroud*;

To Rob Ferguson and Cambridge Mountaineering for *Why?*;

To Tory Stempf and Mountain for *Pinball Wizards*;

To William Collins Sons Company, Ltd. for *The Last Day on the Eiger Direct* from 'Eiger Direct';

To Chris Jones and Sierra Club Books (Ascent) for *North Twin, North Face*;

To James Marshall and The Scottish Mountaineering Club Journal for *Garde de Glace, The Orion Face* and *In the Groove*;

To Jim Perrin and Rocksport (Holmes McDougall) for *Style is the Man*;

To Allan Austin and The Yorkshire Mountaineering Club Journal for *A Tiger's Fling*;

To the Climbers' Club for quotes from the Tryfan and Idwal guides and for obituary notes on J. M. Archer Thomson;

To Pat Ament and Mountain for *The Black Canyon with Kor*;

To T. I. M. Lewis and Rocksport (Holmes McDougall) for *Clothes - A Mode of Communication*;

To The Scottish Mountaineering Club Journal and Mrs. Smith for *A Week in the Hills*;

To Peter Harding and The Rucksack Club Journal for *A Meeting With Dolphin*;

To Al Manson and Leeds University Mountaineering Club Journal for *All Our Yesterdays*;

To Mrs. Elizabeth Patey and Mountain for *Apes or Ballerinas?* and *The Art of Climbing Down Gracefully* (also published in 'One Man's Mountains', Gollancz, London, 1972;

To Robin Campbell and Mountain for *Climbing Ethics* and *Climb to the Lost World*;

To Royal Robbins and Sierra Club Books (Ascent) for *Tis-sa-ack*;

To Reinhold Messner and Mountain for *Murder of the Impossible*;

To Yvon Chouinard and Sierra Club Books (Ascent) for *Coonyard Mouths Off*;

To Royal Robbins and Mountain Gazette for *A Review of Downward Bound*;

To Harold Drasdo and The Climbers' Club Journal for *Cae Coch Quarry* from 'Punch-Up at the Padarn Lake';

To Harold Drasdo and Mountain for *In Praise of Cheating*;
To Keith Myhill and Mountain for *The Future of Gritstone*;
To Ed Drummond and Mountain for *Drumstick Strikes Back*;
To Russell Taylor and Thrutch for *The Handicap Committee*;
To The Countess of Essex and The Fell and Rock Journal for *Expediency* from 'Mechanised Mountaineering';
To Mike Thompson and Mountain for *Out With the Boys Again* and *Annapurna High Life*;
To Doug Scott and Mountain for *A Bivouac on Everest* from 'Everest: South-West Face Climbed';
To Pete Boardman and Mountain Life (Holmes McDougall) for *Everest is Not a Private Affair*;
To Gary Bocarde and Climbing for *Climb of Climbs*;
To David Cox and Mountain for *Some Comments on an Everest Book*;
To The American Alpine Club Journal, Al Read and Lou Reichardt for *The Dhaulagiri Avalanche*;
To Ken Wilson and Mountain for *A Second Talk With Messner*;
To The Climbers' Club Journal for *A Short Siesta on the Upper Slopes*;
To Doug Scott and Mountain for *A Crawl Down the Ogre*;
To The Rucksack Club Journal for *Boulder Trundling* and *Of Bogs, Swamps and Quagmires*;
To G. J. F. Dutton and The Scottish Mountaineering Club Journal for *The Craggie* and *A Good Clean Break*;
To The Guardian and Michael Parkin for *The Peak of Achievement*;
To Sheridan Anderson for *Wolfinger Moves*;
To Iain Ogilvie and The Scottish Mountaineering Club Journal for *Maintaining the Spirit*;
To Sir Douglas Busk and Mountain for *The Young Shavers*;
To David Bentley and Climbing for *Stogams Opape interviews Zeke Bottomley*;
To Harold Drasdo for *Climbing As Art* from Ascent and *Has Mountain Education a Future?* from 'Education and the Mountain Centres';
To Iain Smart and The Scottish Mountaineering Club Journal for *For England Read Middlesex*;
To Anne Marie Rizzi and Mountain for *Hands*;
To John Shorter and David Hewlett and Mountain for letters in response to 'Hands';
To Andrew Ross for *Bear Hunt on the Blosseville Coast*;
To The Climbers' Club Journal and Rev. S. Z. Edwards for *Scenery For A Murder*;
To Jim Sinclair and The Canadian Alpine Journal for *Sometimes You Know – Sometimes You Don't*;
To Bob Barton and Cambridge Mountaineering for *Breaking Through*;
To Off Belay and Mike Quigley for *Falling*;
To Robin Campbell and The Scottish Mountaineering Club Journal for *Dougal Haston, Cumha Dughall*;
To Martin Boysen and Mountain for 'Fissure Boysen' from *Last Trango*;
To Jeffrey Long and Climbing for *The Ice Climber*;
To Lesley and Ed Fulton and Mountain for *Involuntary Rescue*;
To Geoffrey Childs and Climbing for *The Flesh Eaters*;
To Pat Littlejohn and Mountain for *Grand Canyon Climb*;
To Laura Jasch and Climbing and Off Belay for *Warning Record* and *Climbing Restrictions in the Midwest*;
To Laura and Guy Waterman and Off Belay for *Mt. Kathadin, Time for a Change*;
To Larry Kuzniar and Mountain for *It's a 5.10 Mantel Into Heaven*;
To Robin Hodgkin and The Climbers' Club Journal for *Skills and Safety*;
To Harold Drasdo and The Alpine Journal for *Margins of Safety*;
To Mountain for *The Cairngorm Tragedy*;
To Tom Price and Mountain for *Bridging the Gap* and *Adventure by Numbers*;
To Sir Jack Longland, Peter Wood and Robin Hodgkin for letters about Educational Climbing;
To Colin Mortlock for 'The Philosophy of Adventure Education' from *Adventure Education and Outdoor Pursuits*;
To The British Mountaineering Council for *The Hunt Report – Annexe A*;
To Thomas Nelson and Son for *Beginnings* from 'Let's Go Climbing!';
To Sheridan Anderson and the magazines, Summit, Off Belay, Ascent, Mountain, Mountain Gazette, North American Climber and Vulgarian Digest for twenty-seven cartoons in the text;
To the photographers for the 2006 edition: Ray Wood, Michael Kennedy, Daniele Chiappa, John Harwood, Heli Wagner, Tony Riley, John Powell and Reinhold Messner.

Acknowledgements are also due to those who assisted with advice and other services – Sue Jones, Llyn Jones, Angela Nicholas, Jim Perrin, Moira Irvine, Bill Brooker, Mike Pearson, Michael Kennedy and Allen Steck; *and in 2006:* Harold Drasdo, Robin Campbell, Geoff Dutton, Brian Wyvill, Margaret Body, Gloria Wilson and Don Sargeant (map on p.503).

Note for 2006: The magazines: Mountain Gazette, Vulgarian Digest, Off Belay, Crags, Summit, Rocksport, Mountain, Mountain Life, Thrutch and North American Climber are all now defunct, or absorbed into other magazines. Virtually all the journals continue to publish, though some appear spasmodically.

They often have that strange smile
and a faraway look in their eyes.

NOTES ABOUT THE ARTICLES

Mirror, Mirror
The first ascent of Arch Wall (4500ft/Grade 6/A5), Trollrygen North Face, Norway, by Ed Drummond and Hugh Drummond (unrelated) in 1972. The climb took twenty days to complete.

The Bat and the Wicked
The first ascent of the Bat (1000ft/E2) on Carn Dearg Buttress, Ben Nevis, in September 1959 – one of a series of major rock climbs pioneered at this time by Robin Smith and his friends. The article was also important – its style much imitated, particularly in University Journals. In 1979 the event was made into a film: *The Bat*, by Jim Curran, with Rab Carrington and Brian Hall.

The Greatest Climber in the World and *Pumping Sandstone*
Bouldering has always been an aspect of climbing. Two intense boulder scenes have been in the forests around Fontainebleau (with a natural extension to Chamonix in summer) and in the Yosemite Valley and the valleys of Colorado in the United States. These two articles reflect that traditional dynamism. *A note for 2006*: These articles were surprisingly prescient as, aided by the invention of the bouldering mat, during the 1990s and the early 2000s bouldering became a far more central activity boasting more technical interest, and much of the daring and camaraderie and environmental pleasure offered by the mainstream themes.

I Feel Rock
Accounts of nine varied rock climbs from around the world. Yosemite region: Moratorium, El Capitan, (560ft, E4/5.11); Reed Pinnacle Direct (280ft/E1/5.9); Lunatic Fringe, (200ft/E2/5.10); Regular Route, Fairview Dome, Tuolumne Meadows (1500ft/HVS/5.8). Yorkshire: Claws, Kilnsey Crag (200ft/E5/5.12); Wellington Crack, Ilkley (50ft/E4/5.11). Cornwall: Darkinbad the Bright-dayler, Pentire Head, Cornwall (230ft/E4/5.11). Iran: South Face of Kuh i Parau (1500ft/ HVS/5.8). France: L'Ange (The Angel), Le Saussois (E3/5.10/2pts aid).

Surely We're Off the Route? (A Swansong)
Written during a period of poor health, the essay deals with easy climbs in the Snowdon area. Ten years later Fitzgerald was still 'going strong' and on his instructions we shortened the title.

Lazy Men's Ways
Dramatic events on the Cromlech Girdle (755ft/E2), one of the top Welsh climbs of the 1950s.

The Great Wall
An account of the fifth ascent of the most celebrated climb on Clogwyn du'r Arddu by a climber who 'burst' onto the Welsh scene with a number of controversial ascents in the mid 1960s.

A Night Out
Collister's article was first published anonymously as King's College Chapel chimney is one of the great forbidden challenges for the Cambridge night climber.

A Longing for Wales
Pete Crew and Barry Ingle, writing as S. Gonzales, describe a Lake District raiding weekend with ascents of Dovedale Groove and Extol, and the first ascent of Hiraeth – all on Dove Crag.

El Cap Update, The Walrus and the Carpenter
The first article, compiled from Burton's two letters sent to *Mountain*, describes the lure of hard aid climbing on new El Capitan routes. The second covers an English ascent of Yosemite's North America Wall, a climb targeted by the pushier European big wall contenders.

True Grit
Written at a time when Limestone climbing was in vogue in the Derbyshire area and Gritstone seemed to have been worked out. A Gritstone revival soon followed and Derbyshire and Yorkshire experienced a prolonged period of new route activity on Gritstone and Limestone.

A Face: A Friend
The penultimate climb of Colin Taylor. Two days later he died on the Obergabelhorn.

Goofy's Last Climb
A 1960 ascent of the North Rib (von Schumacher/Amstutz) of the Gross Fiescherhorn by Robin Smith and Brian Wakefield. It was thought that they climbed difficult Welzenbach/Tillman route but Wakefield had urged caution and they took a less committing rib line further right.

The Douche – A Tale of Original Sin
A developing romantic adventure enjoyed by a man well-known for his epic ski jumps off El Capitan and Mt. Asgard the latter featuring in the James Bond film – *The Spy Who Loved Me*.

Pinball Wizards
Inspired by the alpine ice-climbing described in Mountain 27, Stempf and Markel set off from Wisconsin (September, 1974) to make an adventurous first ascent on the Breithorn North Face.

North Twin: North Face
The 1970s partnership of George Lowe and Chris Jones made a number of major alpine first ascents in the Canadian Rockies. The North Twin climb (5000ft/Grade 6/5.8/A3), made during six days in August, 1974, was their hardest, and has been described as Canada's answer to the Eigerwand. *Note for 2006:* Recent ascents of this face have endorsed its reputation.

The Old Man and the Mountains, Garde de Glace, The Orion Face
This famous 'triptych' of articles, the first by Smith and the other two by Marshall, describe their celebrated 'route-bagging' week on Ben Nevis in the winter of 1960.

A Tiger's Fling
The 1961 first ascent of Flanker (E1) on Heron Crag, Eskdale by Allan Austin and Eric Metcalf.

Description of routes from the Idwal and Tryfan Guides
The Tryfan guidebook was written in collaboration with Wilfrid Noyce, but the writing seems to bear the unmistakeable Edwards stamp of studied obscurity, which is a constant source of delight to aficionados of his work.

A Week in the Hills
This short article is considered by students of Smith's work to be his finest piece of writing.

The Black Canyon With Kor
Since Layton Kor gave up climbing after the Eiger Direct episode, he has become a living legend in his home state of Colorado. Among his early climbs, none are more admired than his remarkable series of explorations in Gunnison's Black Canyon. Ament depicts the intensity of Kor's dynamism while describing one of these ascents. After his withdrawal from climbing Kor concerned himself mainly with devout religious study.

A Meeting With Dolphin
Peter Harding and Arthur Dolphin were the top English rock climbers of the late 1940s.

All Our Yesterdays
In the early 1970s Leeds-based climbers, led by John Syrett, Ken Wood and Al Manson, were very actively grabbing new routes on Yorkshire gritstone. Hank Pasquill from Lancashire made a number of early repeat raids into Yorkshire and finally made the first ascent of Almscliff's Goblin's Eyes to the chagrin of locals.

The Art of Climbing Down Gracefully
One of a series of articles that Patey wrote specially for *Mountain* before his death and published posthumously in both *Mountain* and the book *One Man's Mountains*. Both book and magazine carried slightly different versions, and this is the first time that the full text has been published.

Tis-sa-ack
Robbins tackles the taboo subject of emotion between climbers (in this case, mainly dislike). The climb, a direct line up the North-West Face of Half Dome (Grade 6/5.9/A4/110 bolts), involved much bolting. Coming just before the controversial Dawn Wall ascent, both climbs triggered a debate on the limits of acceptable bolting in Yosemite.

Murder of the Impossible
An early essay by Reinhold Messner written at a time when some Dolomite climbers were making pointlessly bolted Direttissimas. Messner's crusade against these climbs, backed by other fine climbers, was locally influential and drew world attention to his polemical bent.

Arms Like a Fly
Pete Livesey played a major role in the freeing of many previously aided Limestone routes in Yorkshire and Derbyshire in the 1970s. This article describes one of his first successes.

The Future of Gritstone and Drumstick Strikes Back
The controversial first ascent of The Linden (E6, 6b) on Curbar Edge led to this biting exchange about using unconventional tactics when gritstone ethics were undergoing close scrutiny.

Expediency
This piece was extracted from Smythe's *Mechanised Mountaineering* (1942). British criticism of 'fanatical Münich mechanisation' was at its height at this time. Having debated that, Smythe digressed to urge a purer approach on Everest bids. His advice to eshew bottled-oxygen was not heeded, but today it has a surprisingly avant-garde flavour. *A note for 2006:* Smythe's climbs showed him to be a keen practitioner of an alpine-style approach to high mountain climbing. He made the best pre-war Everest attempt (sans bottled oxygen) reaching 28,100ft, as had Norton, Wyn-Harris and Wager – but at 11am when still going well. He judged it wise to retreat as he was alone. His alpine-style first ascents of Avalanche Peak (1931), and Deoban, Nilgiri Parbat and Mana Peak (1937) were ventures more in line with those of today's practitioners.

A Bivouac on Everest
Doug Scott's description of his night out with Dougal Haston after completing of the South-West Face in 1975, an event that hastened the trend to more adventurous expedition tactics.

Annapurna High Life and *Out With the Boys Again*
Mike Thompson's observations on the often farcical contradictions of big expeditions formed a welcome relief to the indigestible diet of backslapping publicity that these projects inevitably generate. It is surprising that these writing skills were not deployed in the official writings, but iconoclasm sits uneasily with the orthodox heroic account. *Out With The Boys Again* was written as a contribution to *Everest - The Hard Way* but was considered so subversive that it was left out.

Climb of Climbs and *Mac the Belly talks to Cassius Bonafide*
Two 'Expedition Lampoons'. In order to raise money expedition leaders are often compelled to indulge in popular promotion campaigns that frequently become so crass that response is essential. The satirists act as antibodies here, and the Expedition leader, enmeshed in a web of fund-raising and media-adulation is hopefully purged in the eyes of his peer group.

The Dhaulagiri Avalanche
The American 1970 Expedition had a 'wipe-out' in the early stages. Reichardt's miraculous escape serves as a reminder of the dangers on expeditions to the greater ranges.

A Second Talk With Messner
Mountain's first interview with Reinhold Messner came after his Alpine climbs and the Nanga Parbat epic. This second interview took place when he was at the height of his powers and

influence following a number of major Himalayan climbs. In the two seasons that followed after failures on Dhaulagiri and Everest he succeeded in making ascents, without oxygen, of Everest (with Peter Habeler) and Nanga Parbat (solo). *A note for 2006:* Messner continued to solo Everest by the North Face and become the first person to complete all the 8000m peaks. Since then he has maintained a high profile as a popular polemicist, and Green politician. This high profile recently led to a revival of the 1970 Nanga Parbat controversies and a search for his brother's remains. These were found in a position that confirmed the general thrust of his account.

Joe Beige Meets Godzilla and *Climb to the Lost World*
Post-expedition lampoons of the British ascent of Roriama in 1974. This rock peak in the South American jungle had been the subject of Conan Doyle's 'Lost World' saga and thus prompted such bizarre media attention (in the U.K.) that assessment of it's importance as a mountaineering objective was almost impossible. Nobody, least of all the participants, seemed to mind, and the show-biz image of the trip was enthusiastically echoed by the satirists. *A note for 2006*: More recently these jungle buttes (tepuis) have attracted the attention of leading rock climbers and some very long climbs of great difficulty (both aid and free) have been made.

A Crawl Down the Ogre
Doug Scott's account of the near disaster that followed the first ascent of the Ogre in the Karakoram in 1977. *A note for 2006:* There have since been twenty-four attempts to climb the Ogre with only one success (in 2001) when Thomas Huber, Urs Stoecker and Iwan Wolf reached the summit by a route up the Pillar to the right of the original route and then taking the Bonington/Estcourt line up South Face to join the first ascent line up the summit tower. The mountain still awaits an alpine-style ascent.

The Craggie and *A Good Clean Break*
Short stories about The Doctor, the narrator and the Apprentice – the fictitious inventions of Geoffrey Dutton – whose activities and adventures touch every aspect of Scottish highland activity. Dutton, sometime editor of the SMCJ, was (with Robin Campbell), largely responsible for its reputation for penetrating wit throughout the 1960s and early '70s. Regular Doctor stories enlivened many subsequent SMCJs and are now collected in a popular book. Dutton can also be credited (again with Campbell) for promoting Robin Smith's articles to a wider audience.

The Young Shavers
This is part of a longer article in which Sir Douglas Busk describes the personalities and the machinations in the Alpine Club in the 1930s, '40s and '50s.

Doing it for the Perks and *For England Read Middlesex*
It is surprising, in retrospect, that so little has been written about the battles to emancipate some of the traditional all-male British clubs in the 1960s and '70s. These two rare vignettes hint at the diversity of opinion on the topic.

Bear Hunt on the Blosseville Coast
Andrew Ross became obsessed with exploration and life in East Greenland in the early 1970s after making the first ascent of Ejnar Mikkelsen Fjeld (with three others) in 1970. Subsequently he lived with the eskimos [Inuit] for long periods and this article (previously unpublished) records some of his adventures.

Scenery for a Murder
John Menlove Edwards is regarded as one of Britain's greatest mountaineering writers and this essay is said to be his finest. Edwards, an outstanding rock-climber, was also a homosexual and a conscientious objector. He lived an increasingly tortured life, racked by feelings of guilt, failure and self-doubt. He eventually committed suicide in 1958. *A note for 2006:* Jim Perrin's book *Menlove* (Gollancz, 1985) submits the Edwards *oeuvre* (climbing, prose, poetry and professional work) to intense study. This was not fully discussed at the time of Geoffrey Sutton's and Wilfrid Noyce's 1961 biography *Samson*, possibly because of homosexual practices were illegal at that time. The footnote in *Samson* thus states 'The most perfect of JME's works ... the editors

will not spoil the enjoyment and interpretation with their own comments.' Those who find the imagery difficult to fathom might usefully refer to Perrin's critique, in which he links it directly to Edwards' continued love for Wilfrid Noyce, at this time unrequited as Noyce had moved on. The trauma for both of them of the Mickledore Grooves accident in 1937 formed, it seems, a major theme in the article.

In the Groove
Marshall, consumed with the details of his austere, yet thorough Ben Nevis guidebook, made a winter attempt (with Elly Moriarty), and first ascent of The Clanger (Grade 4) with brother Ronnie and Robin Campbell in 1967. Marshall-watchers can only speculate on the anecdotal wealth that his coded guidebook subtleties suggest.

Fissure Boysen (from Last Trango)
Boysen's narrow escape took place during the abortive attempt on the Trango Tower in 1975. He returned the following year, climbed his crack without incident, and reached the summit. *A note for 2006:* Trango Tower is now seamed with fine rock routes but the first ascent line is rarely repeated. In 1975 after his harrowing experience, Boysen joined the Everest South-West Face expedition and played a role in the second summit bid.

Skills and Safety
An optimistic summary of the educational value of mountaineering by an educationalist/climber who later became a critic of the developments in mountain education. *A note for 2006:* It is also worth noting Hodgkin's leading role in the first ascent of the South Ridge of Ushba (1937) and his strong attempt on Masherbrum in 1938 which left him badly injured by frostbite.

Margins of Safety
An article that questioned some of the established Mountain Training wisdom. It drew together the threads of a concern about the often naïve understanding of the realities of climbing. This found dramatic, and tragic emphasis in the Cairngorm Tragedy of the following year.

The Cairngorm Tragedy
The magazines covered this cataclysmic event with articles immediately after the enquiry' but it is surprising that very little considered and expert analysis followed in the journals. This article records the facts and adds some comment, and it seems best to reprint it, in the absence of anything better. As this incident formed the basis of so much that followed, its study is essential. The protagonists in the Educational Debate used it to support their own arguments and it seems likely to form a background to the thinking of mountain educationalists for many years to come. As such the article has a clear place in this collection of essays. *Note for 2006:* The Lyme Bay canoeing accident in the early 1990s had a similar impact of the canoeing world and outdoor education in general and a recent caving incident in Yorkshire, during which a school pupil died, may well trigger similar concerns.

Bridging the Gap and Adventure by Numbers
Two articles by one of the leading expert critics of the trends in Outdoor Education.

Correspondence on Educational Climbing
The concerns about Educational Climbing eventually found a focus in the Mountain Leadership Training Board. These letters reflect the divergent views when reforms were demanded.

Philosophy of Mountain Education
This section from Mortlock's booklet *Adventure Education* and *Mountain Pursuits* gives another aspect of the debate. Mortlock wrote his paper in 1973 as a panegyric on mountain education in the face of growing criticisms. His views form the most cogent defence so far assembled by an active climber, for an energetic expansion of adventure training.

Has Outdoor Education a Future?
Drasdo's booklet *Education and the Mountain Centres* followed his earlier article *Margins of Safety*. It poses doubts about Outdoor Education that form another facet of the debate.

Hunt Report: Annexe A
The concern in the climbing world about the trends in Mountain Training after the Cairngorm Tragedy led the BMC to set up a specialist committee under Lord Hunt to study the problem. The Hunt Committee's subsequent report confirmed that there was cause for concern, and advocated detailed reforms. The more general precepts of the report are however worthy of long-term study.

Beginnings
Colin Kirkus's first experiences as a climber contain valuable pointers to mountain educators, for both caution and good training, and as a reminder of the value of adventurous spontaneity. This was the first chapter of an instructional book and Kirkus clearly believed that with good training the close escapes he experienced could have been avoided. The seeds of much of the dispute about Mountain Education in Britain are echoed in this article from the 1940s.

SUBJECT INDEX

ROCK-CLIMBING (UK)

ROCK-CLIMBING (Other Ranges)

ALPINISM/SNOW AND ICE CLIMBING

EXPEDITION CLIMBING

ESSAYS OR COMMENT ON THE WAY WE CLIMB

FICTION

HUMOROUS AND SATIRICAL ITEMS

PEOPLE INDEX

Entries in bold indicate Authors, Cartoonists *(c)*, Photographers *(p)*, Map artists *(m)*.

Those who are the main subjects of the article (eg the climbing partner of the author) have those entries in bold. Others mentioned in the text (including author 'mentions' in other articles) appear in medium type.